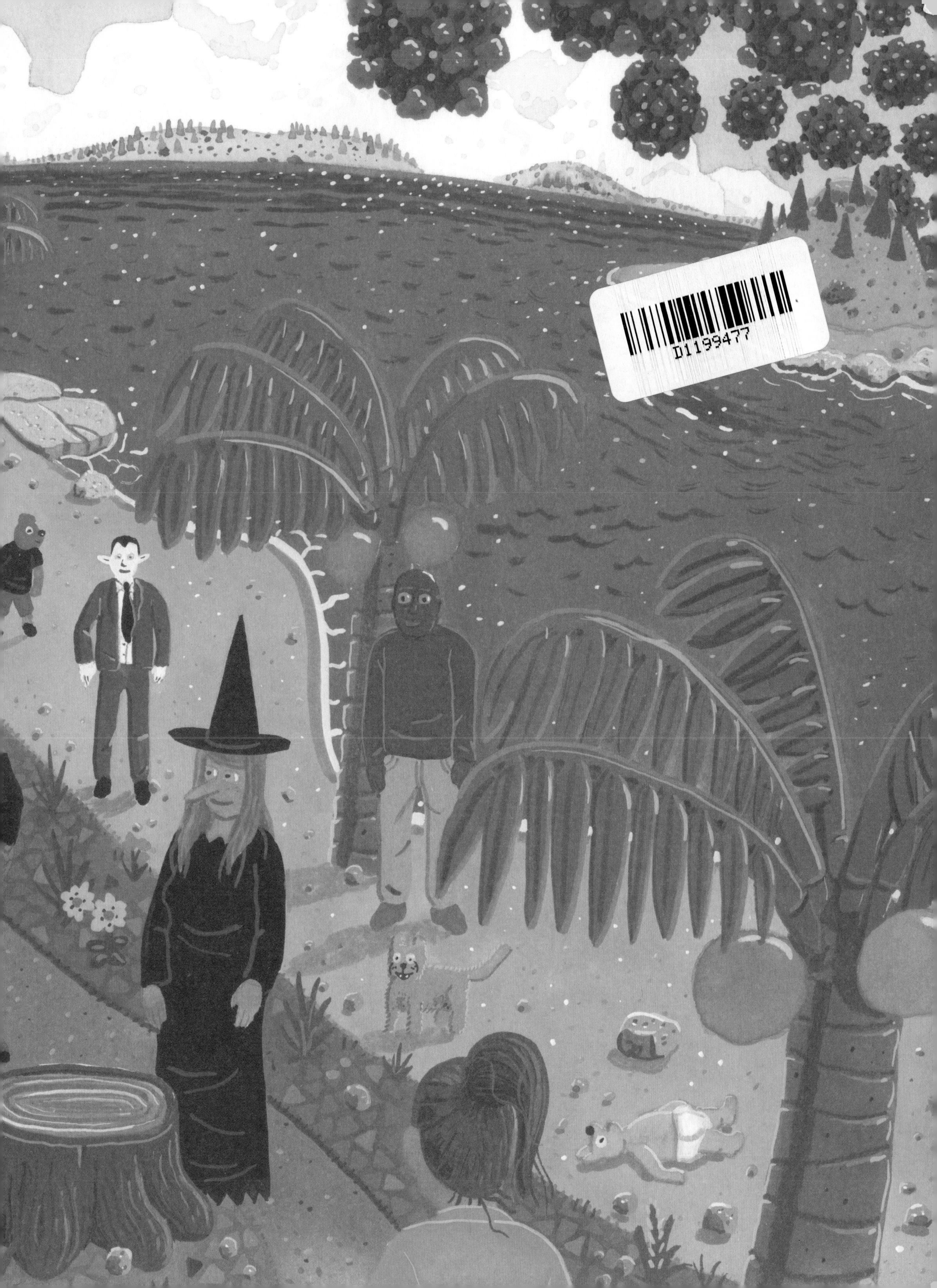

CAST OF CHARACTERS:

MEGG.
WELFARE WITCH.

MOGG.
MEGG'S CRAPPY BOYFRIEND.

OWL.
UPTIGHT STRAIGHT MAN.

WEREWOLF JONES.
RAGING ID.

DIESEL AND JAXON.
SCUMMY CHILDREN.

BOOGER.
TRANSGENDER BOOGEYWOMAN.

MIKE.
PASSIVE WIZARD.

IAN.
SMELLY BEAR.

DRACULA JUNIOR.
GUTTER PHILOSOPHER.

AMELIE.
AGING DRUG-ADDICT.

VALERIA.
EUROPEAN WOMAN.

YOU!
GOD-LIKE OBSERVER.

CONTENTS:
1. CRISIS ZONE (EXTENDED CUT)
271. DIRECTOR'S COMMENTARY
283. EXCLUSIVE EPILOGUE
287. ADVERTISEMENT

WRITTEN AND ILLUSTRATED BY SIMON HANSELMANN.
ORIGINALLY SERIALIZED ONLINE, IN SLIGHTLY DIFFERENT
FORM, FROM MARCH 13TH TO DECEMBER 22ND, 2020.

BOOK DESIGN: SIMON HANSELMANN
EDITOR/ASSOCIATE PUBLISHER: ERIC REYNOLDS
PRODUCTION: PAUL BARESH
PUBLISHER: GARY GROTH

FANTAGRAPHICS BOOKS INC.
7563 LAKE CITY WAY NE
SEATTLE, WASHINGTON, 98115

ISBN 978-1-68396-444-5
LIBRARY OF CONGRESS CONTROL NUMBER 2020949773

FIRST PRINTING: AUGUST 2021
PRINTED IN THAILAND

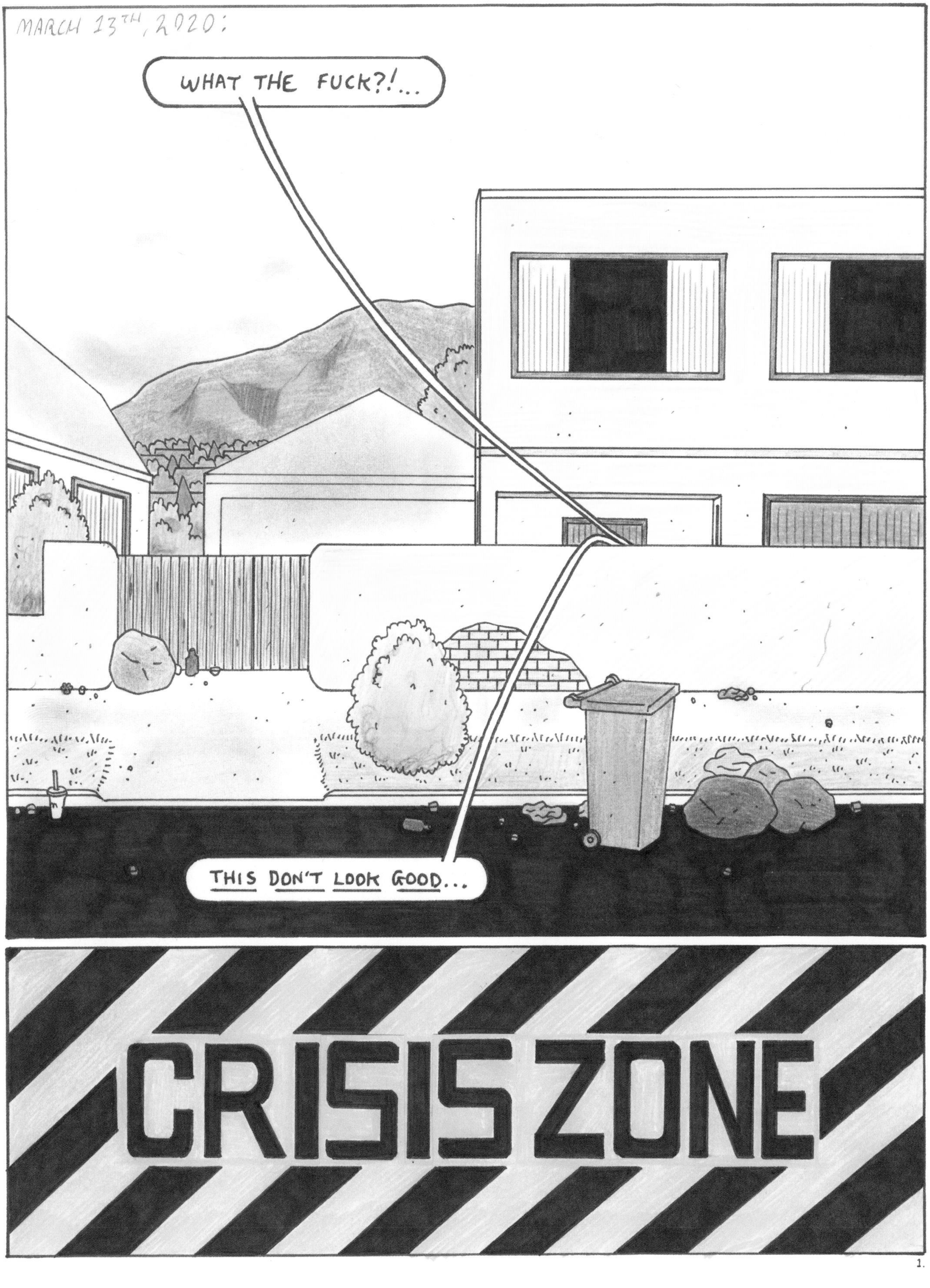
MARCH 13TH, 2020:
WHAT THE FUCK?!...
THIS DON'T LOOK GOOD...
CRISIS ZONE

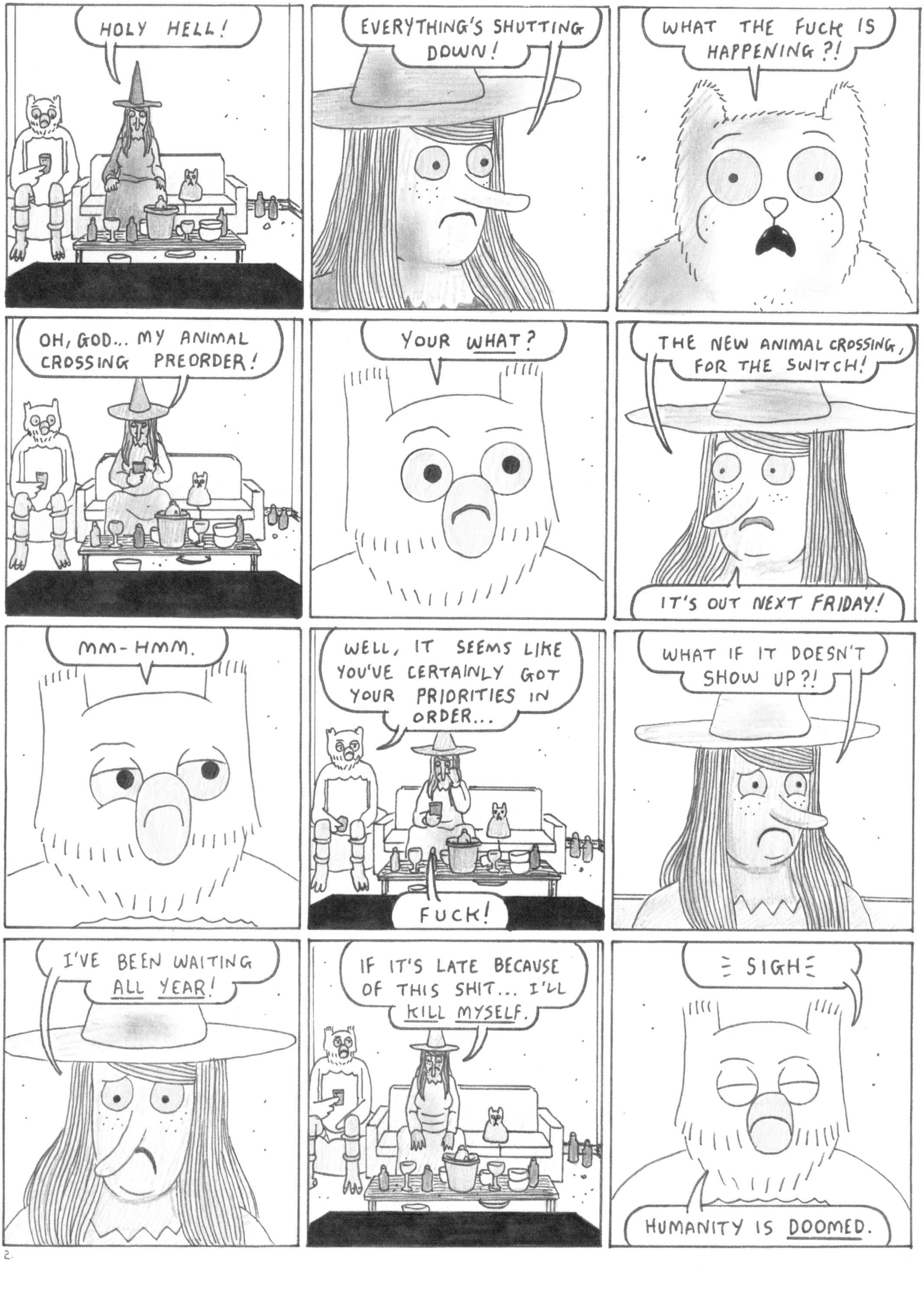
HOLY HELL!
EVERYTHING'S SHUTTING DOWN!
WHAT THE FUCK IS HAPPENING?!
OH, GOD... MY ANIMAL CROSSING PREORDER!
YOUR WHAT?
THE NEW ANIMAL CROSSING, FOR THE SWITCH!
IT'S OUT NEXT FRIDAY!
MM-HMM.
WELL, IT SEEMS LIKE YOU'VE CERTAINLY GOT YOUR PRIORITIES IN ORDER...
FUCK!
WHAT IF IT DOESN'T SHOW UP?!
I'VE BEEN WAITING ALL YEAR!
IF IT'S LATE BECAUSE OF THIS SHIT... I'LL KILL MYSELF.
SIGH
HUMANITY IS DOOMED.

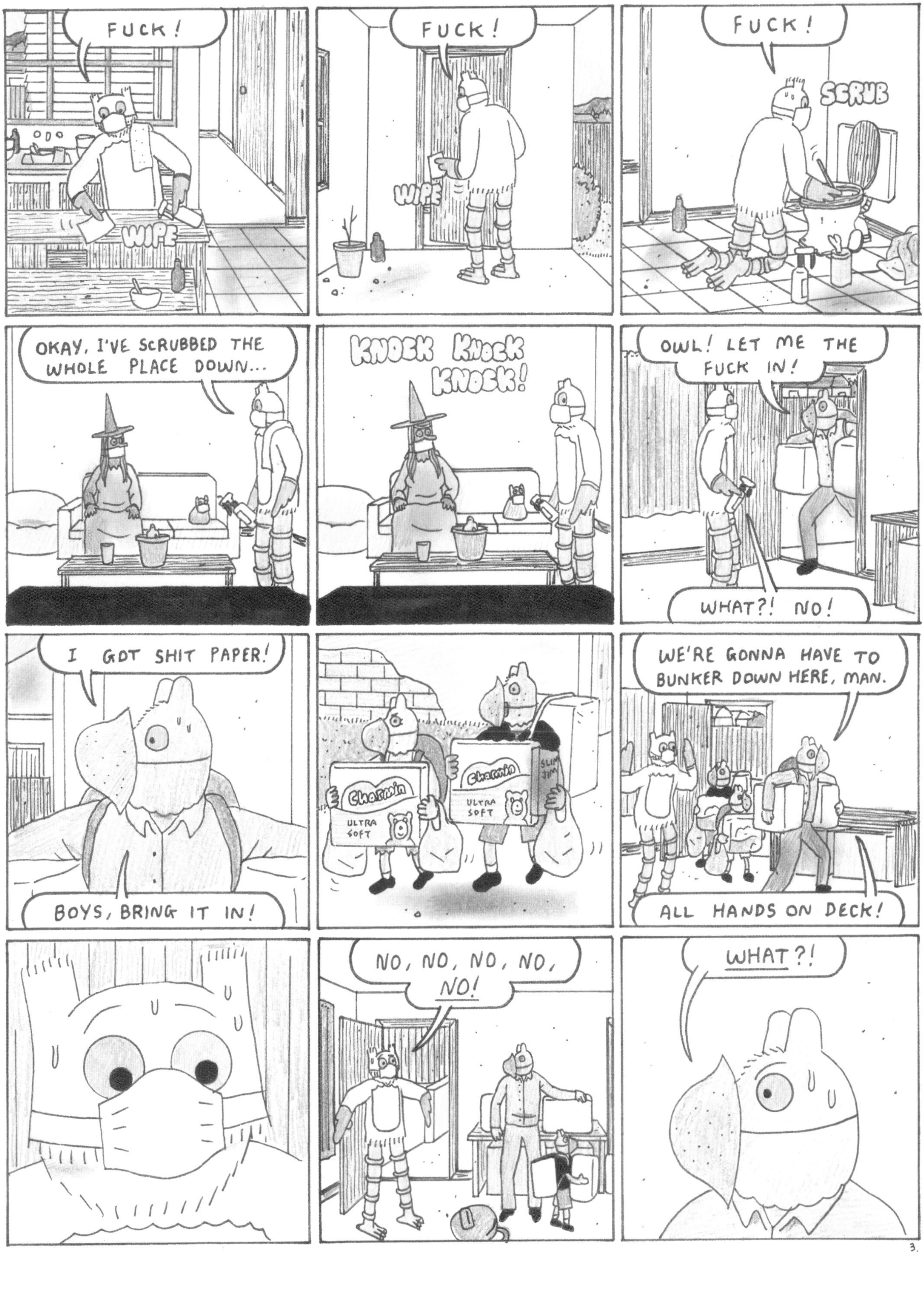
FUCK!
WIPE
FUCK!
WIPE
FUCK!
SCRUB
OKAY, I'VE SCRUBBED THE WHOLE PLACE DOWN...
KNOCK KNOCK KNOCK!
OWL! LET ME THE FUCK IN!
WHAT?! NO!
I GOT SHIT PAPER!
BOYS, BRING IT IN!
Charmin
ULTRA SOFT
Charmin
ULTRA SOFT
SLIM JIM
WE'RE GONNA HAVE TO BUNKER DOWN HERE, MAN.
ALL HANDS ON DECK!
NO, NO, NO, NO, NO!
WHAT?!

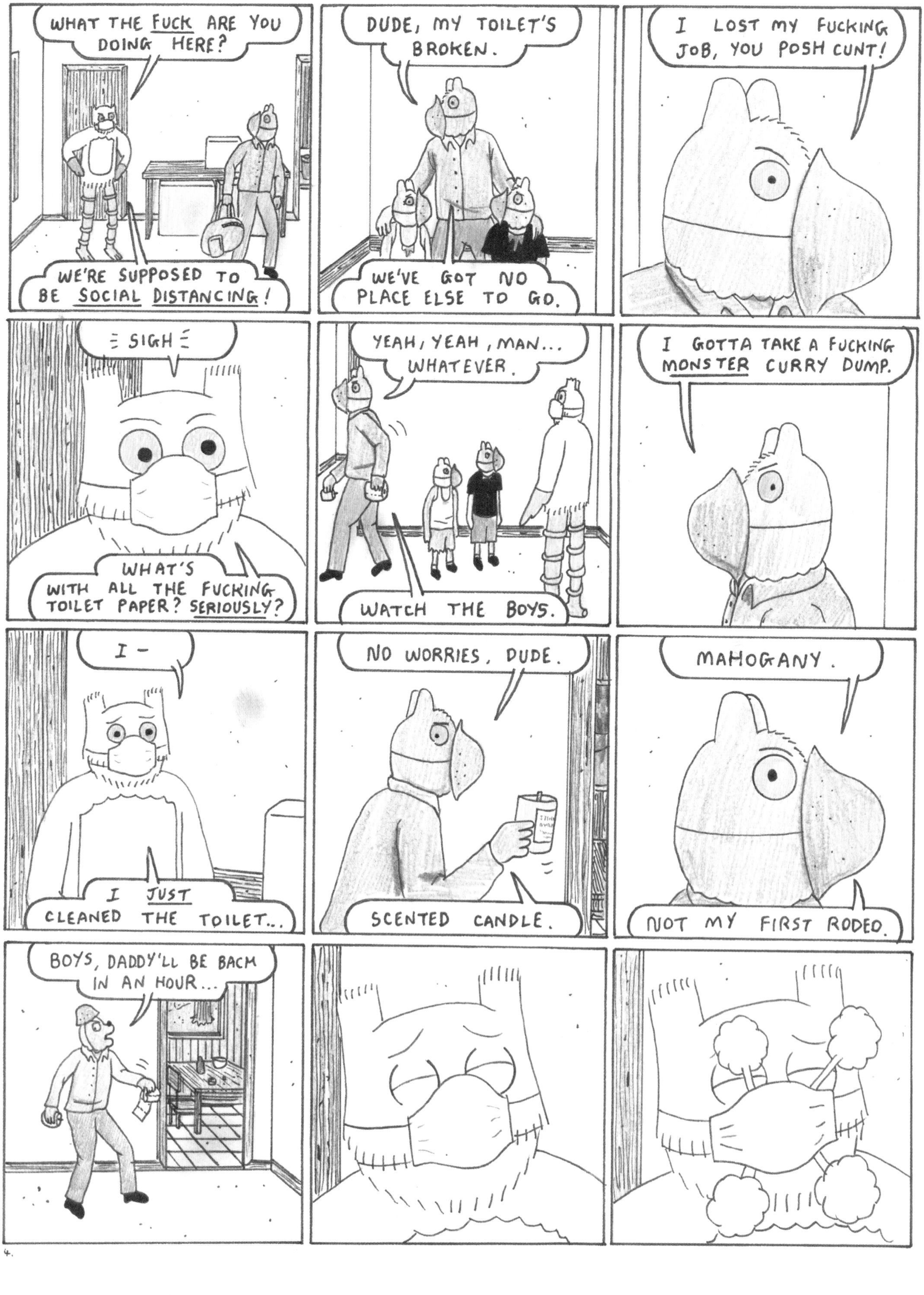
WHAT THE FUCK ARE YOU DOING HERE?
WE'RE SUPPOSED TO BE SOCIAL DISTANCING!
DUDE, MY TOILET'S BROKEN.
WE'VE GOT NO PLACE ELSE TO GO.
I LOST MY FUCKING JOB, YOU POSH CUNT!
SIGH
WHAT'S WITH ALL THE FUCKING TOILET PAPER? SERIOUSLY?
YEAH, YEAH, MAN... WHATEVER.
WATCH THE BOYS.
I GOTTA TAKE A FUCKING MONSTER CURRY DUMP.
I -
I JUST CLEANED THE TOILET...
NO WORRIES, DUDE.
SCENTED CANDLE.
MAHOGANY.
NOT MY FIRST RODEO.
BOYS, DADDY'LL BE BACK IN AN HOUR...

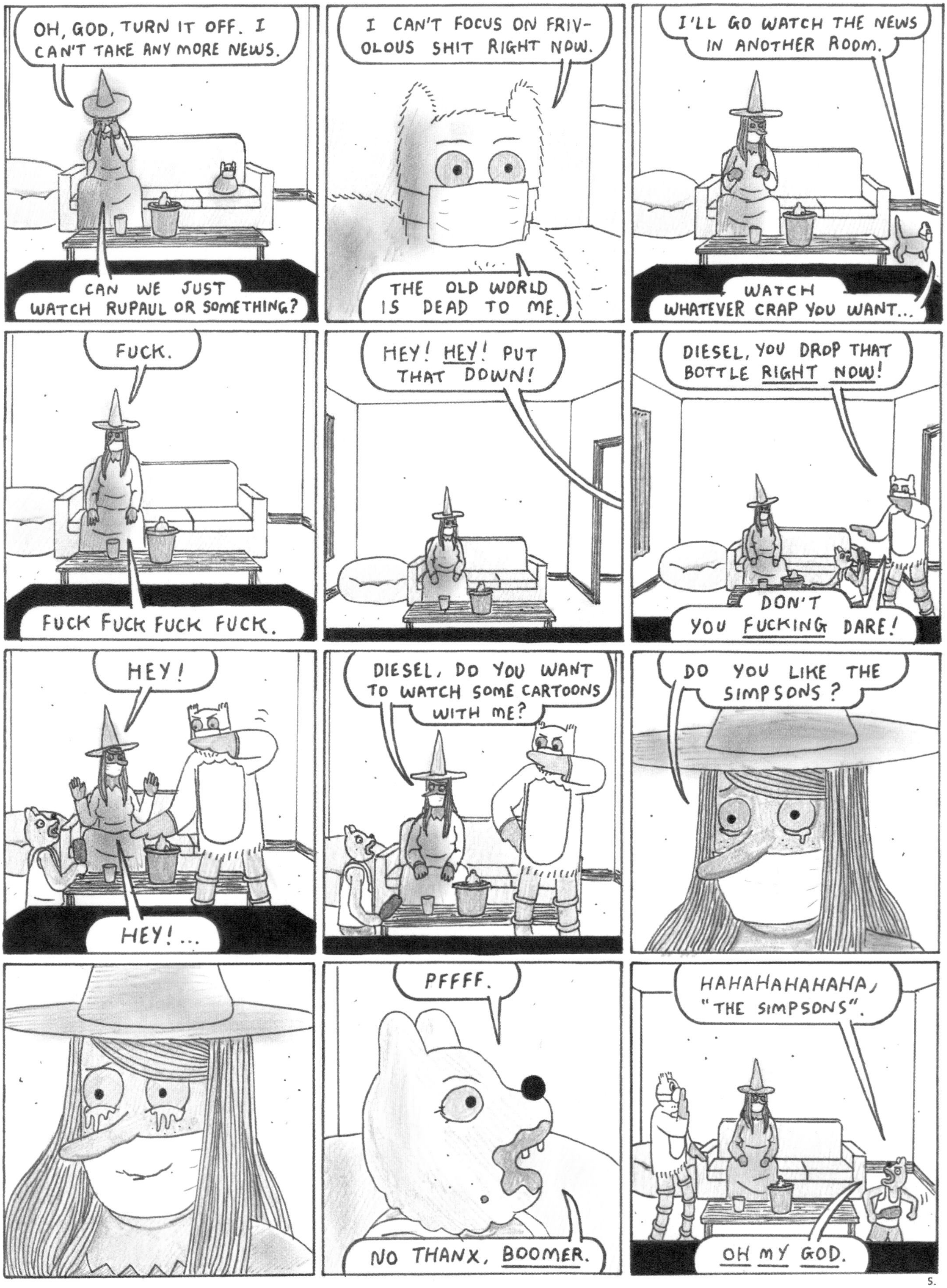
OH, GOD, TURN IT OFF. I CAN'T TAKE ANY MORE NEWS.
CAN WE JUST WATCH RUPAUL OR SOMETHING?
I CAN'T FOCUS ON FRIVOLOUS SHIT RIGHT NOW.
THE OLD WORLD IS DEAD TO ME.
I'LL GO WATCH THE NEWS IN ANOTHER ROOM.
WATCH WHATEVER CRAP YOU WANT...
FUCK.
FUCK FUCK FUCK FUCK.
HEY! HEY! PUT THAT DOWN!
DIESEL, YOU DROP THAT BOTTLE RIGHT NOW!
DON'T YOU FUCKING DARE!
HEY!
HEY! ...
DIESEL, DO YOU WANT TO WATCH SOME CARTOONS WITH ME?
DO YOU LIKE THE SIMPSONS?
PFFFF.
NO THANX, BOOMER.
HAHAHAHAHAHA, "THE SIMPSONS".
OH MY GOD.

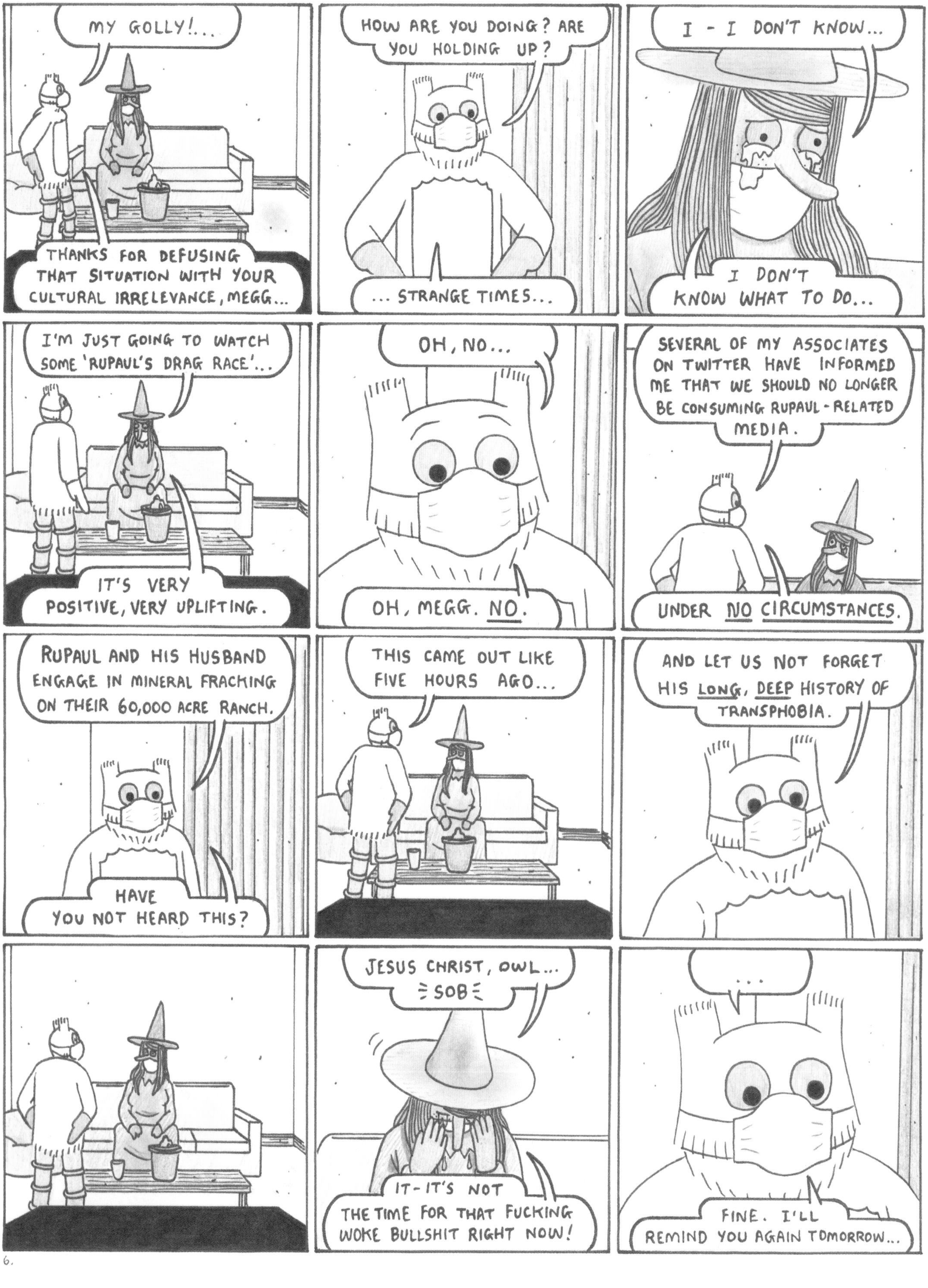

MY GOLLY!...
THANKS FOR DEFUSING THAT SITUATION WITH YOUR CULTURAL IRRELEVANCE, MEGG...
HOW ARE YOU DOING? ARE YOU HOLDING UP?
... STRANGE TIMES...
I - I DON'T KNOW...
I DON'T KNOW WHAT TO DO...
I'M JUST GOING TO WATCH SOME 'RUPAUL'S DRAG RACE'...
IT'S VERY POSITIVE, VERY UPLIFTING.
OH, NO...
OH, MEGG. NO.
SEVERAL OF MY ASSOCIATES ON TWITTER HAVE INFORMED ME THAT WE SHOULD NO LONGER BE CONSUMING RUPAUL-RELATED MEDIA.
UNDER NO CIRCUMSTANCES.
RUPAUL AND HIS HUSBAND ENGAGE IN MINERAL FRACKING ON THEIR 60,000 ACRE RANCH.
HAVE YOU NOT HEARD THIS?
THIS CAME OUT LIKE FIVE HOURS AGO...
AND LET US NOT FORGET HIS LONG, DEEP HISTORY OF TRANSPHOBIA.
JESUS CHRIST, OWL... SOB
IT-IT'S NOT THE TIME FOR THAT FUCKING WOKE BULLSHIT RIGHT NOW!
...
FINE. I'LL REMIND YOU AGAIN TOMORROW...

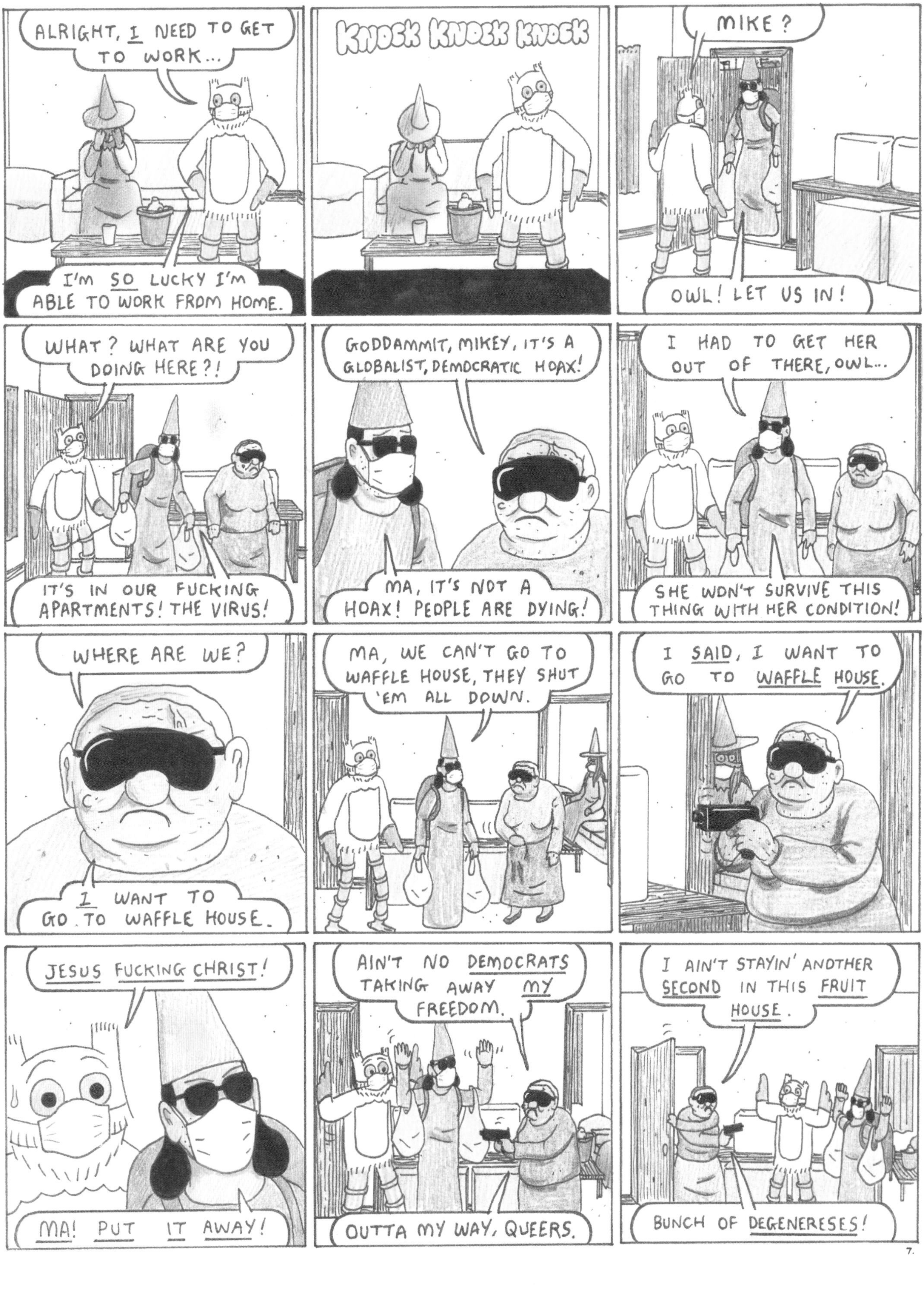
ALRIGHT, I NEED TO GET TO WORK...
I'M SO LUCKY I'M ABLE TO WORK FROM HOME.
KNOCK KNOCK KNOCK
MIKE?
OWL! LET US IN!
WHAT? WHAT ARE YOU DOING HERE?!
IT'S IN OUR FUCKING APARTMENTS! THE VIRUS!
GODDAMMIT, MIKEY, IT'S A GLOBALIST, DEMOCRATIC HOAX!
MA, IT'S NOT A HOAX! PEOPLE ARE DYING!
I HAD TO GET HER OUT OF THERE, OWL...
SHE WON'T SURVIVE THIS THING WITH HER CONDITION!
WHERE ARE WE?
I WANT TO GO TO WAFFLE HOUSE.
MA, WE CAN'T GO TO WAFFLE HOUSE, THEY SHUT 'EM ALL DOWN.
I SAID, I WANT TO GO TO WAFFLE HOUSE.
JESUS FUCKING CHRIST!
MA! PUT IT AWAY!
AIN'T NO DEMOCRATS TAKING AWAY MY FREEDOM.
OUTTA MY WAY, QUEERS.
I AIN'T STAYIN' ANOTHER SECOND IN THIS FRUIT HOUSE.
BUNCH OF DEGENERESES!

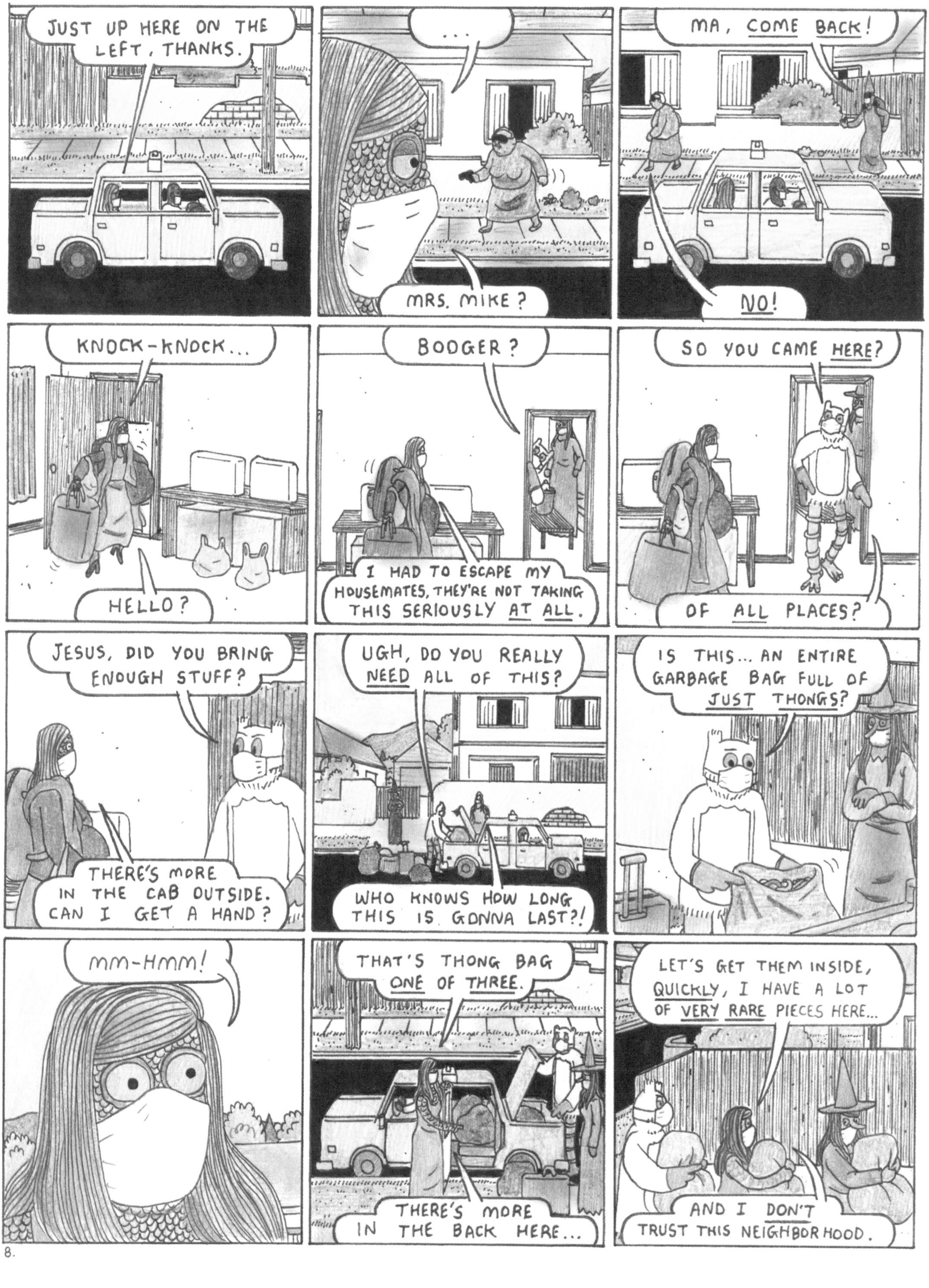
JUST UP HERE ON THE LEFT, THANKS.
...
MRS. MIKE?
MA, COME BACK!
NO!
KNOCK-KNOCK...
HELLO?
BOOGER?
I HAD TO ESCAPE MY HOUSEMATES, THEY'RE NOT TAKING THIS SERIOUSLY AT ALL.
SO YOU CAME HERE?
OF ALL PLACES?
JESUS, DID YOU BRING ENOUGH STUFF?
THERE'S MORE IN THE CAB OUTSIDE. CAN I GET A HAND?
UGH, DO YOU REALLY NEED ALL OF THIS?
WHO KNOWS HOW LONG THIS IS GONNA LAST?!
IS THIS... AN ENTIRE GARBAGE BAG FULL OF JUST THONGS?
MM-HMM!
THAT'S THONG BAG ONE OF THREE.
THERE'S MORE IN THE BACK HERE...
LET'S GET THEM INSIDE, QUICKLY, I HAVE A LOT OF VERY RARE PIECES HERE...
AND I DON'T TRUST THIS NEIGHBORHOOD.

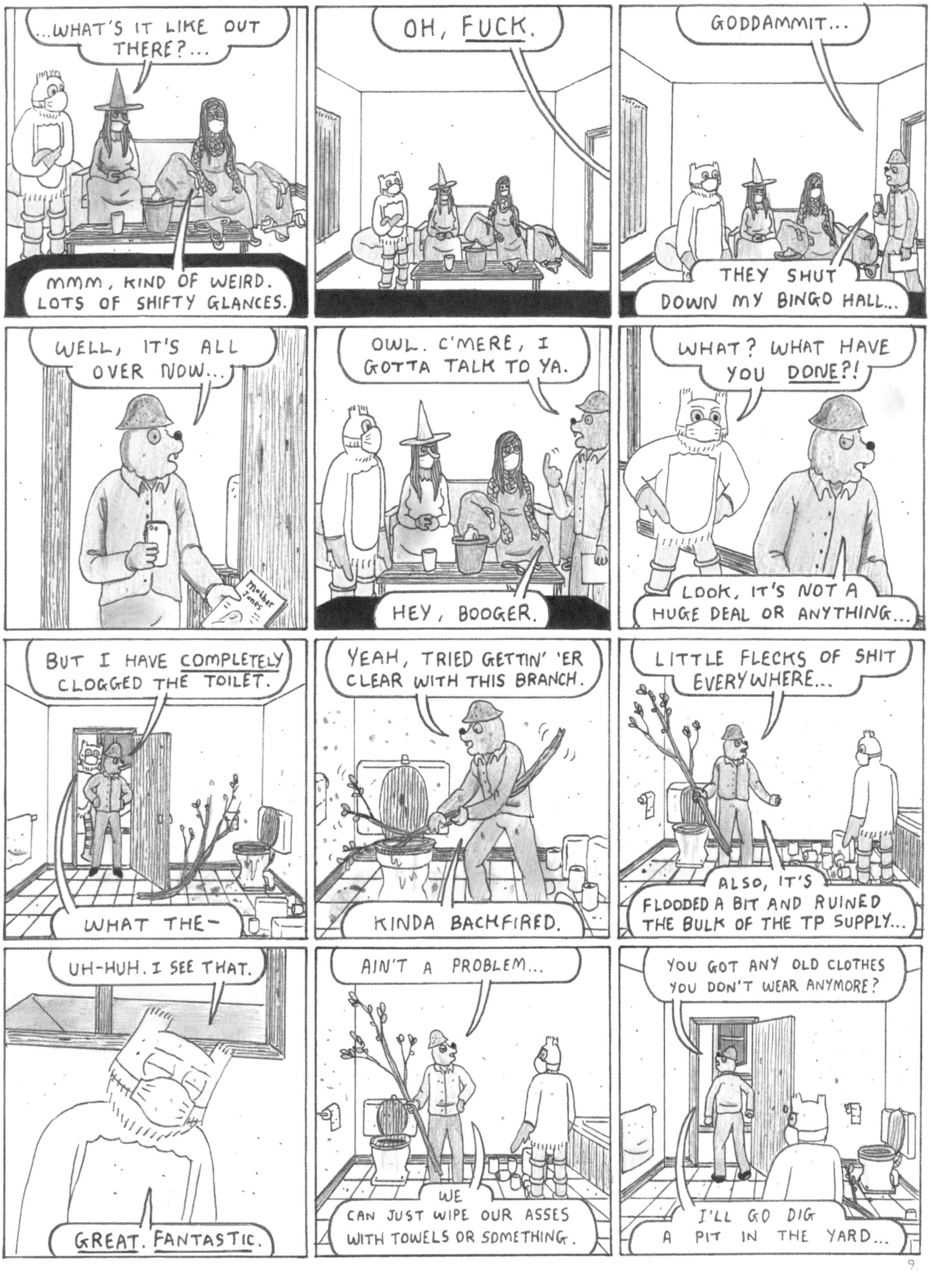

...WHAT'S IT LIKE OUT THERE?...
MMM, KIND OF WEIRD. LOTS OF SHIFTY GLANCES.
OH, FUCK.
GODDAMMIT...
THEY SHUT DOWN MY BINGO HALL...
WELL, IT'S ALL OVER NOW...
Mother Jones
OWL. C'MERE, I GOTTA TALK TO YA.
HEY, BOOGER.
WHAT? WHAT HAVE YOU DONE?!
LOOK, IT'S NOT A HUGE DEAL OR ANYTHING...
BUT I HAVE COMPLETELY CLOGGED THE TOILET.
WHAT THE-
YEAH, TRIED GETTIN' 'ER CLEAR WITH THIS BRANCH.
KINDA BACKFIRED.
LITTLE FLECKS OF SHIT EVERYWHERE...
ALSO, IT'S FLOODED A BIT AND RUINED THE BULK OF THE TP SUPPLY...
UH-HUH. I SEE THAT.
GREAT. FANTASTIC.
AIN'T A PROBLEM...
WE CAN JUST WIPE OUR ASSES WITH TOWELS OR SOMETHING.
YOU GOT ANY OLD CLOTHES YOU DON'T WEAR ANYMORE?
I'LL GO DIG A PIT IN THE YARD...

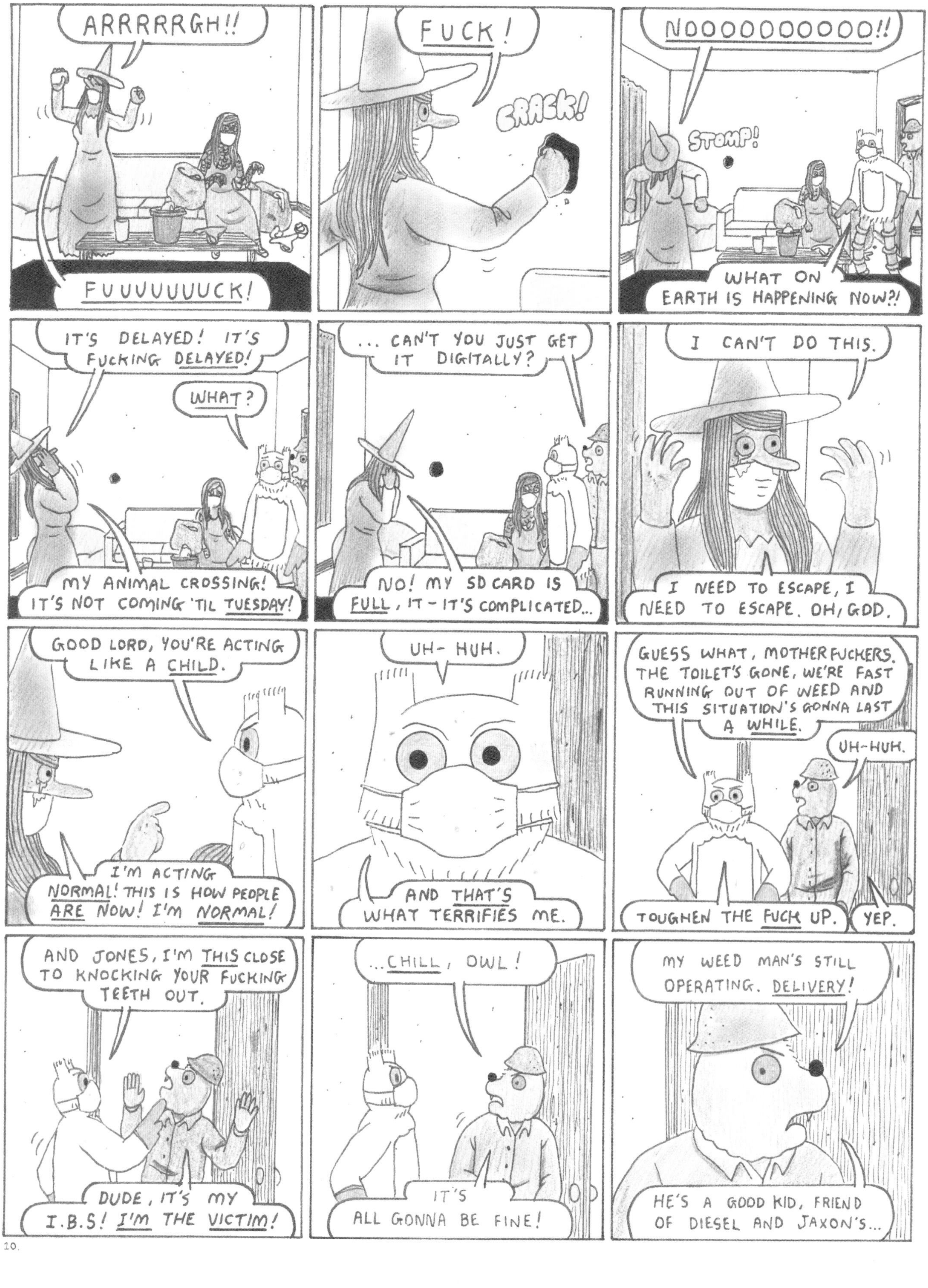

ARRRRRGH!!
FUUUUUUUCK!
FUCK!
CRACK!
NOOOOOOOOOO!!
STOMP!
WHAT ON EARTH IS HAPPENING NOW?!
IT'S DELAYED! IT'S FUCKING DELAYED!
WHAT?
MY ANIMAL CROSSING! IT'S NOT COMING 'TIL TUESDAY!
... CAN'T YOU JUST GET IT DIGITALLY?
NO! MY SD CARD IS FULL, IT - IT'S COMPLICATED...
I CAN'T DO THIS.
I NEED TO ESCAPE, I NEED TO ESCAPE. OH, GOD.
GOOD LORD, YOU'RE ACTING LIKE A CHILD.
I'M ACTING NORMAL! THIS IS HOW PEOPLE ARE NOW! I'M NORMAL!
UH- HUH.
AND THAT'S WHAT TERRIFIES ME.
GUESS WHAT, MOTHERFUCKERS. THE TOILET'S GONE, WE'RE FAST RUNNING OUT OF WEED AND THIS SITUATION'S GONNA LAST A WHILE.
UH-HUH.
TOUGHEN THE FUCK UP.
YEP.
AND JONES, I'M THIS CLOSE TO KNOCKING YOUR FUCKING TEETH OUT.
DUDE, IT'S MY I.B.S! I'M THE VICTIM!
...CHILL, OWL!
IT'S ALL GONNA BE FINE!
MY WEED MAN'S STILL OPERATING. DELIVERY!
HE'S A GOOD KID, FRIEND OF DIESEL AND JAXON'S...

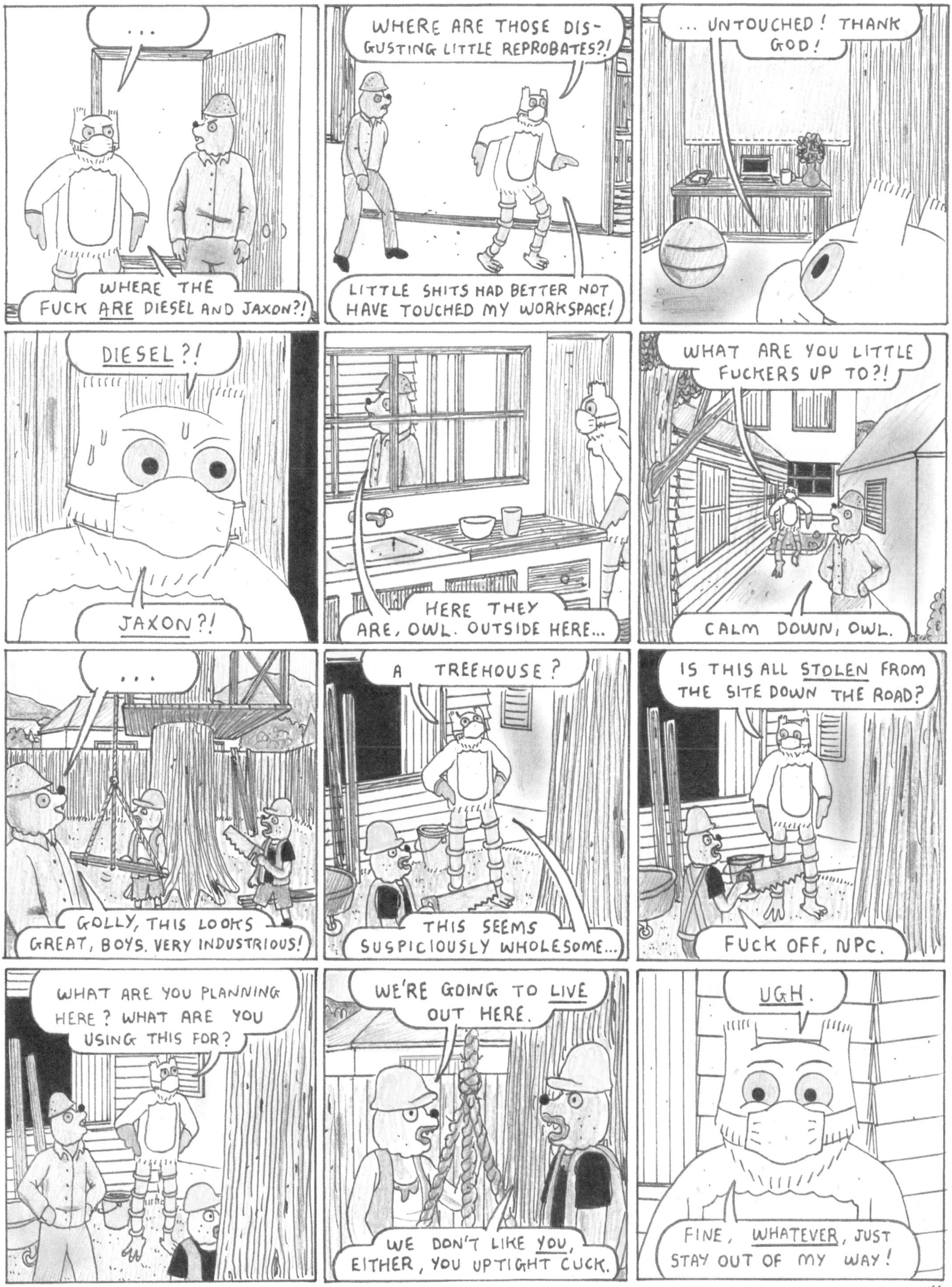
...
WHERE THE FUCK ARE DIESEL AND JAXON?!
WHERE ARE THOSE DISGUSTING LITTLE REPROBATES?!
LITTLE SHITS HAD BETTER NOT HAVE TOUCHED MY WORKSPACE!
... UNTOUCHED! THANK GOD!
DIESEL?!
JAXON?!
HERE THEY ARE, OWL. OUTSIDE HERE...
WHAT ARE YOU LITTLE FUCKERS UP TO?!
CALM DOWN, OWL.
...
GOLLY, THIS LOOKS GREAT, BOYS. VERY INDUSTRIOUS!
A TREEHOUSE?
THIS SEEMS SUSPICIOUSLY WHOLESOME...
IS THIS ALL STOLEN FROM THE SITE DOWN THE ROAD?
FUCK OFF, NPC.
WHAT ARE YOU PLANNING HERE? WHAT ARE YOU USING THIS FOR?
WE'RE GOING TO LIVE OUT HERE.
WE DON'T LIKE YOU, EITHER, YOU UPTIGHT CUCK.
UGH.
FINE, WHATEVER, JUST STAY OUT OF MY WAY!

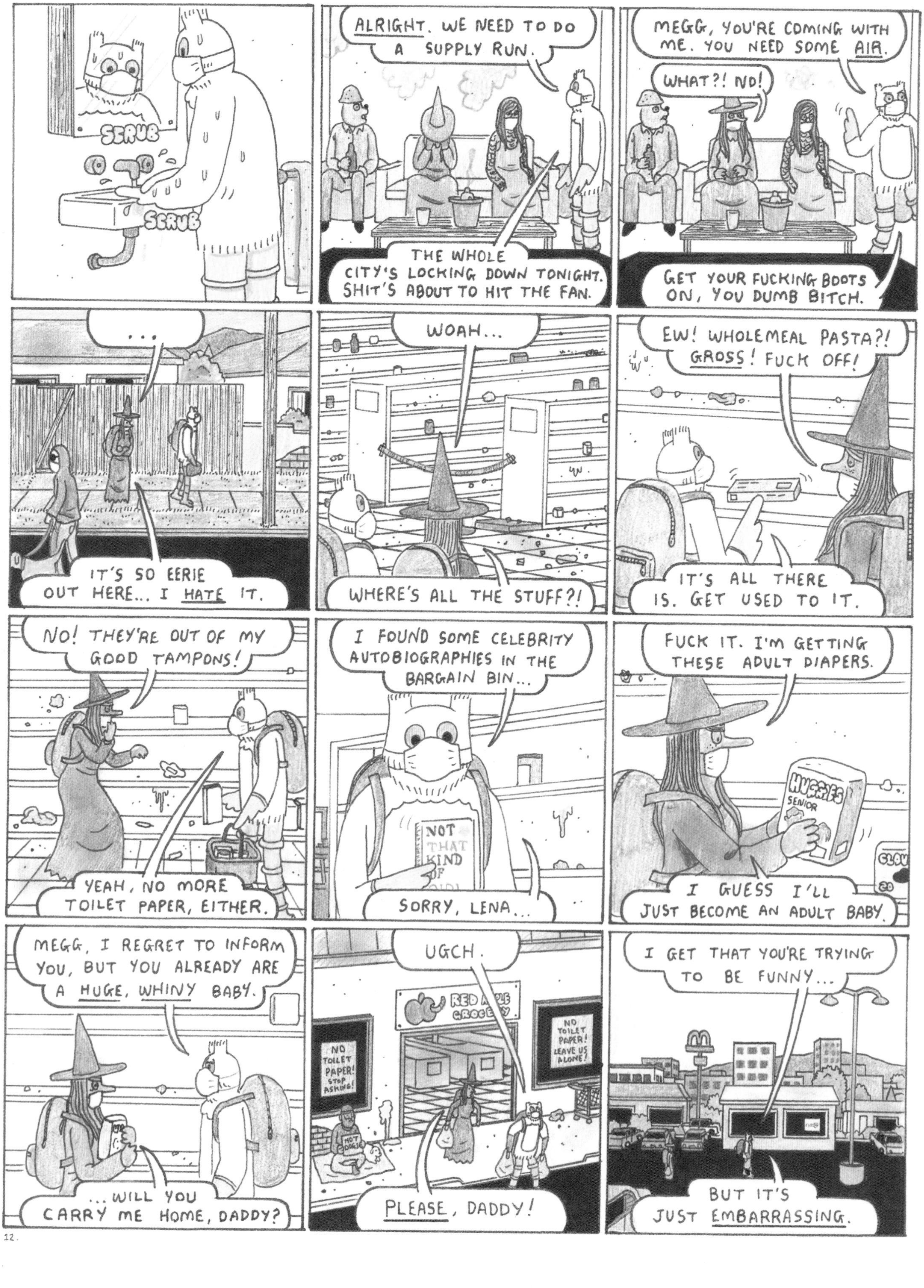
SCRUB
SCRUB
ALRIGHT. WE NEED TO DO A SUPPLY RUN.
THE WHOLE CITY'S LOCKING DOWN TONIGHT. SHIT'S ABOUT TO HIT THE FAN.
MEGG, YOU'RE COMING WITH ME. YOU NEED SOME AIR.
WHAT?! NO!
GET YOUR FUCKING BOOTS ON, YOU DUMB BITCH.
...
IT'S SO EERIE OUT HERE... I HATE IT.
WOAH...
WHERE'S ALL THE STUFF?!
EW! WHOLEMEAL PASTA?! GROSS! FUCK OFF!
IT'S ALL THERE IS. GET USED TO IT.
NO! THEY'RE OUT OF MY GOOD TAMPONS!
YEAH, NO MORE TOILET PAPER, EITHER.
I FOUND SOME CELEBRITY AUTOBIOGRAPHIES IN THE BARGAIN BIN...
NOT THAT KIND
SORRY, LENA...
FUCK IT. I'M GETTING THESE ADULT DIAPERS.
SENIOR
I GUESS I'LL JUST BECOME AN ADULT BABY.
MEGG, I REGRET TO INFORM YOU, BUT YOU ALREADY ARE A HUGE, WHINY BABY.
...WILL YOU CARRY ME HOME, DADDY?
UGCH.
NO TOILET PAPER! STOP ASKING!
NO TOILET PAPER! LEAVE US ALONE!
PLEASE, DADDY!
I GET THAT YOU'RE TRYING TO BE FUNNY...
BUT IT'S JUST EMBARRASSING.

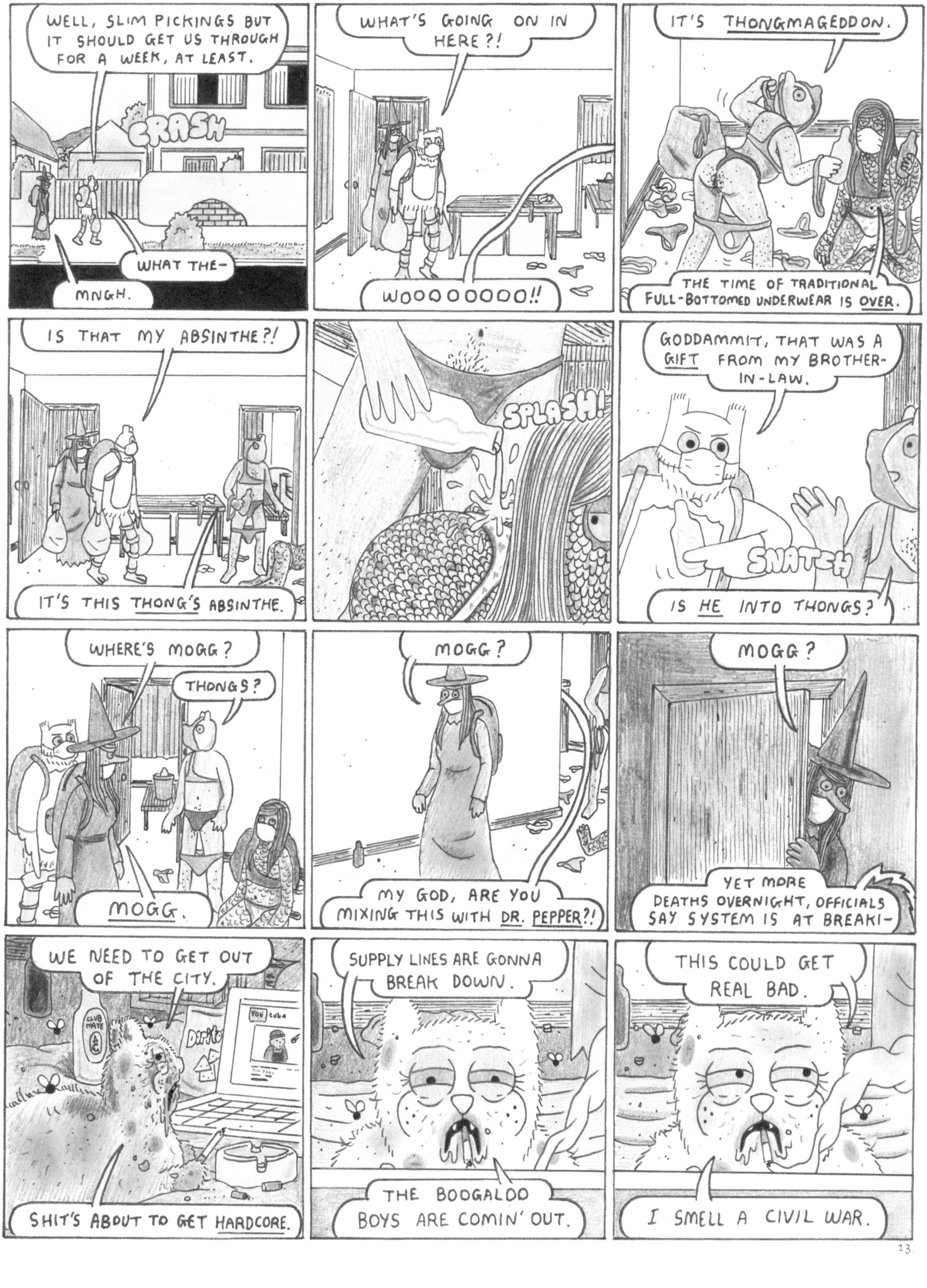
WELL, SLIM PICKINGS BUT IT SHOULD GET US THROUGH FOR A WEEK, AT LEAST.
CRASH
WHAT THE-
MNGH.
WHAT'S GOING ON IN HERE?!
WOOOOOOOO!!
IT'S THONGMAGEDDON.
THE TIME OF TRADITIONAL FULL-BOTTOMED UNDERWEAR IS OVER.
IS THAT MY ABSINTHE?!
IT'S THIS THONG'S ABSINTHE.
SPLASH!
GODDAMMIT, THAT WAS A GIFT FROM MY BROTHER-IN-LAW.
SNATCH
IS HE INTO THONGS?
WHERE'S MOGG?
THONGS?
MOGG.
MOGG?
MY GOD, ARE YOU MIXING THIS WITH DR. PEPPER?!
MOGG?
YET MORE DEATHS OVERNIGHT, OFFICIALS SAY SYSTEM IS AT BREAKI-
WE NEED TO GET OUT OF THE CITY.
CLUB MATE
SHIT'S ABOUT TO GET HARDCORE.
SUPPLY LINES ARE GONNA BREAK DOWN.
THE BOOGALOO BOYS ARE COMIN' OUT.
THIS COULD GET REAL BAD.
I SMELL A CIVIL WAR.

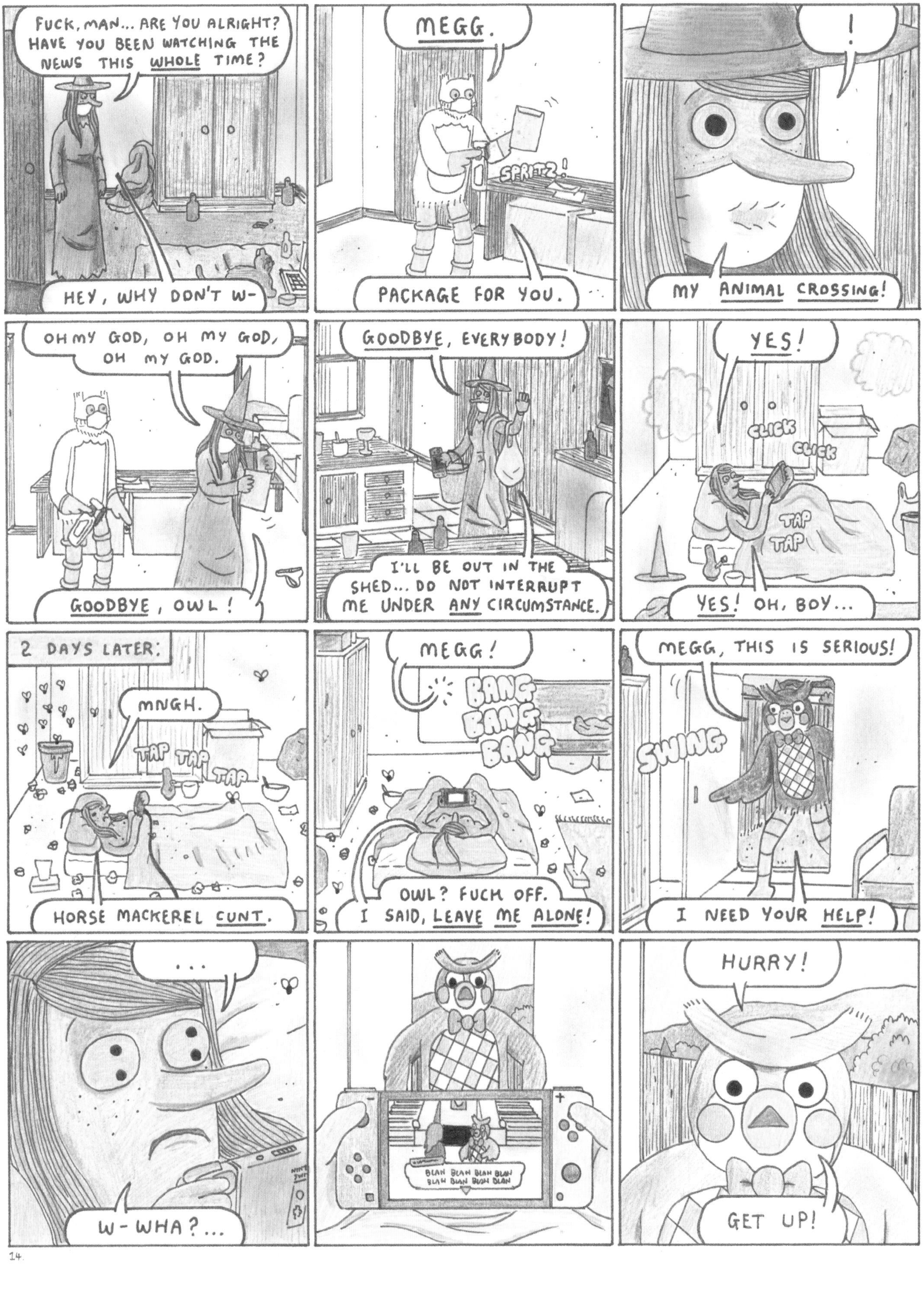

FUCK, MAN... ARE YOU ALRIGHT? HAVE YOU BEEN WATCHING THE NEWS THIS WHOLE TIME?
HEY, WHY DON'T W-
MEGG.
SPRITZ!
PACKAGE FOR YOU.
!
MY ANIMAL CROSSING!
OH MY GOD, OH MY GOD, OH MY GOD.
GOODBYE, OWL!
GOODBYE, EVERYBODY!
I'LL BE OUT IN THE SHED... DO NOT INTERRUPT ME UNDER ANY CIRCUMSTANCE.
YES!
CLICK
CLICK
TAP
TAP
YES! OH, BOY...
2 DAYS LATER:
MNGH.
TAP TAP TAP
HORSE MACKEREL CUNT.
MEGG!
BANG
BANG
BANG
OWL? FUCK OFF. I SAID, LEAVE ME ALONE!
MEGG, THIS IS SERIOUS!
SWING
I NEED YOUR HELP!
...
W-WHA?...
HURRY!
GET UP!

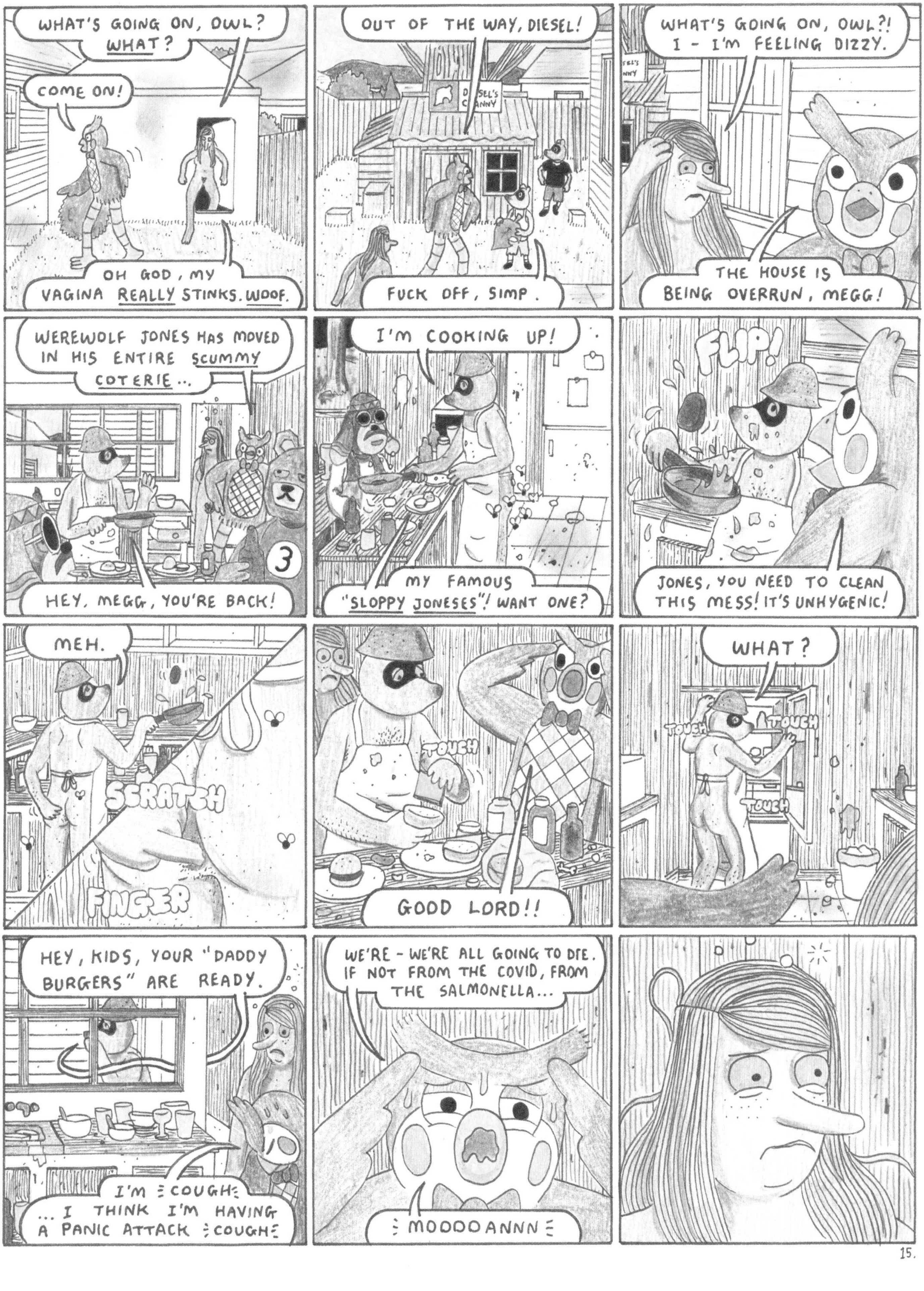
WHAT'S GOING ON, OWL? WHAT?
COME ON!
OH GOD, MY VAGINA REALLY STINKS. WOOF.
OUT OF THE WAY, DIESEL!
FUCK OFF, SIMP.
WHAT'S GOING ON, OWL?! I - I'M FEELING DIZZY.
THE HOUSE IS BEING OVERRUN, MEGG!
WEREWOLF JONES HAS MOVED IN HIS ENTIRE SCUMMY COTERIE...
3
HEY, MEGG, YOU'RE BACK!
I'M COOKING UP!
MY FAMOUS "SLOPPY JONESES"! WANT ONE?
FLIP!
JONES, YOU NEED TO CLEAN THIS MESS! IT'S UNHYGENIC!
MEH.
SCRATCH
FINGER
TOUCH
GOOD LORD!!
WHAT?
TOUCH
TOUCH
TOUCH
HEY, KIDS, YOUR "DADDY BURGERS" ARE READY.
I'M COUGH ... I THINK I'M HAVING A PANIC ATTACK COUGH
WE'RE - WE'RE ALL GOING TO DIE. IF NOT FROM THE COVID, FROM THE SALMONELLA...
MOOOOANNN

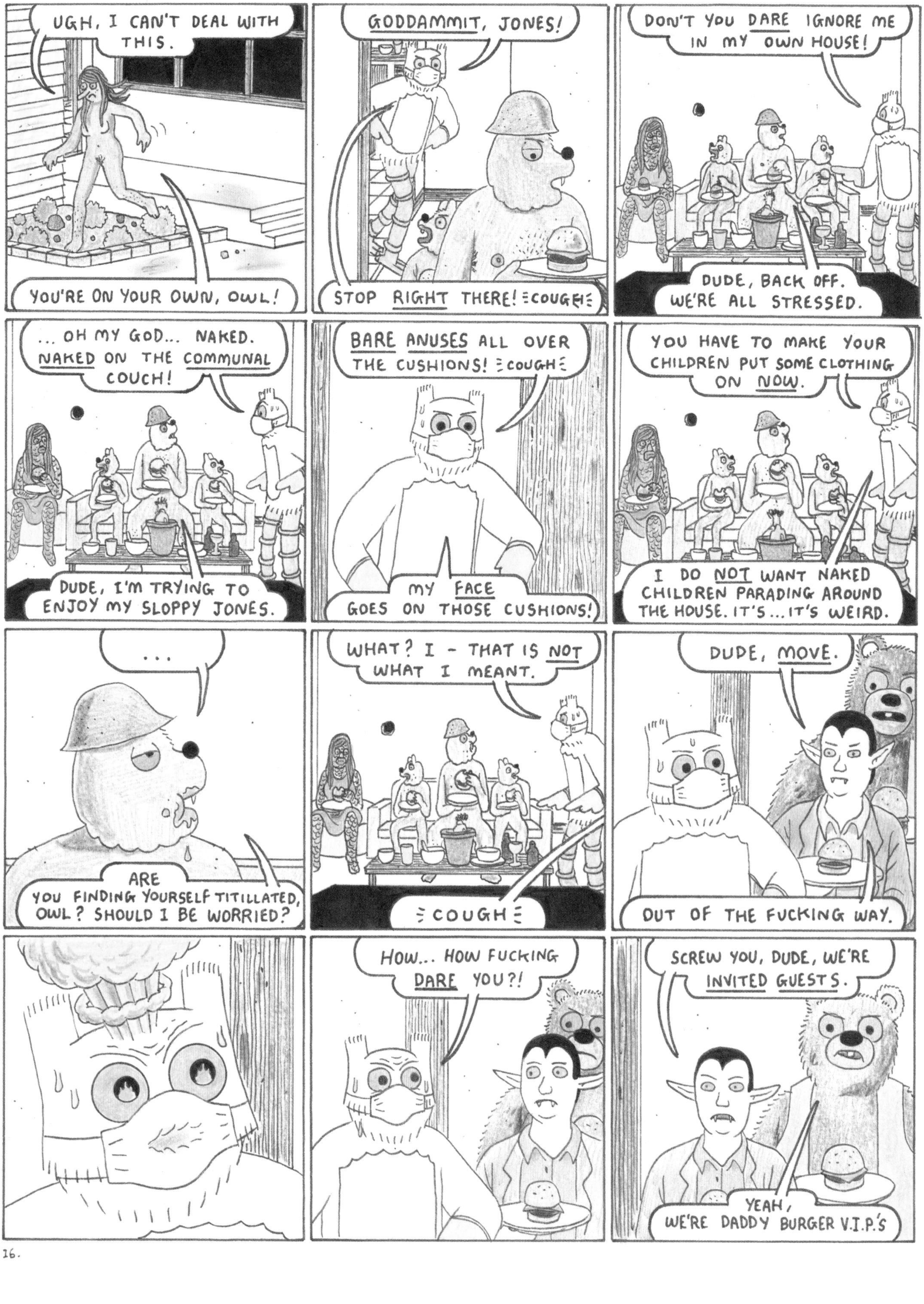
UGH, I CAN'T DEAL WITH THIS.
YOU'RE ON YOUR OWN, OWL!
GODDAMMIT, JONES!
STOP RIGHT THERE! ⁝COUGH⁝
DON'T YOU DARE IGNORE ME IN MY OWN HOUSE!
DUDE, BACK OFF. WE'RE ALL STRESSED.
... OH MY GOD... NAKED. NAKED ON THE COMMUNAL COUCH!
DUDE, I'M TRYING TO ENJOY MY SLOPPY JONES.
BARE ANUSES ALL OVER THE CUSHIONS! ⁝COUGH⁝
MY FACE GOES ON THOSE CUSHIONS!
YOU HAVE TO MAKE YOUR CHILDREN PUT SOME CLOTHING ON NOW.
I DO NOT WANT NAKED CHILDREN PARADING AROUND THE HOUSE. IT'S... IT'S WEIRD.
...
ARE YOU FINDING YOURSELF TITILLATED, OWL? SHOULD I BE WORRIED?
WHAT? I - THAT IS NOT WHAT I MEANT.
⁝COUGH⁝
DUDE, MOVE.
OUT OF THE FUCKING WAY.
HOW... HOW FUCKING DARE YOU?!
SCREW YOU, DUDE, WE'RE INVITED GUESTS.
YEAH, WE'RE DADDY BURGER V.I.P.'S

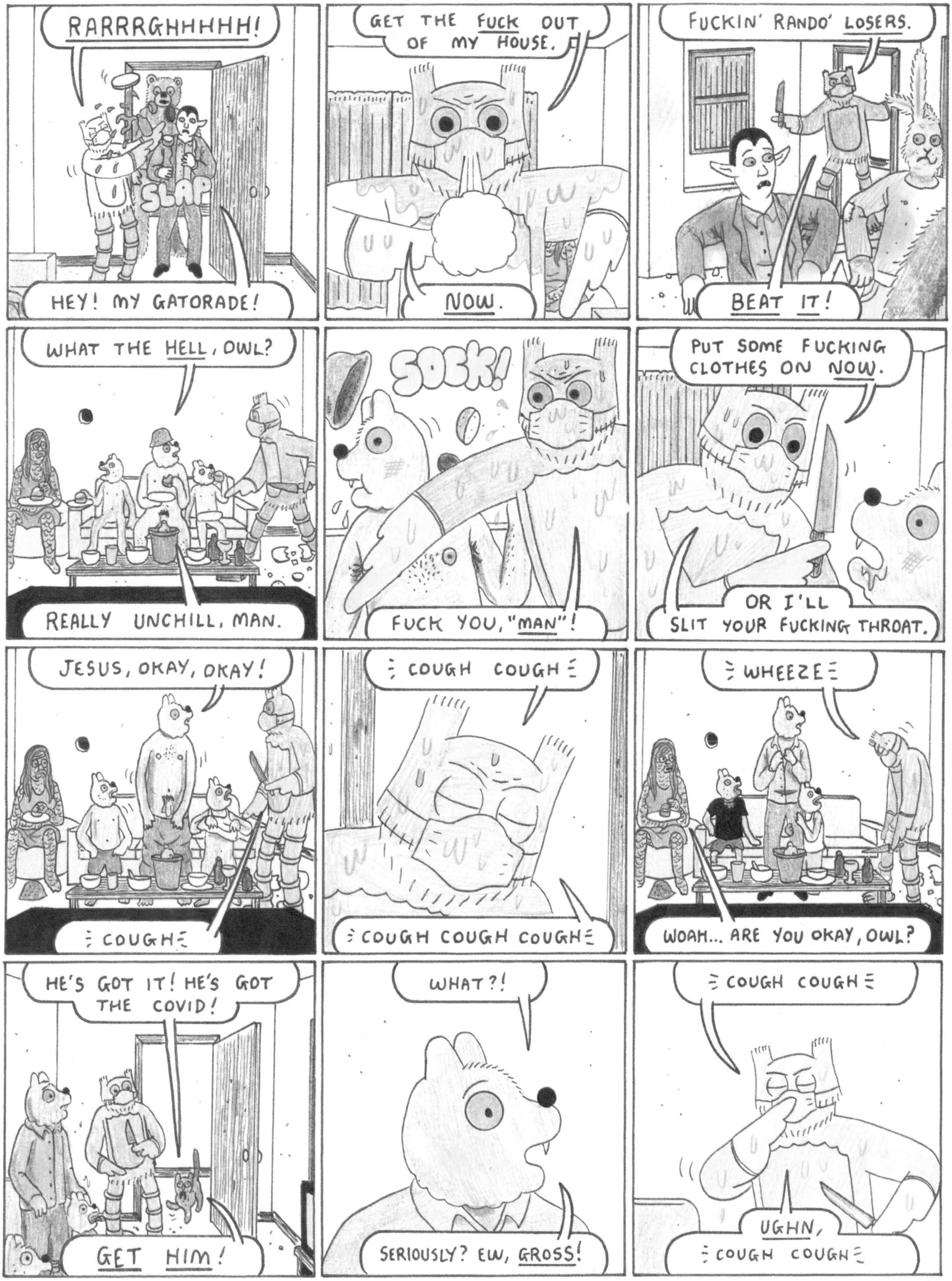
RARRRGHHHHH!
SLAP
HEY! MY GATORADE!
GET THE FUCK OUT OF MY HOUSE.
NOW.
FUCKIN' RANDO' LOSERS.
BEAT IT!
WHAT THE HELL, OWL?
REALLY UNCHILL, MAN.
SOCK!
FUCK YOU, "MAN"!
PUT SOME FUCKING CLOTHES ON NOW.
OR I'LL SLIT YOUR FUCKING THROAT.
JESUS, OKAY, OKAY!
COUGH
COUGH COUGH
COUGH COUGH COUGH
WHEEZE
WOAH... ARE YOU OKAY, OWL?
HE'S GOT IT! HE'S GOT THE COVID!
GET HIM!
WHAT?!
SERIOUSLY? EW, GROSS!
COUGH COUGH
UGHN,
COUGH COUGH

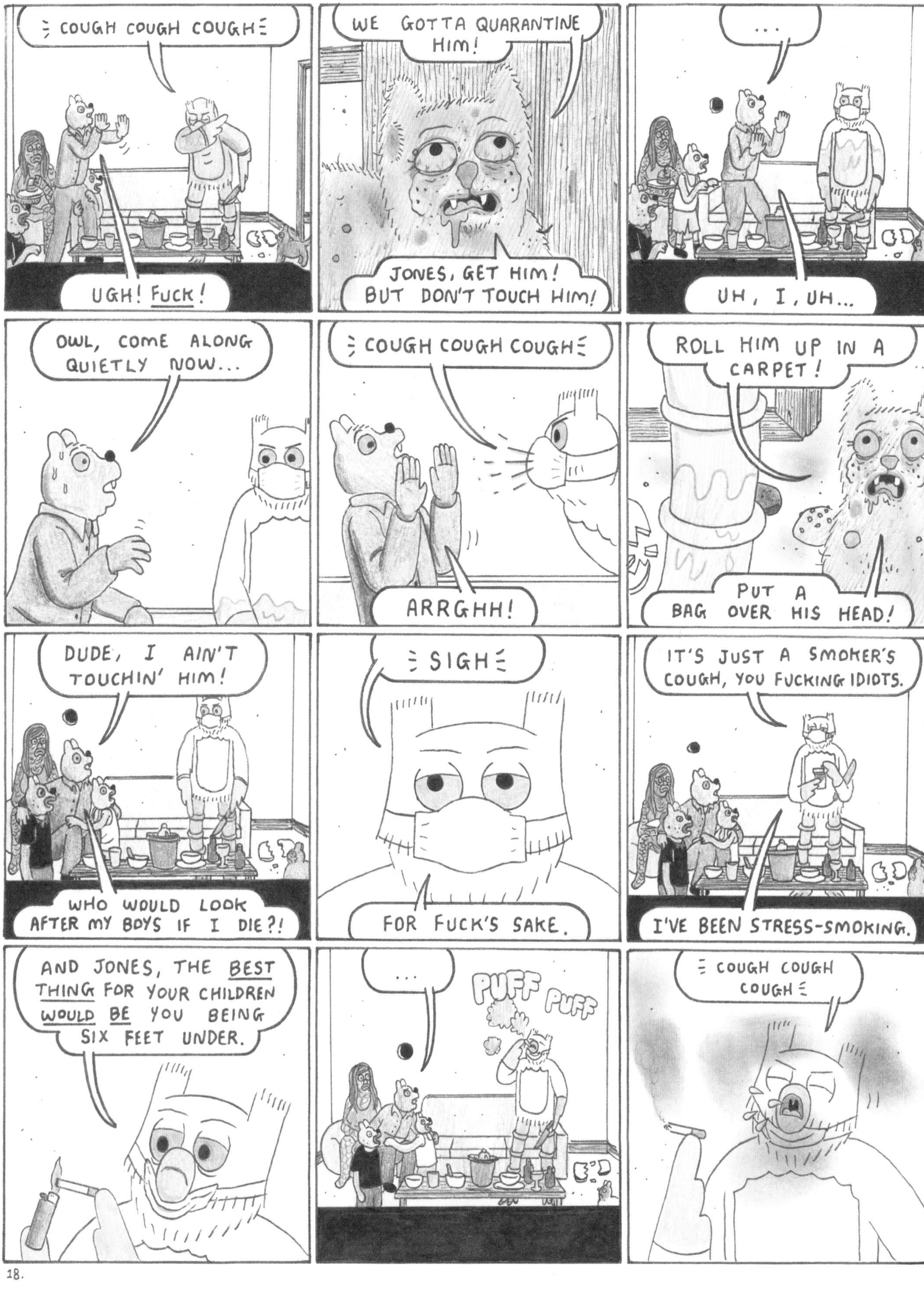
COUGH COUGH COUGH
UGH! FUCK!
WE GOTTA QUARANTINE HIM!
JONES, GET HIM! BUT DON'T TOUCH HIM!
...
UH, I, UH...
OWL, COME ALONG QUIETLY NOW...
COUGH COUGH COUGH
ARRGHH!
ROLL HIM UP IN A CARPET!
PUT A BAG OVER HIS HEAD!
DUDE, I AIN'T TOUCHIN' HIM!
WHO WOULD LOOK AFTER MY BOYS IF I DIE?!
SIGH
FOR FUCK'S SAKE.
IT'S JUST A SMOKER'S COUGH, YOU FUCKING IDIOTS.
I'VE BEEN STRESS-SMOKING.
AND JONES, THE BEST THING FOR YOUR CHILDREN WOULD BE YOU BEING SIX FEET UNDER.
...
PUFF PUFF
COUGH COUGH COUGH

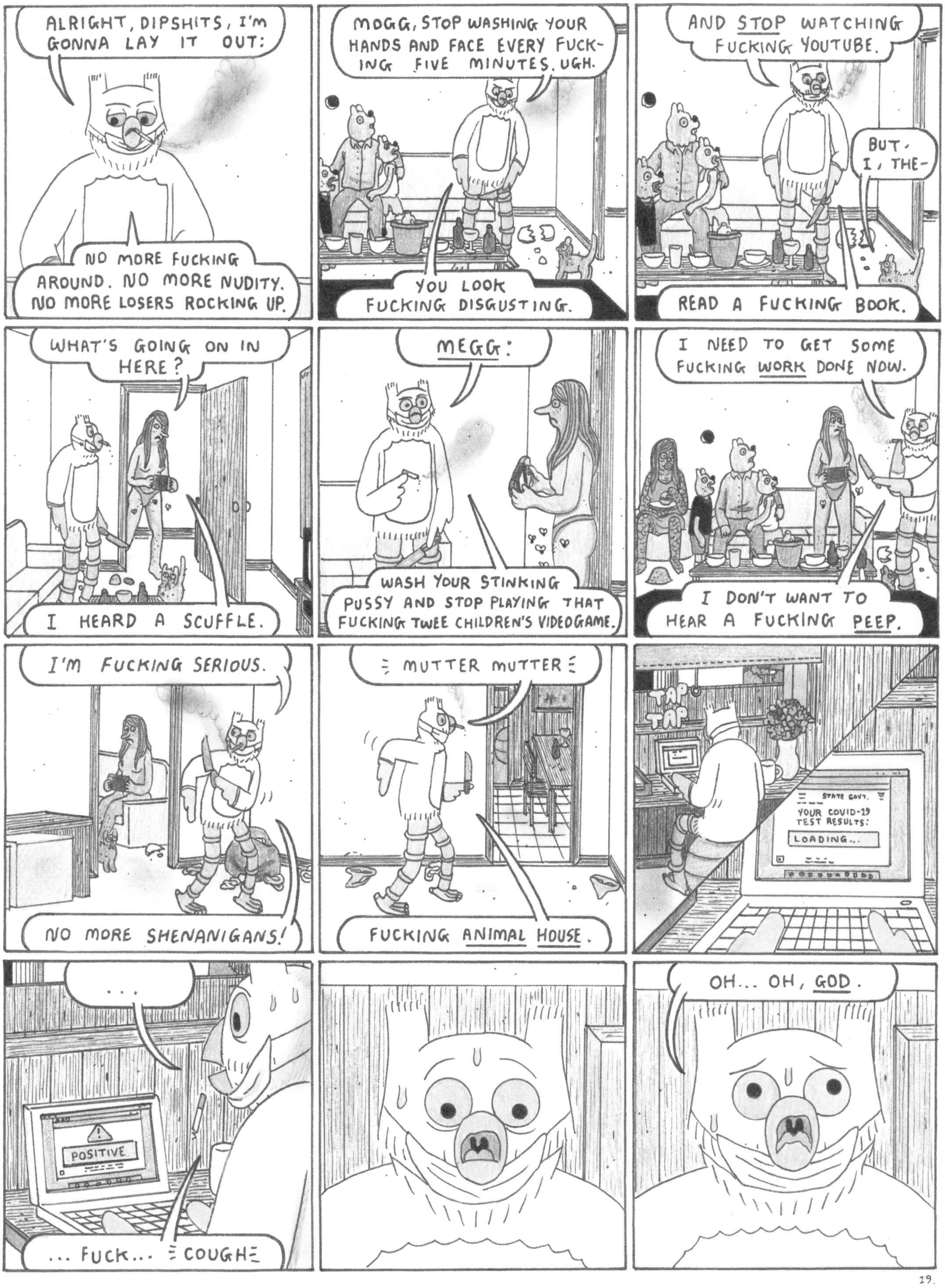
ALRIGHT, DIPSHITS, I'M GONNA LAY IT OUT:
NO MORE FUCKING AROUND. NO MORE NUDITY. NO MORE LOSERS ROCKING UP.
MOGG, STOP WASHING YOUR HANDS AND FACE EVERY FUCK-ING FIVE MINUTES. UGH.
YOU LOOK FUCKING DISGUSTING.
AND STOP WATCHING FUCKING YOUTUBE.
BUT, I, THE-
READ A FUCKING BOOK.
WHAT'S GOING ON IN HERE?
I HEARD A SCUFFLE.
MEGG:
WASH YOUR STINKING PUSSY AND STOP PLAYING THAT FUCKING TWEE CHILDREN'S VIDEOGAME.
I NEED TO GET SOME FUCKING WORK DONE NOW.
I DON'T WANT TO HEAR A FUCKING PEEP.
I'M FUCKING SERIOUS.
NO MORE SHENANIGANS!
MUTTER MUTTER
FUCKING ANIMAL HOUSE.
TAP TAP
STATE GOVT.
YOUR COVID-19 TEST RESULTS:
LOADING...
...
POSITIVE
... FUCK... COUGH
OH... OH, GOD.

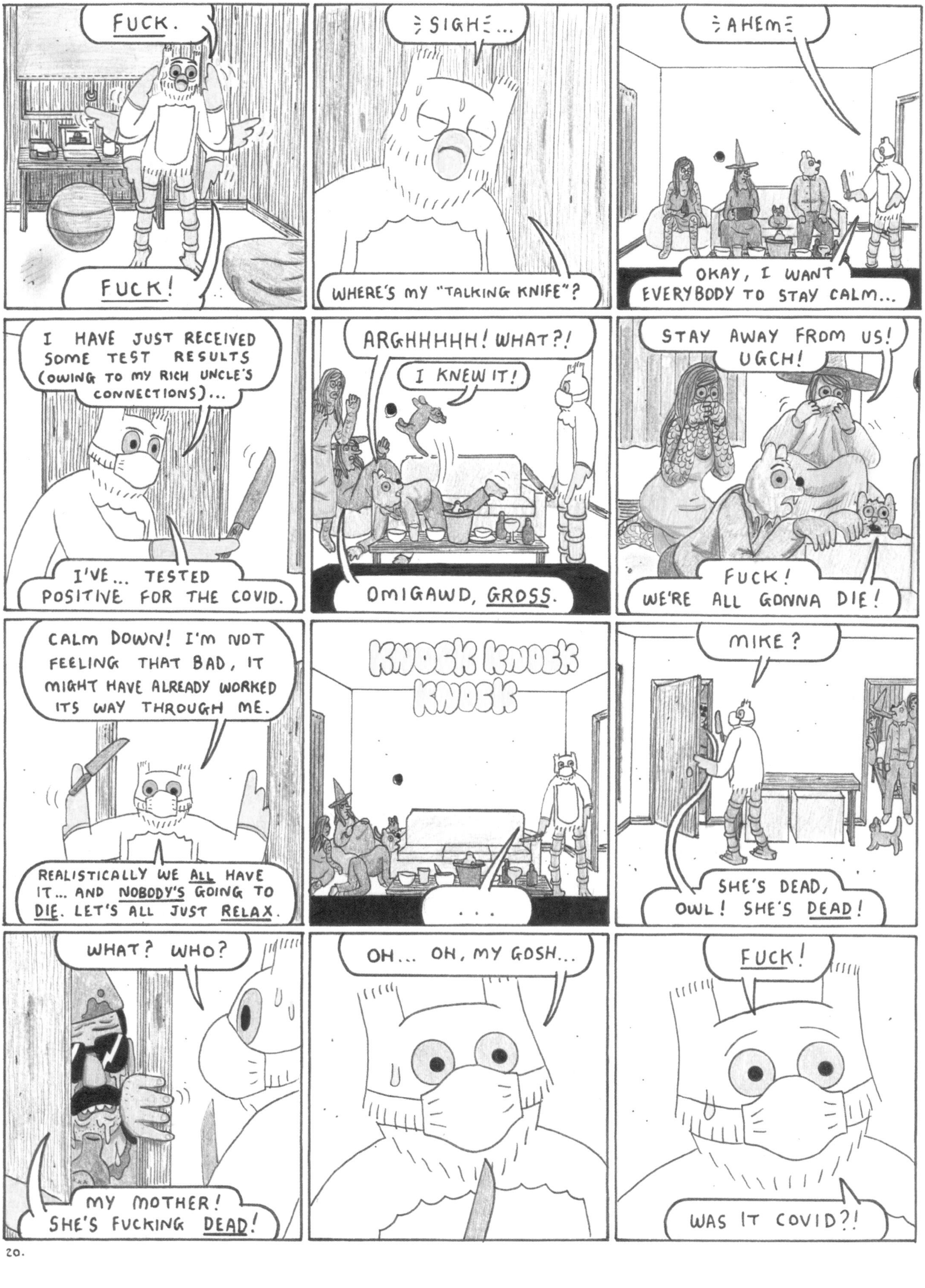
FUCK.
FUCK!
SIGH...
WHERE'S MY "TALKING KNIFE"?
AHEM
OKAY, I WANT EVERYBODY TO STAY CALM...
I HAVE JUST RECEIVED SOME TEST RESULTS (OWING TO MY RICH UNCLE'S CONNECTIONS)...
I'VE... TESTED POSITIVE FOR THE COVID.
ARGHHHHH! WHAT?!
I KNEW IT!
OMIGAWD, GROSS.
STAY AWAY FROM US! UGCH!
FUCK! WE'RE ALL GONNA DIE!
CALM DOWN! I'M NOT FEELING THAT BAD, IT MIGHT HAVE ALREADY WORKED ITS WAY THROUGH ME.
REALISTICALLY WE ALL HAVE IT... AND NOBODY'S GOING TO DIE. LET'S ALL JUST RELAX.
KNOCK KNOCK KNOCK
...
MIKE?
SHE'S DEAD, OWL! SHE'S DEAD!
WHAT? WHO?
MY MOTHER! SHE'S FUCKING DEAD!
OH... OH, MY GOSH...
FUCK!
WAS IT COVID?!

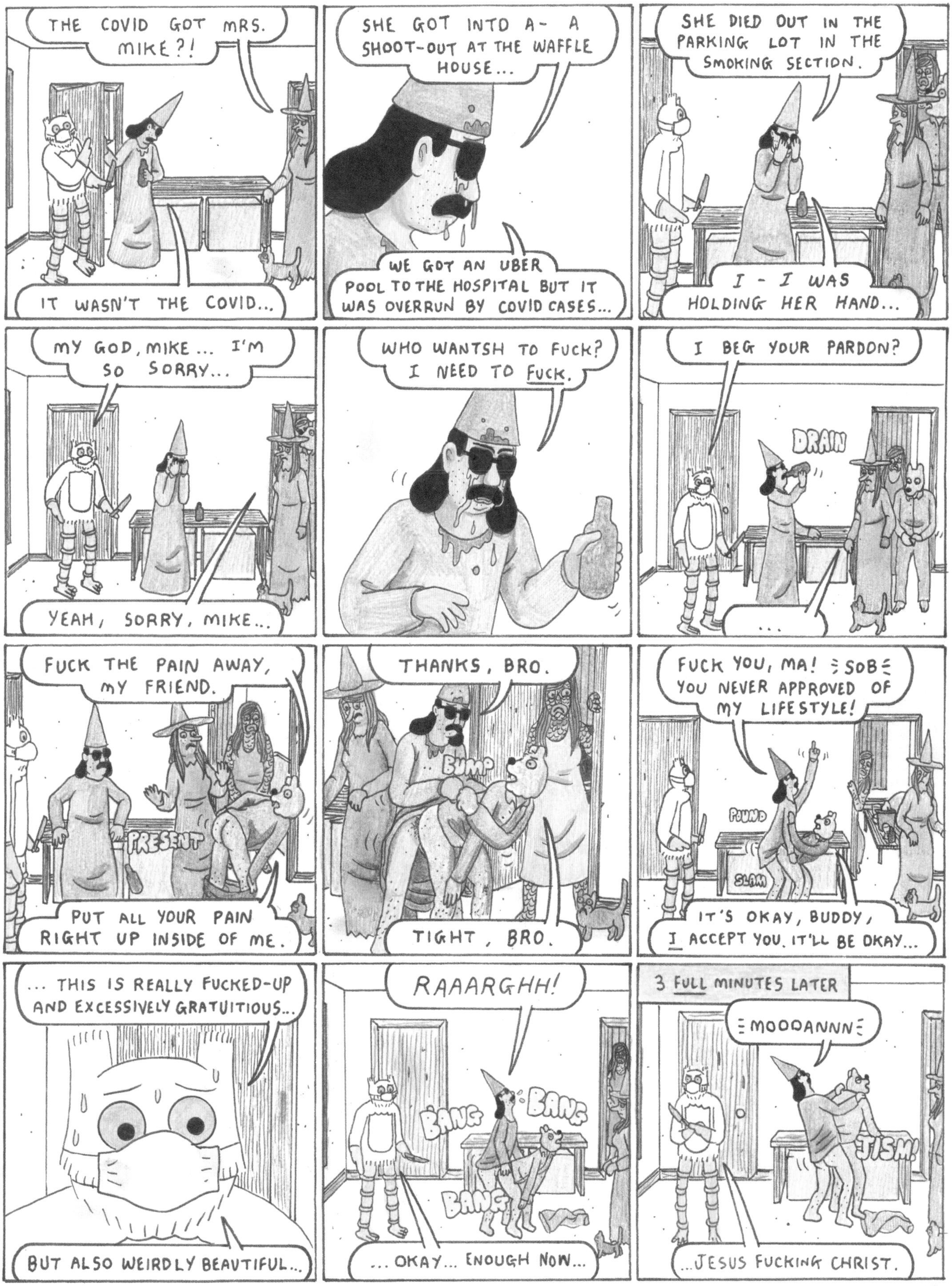
THE COVID GOT MRS. MIKE?!
IT WASN'T THE COVID...
SHE GOT INTO A- A SHOOT-OUT AT THE WAFFLE HOUSE...
WE GOT AN UBER POOL TO THE HOSPITAL BUT IT WAS OVERRUN BY COVID CASES...
SHE DIED OUT IN THE PARKING LOT IN THE SMOKING SECTION.
I - I WAS HOLDING HER HAND...
MY GOD, MIKE... I'M SO SORRY...
YEAH, SORRY, MIKE...
WHO WANTSH TO FUCK? I NEED TO FUCK.
I BEG YOUR PARDON?
DRAIN
...
FUCK THE PAIN AWAY, MY FRIEND.
PRESENT
PUT ALL YOUR PAIN RIGHT UP INSIDE OF ME.
THANKS, BRO.
BUMP
TIGHT, BRO.
FUCK YOU, MA! SOB YOU NEVER APPROVED OF MY LIFESTYLE!
POUND
SLAM
IT'S OKAY, BUDDY, I ACCEPT YOU. IT'LL BE OKAY...
... THIS IS REALLY FUCKED-UP AND EXCESSIVELY GRATUITIOUS...
BUT ALSO WEIRDLY BEAUTIFUL...
RAAARGHH!
BANG
BANG
BANG
... OKAY... ENOUGH NOW...
3 FULL MINUTES LATER
MOOOANNN
JISM!
...JESUS FUCKING CHRIST.

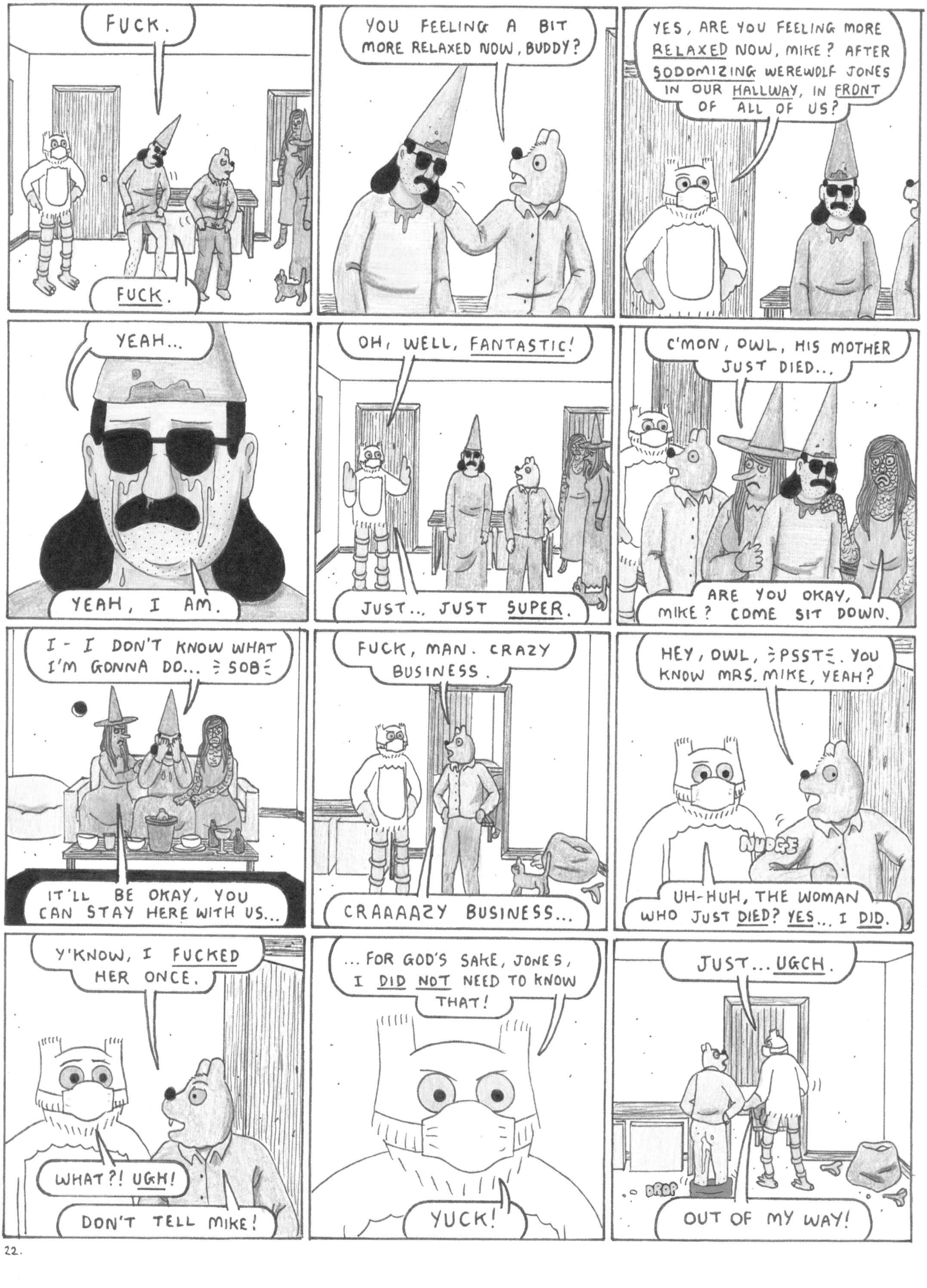

FUCK.
FUCK.
YOU FEELING A BIT MORE RELAXED NOW, BUDDY?
YES, ARE YOU FEELING MORE RELAXED NOW, MIKE? AFTER SODOMIZING WEREWOLF JONES IN OUR HALLWAY, IN FRONT OF ALL OF US?
YEAH...
YEAH, I AM.
OH, WELL, FANTASTIC!
JUST... JUST SUPER.
C'MON, OWL, HIS MOTHER JUST DIED...
ARE YOU OKAY, MIKE? COME SIT DOWN.
I - I DON'T KNOW WHAT I'M GONNA DO... SOB
IT'LL BE OKAY, YOU CAN STAY HERE WITH US...
FUCK, MAN. CRAZY BUSINESS.
CRAAAAZY BUSINESS...
HEY, OWL, PSST. YOU KNOW MRS. MIKE, YEAH?
NUDGE
UH-HUH, THE WOMAN WHO JUST DIED? YES... I DID.
Y'KNOW, I FUCKED HER ONCE.
WHAT?! UGH!
DON'T TELL MIKE!
... FOR GOD'S SAKE, JONES, I DID NOT NEED TO KNOW THAT!
YUCK!
JUST... UGCH.
DROP
OUT OF MY WAY!

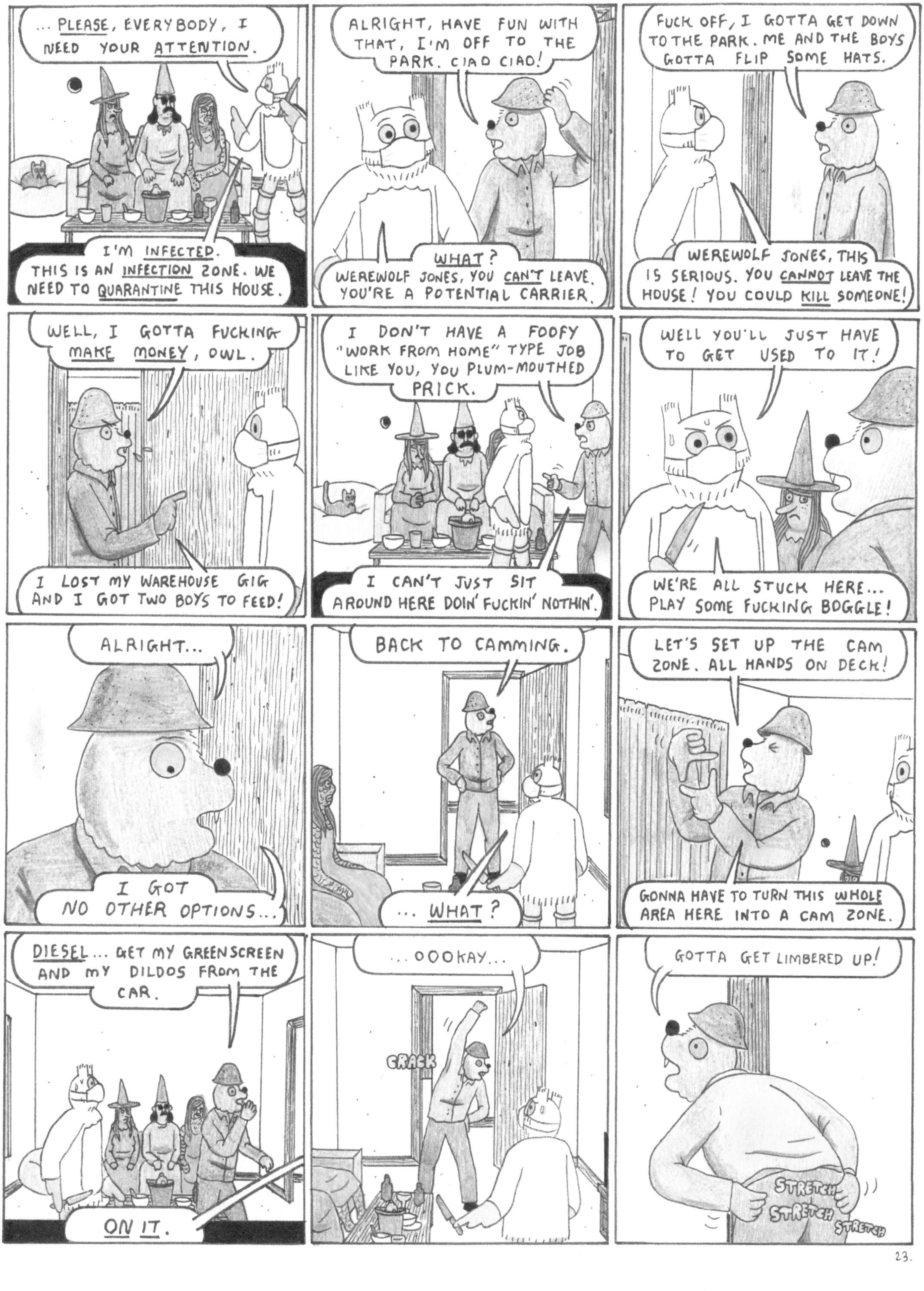
... PLEASE, EVERYBODY, I NEED YOUR ATTENTION.
I'M INFECTED. THIS IS AN INFECTION ZONE. WE NEED TO QUARANTINE THIS HOUSE.
ALRIGHT, HAVE FUN WITH THAT, I'M OFF TO THE PARK. CIAO CIAO!
WHAT? WEREWOLF JONES, YOU CAN'T LEAVE. YOU'RE A POTENTIAL CARRIER.
FUCK OFF, I GOTTA GET DOWN TO THE PARK. ME AND THE BOYS GOTTA FLIP SOME HATS.
WEREWOLF JONES, THIS IS SERIOUS. YOU CANNOT LEAVE THE HOUSE! YOU COULD KILL SOMEONE!
WELL, I GOTTA FUCKING MAKE MONEY, OWL.
I LOST MY WAREHOUSE GIG AND I GOT TWO BOYS TO FEED!
I DON'T HAVE A FOOFY "WORK FROM HOME" TYPE JOB LIKE YOU, YOU PLUM-MOUTHED PRICK.
I CAN'T JUST SIT AROUND HERE DOIN' FUCKIN' NOTHIN'.
WELL YOU'LL JUST HAVE TO GET USED TO IT!
WE'RE ALL STUCK HERE... PLAY SOME FUCKING BOGGLE!
ALRIGHT...
I GOT NO OTHER OPTIONS...
BACK TO CAMMING.
... WHAT?
LET'S SET UP THE CAM ZONE. ALL HANDS ON DECK!
GONNA HAVE TO TURN THIS WHOLE AREA HERE INTO A CAM ZONE.
DIESEL... GET MY GREENSCREEN AND MY DILDOS FROM THE CAR.
ON IT.
...OOOKAY...
CRACK
GOTTA GET LIMBERED UP!
STRETCH
STRETCH
STRETCH

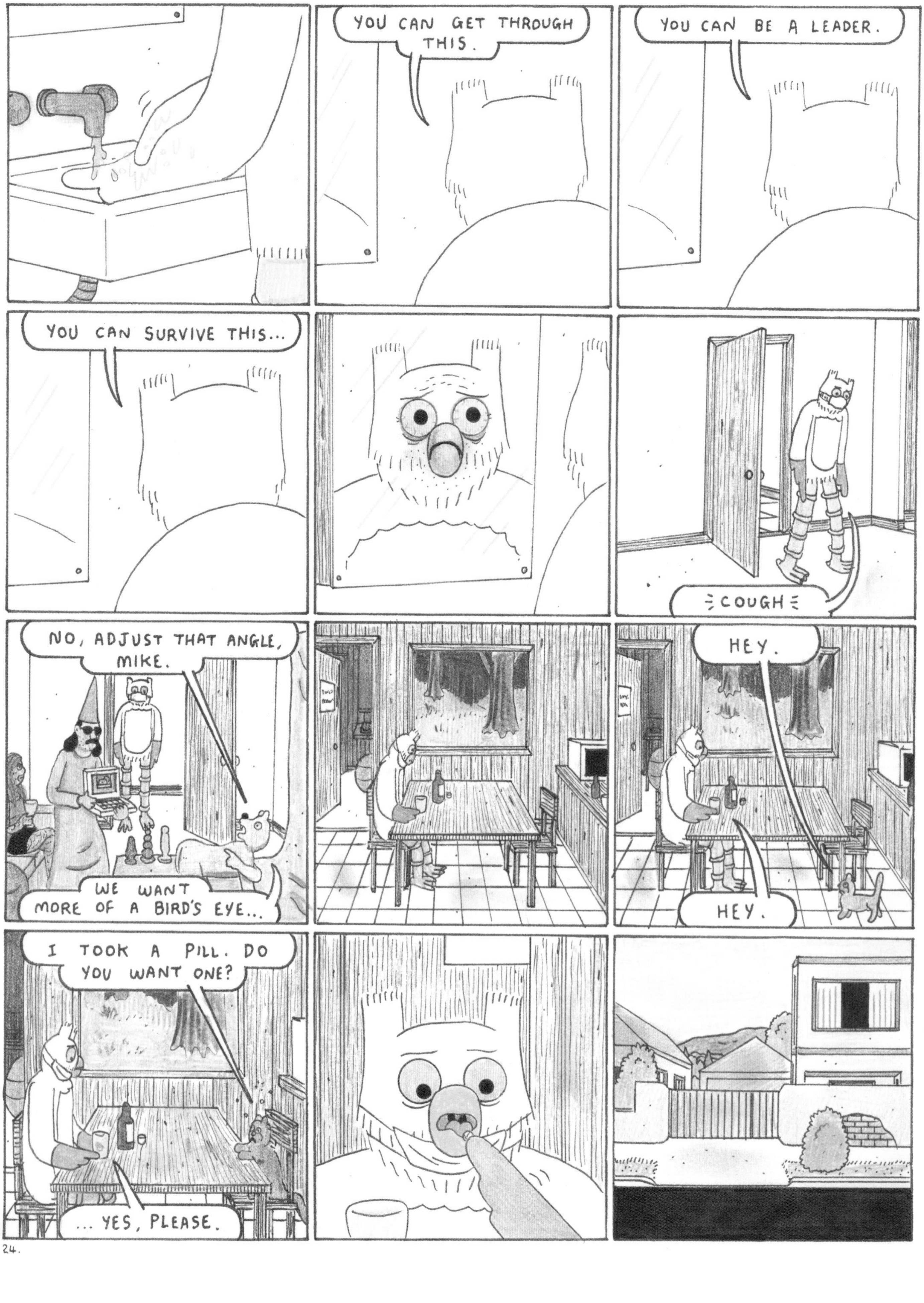
YOU CAN GET THROUGH THIS.
YOU CAN BE A LEADER.
YOU CAN SURVIVE THIS...
COUGH
NO, ADJUST THAT ANGLE, MIKE.
WE WANT MORE OF A BIRD'S EYE...
HEY.
HEY.
I TOOK A PILL. DO YOU WANT ONE?
... YES, PLEASE.

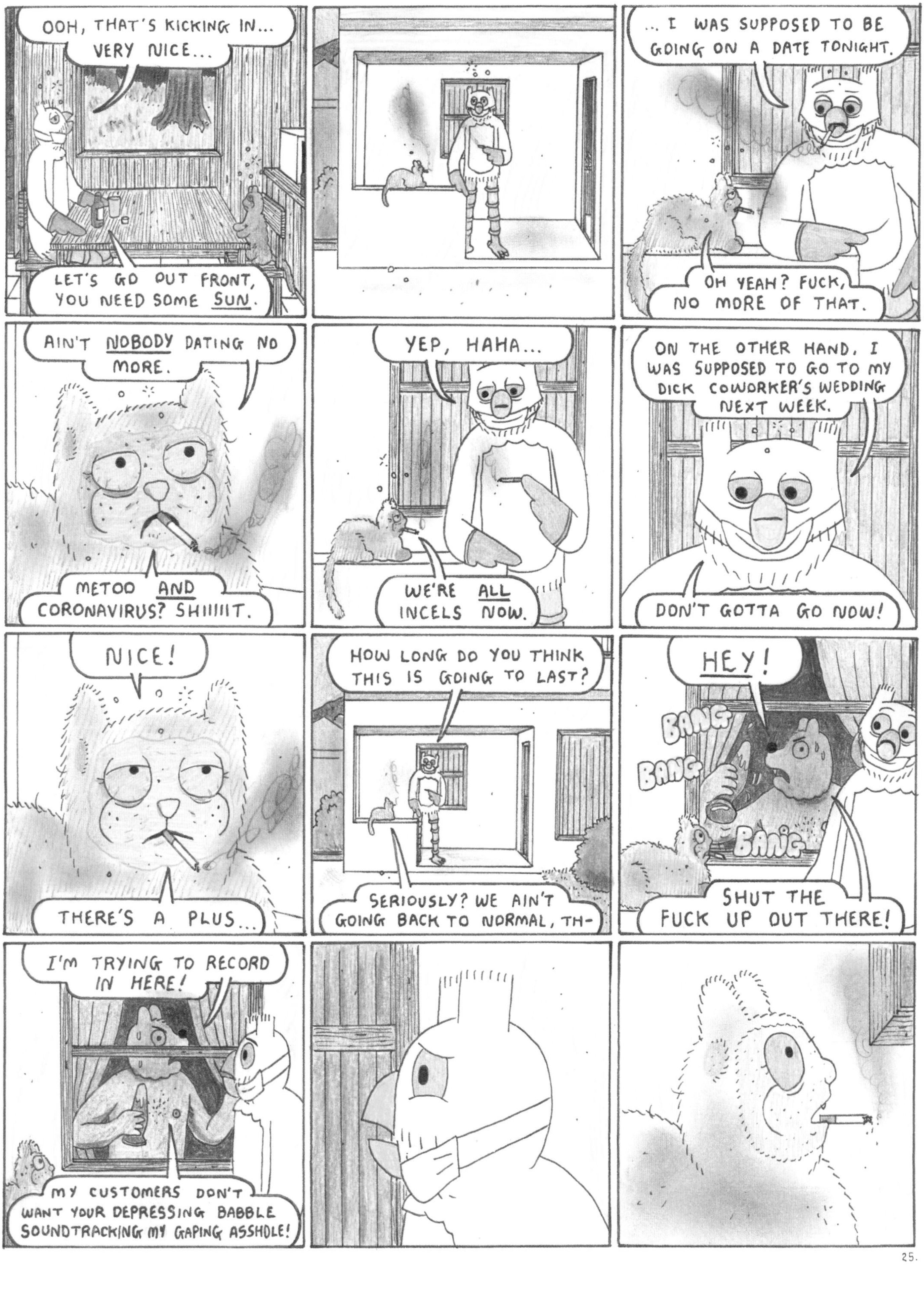

OOH, THAT'S KICKING IN... VERY NICE...
LET'S GO OUT FRONT, YOU NEED SOME SUN.
... I WAS SUPPOSED TO BE GOING ON A DATE TONIGHT.
OH YEAH? FUCK, NO MORE OF THAT.
AIN'T NOBODY DATING NO MORE.
METOO AND CORONAVIRUS? SHIIIIIT.
YEP, HAHA...
WE'RE ALL INCELS NOW.
ON THE OTHER HAND, I WAS SUPPOSED TO GO TO MY DICK COWORKER'S WEDDING NEXT WEEK.
DON'T GOTTA GO NOW!
NICE!
THERE'S A PLUS...
HOW LONG DO YOU THINK THIS IS GOING TO LAST?
SERIOUSLY? WE AIN'T GOING BACK TO NORMAL, TH-
HEY!
BANG
BANG
BANG
SHUT THE FUCK UP OUT THERE!
I'M TRYING TO RECORD IN HERE!
MY CUSTOMERS DON'T WANT YOUR DEPRESSING BABBLE SOUNDTRACKING MY GAPING ASSHOLE!

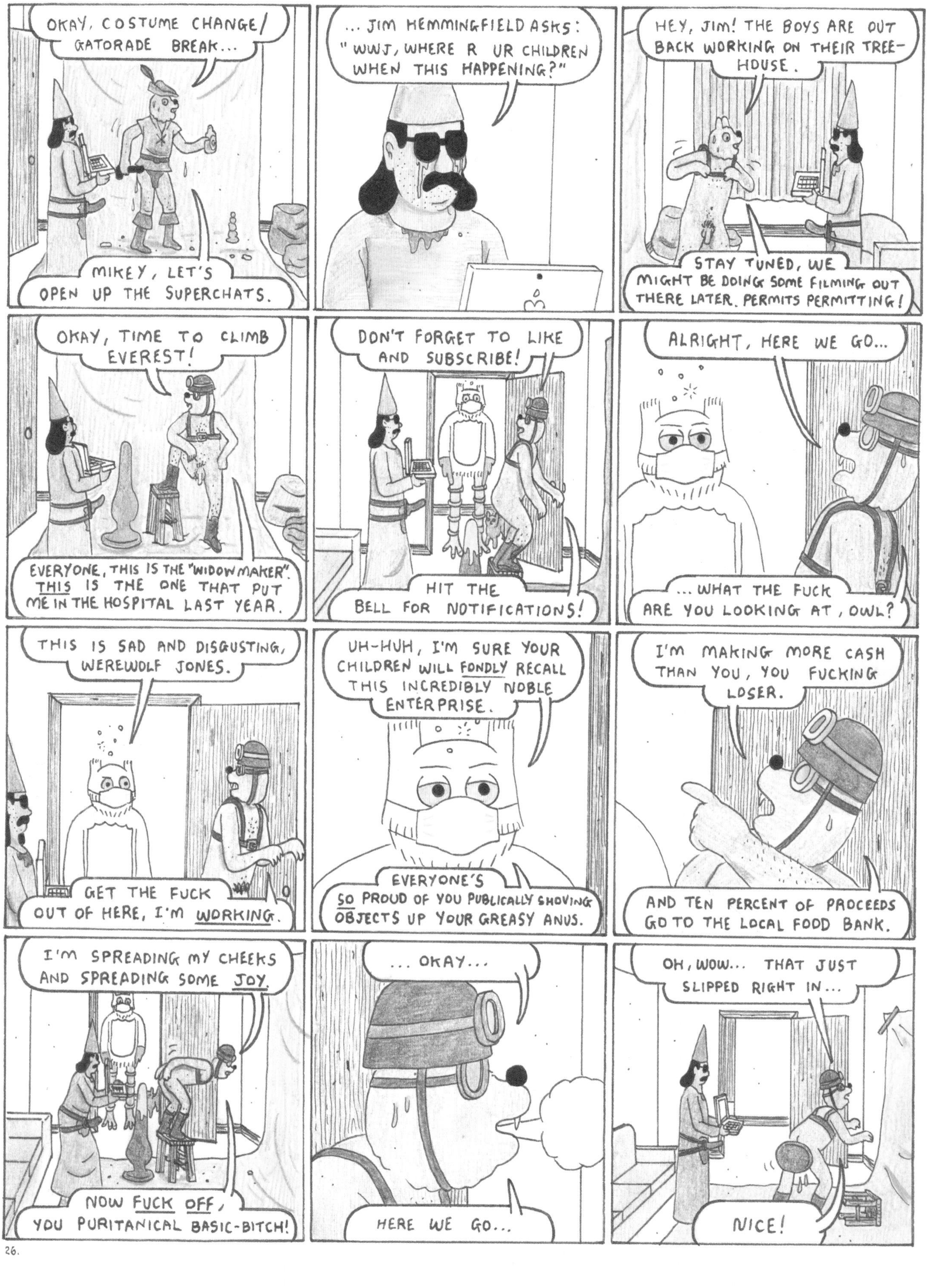
OKAY, COSTUME CHANGE/ GATORADE BREAK...
MIKEY, LET'S OPEN UP THE SUPERCHATS.
... JIM HEMMINGFIELD ASKS: "WWJ, WHERE R UR CHILDREN WHEN THIS HAPPENING?"
HEY, JIM! THE BOYS ARE OUT BACK WORKING ON THEIR TREE-HOUSE.
STAY TUNED, WE MIGHT BE DOING SOME FILMING OUT THERE LATER. PERMITS PERMITTING!
OKAY, TIME TO CLIMB EVEREST!
EVERYONE, THIS IS THE "WIDOWMAKER". THIS IS THE ONE THAT PUT ME IN THE HOSPITAL LAST YEAR.
DON'T FORGET TO LIKE AND SUBSCRIBE!
HIT THE BELL FOR NOTIFICATIONS!
ALRIGHT, HERE WE GO...
... WHAT THE FUCK ARE YOU LOOKING AT, OWL?
THIS IS SAD AND DISGUSTING, WEREWOLF JONES.
GET THE FUCK OUT OF HERE, I'M WORKING.
UH-HUH, I'M SURE YOUR CHILDREN WILL FONDLY RECALL THIS INCREDIBLY NOBLE ENTERPRISE.
EVERYONE'S SO PROUD OF YOU PUBLICALLY SHOVING OBJECTS UP YOUR GREASY ANUS.
I'M MAKING MORE CASH THAN YOU, YOU FUCKING LOSER.
AND TEN PERCENT OF PROCEEDS GO TO THE LOCAL FOOD BANK.
I'M SPREADING MY CHEEKS AND SPREADING SOME JOY.
NOW FUCK OFF, YOU PURITANICAL BASIC-BITCH!
... OKAY...
HERE WE GO...
OH, WOW... THAT JUST SLIPPED RIGHT IN...
NICE!

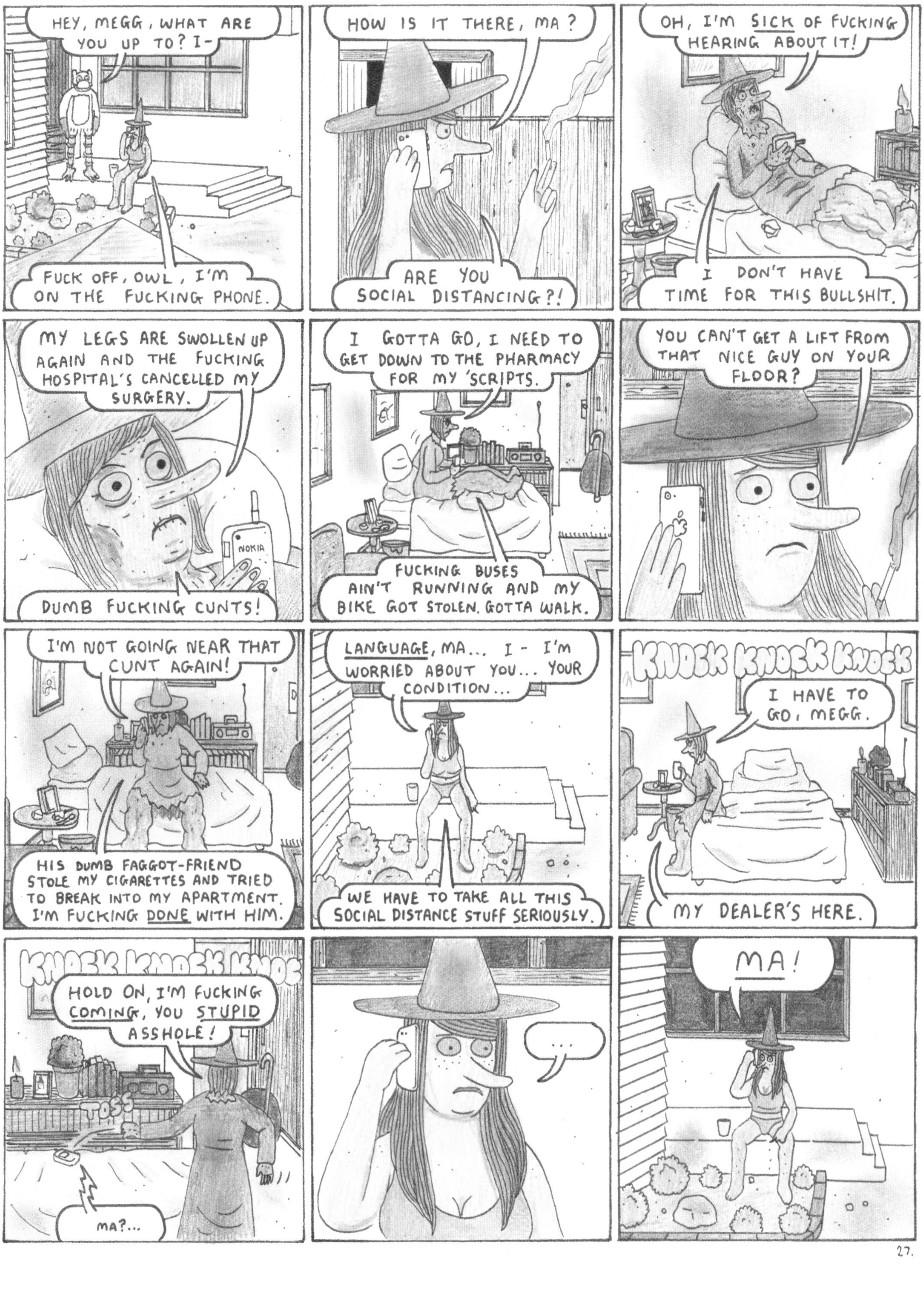
HEY, MEGG, WHAT ARE YOU UP TO? I-
FUCK OFF, OWL, I'M ON THE FUCKING PHONE.
HOW IS IT THERE, MA?
ARE YOU SOCIAL DISTANCING?!
OH, I'M SICK OF FUCKING HEARING ABOUT IT!
I DON'T HAVE TIME FOR THIS BULLSHIT.
MY LEGS ARE SWOLLEN UP AGAIN AND THE FUCKING HOSPITAL'S CANCELLED MY SURGERY.
NOKIA
DUMB FUCKING CUNTS!
I GOTTA GO, I NEED TO GET DOWN TO THE PHARMACY FOR MY 'SCRIPTS.
FUCKING BUSES AIN'T RUNNING AND MY BIKE GOT STOLEN. GOTTA WALK.
YOU CAN'T GET A LIFT FROM THAT NICE GUY ON YOUR FLOOR?
I'M NOT GOING NEAR THAT CUNT AGAIN!
HIS DUMB FAGGOT-FRIEND STOLE MY CIGARETTES AND TRIED TO BREAK INTO MY APARTMENT. I'M FUCKING DONE WITH HIM.
LANGUAGE, MA... I - I'M WORRIED ABOUT YOU... YOUR CONDITION...
WE HAVE TO TAKE ALL THIS SOCIAL DISTANCE STUFF SERIOUSLY.
KNOCK KNOCK KNOCK
I HAVE TO GO, MEGG.
MY DEALER'S HERE.
HOLD ON, I'M FUCKING COMING, YOU STUPID ASSHOLE!
TOSS
MA?...
...
MA!

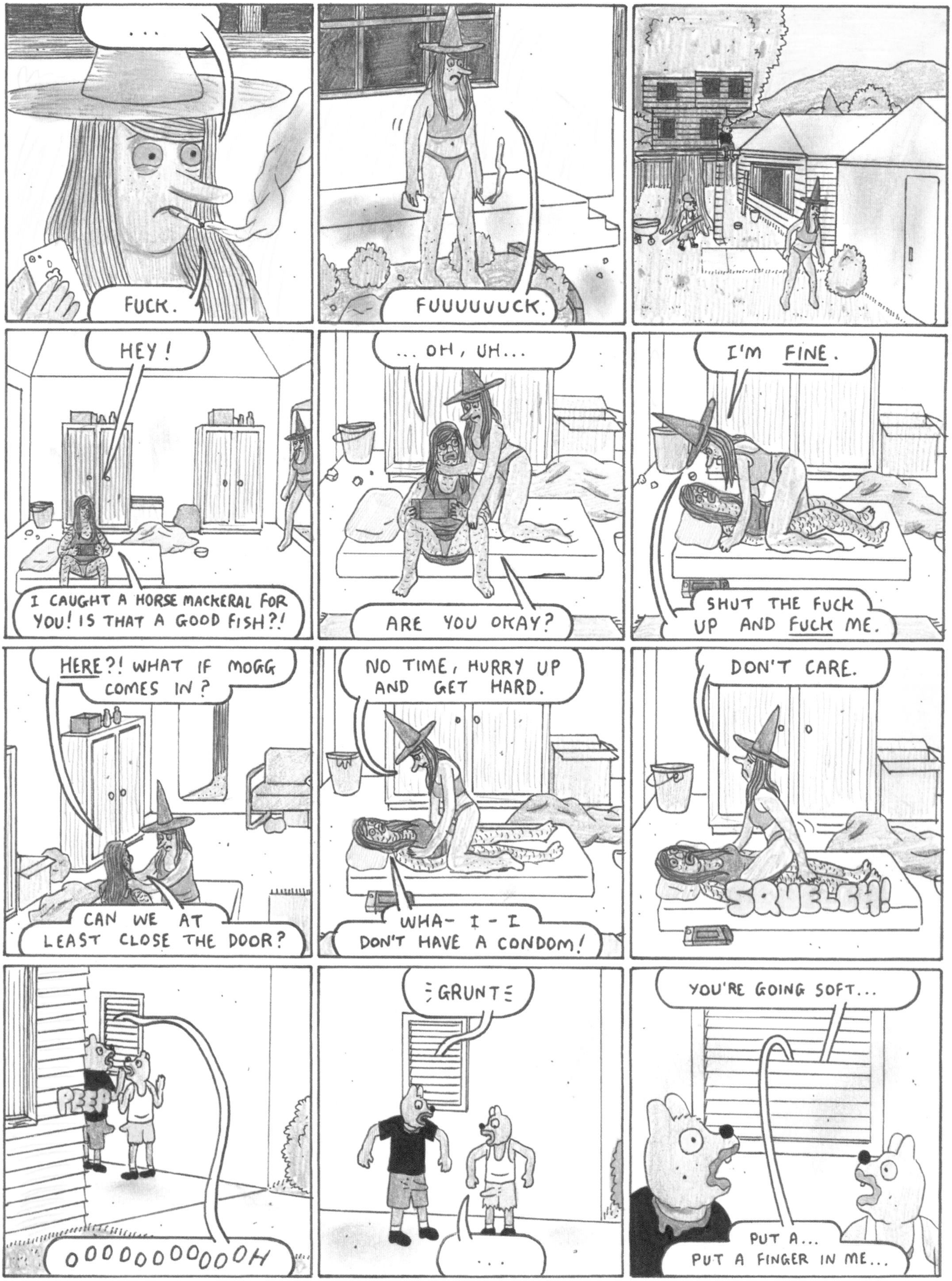
. . .
FUCK.
FUUUUUUCK.
HEY!
I CAUGHT A HORSE MACKERAL FOR YOU! IS THAT A GOOD FISH?!
... OH, UH...
ARE YOU OKAY?
I'M FINE.
SHUT THE FUCK UP AND FUCK ME.
HERE?! WHAT IF MOGG COMES IN?
CAN WE AT LEAST CLOSE THE DOOR?
NO TIME, HURRY UP AND GET HARD.
WHA- I-I DON'T HAVE A CONDOM!
DON'T CARE.
SQUELCH!
PEEP
OOOOOOOOOOOH
GRUNT
. . .
YOU'RE GOING SOFT...
PUT A... PUT A FINGER IN ME...

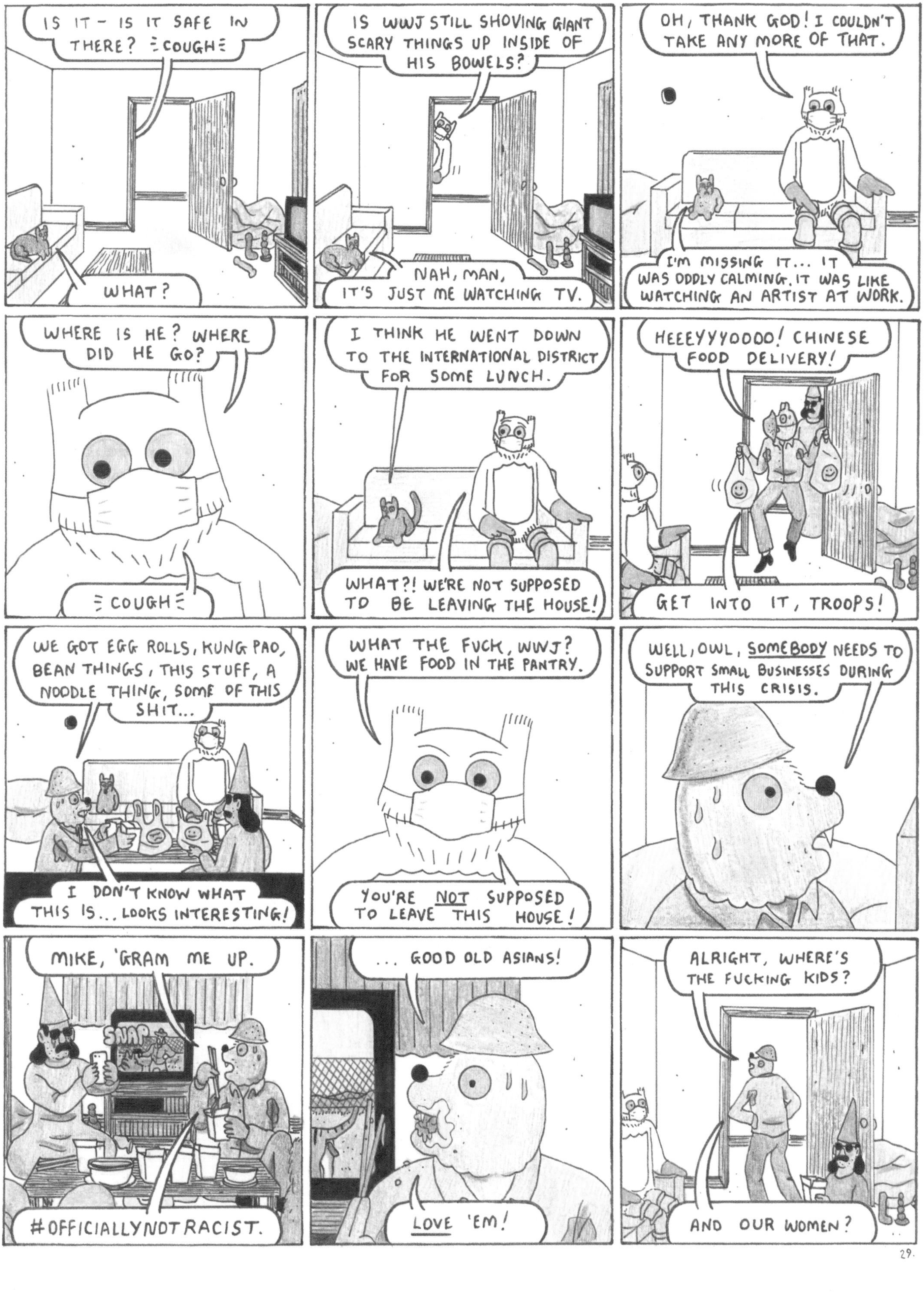
IS IT - IS IT SAFE IN THERE? ≡COUGH≡
WHAT?
IS WWJ STILL SHOVING GIANT SCARY THINGS UP INSIDE OF HIS BOWELS?
NAH, MAN, IT'S JUST ME WATCHING TV.
OH, THANK GOD! I COULDN'T TAKE ANY MORE OF THAT.
I'M MISSING IT... IT WAS ODDLY CALMING. IT WAS LIKE WATCHING AN ARTIST AT WORK.
WHERE IS HE? WHERE DID HE GO?
≡COUGH≡
I THINK HE WENT DOWN TO THE INTERNATIONAL DISTRICT FOR SOME LUNCH.
WHAT?! WE'RE NOT SUPPOSED TO BE LEAVING THE HOUSE!
HEEEYYYOOOO! CHINESE FOOD DELIVERY!
GET INTO IT, TROOPS!
WE GOT EGG ROLLS, KUNG PAO, BEAN THINGS, THIS STUFF, A NOODLE THING, SOME OF THIS SHIT...
I DON'T KNOW WHAT THIS IS... LOOKS INTERESTING!
WHAT THE FUCK, WWJ? WE HAVE FOOD IN THE PANTRY.
YOU'RE NOT SUPPOSED TO LEAVE THIS HOUSE!
WELL, OWL, SOMEBODY NEEDS TO SUPPORT SMALL BUSINESSES DURING THIS CRISIS.
MIKE, 'GRAM ME UP.
SNAP
#OFFICIALLYNOTRACIST.
... GOOD OLD ASIANS!
LOVE 'EM!
ALRIGHT, WHERE'S THE FUCKING KIDS?
AND OUR WOMEN?

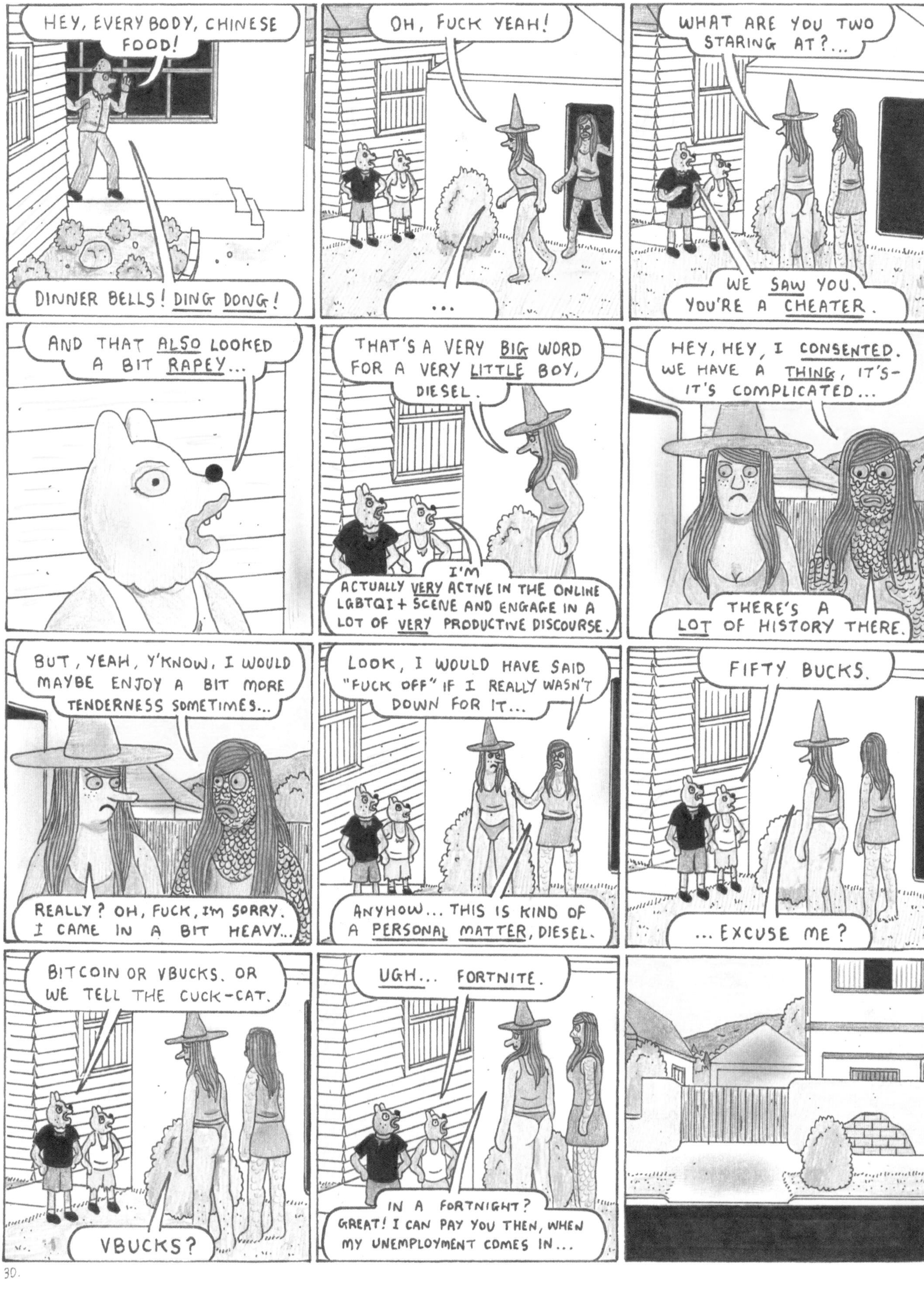
HEY, EVERYBODY, CHINESE FOOD!
DINNER BELLS! DING DONG!
OH, FUCK YEAH!
...
WHAT ARE YOU TWO STARING AT?...
WE SAW YOU. YOU'RE A CHEATER.
AND THAT ALSO LOOKED A BIT RAPEY...
THAT'S A VERY BIG WORD FOR A VERY LITTLE BOY, DIESEL.
I'M ACTUALLY VERY ACTIVE IN THE ONLINE LGBTQI+ SCENE AND ENGAGE IN A LOT OF VERY PRODUCTIVE DISCOURSE.
HEY, HEY, I CONSENTED. WE HAVE A THING, IT'S- IT'S COMPLICATED...
THERE'S A LOT OF HISTORY THERE.
BUT, YEAH, Y'KNOW, I WOULD MAYBE ENJOY A BIT MORE TENDERNESS SOMETIMES...
REALLY? OH, FUCK, I'M SORRY. I CAME IN A BIT HEAVY...
LOOK, I WOULD HAVE SAID "FUCK OFF" IF I REALLY WASN'T DOWN FOR IT...
ANYHOW... THIS IS KIND OF A PERSONAL MATTER, DIESEL.
FIFTY BUCKS.
...EXCUSE ME?
BITCOIN OR VBUCKS. OR WE TELL THE CUCK-CAT.
VBUCKS?
UGH... FORTNITE.
IN A FORTNIGHT? GREAT! I CAN PAY YOU THEN, WHEN MY UNEMPLOYMENT COMES IN...

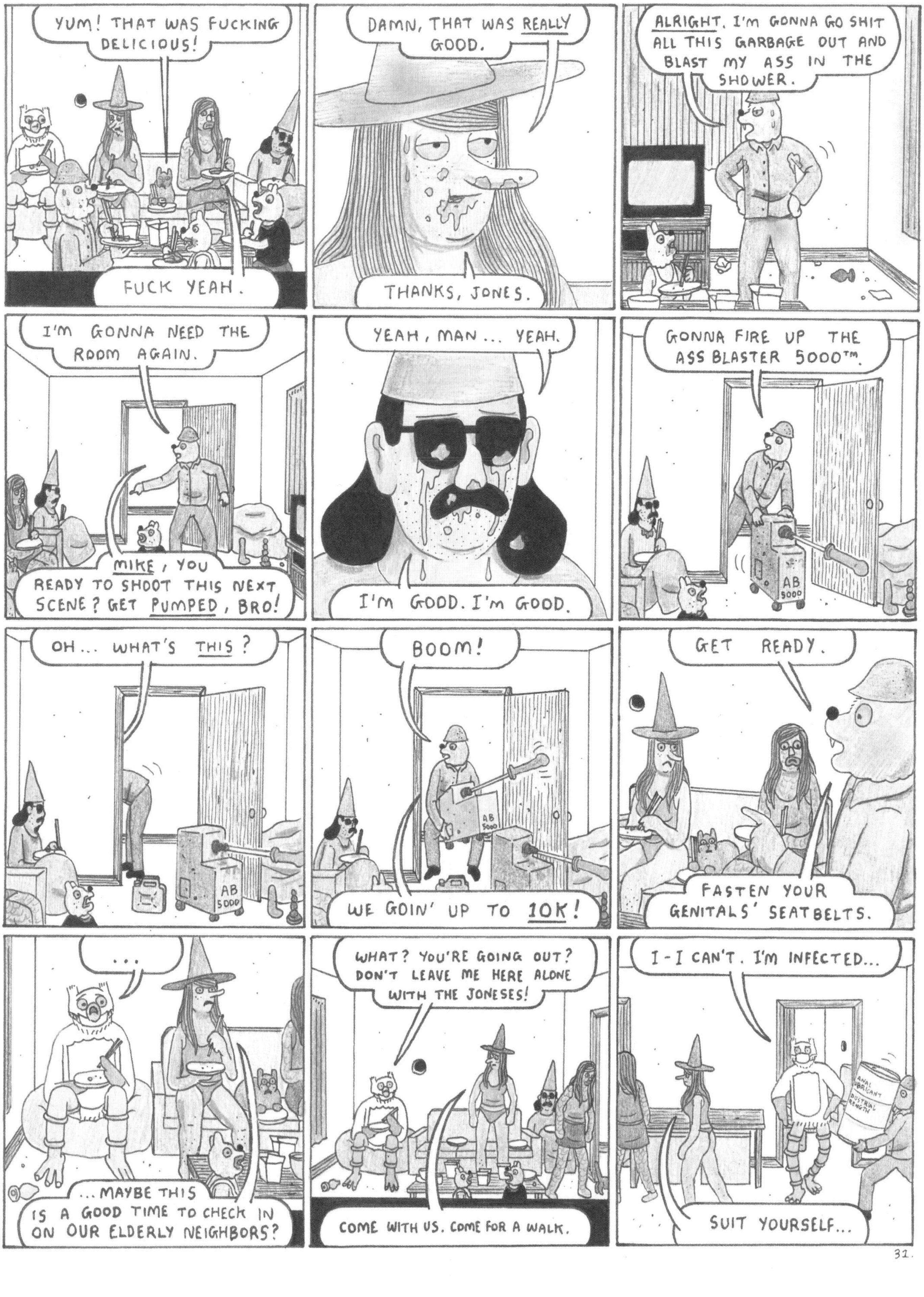
YUM! THAT WAS FUCKING DELICIOUS!
FUCK YEAH.
DAMN, THAT WAS REALLY GOOD.
THANKS, JONES.
ALRIGHT. I'M GONNA GO SHIT ALL THIS GARBAGE OUT AND BLAST MY ASS IN THE SHOWER.
I'M GONNA NEED THE ROOM AGAIN.
MIKE, YOU READY TO SHOOT THIS NEXT SCENE? GET PUMPED, BRO!
YEAH, MAN... YEAH.
I'M GOOD. I'M GOOD.
GONNA FIRE UP THE ASS BLASTER 5000™.
AB 5000
OH... WHAT'S THIS?
AB 5000
BOOM!
AB 5000
WE GOIN' UP TO 10K!
GET READY.
FASTEN YOUR GENITALS' SEATBELTS.
...
...MAYBE THIS IS A GOOD TIME TO CHECK IN ON OUR ELDERLY NEIGHBORS?
WHAT? YOU'RE GOING OUT? DON'T LEAVE ME HERE ALONE WITH THE JONESES!
COME WITH US. COME FOR A WALK.
I-I CAN'T. I'M INFECTED...
SUIT YOURSELF...

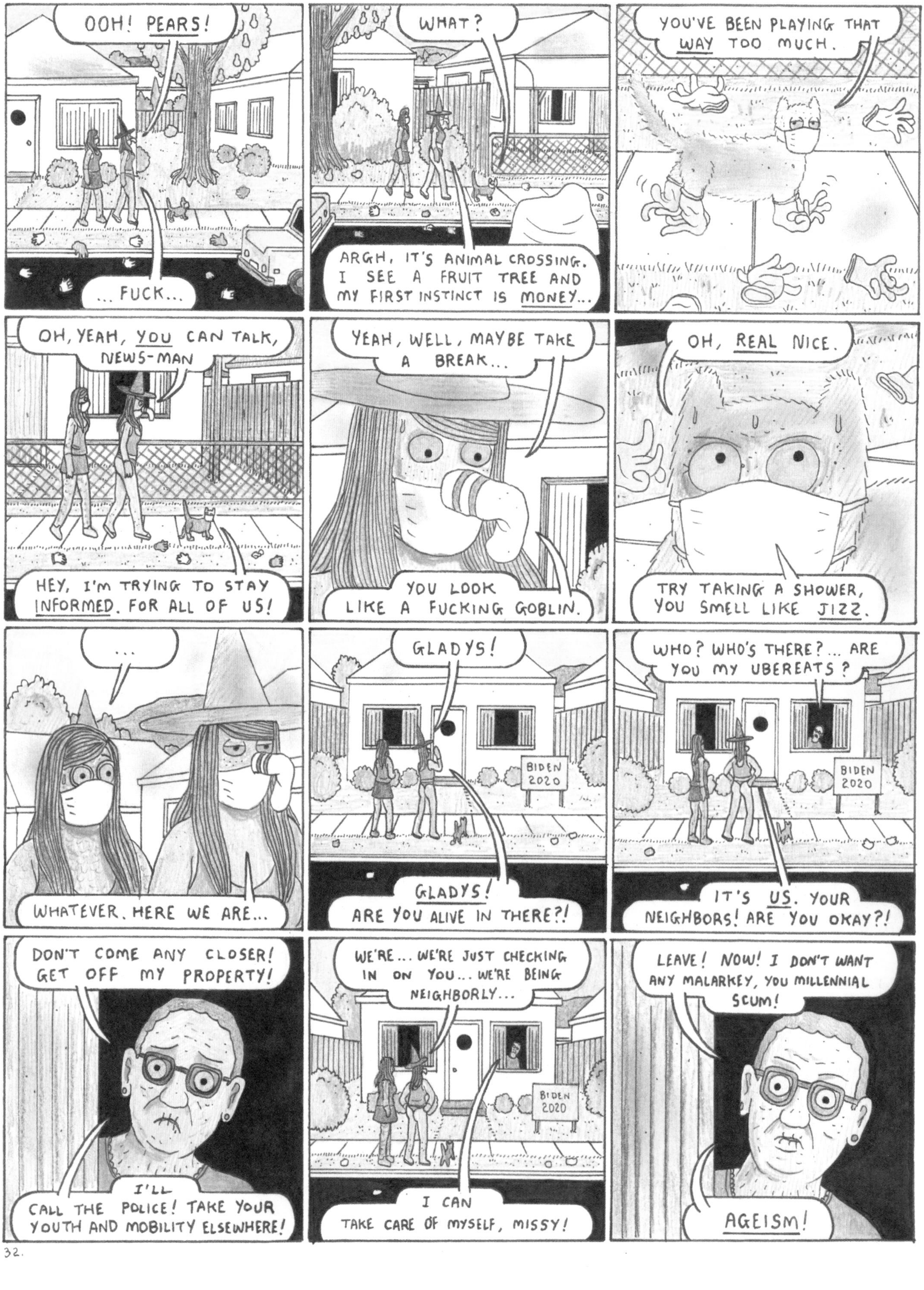
OOH! PEARS!
... FUCK...
WHAT?
ARGH, IT'S ANIMAL CROSSING. I SEE A FRUIT TREE AND MY FIRST INSTINCT IS MONEY...
YOU'VE BEEN PLAYING THAT WAY TOO MUCH.
OH, YEAH, YOU CAN TALK, NEWS-MAN
HEY, I'M TRYING TO STAY INFORMED. FOR ALL OF US!
YEAH, WELL, MAYBE TAKE A BREAK...
YOU LOOK LIKE A FUCKING GOBLIN.
OH, REAL NICE.
TRY TAKING A SHOWER, YOU SMELL LIKE JIZZ.
...
WHATEVER. HERE WE ARE...
GLADYS!
BIDEN 2020
GLADYS! ARE YOU ALIVE IN THERE?!
WHO? WHO'S THERE? ... ARE YOU MY UBEREATS?
BIDEN 2020
IT'S US. YOUR NEIGHBORS! ARE YOU OKAY?!
DON'T COME ANY CLOSER! GET OFF MY PROPERTY!
I'LL CALL THE POLICE! TAKE YOUR YOUTH AND MOBILITY ELSEWHERE!
WE'RE... WE'RE JUST CHECKING IN ON YOU... WE'RE BEING NEIGHBORLY...
BIDEN 2020
I CAN TAKE CARE OF MYSELF, MISSY!
LEAVE! NOW! I DON'T WANT ANY MALARKEY, YOU MILLENNIAL SCUM!
AGEISM!

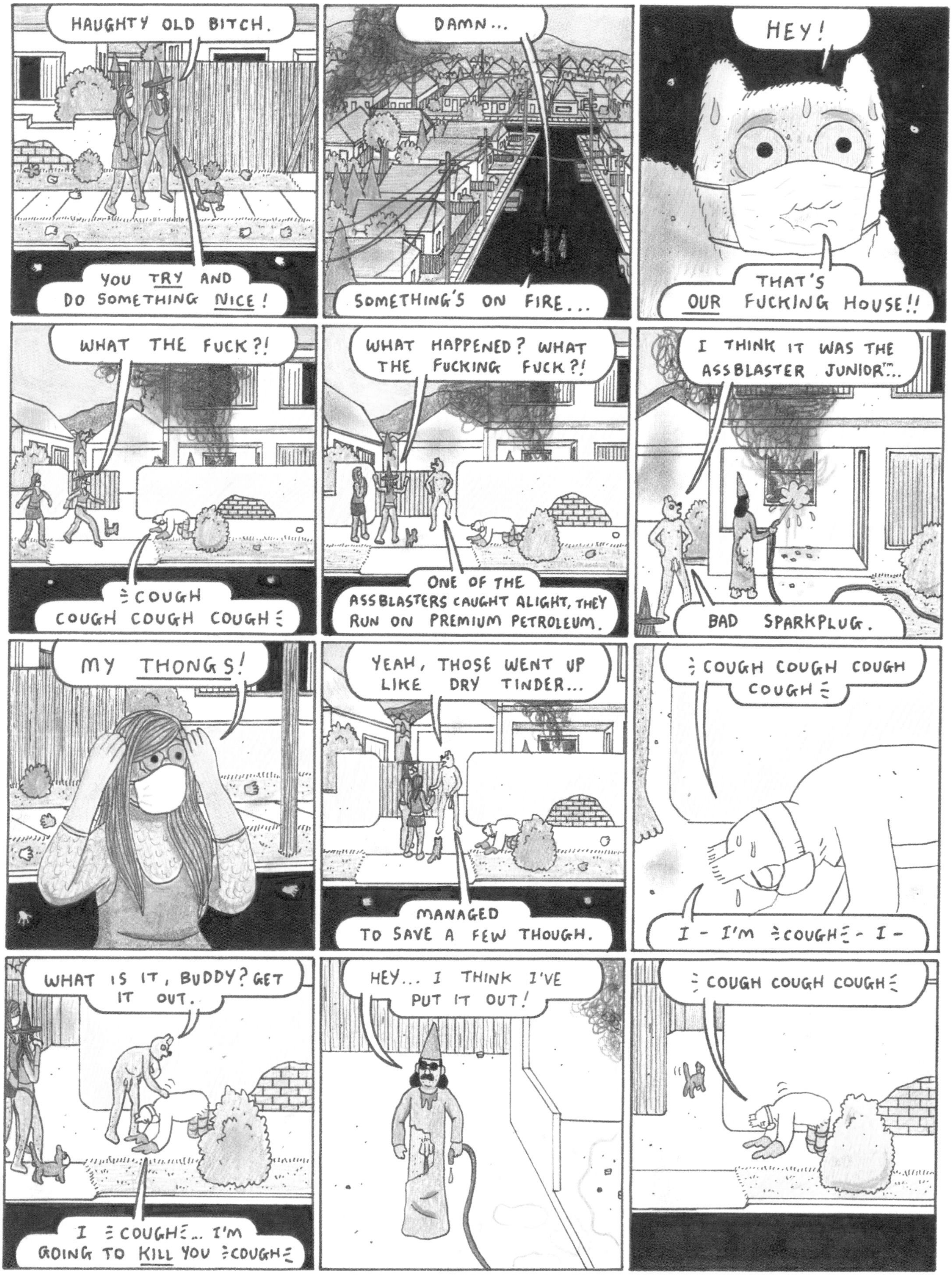
HAUGHTY OLD BITCH.
YOU TRY AND DO SOMETHING NICE!
DAMN...
SOMETHING'S ON FIRE...
HEY!
THAT'S OUR FUCKING HOUSE!!
WHAT THE FUCK?!
COUGH COUGH COUGH COUGH
WHAT HAPPENED? WHAT THE FUCKING FUCK?!
ONE OF THE ASSBLASTERS CAUGHT ALIGHT, THEY RUN ON PREMIUM PETROLEUM.
I THINK IT WAS THE ASSBLASTER JUNIOR™...
BAD SPARKPLUG.
MY THONGS!
YEAH, THOSE WENT UP LIKE DRY TINDER...
MANAGED TO SAVE A FEW THOUGH.
COUGH COUGH COUGH COUGH
I - I'M COUGH - I -
WHAT IS IT, BUDDY? GET IT OUT.
I COUGH... I'M GOING TO KILL YOU COUGH
HEY... I THINK I'VE PUT IT OUT!
COUGH COUGH COUGH

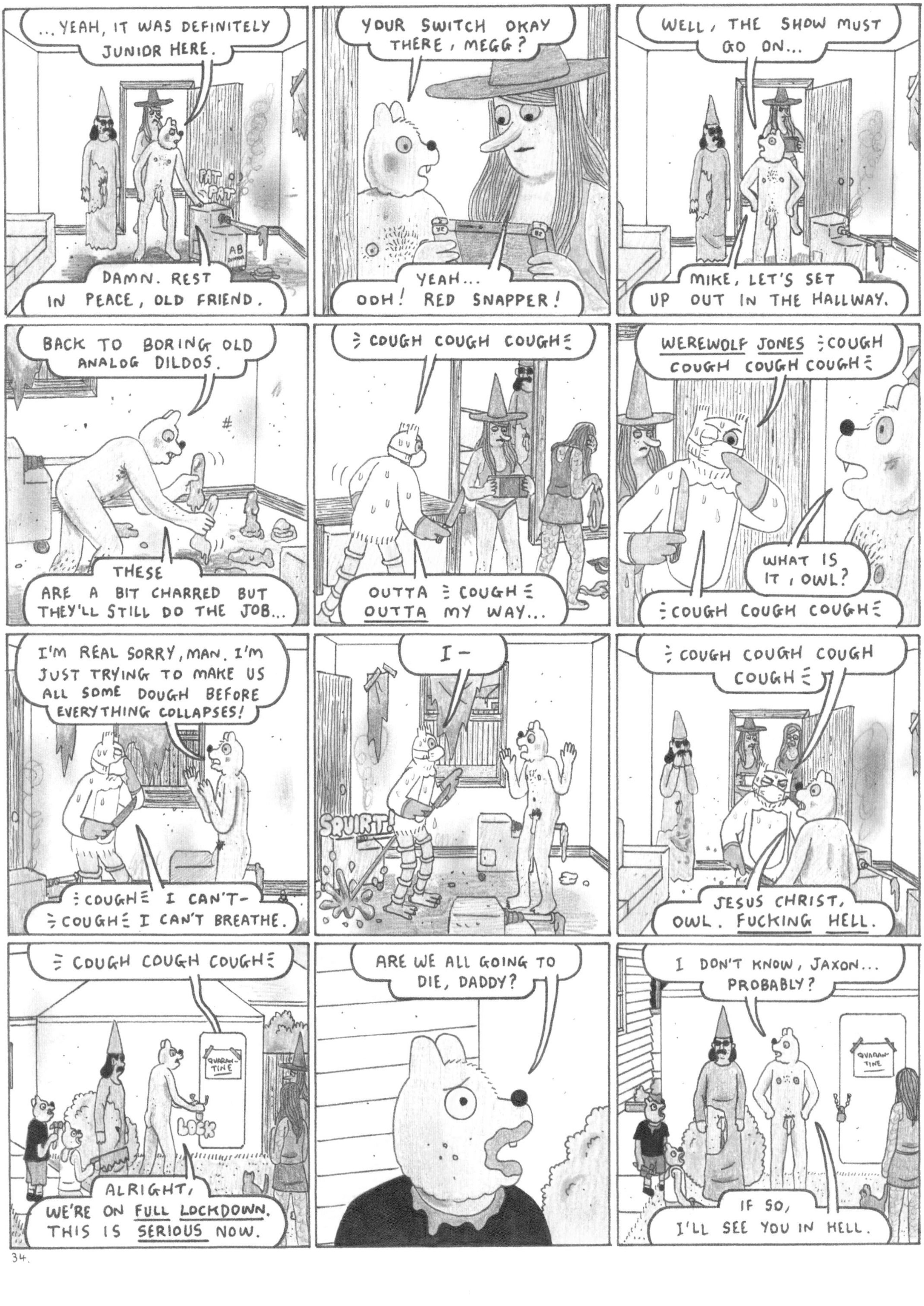
...YEAH, IT WAS DEFINITELY JUNIOR HERE.
PAT PAT
AB
DAMN. REST IN PEACE, OLD FRIEND.
YOUR SWITCH OKAY THERE, MEGG?
YEAH... OOH! RED SNAPPER!
WELL, THE SHOW MUST GO ON...
MIKE, LET'S SET UP OUT IN THE HALLWAY.
BACK TO BORING OLD ANALOG DILDOS.
THESE ARE A BIT CHARRED BUT THEY'LL STILL DO THE JOB...
≋COUGH COUGH COUGH≋
OUTTA ≋COUGH≋ OUTTA MY WAY...
WEREWOLF JONES ≋COUGH COUGH COUGH COUGH≋
WHAT IS IT, OWL?
≋COUGH COUGH COUGH≋
I'M REAL SORRY, MAN. I'M JUST TRYING TO MAKE US ALL SOME DOUGH BEFORE EVERYTHING COLLAPSES!
≋COUGH≋ I CAN'T- ≋COUGH≋ I CAN'T BREATHE.
I-
SQUIRT!
≋COUGH COUGH COUGH COUGH≋
JESUS CHRIST, OWL. FUCKING HELL.
≋COUGH COUGH COUGH≋
QUARAN-TINE
LOCK
ALRIGHT, WE'RE ON FULL LOCKDOWN. THIS IS SERIOUS NOW.
ARE WE ALL GOING TO DIE, DADDY?
I DON'T KNOW, JAXON... PROBABLY?
QUARAN-TINE
IF SO, I'LL SEE YOU IN HELL.

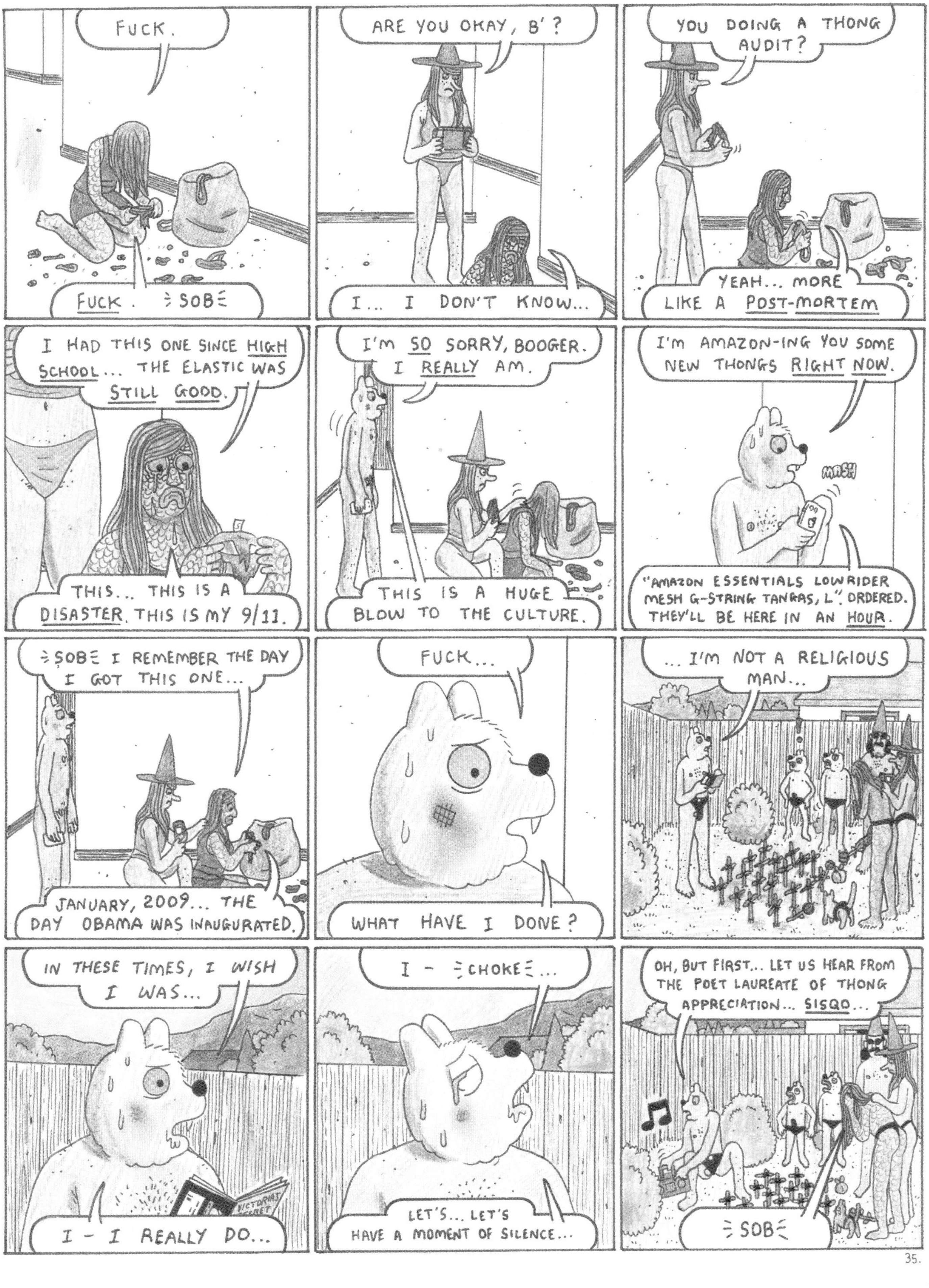
FUCK.
FUCK. ⋮SOB⋮
ARE YOU OKAY, B'?
I... I DON'T KNOW...
YOU DOING A THONG AUDIT?
YEAH... MORE LIKE A POST-MORTEM
I HAD THIS ONE SINCE HIGH SCHOOL... THE ELASTIC WAS STILL GOOD.
THIS... THIS IS A DISASTER. THIS IS MY 9/11.
I'M SO SORRY, BOOGER. I REALLY AM.
THIS IS A HUGE BLOW TO THE CULTURE.
I'M AMAZON-ING YOU SOME NEW THONGS RIGHT NOW.
MASH
"AMAZON ESSENTIALS LOWRIDER MESH G-STRING TANGAS, L" ORDERED. THEY'LL BE HERE IN AN HOUR.
⋮SOB⋮ I REMEMBER THE DAY I GOT THIS ONE...
JANUARY, 2009... THE DAY OBAMA WAS INAUGURATED.
FUCK...
WHAT HAVE I DONE?
... I'M NOT A RELIGIOUS MAN...
IN THESE TIMES, I WISH I WAS...
I - I REALLY DO...
VICTORIA'S SECRET
I - ⋮CHOKE⋮...
LET'S... LET'S HAVE A MOMENT OF SILENCE...
OH, BUT FIRST... LET US HEAR FROM THE POET LAUREATE OF THONG APPRECIATION... SISQO...
⋮SOB⋮

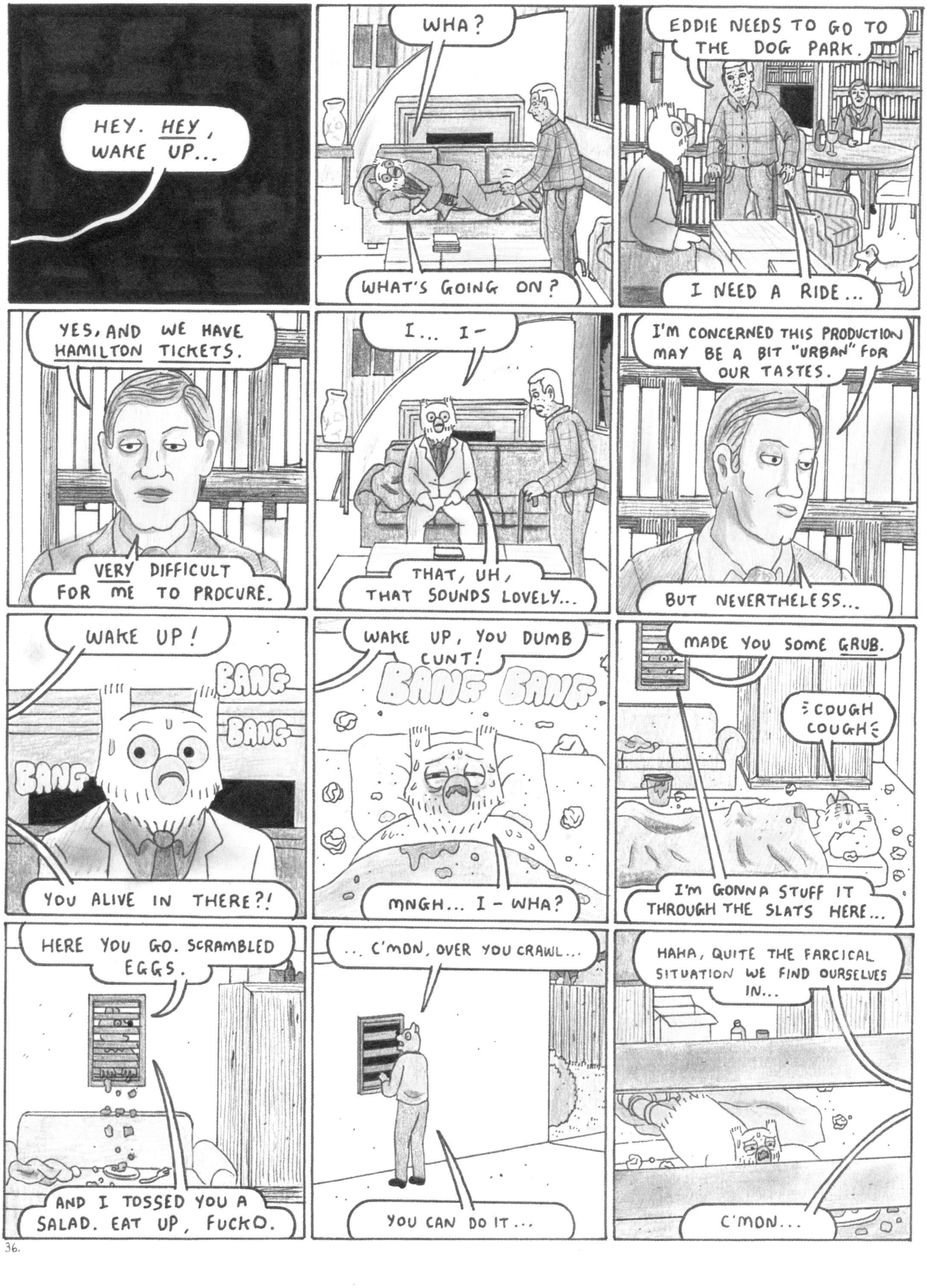
HEY. HEY, WAKE UP...
WHA?
WHAT'S GOING ON?
EDDIE NEEDS TO GO TO THE DOG PARK.
I NEED A RIDE...
YES, AND WE HAVE HAMILTON TICKETS.
VERY DIFFICULT FOR ME TO PROCURE.
I... I-
THAT, UH, THAT SOUNDS LOVELY...
I'M CONCERNED THIS PRODUCTION MAY BE A BIT "URBAN" FOR OUR TASTES.
BUT NEVERTHELESS...
WAKE UP!
BANG
BANG
BANG
YOU ALIVE IN THERE?!
WAKE UP, YOU DUMB CUNT!
BANG BANG
MNGH... I - WHA?
MADE YOU SOME GRUB.
COUGH COUGH
I'M GONNA STUFF IT THROUGH THE SLATS HERE...
HERE YOU GO. SCRAMBLED EGGS.
AND I TOSSED YOU A SALAD. EAT UP, FUCKO.
... C'MON, OVER YOU CRAWL...
YOU CAN DO IT...
HAHA, QUITE THE FARCICAL SITUATION WE FIND OURSELVES IN...
C'MON...

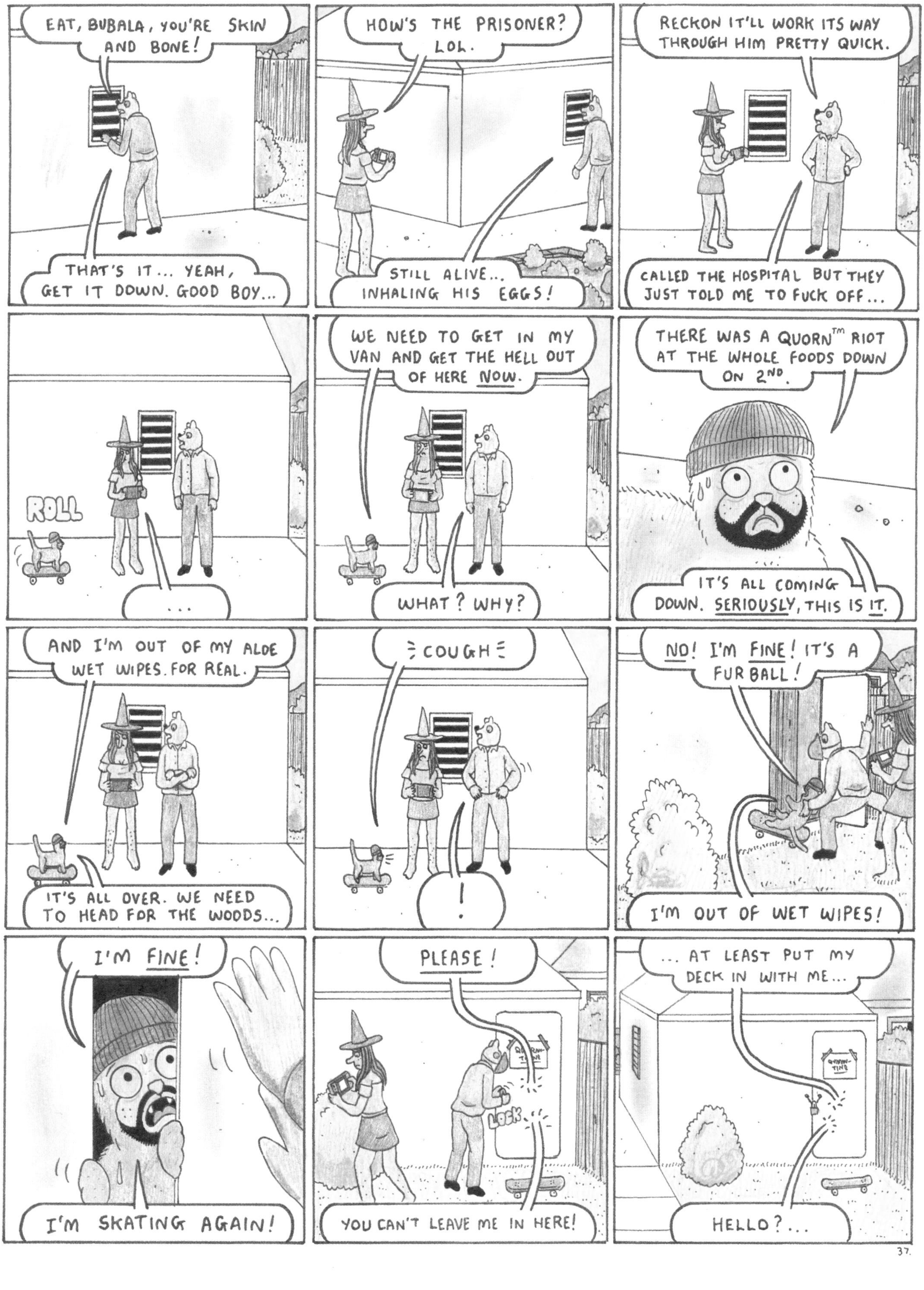
EAT, BUBALA, YOU'RE SKIN AND BONE!
THAT'S IT... YEAH, GET IT DOWN. GOOD BOY...
HOW'S THE PRISONER? LOL.
STILL ALIVE... INHALING HIS EGGS!
RECKON IT'LL WORK ITS WAY THROUGH HIM PRETTY QUICK.
CALLED THE HOSPITAL BUT THEY JUST TOLD ME TO FUCK OFF...
ROLL
...
WE NEED TO GET IN MY VAN AND GET THE HELL OUT OF HERE NOW.
WHAT? WHY?
THERE WAS A QUORN™ RIOT AT THE WHOLE FOODS DOWN ON 2ND.
IT'S ALL COMING DOWN. SERIOUSLY, THIS IS IT.
AND I'M OUT OF MY ALOE WET WIPES. FOR REAL.
IT'S ALL OVER. WE NEED TO HEAD FOR THE WOODS...
COUGH
!
NO! I'M FINE! IT'S A FUR BALL!
I'M OUT OF WET WIPES!
I'M FINE!
I'M SKATING AGAIN!
PLEASE!
LOCK
YOU CAN'T LEAVE ME IN HERE!
... AT LEAST PUT MY DECK IN WITH ME...
HELLO?...

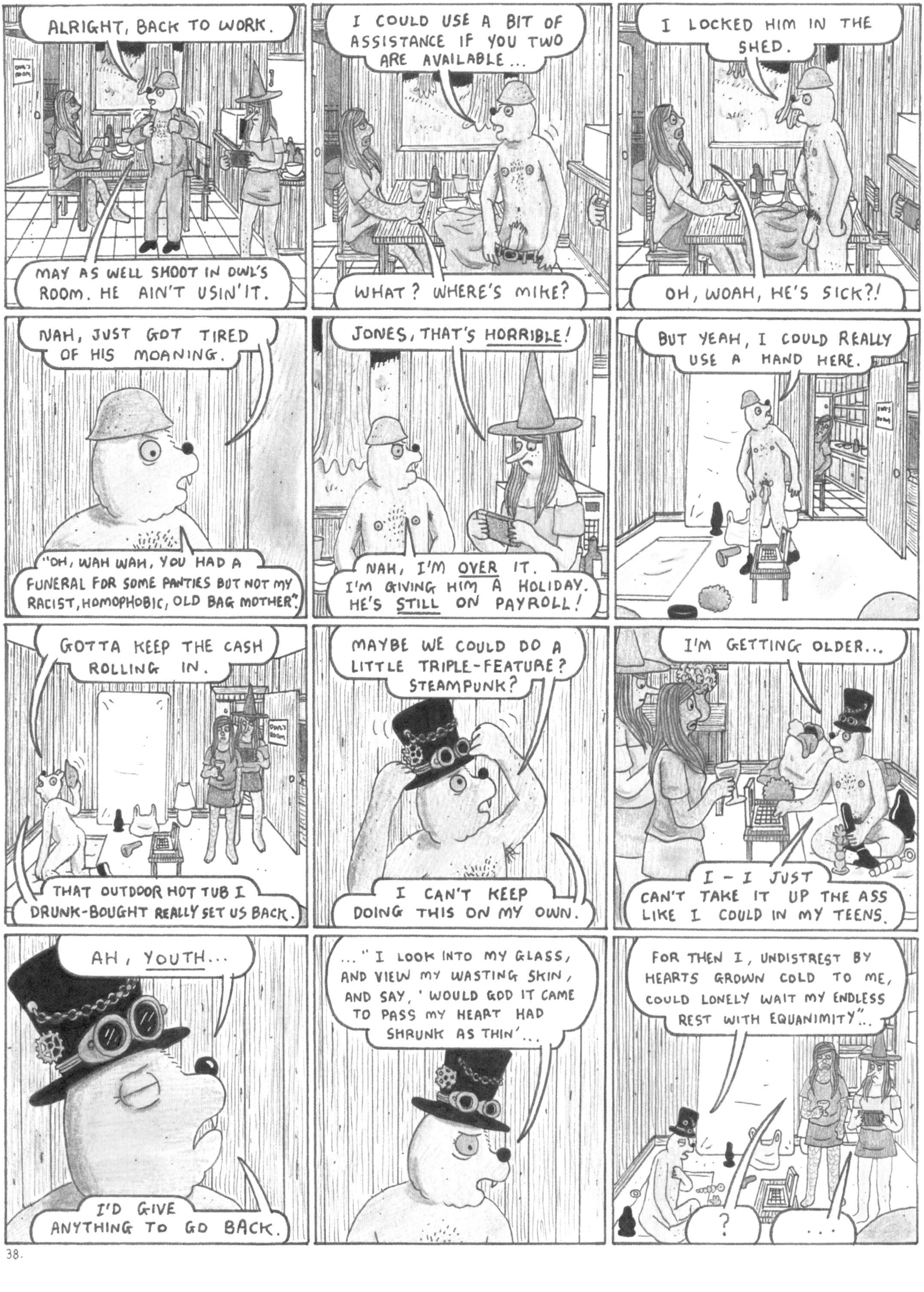
ALRIGHT, BACK TO WORK.
MAY AS WELL SHOOT IN OWL'S ROOM. HE AIN'T USIN' IT.
I COULD USE A BIT OF ASSISTANCE IF YOU TWO ARE AVAILABLE...
WHAT? WHERE'S MIKE?
I LOCKED HIM IN THE SHED.
OH, WOAH, HE'S SICK?!
NAH, JUST GOT TIRED OF HIS MOANING.
"OH, WAH WAH, YOU HAD A FUNERAL FOR SOME PANTIES BUT NOT MY RACIST, HOMOPHOBIC, OLD BAG MOTHER".
JONES, THAT'S HORRIBLE!
NAH, I'M OVER IT. I'M GIVING HIM A HOLIDAY. HE'S STILL ON PAYROLL!
BUT YEAH, I COULD REALLY USE A HAND HERE.
GOTTA KEEP THE CASH ROLLING IN.
THAT OUTDOOR HOT TUB I DRUNK-BOUGHT REALLY SET US BACK.
MAYBE WE COULD DO A LITTLE TRIPLE-FEATURE? STEAMPUNK?
I CAN'T KEEP DOING THIS ON MY OWN.
I'M GETTING OLDER...
I - I JUST CAN'T TAKE IT UP THE ASS LIKE I COULD IN MY TEENS.
AH, YOUTH...
I'D GIVE ANYTHING TO GO BACK.
..."I LOOK INTO MY GLASS, AND VIEW MY WASTING SKIN, AND SAY, 'WOULD GOD IT CAME TO PASS MY HEART HAD SHRUNK AS THIN'...
FOR THEN I, UNDISTREST BY HEARTS GROWN COLD TO ME, COULD LONELY WAIT MY ENDLESS REST WITH EQUANIMITY"...
?
...

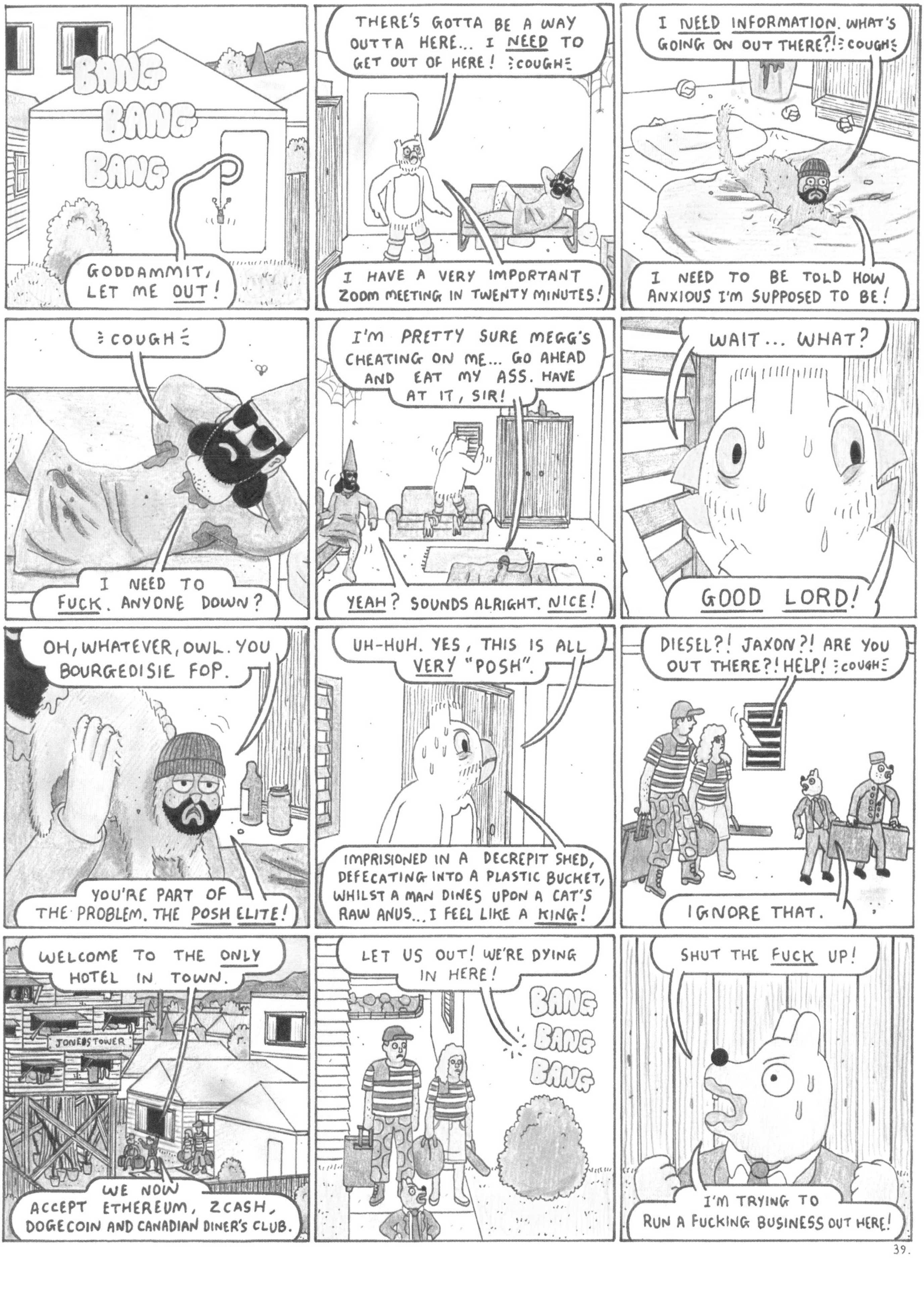
BANG
BANG
BANG
GODDAMMIT, LET ME OUT!
THERE'S GOTTA BE A WAY OUTTA HERE... I NEED TO GET OUT OF HERE! COUGH
I HAVE A VERY IMPORTANT ZOOM MEETING IN TWENTY MINUTES!
I NEED INFORMATION. WHAT'S GOING ON OUT THERE?! COUGH
I NEED TO BE TOLD HOW ANXIOUS I'M SUPPOSED TO BE!
COUGH
I NEED TO FUCK. ANYONE DOWN?
I'M PRETTY SURE MEGG'S CHEATING ON ME... GO AHEAD AND EAT MY ASS. HAVE AT IT, SIR!
YEAH? SOUNDS ALRIGHT. NICE!
WAIT... WHAT?
GOOD LORD!
OH, WHATEVER, OWL. YOU BOURGEOISIE FOP.
YOU'RE PART OF THE PROBLEM. THE POSH ELITE!
UH-HUH. YES, THIS IS ALL VERY "POSH".
IMPRISIONED IN A DECREPIT SHED, DEFECATING INTO A PLASTIC BUCKET, WHILST A MAN DINES UPON A CAT'S RAW ANUS... I FEEL LIKE A KING!
DIESEL?! JAXON?! ARE YOU OUT THERE?! HELP! COUGH
IGNORE THAT.
WELCOME TO THE ONLY HOTEL IN TOWN.
JONES'S TOWER
WE NOW ACCEPT ETHEREUM, ZCASH, DOGECOIN AND CANADIAN DINER'S CLUB.
LET US OUT! WE'RE DYING IN HERE!
BANG
BANG
BANG
SHUT THE FUCK UP!
I'M TRYING TO RUN A FUCKING BUSINESS OUT HERE!

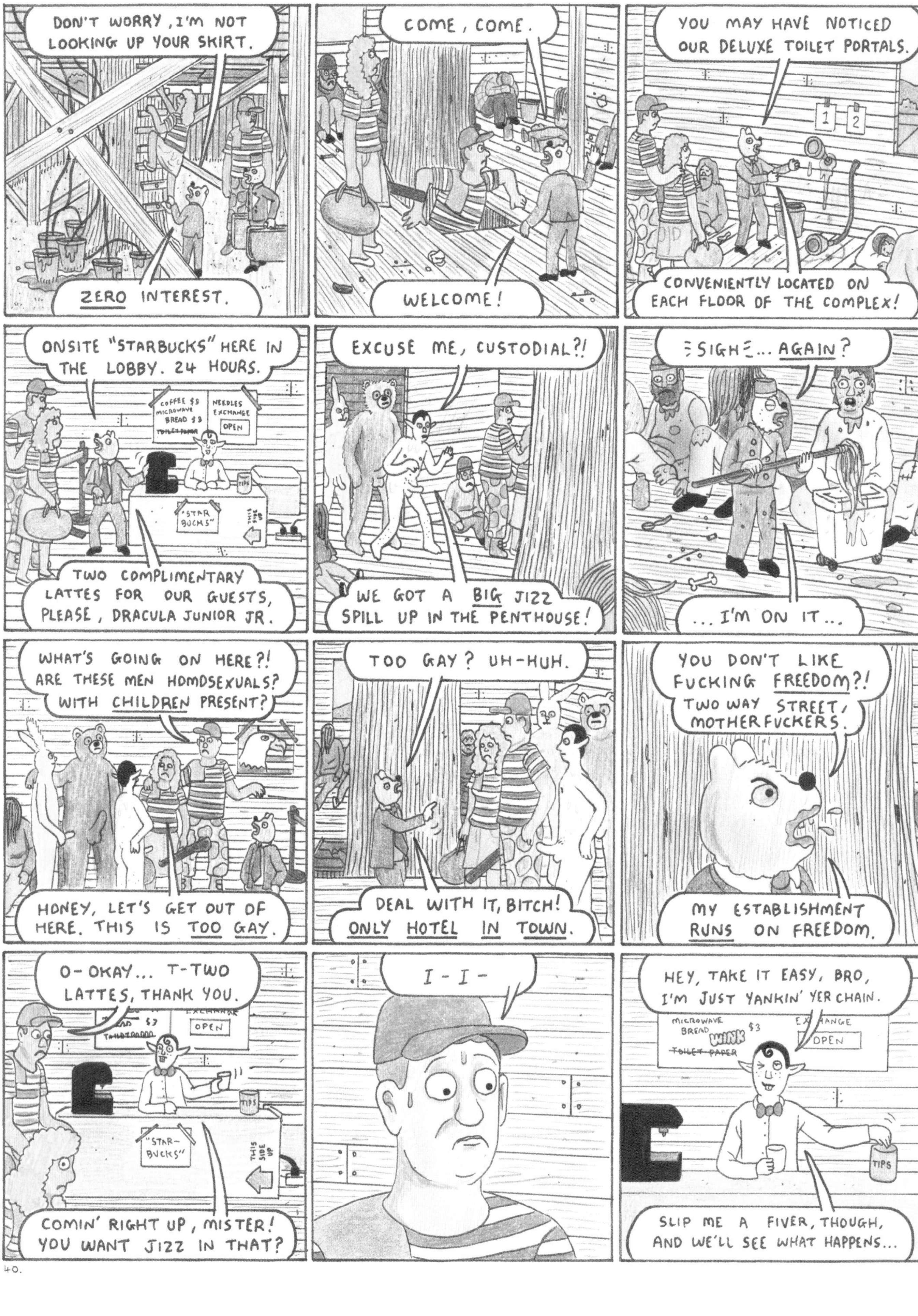
DON'T WORRY, I'M NOT LOOKING UP YOUR SKIRT.
ZERO INTEREST.
COME, COME.
WELCOME!
YOU MAY HAVE NOTICED OUR DELUXE TOILET PORTALS.
1
2
CONVENIENTLY LOCATED ON EACH FLOOR OF THE COMPLEX!
ONSITE "STARBUCKS" HERE IN THE LOBBY. 24 HOURS.
COFFEE $5
MICROWAVE BREAD $3
TOILET PAPER
NEEDLES EXCHANGE
OPEN
TIPS
"STAR BUCKS"
THIS SIDE UP
TWO COMPLIMENTARY LATTES FOR OUR GUESTS, PLEASE, DRACULA JUNIOR JR.
EXCUSE ME, CUSTODIAL?!
WE GOT A BIG JIZZ SPILL UP IN THE PENTHOUSE!
≡SIGH≡... AGAIN?
... I'M ON IT...
WHAT'S GOING ON HERE?! ARE THESE MEN HOMOSEXUALS? WITH CHILDREN PRESENT?
HONEY, LET'S GET OUT OF HERE. THIS IS TOO GAY.
TOO GAY? UH-HUH.
DEAL WITH IT, BITCH! ONLY HOTEL IN TOWN.
YOU DON'T LIKE FUCKING FREEDOM?! TWO WAY STREET, MOTHERFUCKERS.
MY ESTABLISHMENT RUNS ON FREEDOM.
O-OKAY... T-TWO LATTES, THANK YOU.
OPEN
TIPS
"STAR-BUCKS"
THIS SIDE UP
COMIN' RIGHT UP, MISTER! YOU WANT JIZZ IN THAT?
I-I-
HEY, TAKE IT EASY, BRO, I'M JUST YANKIN' YER CHAIN.
MICROWAVE BREAD $3
TOILET PAPER
WINK
OPEN
TIPS
SLIP ME A FIVER, THOUGH, AND WE'LL SEE WHAT HAPPENS...

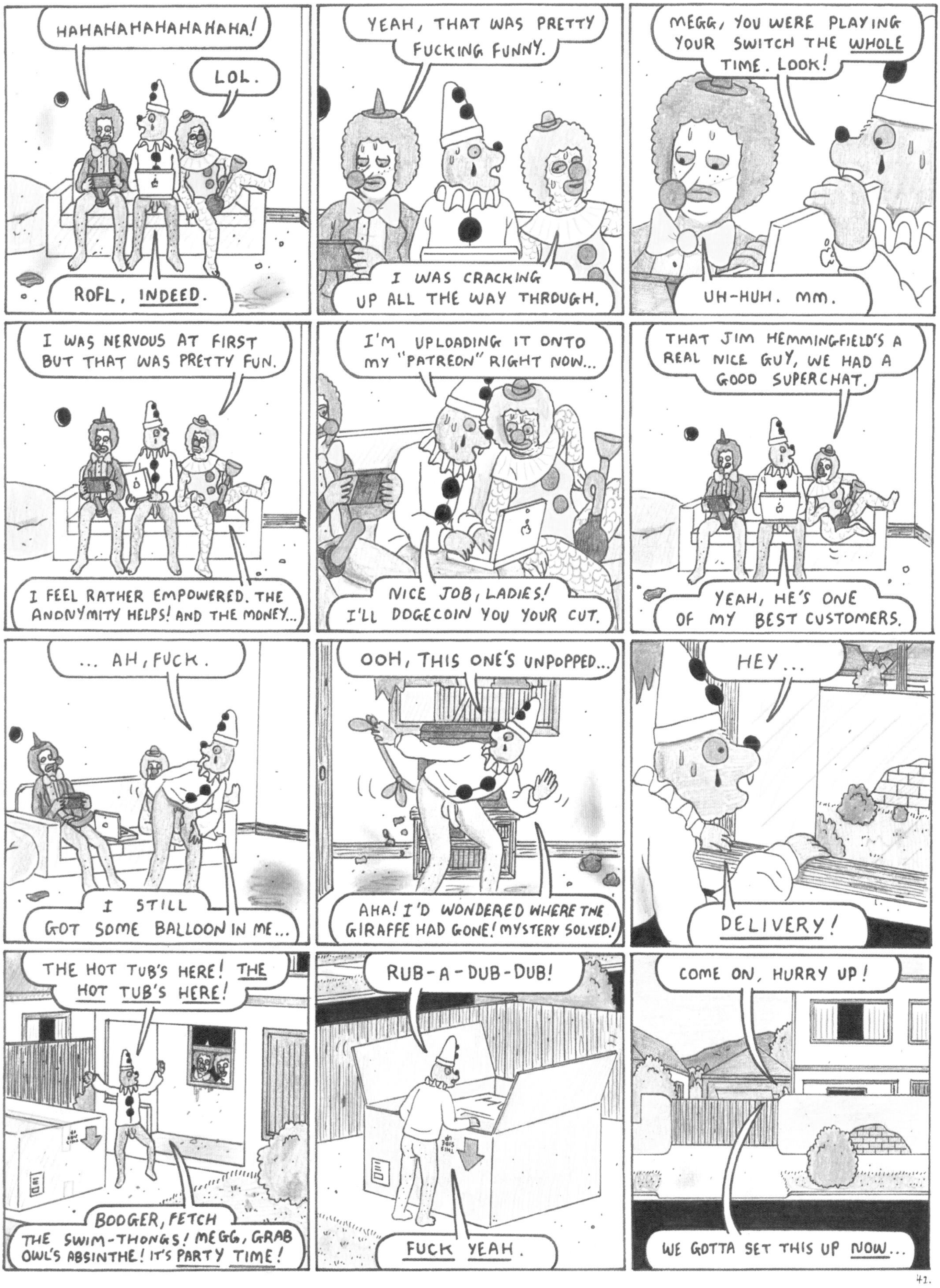
HAHAHAHAHAHAHAHA!
LOL.
ROFL, INDEED.
YEAH, THAT WAS PRETTY FUCKING FUNNY.
I WAS CRACKING UP ALL THE WAY THROUGH.
MEGG, YOU WERE PLAYING YOUR SWITCH THE WHOLE TIME. LOOK!
UH-HUH. MM.
I WAS NERVOUS AT FIRST BUT THAT WAS PRETTY FUN.
I FEEL RATHER EMPOWERED. THE ANONYMITY HELPS! AND THE MONEY...
I'M UPLOADING IT ONTO MY "PATREON" RIGHT NOW...
NICE JOB, LADIES! I'LL DOGECOIN YOU YOUR CUT.
THAT JIM HEMMINGFIELD'S A REAL NICE GUY, WE HAD A GOOD SUPERCHAT.
YEAH, HE'S ONE OF MY BEST CUSTOMERS.
... AH, FUCK.
I STILL GOT SOME BALLOON IN ME...
OOH, THIS ONE'S UNPOPPED...
AHA! I'D WONDERED WHERE THE GIRAFFE HAD GONE! MYSTERY SOLVED!
HEY...
DELIVERY!
THE HOT TUB'S HERE! THE HOT TUB'S HERE!
BODGER, FETCH THE SWIM-THONGS! MEGG, GRAB OWL'S ABSINTHE! IT'S PARTY TIME!
RUB-A-DUB-DUB!
FUCK YEAH.
COME ON, HURRY UP!
WE GOTTA SET THIS UP NOW...

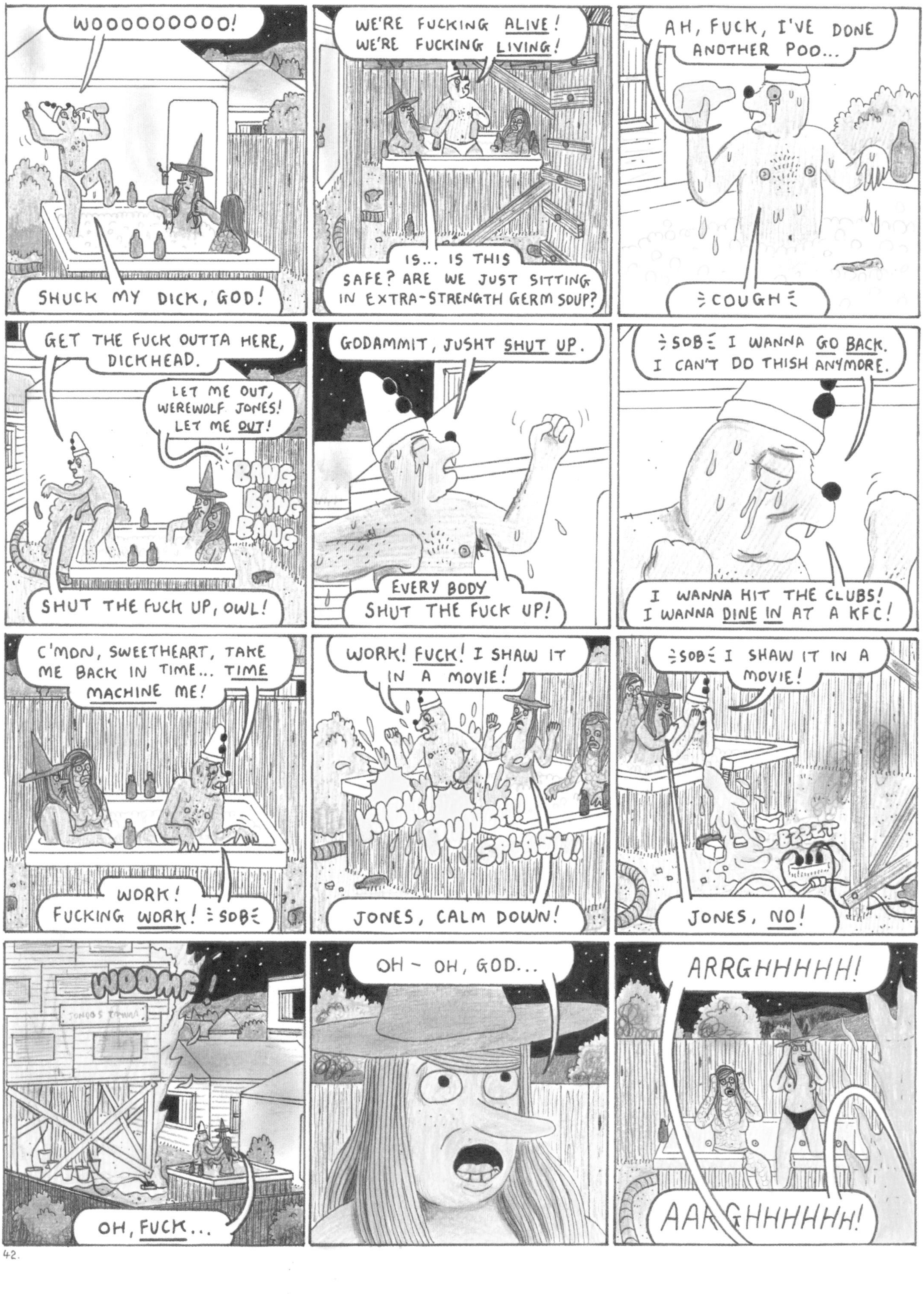
WOOOOOOOOO!
SHUCK MY DICK, GOD!
WE'RE FUCKING ALIVE! WE'RE FUCKING LIVING!
IS... IS THIS SAFE? ARE WE JUST SITTING IN EXTRA-STRENGTH GERM SOUP?
AH, FUCK, I'VE DONE ANOTHER POO...
COUGH
GET THE FUCK OUTTA HERE, DICKHEAD.
LET ME OUT, WEREWOLF JONES! LET ME OUT!
BANG BANG BANG
SHUT THE FUCK UP, OWL!
GODAMMIT, JUSHT SHUT UP.
EVERY BODY SHUT THE FUCK UP!
SOB I WANNA GO BACK. I CAN'T DO THISH ANYMORE.
I WANNA HIT THE CLUBS! I WANNA DINE IN AT A KFC!
C'MON, SWEETHEART, TAKE ME BACK IN TIME... TIME MACHINE ME!
WORK! FUCKING WORK! SOB
WORK! FUCK! I SHAW IT IN A MOVIE!
KICK! PUNCH! SPLASH!
JONES, CALM DOWN!
SOB I SHAW IT IN A MOVIE!
BZZZT
JONES, NO!
WOOMF!
OH, FUCK...
OH - OH, GOD...
ARRGHHHHHH!
AARGHHHHHH!

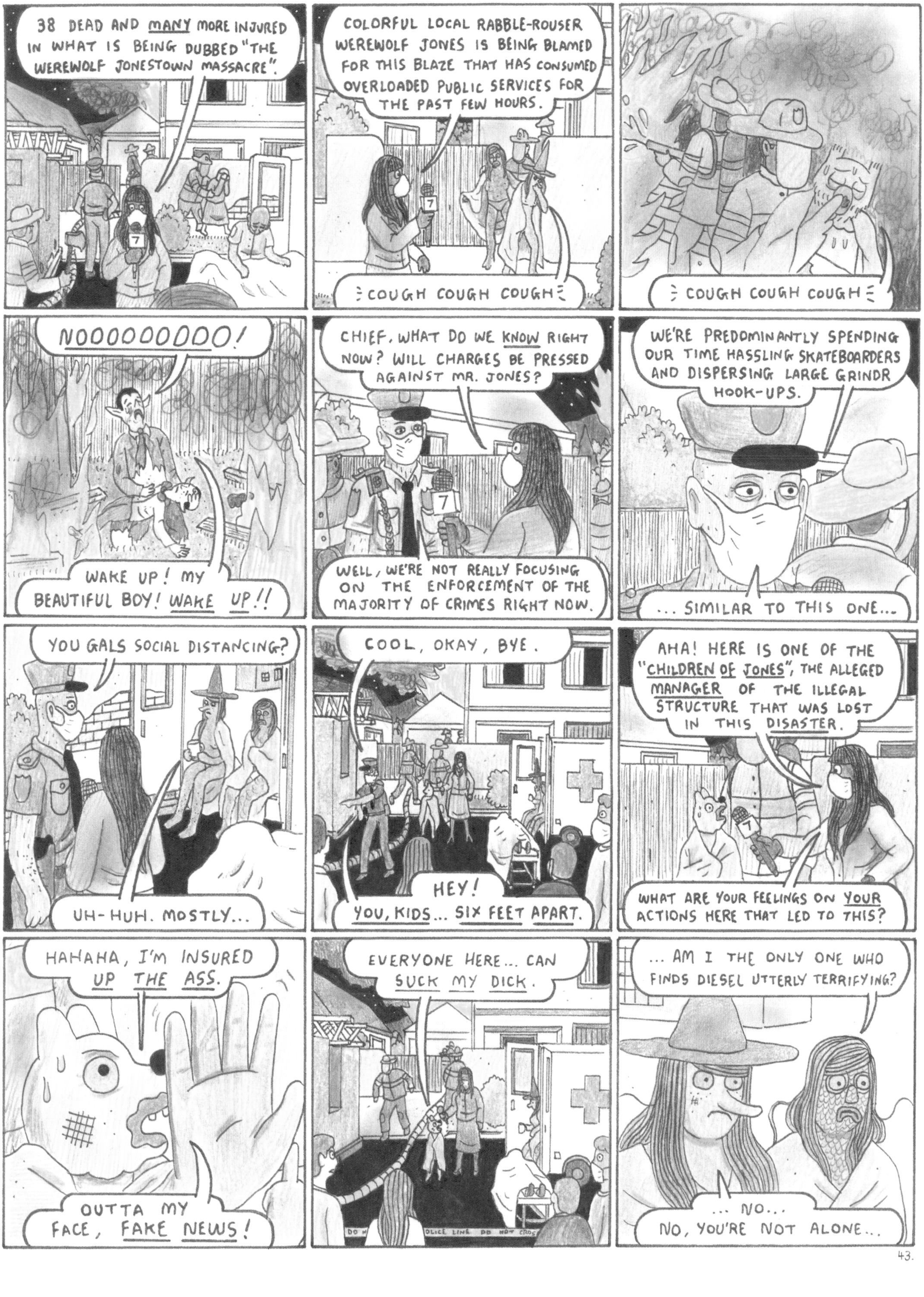
38 DEAD AND MANY MORE INJURED IN WHAT IS BEING DUBBED "THE WEREWOLF JONESTOWN MASSACRE".
COLORFUL LOCAL RABBLE-ROUSER WEREWOLF JONES IS BEING BLAMED FOR THIS BLAZE THAT HAS CONSUMED OVERLOADED PUBLIC SERVICES FOR THE PAST FEW HOURS.
COUGH COUGH COUGH
COUGH COUGH COUGH
NOOOOOOOOO!
WAKE UP! MY BEAUTIFUL BOY! WAKE UP!!
CHIEF, WHAT DO WE KNOW RIGHT NOW? WILL CHARGES BE PRESSED AGAINST MR. JONES?
WELL, WE'RE NOT REALLY FOCUSING ON THE ENFORCEMENT OF THE MAJORITY OF CRIMES RIGHT NOW.
WE'RE PREDOMINANTLY SPENDING OUR TIME HASSLING SKATEBOARDERS AND DISPERSING LARGE GRINDR HOOK-UPS.
... SIMILAR TO THIS ONE...
YOU GALS SOCIAL DISTANCING?
UH-HUH. MOSTLY...
COOL, OKAY, BYE.
HEY!
YOU, KIDS... SIX FEET APART.
AHA! HERE IS ONE OF THE "CHILDREN OF JONES", THE ALLEGED MANAGER OF THE ILLEGAL STRUCTURE THAT WAS LOST IN THIS DISASTER.
WHAT ARE YOUR FEELINGS ON YOUR ACTIONS HERE THAT LED TO THIS?
HAHAHA, I'M INSURED UP THE ASS.
OUTTA MY FACE, FAKE NEWS!
EVERYONE HERE... CAN SUCK MY DICK.
... AM I THE ONLY ONE WHO FINDS DIESEL UTTERLY TERRIFYING?
... NO...
NO, YOU'RE NOT ALONE...

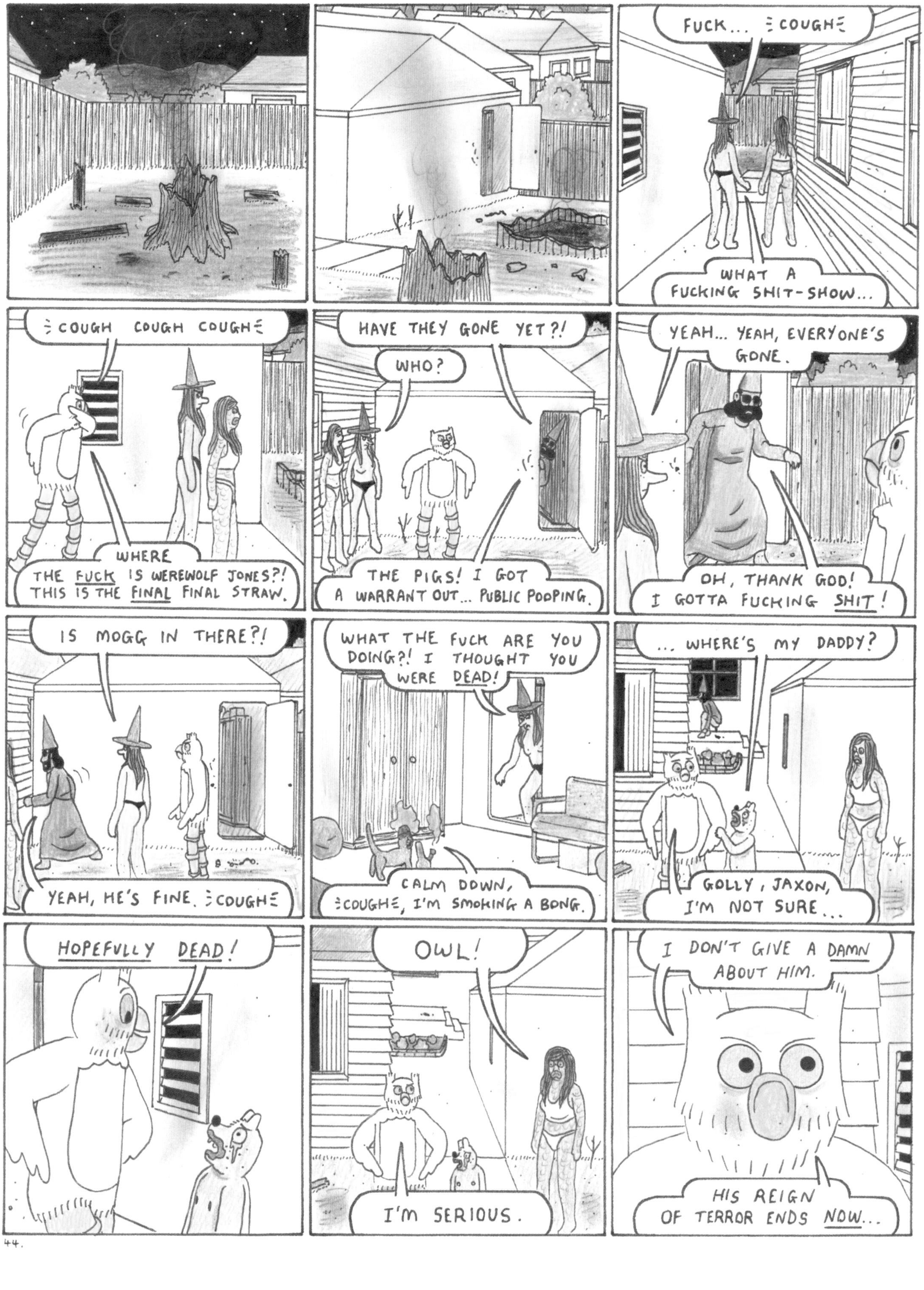
FUCK... ⸗COUGH⸗
WHAT A FUCKING SHIT-SHOW...
⸗COUGH COUGH COUGH⸗
WHERE THE FUCK IS WEREWOLF JONES?! THIS IS THE FINAL FINAL STRAW.
HAVE THEY GONE YET?!
WHO?
THE PIGS! I GOT A WARRANT OUT... PUBLIC POOPING.
YEAH... YEAH, EVERYONE'S GONE.
OH, THANK GOD! I GOTTA FUCKING SHIT!
IS MOGG IN THERE?!
YEAH, HE'S FINE. ⸗COUGH⸗
WHAT THE FUCK ARE YOU DOING?! I THOUGHT YOU WERE DEAD!
CALM DOWN, ⸗COUGH⸗, I'M SMOKING A BONG.
... WHERE'S MY DADDY?
GOLLY, JAXON, I'M NOT SURE...
HOPEFULLY DEAD!
OWL!
I'M SERIOUS.
I DON'T GIVE A DAMN ABOUT HIM.
HIS REIGN OF TERROR ENDS NOW...

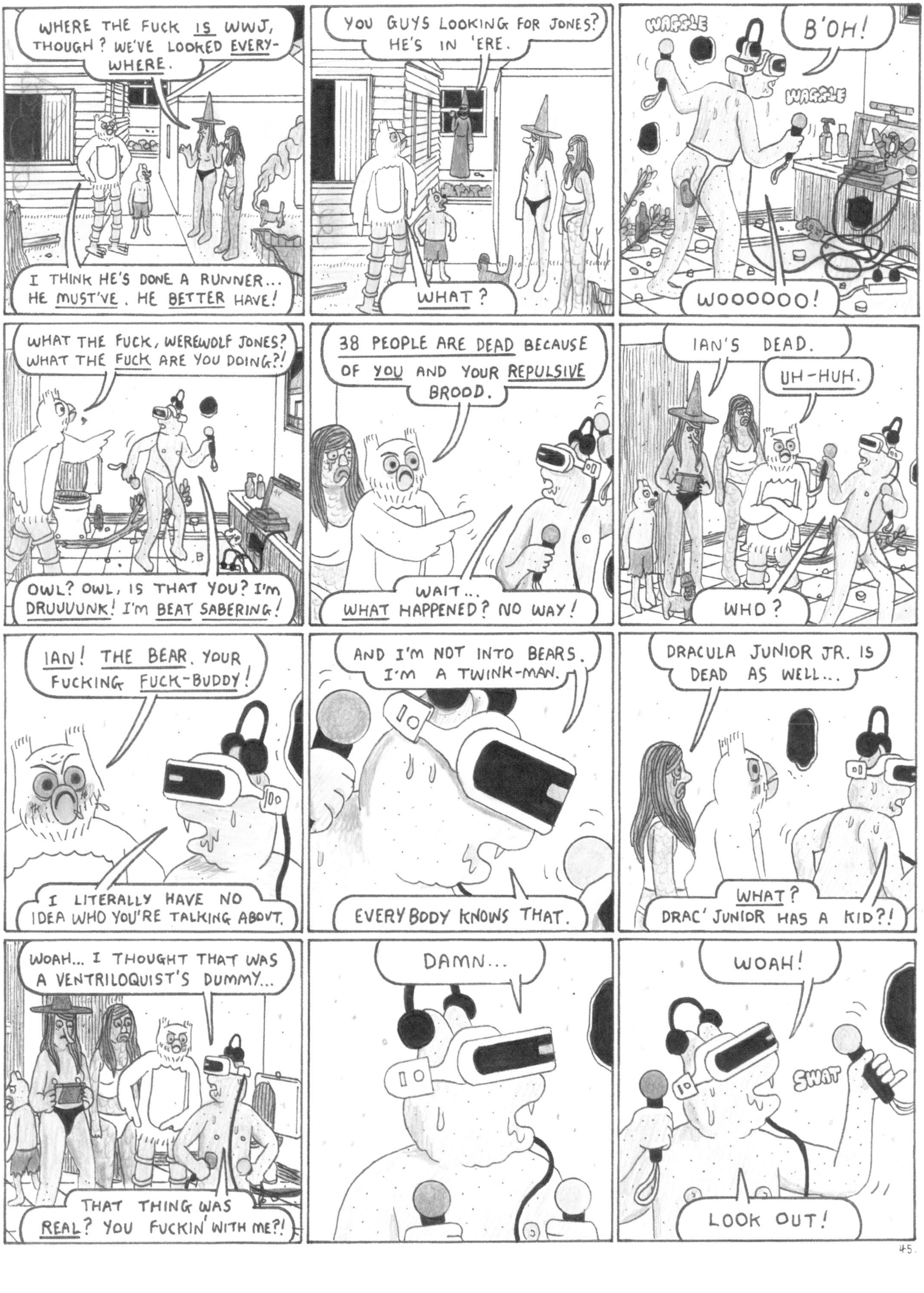
WHERE THE FUCK IS WWJ, THOUGH? WE'VE LOOKED EVERY-WHERE.
I THINK HE'S DONE A RUNNER... HE MUST'VE. HE BETTER HAVE!
YOU GUYS LOOKING FOR JONES? HE'S IN 'ERE.
WHAT?
WAFFLE
B'OH!
WAFFLE
WOOOOOO!
WHAT THE FUCK, WEREWOLF JONES? WHAT THE FUCK ARE YOU DOING?!
OWL? OWL, IS THAT YOU? I'M DRUUUUNK! I'M BEAT SABERING!
38 PEOPLE ARE DEAD BECAUSE OF YOU AND YOUR REPULSIVE BROOD.
WAIT... WHAT HAPPENED? NO WAY!
IAN'S DEAD.
UH-HUH.
WHO?
IAN! THE BEAR. YOUR FUCKING FUCK-BUDDY!
I LITERALLY HAVE NO IDEA WHO YOU'RE TALKING ABOUT.
AND I'M NOT INTO BEARS. I'M A TWINK-MAN.
EVERYBODY KNOWS THAT.
DRACULA JUNIOR JR. IS DEAD AS WELL...
WHAT? DRAC' JUNIOR HAS A KID?!
WOAH... I THOUGHT THAT WAS A VENTRILOQUIST'S DUMMY...
THAT THING WAS REAL? YOU FUCKIN' WITH ME?!
DAMN...
WOAH!
SWAT
LOOK OUT!

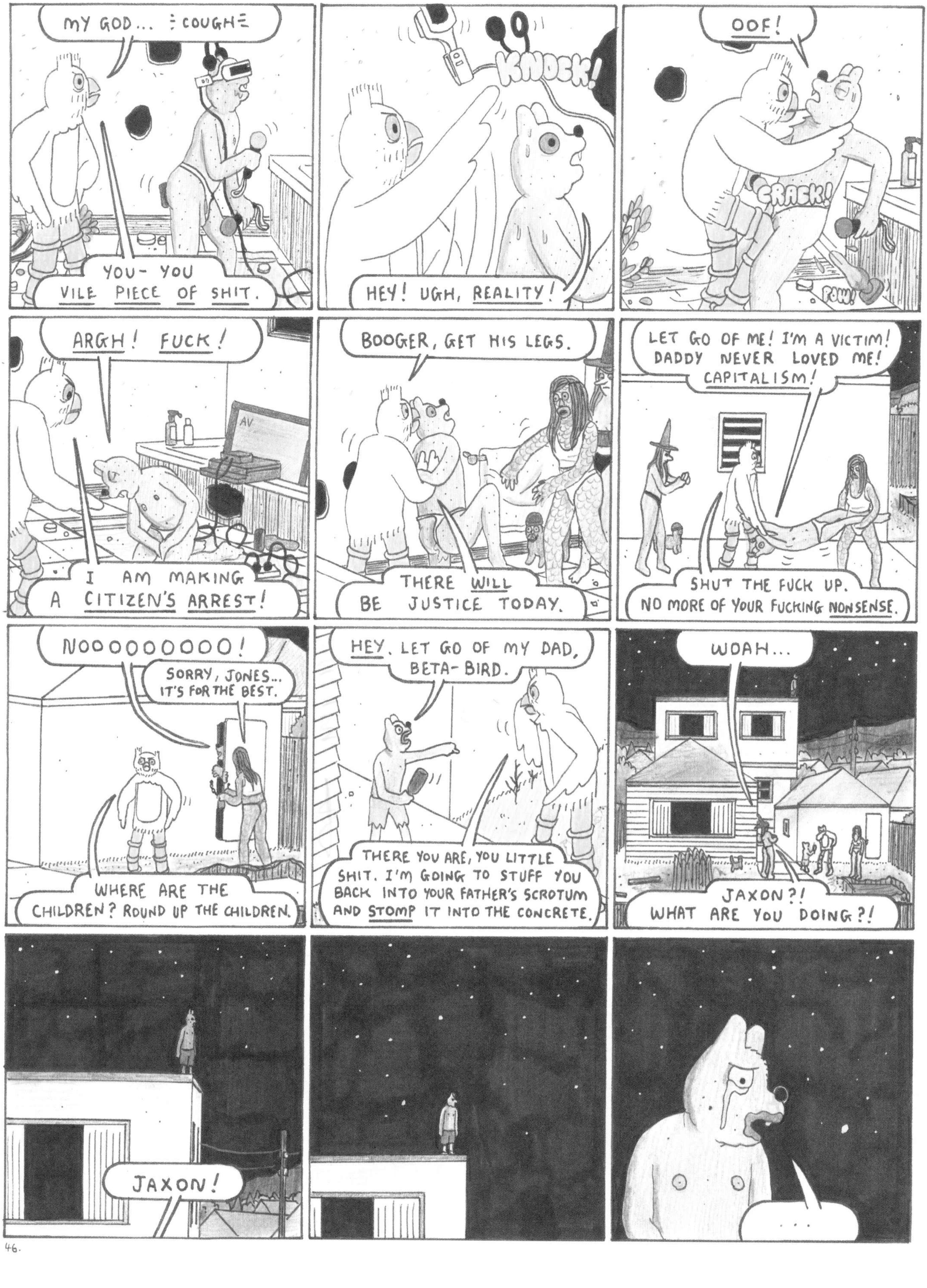
MY GOD... =COUGH=
YOU- YOU VILE PIECE OF SHIT.
KNOCK!
HEY! UGH, REALITY!
OOF!
CRACK!
POW!
ARGH! FUCK!
I AM MAKING A CITIZEN'S ARREST!
BOOGER, GET HIS LEGS.
THERE WILL BE JUSTICE TODAY.
LET GO OF ME! I'M A VICTIM! DADDY NEVER LOVED ME! CAPITALISM!
SHUT THE FUCK UP. NO MORE OF YOUR FUCKING NONSENSE.
NOOOOOOOOO!
SORRY, JONES... IT'S FOR THE BEST.
WHERE ARE THE CHILDREN? ROUND UP THE CHILDREN.
HEY. LET GO OF MY DAD, BETA-BIRD.
THERE YOU ARE, YOU LITTLE SHIT. I'M GOING TO STUFF YOU BACK INTO YOUR FATHER'S SCROTUM AND STOMP IT INTO THE CONCRETE.
WOAH...
JAXON?! WHAT ARE YOU DOING?!
JAXON!
...

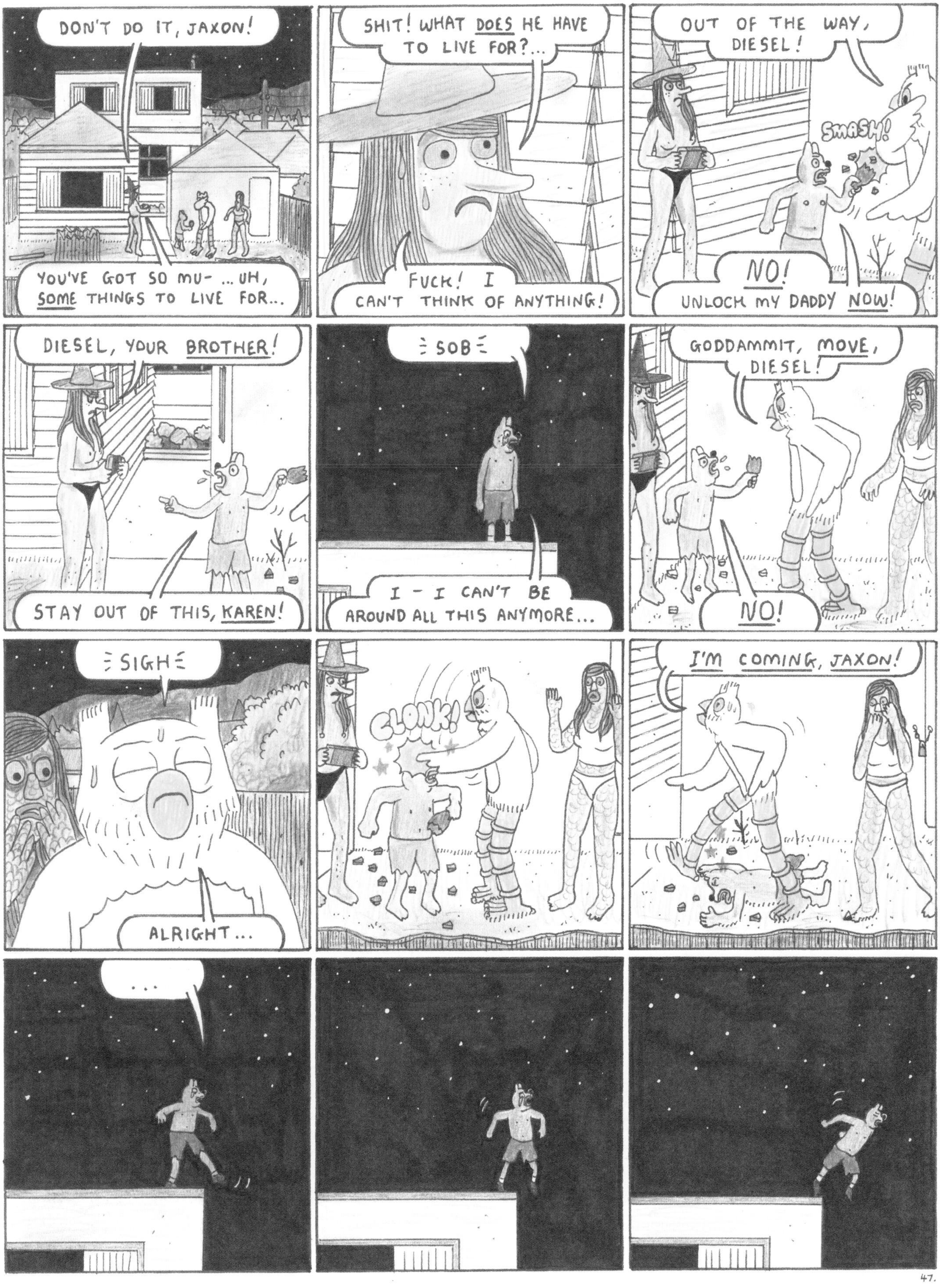
DON'T DO IT, JAXON!
YOU'VE GOT SO MU- ...UH, SOME THINGS TO LIVE FOR...
SHIT! WHAT DOES HE HAVE TO LIVE FOR?...
FUCK! I CAN'T THINK OF ANYTHING!
OUT OF THE WAY, DIESEL!
SMASH!
NO!
UNLOCK MY DADDY NOW!
DIESEL, YOUR BROTHER!
STAY OUT OF THIS, KAREN!
SOB
I - I CAN'T BE AROUND ALL THIS ANYMORE...
GODDAMMIT, MOVE, DIESEL!
NO!
SIGH
ALRIGHT...
CLONK!
I'M COMING, JAXON!
...

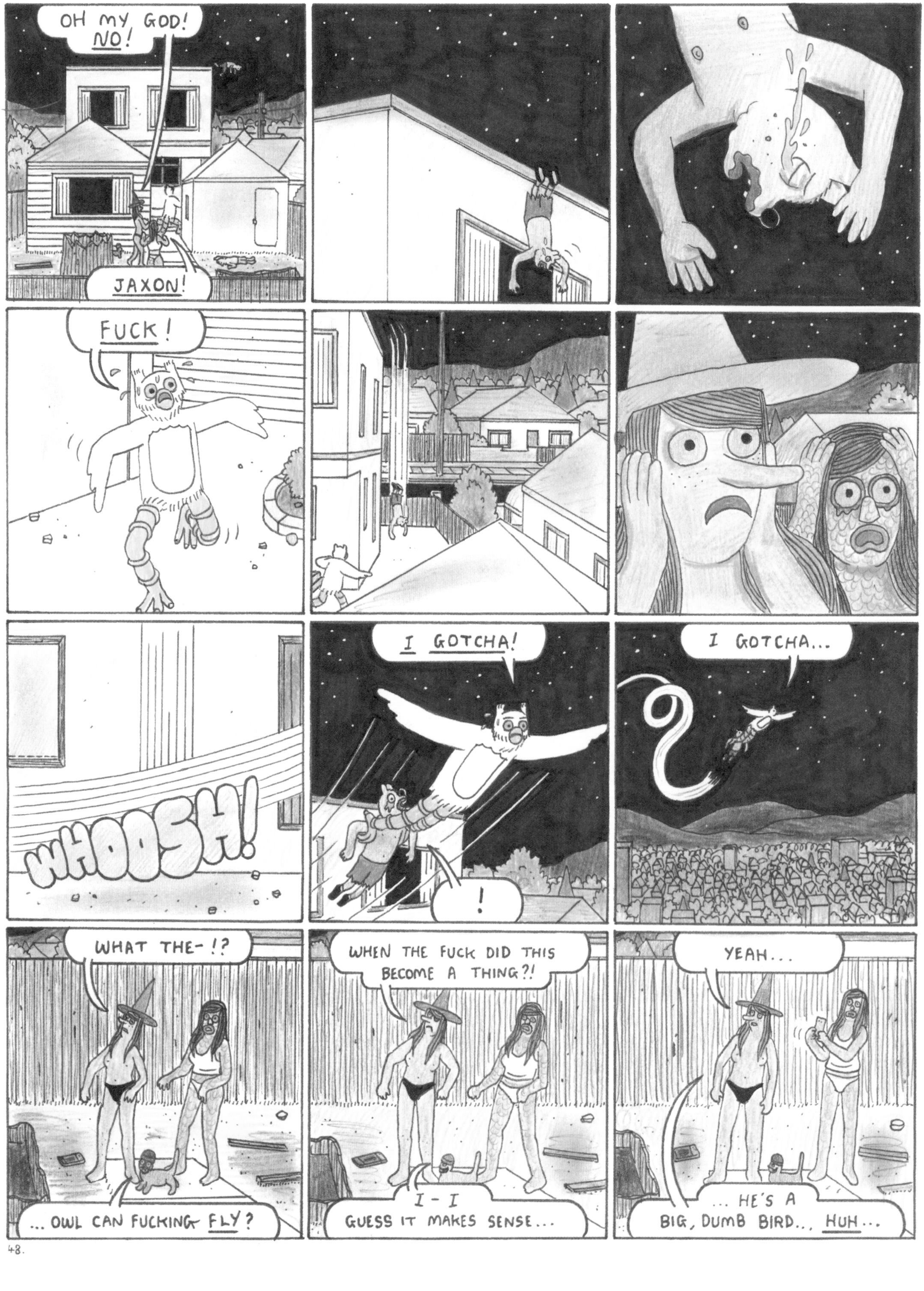
OH MY GOD! NO!
JAXON!
FUCK!
WHOOSH!
I GOTCHA!
!
I GOTCHA...
WHAT THE-!?
... OWL CAN FUCKING FLY?
WHEN THE FUCK DID THIS BECOME A THING?!
I-I GUESS IT MAKES SENSE...
YEAH...
... HE'S A BIG, DUMB BIRD..., HUH...

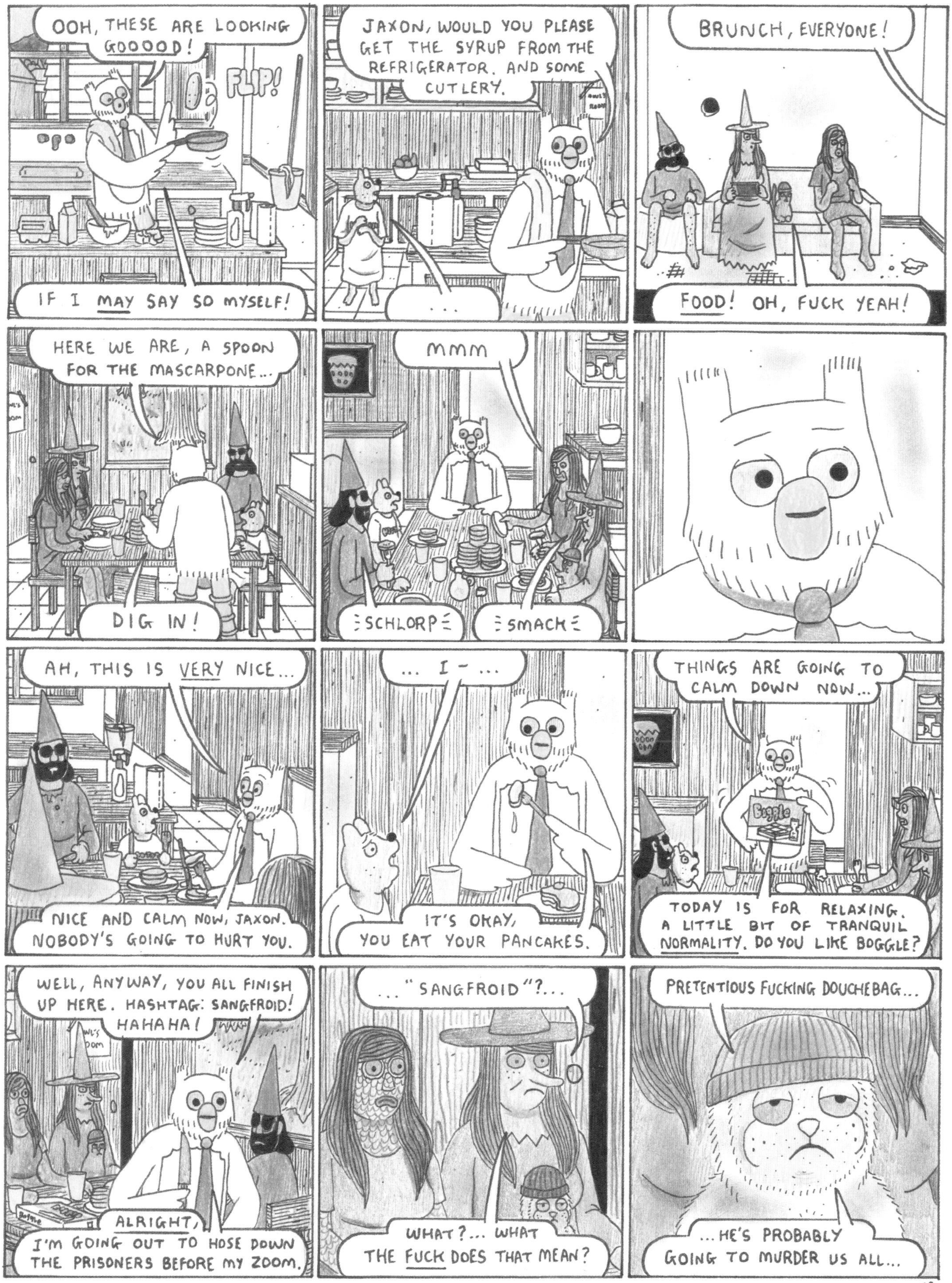

OOH, THESE ARE LOOKING GOOOOD!
FLIP!
IF I MAY SAY SO MYSELF!
JAXON, WOULD YOU PLEASE GET THE SYRUP FROM THE REFRIGERATOR. AND SOME CUTLERY.
...
BRUNCH, EVERYONE!
FOOD! OH, FUCK YEAH!
HERE WE ARE, A SPOON FOR THE MASCARPONE...
DIG IN!
MMM
SCHLORP
SMACK
AH, THIS IS VERY NICE...
NICE AND CALM NOW, JAXON. NOBODY'S GOING TO HURT YOU.
... I - ...
IT'S OKAY, YOU EAT YOUR PANCAKES.
THINGS ARE GOING TO CALM DOWN NOW...
Boggle
TODAY IS FOR RELAXING. A LITTLE BIT OF TRANQUIL NORMALITY. DO YOU LIKE BOGGLE?
WELL, ANYWAY, YOU ALL FINISH UP HERE. HASHTAG: SANGFROID! HAHAHA!
ALRIGHT, I'M GOING OUT TO HOSE DOWN THE PRISONERS BEFORE MY ZOOM.
..."SANGFROID"?...
WHAT?... WHAT THE FUCK DOES THAT MEAN?
PRETENTIOUS FUCKING DOUCHEBAG...
...HE'S PROBABLY GOING TO MURDER US ALL...

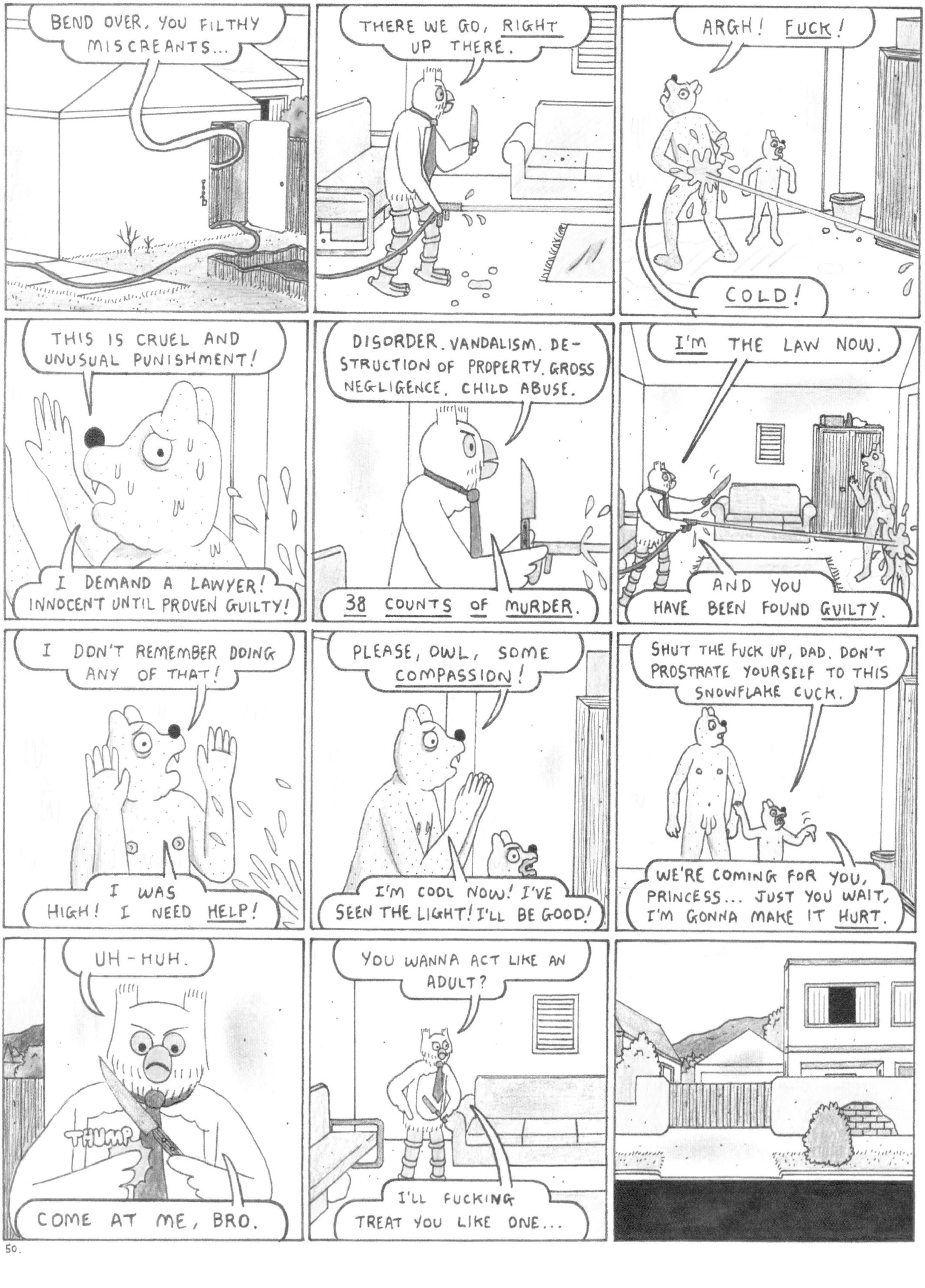
BEND OVER, YOU FILTHY MISCREANTS...
THERE WE GO, RIGHT UP THERE.
ARGH! FUCK!
COLD!
THIS IS CRUEL AND UNUSUAL PUNISHMENT!
I DEMAND A LAWYER! INNOCENT UNTIL PROVEN GUILTY!
DISORDER. VANDALISM. DESTRUCTION OF PROPERTY. GROSS NEGLIGENCE. CHILD ABUSE.
38 COUNTS OF MURDER.
I'M THE LAW NOW.
AND YOU HAVE BEEN FOUND GUILTY.
I DON'T REMEMBER DOING ANY OF THAT!
I WAS HIGH! I NEED HELP!
PLEASE, OWL, SOME COMPASSION!
I'M COOL NOW! I'VE SEEN THE LIGHT! I'LL BE GOOD!
SHUT THE FUCK UP, DAD. DON'T PROSTRATE YOURSELF TO THIS SNOWFLAKE CUCK.
WE'RE COMING FOR YOU, PRINCESS... JUST YOU WAIT, I'M GONNA MAKE IT HURT.
UH-HUH.
THUMP
COME AT ME, BRO.
YOU WANNA ACT LIKE AN ADULT?
I'LL FUCKING TREAT YOU LIKE ONE...

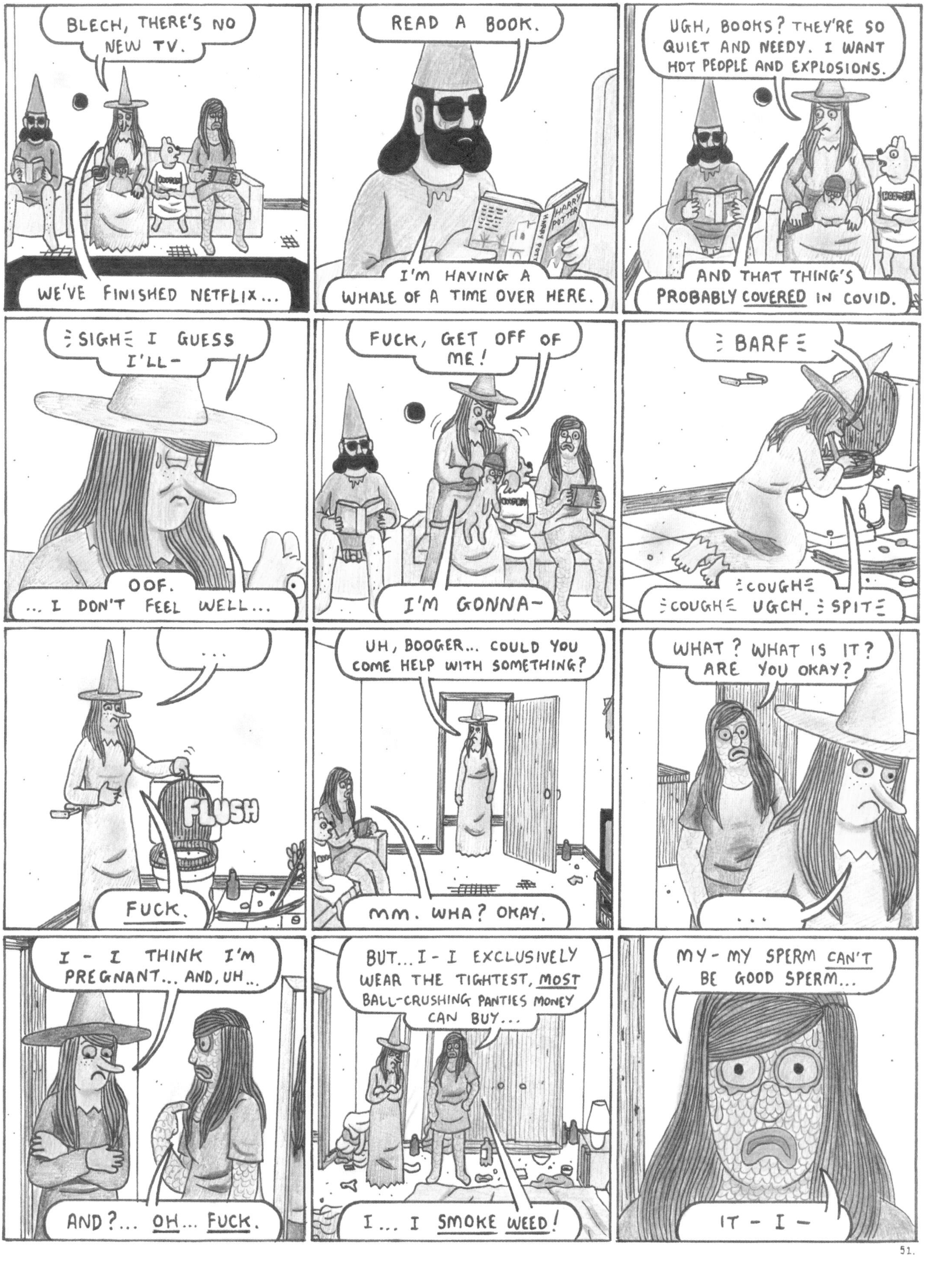
BLECH, THERE'S NO NEW TV.
WE'VE FINISHED NETFLIX...
READ A BOOK.
HARRY POTTER
I'M HAVING A WHALE OF A TIME OVER HERE.
UGH, BOOKS? THEY'RE SO QUIET AND NEEDY. I WANT HOT PEOPLE AND EXPLOSIONS.
AND THAT THING'S PROBABLY COVERED IN COVID.
≡SIGH≡ I GUESS I'LL-
OOF. ... I DON'T FEEL WELL...
FUCK, GET OFF OF ME!
I'M GONNA-
≡BARF≡
≡COUGH≡ ≡COUGH≡ UGCH. ≡SPIT≡
...
FLUSH
FUCK.
UH, BOOGER... COULD YOU COME HELP WITH SOMETHING?
MM. WHA? OKAY.
WHAT? WHAT IS IT? ARE YOU OKAY?
...
I - I THINK I'M PREGNANT... AND, UH...
AND?... OH... FUCK.
BUT... I - I EXCLUSIVELY WEAR THE TIGHTEST, MOST BALL-CRUSHING PANTIES MONEY CAN BUY...
I... I SMOKE WEED!
MY - MY SPERM CAN'T BE GOOD SPERM...
IT - I -

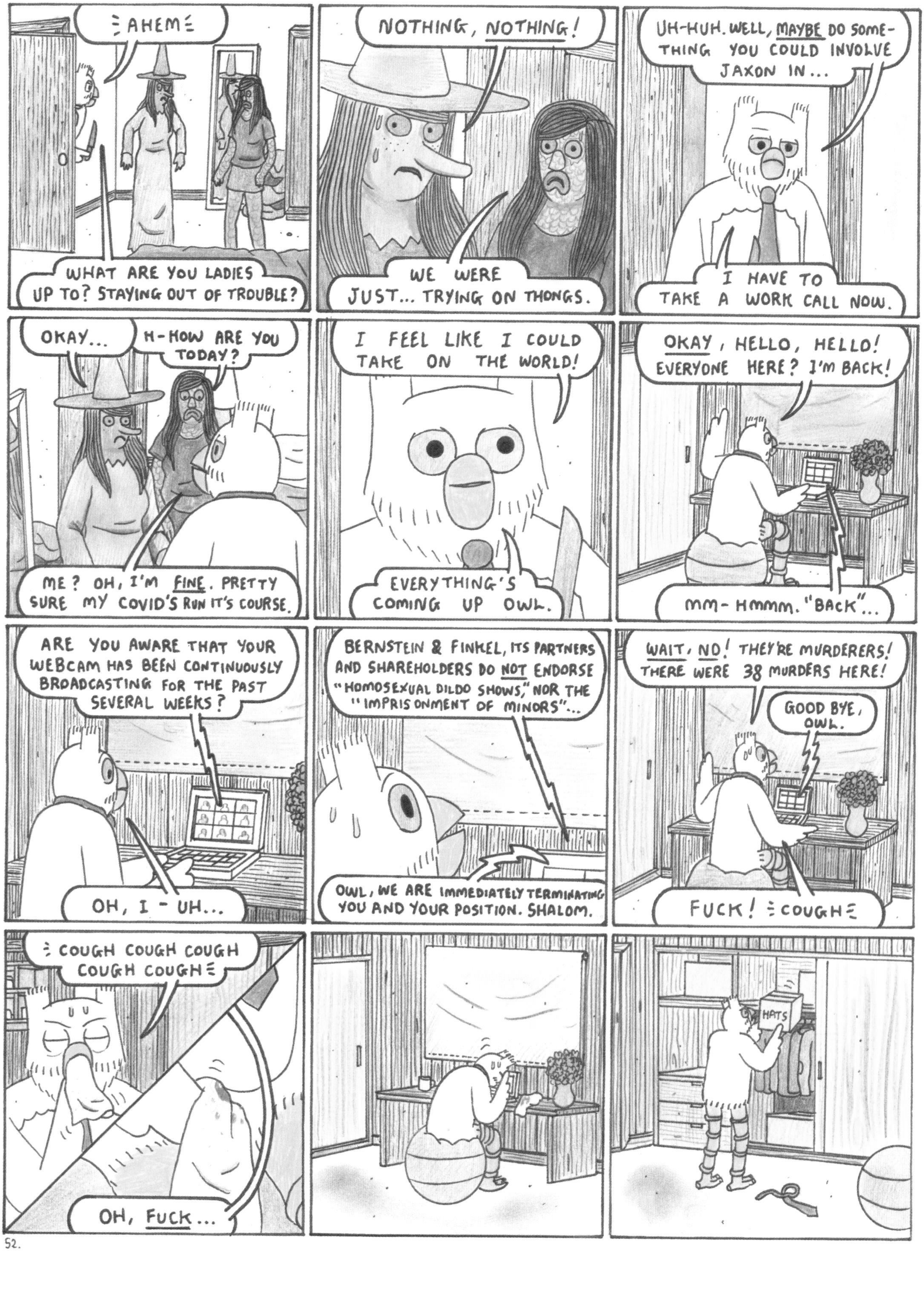
AHEM
WHAT ARE YOU LADIES UP TO? STAYING OUT OF TROUBLE?
NOTHING, NOTHING!
WE WERE JUST... TRYING ON THONGS.
UH-HUH. WELL, MAYBE DO SOMETHING YOU COULD INVOLVE JAXON IN...
I HAVE TO TAKE A WORK CALL NOW.
OKAY...
H-HOW ARE YOU TODAY?
ME? OH, I'M FINE. PRETTY SURE MY COVID'S RUN IT'S COURSE.
I FEEL LIKE I COULD TAKE ON THE WORLD!
EVERYTHING'S COMING UP OWL.
OKAY, HELLO, HELLO! EVERYONE HERE? I'M BACK!
MM-HMMM. "BACK"...
ARE YOU AWARE THAT YOUR WEBCAM HAS BEEN CONTINUOUSLY BROADCASTING FOR THE PAST SEVERAL WEEKS?
OH, I - UH...
BERNSTEIN & FINKEL, ITS PARTNERS AND SHAREHOLDERS DO NOT ENDORSE "HOMOSEXUAL DILDO SHOWS," NOR THE "IMPRISONMENT OF MINORS"...
OWL, WE ARE IMMEDIATELY TERMINATING YOU AND YOUR POSITION. SHALOM.
WAIT, NO! THEY'RE MURDERERS! THERE WERE 38 MURDERS HERE!
GOOD BYE, OWL.
FUCK! COUGH
COUGH COUGH COUGH COUGH COUGH
OH, FUCK...
HATS

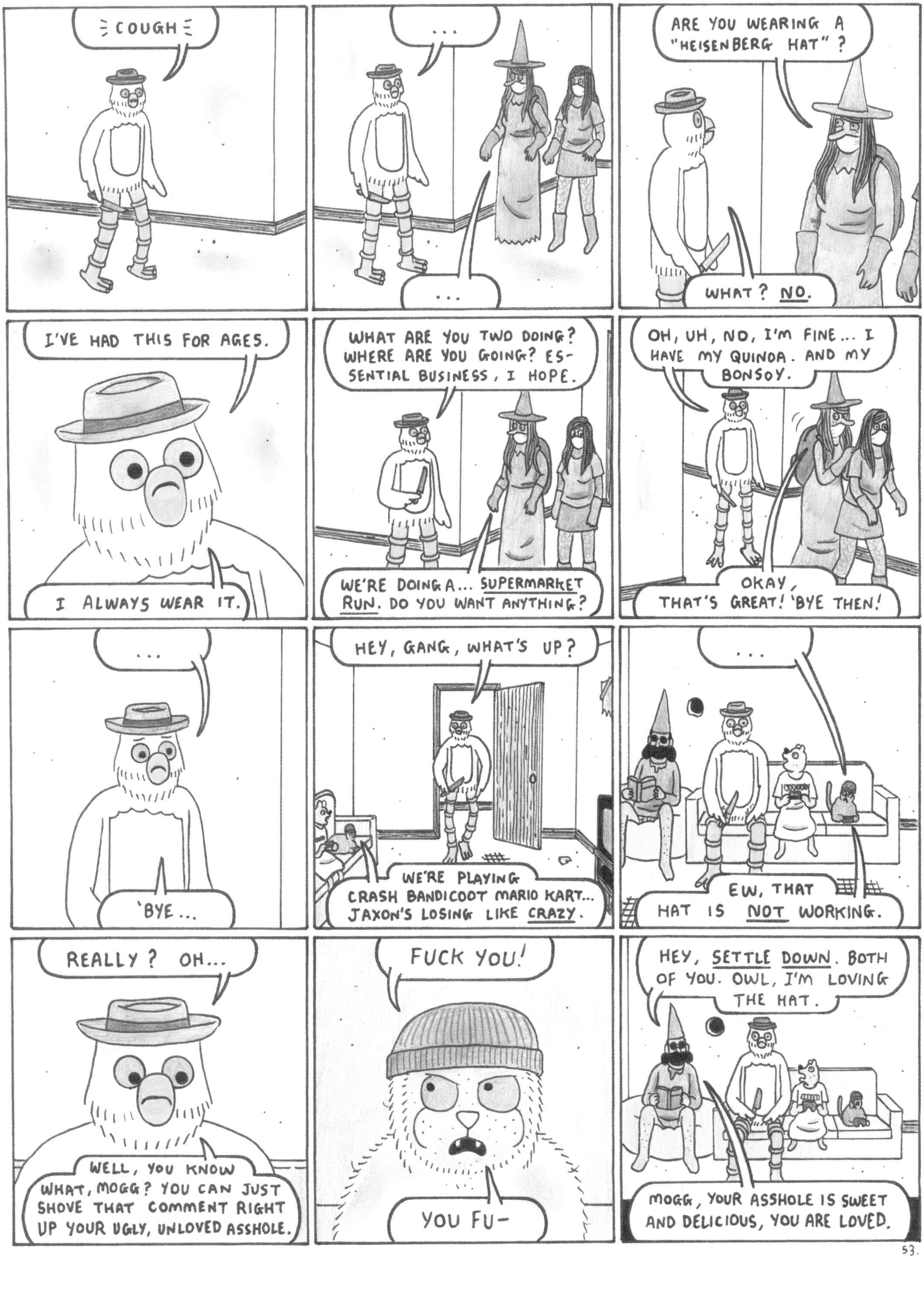
COUGH
...
...
ARE YOU WEARING A "HEISENBERG HAT"?
WHAT? NO.
I'VE HAD THIS FOR AGES.
I ALWAYS WEAR IT.
WHAT ARE YOU TWO DOING? WHERE ARE YOU GOING? ES-SENTIAL BUSINESS, I HOPE.
WE'RE DOING A... SUPERMARKET RUN. DO YOU WANT ANYTHING?
OH, UH, NO, I'M FINE... I HAVE MY QUINOA. AND MY BONSOY.
OKAY, THAT'S GREAT! 'BYE THEN!
...
'BYE...
HEY, GANG, WHAT'S UP?
WE'RE PLAYING CRASH BANDICOOT MARIO KART... JAXON'S LOSING LIKE CRAZY.
...
EW, THAT HAT IS NOT WORKING.
REALLY? OH...
WELL, YOU KNOW WHAT, MOGG? YOU CAN JUST SHOVE THAT COMMENT RIGHT UP YOUR UGLY, UNLOVED ASSHOLE.
FUCK YOU!
YOU FU-
HEY, SETTLE DOWN. BOTH OF YOU. OWL, I'M LOVING THE HAT.
MOGG, YOUR ASSHOLE IS SWEET AND DELICIOUS, YOU ARE LOVED.

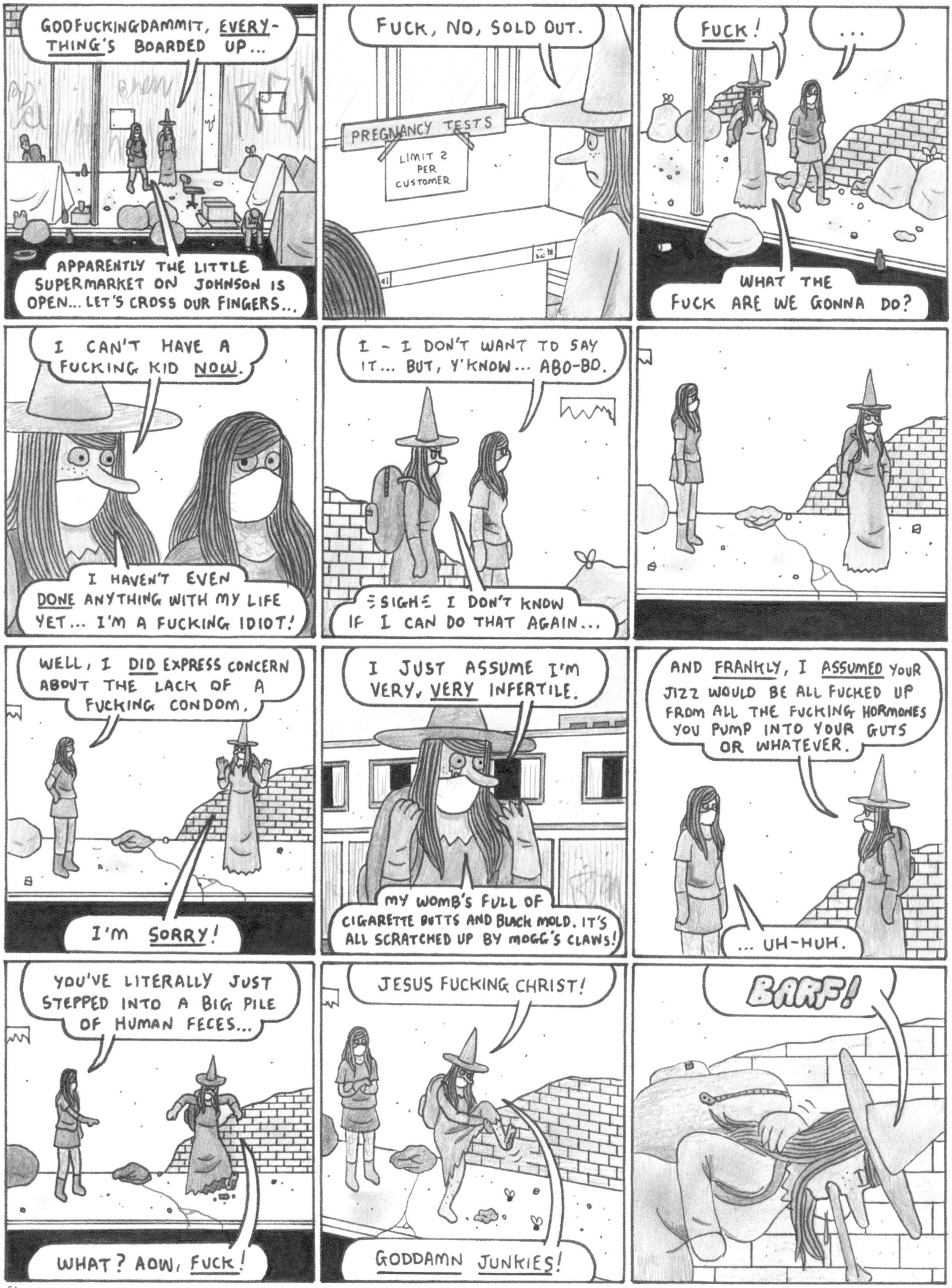
GODFUCKINGDAMMIT, EVERYTHING'S BOARDED UP...
APPARENTLY THE LITTLE SUPERMARKET ON JOHNSON IS OPEN... LET'S CROSS OUR FINGERS...
FUCK, NO, SOLD OUT.
PREGNANCY TESTS
LIMIT 2 PER CUSTOMER
FUCK!
...
WHAT THE FUCK ARE WE GONNA DO?
I CAN'T HAVE A FUCKING KID NOW.
I HAVEN'T EVEN DONE ANYTHING WITH MY LIFE YET... I'M A FUCKING IDIOT!
I - I DON'T WANT TO SAY IT... BUT, Y'KNOW... ABO-BO.
SIGH I DON'T KNOW IF I CAN DO THAT AGAIN...
WELL, I DID EXPRESS CONCERN ABOUT THE LACK OF A FUCKING CONDOM.
I'M SORRY!
I JUST ASSUME I'M VERY, VERY INFERTILE.
MY WOMB'S FULL OF CIGARETTE BUTTS AND BLACK MOLD. IT'S ALL SCRATCHED UP BY MOGG'S CLAWS!
AND FRANKLY, I ASSUMED YOUR JIZZ WOULD BE ALL FUCKED UP FROM ALL THE FUCKING HORMONES YOU PUMP INTO YOUR GUTS OR WHATEVER.
... UH-HUH.
YOU'VE LITERALLY JUST STEPPED INTO A BIG PILE OF HUMAN FECES...
WHAT? AOW, FUCK!
JESUS FUCKING CHRIST!
GODDAMN JUNKIES!
BARF!

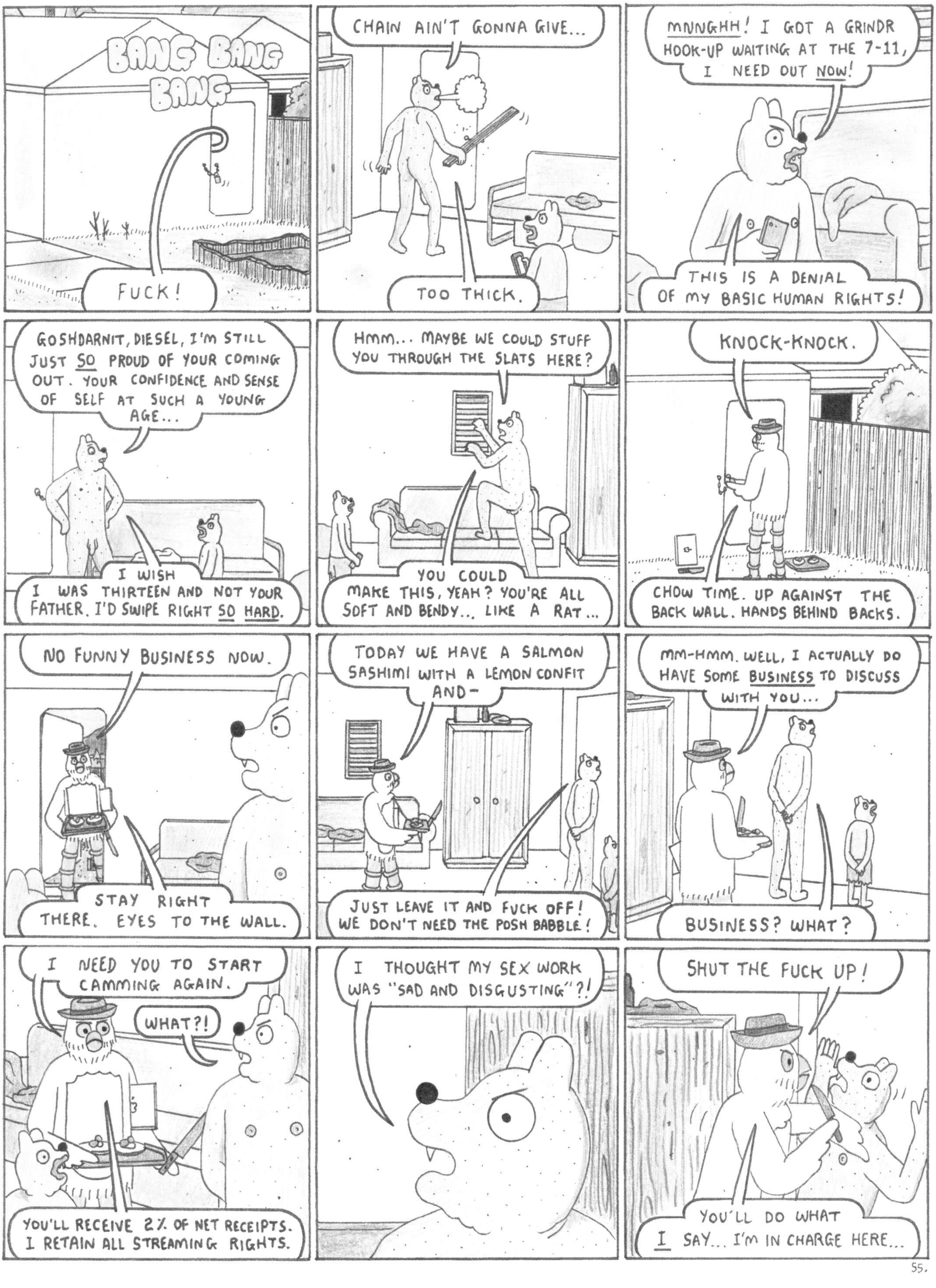
BANG BANG BANG
FUCK!
CHAIN AIN'T GONNA GIVE...
TOO THICK.
MNNGHH! I GOT A GRINDR HOOK-UP WAITING AT THE 7-11, I NEED OUT NOW!
THIS IS A DENIAL OF MY BASIC HUMAN RIGHTS!
GOSHDARNIT, DIESEL, I'M STILL JUST SO PROUD OF YOUR COMING OUT. YOUR CONFIDENCE AND SENSE OF SELF AT SUCH A YOUNG AGE...
I WISH I WAS THIRTEEN AND NOT YOUR FATHER. I'D SWIPE RIGHT SO HARD.
HMM... MAYBE WE COULD STUFF YOU THROUGH THE SLATS HERE?
YOU COULD MAKE THIS, YEAH? YOU'RE ALL SOFT AND BENDY... LIKE A RAT...
KNOCK-KNOCK.
CHOW TIME. UP AGAINST THE BACK WALL. HANDS BEHIND BACKS.
NO FUNNY BUSINESS NOW.
STAY RIGHT THERE. EYES TO THE WALL.
TODAY WE HAVE A SALMON SASHIMI WITH A LEMON CONFIT AND-
JUST LEAVE IT AND FUCK OFF! WE DON'T NEED THE POSH BABBLE!
MM-HMM. WELL, I ACTUALLY DO HAVE SOME BUSINESS TO DISCUSS WITH YOU...
BUSINESS? WHAT?
I NEED YOU TO START CAMMING AGAIN.
WHAT?!
YOU'LL RECEIVE 2% OF NET RECEIPTS. I RETAIN ALL STREAMING RIGHTS.
I THOUGHT MY SEX WORK WAS "SAD AND DISGUSTING"?!
SHUT THE FUCK UP!
YOU'LL DO WHAT I SAY... I'M IN CHARGE HERE...

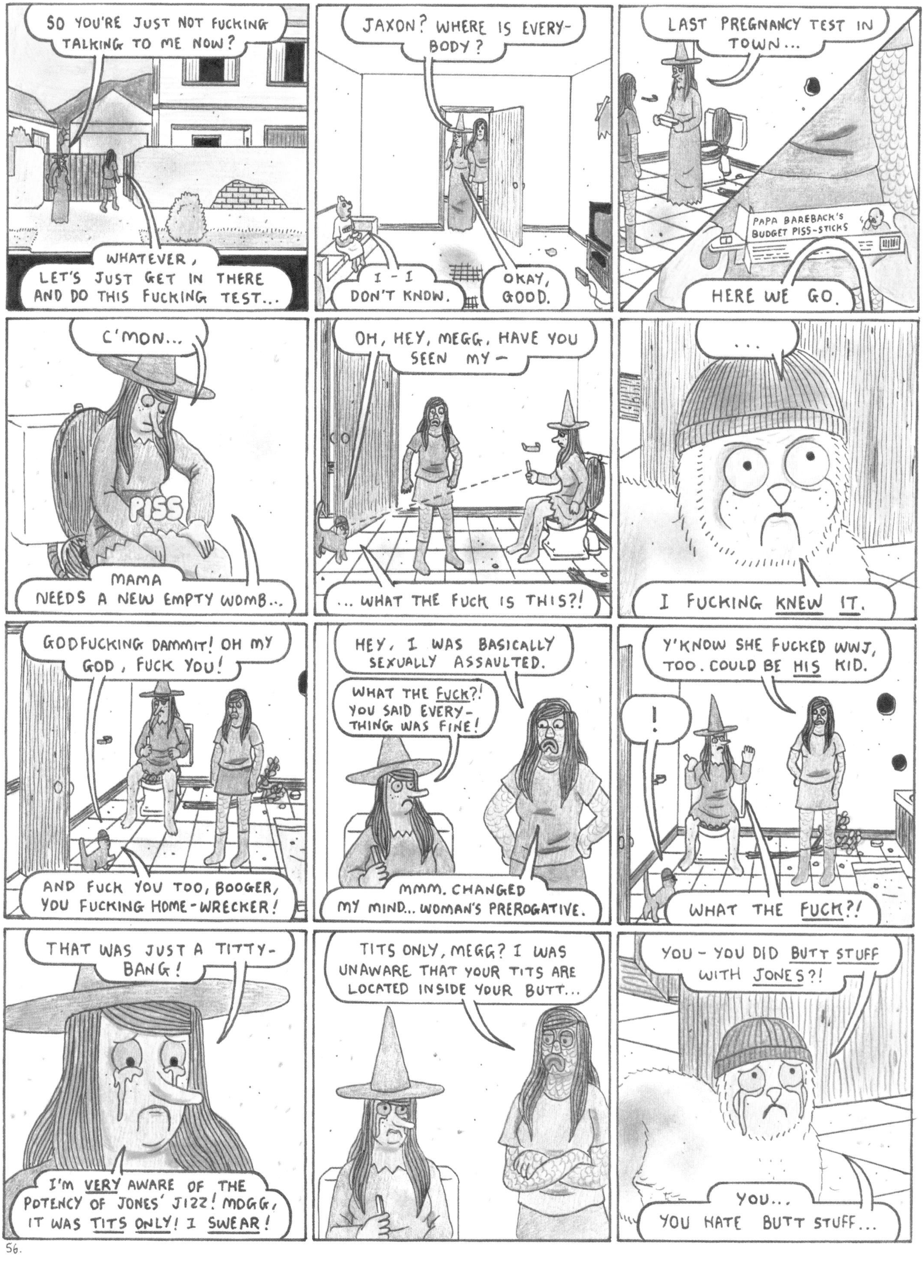
SO YOU'RE JUST NOT FUCKING TALKING TO ME NOW?
WHATEVER, LET'S JUST GET IN THERE AND DO THIS FUCKING TEST...
JAXON? WHERE IS EVERY-BODY?
I - I DON'T KNOW.
OKAY, GOOD.
LAST PREGNANCY TEST IN TOWN...
PAPA BAREBACK'S BUDGET PISS-STICKS
HERE WE GO.
C'MON...
PISS
MAMA NEEDS A NEW EMPTY WOMB...
OH, HEY, MEGG, HAVE YOU SEEN MY—
... WHAT THE FUCK IS THIS?!
...
I FUCKING KNEW IT.
GODFUCKING DAMMIT! OH MY GOD, FUCK YOU!
AND FUCK YOU TOO, BOOGER, YOU FUCKING HOME-WRECKER!
HEY, I WAS BASICALLY SEXUALLY ASSAULTED.
WHAT THE FUCK?! YOU SAID EVERY-THING WAS FINE!
MMM. CHANGED MY MIND... WOMAN'S PREROGATIVE.
Y'KNOW SHE FUCKED WWJ, TOO. COULD BE HIS KID.
!
WHAT THE FUCK?!
THAT WAS JUST A TITTY-BANG!
I'M VERY AWARE OF THE POTENCY OF JONES' JIZZ! MOGG, IT WAS TITS ONLY! I SWEAR!
TITS ONLY, MEGG? I WAS UNAWARE THAT YOUR TITS ARE LOCATED INSIDE YOUR BUTT...
YOU - YOU DID BUTT STUFF WITH JONES?!
YOU... YOU HATE BUTT STUFF...

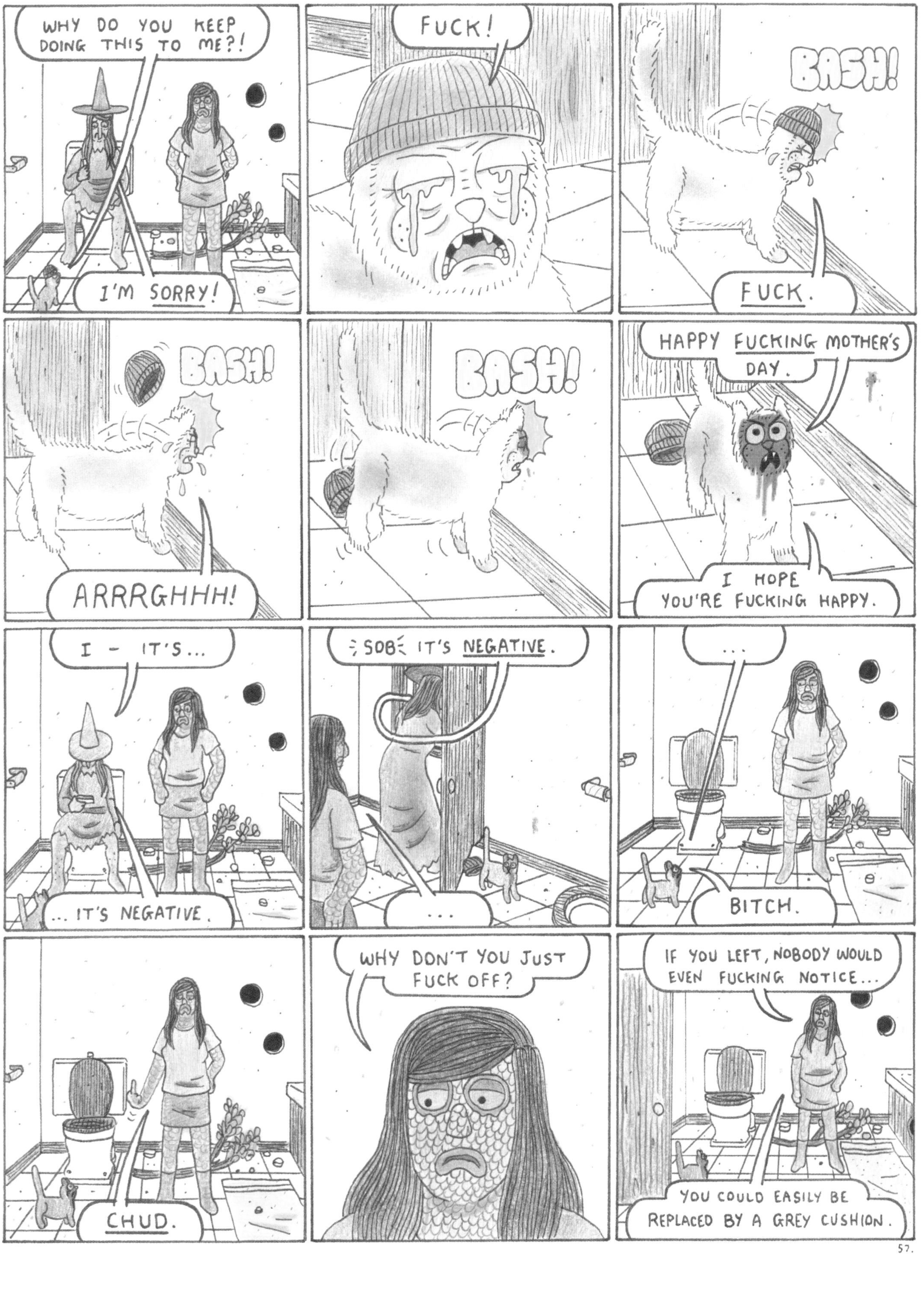
WHY DO YOU KEEP DOING THIS TO ME?!
I'M SORRY!
FUCK!
BASH!
FUCK.
BASH!
ARRRGHHH!
BASH!
HAPPY FUCKING MOTHER'S DAY.
I HOPE YOU'RE FUCKING HAPPY.
I - IT'S...
... IT'S NEGATIVE.
SOB IT'S NEGATIVE.
...
...
BITCH.
CHUD.
WHY DON'T YOU JUST FUCK OFF?
IF YOU LEFT, NOBODY WOULD EVEN FUCKING NOTICE...
YOU COULD EASILY BE REPLACED BY A GREY CUSHION.

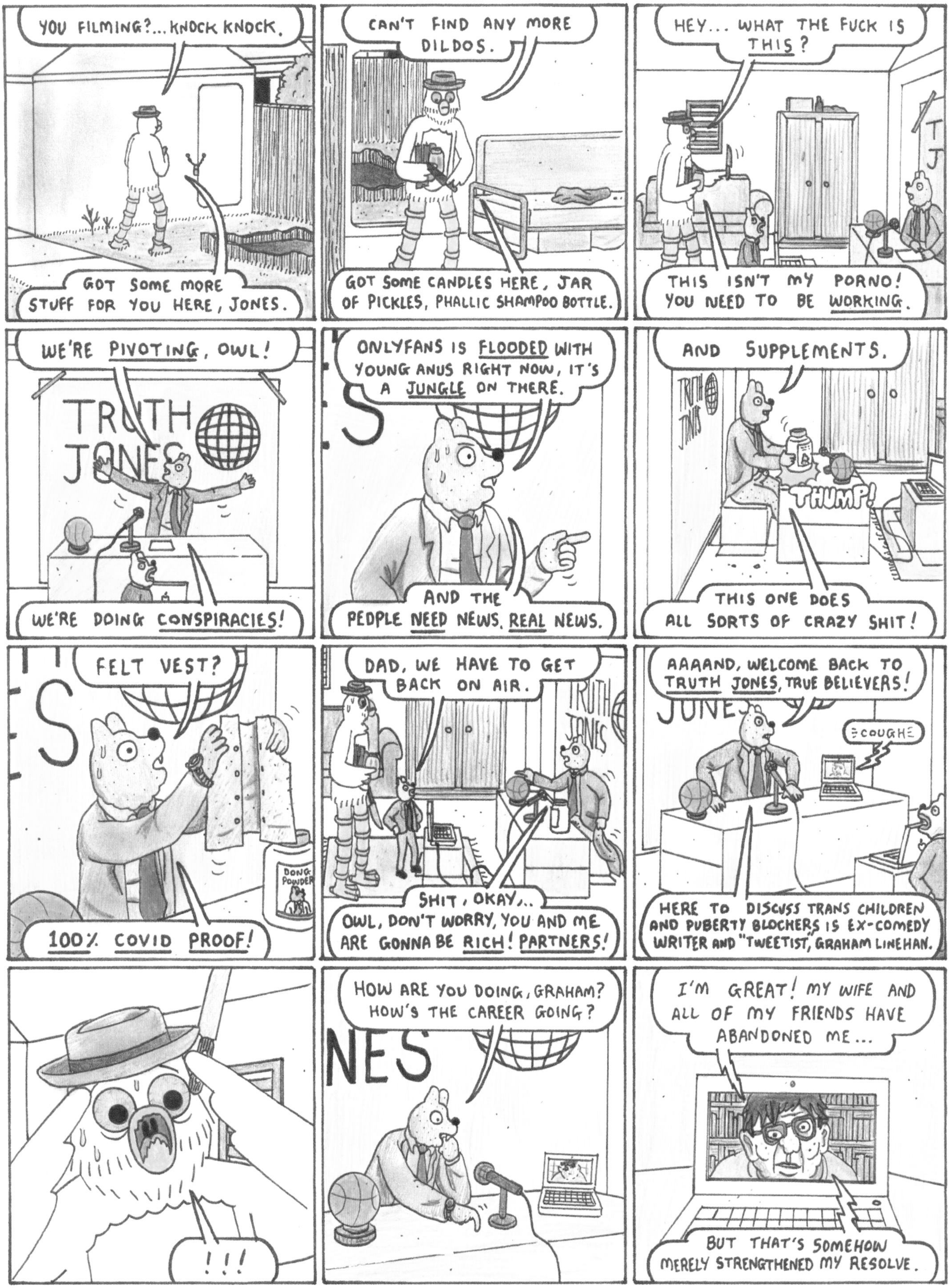
YOU FILMING?... KNOCK KNOCK.
GOT SOME MORE STUFF FOR YOU HERE, JONES.
CAN'T FIND ANY MORE DILDOS.
GOT SOME CANDLES HERE, JAR OF PICKLES, PHALLIC SHAMPOO BOTTLE.
HEY... WHAT THE FUCK IS THIS?
THIS ISN'T MY PORNO! YOU NEED TO BE WORKING.
WE'RE PIVOTING, OWL!
TRUTH JONES
WE'RE DOING CONSPIRACIES!
ONLYFANS IS FLOODED WITH YOUNG ANUS RIGHT NOW, IT'S A JUNGLE ON THERE.
AND THE PEOPLE NEED NEWS. REAL NEWS.
AND SUPPLEMENTS.
THUMP!
THIS ONE DOES ALL SORTS OF CRAZY SHIT!
FELT VEST?
DONG POWDER
100% COVID PROOF!
DAD, WE HAVE TO GET BACK ON AIR.
TRUTH JONES
SHIT, OKAY...
OWL, DON'T WORRY, YOU AND ME ARE GONNA BE RICH! PARTNERS!
AAAAND, WELCOME BACK TO TRUTH JONES, TRUE BELIEVERS!
≡COUGH≡
HERE TO DISCUSS TRANS CHILDREN AND PUBERTY BLOCKERS IS EX-COMEDY WRITER AND "TWEETIST," GRAHAM LINEHAN.
!!!
HOW ARE YOU DOING, GRAHAM? HOW'S THE CAREER GOING?
I'M GREAT! MY WIFE AND ALL OF MY FRIENDS HAVE ABANDONED ME...
BUT THAT'S SOMEHOW MERELY STRENGTHENED MY RESOLVE.

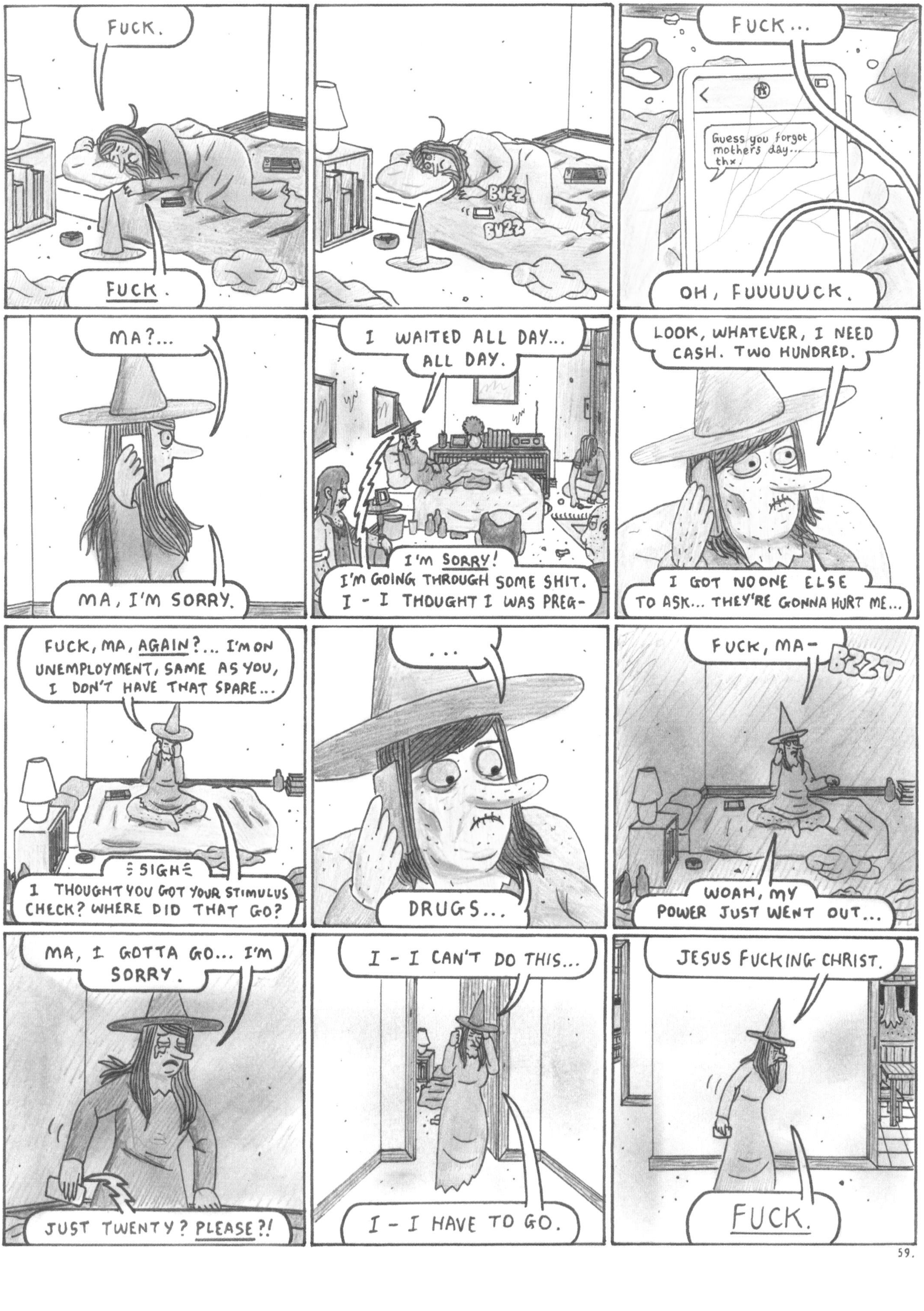
FUCK.
FUCK.
BUZZ
BUZZ
FUCK...
Guess you forgot mothers day... thx.
OH, FUUUUUCK.
MA?...
MA, I'M SORRY.
I WAITED ALL DAY... ALL DAY.
I'M SORRY! I'M GOING THROUGH SOME SHIT. I - I THOUGHT I WAS PREG-
LOOK, WHATEVER, I NEED CASH. TWO HUNDRED.
I GOT NOONE ELSE TO ASK... THEY'RE GONNA HURT ME...
FUCK, MA, AGAIN?... I'M ON UNEMPLOYMENT, SAME AS YOU, I DON'T HAVE THAT SPARE...
SIGH
I THOUGHT YOU GOT YOUR STIMULUS CHECK? WHERE DID THAT GO?
...
DRUGS...
FUCK, MA-
BZZT
WOAH, MY POWER JUST WENT OUT...
MA, I GOTTA GO... I'M SORRY.
JUST TWENTY? PLEASE?!
I - I CAN'T DO THIS...
I - I HAVE TO GO.
JESUS FUCKING CHRIST.
FUCK.

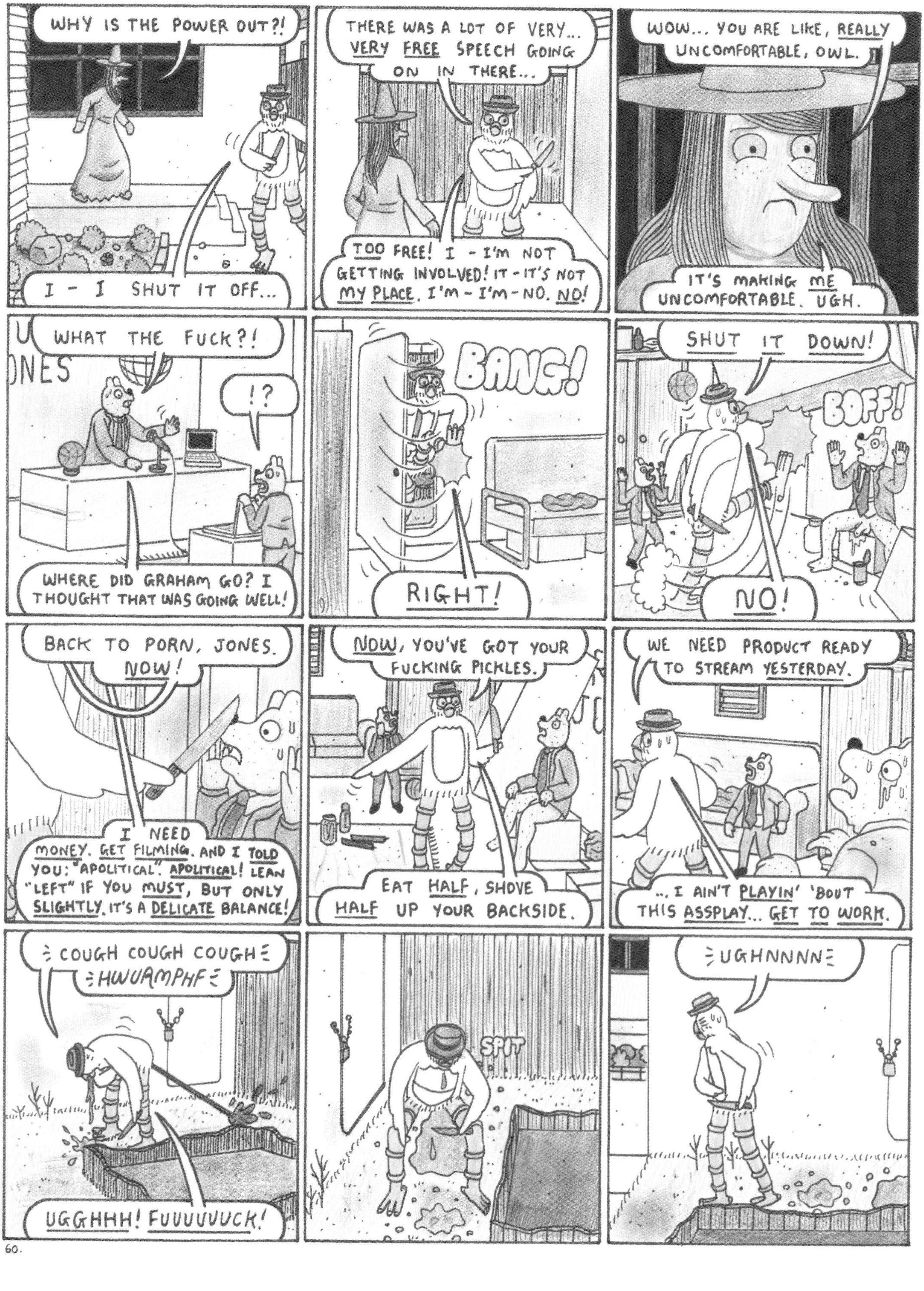
WHY IS THE POWER OUT?!
I - I SHUT IT OFF...
THERE WAS A LOT OF VERY... VERY FREE SPEECH GOING ON IN THERE...
TOO FREE! I - I'M NOT GETTING INVOLVED! IT - IT'S NOT MY PLACE. I'M - I'M - NO. NO!
WOW... YOU ARE LIKE, REALLY UNCOMFORTABLE, OWL.
IT'S MAKING ME UNCOMFORTABLE. UGH.
WHAT THE FUCK?!
!?
WHERE DID GRAHAM GO? I THOUGHT THAT WAS GOING WELL!
BANG!
RIGHT!
SHUT IT DOWN!
BOFF!
NO!
BACK TO PORN, JONES. NOW!
I NEED MONEY. GET FILMING. AND I TOLD YOU: "APOLITICAL". APOLITICAL! LEAN "LEFT" IF YOU MUST, BUT ONLY SLIGHTLY. IT'S A DELICATE BALANCE!
NOW, YOU'VE GOT YOUR FUCKING PICKLES.
EAT HALF, SHOVE HALF UP YOUR BACKSIDE.
WE NEED PRODUCT READY TO STREAM YESTERDAY.
...I AIN'T PLAYIN' 'BOUT THIS ASSPLAY... GET TO WORK.
COUGH COUGH COUGH
HWUAMPHF
UGGHHH! FUUUUUUCK!
SPIT
UGHNNNN

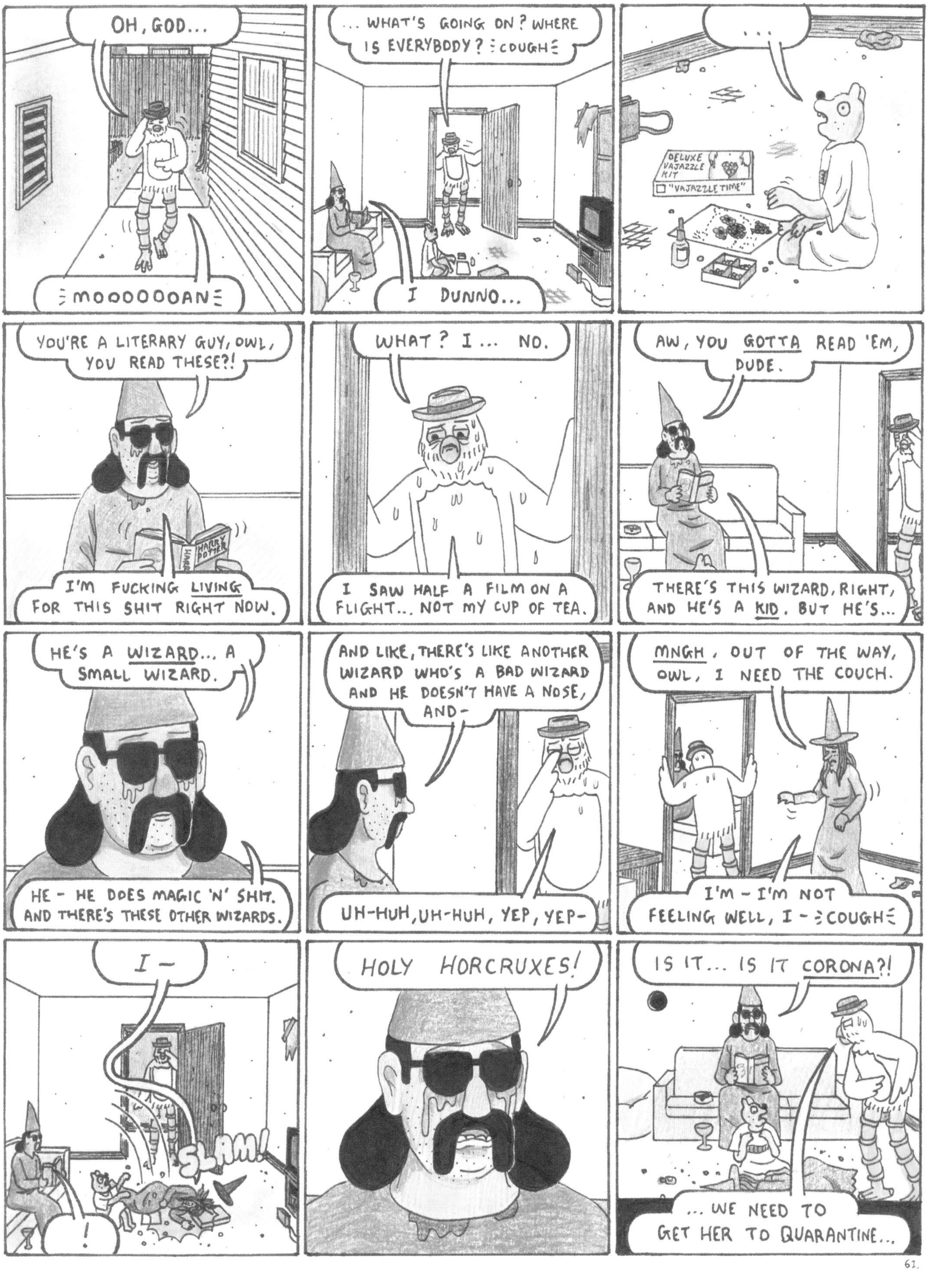
OH, GOD...
MOOOOOOAN
... WHAT'S GOING ON? WHERE IS EVERYBODY? COUGH
I DUNNO...
...
DELUXE VAJAZZLE KIT
"VAJAZZLE TIME"
YOU'RE A LITERARY GUY, OWL, YOU READ THESE?!
HARRY POTTER
I'M FUCKING LIVING FOR THIS SHIT RIGHT NOW.
WHAT? I... NO.
I SAW HALF A FILM ON A FLIGHT... NOT MY CUP OF TEA.
AW, YOU GOTTA READ 'EM, DUDE.
THERE'S THIS WIZARD, RIGHT, AND HE'S A KID. BUT HE'S...
HE'S A WIZARD... A SMALL WIZARD.
HE - HE DOES MAGIC 'N' SHIT. AND THERE'S THESE OTHER WIZARDS.
AND LIKE, THERE'S LIKE ANOTHER WIZARD WHO'S A BAD WIZARD AND HE DOESN'T HAVE A NOSE, AND-
UH-HUH, UH-HUH, YEP, YEP-
MNGH, OUT OF THE WAY, OWL, I NEED THE COUCH.
I'M - I'M NOT FEELING WELL, I - COUGH
I -
SLAM!
!
HOLY HORCRUXES!
IS IT... IS IT CORONA?!
... WE NEED TO GET HER TO QUARANTINE...

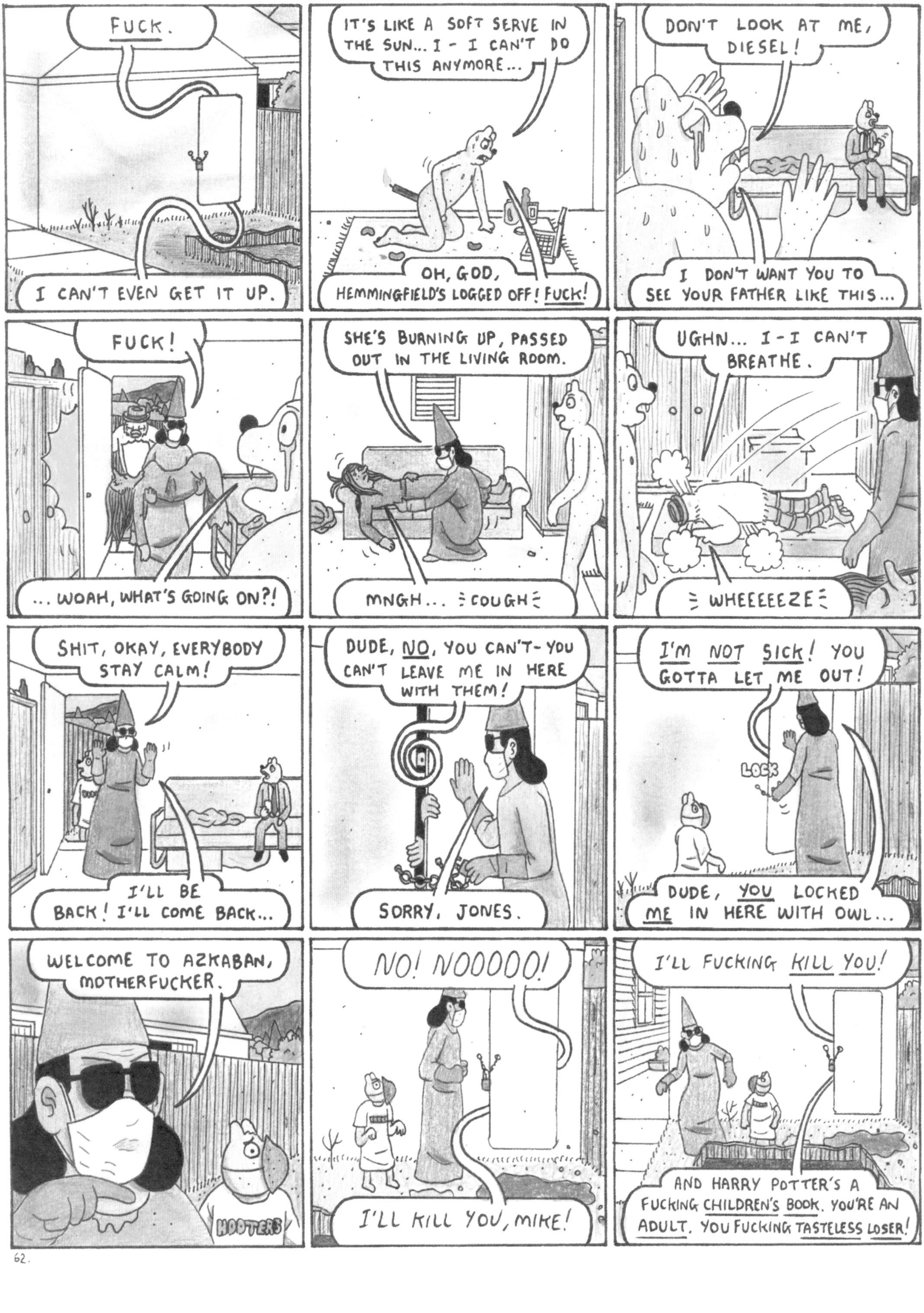
FUCK.
I CAN'T EVEN GET IT UP.
IT'S LIKE A SOFT SERVE IN THE SUN... I - I CAN'T DO THIS ANYMORE...
OH, GOD, HEMMINGFIELD'S LOGGED OFF! FUCK!
DON'T LOOK AT ME, DIESEL!
I DON'T WANT YOU TO SEE YOUR FATHER LIKE THIS...
FUCK!
... WOAH, WHAT'S GOING ON?!
SHE'S BURNING UP, PASSED OUT IN THE LIVING ROOM.
MNGH... COUGH
UGHN... I-I CAN'T BREATHE.
WHEEEEEZE
SHIT, OKAY, EVERYBODY STAY CALM!
I'LL BE BACK! I'LL COME BACK...
DUDE, NO, YOU CAN'T- YOU CAN'T LEAVE ME IN HERE WITH THEM!
SORRY, JONES.
I'M NOT SICK! YOU GOTTA LET ME OUT!
LOCK
DUDE, YOU LOCKED ME IN HERE WITH OWL...
WELCOME TO AZKABAN, MOTHERFUCKER.
HOOTERS
NO! NOOOOO!
I'LL KILL YOU, MIKE!
I'LL FUCKING KILL YOU!
AND HARRY POTTER'S A FUCKING CHILDREN'S BOOK. YOU'RE AN ADULT. YOU FUCKING TASTELESS LOSER!

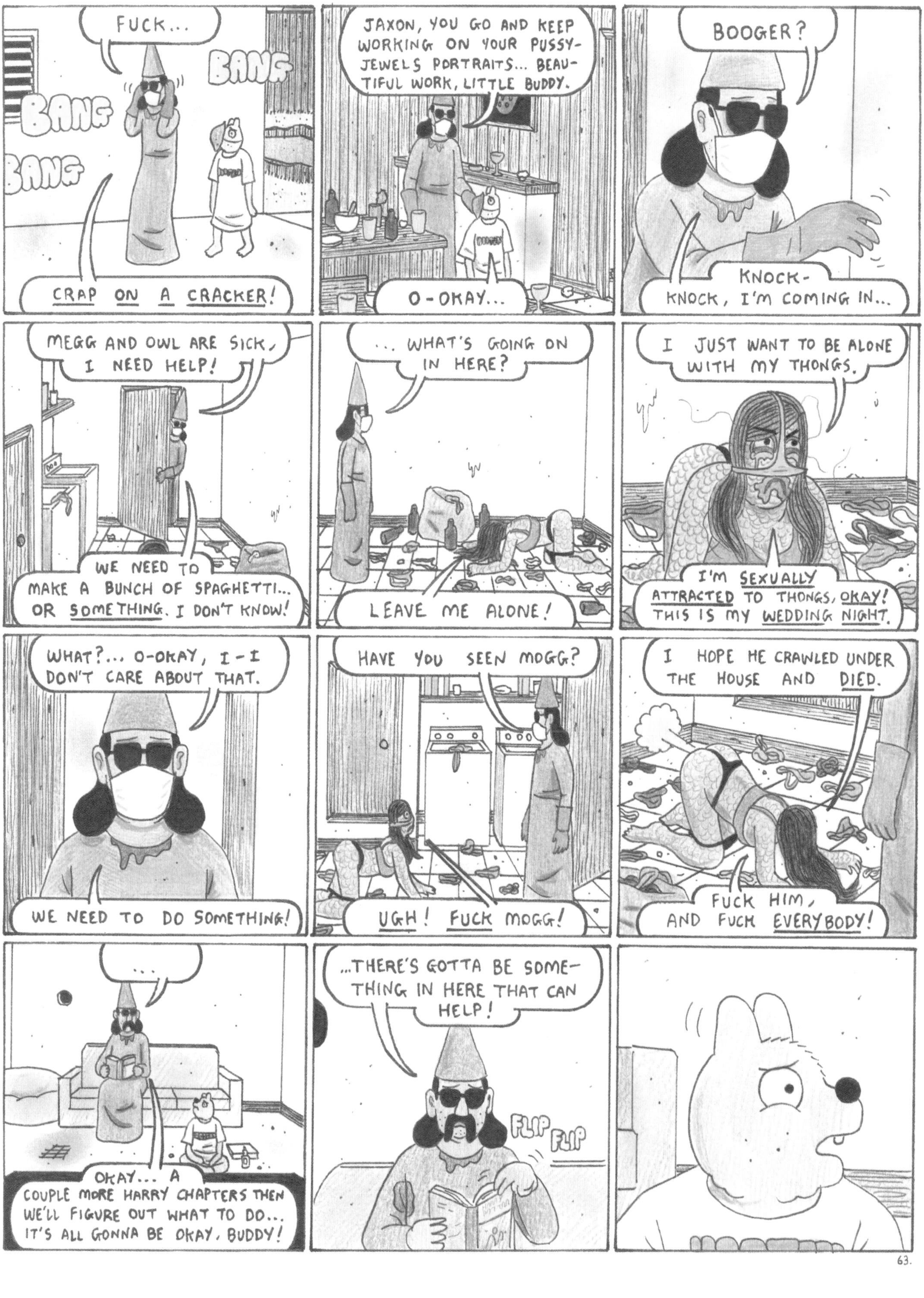

FUCK...
BANG
BANG
BANG
CRAP ON A CRACKER!
JAXON, YOU GO AND KEEP WORKING ON YOUR PUSSY-JEWELS PORTRAITS... BEAUTIFUL WORK, LITTLE BUDDY.
O-OKAY...
BOOGER?
KNOCK-KNOCK, I'M COMING IN...
MEGG AND OWL ARE SICK, I NEED HELP!
WE NEED TO MAKE A BUNCH OF SPAGHETTI... OR SOMETHING. I DON'T KNOW!
... WHAT'S GOING ON IN HERE?
LEAVE ME ALONE!
I JUST WANT TO BE ALONE WITH MY THONGS.
I'M SEXUALLY ATTRACTED TO THONGS, OKAY! THIS IS MY WEDDING NIGHT.
WHAT?... O-OKAY, I-I DON'T CARE ABOUT THAT.
WE NEED TO DO SOMETHING!
HAVE YOU SEEN MOGG?
UGH! FUCK MOGG!
I HOPE HE CRAWLED UNDER THE HOUSE AND DIED.
FUCK HIM, AND FUCK EVERYBODY!
...
OKAY... A COUPLE MORE HARRY CHAPTERS THEN WE'LL FIGURE OUT WHAT TO DO... IT'S ALL GONNA BE OKAY, BUDDY!
...THERE'S GOTTA BE SOMETHING IN HERE THAT CAN HELP!
FLIP FLIP

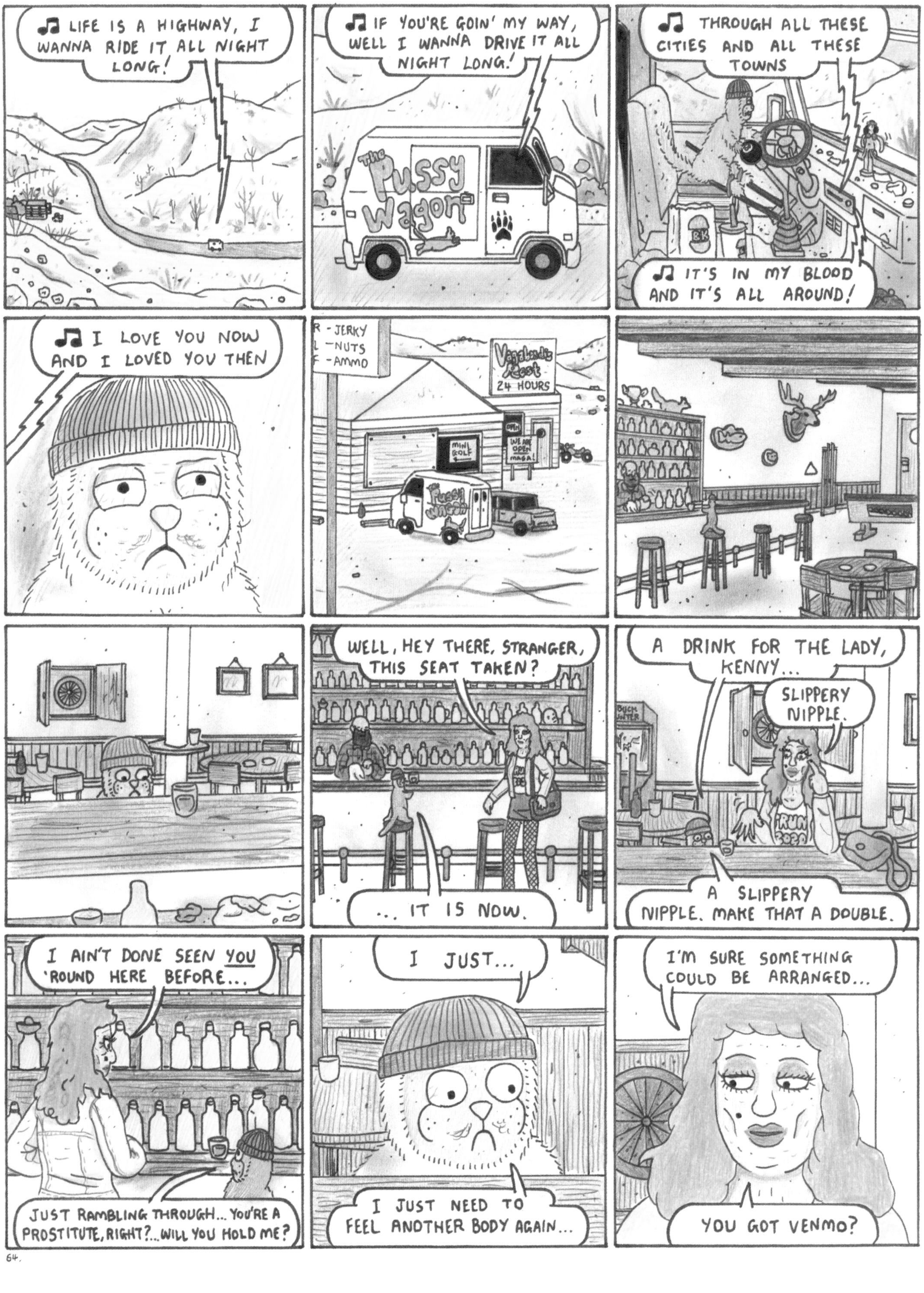
♫ LIFE IS A HIGHWAY, I WANNA RIDE IT ALL NIGHT LONG!
♫ IF YOU'RE GOIN' MY WAY, WELL I WANNA DRIVE IT ALL NIGHT LONG!
The Pussy Wagon
♫ THROUGH ALL THESE CITIES AND ALL THESE TOWNS
♫ IT'S IN MY BLOOD AND IT'S ALL AROUND!
♫ I LOVE YOU NOW AND I LOVED YOU THEN
R - JERKY
L - NUTS
F - AMMO
24 HOURS
MINI GOLF
WE ARE OPEN
WELL, HEY THERE, STRANGER, THIS SEAT TAKEN?
... IT IS NOW.
A DRINK FOR THE LADY, KENNY...
SLIPPERY NIPPLE.
A SLIPPERY NIPPLE. MAKE THAT A DOUBLE.
RUN 2020
I AIN'T DONE SEEN YOU 'ROUND HERE BEFORE...
JUST RAMBLING THROUGH... YOU'RE A PROSTITUTE, RIGHT?... WILL YOU HOLD ME?
I JUST...
I JUST NEED TO FEEL ANOTHER BODY AGAIN...
I'M SURE SOMETHING COULD BE ARRANGED...
YOU GOT VENMO?

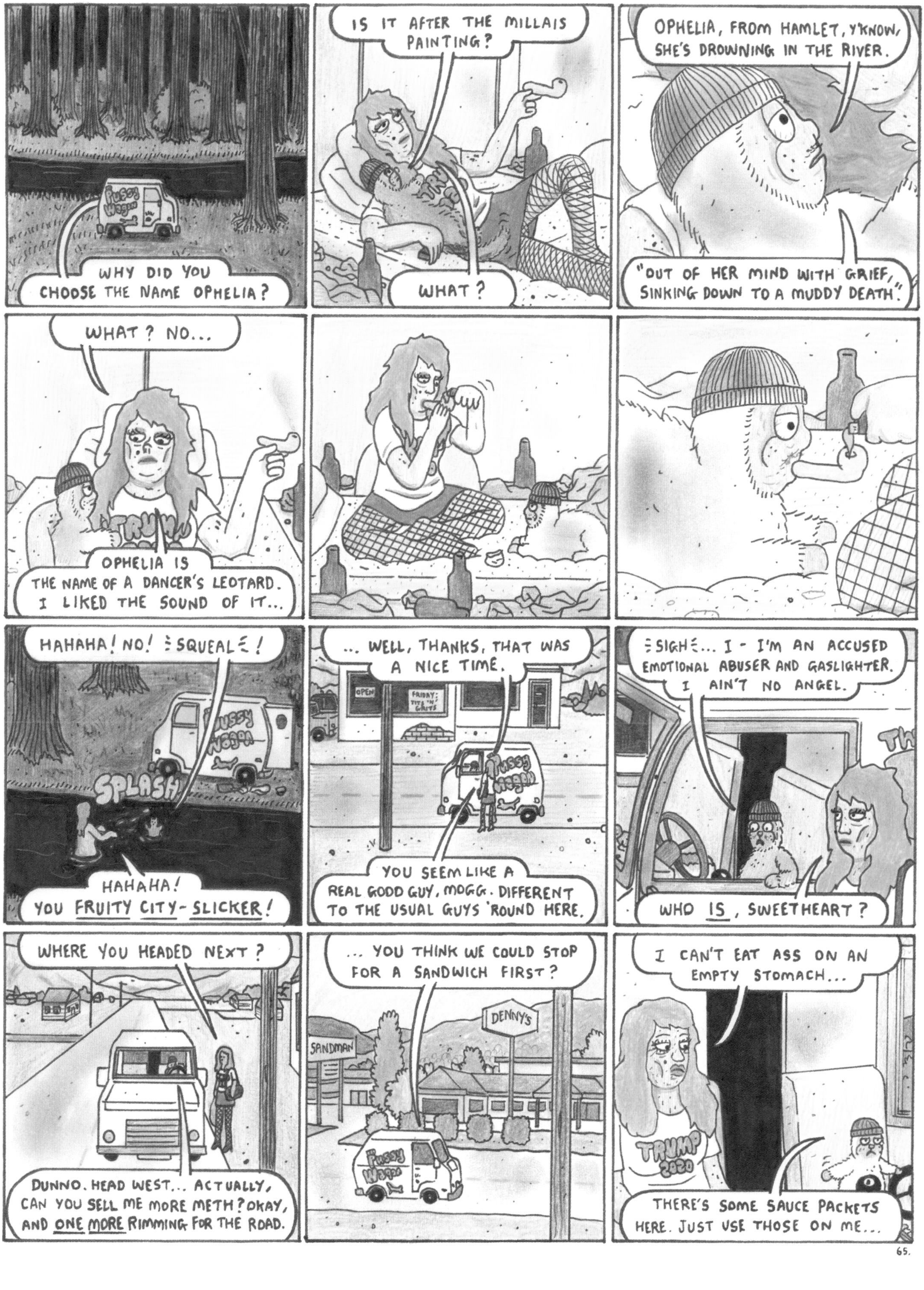
WHY DID YOU CHOOSE THE NAME OPHELIA?
IS IT AFTER THE MILLAIS PAINTING?
WHAT?
OPHELIA, FROM HAMLET, Y'KNOW, SHE'S DROWNING IN THE RIVER.
"OUT OF HER MIND WITH GRIEF, SINKING DOWN TO A MUDDY DEATH".
WHAT? NO...
OPHELIA IS THE NAME OF A DANCER'S LEOTARD. I LIKED THE SOUND OF IT...
HAHAHA! NO! ≡SQUEAL≡!
SPLASH
HAHAHA! YOU FRUITY CITY-SLICKER!
... WELL, THANKS, THAT WAS A NICE TIME.
OPEN
YOU SEEM LIKE A REAL GOOD GUY, MOGG. DIFFERENT TO THE USUAL GUYS 'ROUND HERE.
≡SIGH≡... I - I'M AN ACCUSED EMOTIONAL ABUSER AND GASLIGHTER. I AIN'T NO ANGEL.
WHO IS, SWEETHEART?
WHERE YOU HEADED NEXT?
DUNNO. HEAD WEST... ACTUALLY, CAN YOU SELL ME MORE METH? OKAY, AND ONE MORE RIMMING FOR THE ROAD.
... YOU THINK WE COULD STOP FOR A SANDWICH FIRST?
DENNY'S
SANDMAN
I CAN'T EAT ASS ON AN EMPTY STOMACH...
TRUMP 2020
THERE'S SOME SAUCE PACKETS HERE. JUST USE THOSE ON ME...

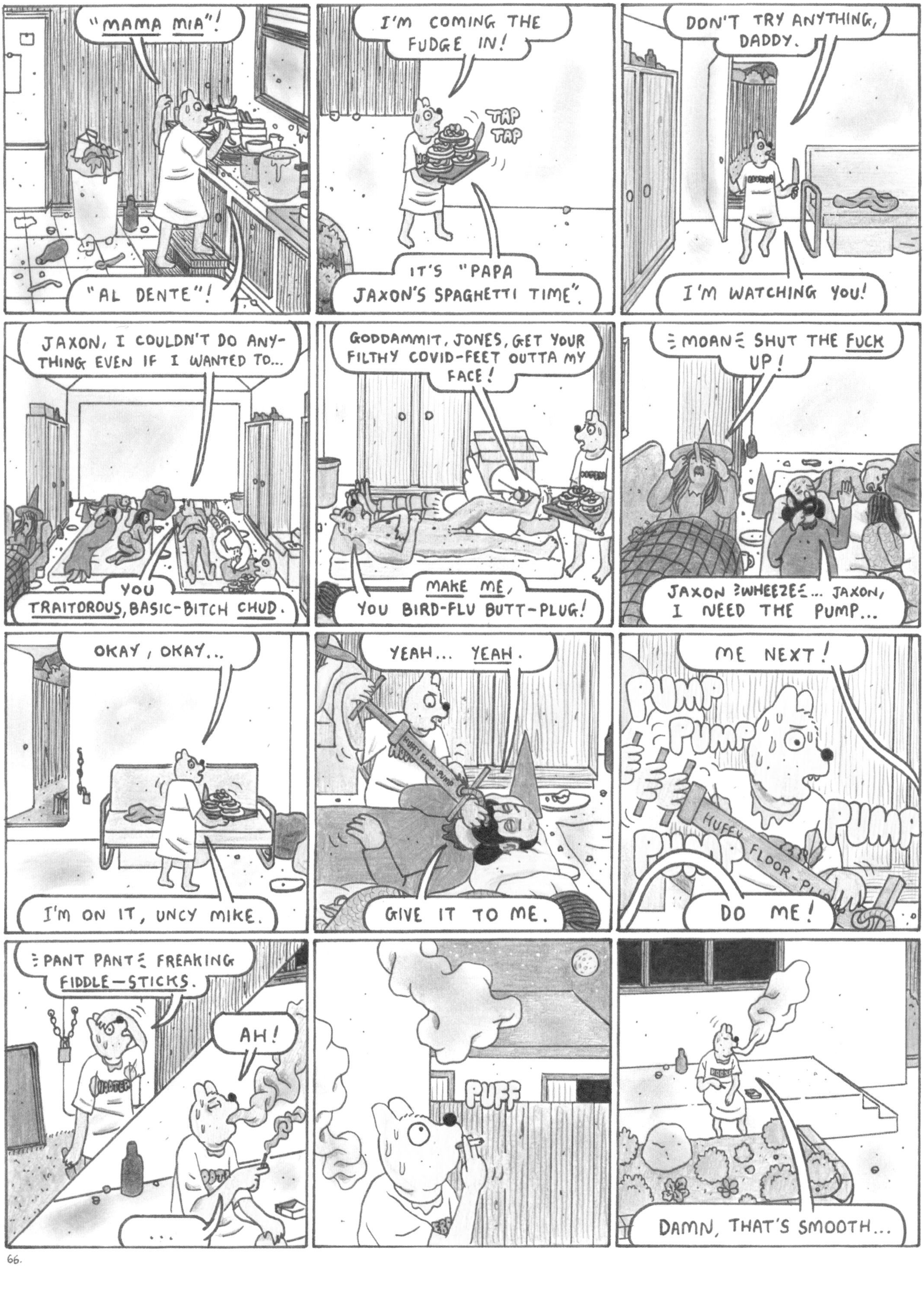
"MAMA MIA"!
"AL DENTE"!
I'M COMING THE FUDGE IN!
TAP TAP
IT'S "PAPA JAXON'S SPAGHETTI TIME".
DON'T TRY ANYTHING, DADDY.
I'M WATCHING YOU!
JAXON, I COULDN'T DO ANYTHING EVEN IF I WANTED TO...
YOU TRAITOROUS, BASIC-BITCH CHUD.
GODDAMMIT, JONES, GET YOUR FILTHY COVID-FEET OUTTA MY FACE!
MAKE ME, YOU BIRD-FLU BUTT-PLUG!
MOAN SHUT THE FUCK UP!
JAXON WHEEZE... JAXON, I NEED THE PUMP...
OKAY, OKAY...
I'M ON IT, UNCY MIKE.
YEAH... YEAH.
HUFFY FLOOR-PUMP
GIVE IT TO ME.
ME NEXT!
PUMP PUMP
PUMP PUMP
HUFFY FLOOR-PU
DO ME!
PANT PANT FREAKING FIDDLE-STICKS.
AH!
...
PUFF
DAMN, THAT'S SMOOTH...

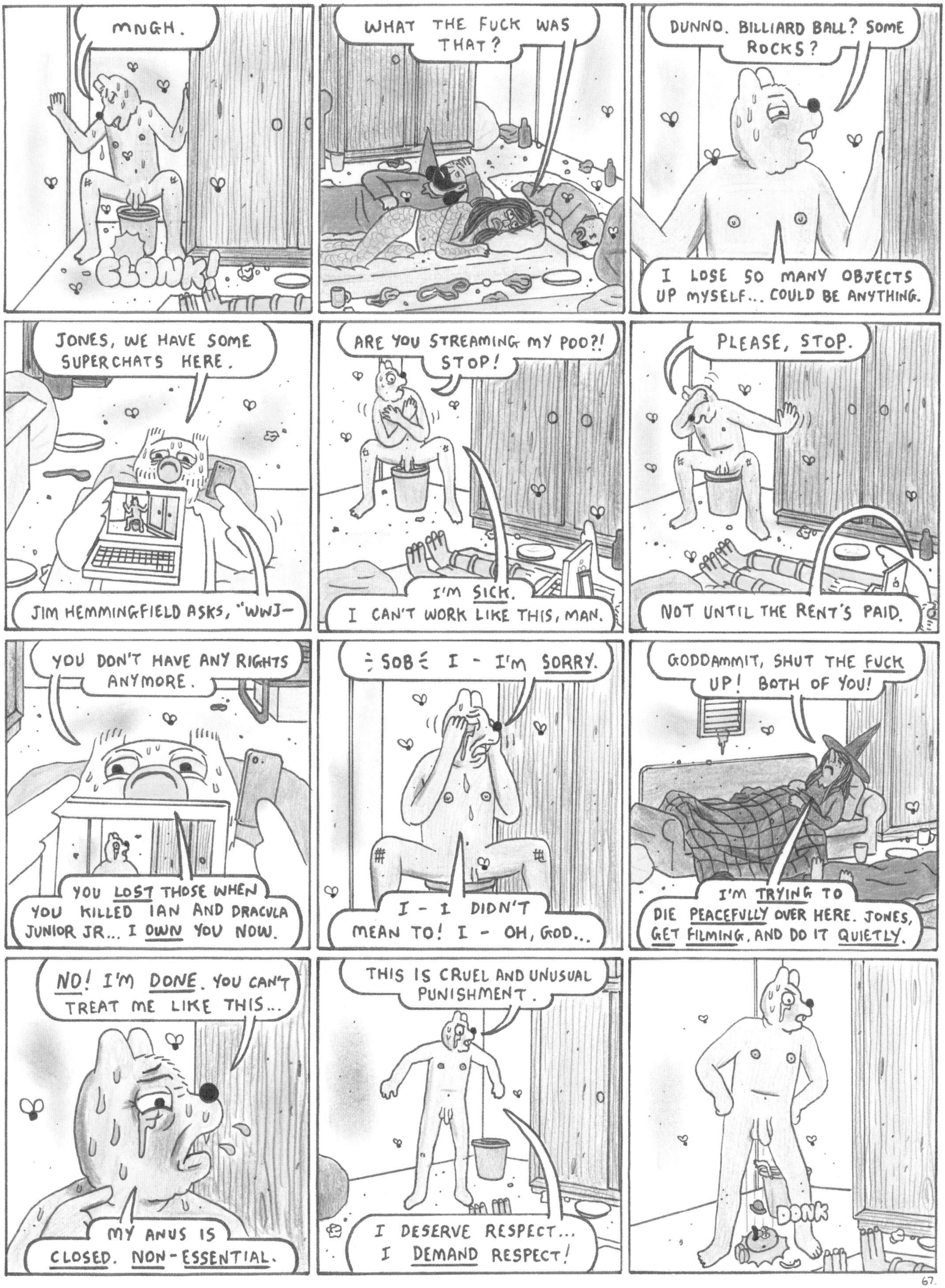
MNGH.
CLONK!
WHAT THE FUCK WAS THAT?
DUNNO. BILLIARD BALL? SOME ROCKS?
I LOSE SO MANY OBJECTS UP MYSELF... COULD BE ANYTHING.
JONES, WE HAVE SOME SUPERCHATS HERE.
JIM HEMMINGFIELD ASKS, "WWJ—
ARE YOU STREAMING MY POO?! STOP!
I'M SICK. I CAN'T WORK LIKE THIS, MAN.
PLEASE, STOP.
NOT UNTIL THE RENT'S PAID.
YOU DON'T HAVE ANY RIGHTS ANYMORE.
YOU LOST THOSE WHEN YOU KILLED IAN AND DRACULA JUNIOR JR... I OWN YOU NOW.
SOB I - I'M SORRY.
I - I DIDN'T MEAN TO! I - OH, GOD...
GODDAMMIT, SHUT THE FUCK UP! BOTH OF YOU!
I'M TRYING TO DIE PEACEFULLY OVER HERE. JONES, GET FILMING, AND DO IT QUIETLY.
NO! I'M DONE. YOU CAN'T TREAT ME LIKE THIS...
MY ANUS IS CLOSED. NON-ESSENTIAL.
THIS IS CRUEL AND UNUSUAL PUNISHMENT.
I DESERVE RESPECT... I DEMAND RESPECT!
DONK

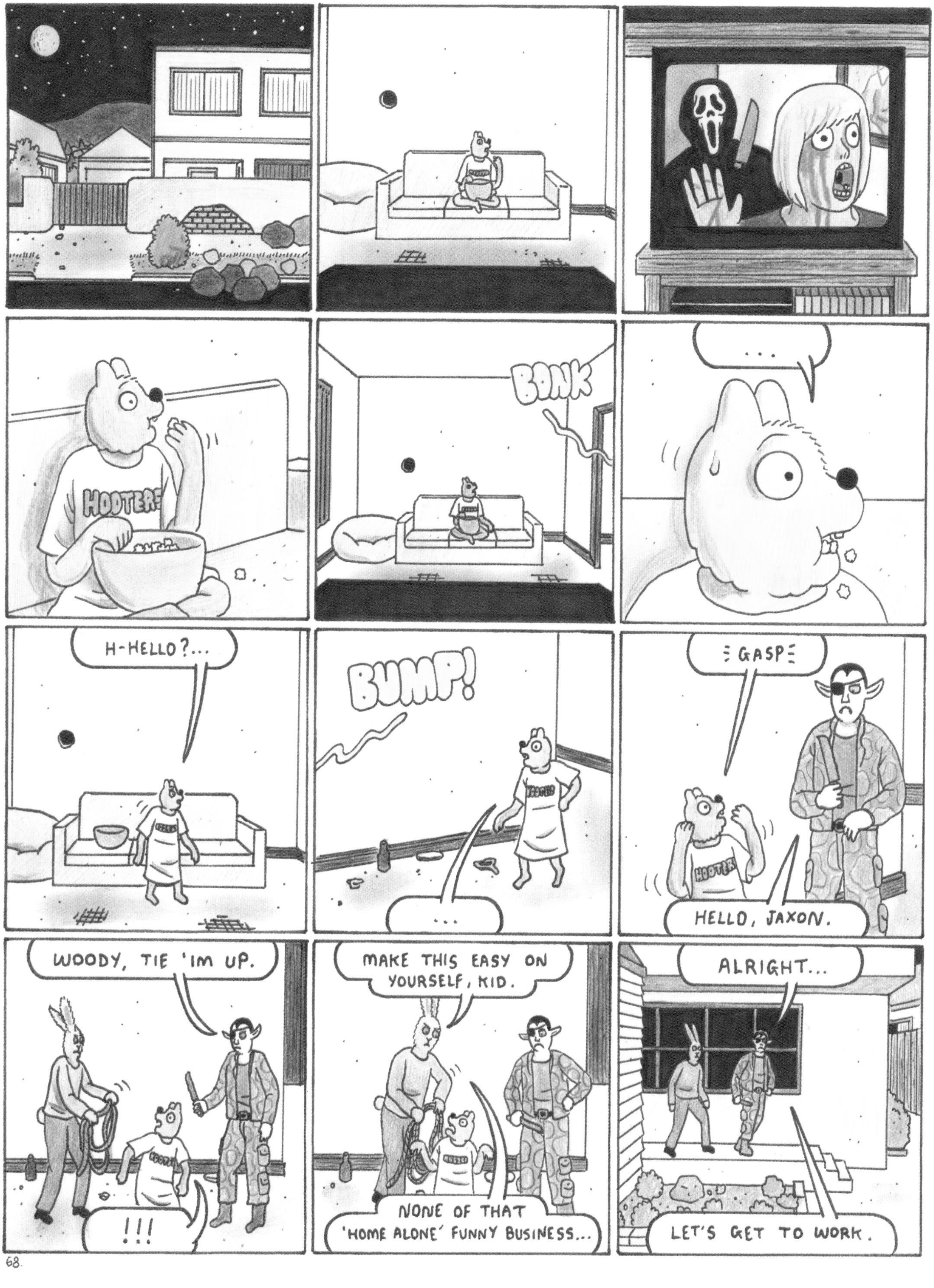
BONK
...
H-HELLO?...
BUMP!
...
GASP
HELLO, JAXON.
WOODY, TIE 'IM UP.
!!!
MAKE THIS EASY ON YOURSELF, KID.
NONE OF THAT 'HOME ALONE' FUNNY BUSINESS...
ALRIGHT...
LET'S GET TO WORK.

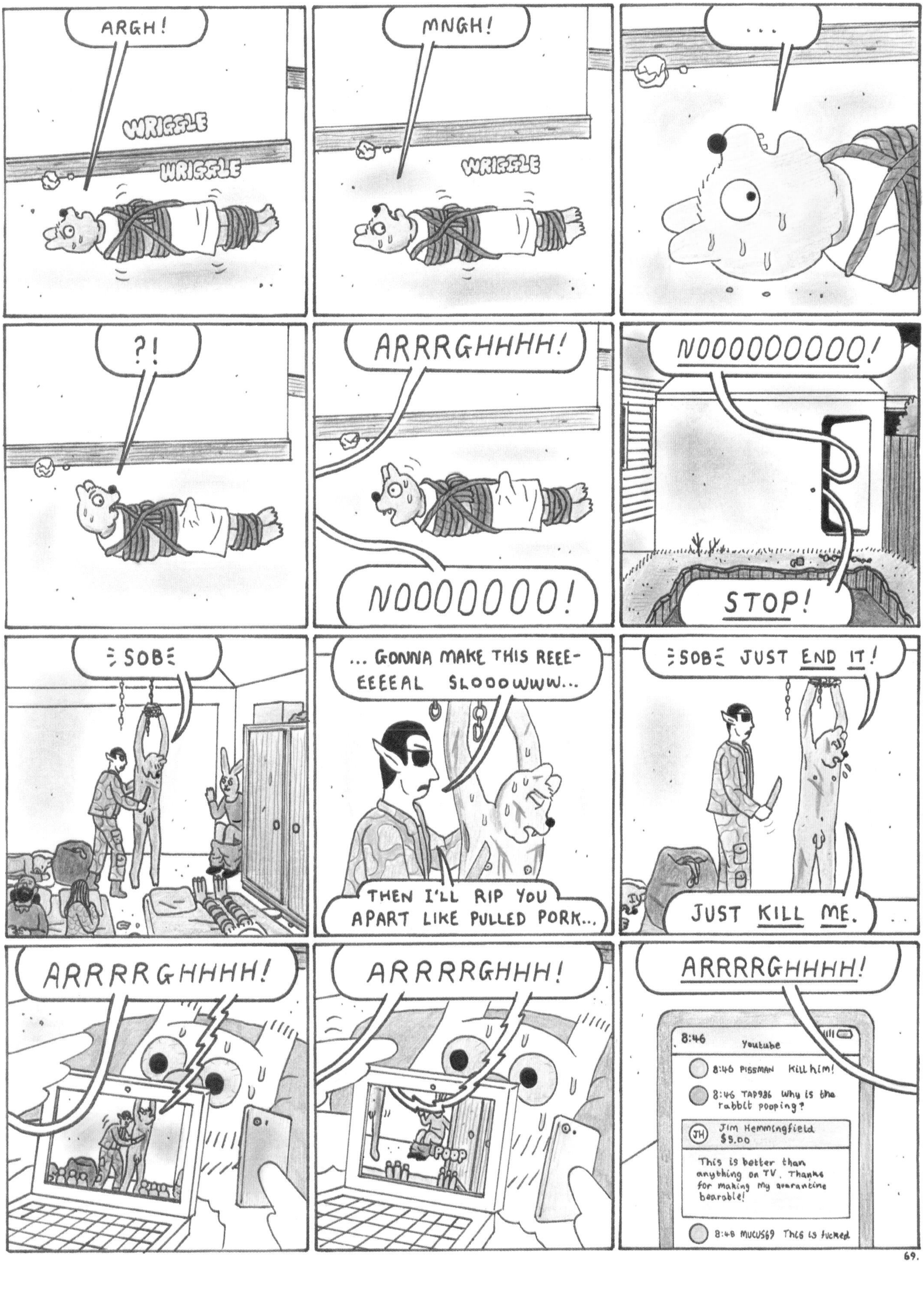
ARGH!
WRIGGLE
WRIGGLE
MNGH!
WRIGGLE
...
?!
ARRRGHHHH!
NOOOOOOO!
NOOOOOOOOO!
STOP!
SOB
... GONNA MAKE THIS REEE-EEEEAL SLOOOWWW...
THEN I'LL RIP YOU APART LIKE PULLED PORK...
SOB JUST END IT!
JUST KILL ME.
ARRRRGHHHH!
ARRRRGHHH!
POOP
ARRRRGHHHH!
8:46
Youtube
8:46 PISSMAN Kill him!
8:46 TAP986 Why is the rabbit pooping?
JH Jim Hemmingfield $5.00
This is better than anything on TV. Thanks for making my quarantine bearable!
8:48 MUCUS69 This is fucked

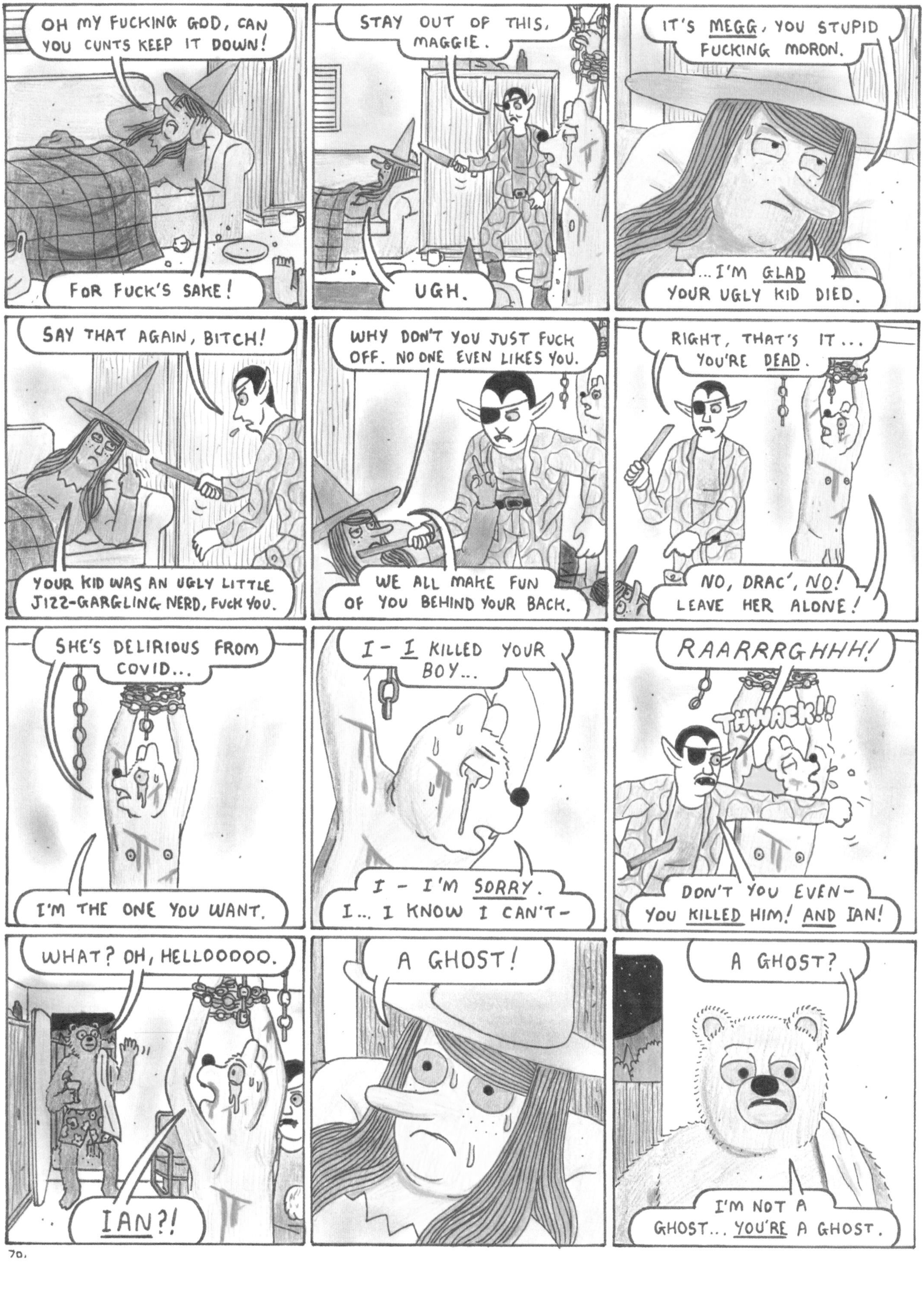
OH MY FUCKING GOD, CAN YOU CUNTS KEEP IT DOWN!
FOR FUCK'S SAKE!
STAY OUT OF THIS, MAGGIE.
UGH.
IT'S MEGG, YOU STUPID FUCKING MORON.
...I'M GLAD YOUR UGLY KID DIED.
SAY THAT AGAIN, BITCH!
YOUR KID WAS AN UGLY LITTLE JIZZ-GARGLING NERD. FUCK YOU.
WHY DON'T YOU JUST FUCK OFF. NO ONE EVEN LIKES YOU.
WE ALL MAKE FUN OF YOU BEHIND YOUR BACK.
RIGHT, THAT'S IT... YOU'RE DEAD.
NO, DRAC', NO! LEAVE HER ALONE!
SHE'S DELIRIOUS FROM COVID...
I'M THE ONE YOU WANT.
I- I KILLED YOUR BOY...
I - I'M SORRY. I... I KNOW I CAN'T-
RAARRRGHHH!
THWACK!!
DON'T YOU EVEN- YOU KILLED HIM! AND IAN!
WHAT? OH, HELLOOOOO.
IAN?!
A GHOST!
A GHOST?
I'M NOT A GHOST... YOU'RE A GHOST.

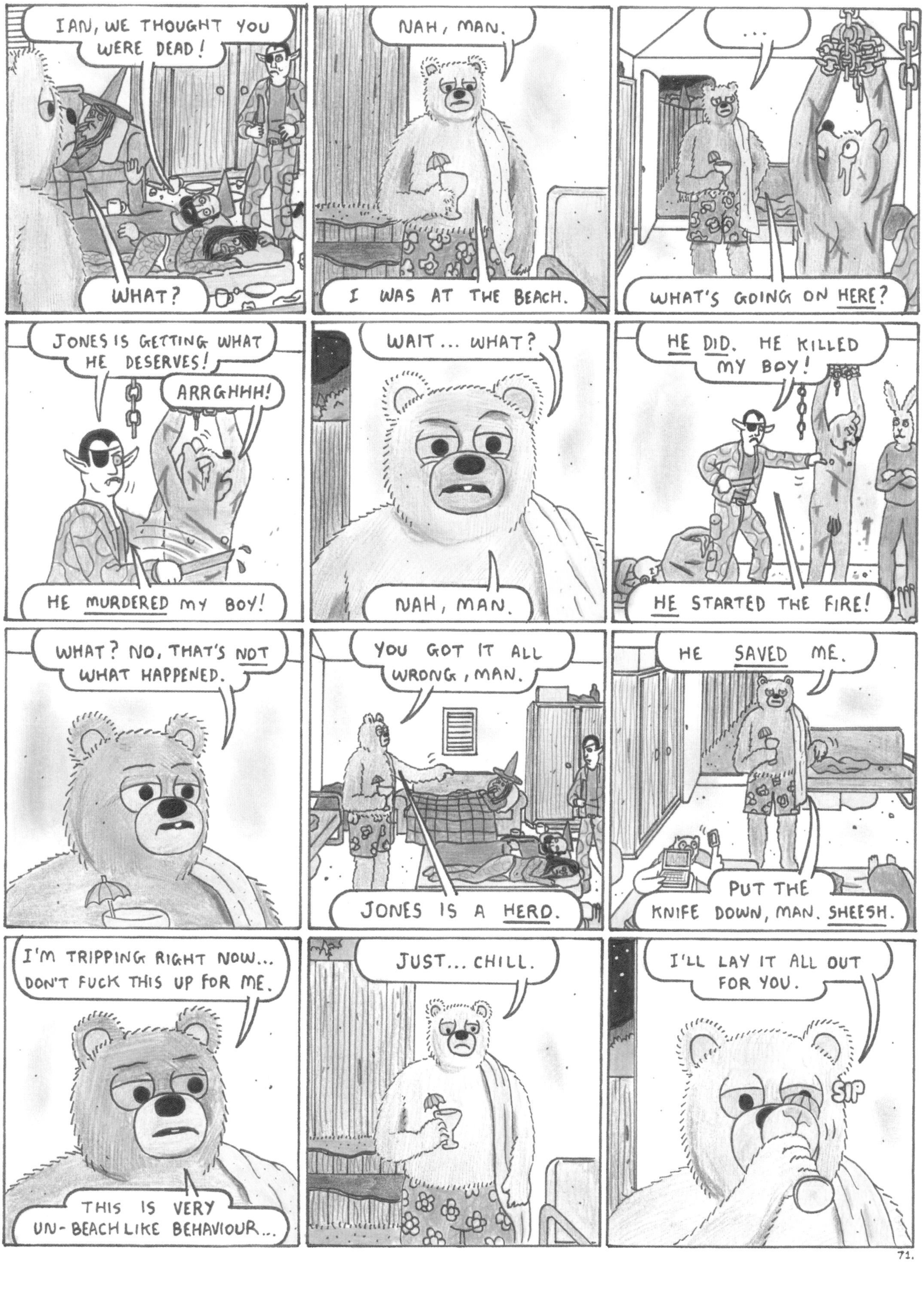
IAN, WE THOUGHT YOU WERE DEAD!
WHAT?
NAH, MAN.
I WAS AT THE BEACH.
...
WHAT'S GOING ON HERE?
JONES IS GETTING WHAT HE DESERVES!
ARRGHHH!
HE MURDERED MY BOY!
WAIT... WHAT?
NAH, MAN.
HE DID. HE KILLED MY BOY!
HE STARTED THE FIRE!
WHAT? NO, THAT'S NOT WHAT HAPPENED.
YOU GOT IT ALL WRONG, MAN.
JONES IS A HERO.
HE SAVED ME.
PUT THE KNIFE DOWN, MAN. SHEESH.
I'M TRIPPING RIGHT NOW... DON'T FUCK THIS UP FOR ME.
THIS IS VERY UN-BEACH LIKE BEHAVIOUR...
JUST... CHILL.
I'LL LAY IT ALL OUT FOR YOU.
SIP

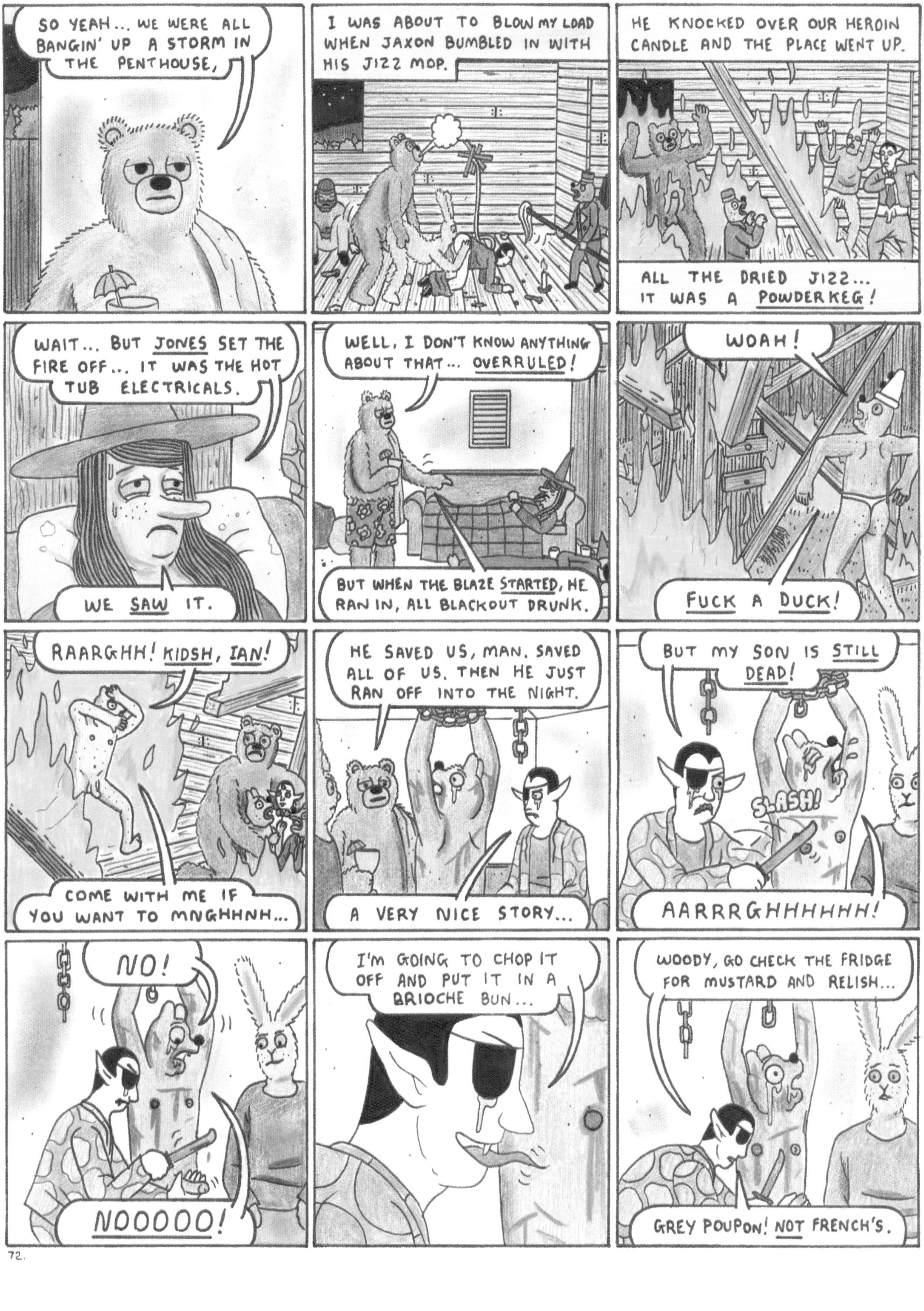
SO YEAH... WE WERE ALL BANGIN' UP A STORM IN THE PENTHOUSE,
I WAS ABOUT TO BLOW MY LOAD WHEN JAXON BUMBLED IN WITH HIS JIZZ MOP.
HE KNOCKED OVER OUR HEROIN CANDLE AND THE PLACE WENT UP.
ALL THE DRIED JIZZ... IT WAS A POWDERKEG!
WAIT... BUT JONES SET THE FIRE OFF... IT WAS THE HOT TUB ELECTRICALS.
WE SAW IT.
WELL, I DON'T KNOW ANYTHING ABOUT THAT... OVERRULED!
BUT WHEN THE BLAZE STARTED, HE RAN IN, ALL BLACKOUT DRUNK.
WOAH!
FUCK A DUCK!
RAARGHH! KIDSH, IAN!
COME WITH ME IF YOU WANT TO MNGHHNH...
HE SAVED US, MAN. SAVED ALL OF US. THEN HE JUST RAN OFF INTO THE NIGHT.
A VERY NICE STORY...
BUT MY SON IS STILL DEAD!
SLASH!
AARRRGHHHHHH!
NO!
NOOOOO!
I'M GOING TO CHOP IT OFF AND PUT IT IN A BRIOCHE BUN...
WOODY, GO CHECK THE FRIDGE FOR MUSTARD AND RELISH...
GREY POUPON! NOT FRENCH'S.

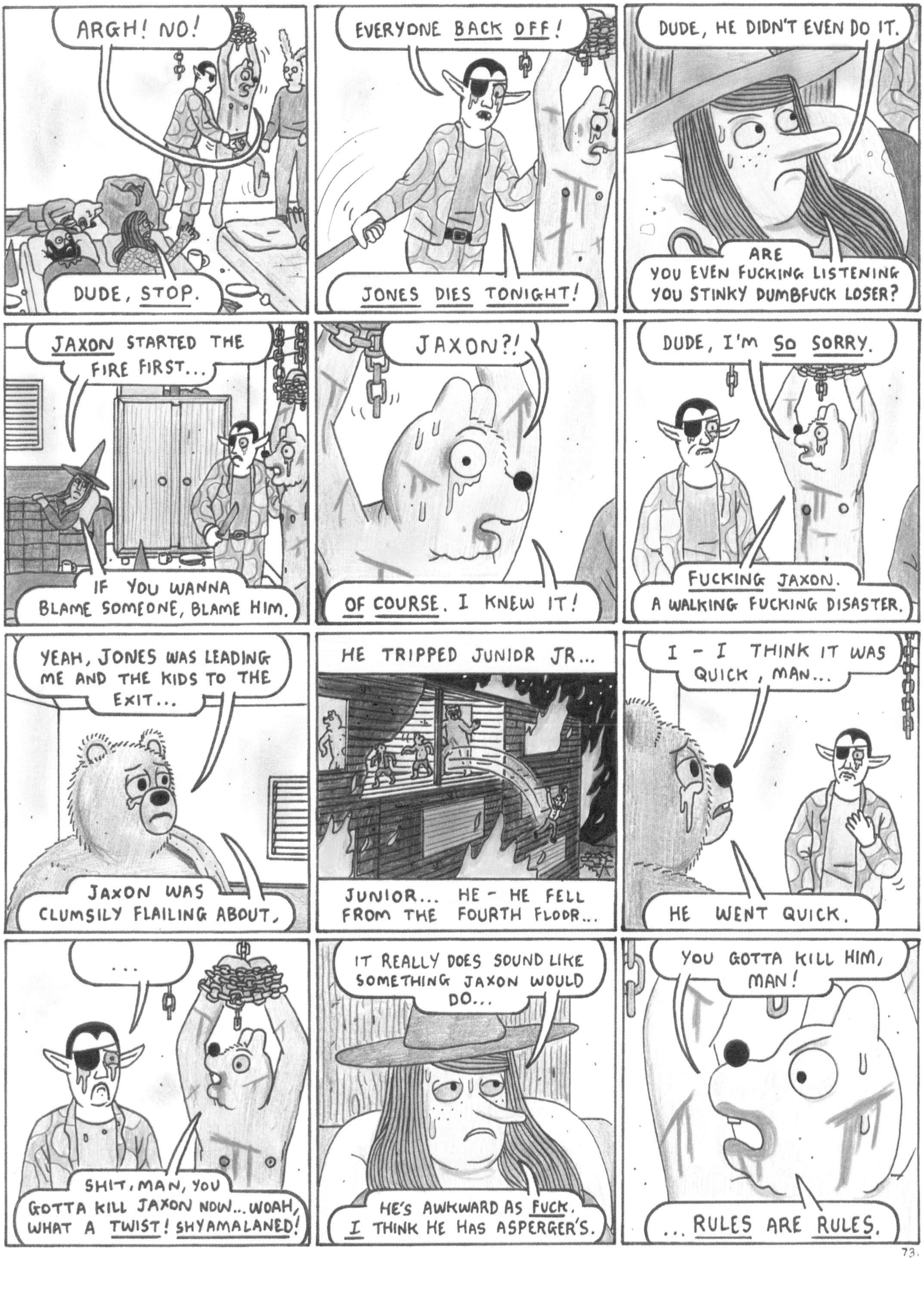
ARGH! NO!
DUDE, STOP.
EVERYONE BACK OFF!
JONES DIES TONIGHT!
DUDE, HE DIDN'T EVEN DO IT.
ARE YOU EVEN FUCKING LISTENING YOU STINKY DUMBFUCK LOSER?
JAXON STARTED THE FIRE FIRST...
IF YOU WANNA BLAME SOMEONE, BLAME HIM.
JAXON?!
OF COURSE. I KNEW IT!
DUDE, I'M SO SORRY.
FUCKING JAXON. A WALKING FUCKING DISASTER.
YEAH, JONES WAS LEADING ME AND THE KIDS TO THE EXIT...
JAXON WAS CLUMSILY FLAILING ABOUT,
HE TRIPPED JUNIOR JR...
JUNIOR... HE - HE FELL FROM THE FOURTH FLOOR...
I - I THINK IT WAS QUICK, MAN...
HE WENT QUICK.
...
SHIT, MAN, YOU GOTTA KILL JAXON NOW... WOAH, WHAT A TWIST! SHYAMALANED!
IT REALLY DOES SOUND LIKE SOMETHING JAXON WOULD DO...
HE'S AWKWARD AS FUCK. I THINK HE HAS ASPERGER'S.
YOU GOTTA KILL HIM, MAN!
... RULES ARE RULES.

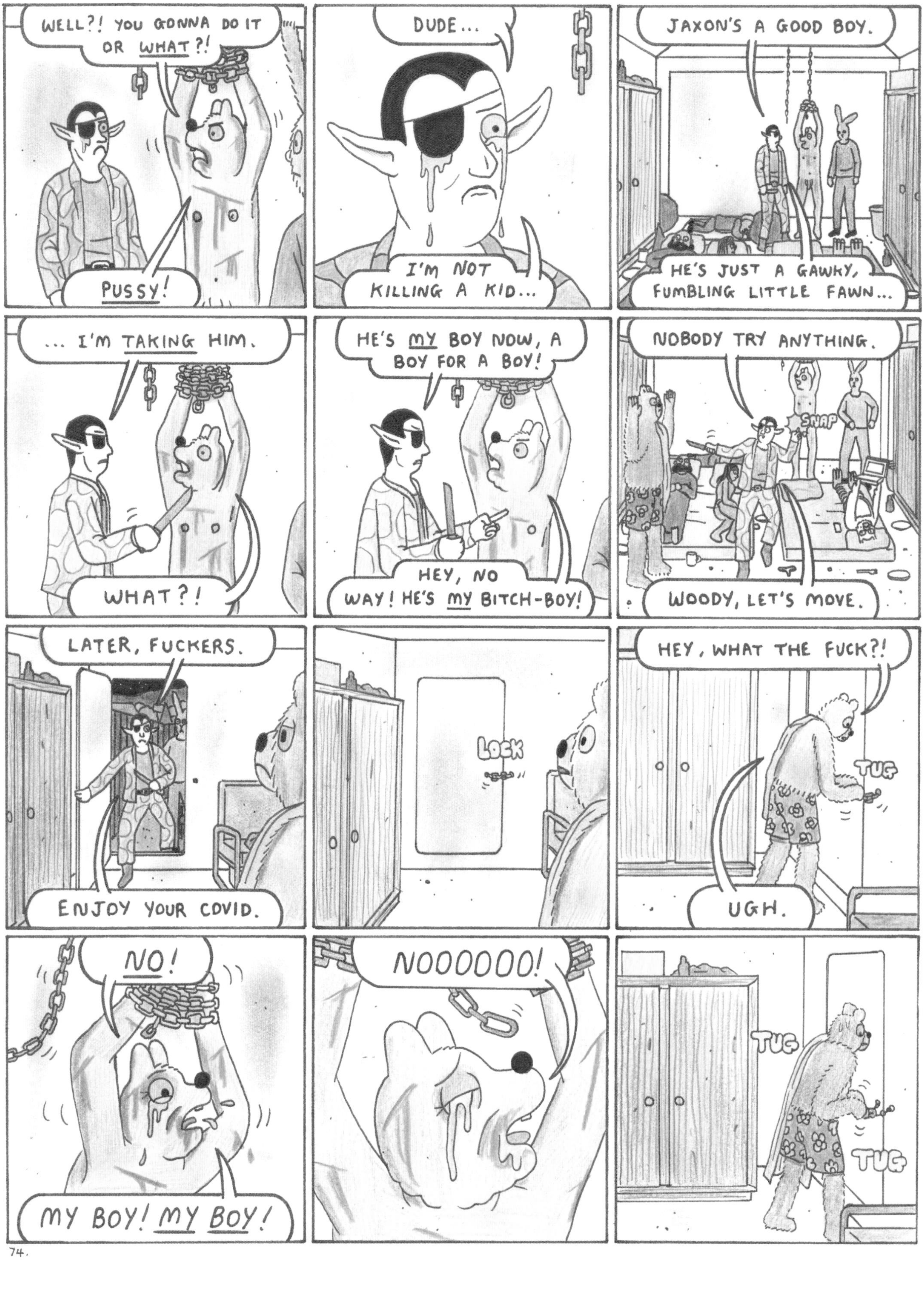
WELL?! YOU GONNA DO IT OR WHAT?!
PUSSY!
DUDE...
I'M NOT KILLING A KID...
JAXON'S A GOOD BOY.
HE'S JUST A GAWKY, FUMBLING LITTLE FAWN...
... I'M TAKING HIM.
WHAT?!
HE'S MY BOY NOW, A BOY FOR A BOY!
HEY, NO WAY! HE'S MY BITCH-BOY!
NOBODY TRY ANYTHING.
SNAP
WOODY, LET'S MOVE.
LATER, FUCKERS.
ENJOY YOUR COVID.
LOCK
HEY, WHAT THE FUCK?!
TUG
UGH.
NO!
MY BOY! MY BOY!
NOOOOOO!
TUG
TUG

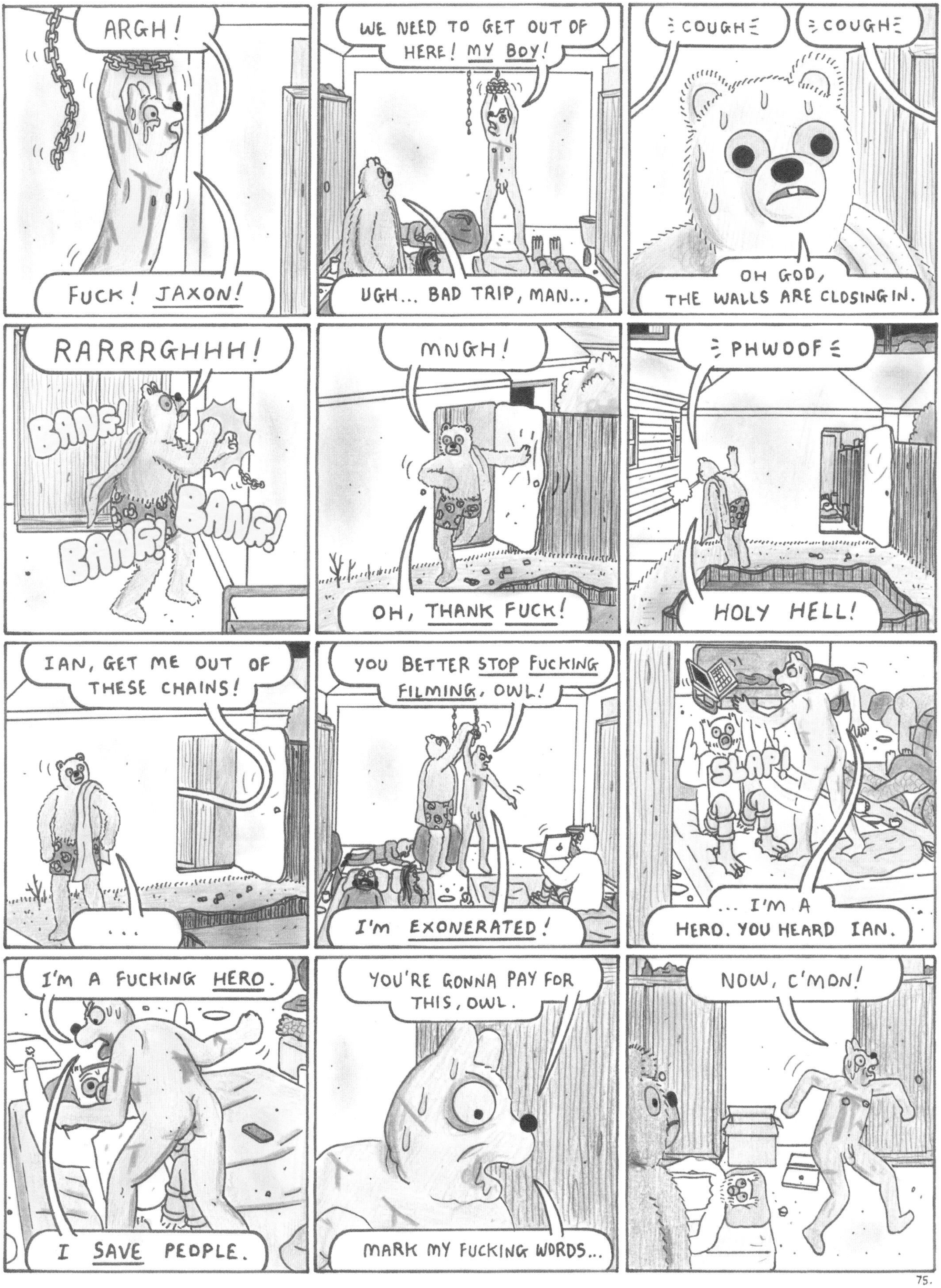
ARGH!
FUCK! JAXON!
WE NEED TO GET OUT OF HERE! MY BOY!
UGH... BAD TRIP, MAN...
COUGH
COUGH
OH GOD, THE WALLS ARE CLOSING IN.
RARRRGHHH!
BANG!
BANG!
BANG!
MNGH!
OH, THANK FUCK!
PHWOOF
HOLY HELL!
IAN, GET ME OUT OF THESE CHAINS!
...
YOU BETTER STOP FUCKING FILMING, OWL!
I'M EXONERATED!
SLAP!
... I'M A HERO. YOU HEARD IAN.
I'M A FUCKING HERO.
I SAVE PEOPLE.
YOU'RE GONNA PAY FOR THIS, OWL.
MARK MY FUCKING WORDS...
NOW, C'MON!

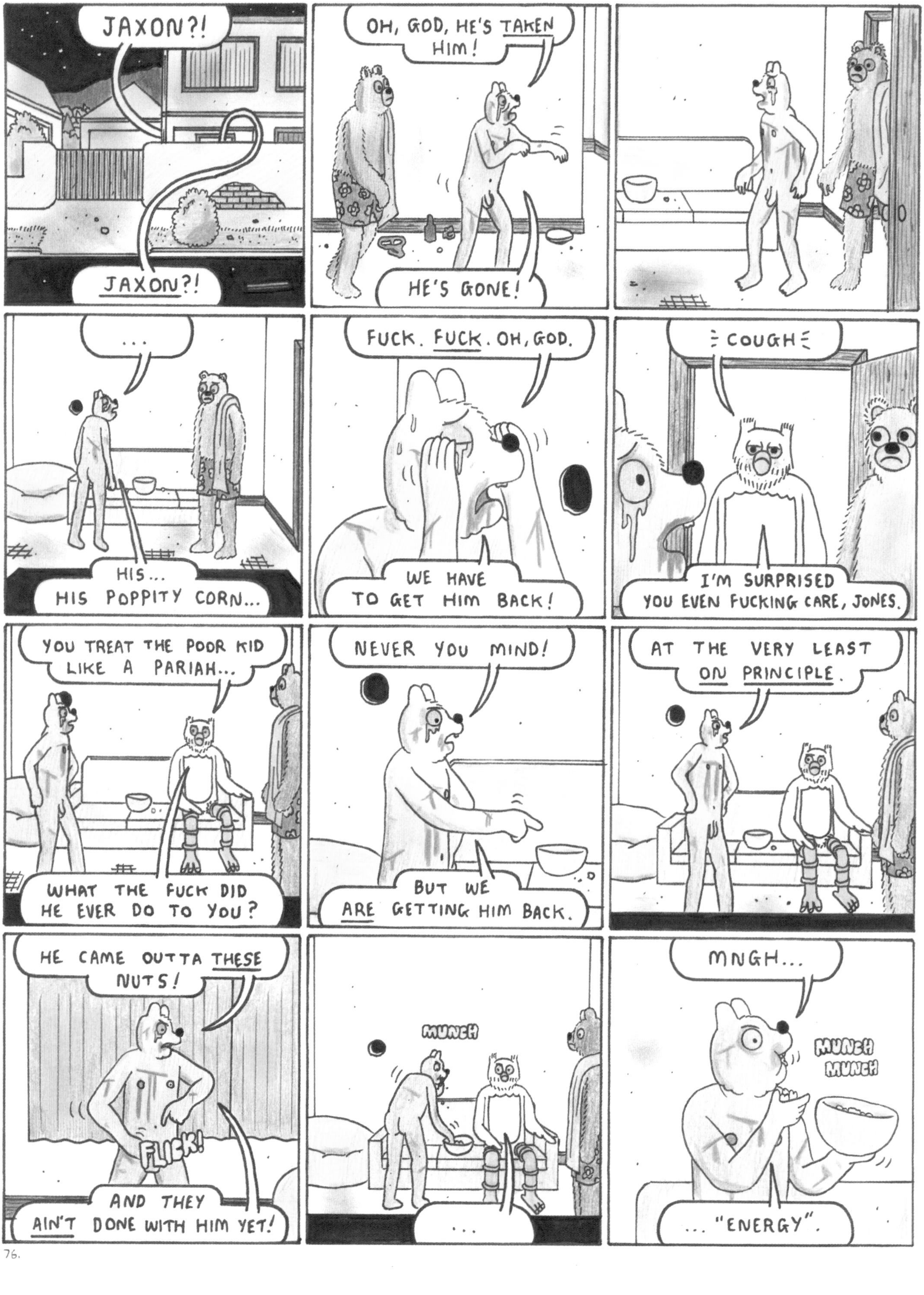
JAXON?!
JAXON?!
OH, GOD, HE'S TAKEN HIM!
HE'S GONE!
...
HIS... HIS POPPITY CORN...
FUCK. FUCK. OH, GOD.
WE HAVE TO GET HIM BACK!
COUGH
I'M SURPRISED YOU EVEN FUCKING CARE, JONES.
YOU TREAT THE POOR KID LIKE A PARIAH...
WHAT THE FUCK DID HE EVER DO TO YOU?
NEVER YOU MIND!
BUT WE ARE GETTING HIM BACK.
AT THE VERY LEAST ON PRINCIPLE.
HE CAME OUTTA THESE NUTS!
FLICK!
AND THEY AIN'T DONE WITH HIM YET!
MUNCH
...
MNGH...
MUNCH MUNCH
... "ENERGY".

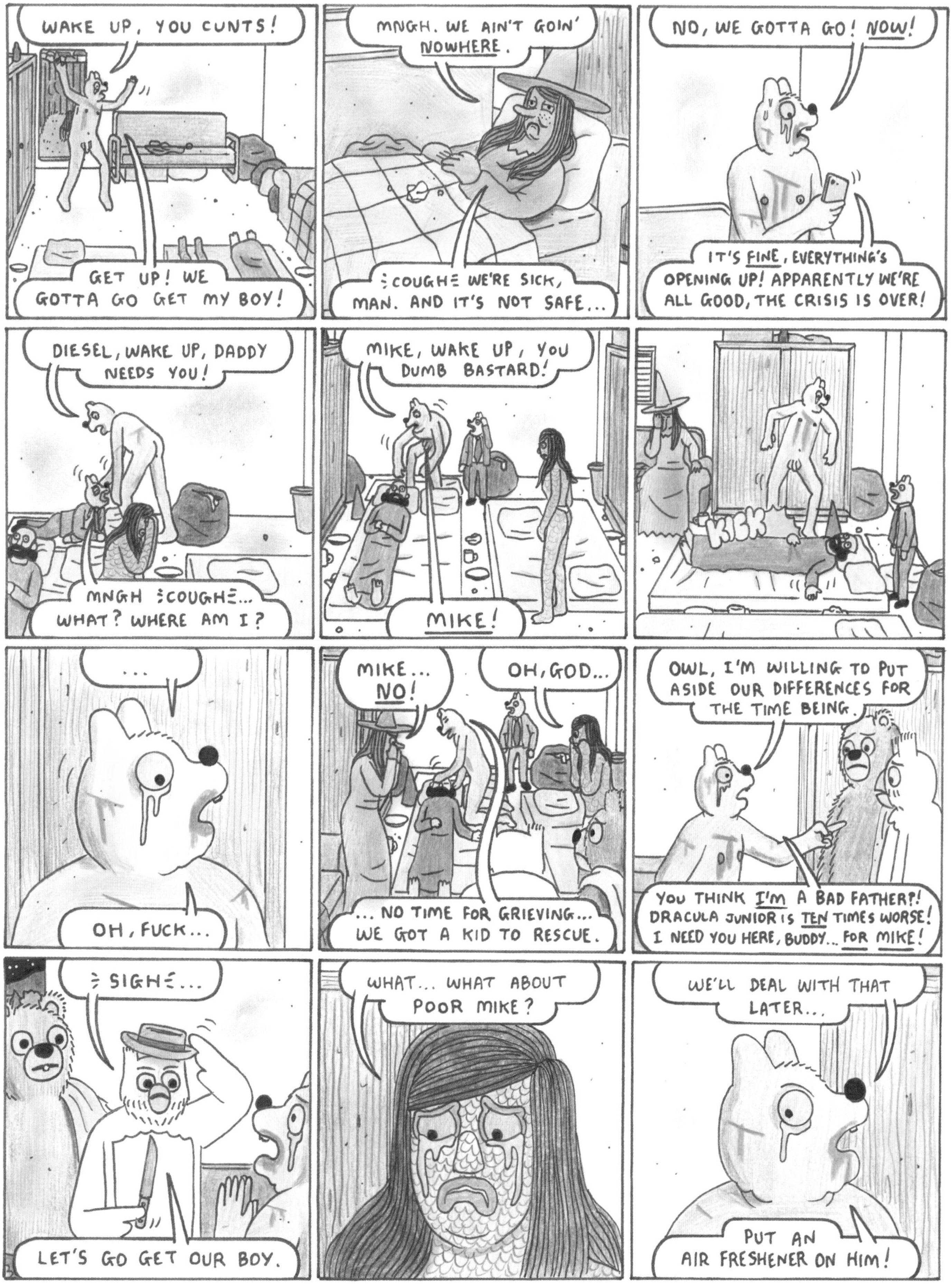
WAKE UP, YOU CUNTS!
GET UP! WE GOTTA GO GET MY BOY!
MNGH. WE AIN'T GOIN' NOWHERE.
=COUGH= WE'RE SICK, MAN. AND IT'S NOT SAFE...
NO, WE GOTTA GO! NOW!
IT'S FINE, EVERYTHING'S OPENING UP! APPARENTLY WE'RE ALL GOOD, THE CRISIS IS OVER!
DIESEL, WAKE UP, DADDY NEEDS YOU!
MNGH =COUGH=... WHAT? WHERE AM I?
MIKE, WAKE UP, YOU DUMB BASTARD!
MIKE!
KICK
...
OH, FUCK...
MIKE... NO!
OH, GOD...
... NO TIME FOR GRIEVING... WE GOT A KID TO RESCUE.
OWL, I'M WILLING TO PUT ASIDE OUR DIFFERENCES FOR THE TIME BEING.
YOU THINK I'M A BAD FATHER?! DRACULA JUNIOR IS TEN TIMES WORSE! I NEED YOU HERE, BUDDY... FOR MIKE!
=SIGH=...
LET'S GO GET OUR BOY.
WHAT... WHAT ABOUT POOR MIKE?
WE'LL DEAL WITH THAT LATER...
PUT AN AIR FRESHENER ON HIM!

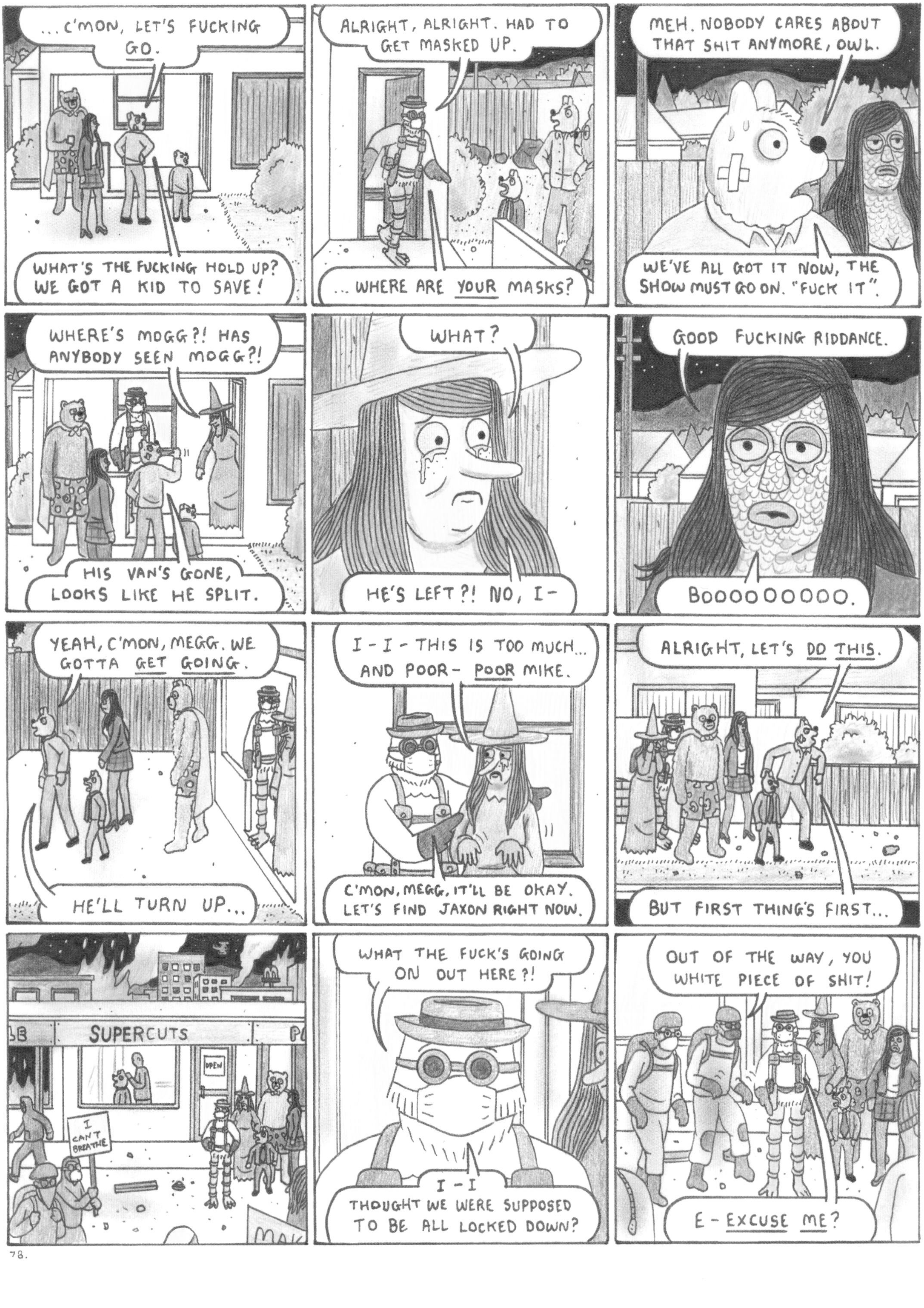
...C'MON, LET'S FUCKING GO.
WHAT'S THE FUCKING HOLD UP? WE GOT A KID TO SAVE!
ALRIGHT, ALRIGHT. HAD TO GET MASKED UP.
...WHERE ARE YOUR MASKS?
MEH. NOBODY CARES ABOUT THAT SHIT ANYMORE, OWL.
WE'VE ALL GOT IT NOW, THE SHOW MUST GO ON. "FUCK IT".
WHERE'S MOGG?! HAS ANYBODY SEEN MOGG?!
HIS VAN'S GONE, LOOKS LIKE HE SPLIT.
WHAT?
HE'S LEFT?! NO, I-
GOOD FUCKING RIDDANCE.
BOOOOOOOOO.
YEAH, C'MON, MEGG. WE GOTTA GET GOING.
HE'LL TURN UP...
I-I-THIS IS TOO MUCH... AND POOR- POOR MIKE.
C'MON, MEGG, IT'LL BE OKAY. LET'S FIND JAXON RIGHT NOW.
ALRIGHT, LET'S DO THIS.
BUT FIRST THING'S FIRST...
SUPERCUTS
OPEN
I CAN'T BREATHE
WHAT THE FUCK'S GOING ON OUT HERE?!
I-I THOUGHT WE WERE SUPPOSED TO BE ALL LOCKED DOWN?
OUT OF THE WAY, YOU WHITE PIECE OF SHIT!
E-EXCUSE ME?

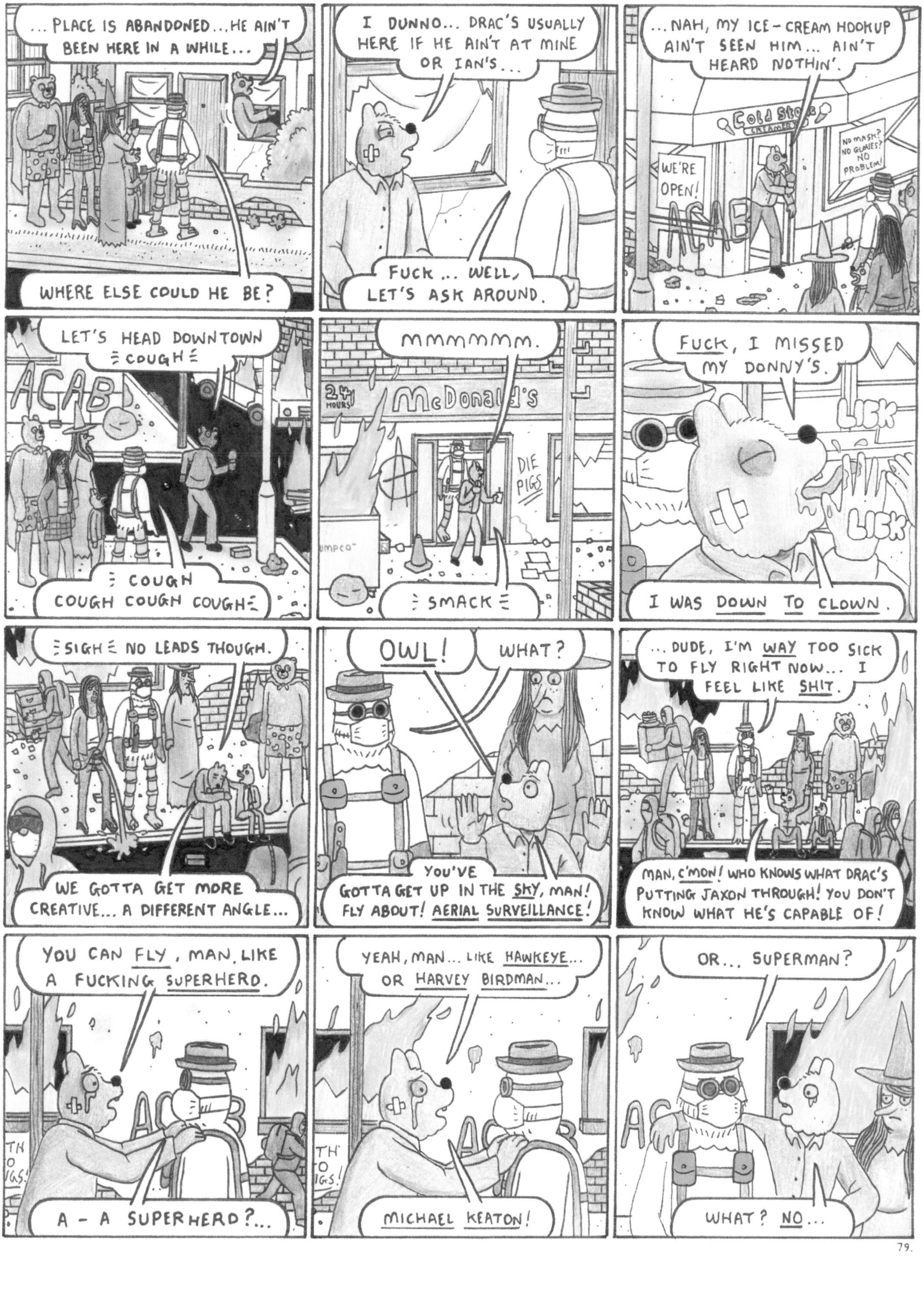
...PLACE IS ABANDONED... HE AIN'T BEEN HERE IN A WHILE...
WHERE ELSE COULD HE BE?
I DUNNO... DRAC'S USUALLY HERE IF HE AIN'T AT MINE OR IAN'S...
FUCK... WELL, LET'S ASK AROUND.
...NAH, MY ICE-CREAM HOOKUP AIN'T SEEN HIM... AIN'T HEARD NOTHIN'.
Cold Stone CREAMERY
WE'RE OPEN!
NO MASK? NO GLOVES? NO PROBLEM!
ACAB
LET'S HEAD DOWNTOWN ⁝COUGH⁝
ACAB
⁝COUGH COUGH COUGH COUGH⁝
MMMMMM.
24 HOURS
McDonald's
DIE PIGS
⁝SMACK⁝
FUCK, I MISSED MY DONNY'S.
LICK
LICK
I WAS DOWN TO CLOWN.
⁝SIGH⁝ NO LEADS THOUGH.
WE GOTTA GET MORE CREATIVE... A DIFFERENT ANGLE...
OWL!
WHAT?
YOU'VE GOTTA GET UP IN THE SKY, MAN! FLY ABOUT! AERIAL SURVEILLANCE!
...DUDE, I'M WAY TOO SICK TO FLY RIGHT NOW... I FEEL LIKE SHIT.
MAN, C'MON! WHO KNOWS WHAT DRAC'S PUTTING JAXON THROUGH! YOU DON'T KNOW WHAT HE'S CAPABLE OF!
YOU CAN FLY, MAN, LIKE A FUCKING SUPERHERO.
A-A SUPERHERO?...
YEAH, MAN... LIKE HAWKEYE... OR HARVEY BIRDMAN...
MICHAEL KEATON!
OR... SUPERMAN?
WHAT? NO...

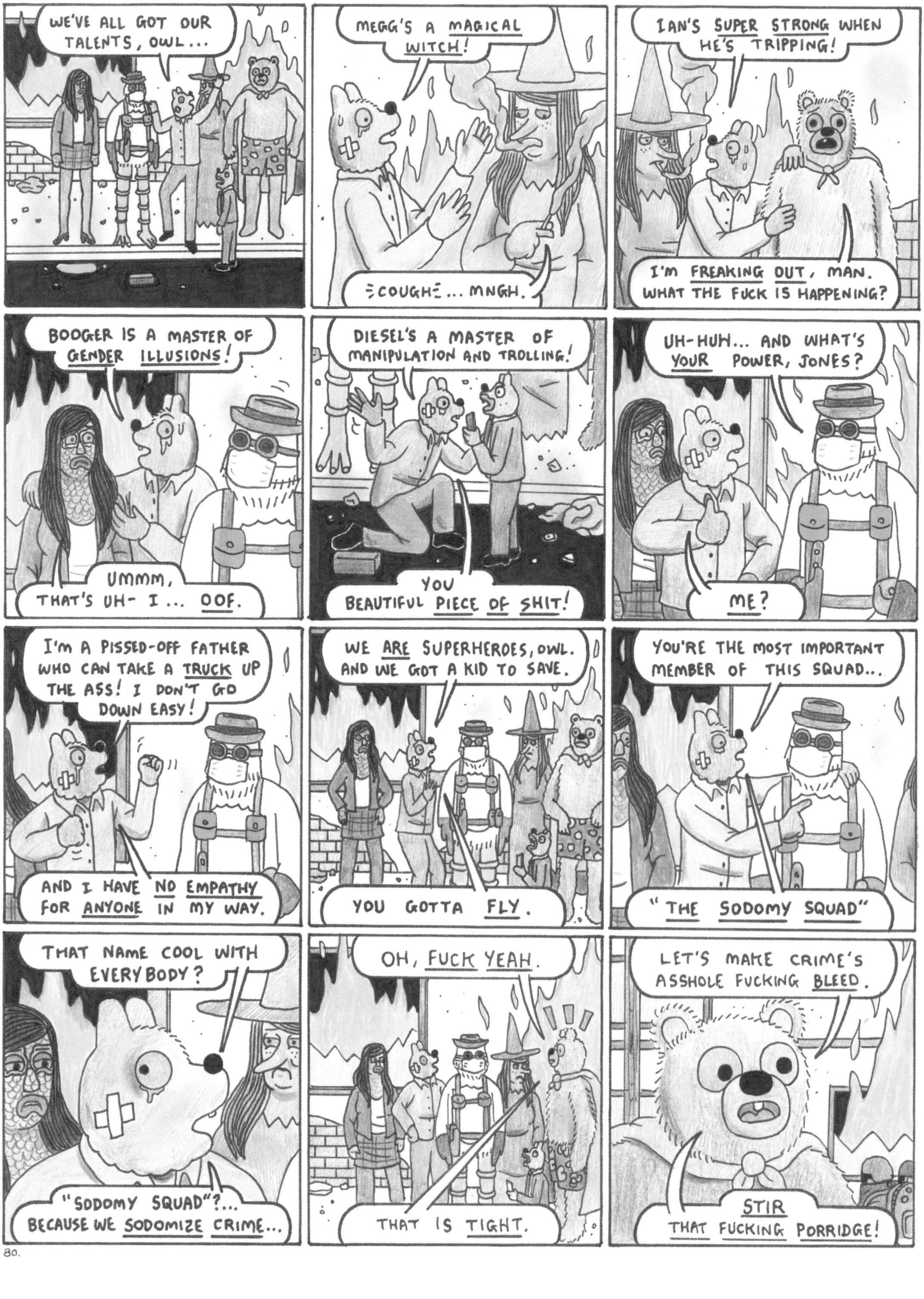
WE'VE ALL GOT OUR TALENTS, OWL...
MEGG'S A MAGICAL WITCH!
≈COUGH≈ ... MNGH.
IAN'S SUPER STRONG WHEN HE'S TRIPPING!
I'M FREAKING OUT, MAN. WHAT THE FUCK IS HAPPENING?
BOOGER IS A MASTER OF GENDER ILLUSIONS!
UMMM, THAT'S UH- I... OOF.
DIESEL'S A MASTER OF MANIPULATION AND TROLLING!
YOU BEAUTIFUL PIECE OF SHIT!
UH-HUH... AND WHAT'S YOUR POWER, JONES?
ME?
I'M A PISSED-OFF FATHER WHO CAN TAKE A TRUCK UP THE ASS! I DON'T GO DOWN EASY!
AND I HAVE NO EMPATHY FOR ANYONE IN MY WAY.
WE ARE SUPERHEROES, OWL. AND WE GOT A KID TO SAVE.
YOU GOTTA FLY.
YOU'RE THE MOST IMPORTANT MEMBER OF THIS SQUAD...
"THE SODOMY SQUAD"
THAT NAME COOL WITH EVERYBODY?
"SODOMY SQUAD"?... BECAUSE WE SODOMIZE CRIME...
OH, FUCK YEAH.
THAT IS TIGHT.
LET'S MAKE CRIME'S ASSHOLE FUCKING BLEED.
STIR THAT FUCKING PORRIDGE!

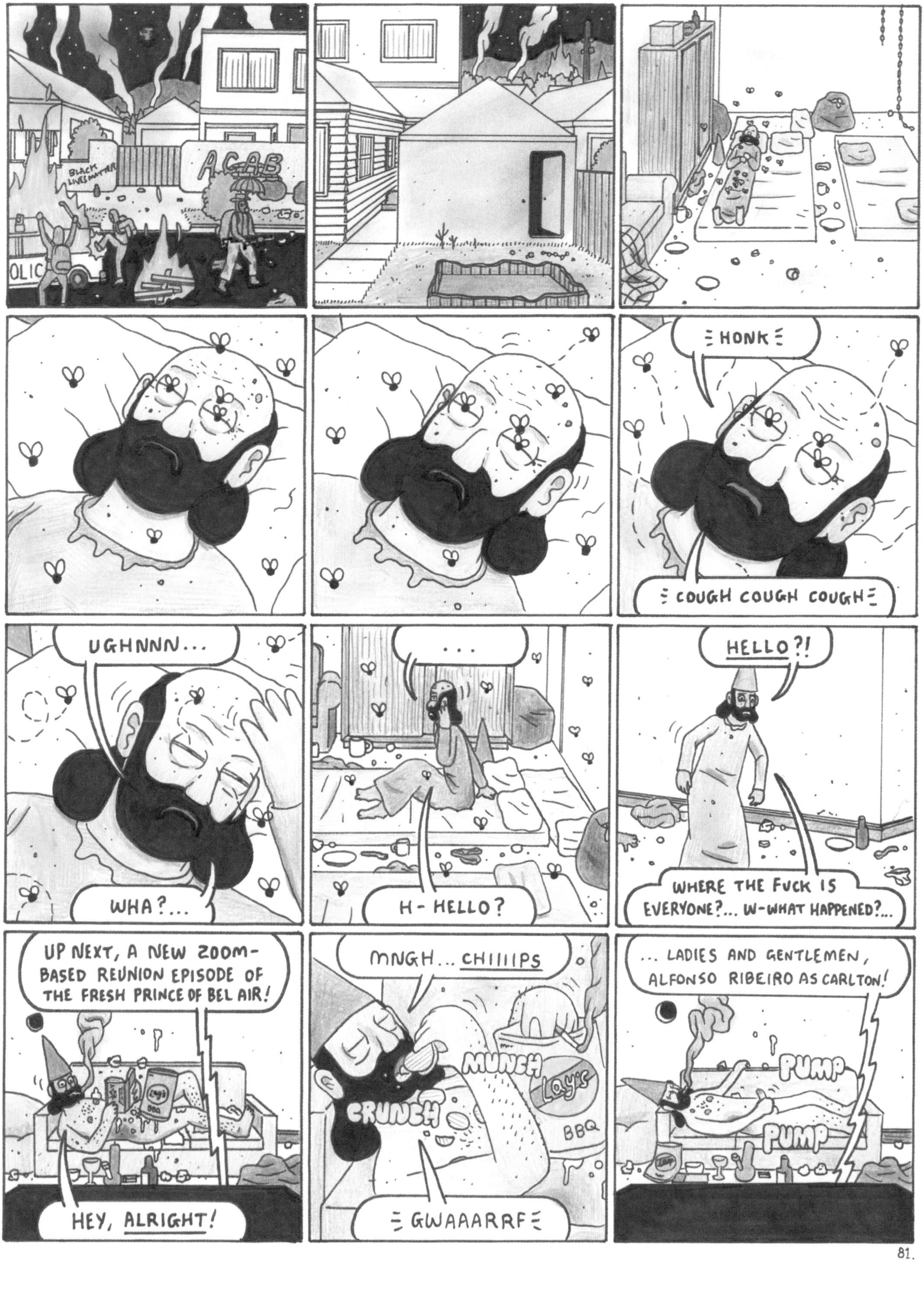

BLACK LIVES MATTER
A.C.A.B
OLIC
HONK
COUGH COUGH COUGH
UGHNNN...
WHA?...
...
H-HELLO?
HELLO?!
WHERE THE FUCK IS EVERYONE?... W-WHAT HAPPENED?...
UP NEXT, A NEW ZOOM-BASED REUNION EPISODE OF THE FRESH PRINCE OF BEL AIR!
HEY, ALRIGHT!
MNGH... CHIIIIPS
MUNCH
CRUNCH
Lay's
BBQ
GWAAARRF
... LADIES AND GENTLEMEN, ALFONSO RIBEIRO AS CARLTON!
PUMP
PUMP

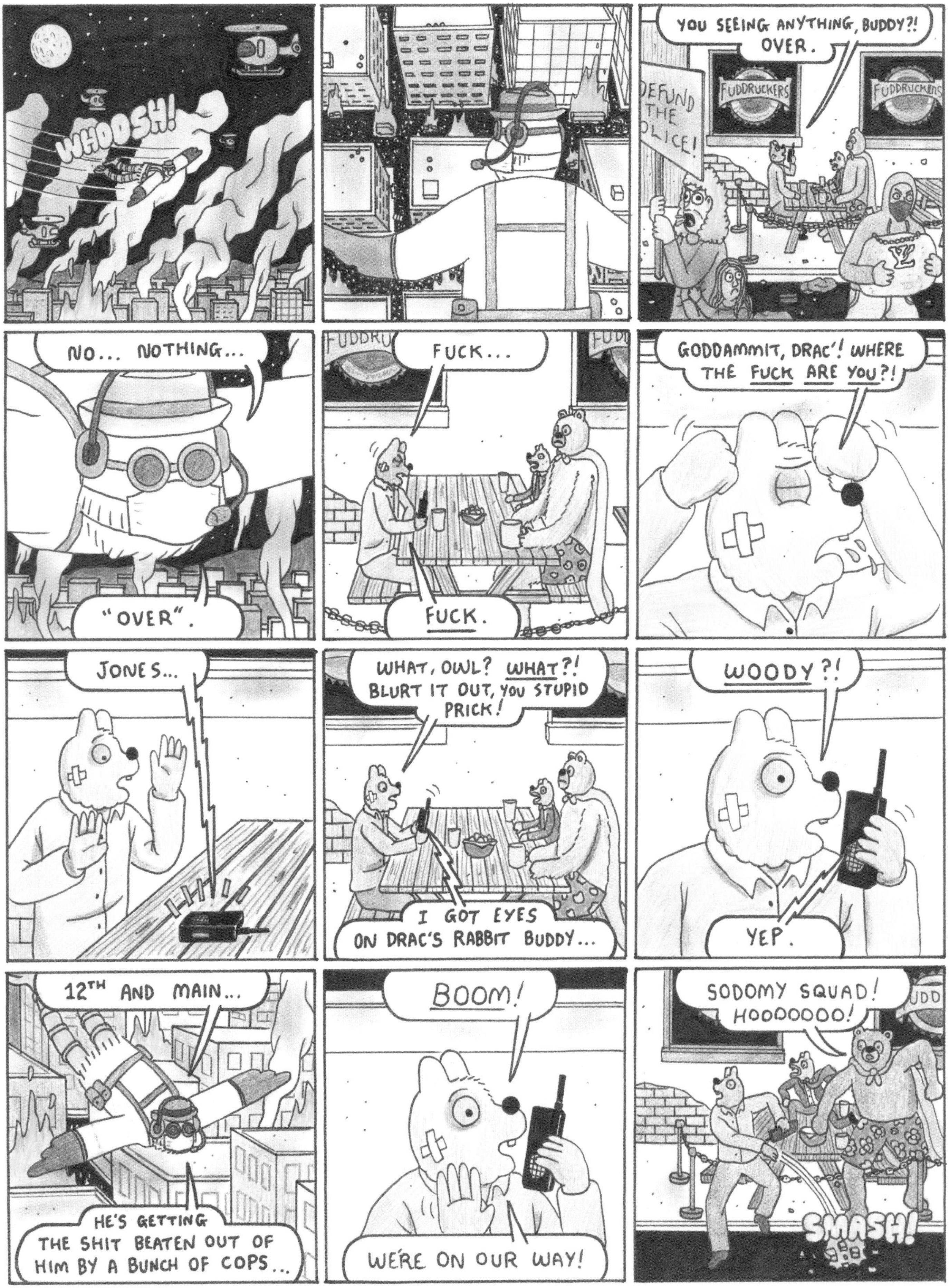
WHOOSH!
YOU SEEING ANYTHING, BUDDY?! OVER.
FUDDRUCKERS
FUDDRUCKERS
DEFUND THE POLICE!
NO... NOTHING...
"OVER".
FUCK...
FUCK.
GODDAMMIT, DRAC'! WHERE THE FUCK ARE YOU?!
JONES...
WHAT, OWL? WHAT?! BLURT IT OUT, YOU STUPID PRICK!
I GOT EYES ON DRAC'S RABBIT BUDDY...
WOODY?!
YEP.
12TH AND MAIN...
HE'S GETTING THE SHIT BEATEN OUT OF HIM BY A BUNCH OF COPS...
BOOM!
WE'RE ON OUR WAY!
SODOMY SQUAD! HOOOOOOO!
SMASH!

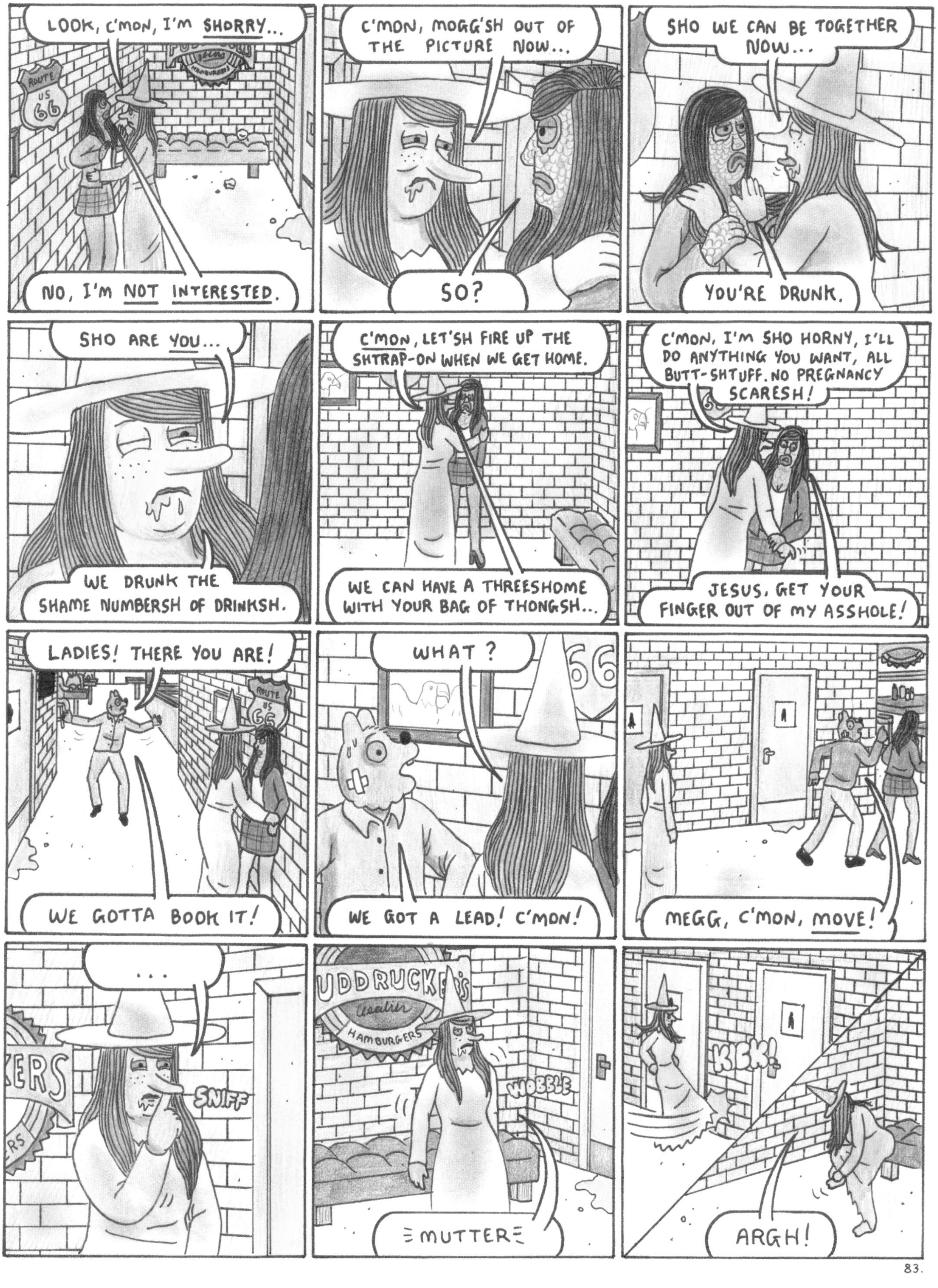

LOOK, C'MON, I'M SHORRY...
ROUTE US 66
NO, I'M NOT INTERESTED.
C'MON, MOGG'SH OUT OF THE PICTURE NOW...
SO?
SHO WE CAN BE TOGETHER NOW...
YOU'RE DRUNK.
SHO ARE YOU...
WE DRUNK THE SHAME NUMBERSH OF DRINKSH.
C'MON, LET'SH FIRE UP THE SHTRAP-ON WHEN WE GET HOME.
WE CAN HAVE A THREESHOME WITH YOUR BAG OF THONGSH...
C'MON, I'M SHO HORNY, I'LL DO ANYTHING YOU WANT, ALL BUTT-SHTUFF. NO PREGNANCY SCARESH!
JESUS, GET YOUR FINGER OUT OF MY ASSHOLE!
LADIES! THERE YOU ARE!
ROUTE US 66
WE GOTTA BOOK IT!
WHAT?
WE GOT A LEAD! C'MON!
MEGG, C'MON, MOVE!
...
SNIFF
UDDRUCKER'S
HAMBURGERS
WOBBLE
MUTTER
KEK!
ARGH!

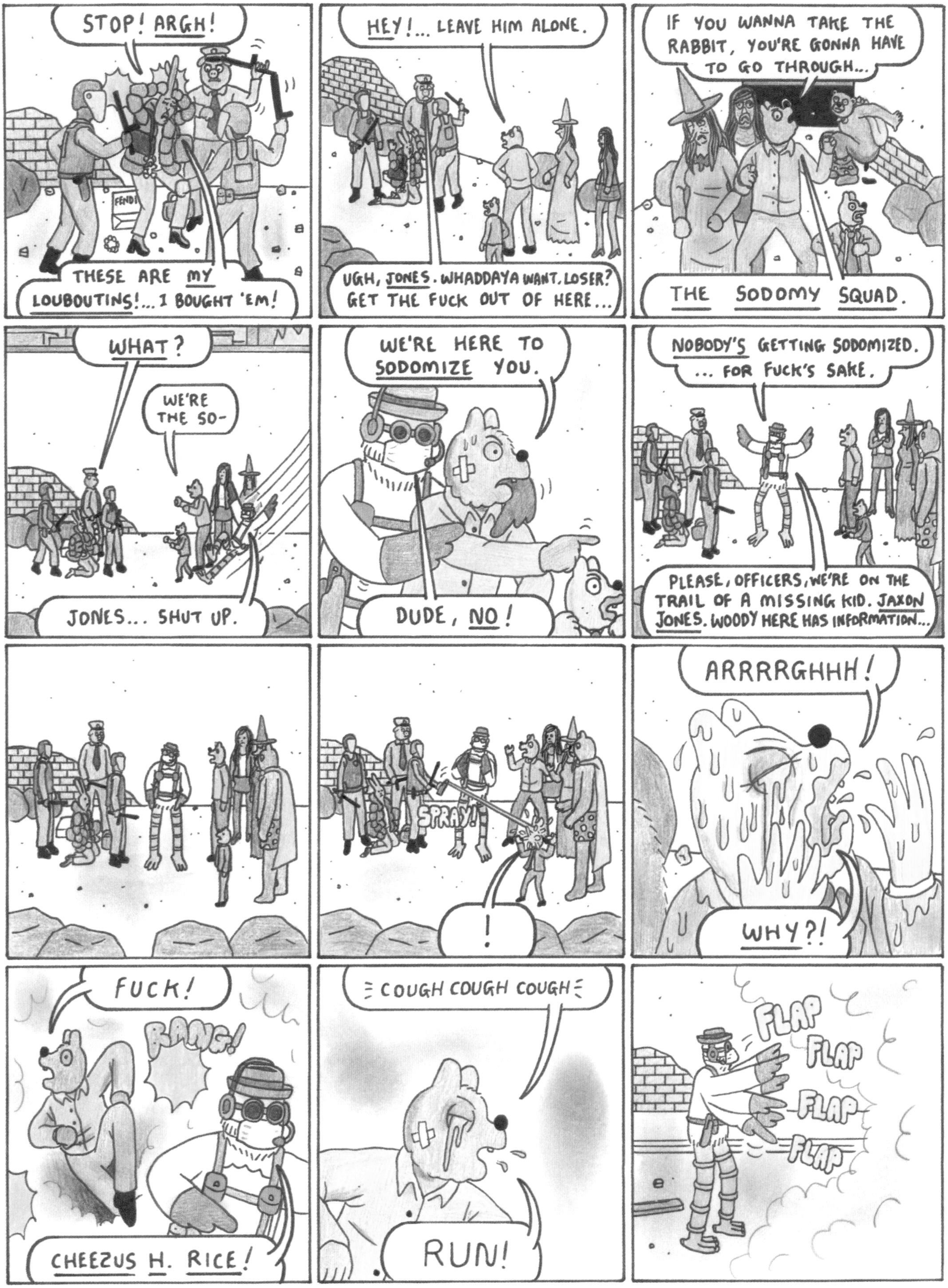
STOP! ARGH!
THESE ARE MY LOUBOUTINS!... I BOUGHT 'EM!
FENDI
HEY!... LEAVE HIM ALONE.
UGH, JONES. WHADDAYA WANT, LOSER? GET THE FUCK OUT OF HERE...
IF YOU WANNA TAKE THE RABBIT, YOU'RE GONNA HAVE TO GO THROUGH...
THE SODOMY SQUAD.
WHAT?
WE'RE THE SO-
JONES... SHUT UP.
WE'RE HERE TO SODOMIZE YOU.
DUDE, NO!
NOBODY'S GETTING SODOMIZED. ... FOR FUCK'S SAKE.
PLEASE, OFFICERS, WE'RE ON THE TRAIL OF A MISSING KID. JAXON JONES. WOODY HERE HAS INFORMATION...
SPRAY!
!
ARRRRGHHH!
WHY?!
FUCK!
BANG!
CHEEZUS H. RICE!
COUGH COUGH COUGH
RUN!
FLAP
FLAP
FLAP
FLAP

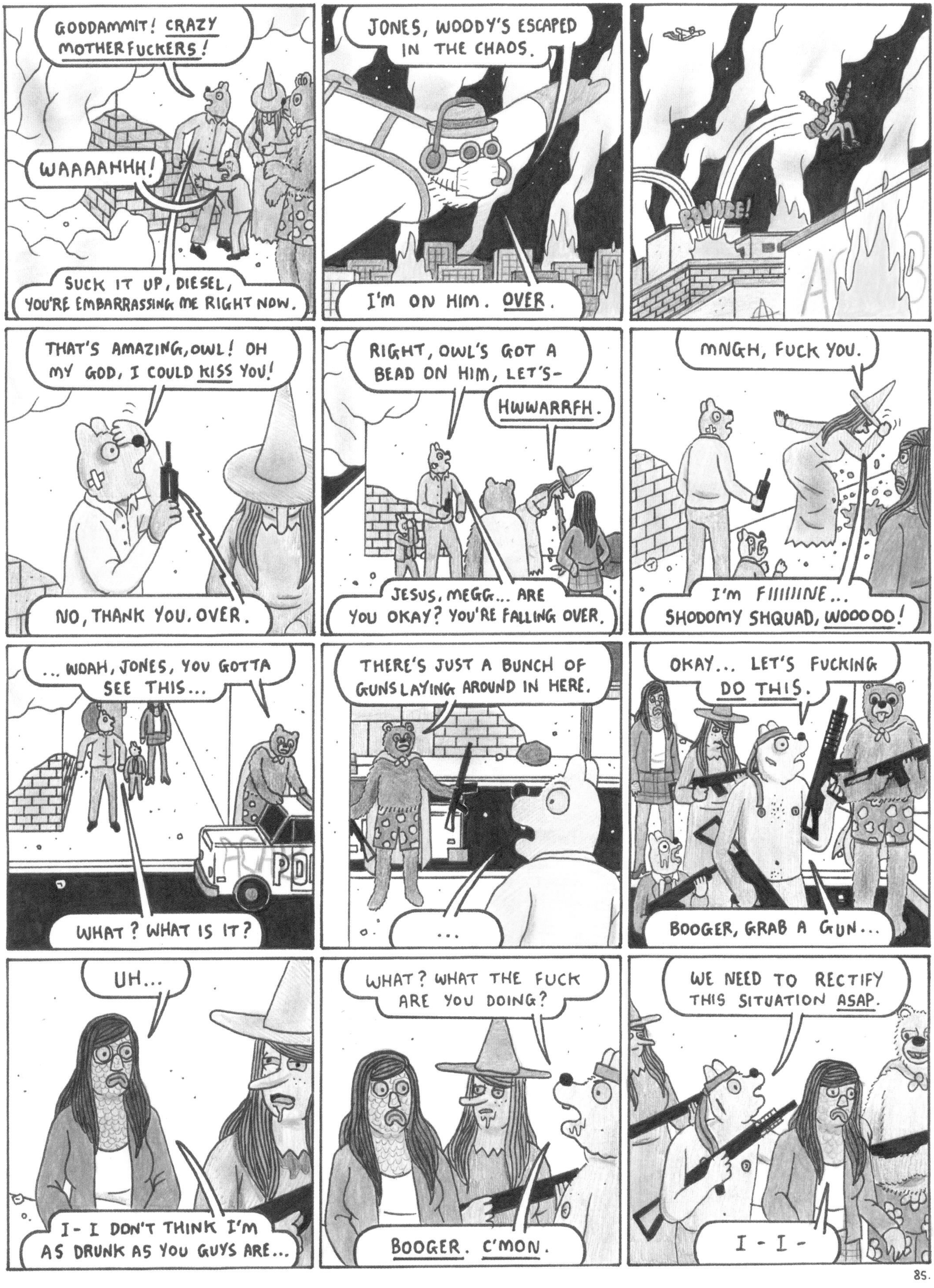

GODDAMMIT! CRAZY MOTHERFUCKERS!
WAAAAHHH!
SUCK IT UP, DIESEL, YOU'RE EMBARRASSING ME RIGHT NOW.
JONES, WOODY'S ESCAPED IN THE CHAOS.
I'M ON HIM. OVER.
BOUNCE!
THAT'S AMAZING, OWL! OH MY GOD, I COULD KISS YOU!
NO, THANK YOU. OVER.
RIGHT, OWL'S GOT A BEAD ON HIM, LET'S-
HWWARRFH.
JESUS, MEGG... ARE YOU OKAY? YOU'RE FALLING OVER.
MNGH, FUCK YOU.
I'M FIIIIIINE... SHODOMY SHQUAD, WOOOOO!
... WOAH, JONES, YOU GOTTA SEE THIS...
WHAT? WHAT IS IT?
THERE'S JUST A BUNCH OF GUNS LAYING AROUND IN HERE.
...
OKAY... LET'S FUCKING DO THIS.
BOOGER, GRAB A GUN...
UH...
I- I DON'T THINK I'M AS DRUNK AS YOU GUYS ARE...
WHAT? WHAT THE FUCK ARE YOU DOING?
BOOGER. C'MON.
WE NEED TO RECTIFY THIS SITUATION ASAP.
I - I -

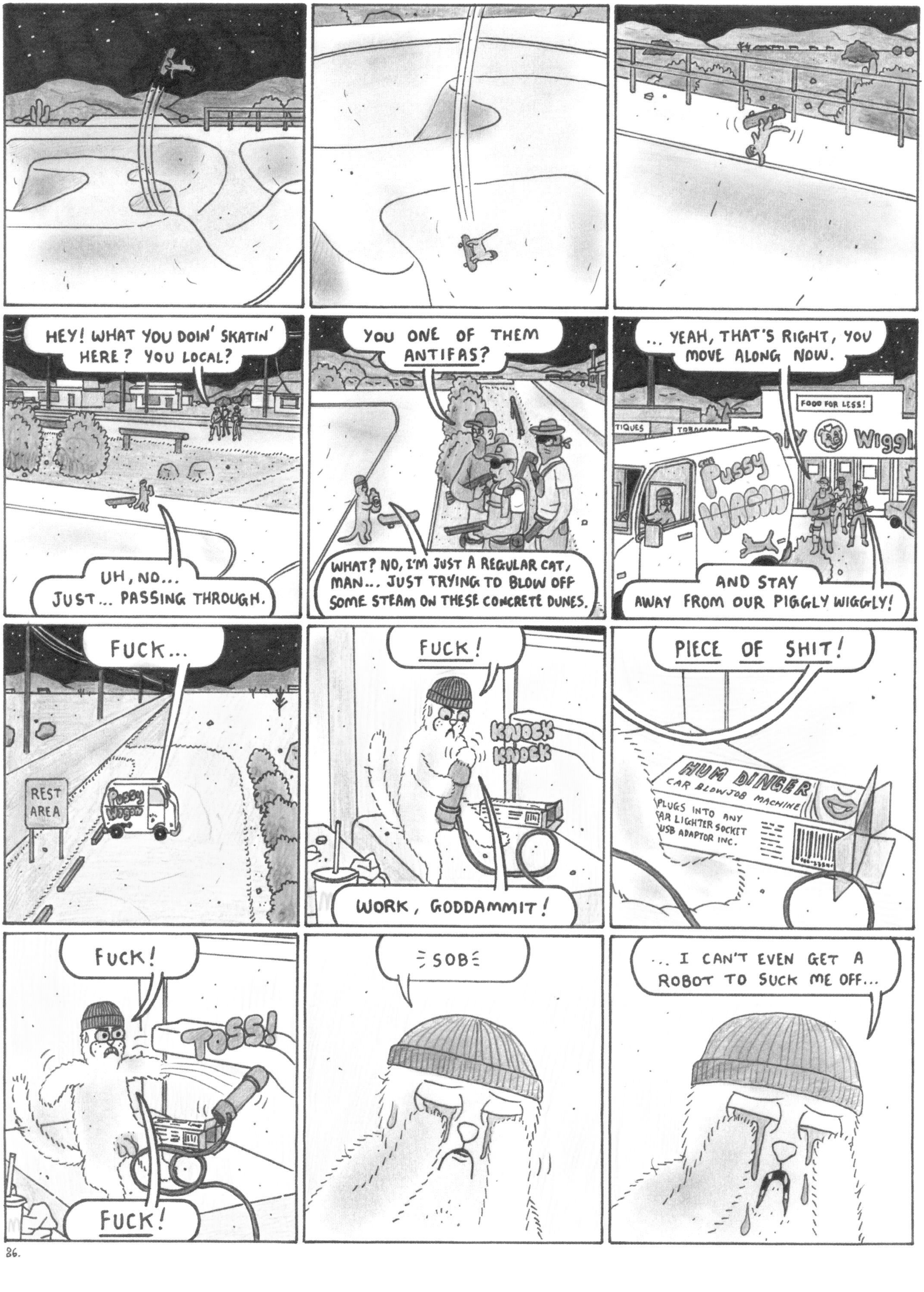

HEY! WHAT YOU DOIN' SKATIN' HERE? YOU LOCAL?
UH, NO... JUST... PASSING THROUGH.
YOU ONE OF THEM ANTIFAS?
WHAT? NO, I'M JUST A REGULAR CAT, MAN... JUST TRYING TO BLOW OFF SOME STEAM ON THESE CONCRETE DUNES.
... YEAH, THAT'S RIGHT, YOU MOVE ALONG NOW.
FOOD FOR LESS!
THE Pussy WAGON
AND STAY AWAY FROM OUR PIGGLY WIGGLY!
FUCK...
REST AREA
Pussy Wagon
FUCK!
KNOCK KNOCK
WORK, GODDAMMIT!
PIECE OF SHIT!
HUM DINGER
CAR BLOWJOB MACHINE
PLUGS INTO ANY CAR LIGHTER SOCKET
USB ADAPTOR INC.
FUCK!
TOSS!
FUCK!
SOB
... I CAN'T EVEN GET A ROBOT TO SUCK ME OFF...

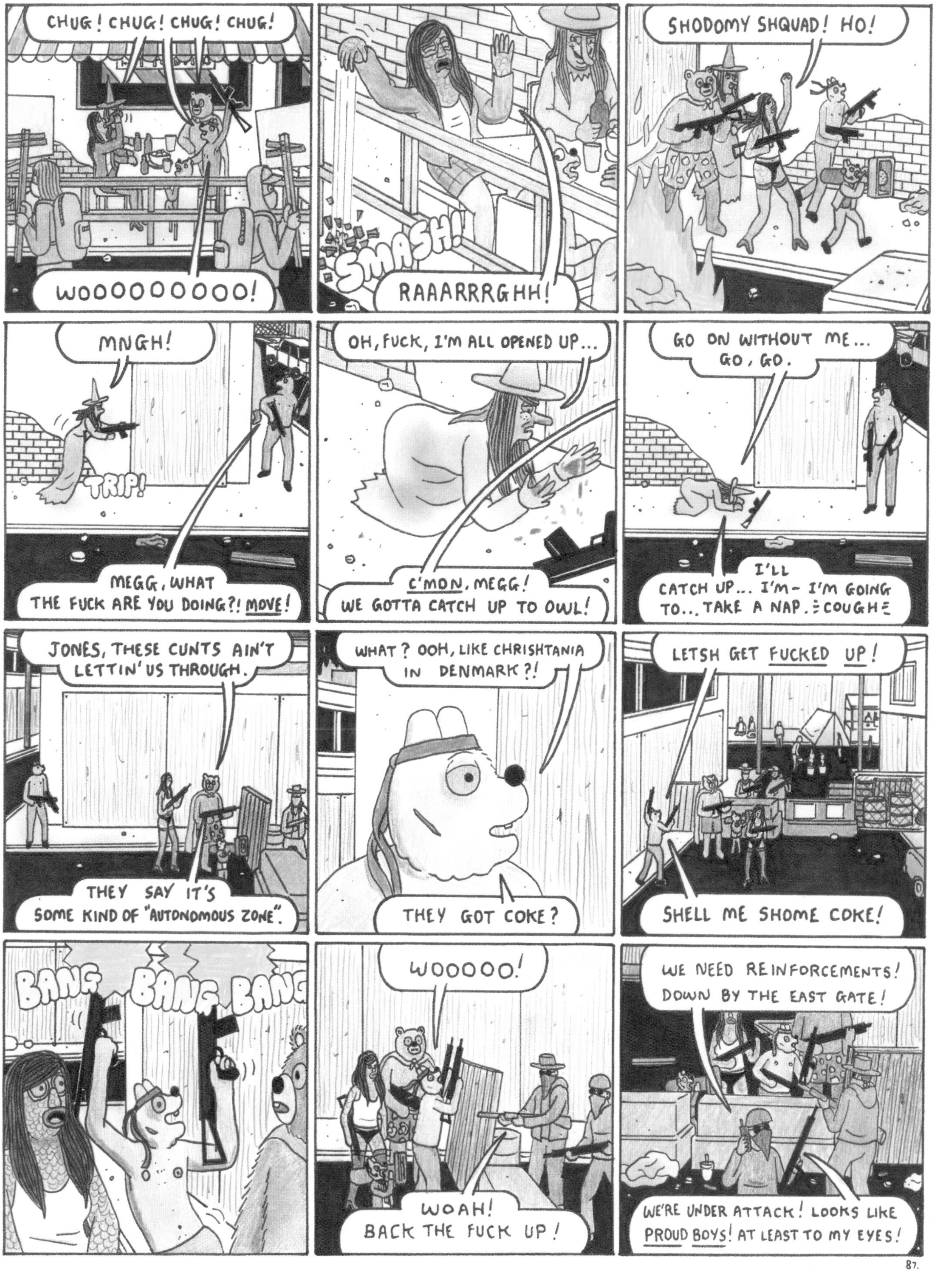
CHUG! CHUG! CHUG! CHUG!
WOOOOOOOOO!
SMASH!
RAAARRRGHH!
SHODOMY SHQUAD! HO!
MNGH!
TRIP!
MEGG, WHAT THE FUCK ARE YOU DOING?! MOVE!
OH, FUCK, I'M ALL OPENED UP...
C'MON, MEGG! WE GOTTA CATCH UP TO OWL!
GO ON WITHOUT ME... GO, GO.
I'LL CATCH UP... I'M- I'M GOING TO... TAKE A NAP. =COUGH=
JONES, THESE CUNTS AIN'T LETTIN' US THROUGH.
THEY SAY IT'S SOME KIND OF "AUTONOMOUS ZONE".
WHAT? OOH, LIKE CHRISHTANIA IN DENMARK?!
THEY GOT COKE?
LETSH GET FUCKED UP!
SHELL ME SHOME COKE!
BANG BANG BANG
WOOOOO!
WOAH! BACK THE FUCK UP!
WE NEED REINFORCEMENTS! DOWN BY THE EAST GATE!
WE'RE UNDER ATTACK! LOOKS LIKE PROUD BOYS! AT LEAST TO MY EYES!

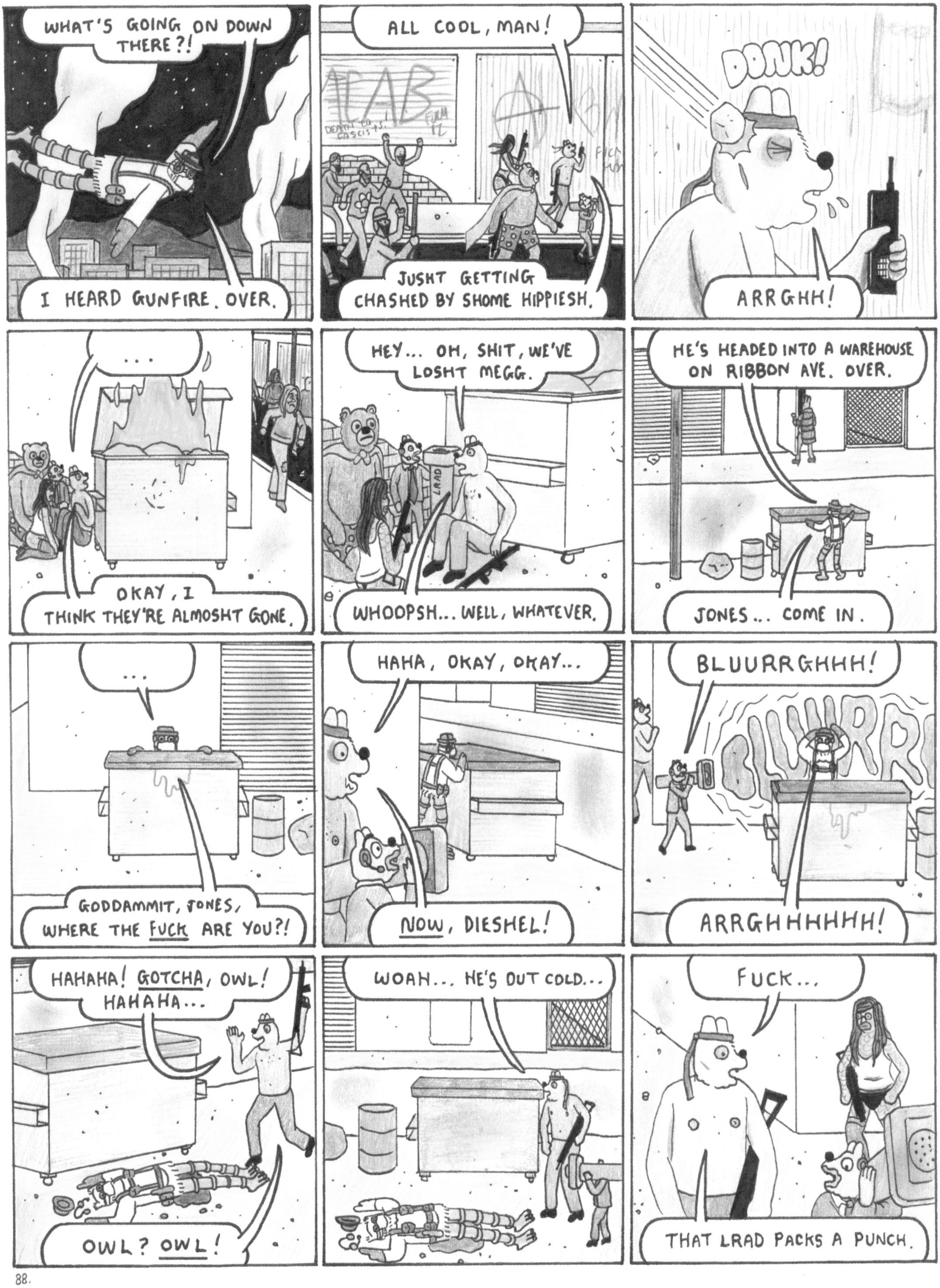

WHAT'S GOING ON DOWN THERE?!
I HEARD GUNFIRE. OVER.
ALL COOL, MAN!
ACAB
JUSHT GETTING CHASHED BY SHOME HIPPIESH.
DONK!
ARRGHH!
...
OKAY, I THINK THEY'RE ALMOSHT GONE.
HEY... OH, SHIT, WE'VE LOSHT MEGG.
LRAD
WHOOPSH... WELL, WHATEVER.
HE'S HEADED INTO A WAREHOUSE ON RIBBON AVE. OVER.
JONES... COME IN.
...
GODDAMMIT, JONES, WHERE THE FUCK ARE YOU?!
HAHA, OKAY, OKAY...
NOW, DIESHEL!
BLUURRGHHH!
ARRGHHHHHH!
HAHAHA! GOTCHA, OWL! HAHAHA...
OWL? OWL!
WOAH... HE'S OUT COLD...
FUCK...
THAT LRAD PACKS A PUNCH.

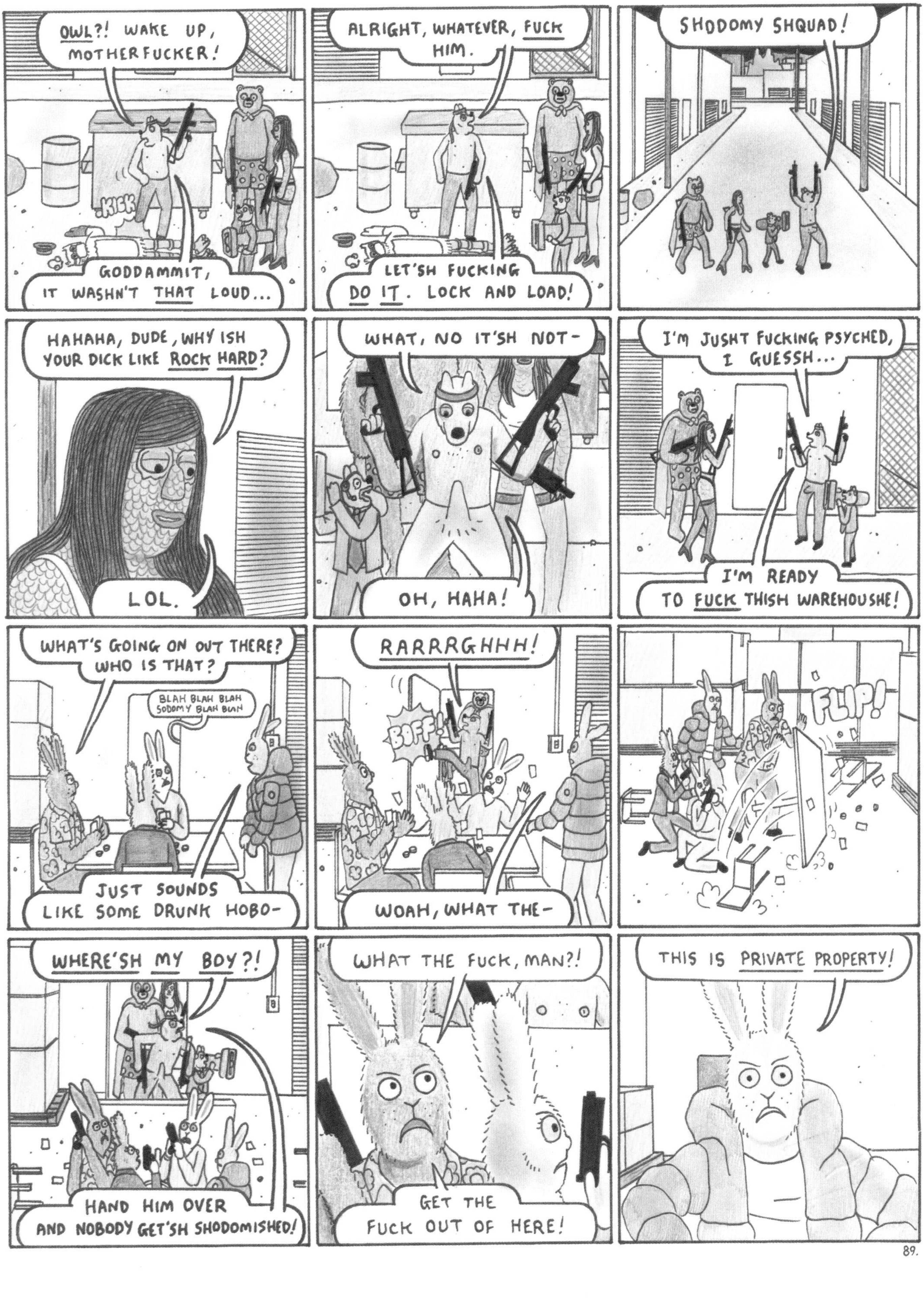

OWL?! WAKE UP, MOTHERFUCKER!
KICK
GODDAMMIT, IT WASHN'T THAT LOUD...
ALRIGHT, WHATEVER, FUCK HIM.
LET'SH FUCKING DO IT. LOCK AND LOAD!
SHODOMY SHQUAD!
HAHAHA, DUDE, WHY ISH YOUR DICK LIKE ROCK HARD?
LOL.
WHAT, NO IT'SH NOT-
OH, HAHA!
I'M JUSHT FUCKING PSYCHED, I GUESSH...
I'M READY TO FUCK THISH WAREHOUSHE!
WHAT'S GOING ON OUT THERE? WHO IS THAT?
BLAH BLAH BLAH SODOMY BLAH BLAH
JUST SOUNDS LIKE SOME DRUNK HOBO-
RARRRGHHH!
BOFF!
WOAH, WHAT THE-
FLIP!
WHERE'SH MY BOY?!
HAND HIM OVER AND NOBODY GET'SH SHODOMISHED!
WHAT THE FUCK, MAN?!
GET THE FUCK OUT OF HERE!
THIS IS PRIVATE PROPERTY!

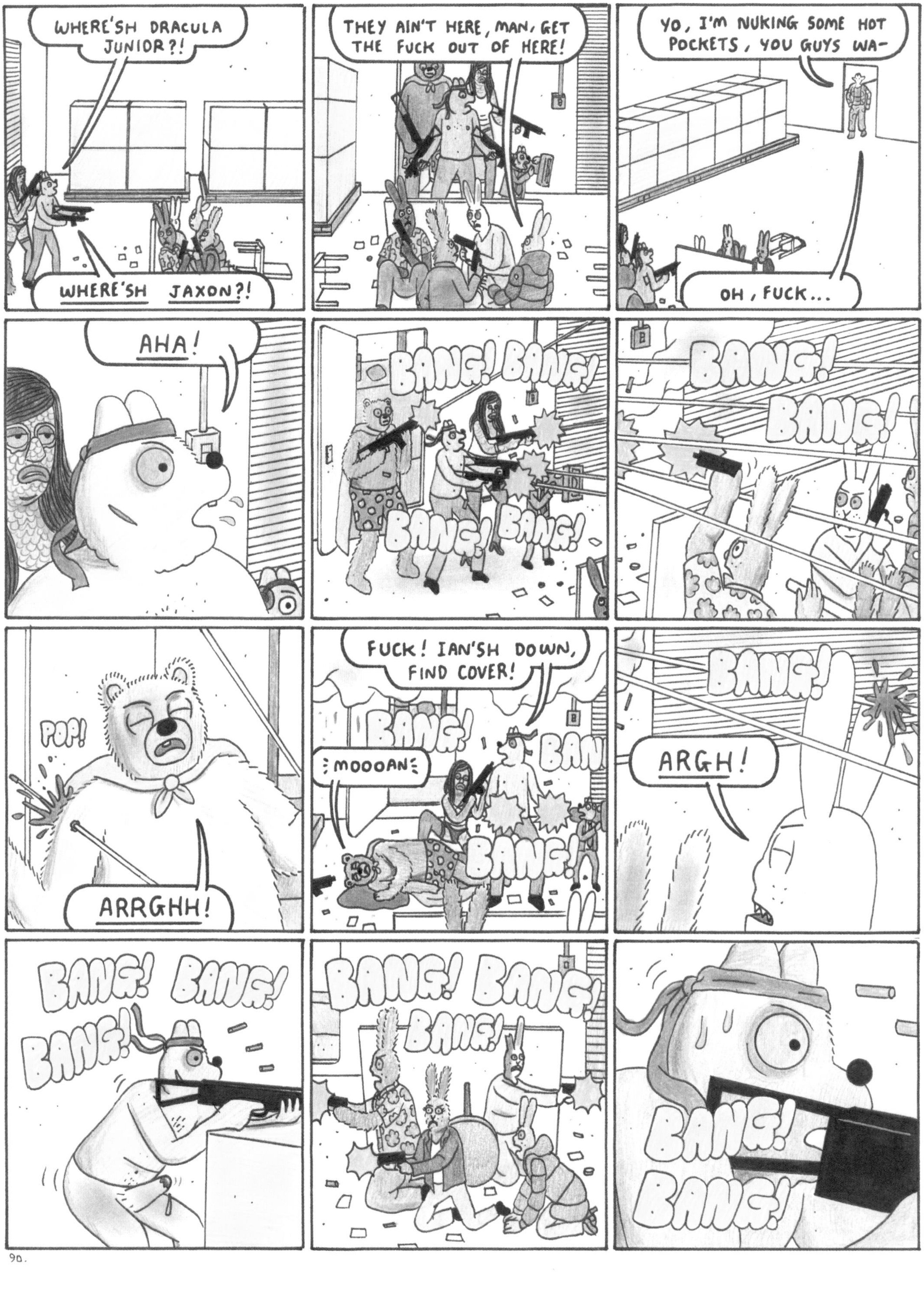

WHERE'SH DRACULA JUNIOR?!
WHERE'SH JAXON?!
THEY AIN'T HERE, MAN, GET THE FUCK OUT OF HERE!
YO, I'M NUKING SOME HOT POCKETS, YOU GUYS WA-
OH, FUCK...
AHA!
BANG! BANG!
BANG! BANG!
BANG!
BANG!
POP!
ARRGHH!
FUCK! IAN'SH DOWN, FIND COVER!
BANG!
MOOOAN
BAN
BANG!
BANG!
ARGH!
BANG! BANG!
BANG!
BANG! BANG!
BANG!
BANG!
BANG!

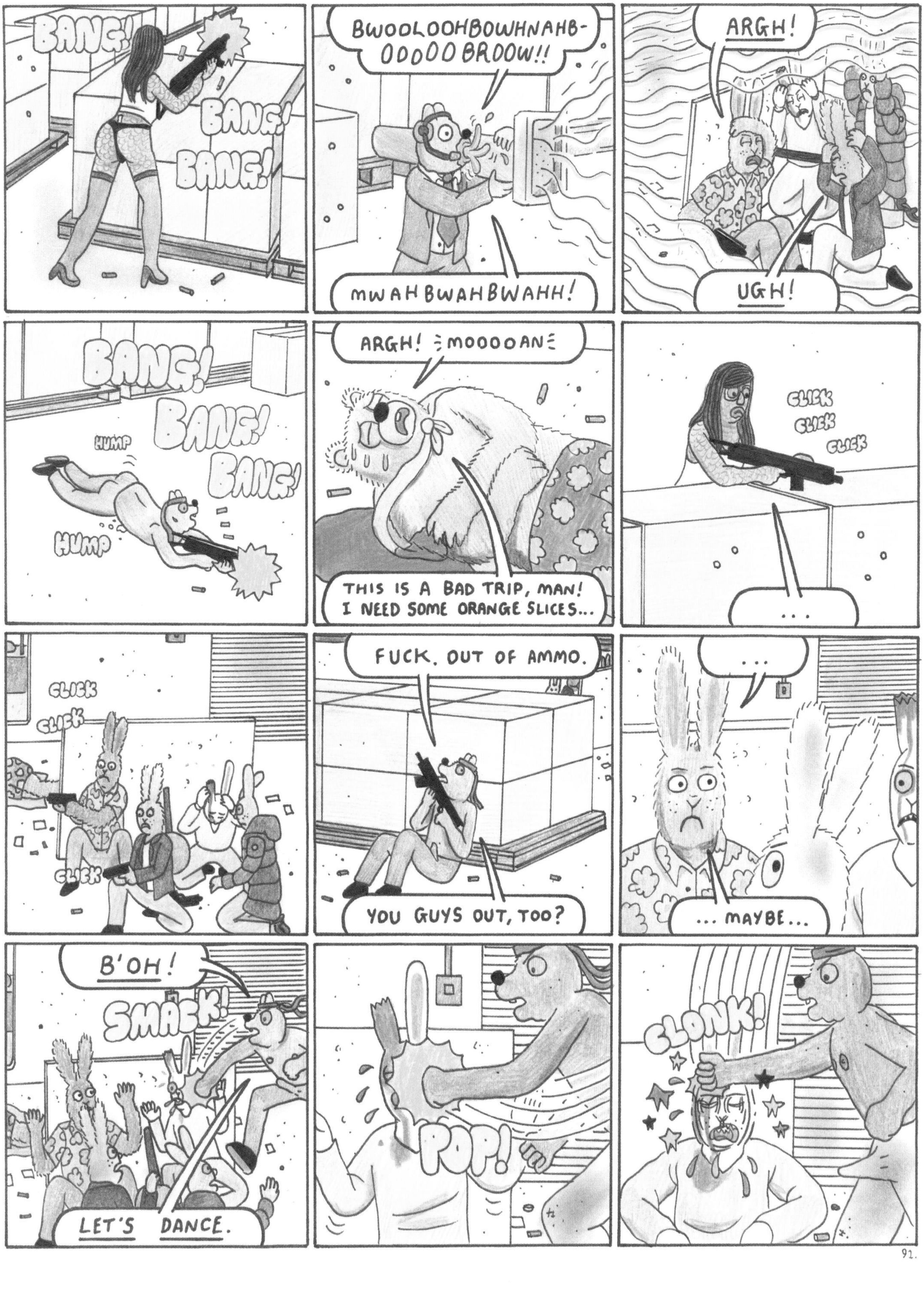

BANG!
BANG!
BANG!
BWOOLOOHBOWHNAHB-OOOOO BROOW!!
MWAHBWAHBWAHH!
ARGH!
UGH!
BANG!
BANG!
BANG!
HUMP
HUMP
ARGH! MOOOOAN
THIS IS A BAD TRIP, MAN! I NEED SOME ORANGE SLICES...
CLICK
CLICK
CLICK
...
CLICK
CLICK
CLICK
FUCK. OUT OF AMMO.
YOU GUYS OUT, TOO?
...
... MAYBE...
B'OH!
SMACK!
LET'S DANCE.
POP!
CLONK!

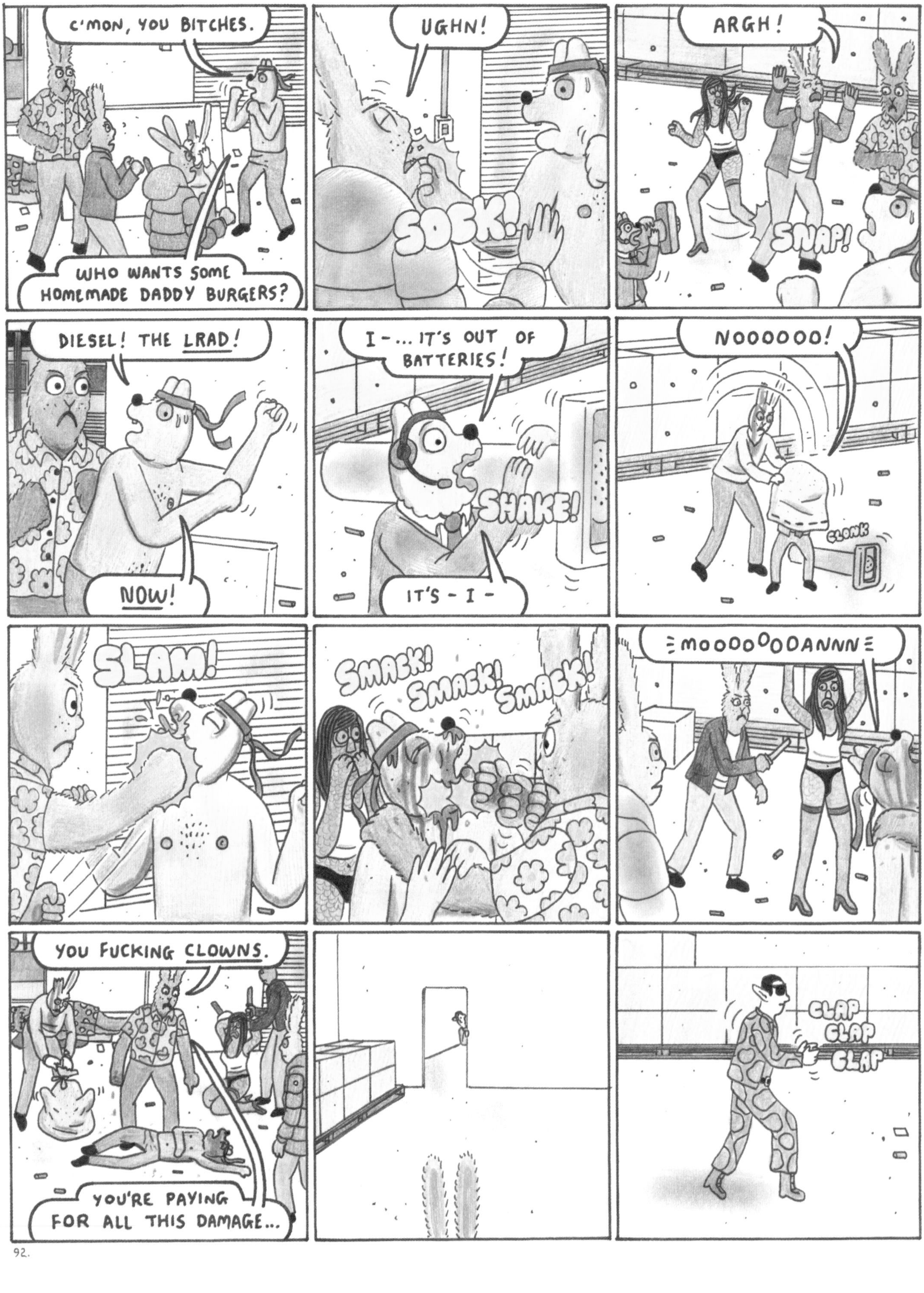
C'MON, YOU BITCHES.
WHO WANTS SOME HOMEMADE DADDY BURGERS?
UGHN!
SOCK!
ARGH!
SNAP!
DIESEL! THE LRAD!
NOW!
I-... IT'S OUT OF BATTERIES!
SHAKE!
IT'S - I -
NOOOOOO!
CLONK
SLAM!
SMACK! SMACK! SMACK!
MOOOOOOOANNN
YOU FUCKING CLOWNS.
YOU'RE PAYING FOR ALL THIS DAMAGE...
CLAP CLAP CLAP

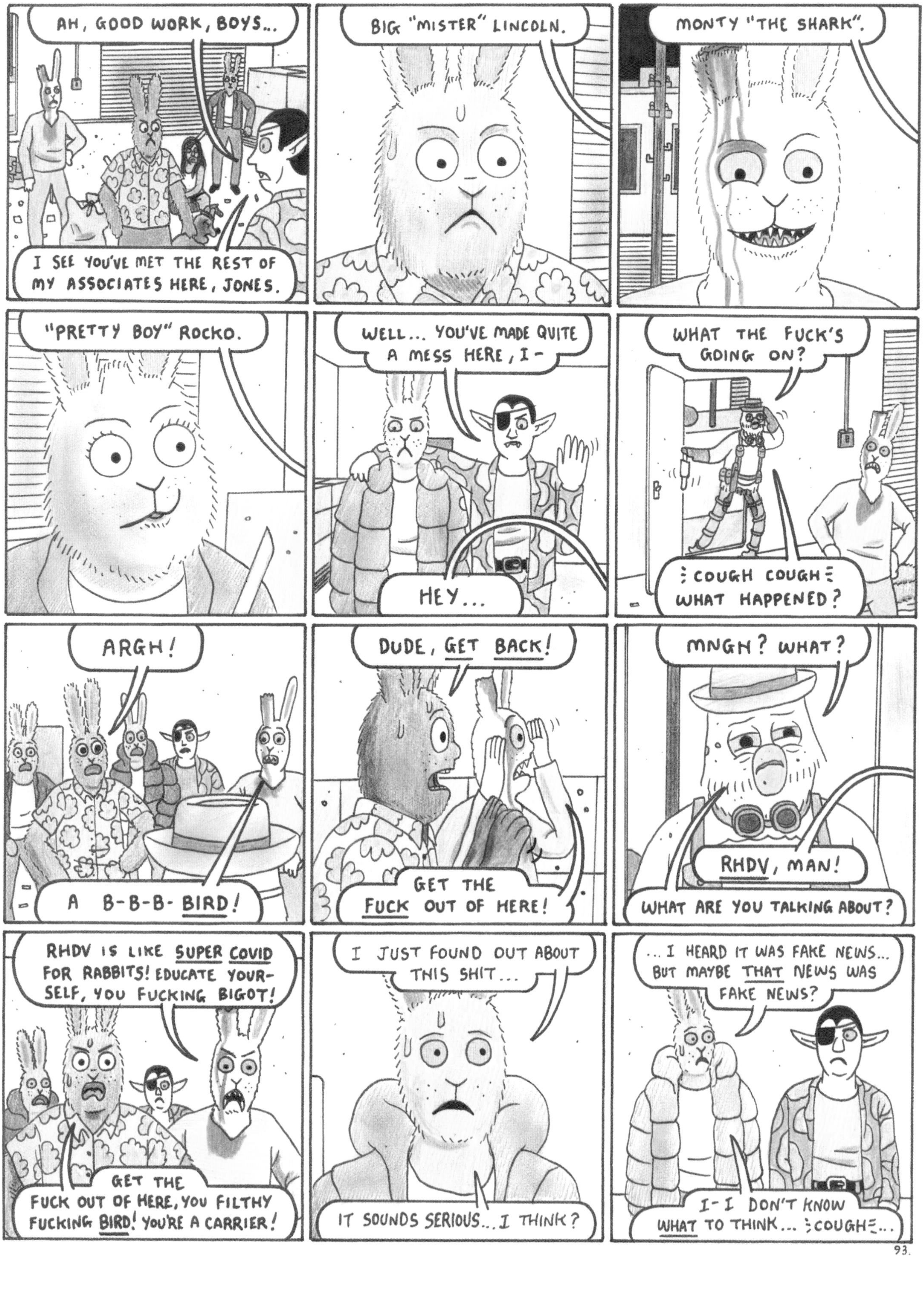

AH, GOOD WORK, BOYS...
I SEE YOU'VE MET THE REST OF MY ASSOCIATES HERE, JONES.
BIG "MISTER" LINCOLN.
MONTY "THE SHARK".
"PRETTY BOY" ROCKO.
WELL... YOU'VE MADE QUITE A MESS HERE, I-
HEY...
WHAT THE FUCK'S GOING ON?
COUGH COUGH WHAT HAPPENED?
ARGH!
A B-B-B- BIRD!
DUDE, GET BACK!
GET THE FUCK OUT OF HERE!
MNGH? WHAT?
RHDV, MAN!
WHAT ARE YOU TALKING ABOUT?
RHDV IS LIKE SUPER COVID FOR RABBITS! EDUCATE YOURSELF, YOU FUCKING BIGOT!
GET THE FUCK OUT OF HERE, YOU FILTHY FUCKING BIRD! YOU'RE A CARRIER!
I JUST FOUND OUT ABOUT THIS SHIT...
IT SOUNDS SERIOUS... I THINK?
...I HEARD IT WAS FAKE NEWS... BUT MAYBE THAT NEWS WAS FAKE NEWS?
I-I DON'T KNOW WHAT TO THINK... COUGH...

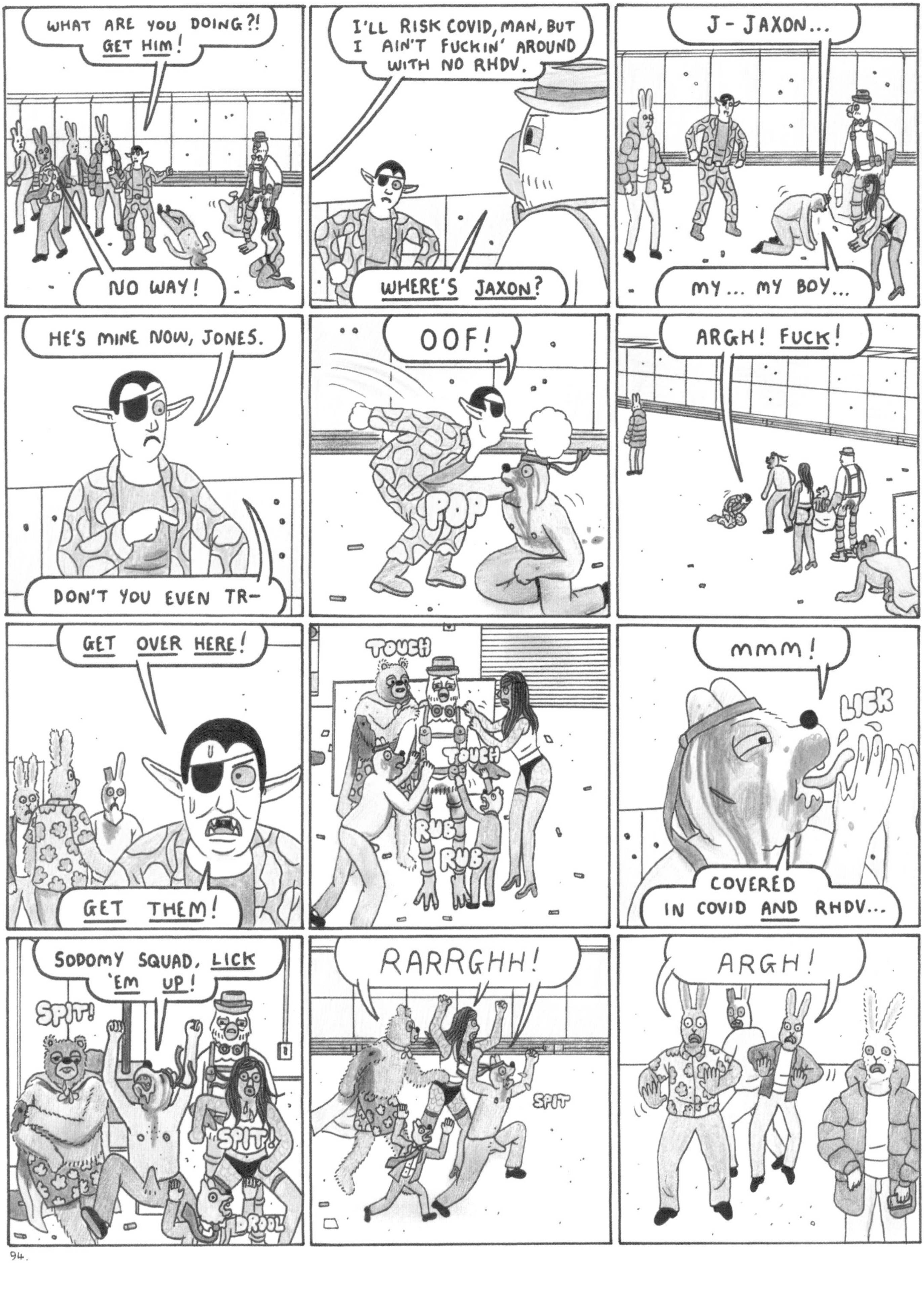
WHAT ARE YOU DOING?! GET HIM!
NO WAY!
I'LL RISK COVID, MAN, BUT I AIN'T FUCKIN' AROUND WITH NO RHDV.
WHERE'S JAXON?
J-JAXON...
MY... MY BOY...
HE'S MINE NOW, JONES.
DON'T YOU EVEN TR-
OOF!
POP
ARGH! FUCK!
GET OVER HERE!
GET THEM!
TOUCH
TOUCH
RUB
RUB
MMM!
LICK
COVERED IN COVID AND RHDV...
SODOMY SQUAD, LICK 'EM UP!
SPIT!
SPIT!
DROOL
RARRGHH!
SPIT
ARGH!

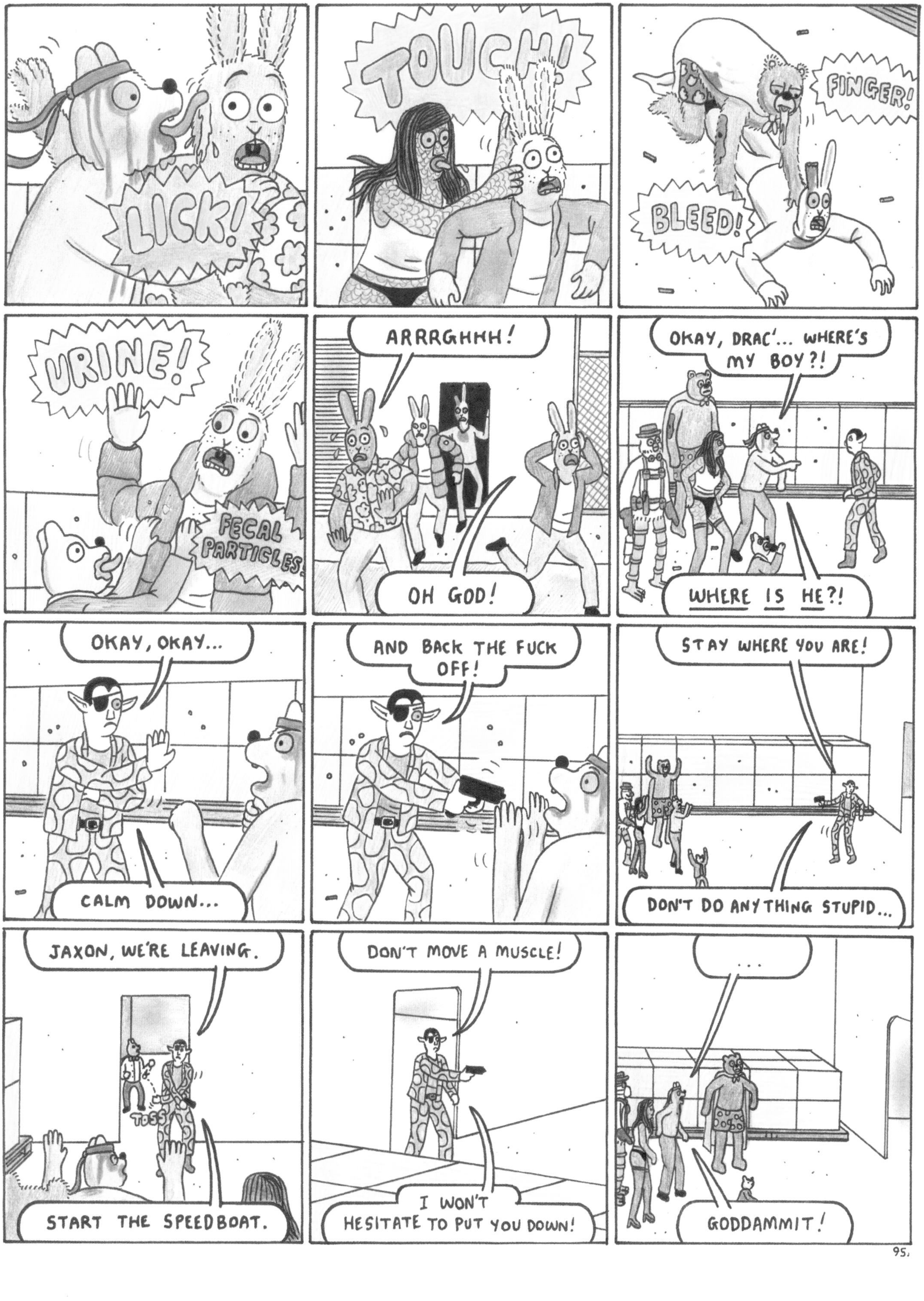
LICK!
TOUCH!
FINGER!
BLEED!
URINE!
FECAL PARTICLES!
ARRRGHHH!
OH GOD!
OKAY, DRAC'... WHERE'S MY BOY?!
WHERE IS HE?!
OKAY, OKAY...
CALM DOWN...
AND BACK THE FUCK OFF!
STAY WHERE YOU ARE!
DON'T DO ANYTHING STUPID...
JAXON, WE'RE LEAVING.
TOSS
START THE SPEEDBOAT.
DON'T MOVE A MUSCLE!
I WON'T HESITATE TO PUT YOU DOWN!
...
GODDAMMIT!

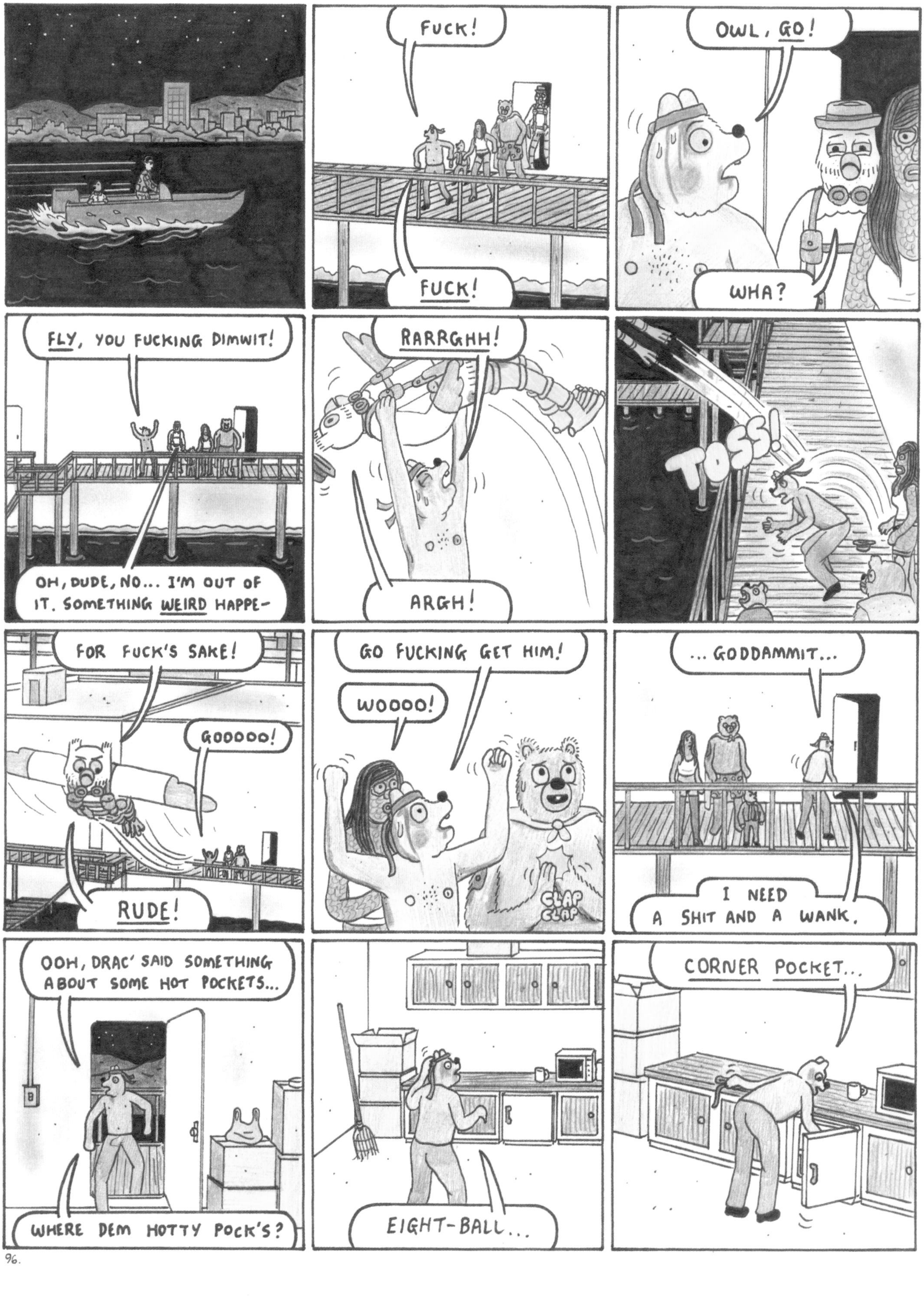
FUCK!
FUCK!
OWL, GO!
WHA?
FLY, YOU FUCKING DIMWIT!
OH, DUDE, NO... I'M OUT OF IT. SOMETHING WEIRD HAPPE-
RARRGHH!
ARGH!
TOSS!
FOR FUCK'S SAKE!
GOOOOO!
RUDE!
GO FUCKING GET HIM!
WOOOO!
CLAP CLAP
...GODDAMMIT...
I NEED A SHIT AND A WANK.
OOH, DRAC' SAID SOMETHING ABOUT SOME HOT POCKETS...
WHERE DEM HOTTY POCK'S?
EIGHT-BALL...
CORNER POCKET...

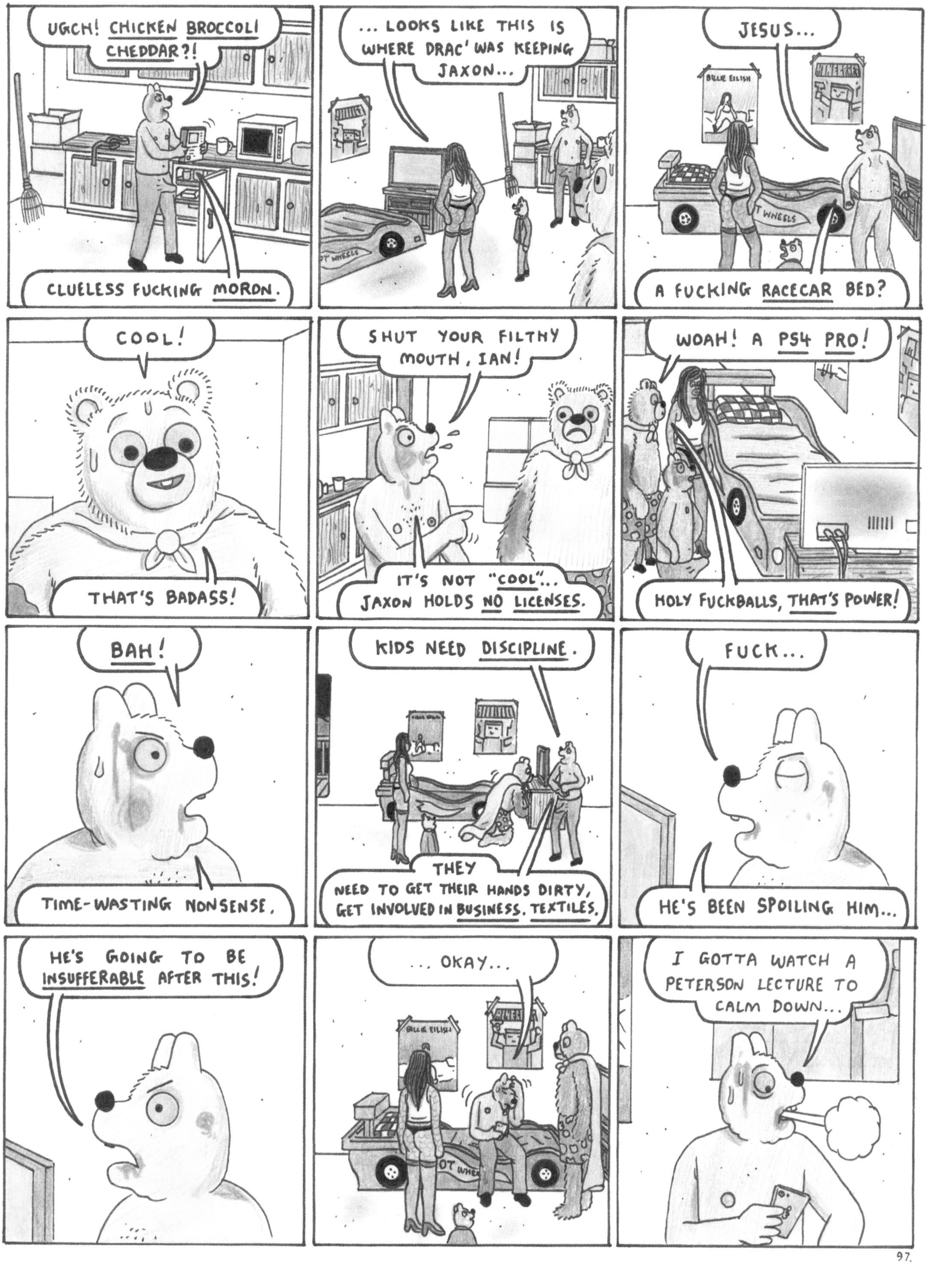
UGCH! CHICKEN BROCCOLI CHEDDAR?!
CLUELESS FUCKING MORON.
... LOOKS LIKE THIS IS WHERE DRAC' WAS KEEPING JAXON...
JESUS...
BILLIE EILISH
A FUCKING RACECAR BED?
COOL!
THAT'S BADASS!
SHUT YOUR FILTHY MOUTH, IAN!
IT'S NOT "COOL"... JAXON HOLDS NO LICENSES.
WOAH! A PS4 PRO!
HOLY FUCKBALLS, THAT'S POWER!
BAH!
TIME-WASTING NONSENSE.
KIDS NEED DISCIPLINE.
THEY NEED TO GET THEIR HANDS DIRTY, GET INVOLVED IN BUSINESS. TEXTILES.
FUCK...
HE'S BEEN SPOILING HIM...
HE'S GOING TO BE INSUFFERABLE AFTER THIS!
... OKAY...
BILLIE EILISH
I GOTTA WATCH A PETERSON LECTURE TO CALM DOWN...

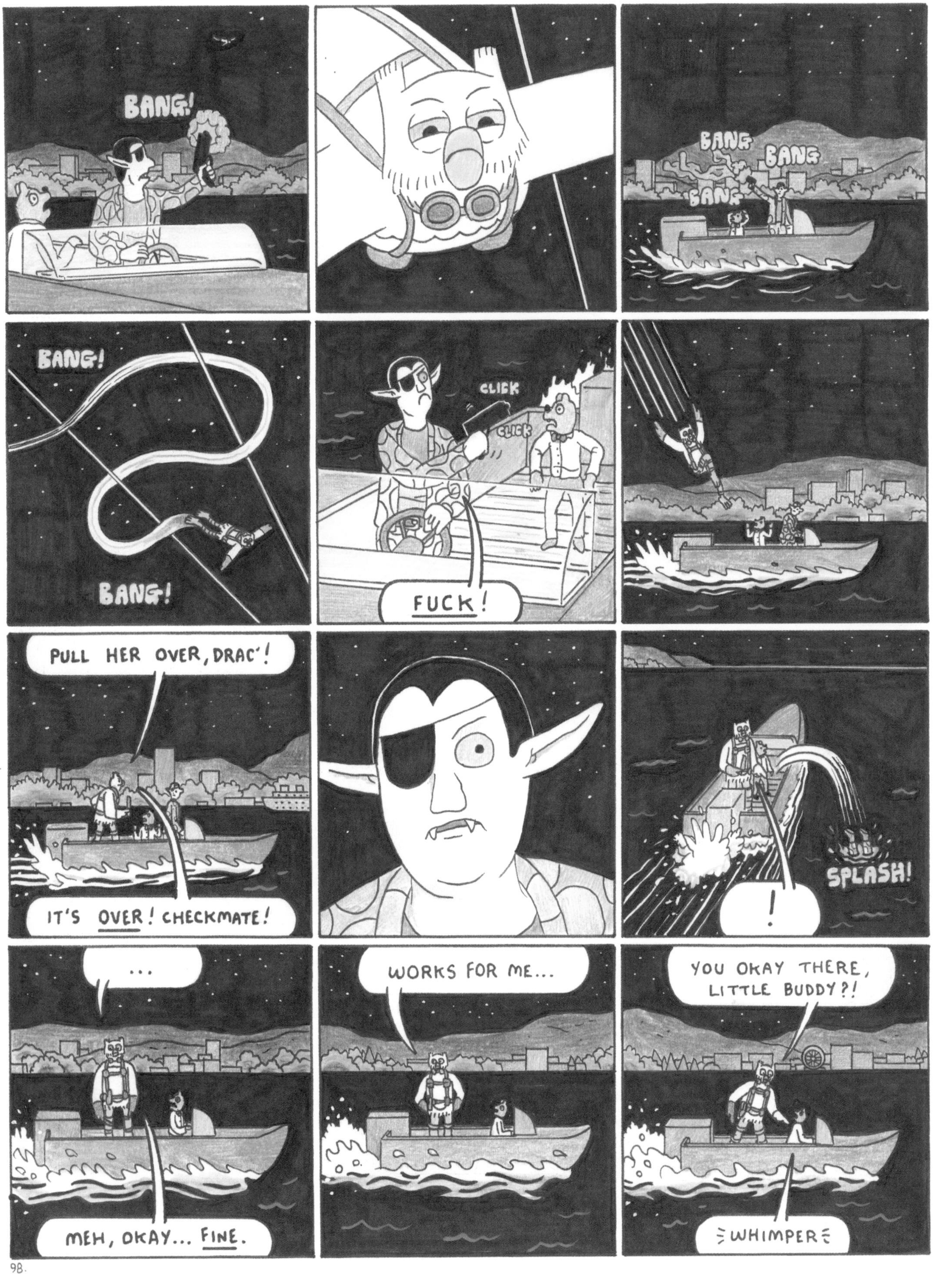
BANG!
BANG
BANG
BANG
BANG!
BANG!
CLICK
CLICK
FUCK!
PULL HER OVER, DRAC'!
IT'S OVER! CHECKMATE!
!
SPLASH!
...
MEH, OKAY... FINE.
WORKS FOR ME...
YOU OKAY THERE, LITTLE BUDDY?!
WHIMPER

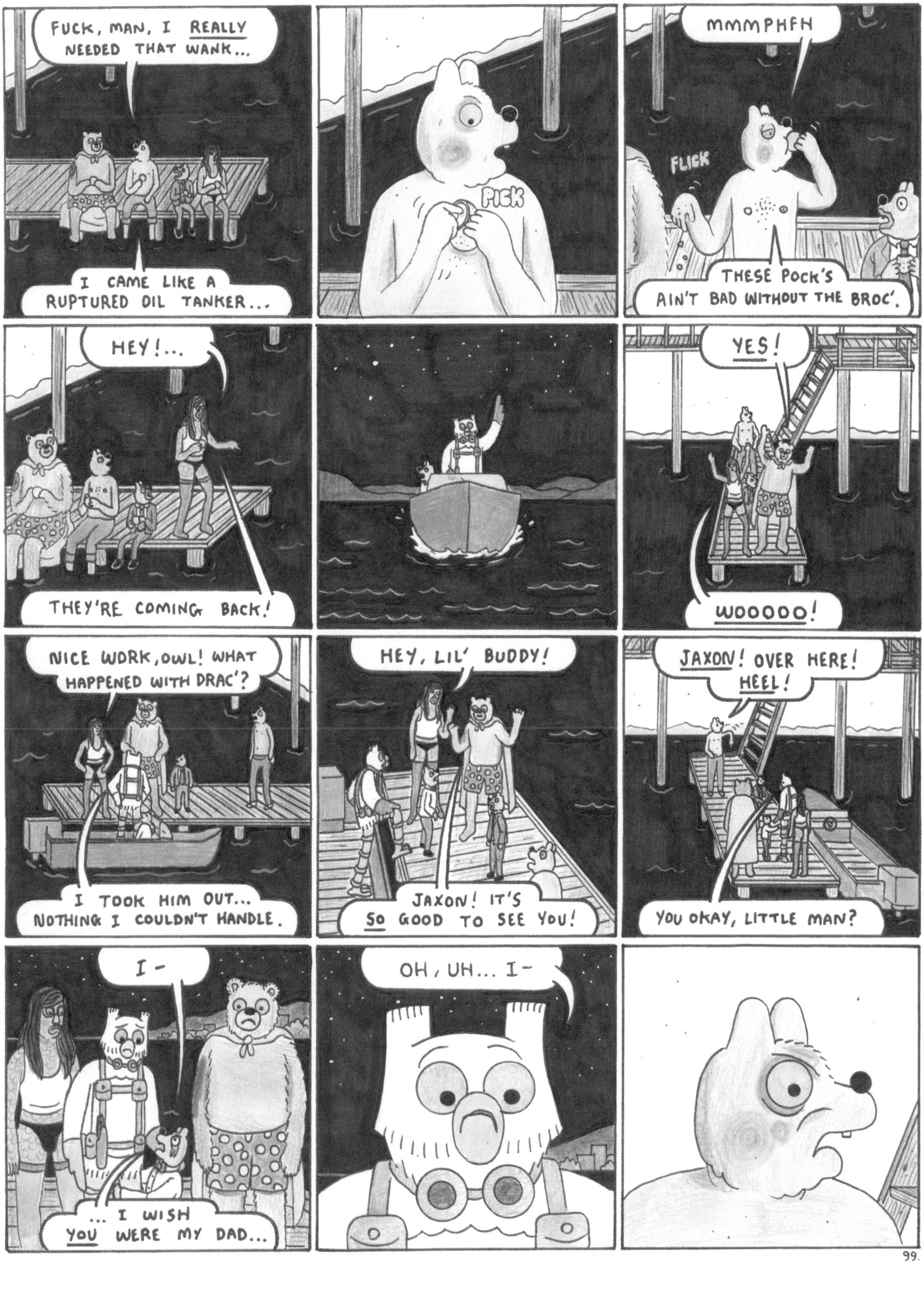
FUCK, MAN, I REALLY NEEDED THAT WANK...
I CAME LIKE A RUPTURED OIL TANKER...
PICK
MMMPHFH
FLICK
THESE POCK'S AIN'T BAD WITHOUT THE BROC'.
HEY!...
THEY'RE COMING BACK!
YES!
WOOOOO!
NICE WORK, OWL! WHAT HAPPENED WITH DRAC'?
I TOOK HIM OUT... NOTHING I COULDN'T HANDLE.
HEY, LIL' BUDDY!
JAXON! IT'S SO GOOD TO SEE YOU!
JAXON! OVER HERE! HEEL!
YOU OKAY, LITTLE MAN?
I-
... I WISH YOU WERE MY DAD...
OH, UH... I-

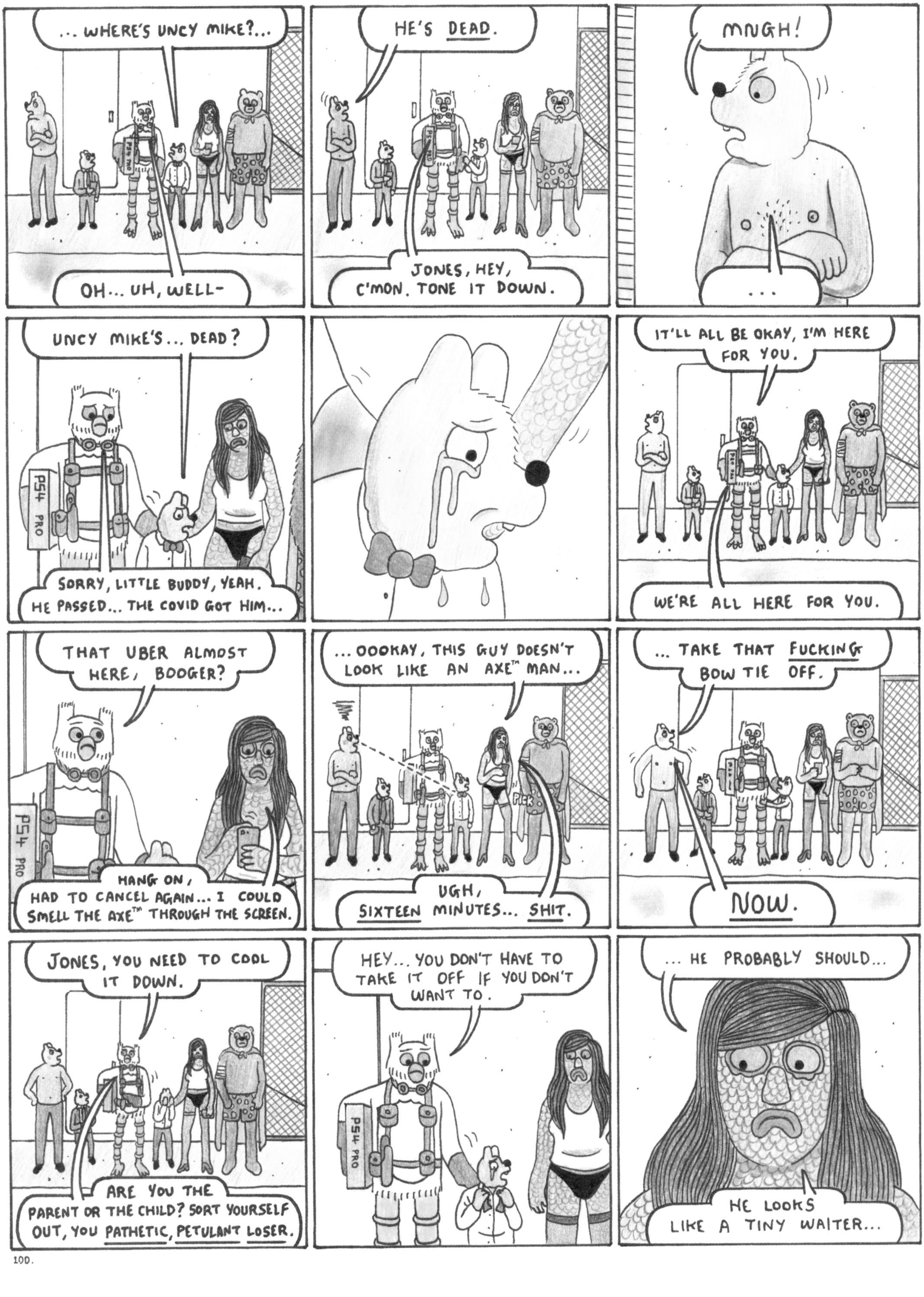

... WHERE'S UNCY MIKE?...
OH... UH, WELL-
HE'S DEAD.
JONES, HEY, C'MON. TONE IT DOWN.
MNGH!
...
UNCY MIKE'S... DEAD?
SORRY, LITTLE BUDDY, YEAH. HE PASSED... THE COVID GOT HIM...
IT'LL ALL BE OKAY, I'M HERE FOR YOU.
WE'RE ALL HERE FOR YOU.
THAT UBER ALMOST HERE, BOOGER?
HANG ON, HAD TO CANCEL AGAIN... I COULD SMELL THE AXE™ THROUGH THE SCREEN.
...OOOKAY, THIS GUY DOESN'T LOOK LIKE AN AXE™ MAN...
PICK
UGH, SIXTEEN MINUTES... SHIT.
... TAKE THAT FUCKING BOW TIE OFF.
NOW.
JONES, YOU NEED TO COOL IT DOWN.
ARE YOU THE PARENT OR THE CHILD? SORT YOURSELF OUT, YOU PATHETIC, PETULANT LOSER.
HEY... YOU DON'T HAVE TO TAKE IT OFF IF YOU DON'T WANT TO.
... HE PROBABLY SHOULD...
HE LOOKS LIKE A TINY WAITER...

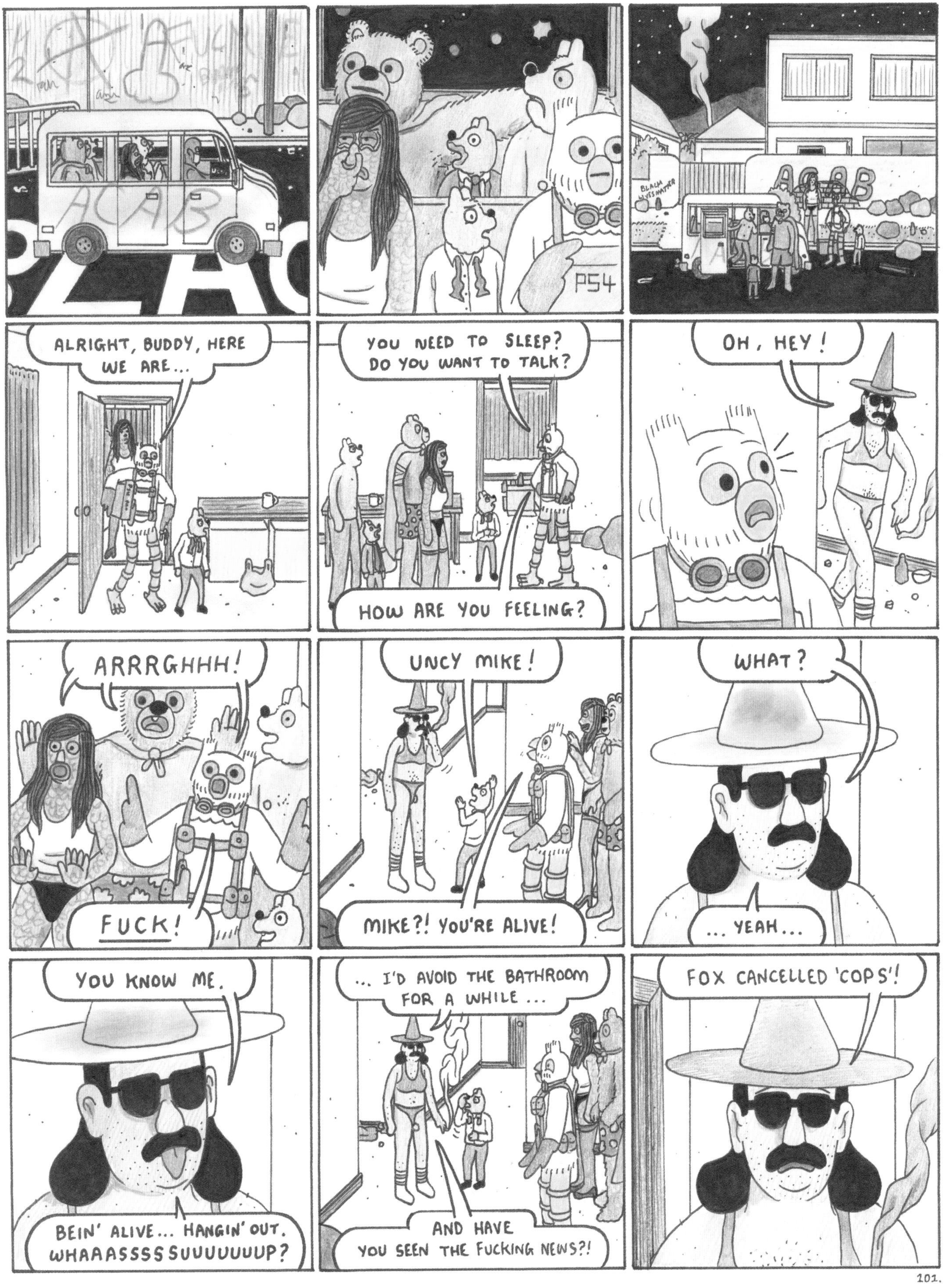
ACAB
PS4
ACAB
ALRIGHT, BUDDY, HERE WE ARE...
YOU NEED TO SLEEP? DO YOU WANT TO TALK?
HOW ARE YOU FEELING?
OH, HEY!
ARRRGHHH!
FUCK!
UNCY MIKE!
MIKE?! YOU'RE ALIVE!
WHAT?
... YEAH...
YOU KNOW ME.
BEIN' ALIVE... HANGIN' OUT. WHAAASSSSSUUUUUUUP?
... I'D AVOID THE BATHROOM FOR A WHILE ...
AND HAVE YOU SEEN THE FUCKING NEWS?!
FOX CANCELLED 'COPS'!

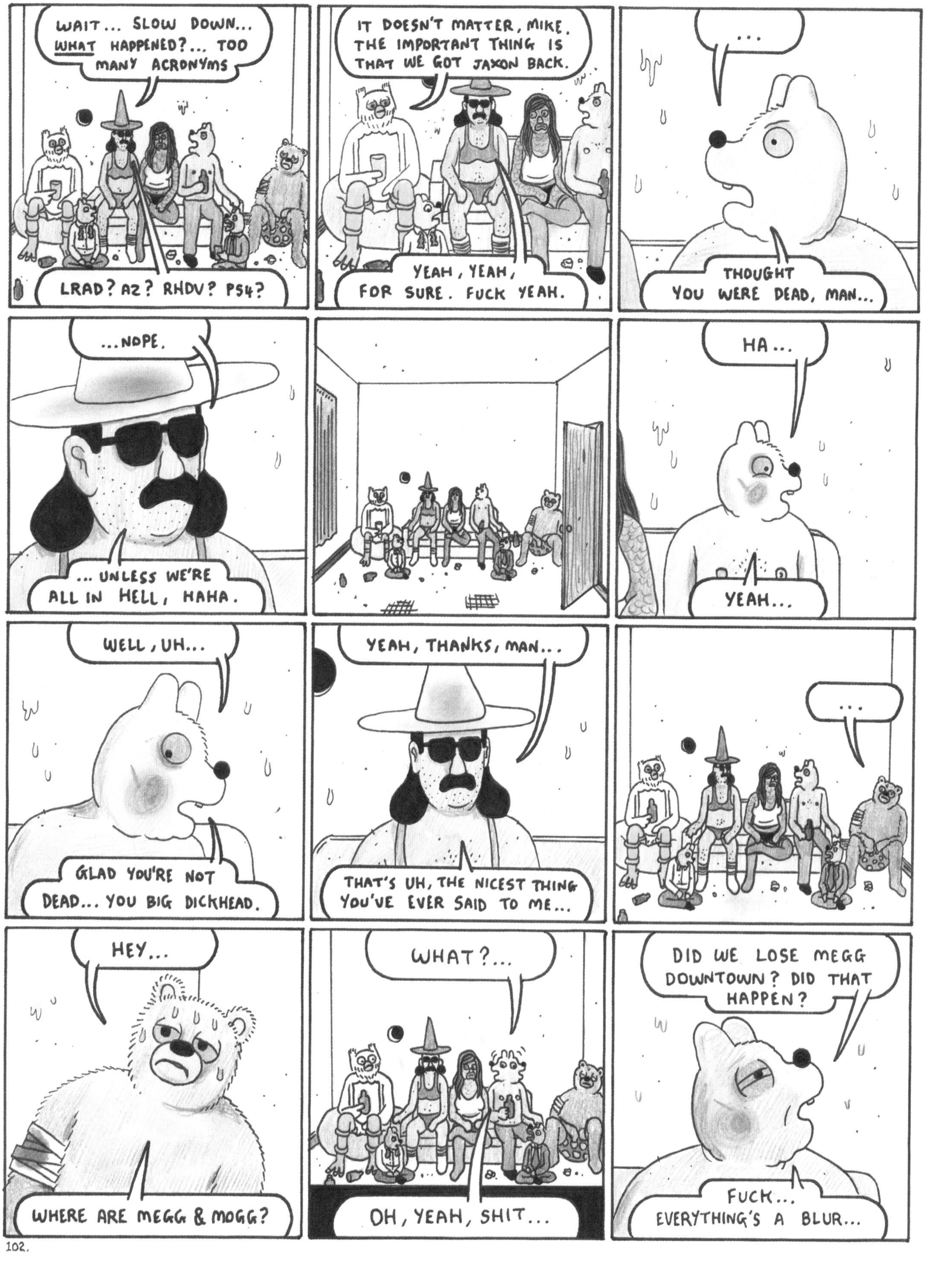

WAIT... SLOW DOWN... WHAT HAPPENED?... TOO MANY ACRONYMS
LRAD? AZ? RHDV? PS4?
IT DOESN'T MATTER, MIKE. THE IMPORTANT THING IS THAT WE GOT JAXON BACK.
YEAH, YEAH, FOR SURE. FUCK YEAH.
...
THOUGHT YOU WERE DEAD, MAN...
...NOPE.
...UNLESS WE'RE ALL IN HELL, HAHA.
HA...
YEAH...
WELL, UH...
GLAD YOU'RE NOT DEAD... YOU BIG DICKHEAD.
YEAH, THANKS, MAN...
THAT'S UH, THE NICEST THING YOU'VE EVER SAID TO ME...
...
HEY...
WHERE ARE MEGG & MOGG?
WHAT?...
OH, YEAH, SHIT...
DID WE LOSE MEGG DOWNTOWN? DID THAT HAPPEN?
FUCK... EVERYTHING'S A BLUR...

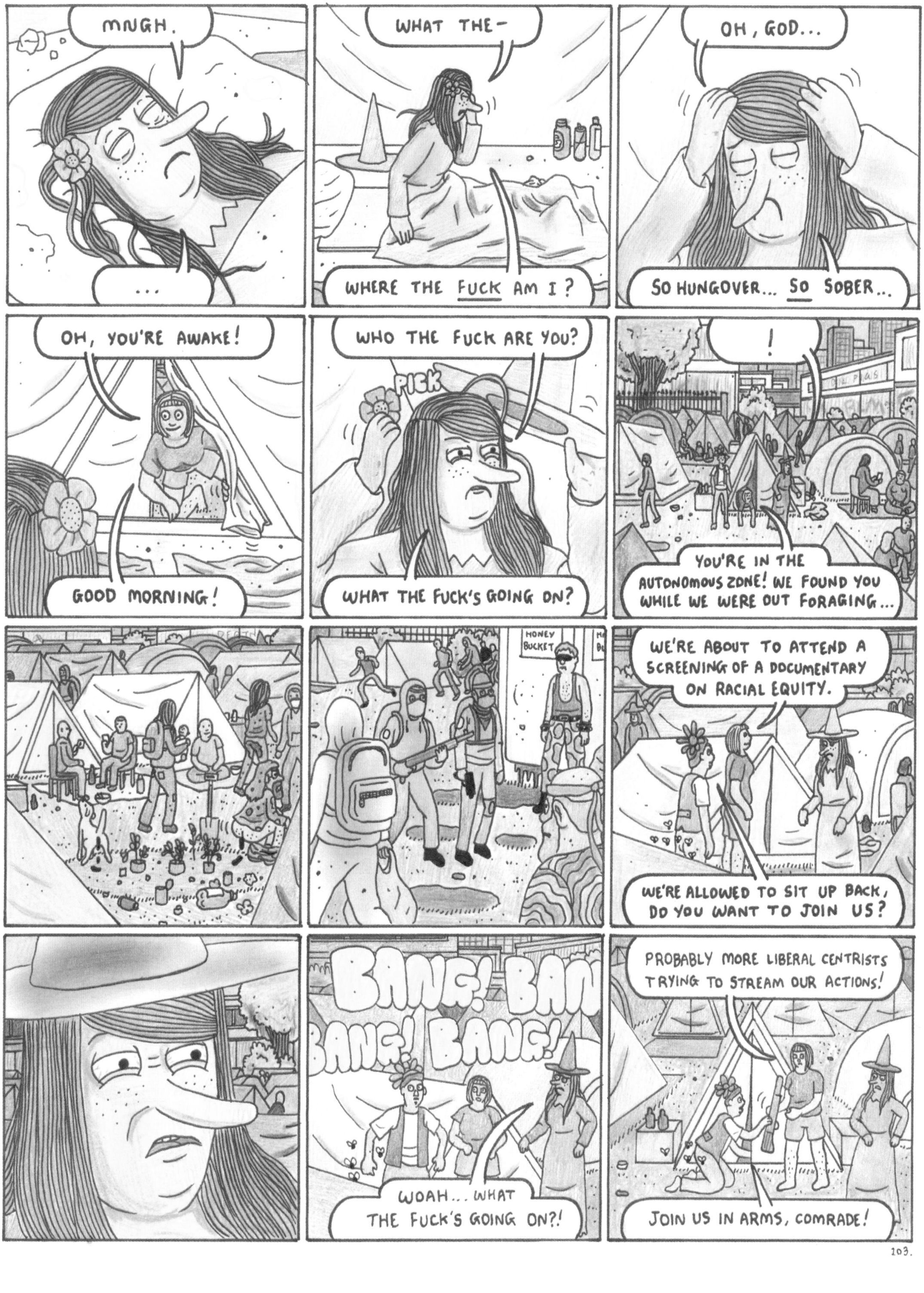
MNGH.
...
WHAT THE-
WHERE THE FUCK AM I?
OH, GOD...
SO HUNGOVER... SO SOBER...
OH, YOU'RE AWAKE!
GOOD MORNING!
WHO THE FUCK ARE YOU?
PICK
WHAT THE FUCK'S GOING ON?
!
YOU'RE IN THE AUTONOMOUS ZONE! WE FOUND YOU WHILE WE WERE OUT FORAGING...
HONEY BUCKET
WE'RE ABOUT TO ATTEND A SCREENING OF A DOCUMENTARY ON RACIAL EQUITY.
WE'RE ALLOWED TO SIT UP BACK, DO YOU WANT TO JOIN US?
BANG! BAN
BANG! BANG!
WOAH... WHAT THE FUCK'S GOING ON?!
PROBABLY MORE LIBERAL CENTRISTS TRYING TO STREAM OUR ACTIONS!
JOIN US IN ARMS, COMRADE!

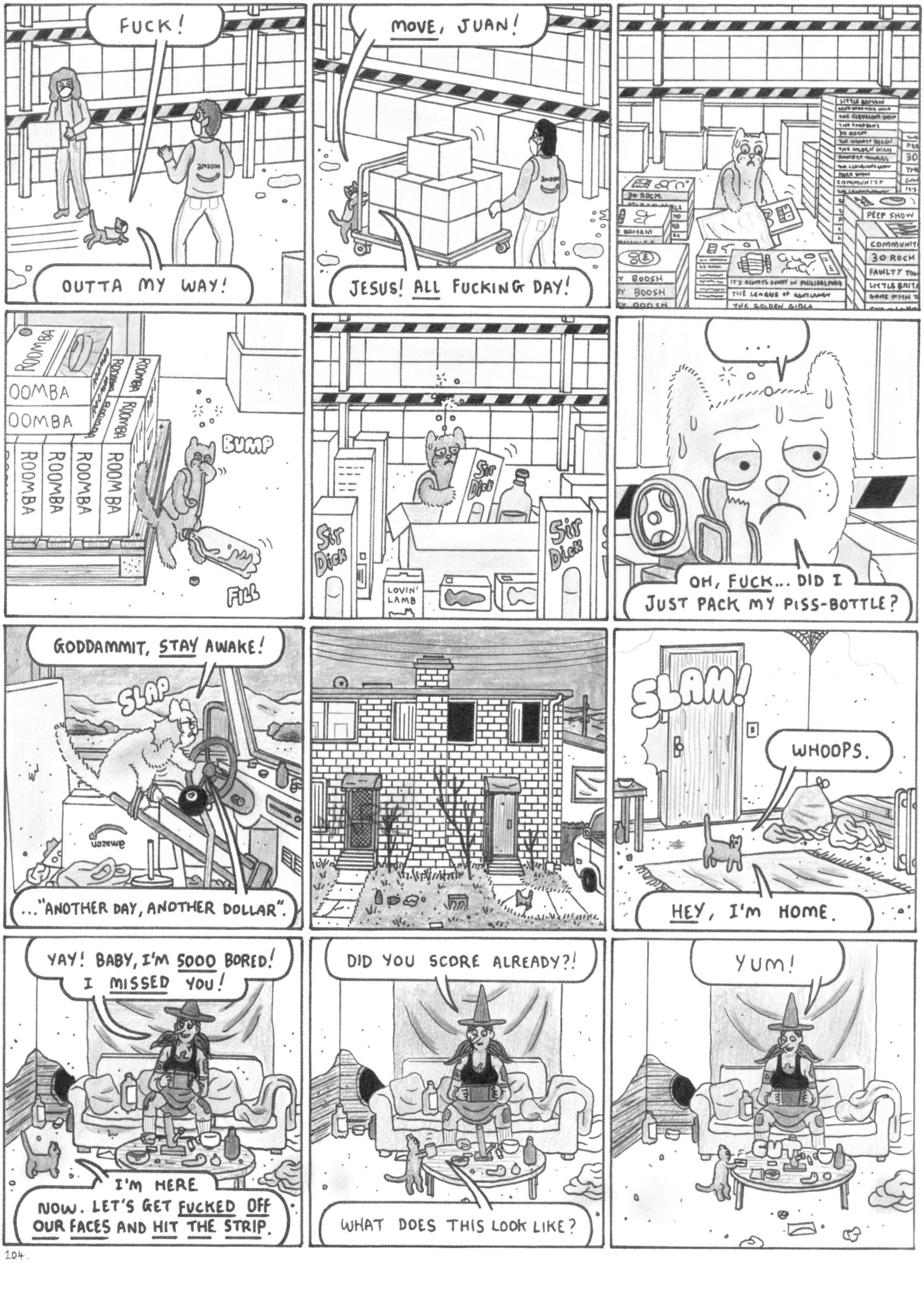
FUCK!
OUTTA MY WAY!
MOVE, JUAN!
JESUS! ALL FUCKING DAY!
PEEP SHOW
30 ROCK
ROOMBA
BUMP
FILL
Sir Dick
LOVIN' LAMB
...
OH, FUCK... DID I JUST PACK MY PISS-BOTTLE?
GODDAMMIT, STAY AWAKE!
SLAP
..."ANOTHER DAY, ANOTHER DOLLAR".
SLAM!
WHOOPS.
HEY, I'M HOME.
YAY! BABY, I'M SOOO BORED! I MISSED YOU!
I'M HERE NOW. LET'S GET FUCKED OFF OUR FACES AND HIT THE STRIP.
DID YOU SCORE ALREADY?!
WHAT DOES THIS LOOK LIKE?
YUM!
CUT

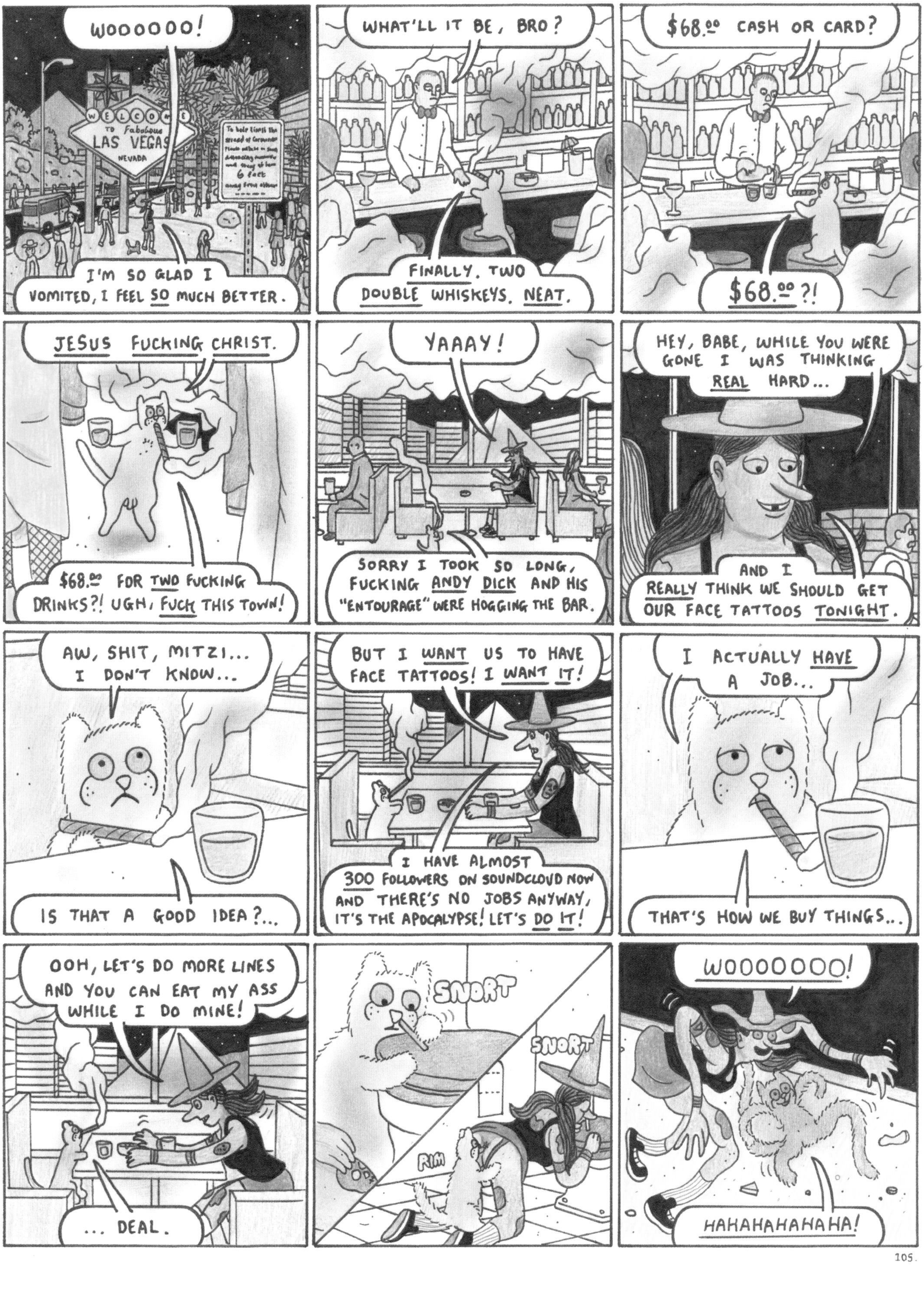
WOOOOOO!
TO Fabulous LAS VEGAS NEVADA
I'M SO GLAD I VOMITED, I FEEL SO MUCH BETTER.
WHAT'LL IT BE, BRO?
FINALLY. TWO DOUBLE WHISKEYS. NEAT.
$68.00 CASH OR CARD?
$68.00?!
JESUS FUCKING CHRIST.
$68.00 FOR TWO FUCKING DRINKS?! UGH, FUCK THIS TOWN!
YAAAY!
SORRY I TOOK SO LONG, FUCKING ANDY DICK AND HIS "ENTOURAGE" WERE HOGGING THE BAR.
HEY, BABE, WHILE YOU WERE GONE I WAS THINKING REAL HARD...
AND I REALLY THINK WE SHOULD GET OUR FACE TATTOOS TONIGHT.
AW, SHIT, MITZI... I DON'T KNOW...
IS THAT A GOOD IDEA?...
BUT I WANT US TO HAVE FACE TATTOOS! I WANT IT!
I HAVE ALMOST 300 FOLLOWERS ON SOUNDCLOUD NOW AND THERE'S NO JOBS ANYWAY, IT'S THE APOCALYPSE! LET'S DO IT!
I ACTUALLY HAVE A JOB...
THAT'S HOW WE BUY THINGS...
OOH, LET'S DO MORE LINES AND YOU CAN EAT MY ASS WHILE I DO MINE!
... DEAL.
SNORT
SNORT
RIM
WOOOOOOO!
HAHAHAHAHAHA!

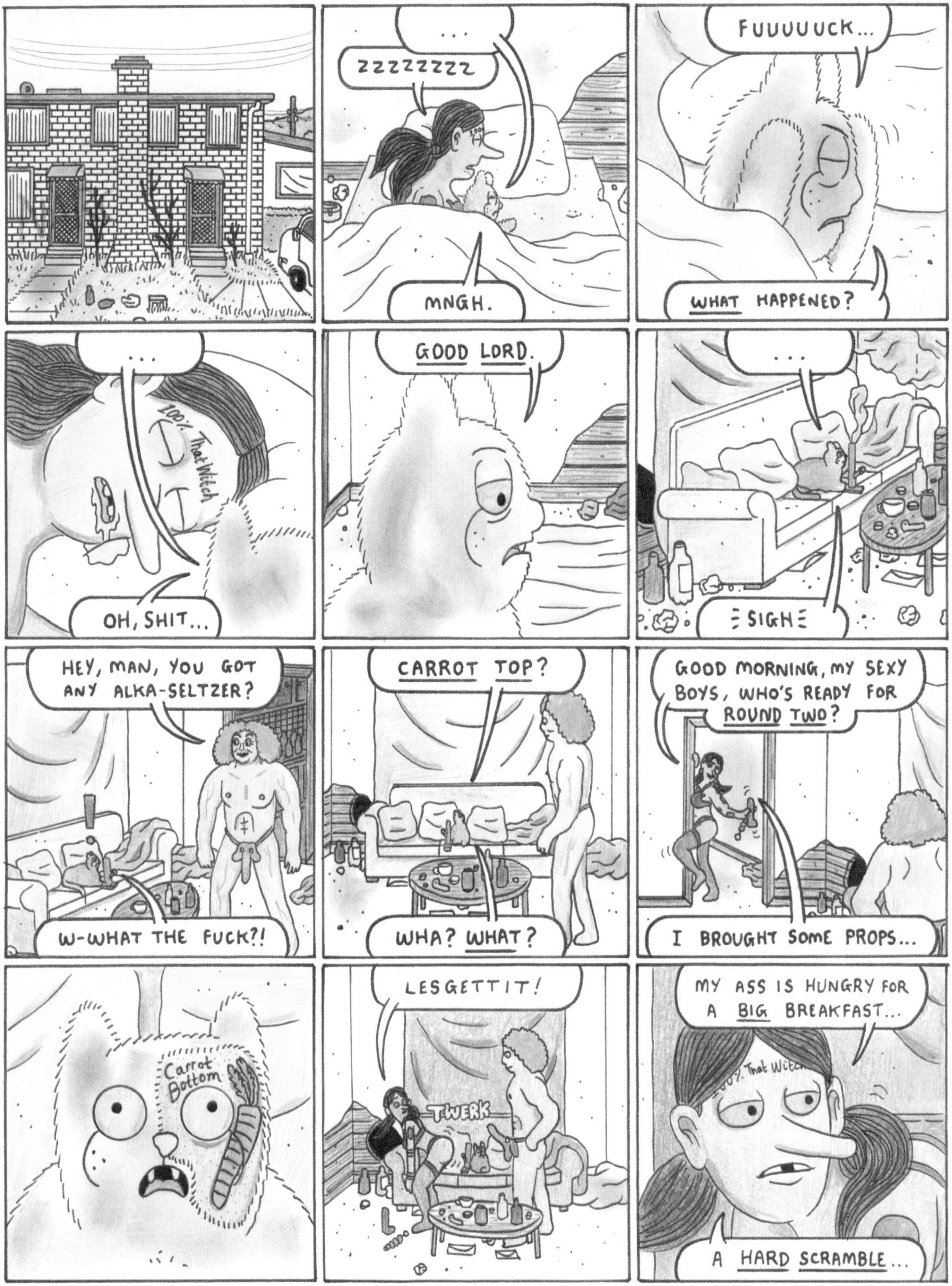

ZZZZZZZZ
...
MNGH.
FUUUUUCK...
WHAT HAPPENED?
...
100% That Witch
OH, SHIT...
GOOD LORD.
...
SIGH
HEY, MAN, YOU GOT ANY ALKA-SELTZER?
W-WHAT THE FUCK?!
CARROT TOP?
WHA? WHAT?
GOOD MORNING, MY SEXY BOYS, WHO'S READY FOR ROUND TWO?
I BROUGHT SOME PROPS...
Carrot Bottom
LESGETTIT!
TWERK
MY ASS IS HUNGRY FOR A BIG BREAKFAST...
A HARD SCRAMBLE...

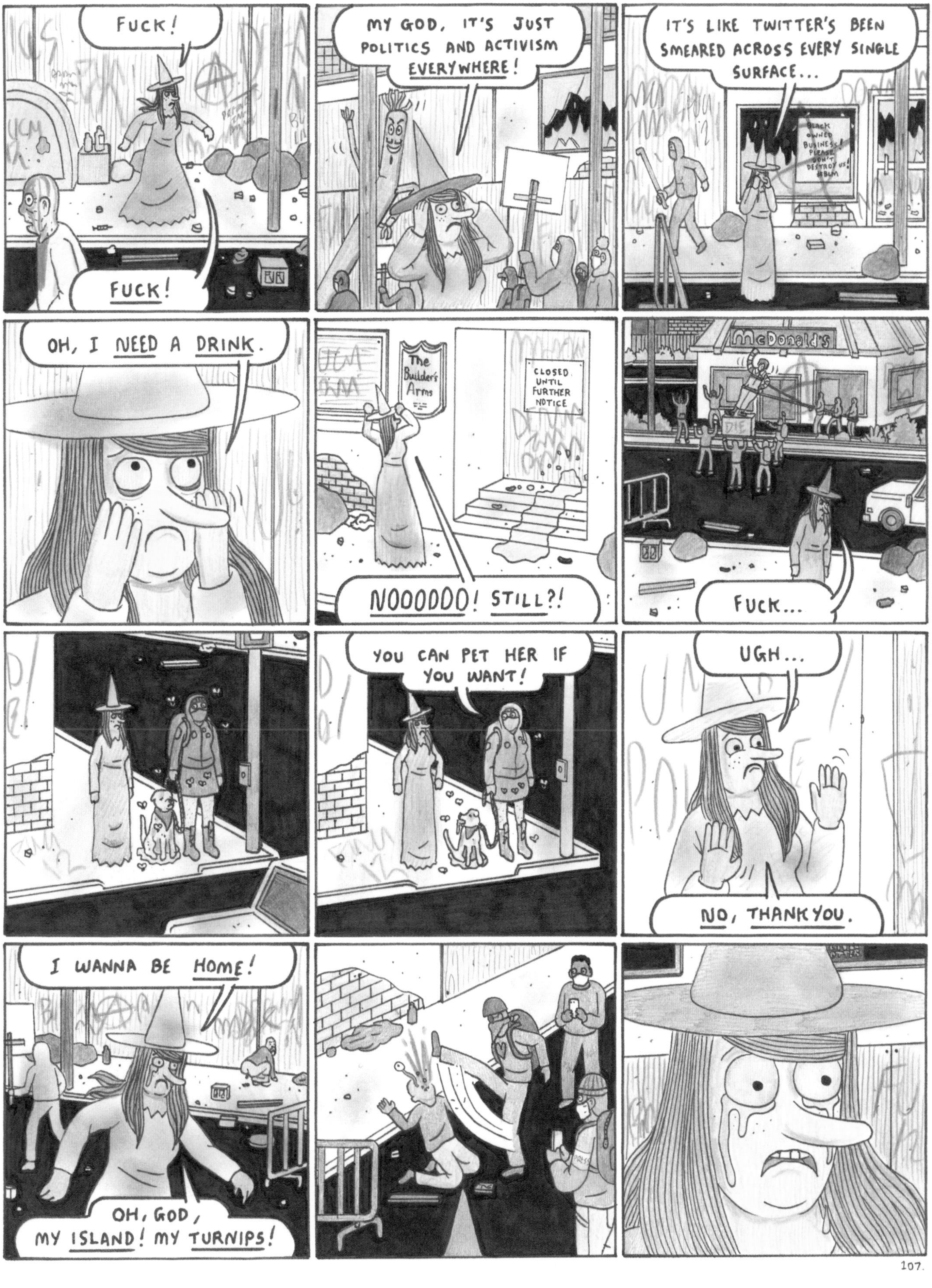
FUCK!
FUCK!
MY GOD, IT'S JUST POLITICS AND ACTIVISM EVERYWHERE!
IT'S LIKE TWITTER'S BEEN SMEARED ACROSS EVERY SINGLE SURFACE...
BLACK OWNED BUSINESS! PLEASE DON'T DESTROY US! #BLM
OH, I NEED A DRINK.
The Builder's Arms
CLOSED UNTIL FURTHER NOTICE
NOOODDO! STILL?!
McDonald's
DIE
FUCK...
YOU CAN PET HER IF YOU WANT!
UGH...
NO, THANK YOU.
I WANNA BE HOME!
OH, GOD, MY ISLAND! MY TURNIPS!

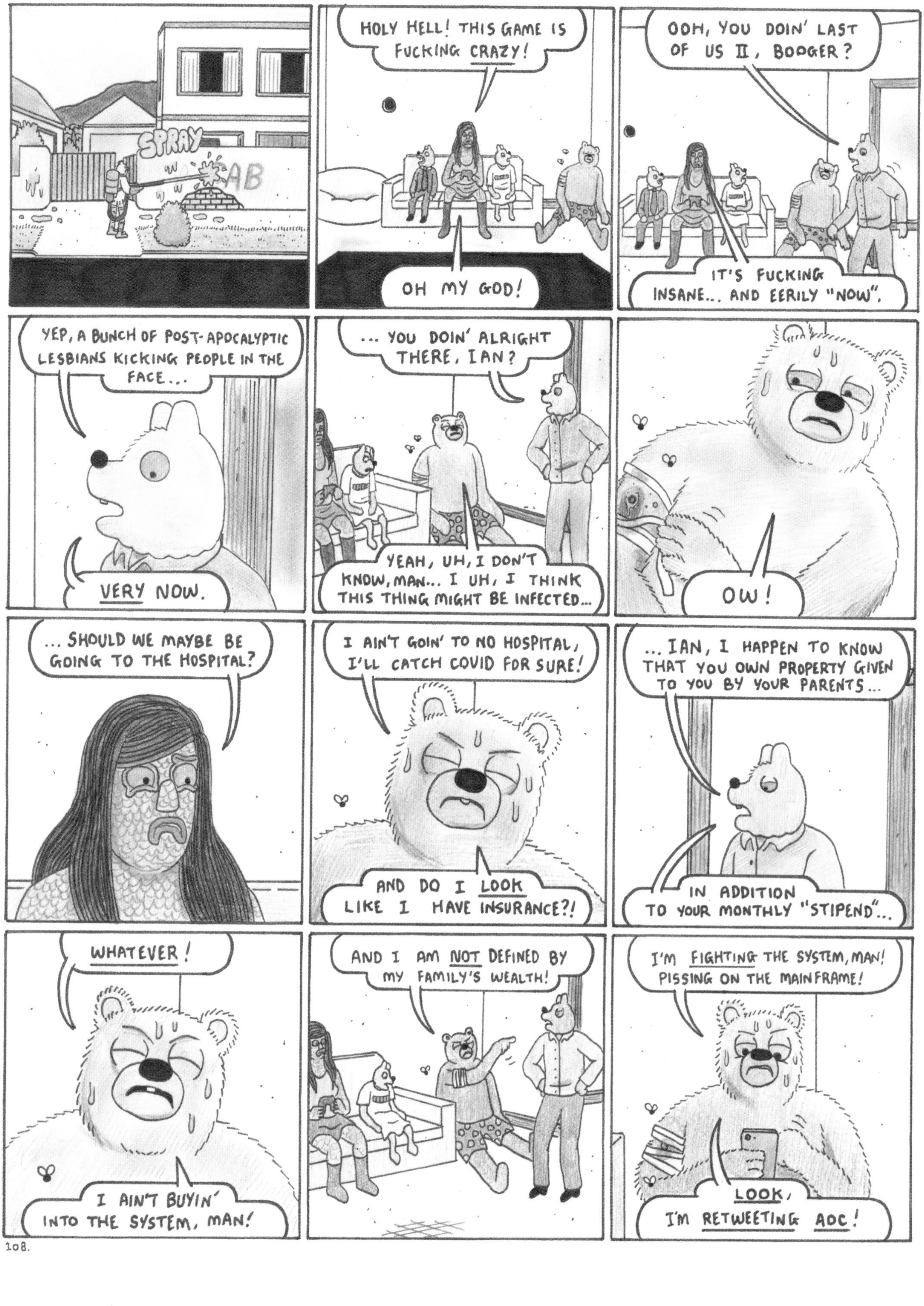
SPRAY
AB
HOLY HELL! THIS GAME IS FUCKING CRAZY!
OH MY GOD!
OOH, YOU DOIN' LAST OF US II, BOOGER?
IT'S FUCKING INSANE... AND EERILY "NOW".
YEP, A BUNCH OF POST-APOCALYPTIC LESBIANS KICKING PEOPLE IN THE FACE...
VERY NOW.
... YOU DOIN' ALRIGHT THERE, IAN?
YEAH, UH, I DON'T KNOW, MAN... I UH, I THINK THIS THING MIGHT BE INFECTED...
OW!
... SHOULD WE MAYBE BE GOING TO THE HOSPITAL?
I AIN'T GOIN' TO NO HOSPITAL, I'LL CATCH COVID FOR SURE!
AND DO I LOOK LIKE I HAVE INSURANCE?!
... IAN, I HAPPEN TO KNOW THAT YOU OWN PROPERTY GIVEN TO YOU BY YOUR PARENTS...
IN ADDITION TO YOUR MONTHLY "STIPEND"...
WHATEVER!
I AIN'T BUYIN' INTO THE SYSTEM, MAN!
AND I AM NOT DEFINED BY MY FAMILY'S WEALTH!
I'M FIGHTING THE SYSTEM, MAN! PISSING ON THE MAINFRAME!
LOOK, I'M RETWEETING AOC!

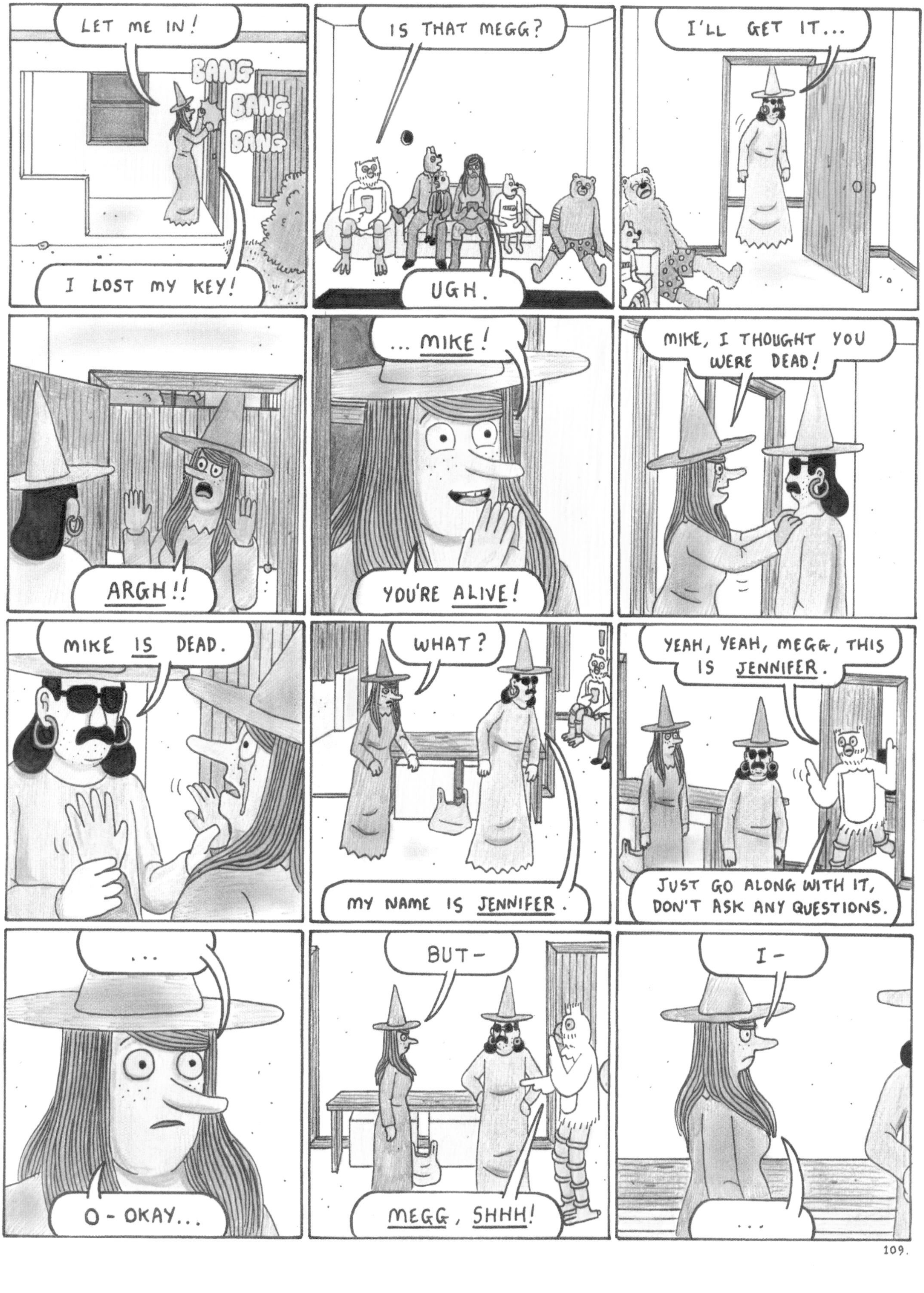
LET ME IN!
BANG
BANG
BANG
I LOST MY KEY!
IS THAT MEGG?
UGH.
I'LL GET IT...
ARGH!!
... MIKE!
YOU'RE ALIVE!
MIKE, I THOUGHT YOU WERE DEAD!
MIKE IS DEAD.
WHAT?
MY NAME IS JENNIFER.
YEAH, YEAH, MEGG, THIS IS JENNIFER.
JUST GO ALONG WITH IT, DON'T ASK ANY QUESTIONS.
...
O-OKAY...
BUT-
MEGG, SHHH!
I-
...

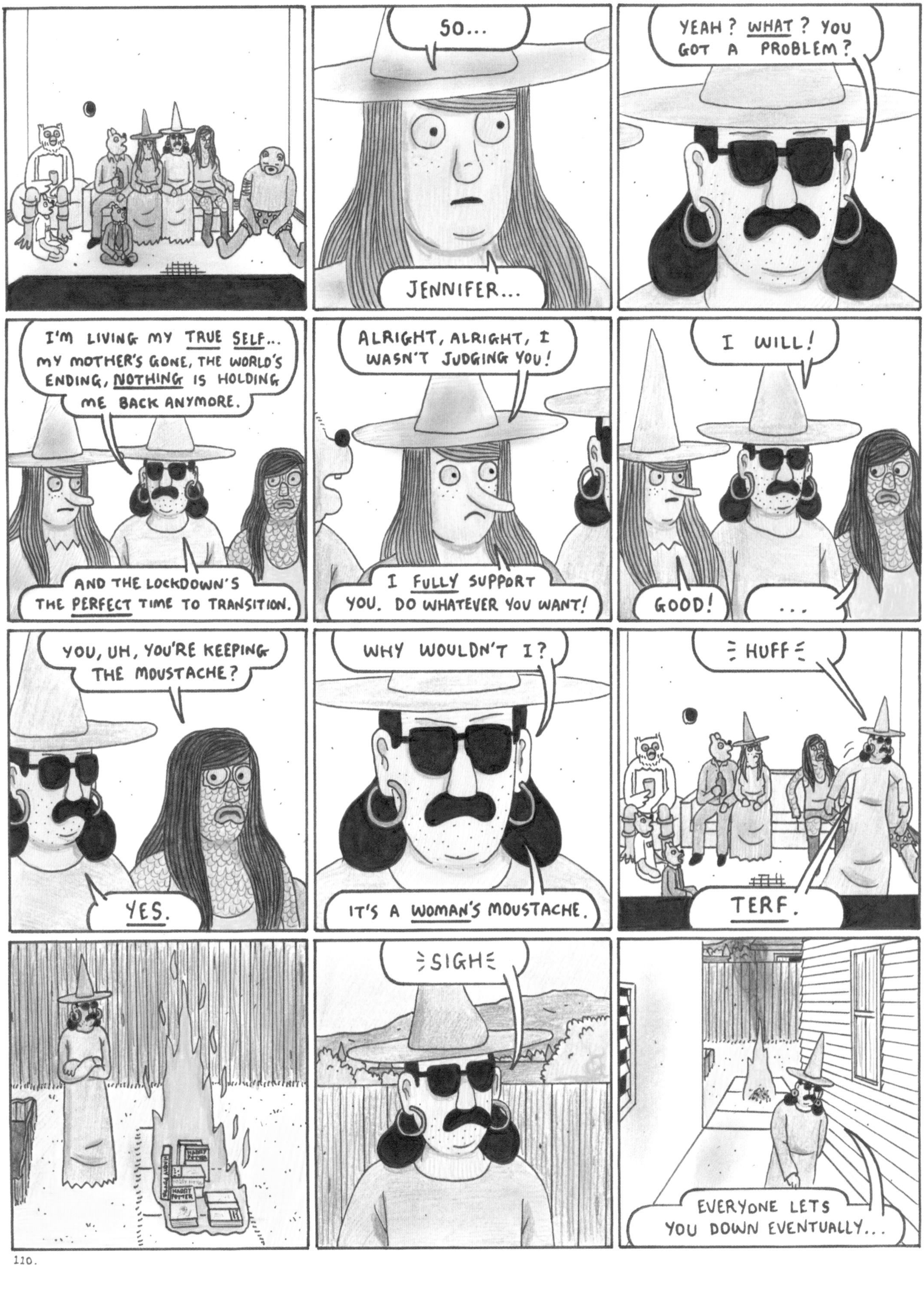
SO...
JENNIFER...
YEAH? WHAT? YOU GOT A PROBLEM?
I'M LIVING MY TRUE SELF... MY MOTHER'S GONE, THE WORLD'S ENDING, NOTHING IS HOLDING ME BACK ANYMORE.
AND THE LOCKDOWN'S THE PERFECT TIME TO TRANSITION.
ALRIGHT, ALRIGHT, I WASN'T JUDGING YOU!
I FULLY SUPPORT YOU. DO WHATEVER YOU WANT!
I WILL!
GOOD!
...
YOU, UH, YOU'RE KEEPING THE MOUSTACHE?
YES.
WHY WOULDN'T I?
IT'S A WOMAN'S MOUSTACHE.
HUFF
TERF.
SIGH
EVERYONE LETS YOU DOWN EVENTUALLY...

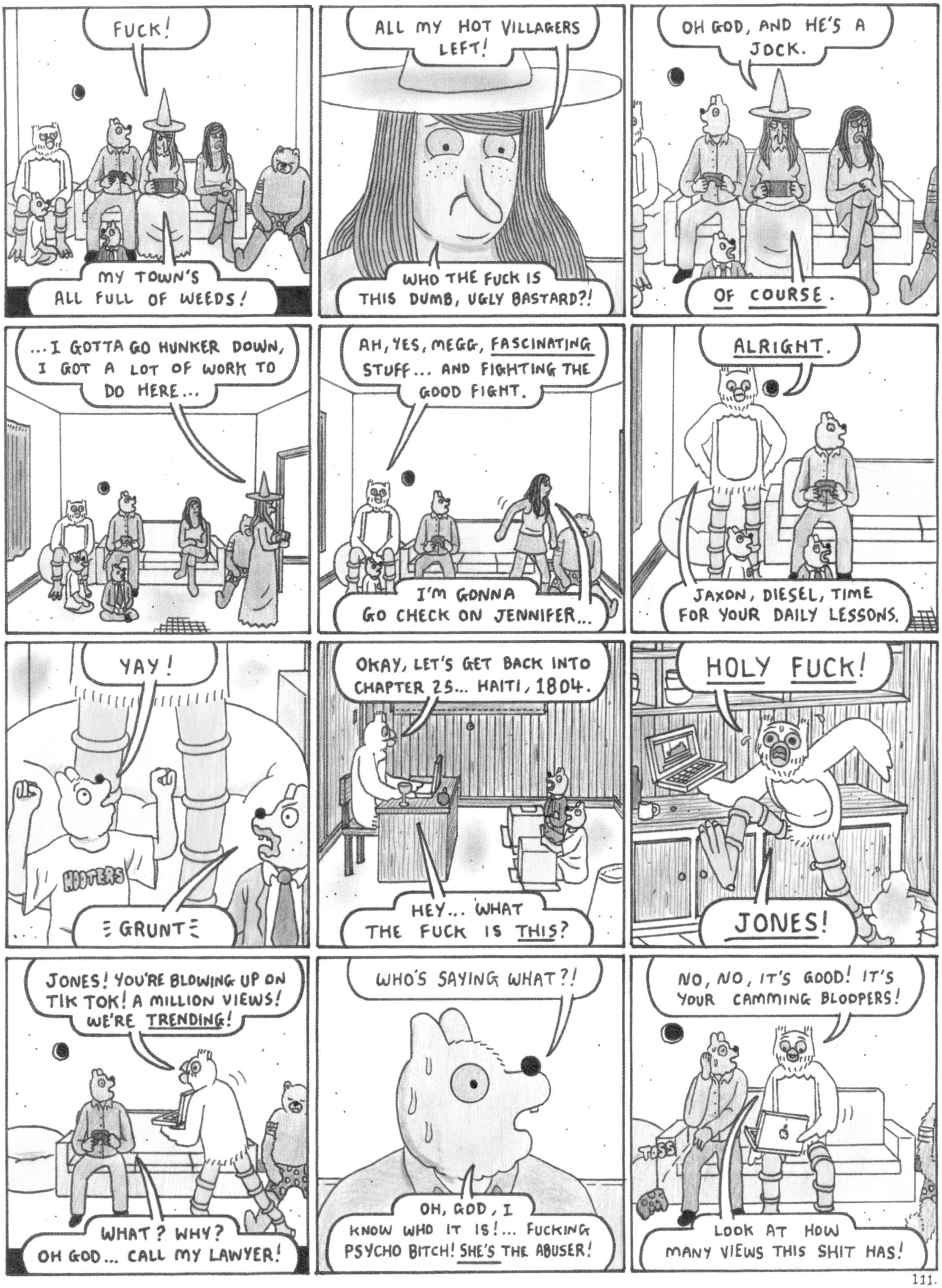
FUCK!
MY TOWN'S ALL FULL OF WEEDS!
ALL MY HOT VILLAGERS LEFT!
WHO THE FUCK IS THIS DUMB, UGLY BASTARD?!
OH GOD, AND HE'S A JOCK.
OF COURSE.
...I GOTTA GO HUNKER DOWN, I GOT A LOT OF WORK TO DO HERE...
AH, YES, MEGG, FASCINATING STUFF... AND FIGHTING THE GOOD FIGHT.
I'M GONNA GO CHECK ON JENNIFER...
ALRIGHT.
JAXON, DIESEL, TIME FOR YOUR DAILY LESSONS.
YAY!
HOOTERS
GRUNT
OKAY, LET'S GET BACK INTO CHAPTER 25... HAITI, 1804.
HEY... WHAT THE FUCK IS THIS?
HOLY FUCK!
JONES!
JONES! YOU'RE BLOWING UP ON TIK TOK! A MILLION VIEWS! WE'RE TRENDING!
WHAT? WHY? OH GOD... CALL MY LAWYER!
WHO'S SAYING WHAT?!
OH, GOD, I KNOW WHO IT IS!... FUCKING PSYCHO BITCH! SHE'S THE ABUSER!
NO, NO, IT'S GOOD! IT'S YOUR CAMMING BLOOPERS!
TOSS
LOOK AT HOW MANY VIEWS THIS SHIT HAS!

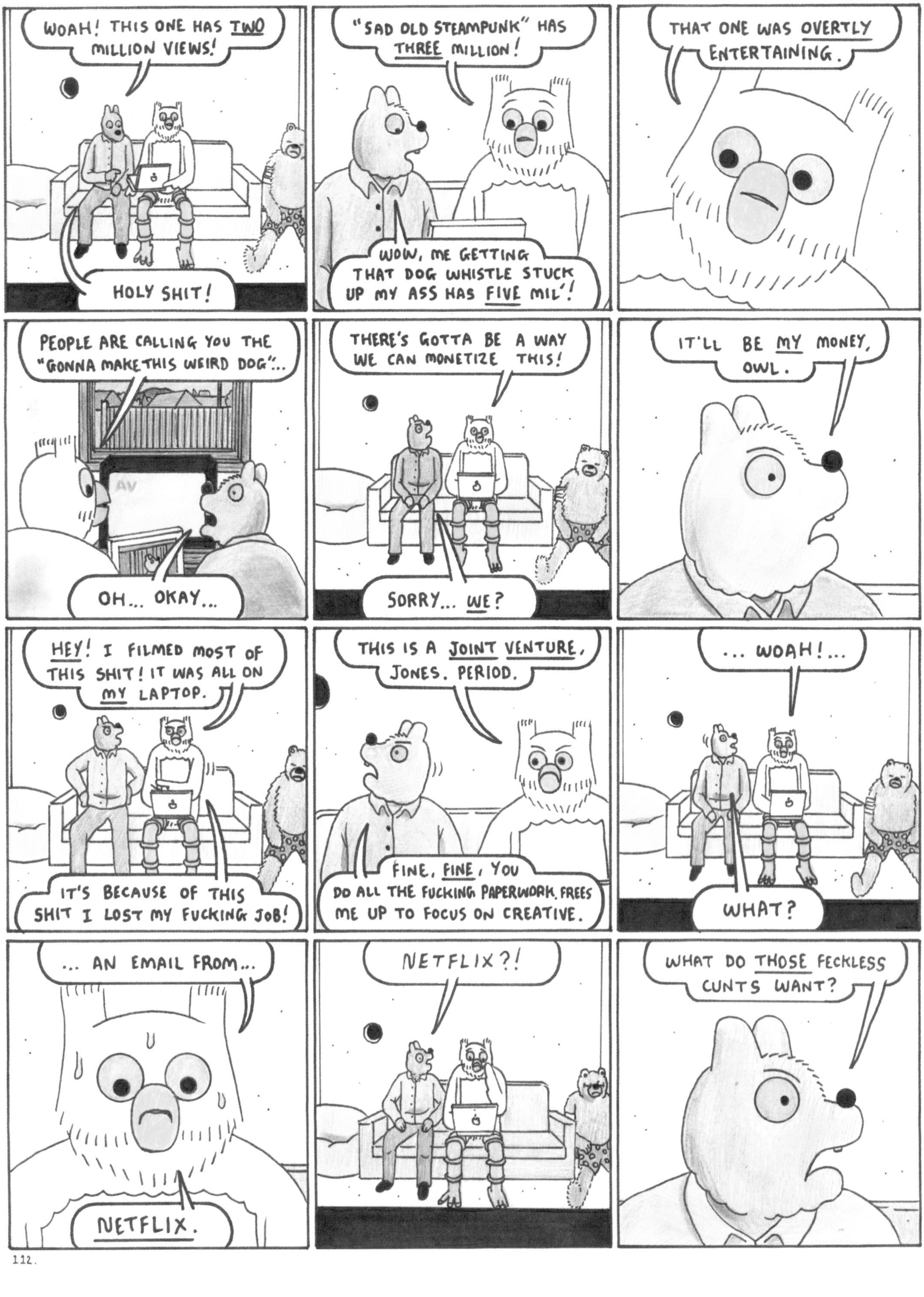
WOAH! THIS ONE HAS TWO MILLION VIEWS!
HOLY SHIT!
"SAD OLD STEAMPUNK" HAS THREE MILLION!
WOW, ME GETTING THAT DOG WHISTLE STUCK UP MY ASS HAS FIVE MIL'!
THAT ONE WAS OVERTLY ENTERTAINING.
PEOPLE ARE CALLING YOU THE "GONNA MAKE THIS WEIRD DOG"...
OH... OKAY...
THERE'S GOTTA BE A WAY WE CAN MONETIZE THIS!
SORRY... WE?
IT'LL BE MY MONEY, OWL.
HEY! I FILMED MOST OF THIS SHIT! IT WAS ALL ON MY LAPTOP.
IT'S BECAUSE OF THIS SHIT I LOST MY FUCKING JOB!
THIS IS A JOINT VENTURE, JONES. PERIOD.
FINE, FINE, YOU DO ALL THE FUCKING PAPERWORK, FREES ME UP TO FOCUS ON CREATIVE.
... WOAH!...
WHAT?
... AN EMAIL FROM...
NETFLIX.
NETFLIX?!
WHAT DO THOSE FECKLESS CUNTS WANT?

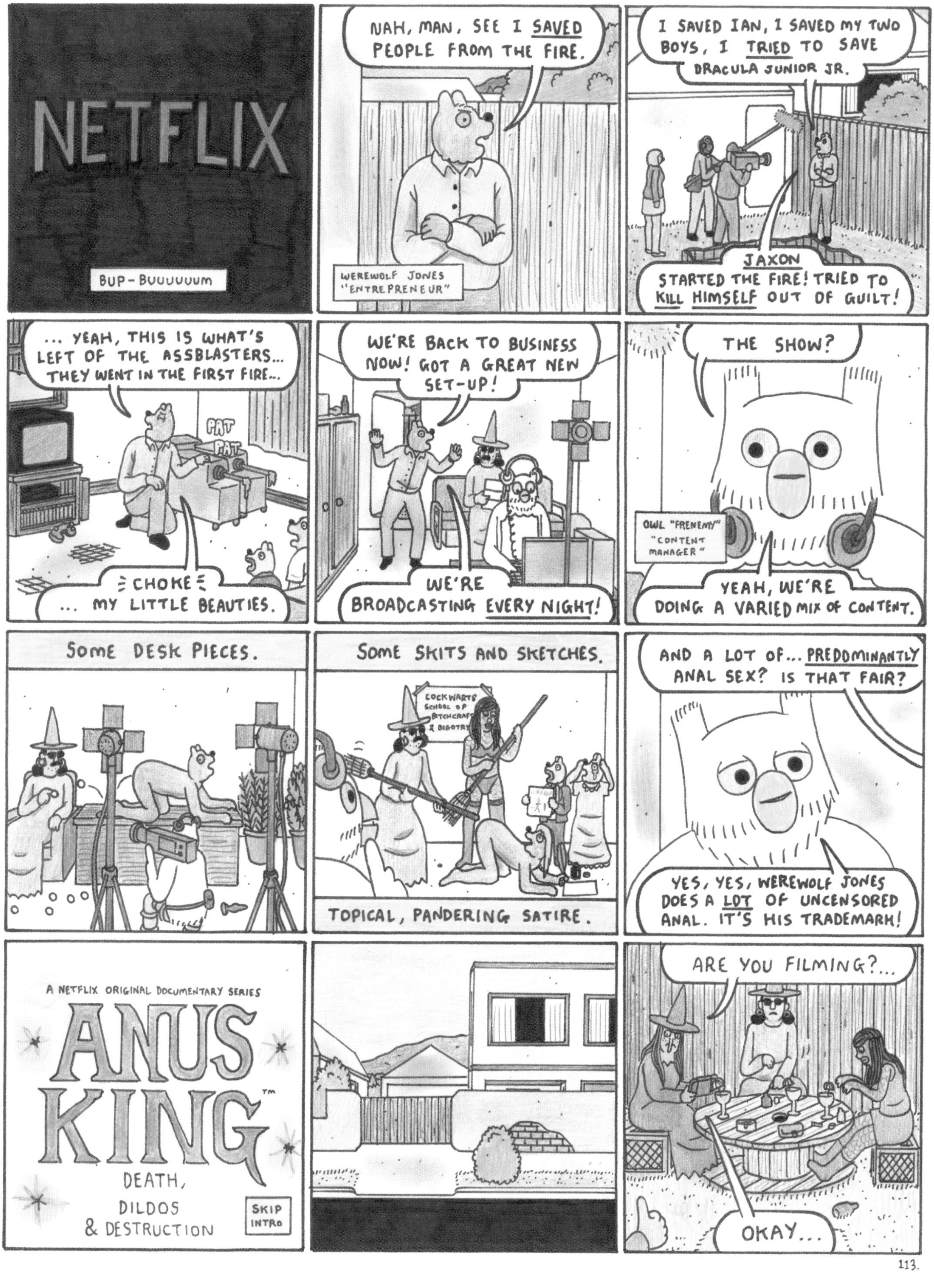
NETFLIX
BUP-BUUUUUUM
NAH, MAN, SEE I SAVED PEOPLE FROM THE FIRE.
WEREWOLF JONES "ENTREPRENEUR"
I SAVED IAN, I SAVED MY TWO BOYS, I TRIED TO SAVE DRACULA JUNIOR JR.
JAXON STARTED THE FIRE! TRIED TO KILL HIMSELF OUT OF GUILT!
... YEAH, THIS IS WHAT'S LEFT OF THE ASSBLASTERS... THEY WENT IN THE FIRST FIRE...
PAT
PAT
CHOKE ... MY LITTLE BEAUTIES.
WE'RE BACK TO BUSINESS NOW! GOT A GREAT NEW SET-UP!
WE'RE BROADCASTING EVERY NIGHT!
THE SHOW?
OWL "FRENEMY" "CONTENT MANAGER"
YEAH, WE'RE DOING A VARIED MIX OF CONTENT.
SOME DESK PIECES.
SOME SKITS AND SKETCHES.
COCKWARTS SCHOOL OF BITCHCRAFT & BIGOTRY
TOPICAL, PANDERING SATIRE.
AND A LOT OF... PREDOMINANTLY ANAL SEX? IS THAT FAIR?
YES, YES, WEREWOLF JONES DOES A LOT OF UNCENSORED ANAL. IT'S HIS TRADEMARK!
A NETFLIX ORIGINAL DOCUMENTARY SERIES
ANUS KING™
DEATH, DILDOS & DESTRUCTION
SKIP INTRO
ARE YOU FILMING?...
OKAY...

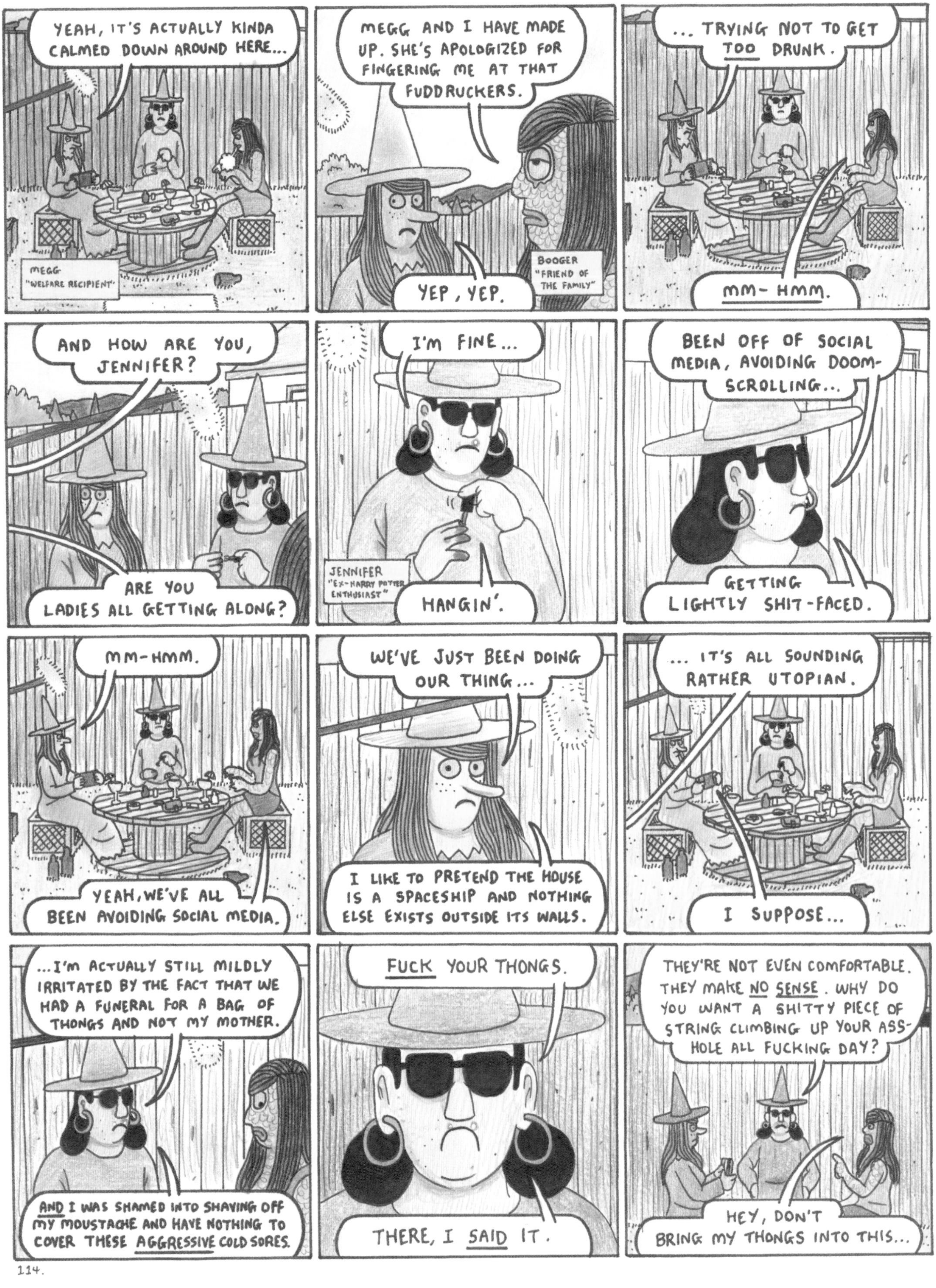
YEAH, IT'S ACTUALLY KINDA CALMED DOWN AROUND HERE...
MEGG "WELFARE RECIPIENT"
MEGG AND I HAVE MADE UP. SHE'S APOLOGIZED FOR FINGERING ME AT THAT FUDDRUCKERS.
YEP, YEP.
BOOGER "FRIEND OF THE FAMILY"
... TRYING NOT TO GET TOO DRUNK.
MM-HMM.
AND HOW ARE YOU, JENNIFER?
ARE YOU LADIES ALL GETTING ALONG?
I'M FINE...
HANGIN'.
JENNIFER "EX-HARRY POTTER ENTHUSIAST"
BEEN OFF OF SOCIAL MEDIA, AVOIDING DOOM-SCROLLING...
GETTING LIGHTLY SHIT-FACED.
MM-HMM.
YEAH, WE'VE ALL BEEN AVOIDING SOCIAL MEDIA.
WE'VE JUST BEEN DOING OUR THING...
I LIKE TO PRETEND THE HOUSE IS A SPACESHIP AND NOTHING ELSE EXISTS OUTSIDE ITS WALLS.
... IT'S ALL SOUNDING RATHER UTOPIAN.
I SUPPOSE...
...I'M ACTUALLY STILL MILDLY IRRITATED BY THE FACT THAT WE HAD A FUNERAL FOR A BAG OF THONGS AND NOT MY MOTHER.
AND I WAS SHAMED INTO SHAVING OFF MY MOUSTACHE AND HAVE NOTHING TO COVER THESE AGGRESSIVE COLD SORES.
FUCK YOUR THONGS.
THERE, I SAID IT.
THEY'RE NOT EVEN COMFORTABLE. THEY MAKE NO SENSE. WHY DO YOU WANT A SHITTY PIECE OF STRING CLIMBING UP YOUR ASS-HOLE ALL FUCKING DAY?
HEY, DON'T BRING MY THONGS INTO THIS...

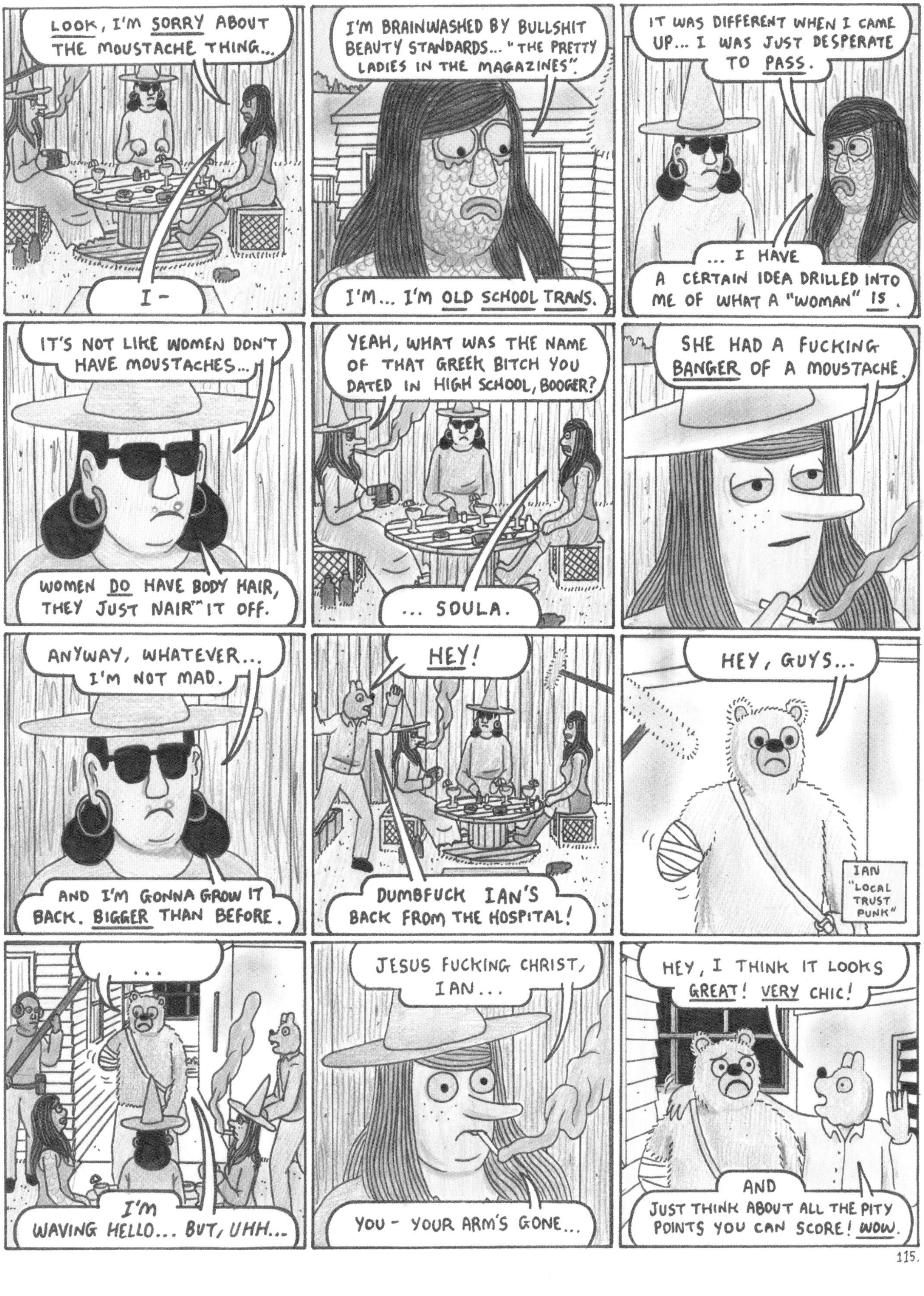
LOOK, I'M SORRY ABOUT THE MOUSTACHE THING...
I -
I'M BRAINWASHED BY BULLSHIT BEAUTY STANDARDS... "THE PRETTY LADIES IN THE MAGAZINES".
I'M... I'M OLD SCHOOL TRANS.
IT WAS DIFFERENT WHEN I CAME UP... I WAS JUST DESPERATE TO PASS.
... I HAVE A CERTAIN IDEA DRILLED INTO ME OF WHAT A "WOMAN" IS.
IT'S NOT LIKE WOMEN DON'T HAVE MOUSTACHES...
WOMEN DO HAVE BODY HAIR, THEY JUST NAIR™ IT OFF.
YEAH, WHAT WAS THE NAME OF THAT GREEK BITCH YOU DATED IN HIGH SCHOOL, BOOGER?
... SOULA.
SHE HAD A FUCKING BANGER OF A MOUSTACHE.
ANYWAY, WHATEVER... I'M NOT MAD.
AND I'M GONNA GROW IT BACK. BIGGER THAN BEFORE.
HEY!
DUMBFUCK IAN'S BACK FROM THE HOSPITAL!
HEY, GUYS...
IAN "LOCAL TRUST PUNK"
...
I'M WAVING HELLO... BUT, UHH...
JESUS FUCKING CHRIST, IAN...
YOU - YOUR ARM'S GONE...
HEY, I THINK IT LOOKS GREAT! VERY CHIC!
AND JUST THINK ABOUT ALL THE PITY POINTS YOU CAN SCORE! WOW.

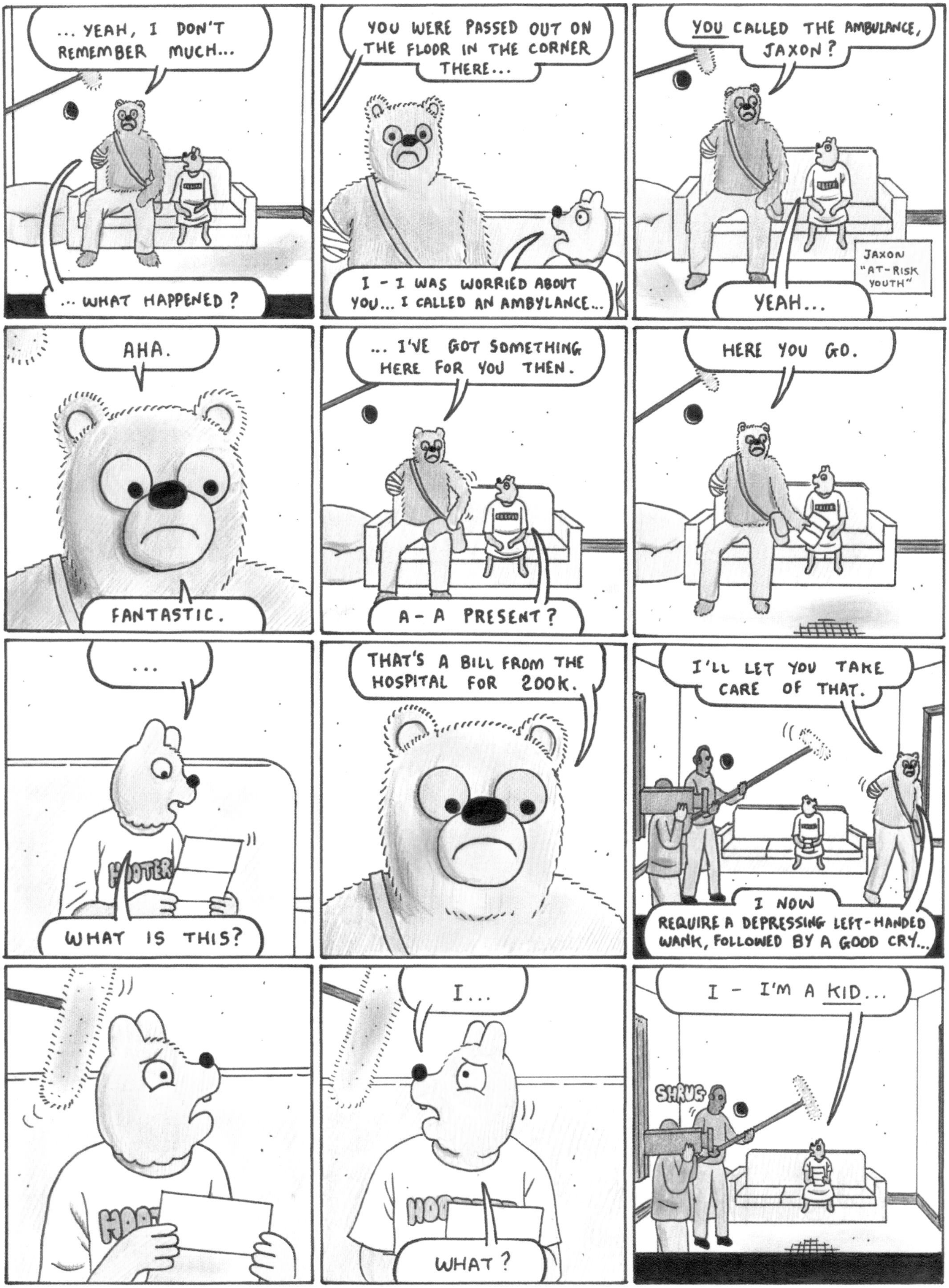
... YEAH, I DON'T REMEMBER MUCH...
... WHAT HAPPENED?
YOU WERE PASSED OUT ON THE FLOOR IN THE CORNER THERE...
I - I WAS WORRIED ABOUT YOU... I CALLED AN AMBYLANCE...
YOU CALLED THE AMBULANCE, JAXON?
JAXON "AT-RISK YOUTH"
YEAH...
AHA.
FANTASTIC.
... I'VE GOT SOMETHING HERE FOR YOU THEN.
A- A PRESENT?
HERE YOU GO.
...
WHAT IS THIS?
THAT'S A BILL FROM THE HOSPITAL FOR 200K.
I'LL LET YOU TAKE CARE OF THAT.
I NOW REQUIRE A DEPRESSING LEFT-HANDED WANK, FOLLOWED BY A GOOD CRY...
I...
WHAT?
SHRUG
I - I'M A KID...

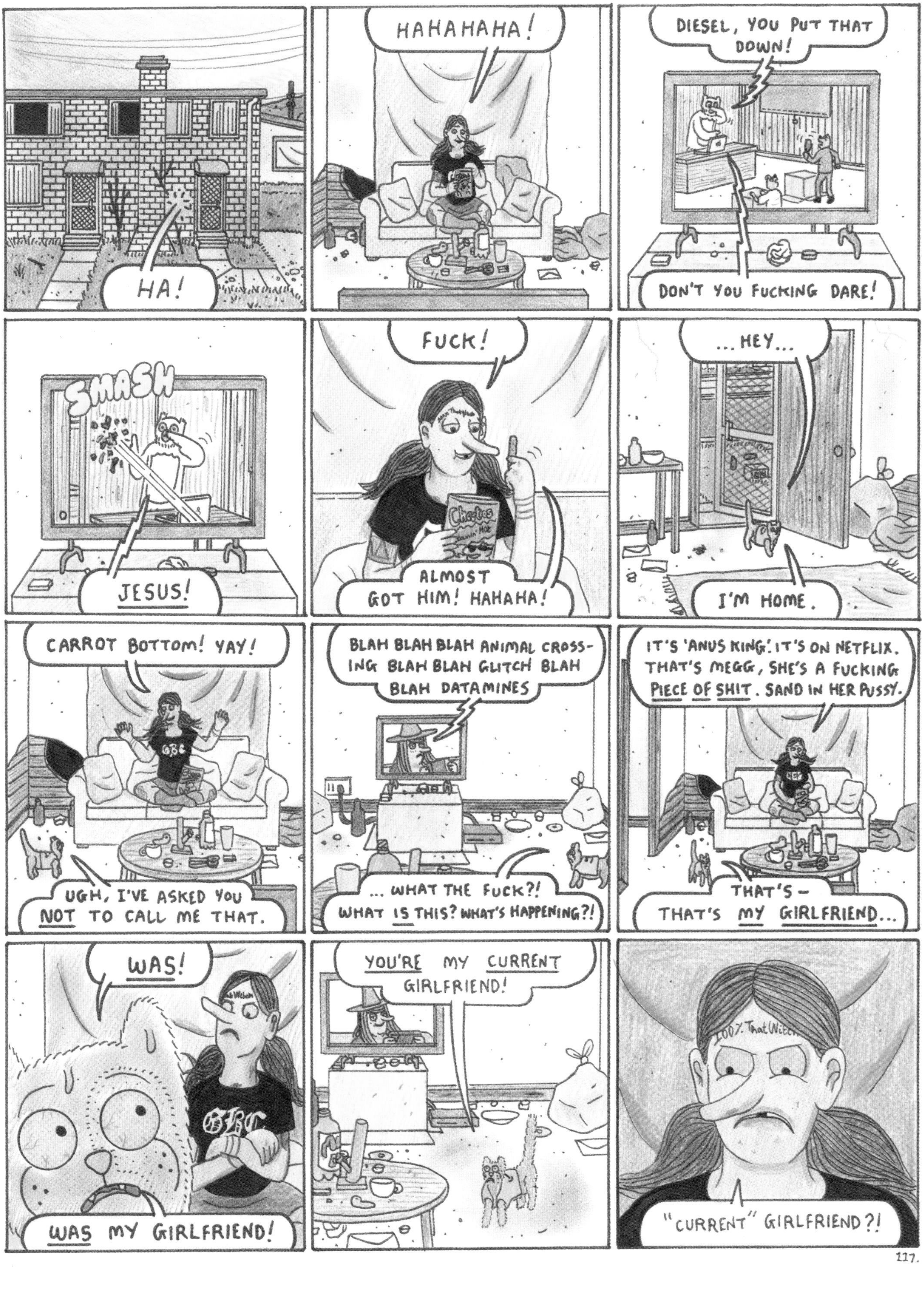
HA!
HAHAHAHA!
DIESEL, YOU PUT THAT DOWN!
DON'T YOU FUCKING DARE!
SMASH
JESUS!
FUCK!
ALMOST GOT HIM! HAHAHA!
... HEY...
I'M HOME.
CARROT BOTTOM! YAY!
UGH, I'VE ASKED YOU NOT TO CALL ME THAT.
BLAH BLAH BLAH ANIMAL CROSSING BLAH BLAH GLITCH BLAH BLAH DATAMINES
... WHAT THE FUCK?! WHAT IS THIS? WHAT'S HAPPENING?!
IT'S 'ANUS KING'. IT'S ON NETFLIX. THAT'S MEGG, SHE'S A FUCKING PIECE OF SHIT. SAND IN HER PUSSY.
THAT'S — THAT'S MY GIRLFRIEND...
WAS!
WAS MY GIRLFRIEND!
YOU'RE MY CURRENT GIRLFRIEND!
100% That Witch
"CURRENT" GIRLFRIEND?!

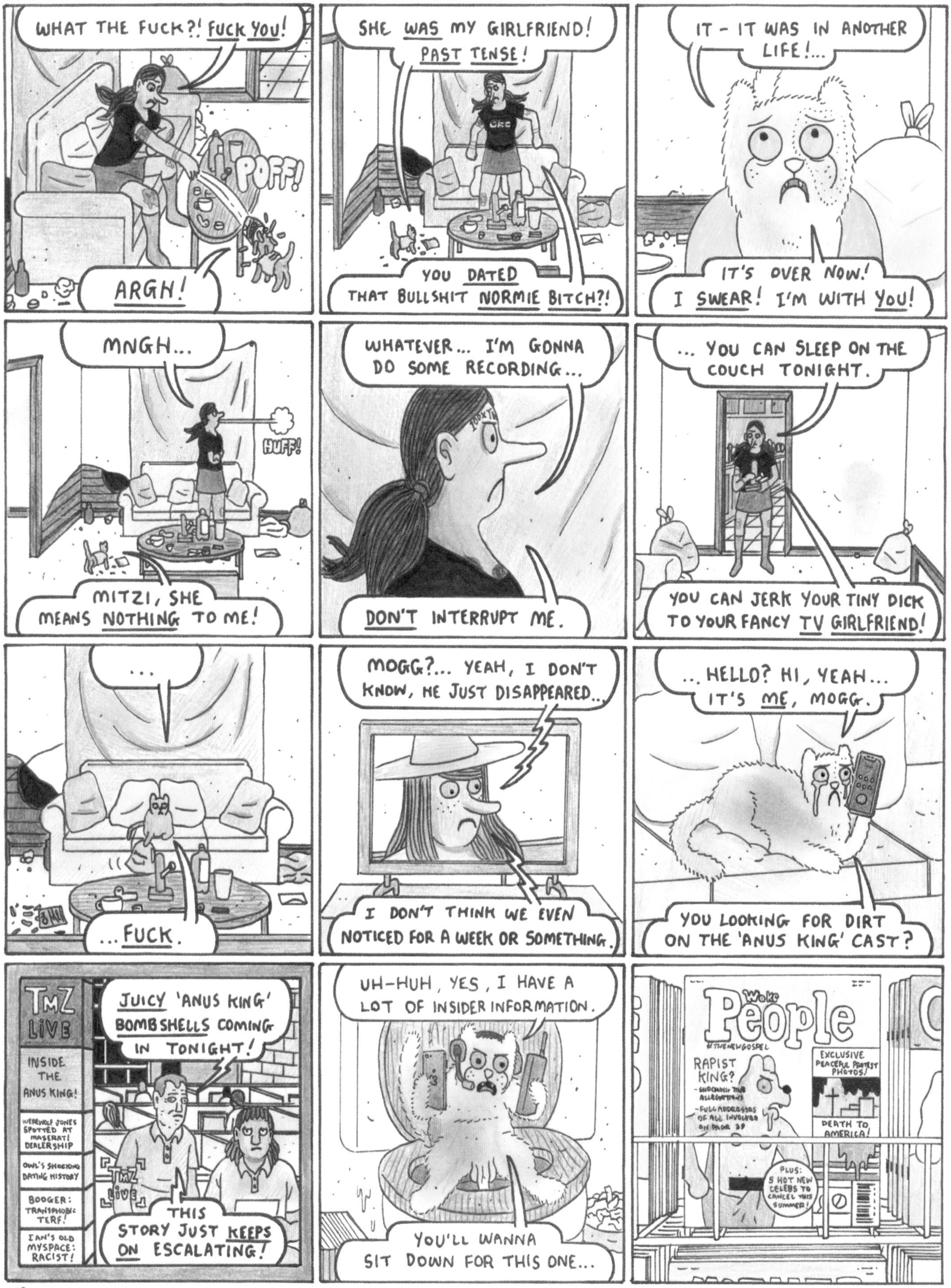
WHAT THE FUCK?! FUCK YOU!
POFF!
ARGH!
SHE WAS MY GIRLFRIEND! PAST TENSE!
YOU DATED THAT BULLSHIT NORMIE BITCH?!
IT - IT WAS IN ANOTHER LIFE!...
IT'S OVER NOW! I SWEAR! I'M WITH YOU!
MNGH...
HUFF!
MITZI, SHE MEANS NOTHING TO ME!
WHATEVER... I'M GONNA DO SOME RECORDING...
DON'T INTERRUPT ME.
... YOU CAN SLEEP ON THE COUCH TONIGHT.
YOU CAN JERK YOUR TINY DICK TO YOUR FANCY TV GIRLFRIEND!
...
... FUCK.
MOGG?... YEAH, I DON'T KNOW, HE JUST DISAPPEARED...
I DON'T THINK WE EVEN NOTICED FOR A WEEK OR SOMETHING.
... HELLO? HI, YEAH... IT'S ME, MOGG.
YOU LOOKING FOR DIRT ON THE 'ANUS KING' CAST?
TMZ LIVE
INSIDE THE ANUS KING!
WEREWOLF JONES SPOTTED AT MASERATI DEALERSHIP
OWL'S SHOCKING DATING HISTORY
BOOGER: TRANSPHOBIC TERF!
IAN'S OLD MYSPACE: RACIST!
JUICY 'ANUS KING' BOMBSHELLS COMING IN TONIGHT!
TMZ LIVE
THIS STORY JUST KEEPS ON ESCALATING!
UH-HUH, YES, I HAVE A LOT OF INSIDER INFORMATION.
YOU'LL WANNA SIT DOWN FOR THIS ONE...
Woke People
#THENEWGOSPEL
RAPIST KING?
EXCLUSIVE PEACEFUL PROTEST PHOTOS!
DEATH TO AMERICA!
PLUS: 5 HOT NEW CELEBS TO CANCEL THIS SUMMER!

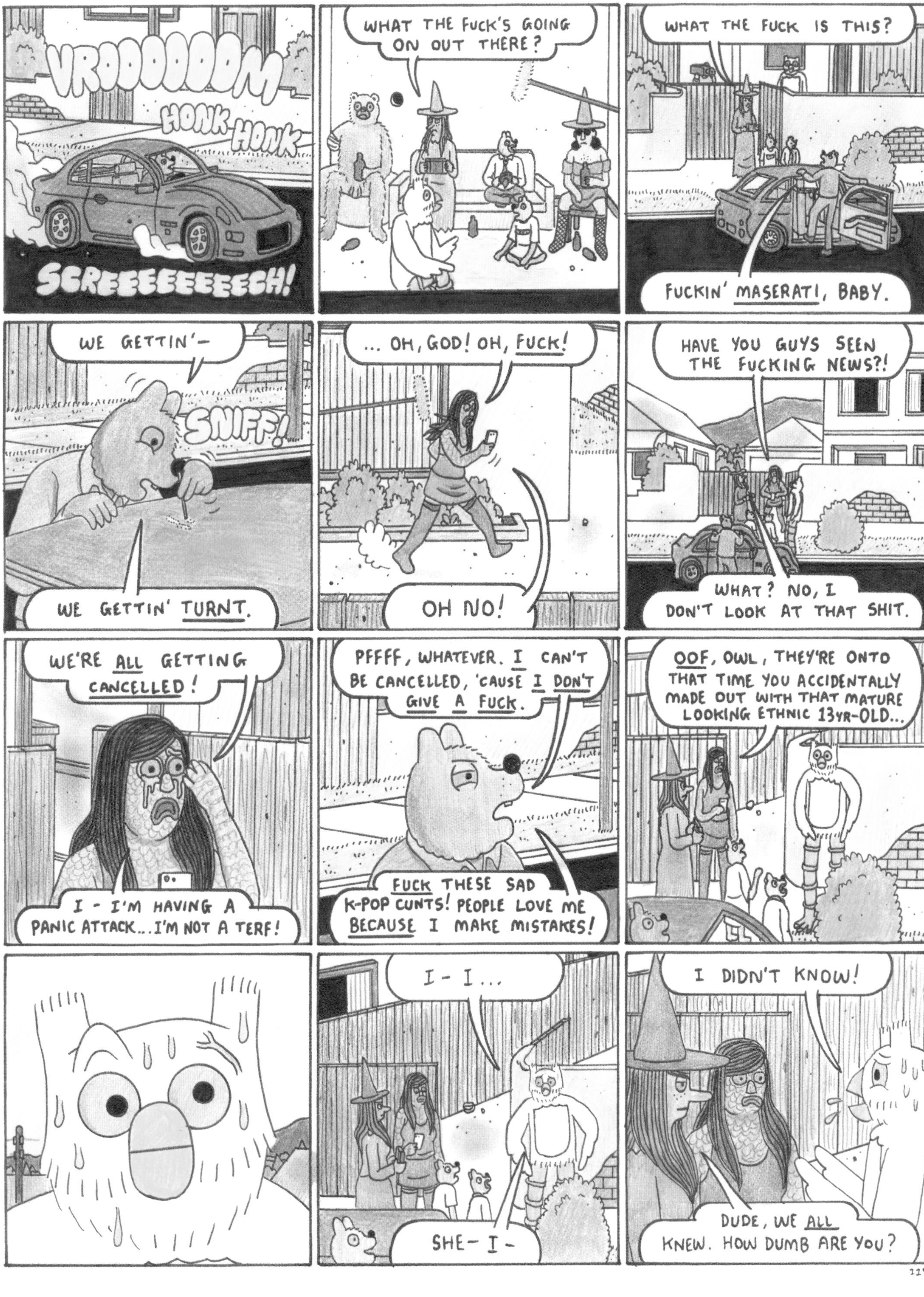
VROOOOOOOM
HONK-HONK
SCREEEEEEEEECH!
WHAT THE FUCK'S GOING ON OUT THERE?
WHAT THE FUCK IS THIS?
FUCKIN' MASERATI, BABY.
WE GETTIN'—
SNIFF!
WE GETTIN' TURNT.
... OH, GOD! OH, FUCK!
OH NO!
HAVE YOU GUYS SEEN THE FUCKING NEWS?!
WHAT? NO, I DON'T LOOK AT THAT SHIT.
WE'RE ALL GETTING CANCELLED!
I - I'M HAVING A PANIC ATTACK... I'M NOT A TERF!
PFFFF, WHATEVER. I CAN'T BE CANCELLED, 'CAUSE I DON'T GIVE A FUCK.
FUCK THESE SAD K-POP CUNTS! PEOPLE LOVE ME BECAUSE I MAKE MISTAKES!
OOF, OWL, THEY'RE ONTO THAT TIME YOU ACCIDENTALLY MADE OUT WITH THAT MATURE LOOKING ETHNIC 13YR-OLD...
I - I...
SHE— I -
I DIDN'T KNOW!
DUDE, WE ALL KNEW. HOW DUMB ARE YOU?

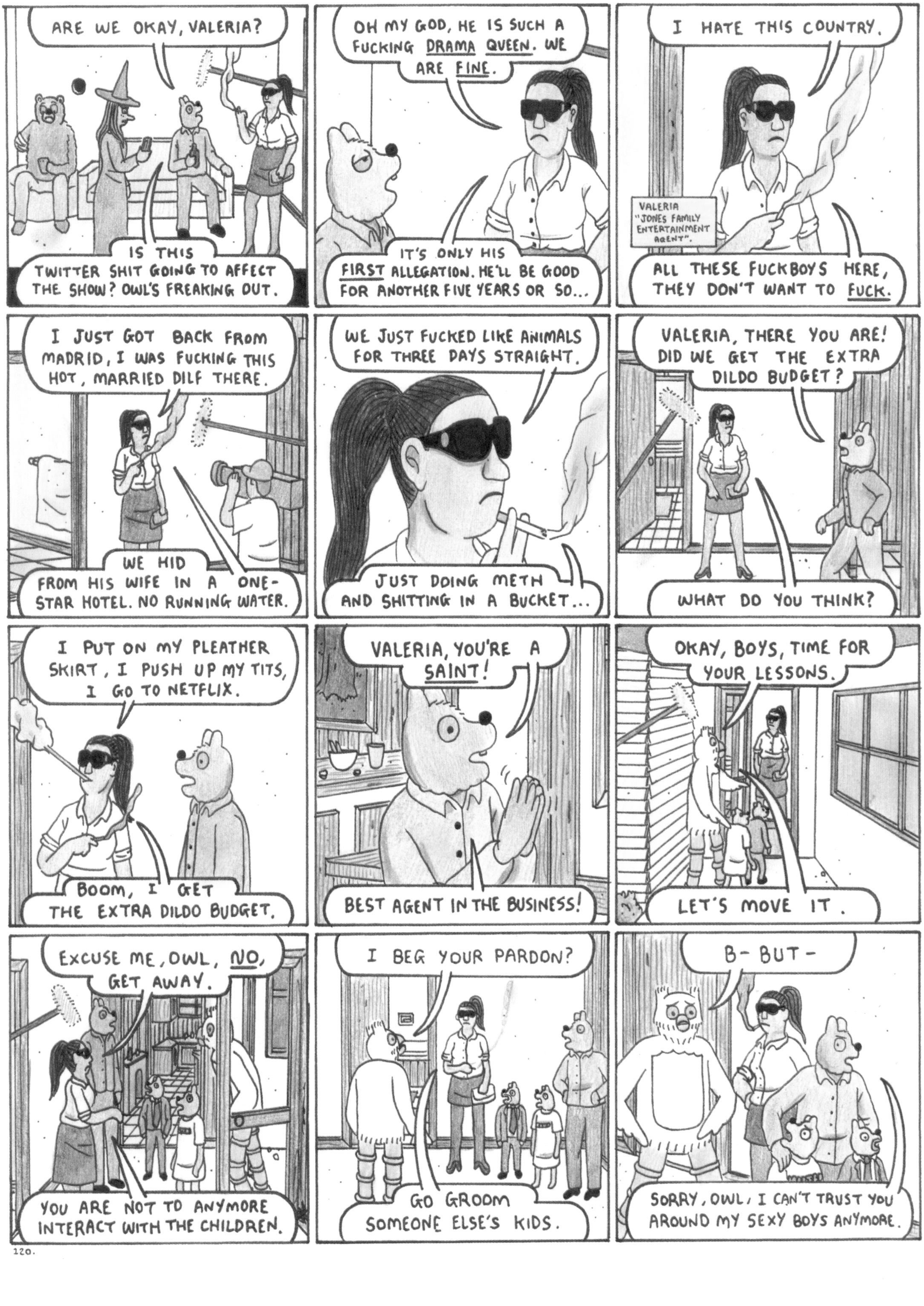
ARE WE OKAY, VALERIA?
IS THIS TWITTER SHIT GOING TO AFFECT THE SHOW? OWL'S FREAKING OUT.
OH MY GOD, HE IS SUCH A FUCKING DRAMA QUEEN. WE ARE FINE.
IT'S ONLY HIS FIRST ALLEGATION. HE'LL BE GOOD FOR ANOTHER FIVE YEARS OR SO...
I HATE THIS COUNTRY.
VALERIA "JONES FAMILY ENTERTAINMENT AGENT".
ALL THESE FUCKBOYS HERE, THEY DON'T WANT TO FUCK.
I JUST GOT BACK FROM MADRID, I WAS FUCKING THIS HOT, MARRIED DILF THERE.
WE HID FROM HIS WIFE IN A ONE-STAR HOTEL. NO RUNNING WATER.
WE JUST FUCKED LIKE ANIMALS FOR THREE DAYS STRAIGHT.
JUST DOING METH AND SHITTING IN A BUCKET...
VALERIA, THERE YOU ARE! DID WE GET THE EXTRA DILDO BUDGET?
WHAT DO YOU THINK?
I PUT ON MY PLEATHER SKIRT, I PUSH UP MY TITS, I GO TO NETFLIX.
BOOM, I GET THE EXTRA DILDO BUDGET.
VALERIA, YOU'RE A SAINT!
BEST AGENT IN THE BUSINESS!
OKAY, BOYS, TIME FOR YOUR LESSONS.
LET'S MOVE IT.
EXCUSE ME, OWL, NO, GET AWAY.
YOU ARE NOT TO ANYMORE INTERACT WITH THE CHILDREN.
I BEG YOUR PARDON?
GO GROOM SOMEONE ELSE'S KIDS.
B- BUT-
SORRY, OWL, I CAN'T TRUST YOU AROUND MY SEXY BOYS ANYMORE.

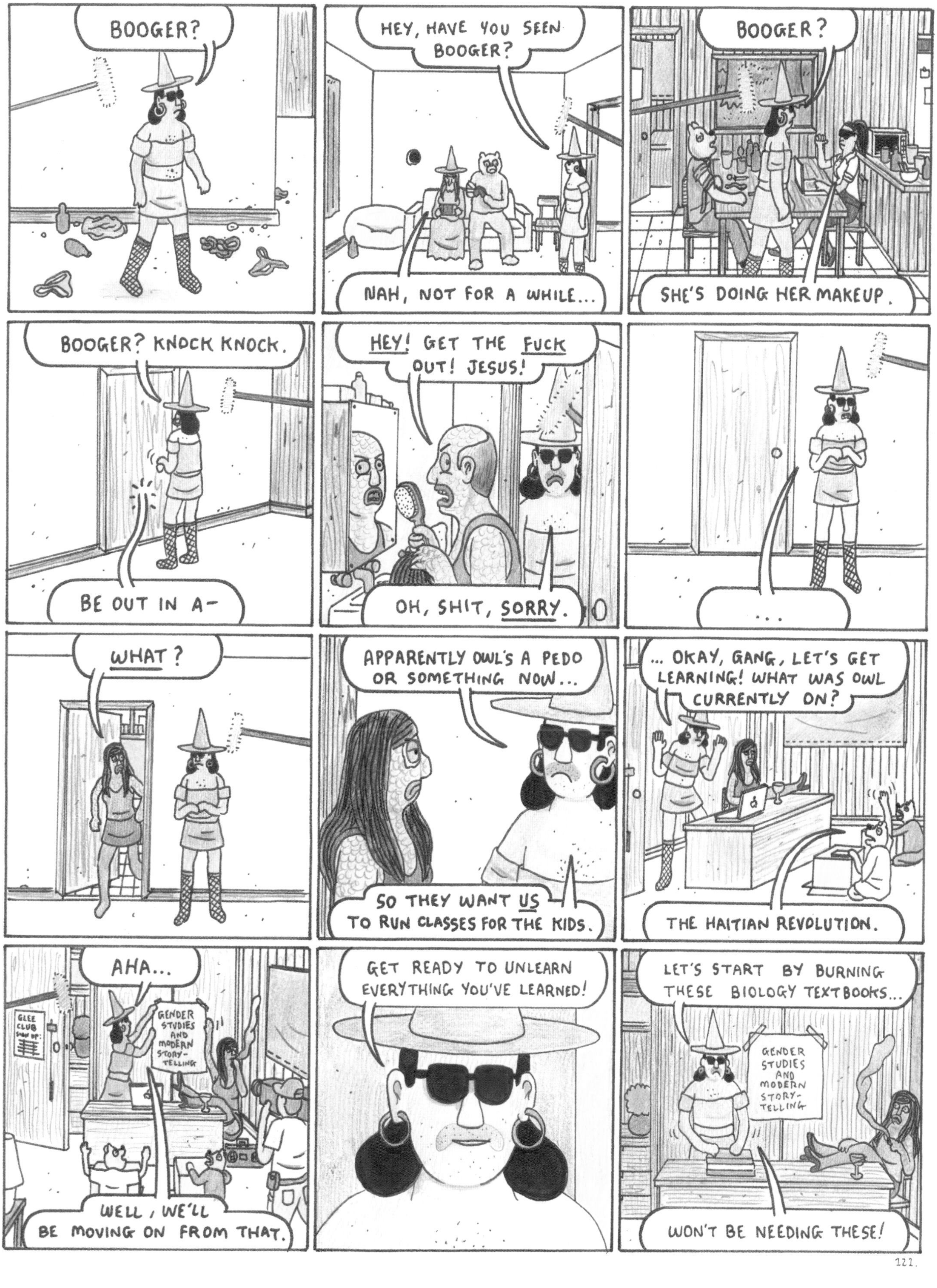
BOOGER?
HEY, HAVE YOU SEEN BOOGER?
NAH, NOT FOR A WHILE...
BOOGER?
SHE'S DOING HER MAKEUP.
BOOGER? KNOCK KNOCK.
BE OUT IN A-
HEY! GET THE FUCK OUT! JESUS!
OH, SHIT, SORRY.
...
WHAT?
APPARENTLY OWL'S A PEDO OR SOMETHING NOW...
SO THEY WANT US TO RUN CLASSES FOR THE KIDS.
... OKAY, GANG, LET'S GET LEARNING! WHAT WAS OWL CURRENTLY ON?
THE HAITIAN REVOLUTION.
AHA...
GLEE CLUB SIGN UP:
GENDER STUDIES AND MODERN STORY-TELLING
WELL, WE'LL BE MOVING ON FROM THAT.
GET READY TO UNLEARN EVERYTHING YOU'VE LEARNED!
LET'S START BY BURNING THESE BIOLOGY TEXTBOOKS...
GENDER STUDIES AND MODERN STORY-TELLING
WON'T BE NEEDING THESE!

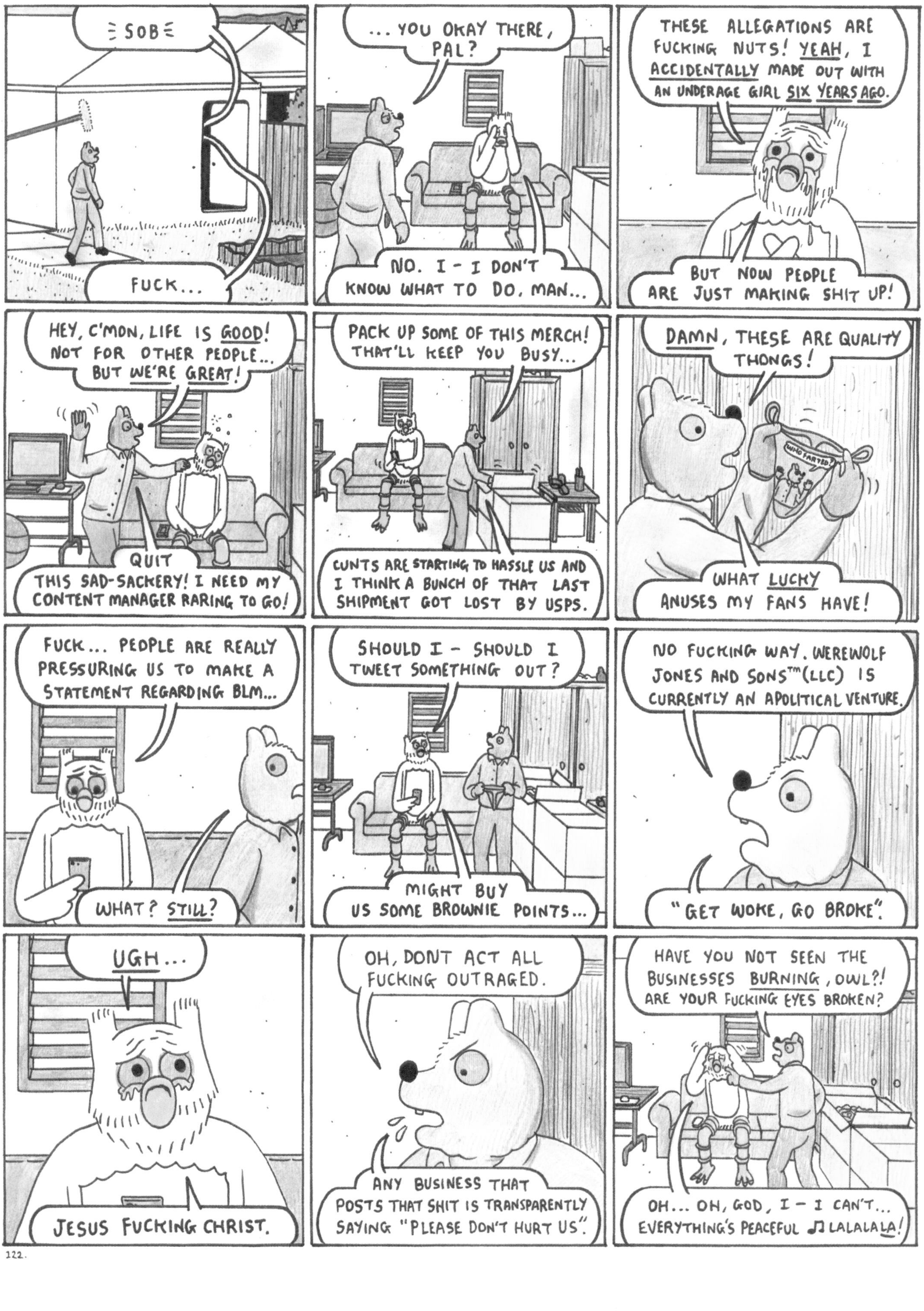
SOB
FUCK...
... YOU OKAY THERE, PAL?
NO. I - I DON'T KNOW WHAT TO DO, MAN...
THESE ALLEGATIONS ARE FUCKING NUTS! YEAH, I ACCIDENTALLY MADE OUT WITH AN UNDERAGE GIRL SIX YEARS AGO.
BUT NOW PEOPLE ARE JUST MAKING SHIT UP!
HEY, C'MON, LIFE IS GOOD! NOT FOR OTHER PEOPLE... BUT WE'RE GREAT!
QUIT THIS SAD-SACKERY! I NEED MY CONTENT MANAGER RARING TO GO!
PACK UP SOME OF THIS MERCH! THAT'LL KEEP YOU BUSY...
CUNTS ARE STARTING TO HASSLE US AND I THINK A BUNCH OF THAT LAST SHIPMENT GOT LOST BY USPS.
DAMN, THESE ARE QUALITY THONGS!
WHAT LUCKY ANUSES MY FANS HAVE!
FUCK... PEOPLE ARE REALLY PRESSURING US TO MAKE A STATEMENT REGARDING BLM...
WHAT? STILL?
SHOULD I - SHOULD I TWEET SOMETHING OUT?
MIGHT BUY US SOME BROWNIE POINTS...
NO FUCKING WAY. WEREWOLF JONES AND SONS™ (LLC) IS CURRENTLY AN APOLITICAL VENTURE.
"GET WOKE, GO BROKE".
UGH...
JESUS FUCKING CHRIST.
OH, DONT ACT ALL FUCKING OUTRAGED.
ANY BUSINESS THAT POSTS THAT SHIT IS TRANSPARENTLY SAYING "PLEASE DON'T HURT US".
HAVE YOU NOT SEEN THE BUSINESSES BURNING, OWL?! ARE YOUR FUCKING EYES BROKEN?
OH... OH, GOD, I - I CAN'T... EVERYTHING'S PEACEFUL ♫ LALALALA!

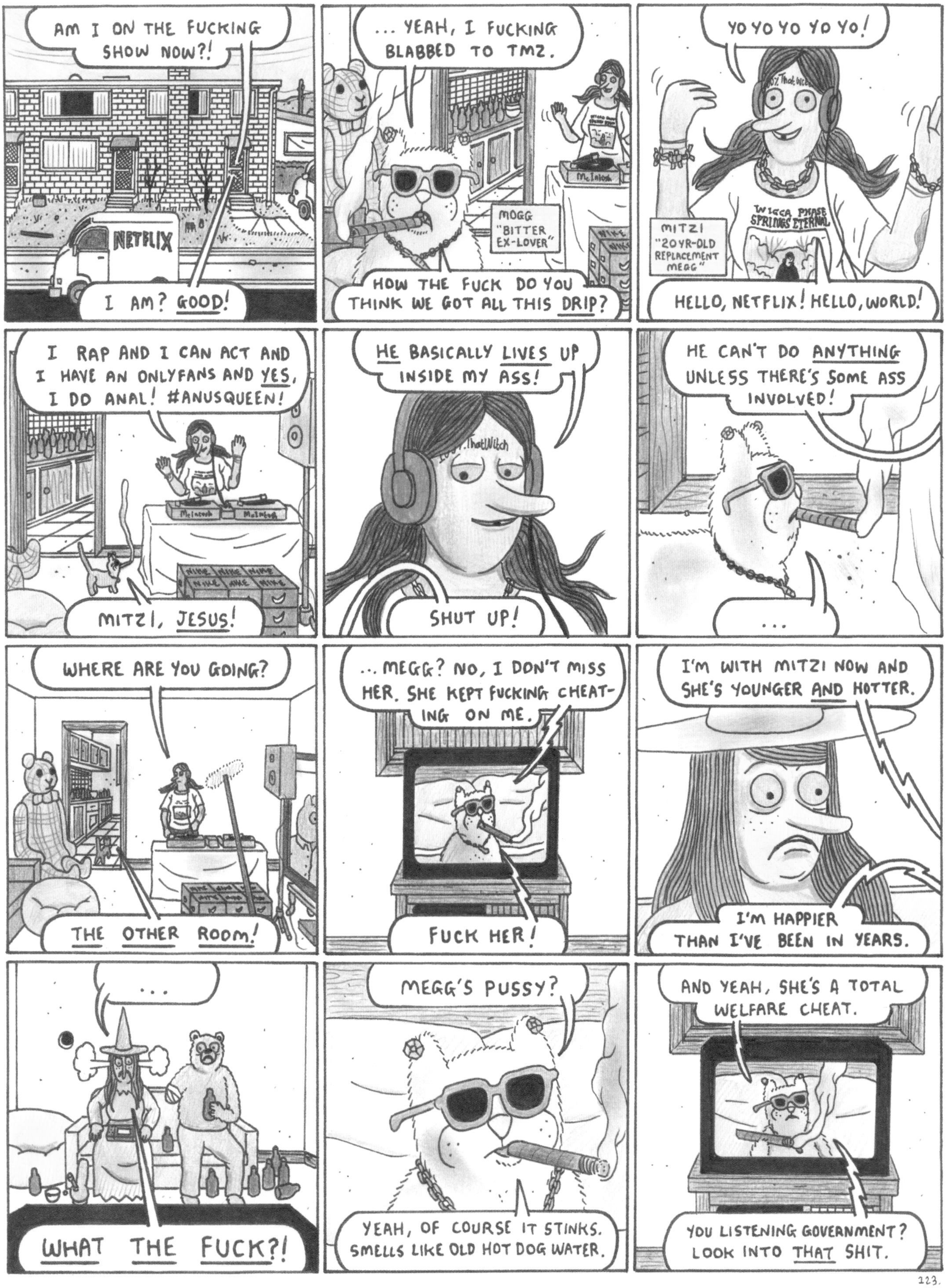

AM I ON THE FUCKING SHOW NOW?!
NETFLIX
I AM? GOOD!
... YEAH, I FUCKING BLABBED TO TMZ.
MOGG "BITTER EX-LOVER"
HOW THE FUCK DO YOU THINK WE GOT ALL THIS DRIP?
YO YO YO YO YO!
WICCA PHASE SPRINGS ETERNAL
MITZI "20YR-OLD REPLACEMENT MEGG"
HELLO, NETFLIX! HELLO, WORLD!
I RAP AND I CAN ACT AND I HAVE AN ONLYFANS AND YES, I DO ANAL! #ANUSQUEEN!
MITZI, JESUS!
HE BASICALLY LIVES UP INSIDE MY ASS!
100% That Witch
SHUT UP!
HE CAN'T DO ANYTHING UNLESS THERE'S SOME ASS INVOLVED!
...
WHERE ARE YOU GOING?
THE OTHER ROOM!
... MEGG? NO, I DON'T MISS HER. SHE KEPT FUCKING CHEATING ON ME.
FUCK HER!
I'M WITH MITZI NOW AND SHE'S YOUNGER AND HOTTER.
I'M HAPPIER THAN I'VE BEEN IN YEARS.
...
WHAT THE FUCK?!
MEGG'S PUSSY?
YEAH, OF COURSE IT STINKS. SMELLS LIKE OLD HOT DOG WATER.
AND YEAH, SHE'S A TOTAL WELFARE CHEAT.
YOU LISTENING GOVERNMENT? LOOK INTO THAT SHIT.

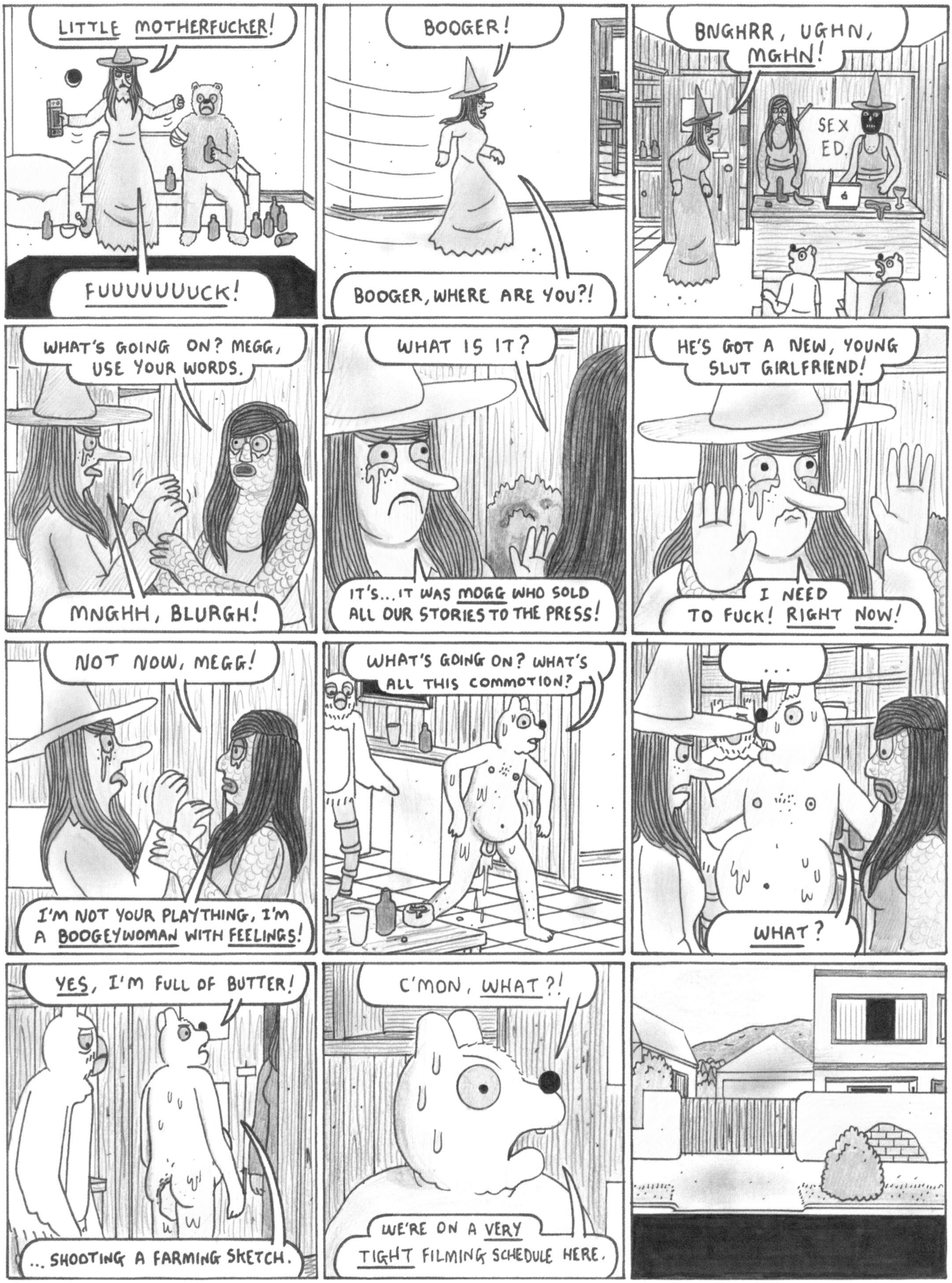
LITTLE MOTHERFUCKER!
FUUUUUUUCK!
BOOGER!
BOOGER, WHERE ARE YOU?!
BNGHRR, UGHN, MGHN!
SEX ED.
WHAT'S GOING ON? MEGG, USE YOUR WORDS.
MNGHH, BLURGH!
WHAT IS IT?
IT'S... IT WAS MOGG WHO SOLD ALL OUR STORIES TO THE PRESS!
HE'S GOT A NEW, YOUNG SLUT GIRLFRIEND!
I NEED TO FUCK! RIGHT NOW!
NOT NOW, MEGG!
I'M NOT YOUR PLAYTHING, I'M A BOOGEYWOMAN WITH FEELINGS!
WHAT'S GOING ON? WHAT'S ALL THIS COMMOTION?
...
WHAT?
YES, I'M FULL OF BUTTER!
... SHOOTING A FARMING SKETCH.
C'MON, WHAT?!
WE'RE ON A VERY TIGHT FILMING SCHEDULE HERE.

Panel 1: TWO CAN PLAY AT THAT GAME! ... LET'S SEE HOW HE LIKES IT!

Panel 2: MOGG SEXUALLY ASSAULTED ME IN 2014. I WAS ASLEEP AND I AWOKE TO FIND HIM FEASTING UPON MY RECTUM. ... HOW COULD I CONSENT?! I WAS ASLEEP!

Panel 3: BOOM! ... SLAM DUNK. RETWEET THAT.

Panel 4: DIDN'T YOU TELL ME THAT ONCE, MOGG "PRETENDED" TO BE A "PEDOPHILE" AND BROKE INTO A CHILDREN'S DANCE CLASS? ... YES. AND HE URINATED INTO A CUP AND MADE ME THROW IT AT A SECURITY GUARD.

Panel 5: DISGUSTING! ... THAT'S SOME SICK STUFF! I NEVER!

Panel 6: OWL, I BELIEVE, ONCE, MOGG DEFECATED INTO YOUR FOOD AS A "PRANK"... ... HE COULD HAVE KILLED HIM!

Panel 7: WHAT?... YEAH... ... WHATEVER... I DON'T KNOW...

Panel 8: AY YO, ONE TIME I WAS OUT OF IT AND TOUCHING MOGG'S BELLY AND HE JUST WENT FUCKING NUTS. SCRATCHED ME UP REAL BAD. ... MMM... WELL, IT KINDA SOUNDS LIKE YOU ASSAULTED HIM, IAN...

Panel 9: ... I FUCKED HIM ONCE. ... HE HAS A VERY PRETTY DICK. VERY WHOLESOME. "ALL AMERICAN".

Panel 10: ... THEY SAID WHAT?! ... ...YEAH, IT'S ALL TRUE! THAT AIN'T THE HALF OF IT! I'M A BAD BOY! BREDDOW™!

Panel 11: I OWN ALL OF MY SHIT

Panel 12: I DARE THEM TO DO THE SAME— ... UGHN!! ... OH, DAMN!

125.

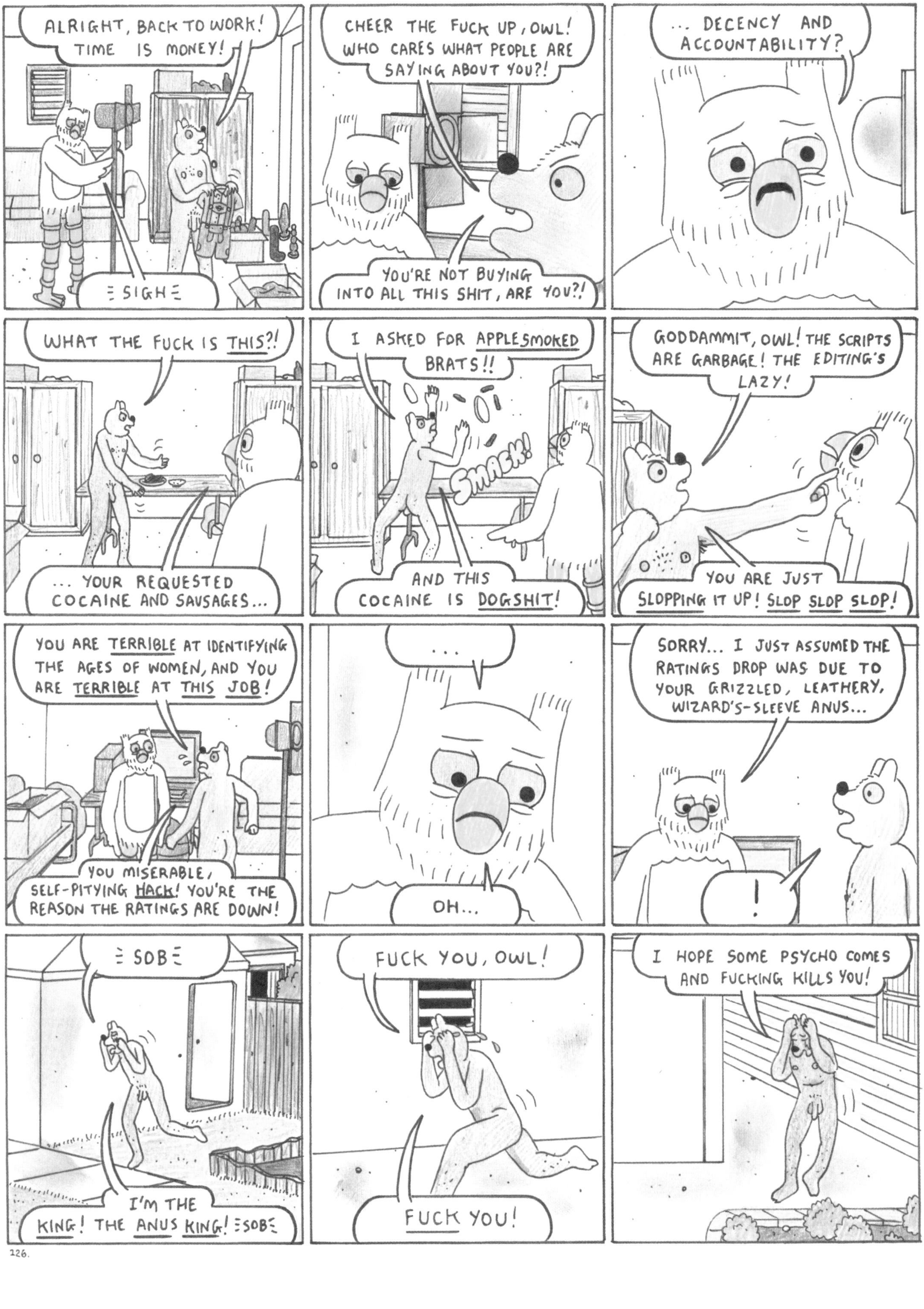
ALRIGHT, BACK TO WORK! TIME IS MONEY!
≡ SIGH ≡
CHEER THE FUCK UP, OWL! WHO CARES WHAT PEOPLE ARE SAYING ABOUT YOU?!
YOU'RE NOT BUYING INTO ALL THIS SHIT, ARE YOU?!
... DECENCY AND ACCOUNTABILITY?
WHAT THE FUCK IS THIS?!
... YOUR REQUESTED COCAINE AND SAUSAGES...
I ASKED FOR APPLESMOKED BRATS!!
SMACK!
AND THIS COCAINE IS DOGSHIT!
GODDAMMIT, OWL! THE SCRIPTS ARE GARBAGE! THE EDITING'S LAZY!
YOU ARE JUST SLOPPING IT UP! SLOP SLOP SLOP!
YOU ARE TERRIBLE AT IDENTIFYING THE AGES OF WOMEN, AND YOU ARE TERRIBLE AT THIS JOB!
YOU MISERABLE, SELF-PITYING HACK! YOU'RE THE REASON THE RATINGS ARE DOWN!
...
OH...
SORRY... I JUST ASSUMED THE RATINGS DROP WAS DUE TO YOUR GRIZZLED, LEATHERY, WIZARD'S-SLEEVE ANUS...
!
≡ SOB ≡
I'M THE KING! THE ANUS KING! ≡SOB≡
FUCK YOU, OWL!
FUCK YOU!
I HOPE SOME PSYCHO COMES AND FUCKING KILLS YOU!

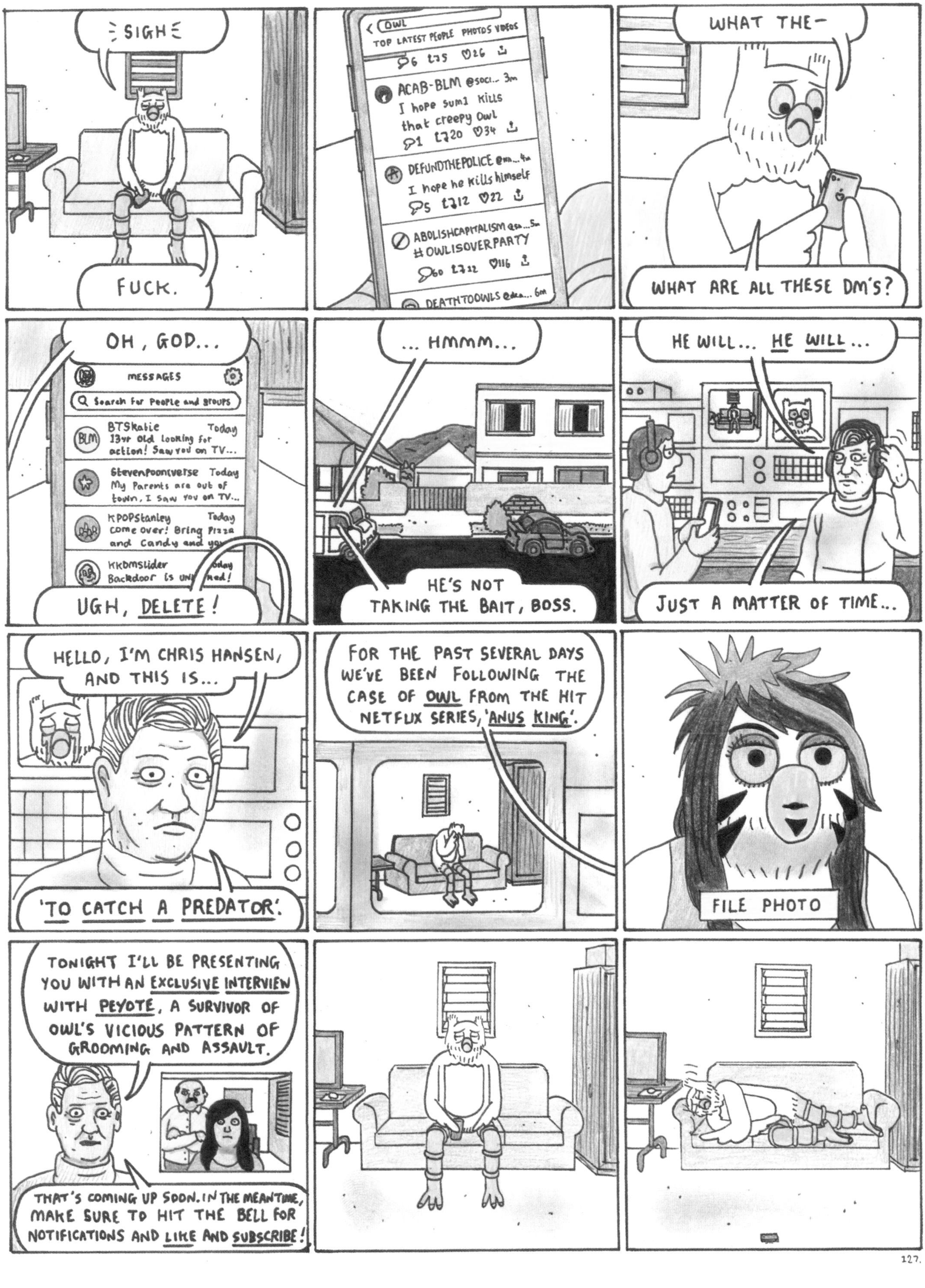
SIGH
FUCK.
OWL
TOP LATEST PEOPLE PHOTOS VIDEOS
ACAB-BLM
I hope sum1 kills that creepy Owl
DEFUNDTHEPOLICE
I hope he kills himself
ABOLISHCAPITALISM
#OWLISOVERPARTY
DEATHTOOWLS
WHAT THE-
WHAT ARE ALL THESE DM'S?
OH, GOD...
MESSAGES
Search for people and groups
BTSkatie Today
13yr old looking for action! Saw you on TV...
Stevenpoonıverse Today
My parents are out of town, I saw you on TV...
KPOPStanley Today
come over! Bring pizza and candy and you
KKbmslider Today
Backdoor is un med!
UGH, DELETE!
... HMMM...
HE'S NOT TAKING THE BAIT, BOSS.
HE WILL... HE WILL...
JUST A MATTER OF TIME...
HELLO, I'M CHRIS HANSEN, AND THIS IS...
'TO CATCH A PREDATOR'.
FOR THE PAST SEVERAL DAYS WE'VE BEEN FOLLOWING THE CASE OF OWL FROM THE HIT NETFLIX SERIES, 'ANUS KING'.
FILE PHOTO
TONIGHT I'LL BE PRESENTING YOU WITH AN EXCLUSIVE INTERVIEW WITH PEYOTE, A SURVIVOR OF OWL'S VICIOUS PATTERN OF GROOMING AND ASSAULT.
THAT'S COMING UP SOON. IN THE MEANTIME, MAKE SURE TO HIT THE BELL FOR NOTIFICATIONS AND LIKE AND SUBSCRIBE!

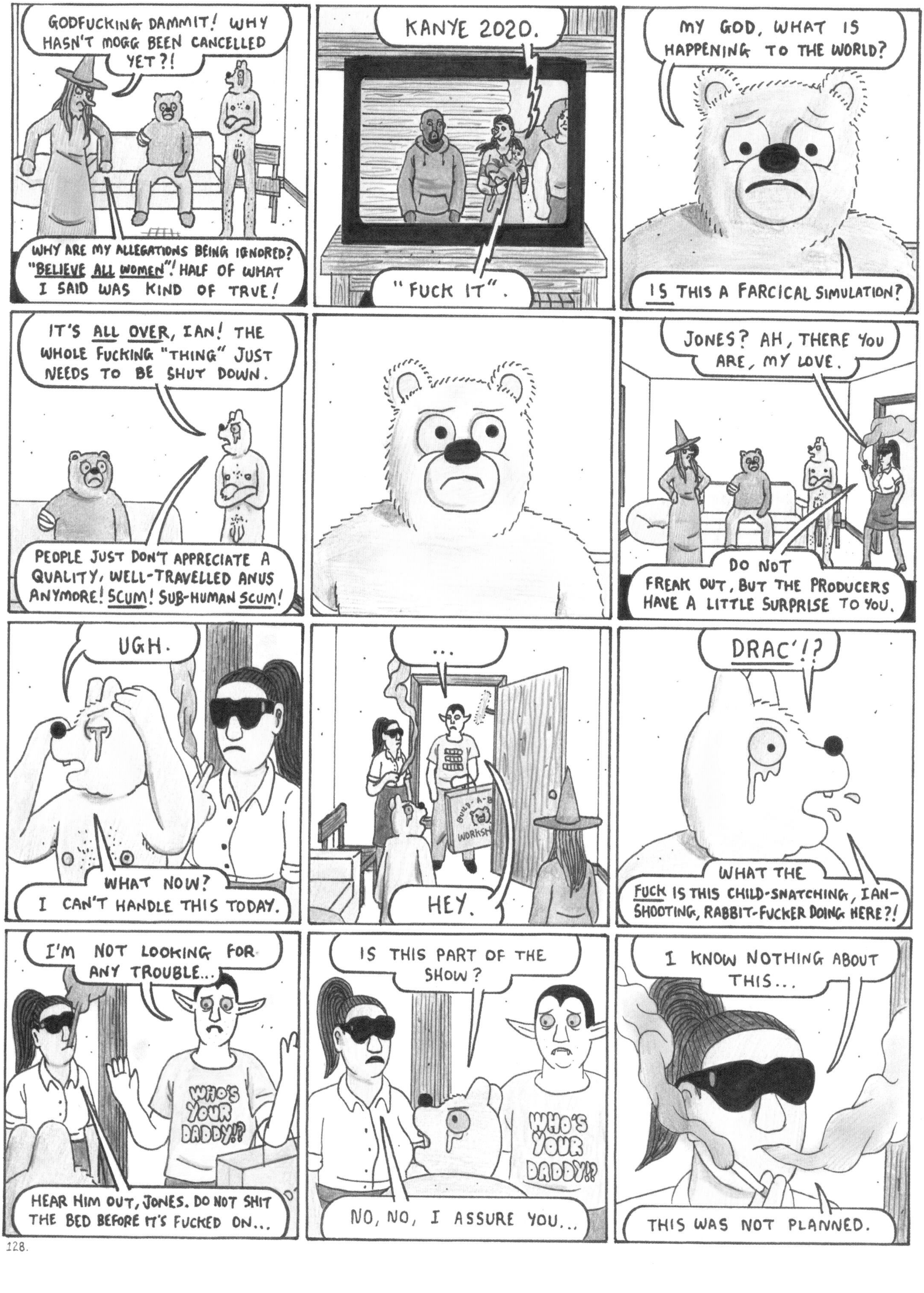
GODFUCKING DAMMIT! WHY HASN'T MOGG BEEN CANCELLED YET?!
WHY ARE MY ALLEGATIONS BEING IGNORED? "BELIEVE ALL WOMEN"! HALF OF WHAT I SAID WAS KIND OF TRUE!
KANYE 2020.
"FUCK IT".
MY GOD, WHAT IS HAPPENING TO THE WORLD?
IS THIS A FARCICAL SIMULATION?
IT'S ALL OVER, IAN! THE WHOLE FUCKING "THING" JUST NEEDS TO BE SHUT DOWN.
PEOPLE JUST DON'T APPRECIATE A QUALITY, WELL-TRAVELLED ANUS ANYMORE! SCUM! SUB-HUMAN SCUM!
JONES? AH, THERE YOU ARE, MY LOVE.
DO NOT FREAK OUT, BUT THE PRODUCERS HAVE A LITTLE SURPRISE TO YOU.
UGH.
WHAT NOW? I CAN'T HANDLE THIS TODAY.
...
HEY.
DRAC'!?
WHAT THE FUCK IS THIS CHILD-SNATCHING, IAN-SHOOTING, RABBIT-FUCKER DOING HERE?!
I'M NOT LOOKING FOR ANY TROUBLE...
WHO'S YOUR DADDY!?
HEAR HIM OUT, JONES. DO NOT SHIT THE BED BEFORE IT'S FUCKED ON...
IS THIS PART OF THE SHOW?
WHO'S YOUR DADDY!?
NO, NO, I ASSURE YOU...
I KNOW NOTHING ABOUT THIS...
THIS WAS NOT PLANNED.

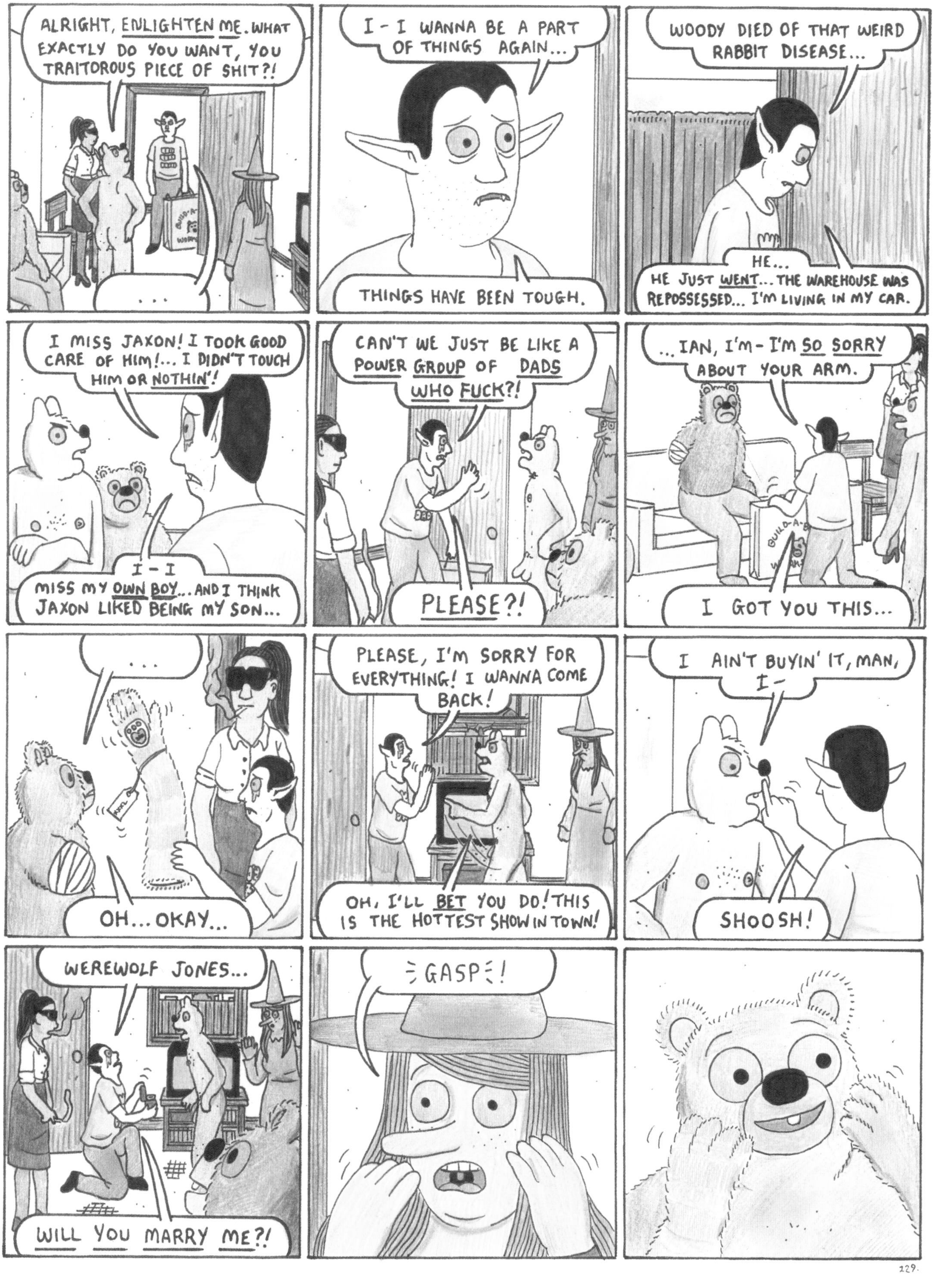

ALRIGHT, ENLIGHTEN ME. WHAT EXACTLY DO YOU WANT, YOU TRAITOROUS PIECE OF SHIT?!
. . .
I - I WANNA BE A PART OF THINGS AGAIN...
THINGS HAVE BEEN TOUGH.
WOODY DIED OF THAT WEIRD RABBIT DISEASE...
HE... HE JUST WENT... THE WAREHOUSE WAS REPOSSESSED... I'M LIVING IN MY CAR.
I MISS JAXON! I TOOK GOOD CARE OF HIM!... I DIDN'T TOUCH HIM OR NOTHIN'!
I - I MISS MY OWN BOY... AND I THINK JAXON LIKED BEING MY SON...
CAN'T WE JUST BE LIKE A POWER GROUP OF DADS WHO FUCK?!
PLEASE?!
... IAN, I'M - I'M SO SORRY ABOUT YOUR ARM.
I GOT YOU THIS...
. . .
OH... OKAY...
PLEASE, I'M SORRY FOR EVERYTHING! I WANNA COME BACK!
OH, I'LL BET YOU DO! THIS IS THE HOTTEST SHOW IN TOWN!
I AIN'T BUYIN' IT, MAN, I-
SHOOSH!
WEREWOLF JONES...
WILL YOU MARRY ME?!
GASP!

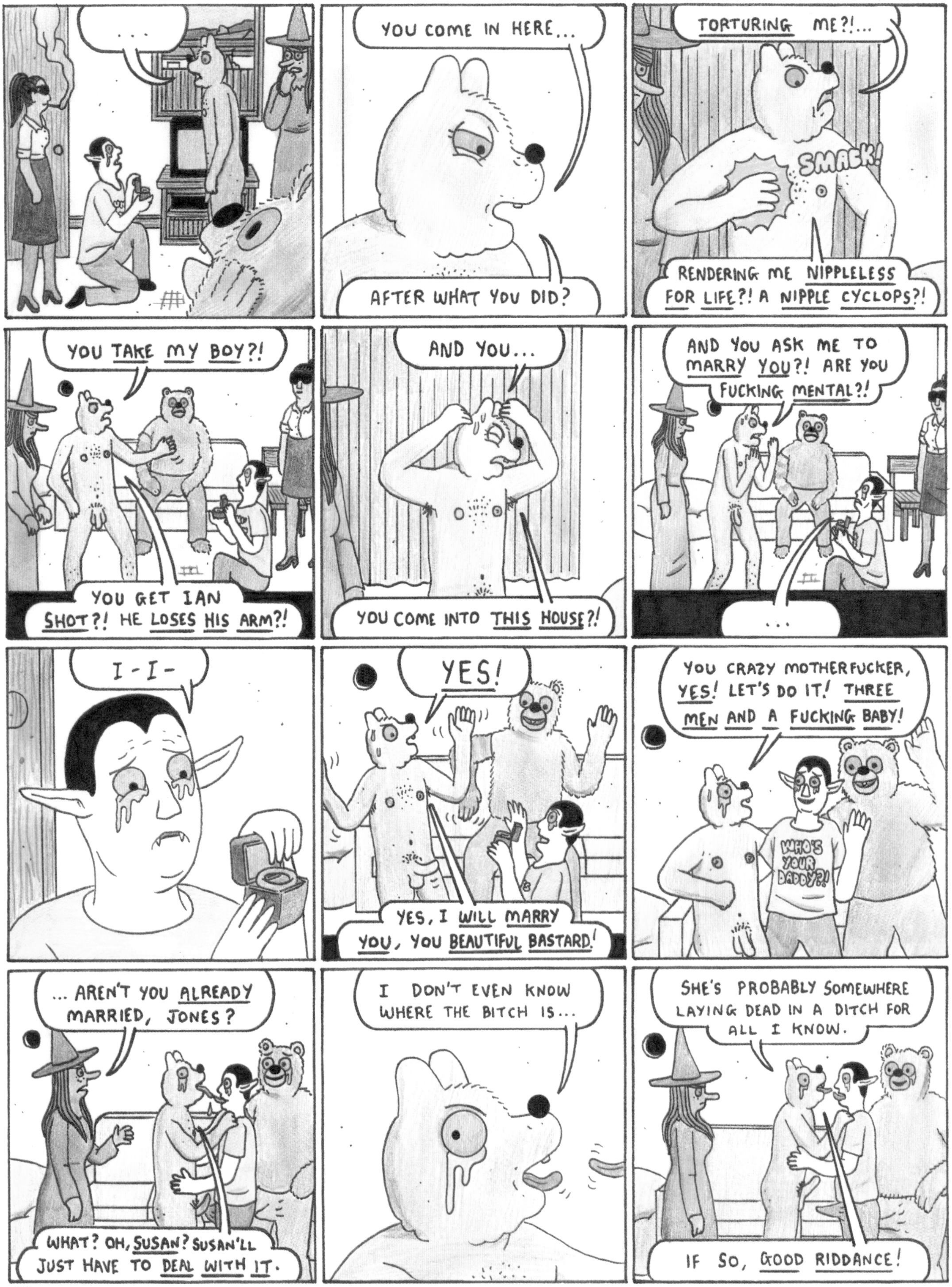
. . .
YOU COME IN HERE...
AFTER WHAT YOU DID?
TORTURING ME?!...
SMACK!
RENDERING ME NIPPLELESS FOR LIFE?! A NIPPLE CYCLOPS?!
YOU TAKE MY BOY?!
YOU GET IAN SHOT?! HE LOSES HIS ARM?!
AND YOU...
YOU COME INTO THIS HOUSE?!
AND YOU ASK ME TO MARRY YOU?! ARE YOU FUCKING MENTAL?!
. . .
I-I-
YES!
YES, I WILL MARRY YOU, YOU BEAUTIFUL BASTARD!
YOU CRAZY MOTHERFUCKER, YES! LET'S DO IT! THREE MEN AND A FUCKING BABY!
WHO'S YOUR DADDY?!
... AREN'T YOU ALREADY MARRIED, JONES?
WHAT? OH, SUSAN? SUSAN'LL JUST HAVE TO DEAL WITH IT.
I DON'T EVEN KNOW WHERE THE BITCH IS...
SHE'S PROBABLY SOMEWHERE LAYING DEAD IN A DITCH FOR ALL I KNOW.
IF SO, GOOD RIDDANCE!

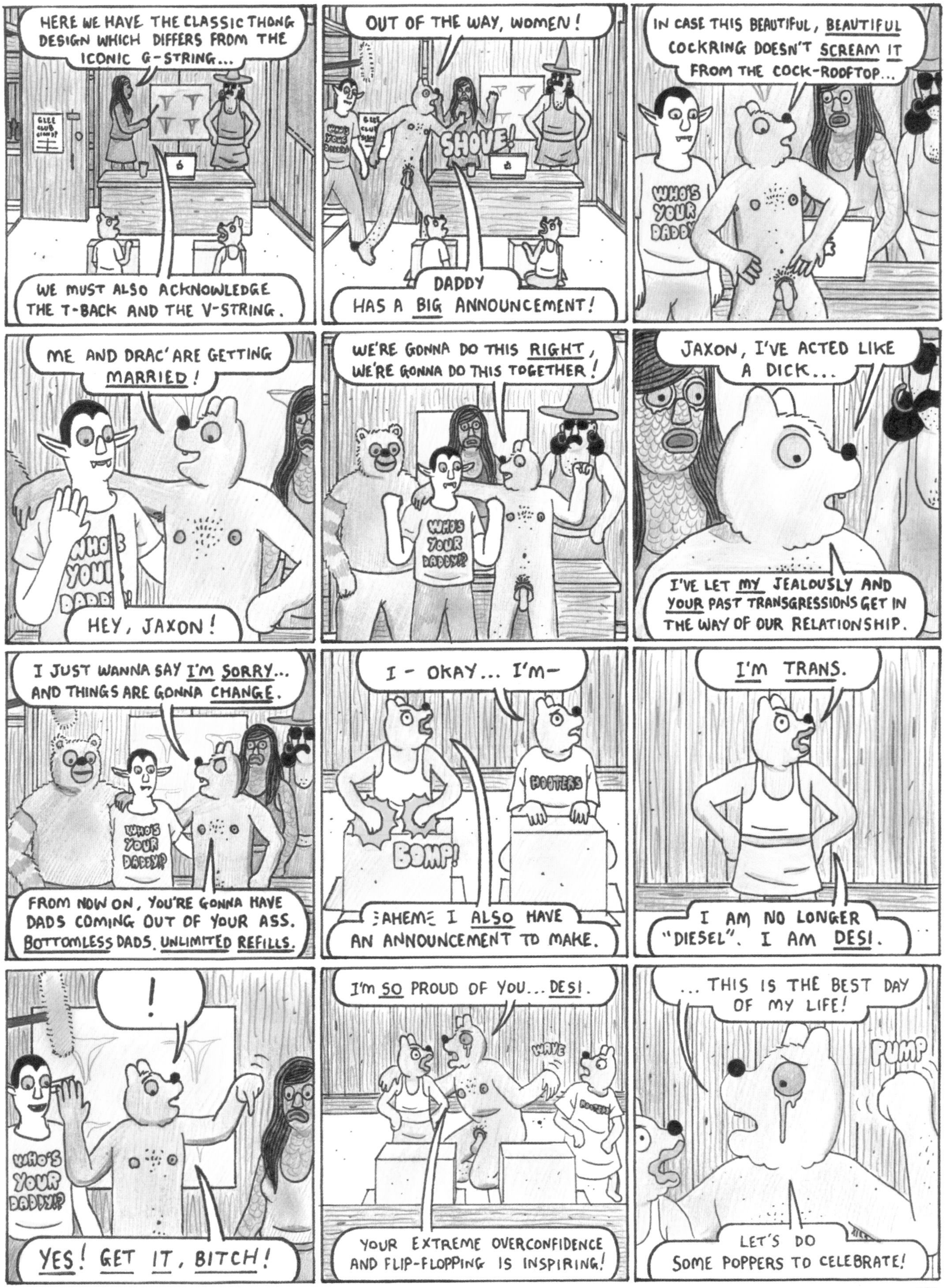
HERE WE HAVE THE CLASSIC THONG DESIGN WHICH DIFFERS FROM THE ICONIC G-STRING...
GLEE CLUB SIGN UP!
WE MUST ALSO ACKNOWLEDGE THE T-BACK AND THE V-STRING.
OUT OF THE WAY, WOMEN!
WHO'S YOUR DADDY
SHOVE!
DADDY HAS A BIG ANNOUNCEMENT!
IN CASE THIS BEAUTIFUL, BEAUTIFUL COCKRING DOESN'T SCREAM IT FROM THE COCK-ROOFTOP...
WHO'S YOUR DADDY
ME AND DRAC' ARE GETTING MARRIED!
HEY, JAXON!
WE'RE GONNA DO THIS RIGHT, WE'RE GONNA DO THIS TOGETHER!
WHO'S YOUR DADDY!?
JAXON, I'VE ACTED LIKE A DICK...
I'VE LET MY JEALOUSLY AND YOUR PAST TRANSGRESSIONS GET IN THE WAY OF OUR RELATIONSHIP.
I JUST WANNA SAY I'M SORRY... AND THINGS ARE GONNA CHANGE.
WHO'S YOUR DADDY!?
FROM NOW ON, YOU'RE GONNA HAVE DADS COMING OUT OF YOUR ASS. BOTTOMLESS DADS. UNLIMITED REFILLS.
I - OKAY... I'M-
HOOTERS
BOMP!
AHEM I ALSO HAVE AN ANNOUNCEMENT TO MAKE.
I'M TRANS.
I AM NO LONGER "DIESEL". I AM DESI.
!
WHO'S YOUR DADDY!?
YES! GET IT, BITCH!
I'M SO PROUD OF YOU... DESI.
WAVE
HOOTERS
YOUR EXTREME OVERCONFIDENCE AND FLIP-FLOPPING IS INSPIRING!
... THIS IS THE BEST DAY OF MY LIFE!
PUMP
LET'S DO SOME POPPERS TO CELEBRATE!

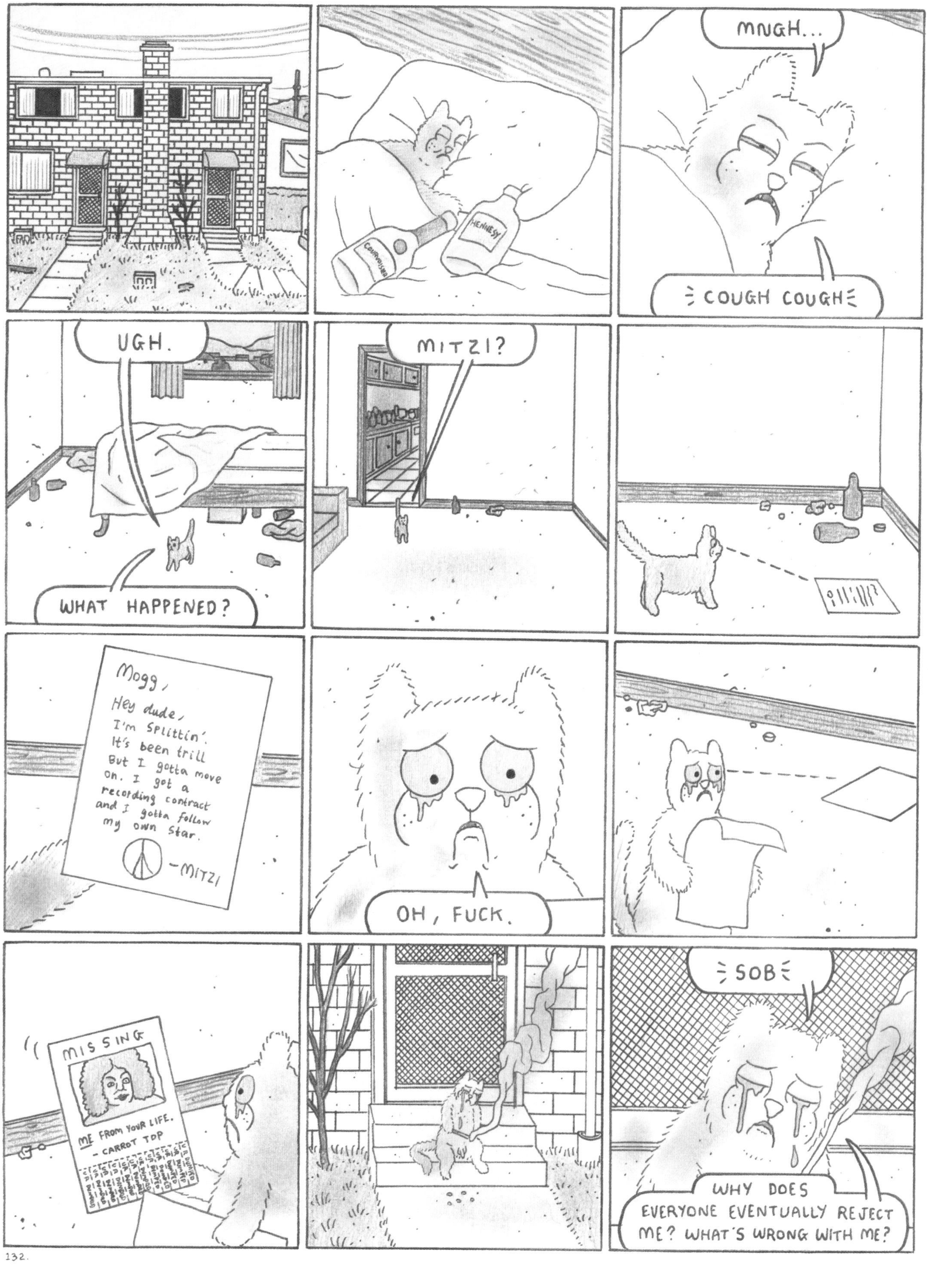
COURVOISIER
HENNESY
MNGH...
COUGH COUGH
UGH.
WHAT HAPPENED?
MITZI?
Mogg,
Hey dude,
I'm splittin'.
It's been trill
But I gotta move
on. I got a
recording contract
and I gotta follow
my own star.
-MITZI
OH, FUCK.
MISSING
ME FROM YOUR LIFE.
- CARROT TOP
SOB
WHY DOES
EVERYONE EVENTUALLY REJECT
ME? WHAT'S WRONG WITH ME?

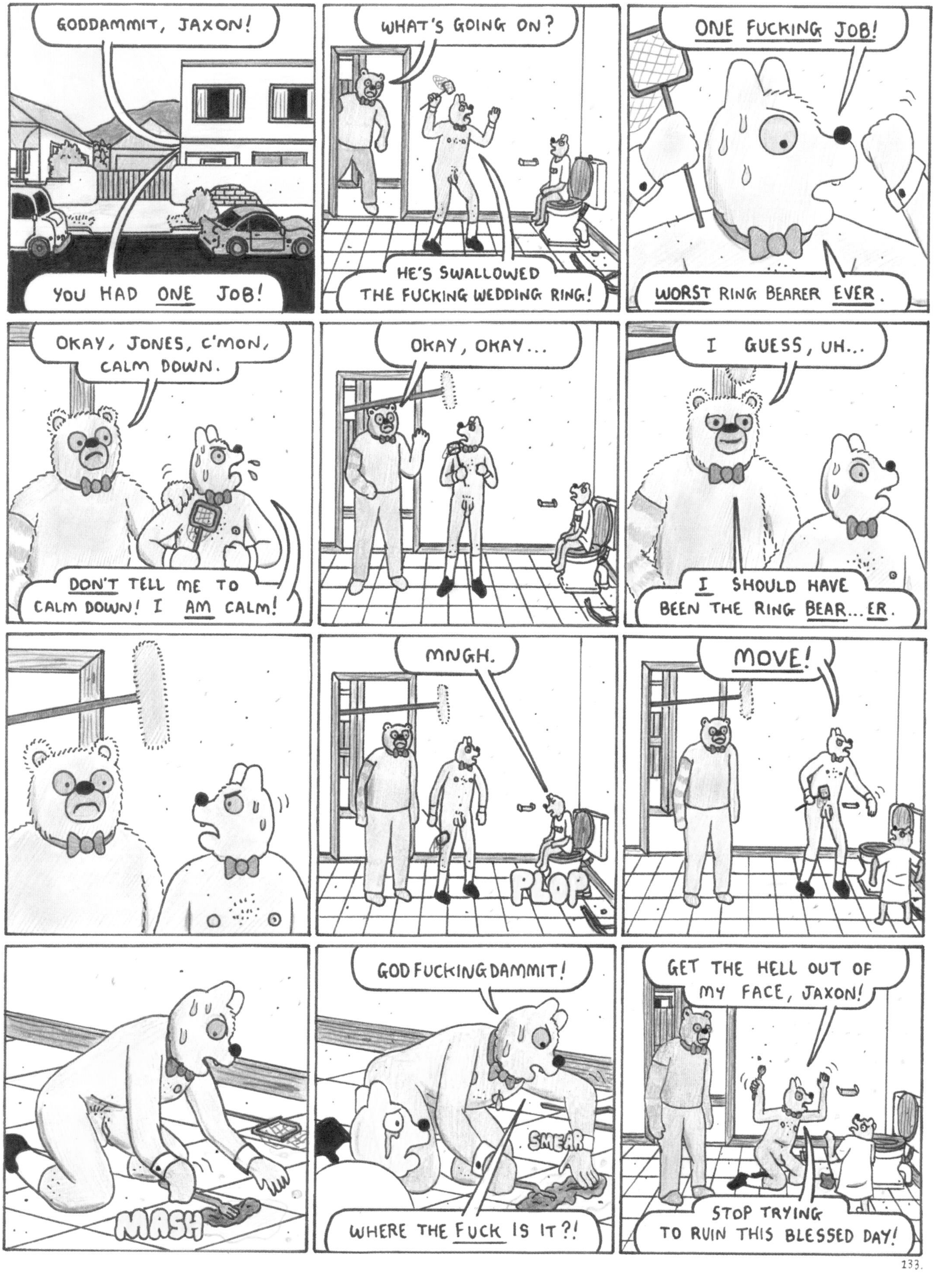
GODDAMMIT, JAXON!
YOU HAD ONE JOB!
WHAT'S GOING ON?
HE'S SWALLOWED THE FUCKING WEDDING RING!
ONE FUCKING JOB!
WORST RING BEARER EVER.
OKAY, JONES, C'MON, CALM DOWN.
DON'T TELL ME TO CALM DOWN! I AM CALM!
OKAY, OKAY...
I GUESS, UH...
I SHOULD HAVE BEEN THE RING BEAR... ER.
MNGH.
PLOP
MOVE!
MASH
GODFUCKINGDAMMIT!
SMEAR
WHERE THE FUCK IS IT?!
GET THE HELL OUT OF MY FACE, JAXON!
STOP TRYING TO RUIN THIS BLESSED DAY!

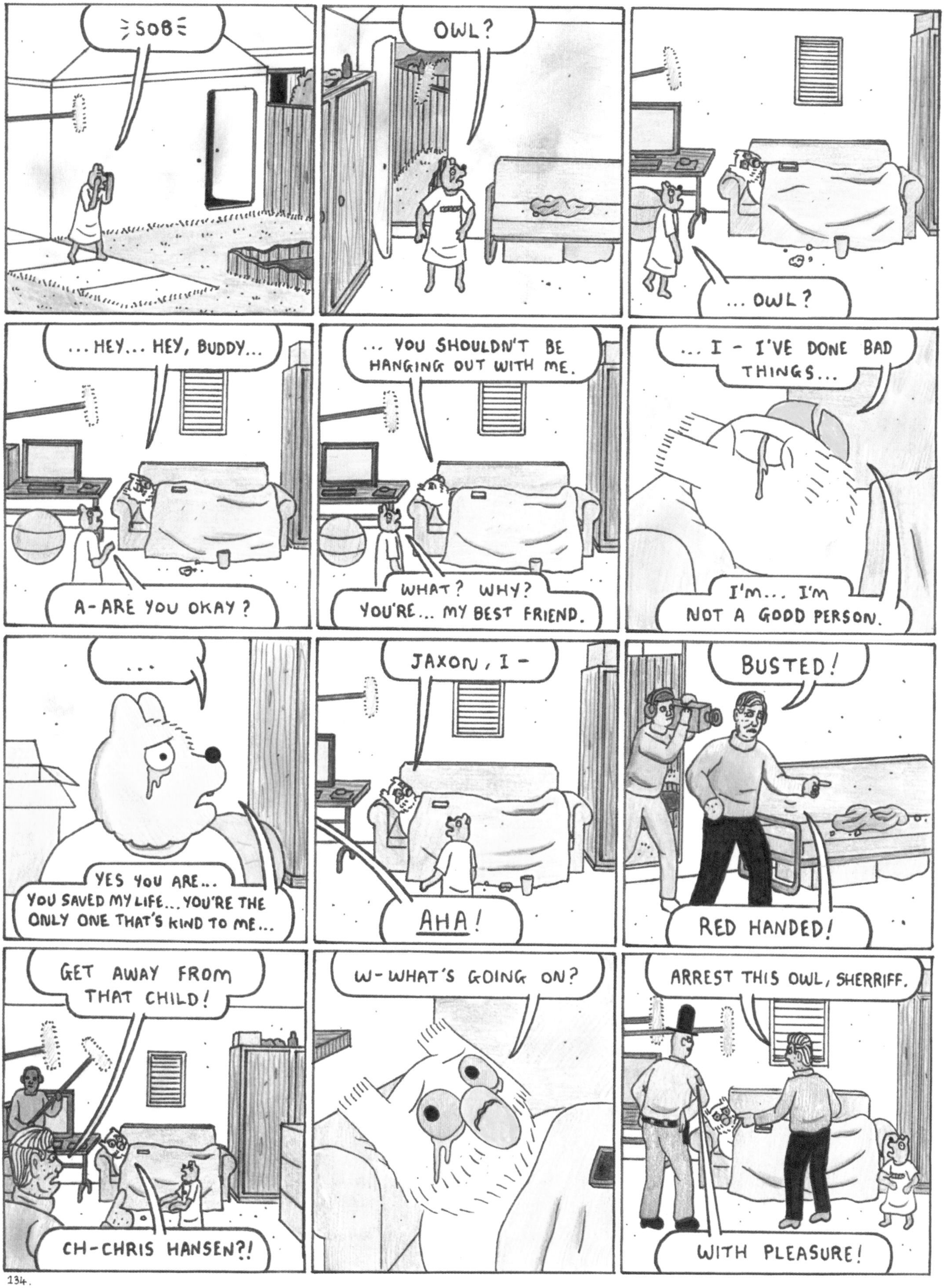
SOB
OWL?
... OWL?
... HEY... HEY, BUDDY...
A-ARE YOU OKAY?
... YOU SHOULDN'T BE HANGING OUT WITH ME.
WHAT? WHY? YOU'RE... MY BEST FRIEND.
... I - I'VE DONE BAD THINGS...
I'M... I'M NOT A GOOD PERSON.
...
YES YOU ARE... YOU SAVED MY LIFE... YOU'RE THE ONLY ONE THAT'S KIND TO ME...
JAXON, I -
AHA!
BUSTED!
RED HANDED!
GET AWAY FROM THAT CHILD!
CH-CHRIS HANSEN?!
W-WHAT'S GOING ON?
ARREST THIS OWL, SHERRIFF.
WITH PLEASURE!

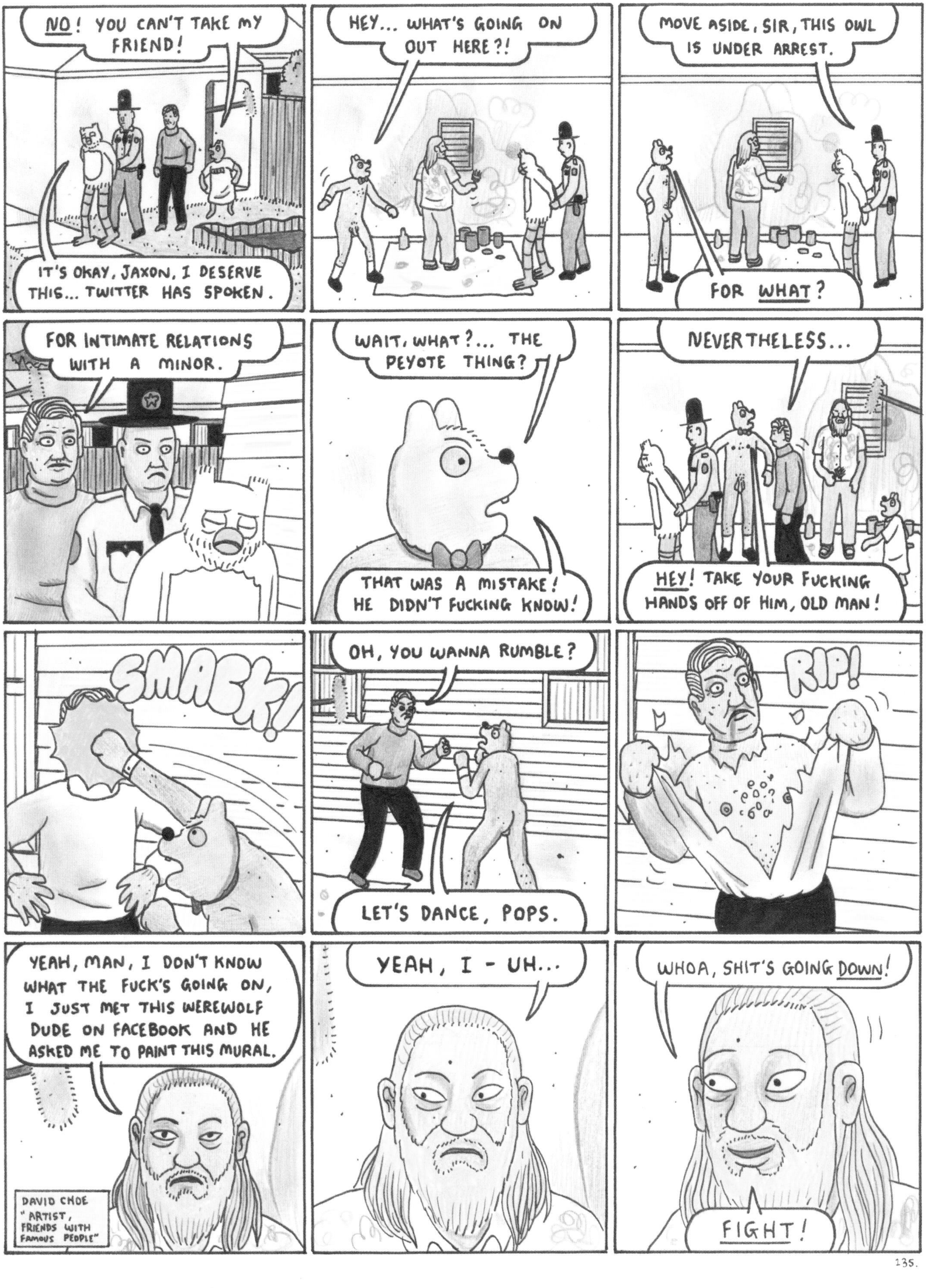
NO! YOU CAN'T TAKE MY FRIEND!
IT'S OKAY, JAXON, I DESERVE THIS... TWITTER HAS SPOKEN.
HEY... WHAT'S GOING ON OUT HERE?!
MOVE ASIDE, SIR, THIS OWL IS UNDER ARREST.
FOR WHAT?
FOR INTIMATE RELATIONS WITH A MINOR.
WAIT, WHAT?... THE PEYOTE THING?
THAT WAS A MISTAKE! HE DIDN'T FUCKING KNOW!
NEVERTHELESS...
HEY! TAKE YOUR FUCKING HANDS OFF OF HIM, OLD MAN!
SMACK!
OH, YOU WANNA RUMBLE?
LET'S DANCE, POPS.
RIP!
YEAH, MAN, I DON'T KNOW WHAT THE FUCK'S GOING ON, I JUST MET THIS WEREWOLF DUDE ON FACEBOOK AND HE ASKED ME TO PAINT THIS MURAL.
DAVID CHOE "ARTIST, FRIENDS WITH FAMOUS PEOPLE"
YEAH, I - UH...
WHOA, SHIT'S GOING DOWN!
FIGHT!

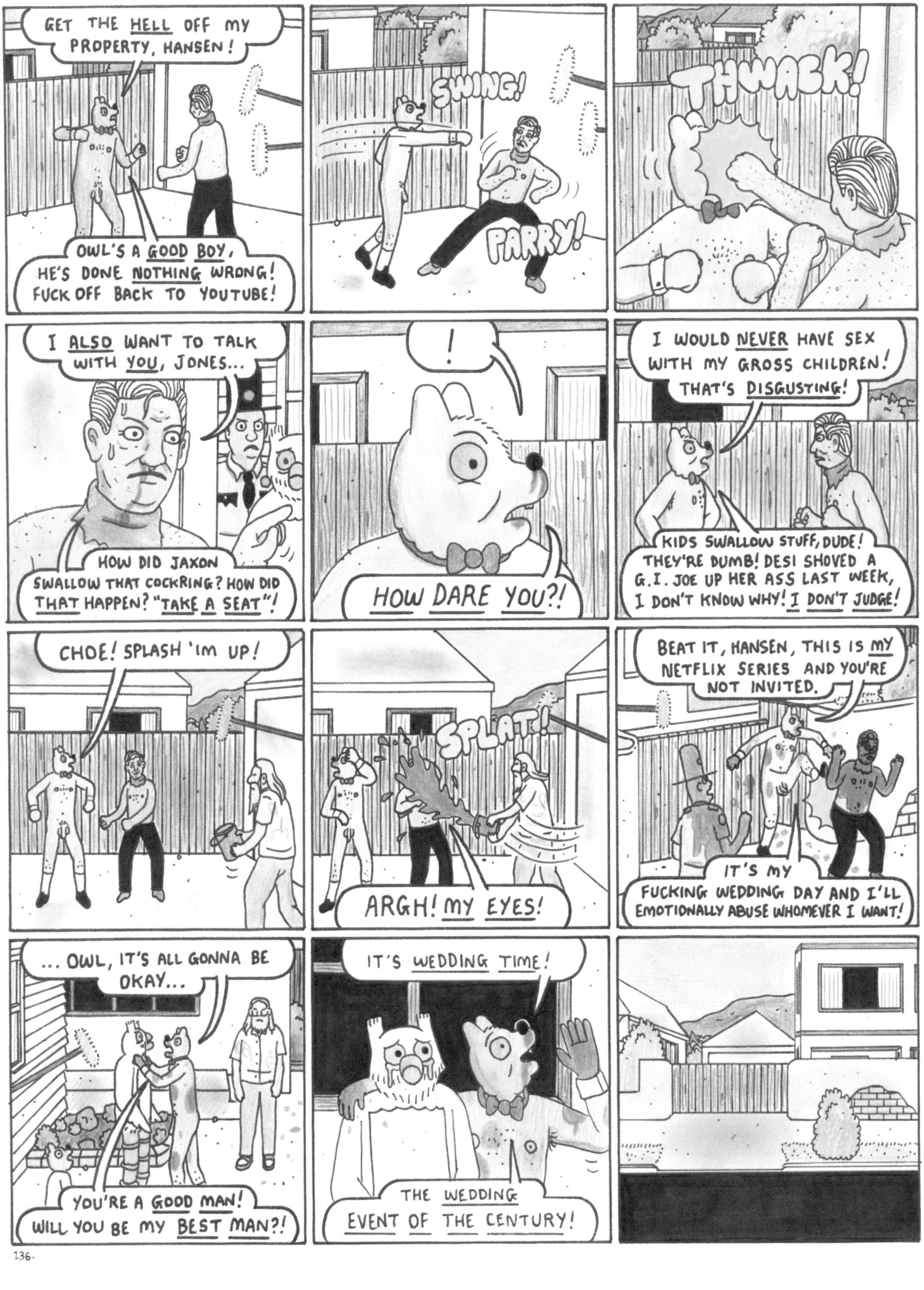
GET THE HELL OFF MY PROPERTY, HANSEN!
OWL'S A GOOD BOY, HE'S DONE NOTHING WRONG! FUCK OFF BACK TO YOUTUBE!
SWING!
PARRY!
THWACK!
I ALSO WANT TO TALK WITH YOU, JONES...
HOW DID JAXON SWALLOW THAT COCKRING? HOW DID THAT HAPPEN? "TAKE A SEAT"!
!
HOW DARE YOU?!
I WOULD NEVER HAVE SEX WITH MY GROSS CHILDREN! THAT'S DISGUSTING!
KIDS SWALLOW STUFF, DUDE! THEY'RE DUMB! DESI SHOVED A G.I. JOE UP HER ASS LAST WEEK, I DON'T KNOW WHY! I DON'T JUDGE!
CHOE! SPLASH 'IM UP!
SPLAT!
ARGH! MY EYES!
BEAT IT, HANSEN, THIS IS MY NETFLIX SERIES AND YOU'RE NOT INVITED.
IT'S MY FUCKING WEDDING DAY AND I'LL EMOTIONALLY ABUSE WHOMEVER I WANT!
... OWL, IT'S ALL GONNA BE OKAY...
YOU'RE A GOOD MAN! WILL YOU BE MY BEST MAN?!
IT'S WEDDING TIME!
THE WEDDING EVENT OF THE CENTURY!

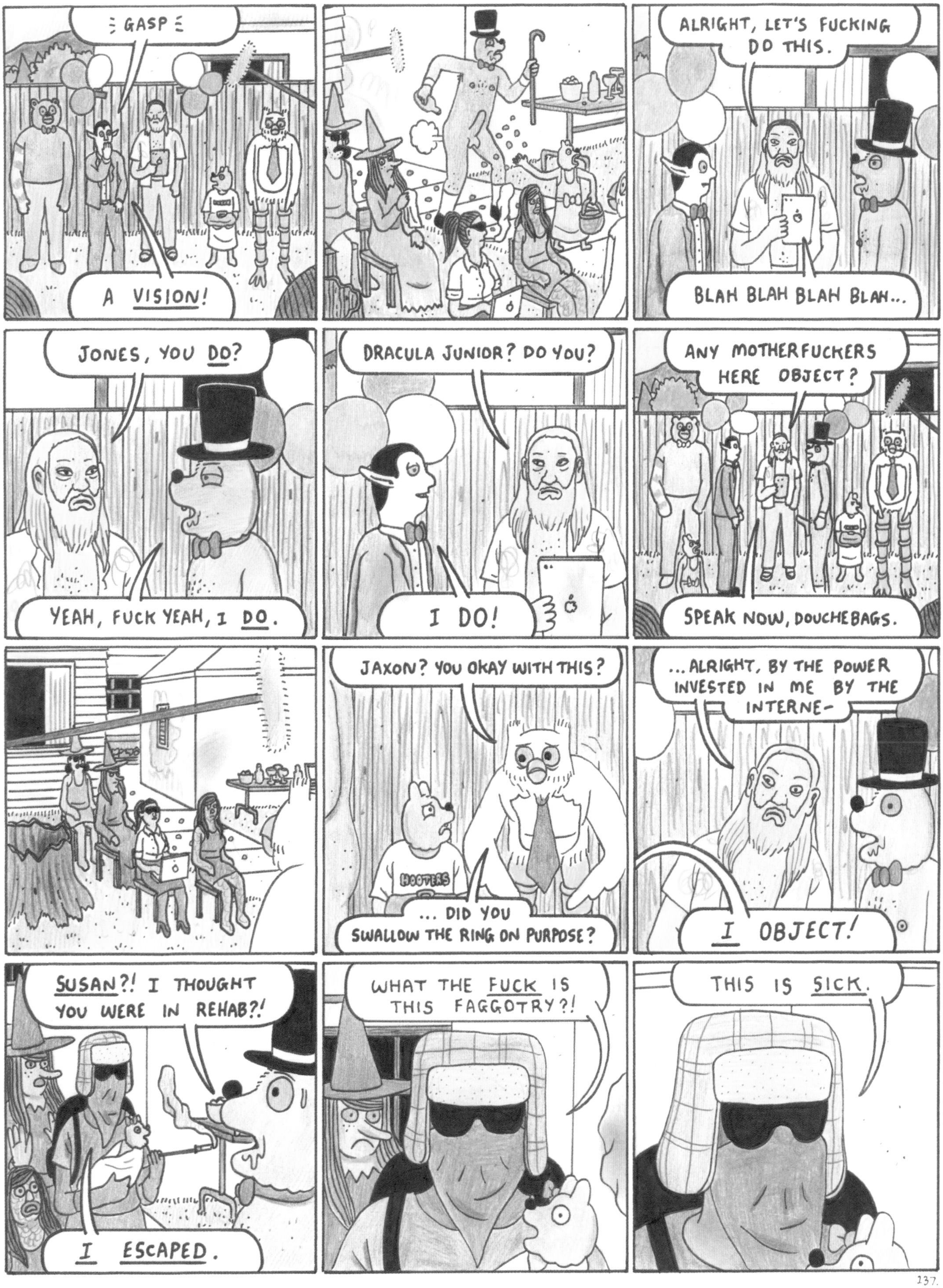

GASP
A VISION!
ALRIGHT, LET'S FUCKING DO THIS.
BLAH BLAH BLAH BLAH...
JONES, YOU DO?
YEAH, FUCK YEAH, I DO.
DRACULA JUNIOR? DO YOU?
I DO!
ANY MOTHERFUCKERS HERE OBJECT?
SPEAK NOW, DOUCHEBAGS.
HOOTERS
JAXON? YOU OKAY WITH THIS?
... DID YOU SWALLOW THE RING ON PURPOSE?
...ALRIGHT, BY THE POWER INVESTED IN ME BY THE INTERNE-
I OBJECT!
SUSAN?! I THOUGHT YOU WERE IN REHAB?!
I ESCAPED.
WHAT THE FUCK IS THIS FAGGOTRY?!
THIS IS SICK.

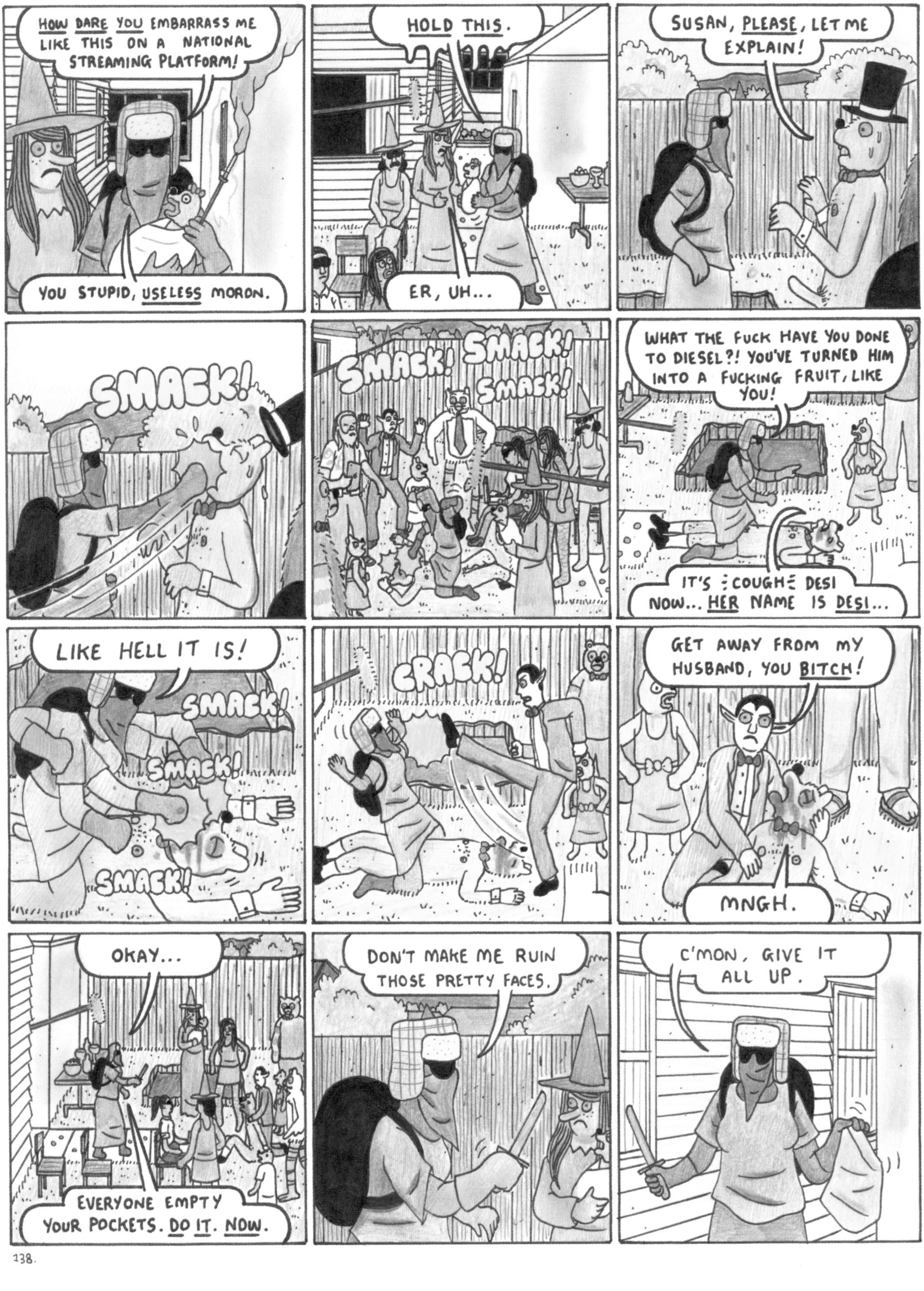

HOW DARE YOU EMBARRASS ME LIKE THIS ON A NATIONAL STREAMING PLATFORM!
YOU STUPID, USELESS MORON.
HOLD THIS.
ER, UH...
SUSAN, PLEASE, LET ME EXPLAIN!
SMACK!
SMACK! SMACK! SMACK!
WHAT THE FUCK HAVE YOU DONE TO DIESEL?! YOU'VE TURNED HIM INTO A FUCKING FRUIT, LIKE YOU!
IT'S COUGH DESI NOW... HER NAME IS DESI...
LIKE HELL IT IS!
SMACK!
SMACK!
SMACK!
CRACK!
GET AWAY FROM MY HUSBAND, YOU BITCH!
MNGH.
OKAY...
EVERYONE EMPTY YOUR POCKETS. DO IT. NOW.
DON'T MAKE ME RUIN THOSE PRETTY FACES.
C'MON, GIVE IT ALL UP.

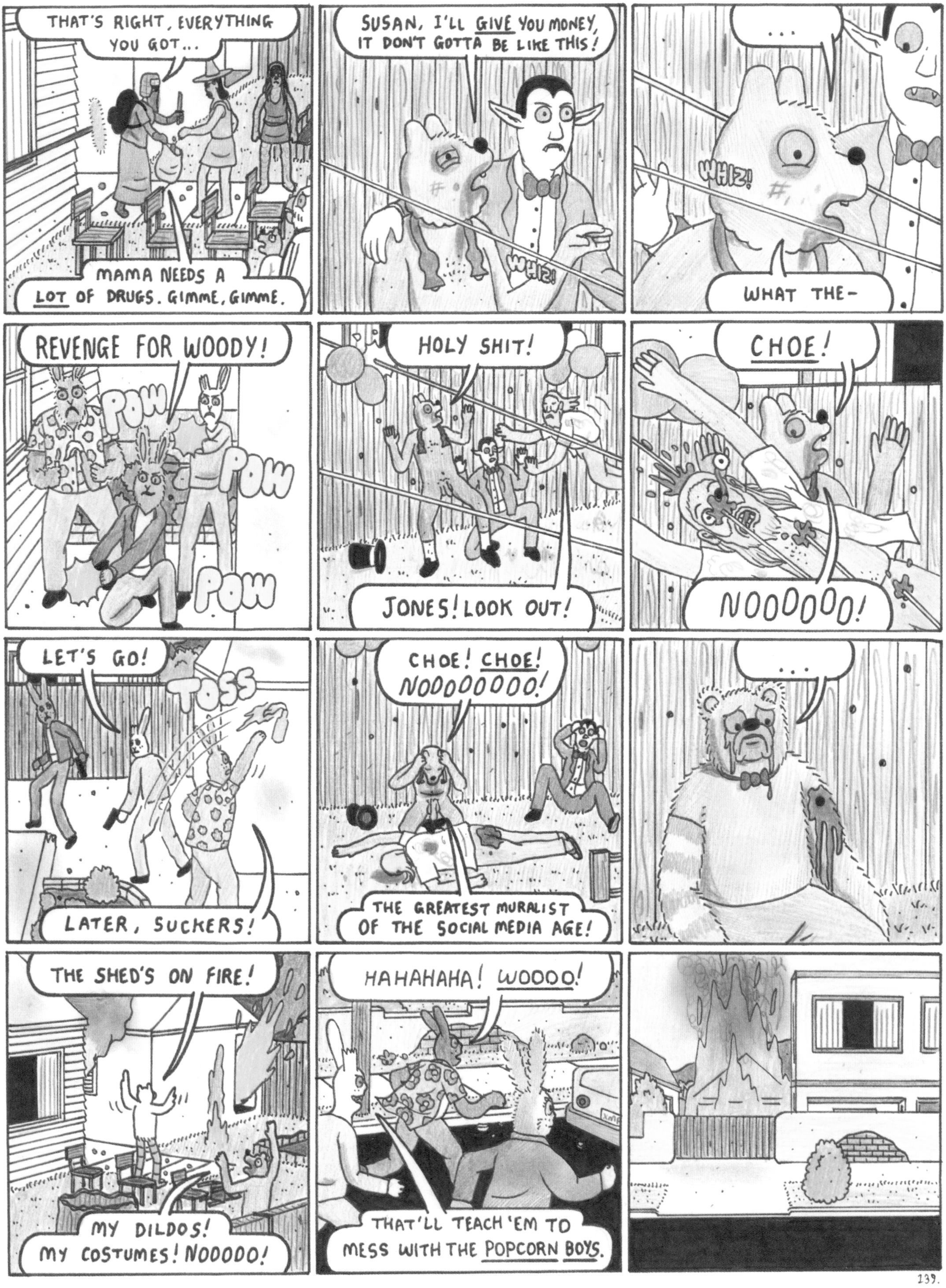
THAT'S RIGHT, EVERYTHING YOU GOT...
MAMA NEEDS A LOT OF DRUGS. GIMME, GIMME.
SUSAN, I'LL GIVE YOU MONEY, IT DON'T GOTTA BE LIKE THIS!
WHIZ!
...
WHIZ!
WHAT THE-
REVENGE FOR WOODY!
POW
POW
POW
HOLY SHIT!
JONES! LOOK OUT!
CHOE!
NOOOOOO!
LET'S GO!
TOSS
LATER, SUCKERS!
CHOE! CHOE! NOOOOOOOO!
THE GREATEST MURALIST OF THE SOCIAL MEDIA AGE!
...
THE SHED'S ON FIRE!
MY DILDOS! MY COSTUMES! NOOOOO!
HAHAHAHA! WOOOO!
THAT'LL TEACH 'EM TO MESS WITH THE POPCORN BOYS.

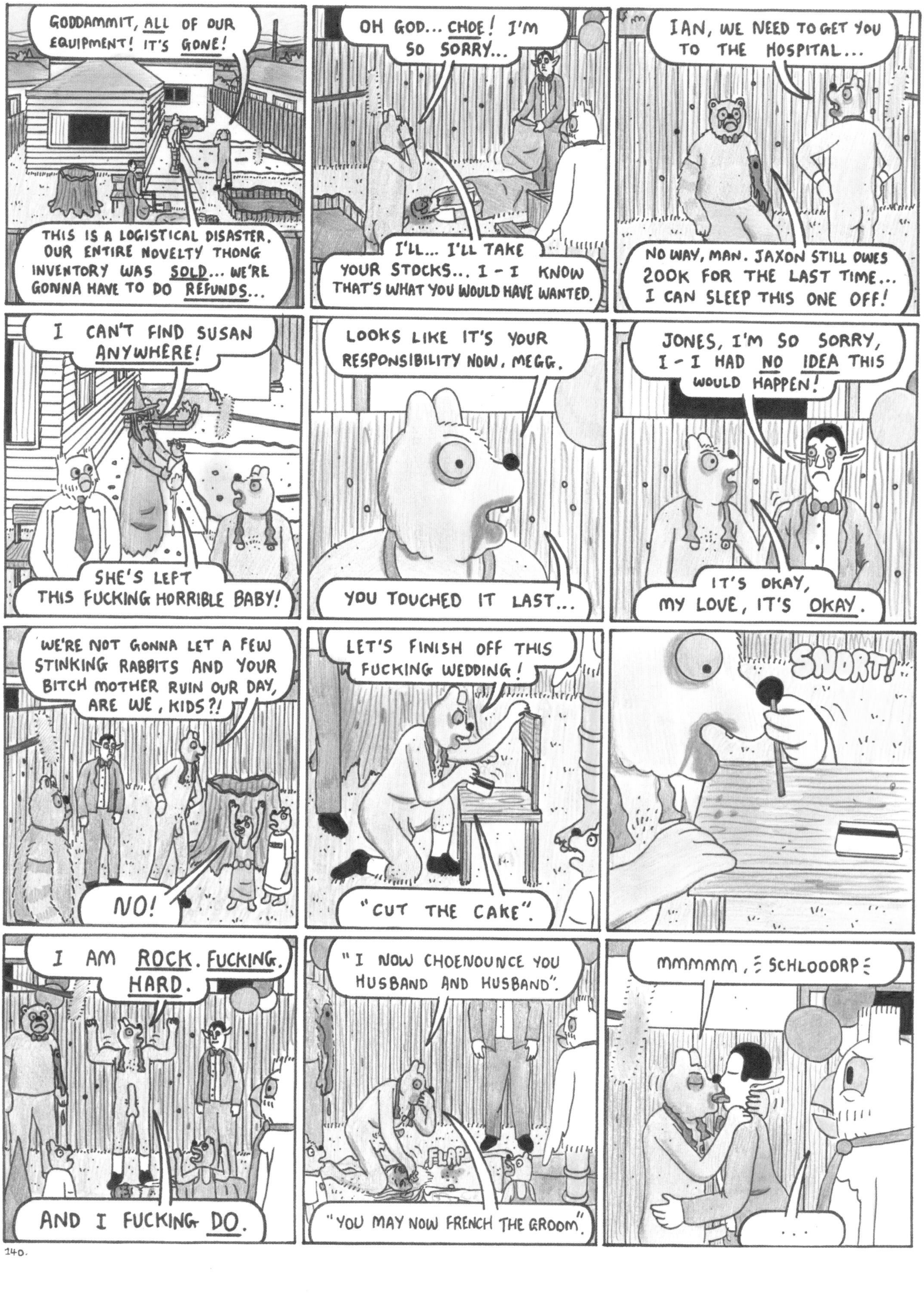
GODDAMMIT, ALL OF OUR EQUIPMENT! IT'S GONE!
THIS IS A LOGISTICAL DISASTER. OUR ENTIRE NOVELTY THONG INVENTORY WAS SOLD... WE'RE GONNA HAVE TO DO REFUNDS...
OH GOD... CHOE! I'M SO SORRY...
I'LL... I'LL TAKE YOUR STOCKS... I - I KNOW THAT'S WHAT YOU WOULD HAVE WANTED.
IAN, WE NEED TO GET YOU TO THE HOSPITAL...
NO WAY, MAN. JAXON STILL OWES 200K FOR THE LAST TIME... I CAN SLEEP THIS ONE OFF!
I CAN'T FIND SUSAN ANYWHERE!
SHE'S LEFT THIS FUCKING HORRIBLE BABY!
LOOKS LIKE IT'S YOUR RESPONSIBILITY NOW, MEGG.
YOU TOUCHED IT LAST...
JONES, I'M SO SORRY, I - I HAD NO IDEA THIS WOULD HAPPEN!
IT'S OKAY, MY LOVE, IT'S OKAY.
WE'RE NOT GONNA LET A FEW STINKING RABBITS AND YOUR BITCH MOTHER RUIN OUR DAY, ARE WE, KIDS?!
NO!
LET'S FINISH OFF THIS FUCKING WEDDING!
"CUT THE CAKE".
SNORT!
I AM ROCK. FUCKING. HARD.
AND I FUCKING DO.
"I NOW CHOENOUNCE YOU HUSBAND AND HUSBAND".
FLAP
"YOU MAY NOW FRENCH THE GROOM".
MMMMM, SCHLOOORP
...

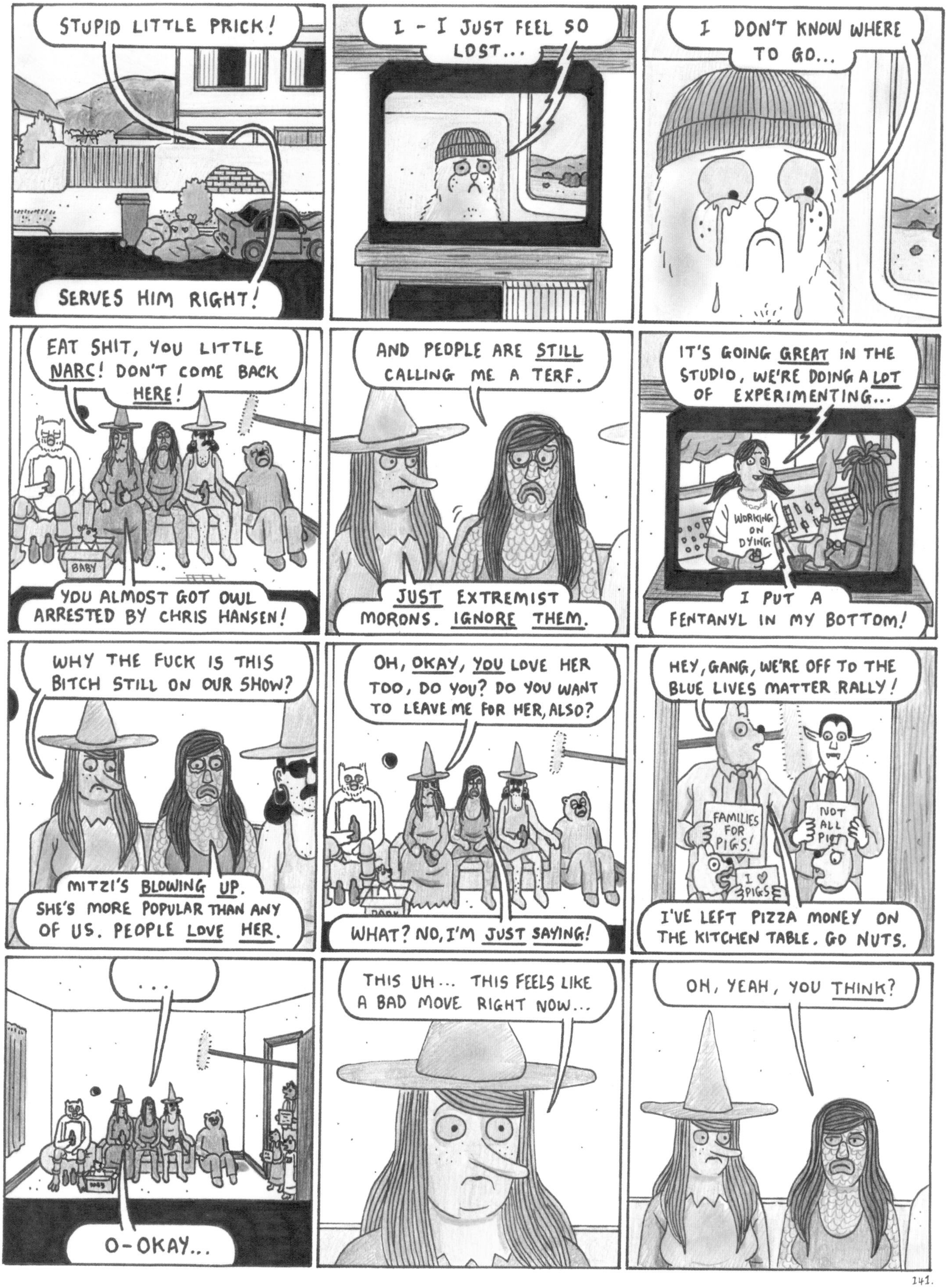

STUPID LITTLE PRICK!
SERVES HIM RIGHT!
I - I JUST FEEL SO LOST...
I DON'T KNOW WHERE TO GO...
EAT SHIT, YOU LITTLE NARC! DON'T COME BACK HERE!
BABY
YOU ALMOST GOT OWL ARRESTED BY CHRIS HANSEN!
AND PEOPLE ARE STILL CALLING ME A TERF.
JUST EXTREMIST MORONS. IGNORE THEM.
IT'S GOING GREAT IN THE STUDIO, WE'RE DOING A LOT OF EXPERIMENTING...
WORKING ON DYING
I PUT A FENTANYL IN MY BOTTOM!
WHY THE FUCK IS THIS BITCH STILL ON OUR SHOW?
MITZI'S BLOWING UP. SHE'S MORE POPULAR THAN ANY OF US. PEOPLE LOVE HER.
OH, OKAY, YOU LOVE HER TOO, DO YOU? DO YOU WANT TO LEAVE ME FOR HER, ALSO?
WHAT? NO, I'M JUST SAYING!
HEY, GANG, WE'RE OFF TO THE BLUE LIVES MATTER RALLY!
FAMILIES FOR PIGS!
I ♡ PIGS
I'VE LEFT PIZZA MONEY ON THE KITCHEN TABLE. GO NUTS.
...
O-OKAY...
THIS UH... THIS FEELS LIKE A BAD MOVE RIGHT NOW...
OH, YEAH, YOU THINK?

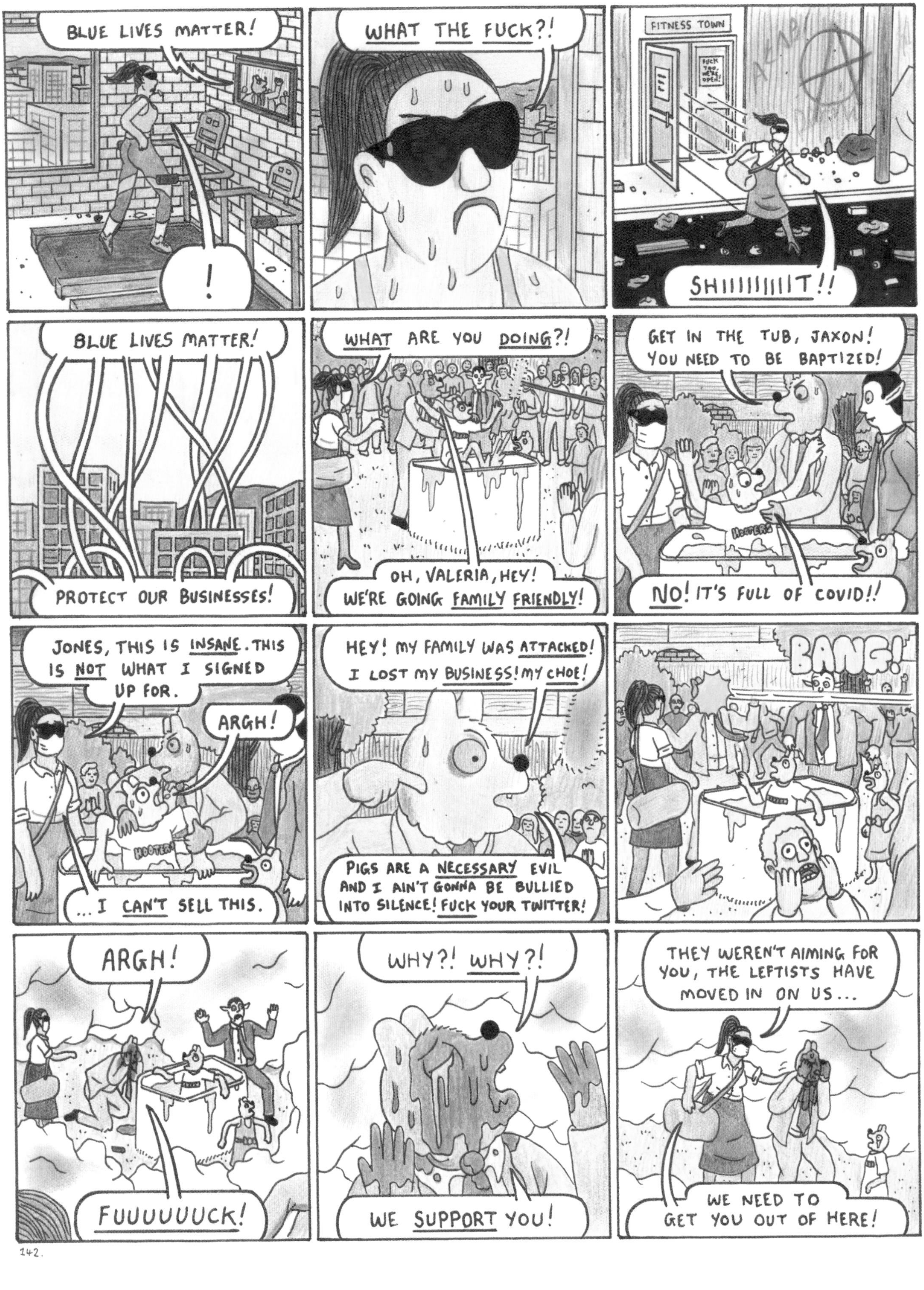
BLUE LIVES MATTER!
!
WHAT THE FUCK?!
FITNESS TOWN
SHIIIIIIIIT!!
BLUE LIVES MATTER!
PROTECT OUR BUSINESSES!
WHAT ARE YOU DOING?!
OH, VALERIA, HEY! WE'RE GOING FAMILY FRIENDLY!
GET IN THE TUB, JAXON! YOU NEED TO BE BAPTIZED!
NO! IT'S FULL OF COVID!!
JONES, THIS IS INSANE. THIS IS NOT WHAT I SIGNED UP FOR.
ARGH!
...I CAN'T SELL THIS.
HEY! MY FAMILY WAS ATTACKED! I LOST MY BUSINESS! MY CHOE!
PIGS ARE A NECESSARY EVIL AND I AIN'T GONNA BE BULLIED INTO SILENCE! FUCK YOUR TWITTER!
BANG!
ARGH!
FUUUUUUCK!
WHY?! WHY?!
WE SUPPORT YOU!
THEY WEREN'T AIMING FOR YOU, THE LEFTISTS HAVE MOVED IN ON US...
WE NEED TO GET YOU OUT OF HERE!

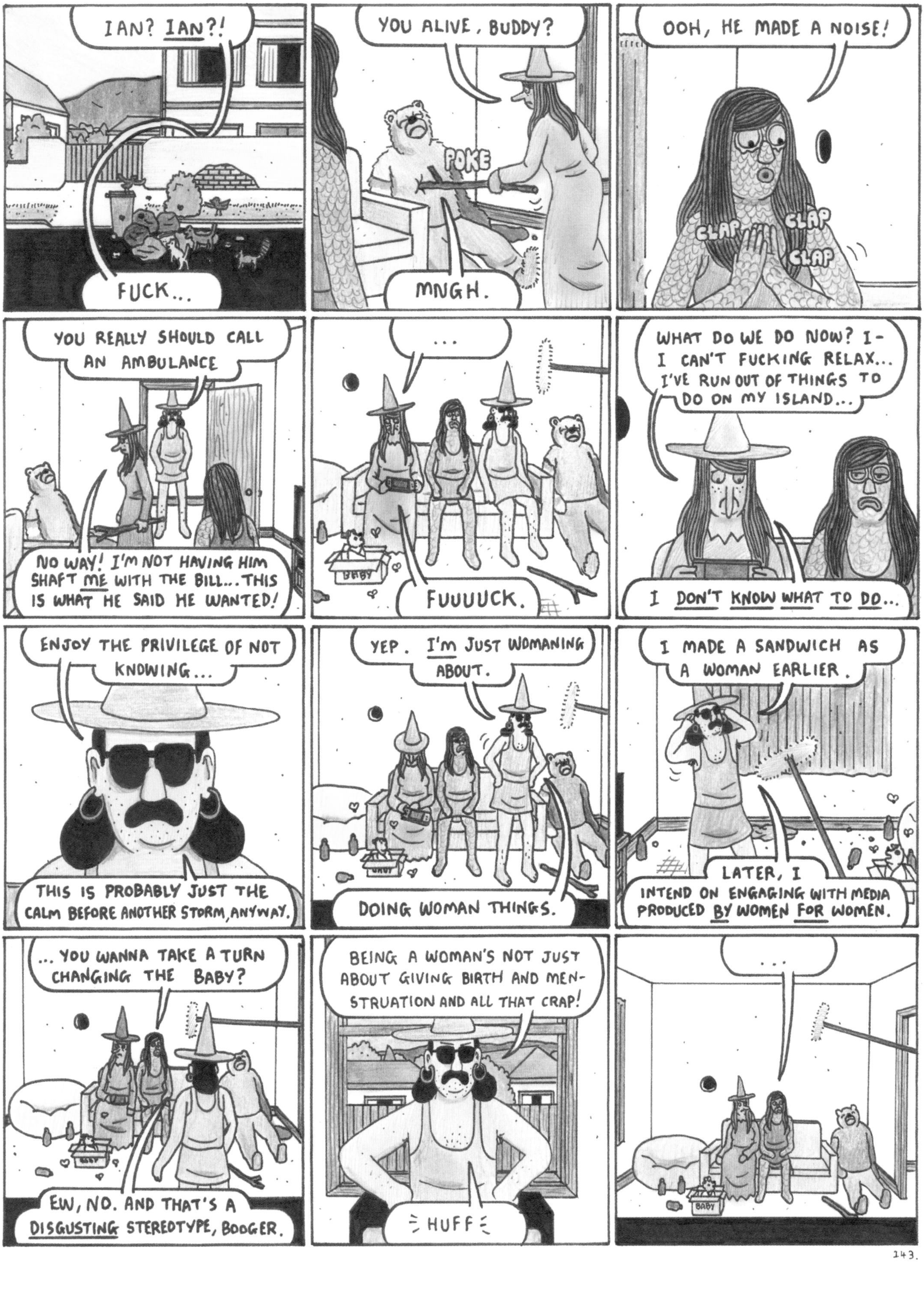
IAN? IAN?!
FUCK...
YOU ALIVE, BUDDY?
POKE
MNGH.
OOH, HE MADE A NOISE!
CLAP CLAP CLAP
YOU REALLY SHOULD CALL AN AMBULANCE
NO WAY! I'M NOT HAVING HIM SHAFT ME WITH THE BILL... THIS IS WHAT HE SAID HE WANTED!
...
FUUUUCK.
BABY
WHAT DO WE DO NOW? I- I CAN'T FUCKING RELAX... I'VE RUN OUT OF THINGS TO DO ON MY ISLAND...
I DON'T KNOW WHAT TO DO...
ENJOY THE PRIVILEGE OF NOT KNOWING...
THIS IS PROBABLY JUST THE CALM BEFORE ANOTHER STORM, ANYWAY.
YEP. I'M JUST WOMANING ABOUT.
DOING WOMAN THINGS.
I MADE A SANDWICH AS A WOMAN EARLIER.
LATER, I INTEND ON ENGAGING WITH MEDIA PRODUCED BY WOMEN FOR WOMEN.
... YOU WANNA TAKE A TURN CHANGING THE BABY?
EW, NO. AND THAT'S A DISGUSTING STEREOTYPE, BOOGER.
BEING A WOMAN'S NOT JUST ABOUT GIVING BIRTH AND MENSTRUATION AND ALL THAT CRAP!
HUFF
...
BABY

Panel 1: ≡SIGH≡... I REALLY SHOULD CALL MY MA... / OH, FUCK... WHEN DID YOU LAST TALK TO HER?

Panel 2: UGH, IT'S BEEN WEEKS. / I THINK MAYBE I'M SUBCONCIOUSLY PUNISHING HER FOR THE LAST TIME...

Panel 3: I - I GOTTA DO IT THOUGH... THE GUILT'S BECOMING CLAUSTROPHOBIC. / OH, SHUT THE FUCK UP!

Panel 4: SLAM!

Panel 5: YOU WERE RIGHT AS ALWAYS! YOU WIN! / IT'S NOT A COMPETITION, JONES, AND I'M NOT TRYING TO FUCK YOUR SHIT.

Panel 6: ...SWEETHEART, I KNOW YOU'RE EXCITED ABOUT THIS WHOLE "PERFECT FAMILY" THING... / BUT YOU ARE HAVING TO... NOT BE SUCH A CUNT ABOUT IT...

Panel 7: IS... IS NETFLIX ANGRY? / NO, NO, ACTUALLY, THE OPPOSITE, THEY WERE QUITE EXCITED ABOUT IT.

Panel 8: WHAT THE FUCK HAPPENED?! / I GOT SHOT IN THE FACE WITH A RUBBER BULLET.

Panel 9: OH, MY GOD! THAT'S HORRIBLE! / ARE YOU OKAY?

Panel 10: I... HAD SOME SENSE KNOCKED INTO ME... / AND IT WAS KIND OF EROTIC! LIKE GETTING SMACKED IN THE FACE BY A BIG, HOT DILDO!

Panel 11: BUT YEAH, WE'RE A CENTRIST FAMILY NOW... / NO MORE SIDE-TAKING, NO MORE TOUGH DECISIONS!

Panel 12: I WASH MY HANDS OF IT ALL. / EVERYBODY CAN FUCK OFF.

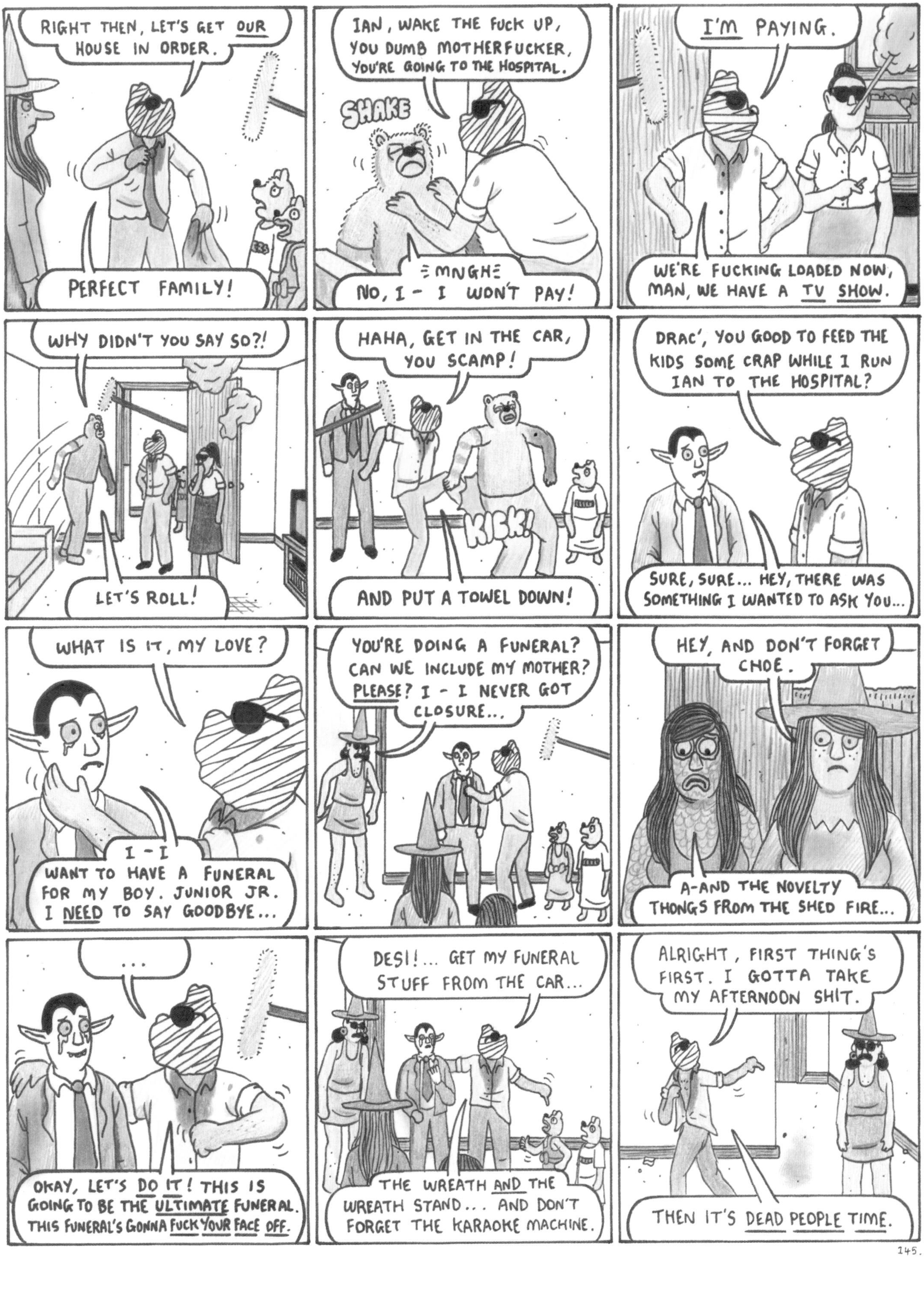
RIGHT THEN, LET'S GET OUR HOUSE IN ORDER.
PERFECT FAMILY!
IAN, WAKE THE FUCK UP, YOU DUMB MOTHERFUCKER, YOU'RE GOING TO THE HOSPITAL.
SHAKE
MNGH
NO, I - I WON'T PAY!
I'M PAYING.
WE'RE FUCKING LOADED NOW, MAN, WE HAVE A TV SHOW.
WHY DIDN'T YOU SAY SO?!
LET'S ROLL!
HAHA, GET IN THE CAR, YOU SCAMP!
KICK!
AND PUT A TOWEL DOWN!
DRAC', YOU GOOD TO FEED THE KIDS SOME CRAP WHILE I RUN IAN TO THE HOSPITAL?
SURE, SURE... HEY, THERE WAS SOMETHING I WANTED TO ASK YOU...
WHAT IS IT, MY LOVE?
I - I WANT TO HAVE A FUNERAL FOR MY BOY. JUNIOR JR. I NEED TO SAY GOODBYE...
YOU'RE DOING A FUNERAL? CAN WE INCLUDE MY MOTHER? PLEASE? I - I NEVER GOT CLOSURE...
HEY, AND DON'T FORGET CHOE.
A-AND THE NOVELTY THONGS FROM THE SHED FIRE...
...
OKAY, LET'S DO IT! THIS IS GOING TO BE THE ULTIMATE FUNERAL. THIS FUNERAL'S GONNA FUCK YOUR FACE OFF.
DESI!... GET MY FUNERAL STUFF FROM THE CAR...
THE WREATH AND THE WREATH STAND... AND DON'T FORGET THE KARAOKE MACHINE.
ALRIGHT, FIRST THING'S FIRST. I GOTTA TAKE MY AFTERNOON SHIT.
THEN IT'S DEAD PEOPLE TIME.

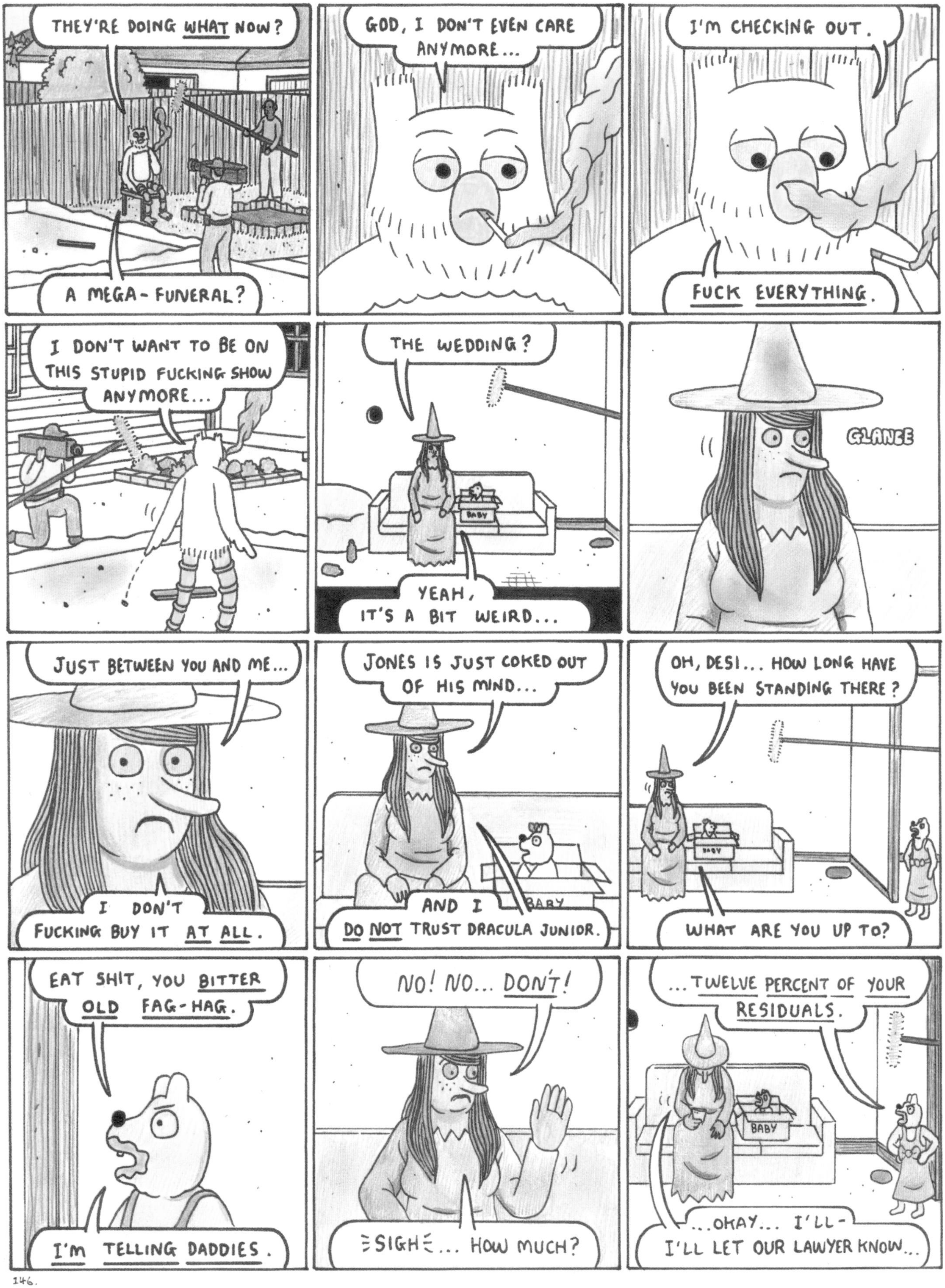
THEY'RE DOING WHAT NOW?
A MEGA-FUNERAL?
GOD, I DON'T EVEN CARE ANYMORE...
I'M CHECKING OUT.
FUCK EVERYTHING.
I DON'T WANT TO BE ON THIS STUPID FUCKING SHOW ANYMORE...
THE WEDDING?
BABY
YEAH, IT'S A BIT WEIRD...
GLANCE
JUST BETWEEN YOU AND ME...
I DON'T FUCKING BUY IT AT ALL.
JONES IS JUST COKED OUT OF HIS MIND...
AND I DO NOT TRUST DRACULA JUNIOR.
BABY
OH, DESI... HOW LONG HAVE YOU BEEN STANDING THERE?
BABY
WHAT ARE YOU UP TO?
EAT SHIT, YOU BITTER OLD FAG-HAG.
I'M TELLING DADDIES.
NO! NO... DON'T!
≡SIGH≡... HOW MUCH?
...TWELVE PERCENT OF YOUR RESIDUALS.
BABY
...OKAY... I'LL- I'LL LET OUR LAWYER KNOW...

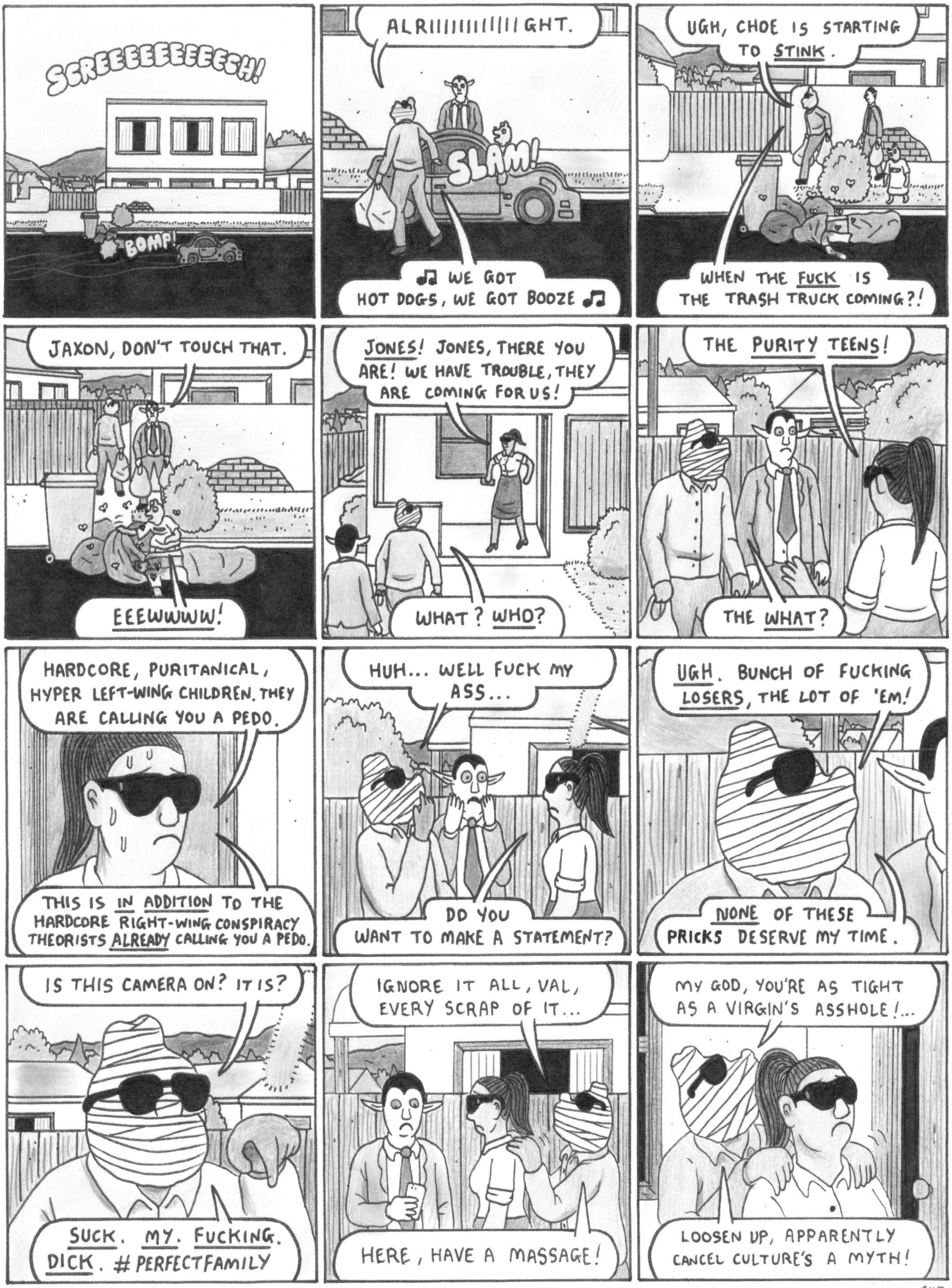
SCREEEEEEEEEECH!
BOMP!
ALRIIIIIIIIIIIIGHT.
SLAM!
♫ WE GOT HOT DOGS, WE GOT BOOZE ♫
UGH, CHOE IS STARTING TO STINK.
WHEN THE FUCK IS THE TRASH TRUCK COMING?!
JAXON, DON'T TOUCH THAT.
EEEWWWW!
JONES! JONES, THERE YOU ARE! WE HAVE TROUBLE, THEY ARE COMING FOR US!
WHAT? WHO?
THE PURITY TEENS!
THE WHAT?
HARDCORE, PURITANICAL, HYPER LEFT-WING CHILDREN. THEY ARE CALLING YOU A PEDO.
THIS IS IN ADDITION TO THE HARDCORE RIGHT-WING CONSPIRACY THEORISTS ALREADY CALLING YOU A PEDO.
HUH... WELL FUCK MY ASS...
DO YOU WANT TO MAKE A STATEMENT?
UGH. BUNCH OF FUCKING LOSERS, THE LOT OF 'EM!
NONE OF THESE PRICKS DESERVE MY TIME.
IS THIS CAMERA ON? IT IS?
SUCK. MY. FUCKING. DICK. #PERFECTFAMILY
IGNORE IT ALL, VAL, EVERY SCRAP OF IT...
HERE, HAVE A MASSAGE!
MY GOD, YOU'RE AS TIGHT AS A VIRGIN'S ASSHOLE!...
LOOSEN UP, APPARENTLY CANCEL CULTURE'S A MYTH!

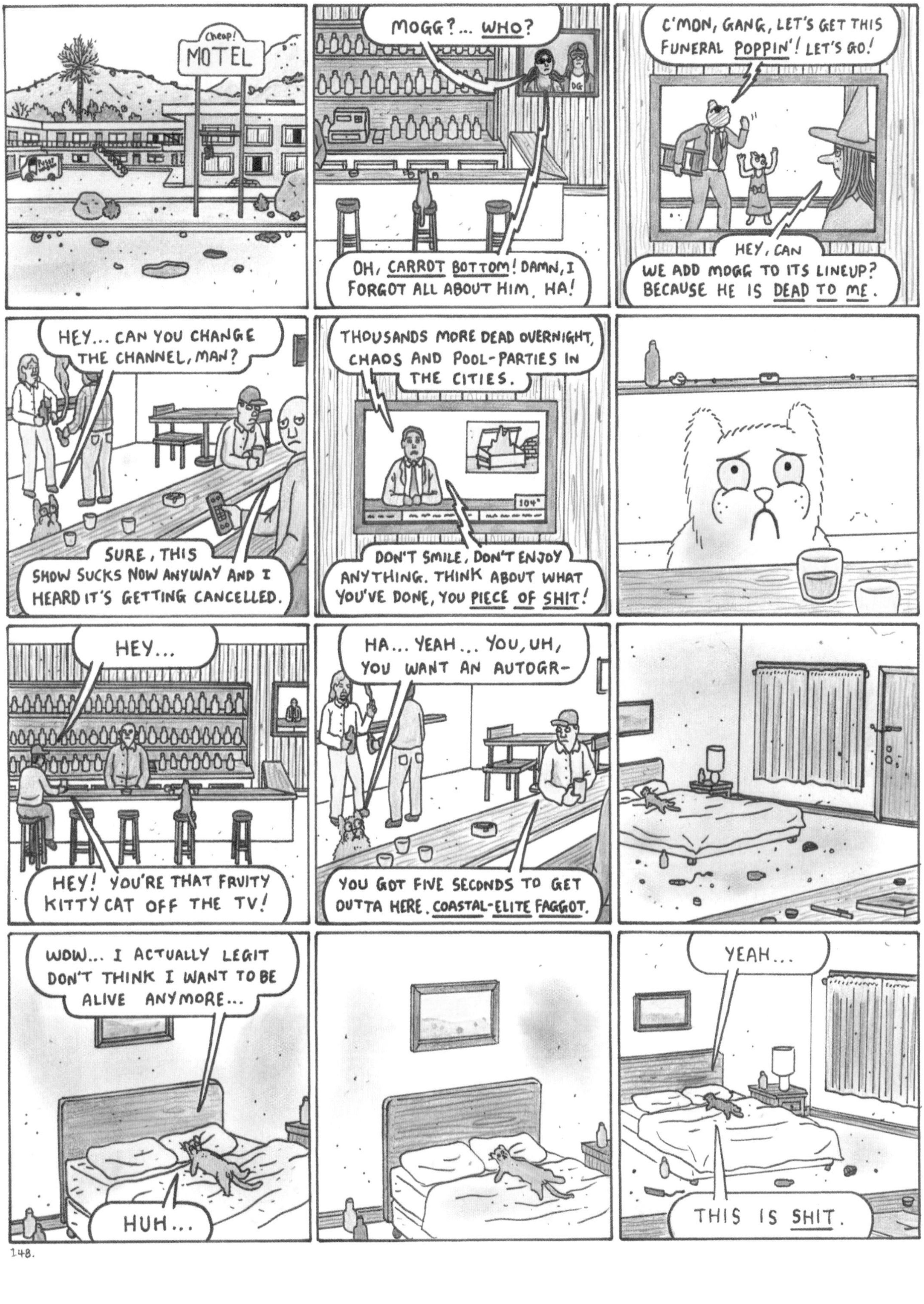
Cheap!
MOTEL
MOGG?... WHO?
DG
OH, CARROT BOTTOM! DAMN, I FORGOT ALL ABOUT HIM. HA!
C'MON, GANG, LET'S GET THIS FUNERAL POPPIN'! LET'S GO!
HEY, CAN WE ADD MOGG TO ITS LINEUP? BECAUSE HE IS DEAD TO ME.
HEY... CAN YOU CHANGE THE CHANNEL, MAN?
SURE, THIS SHOW SUCKS NOW ANYWAY AND I HEARD IT'S GETTING CANCELLED.
THOUSANDS MORE DEAD OVERNIGHT, CHAOS AND POOL-PARTIES IN THE CITIES.
104°
DON'T SMILE, DON'T ENJOY ANYTHING. THINK ABOUT WHAT YOU'VE DONE, YOU PIECE OF SHIT!
HEY...
HEY! YOU'RE THAT FRUITY KITTY CAT OFF THE TV!
HA... YEAH... YOU, UH, YOU WANT AN AUTOGR-
YOU GOT FIVE SECONDS TO GET OUTTA HERE. COASTAL-ELITE FAGGOT.
WOW... I ACTUALLY LEGIT DON'T THINK I WANT TO BE ALIVE ANYMORE...
HUH...
YEAH...
THIS IS SHIT.

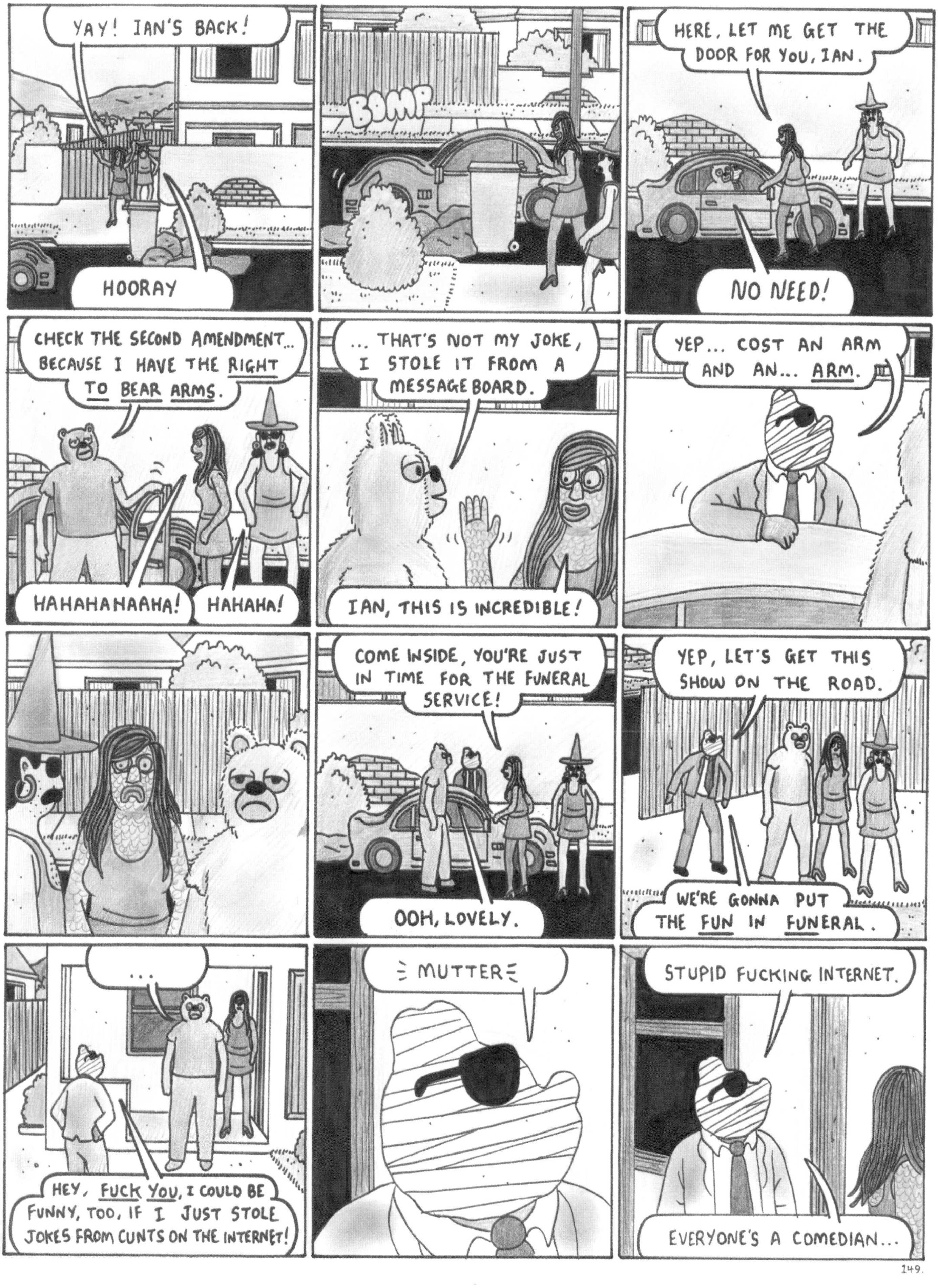
YAY! IAN'S BACK!
HOORAY
BOMP
HERE, LET ME GET THE DOOR FOR YOU, IAN.
NO NEED!
CHECK THE SECOND AMENDMENT... BECAUSE I HAVE THE RIGHT TO BEAR ARMS.
HAHAHAHAAHA!
HAHAHA!
... THAT'S NOT MY JOKE, I STOLE IT FROM A MESSAGE BOARD.
IAN, THIS IS INCREDIBLE!
YEP... COST AN ARM AND AN... ARM.
COME INSIDE, YOU'RE JUST IN TIME FOR THE FUNERAL SERVICE!
OOH, LOVELY.
YEP, LET'S GET THIS SHOW ON THE ROAD.
WE'RE GONNA PUT THE FUN IN FUNERAL.
...
HEY, FUCK YOU, I COULD BE FUNNY, TOO, IF I JUST STOLE JOKES FROM CUNTS ON THE INTERNET!
MUTTER
STUPID FUCKING INTERNET.
EVERYONE'S A COMEDIAN...

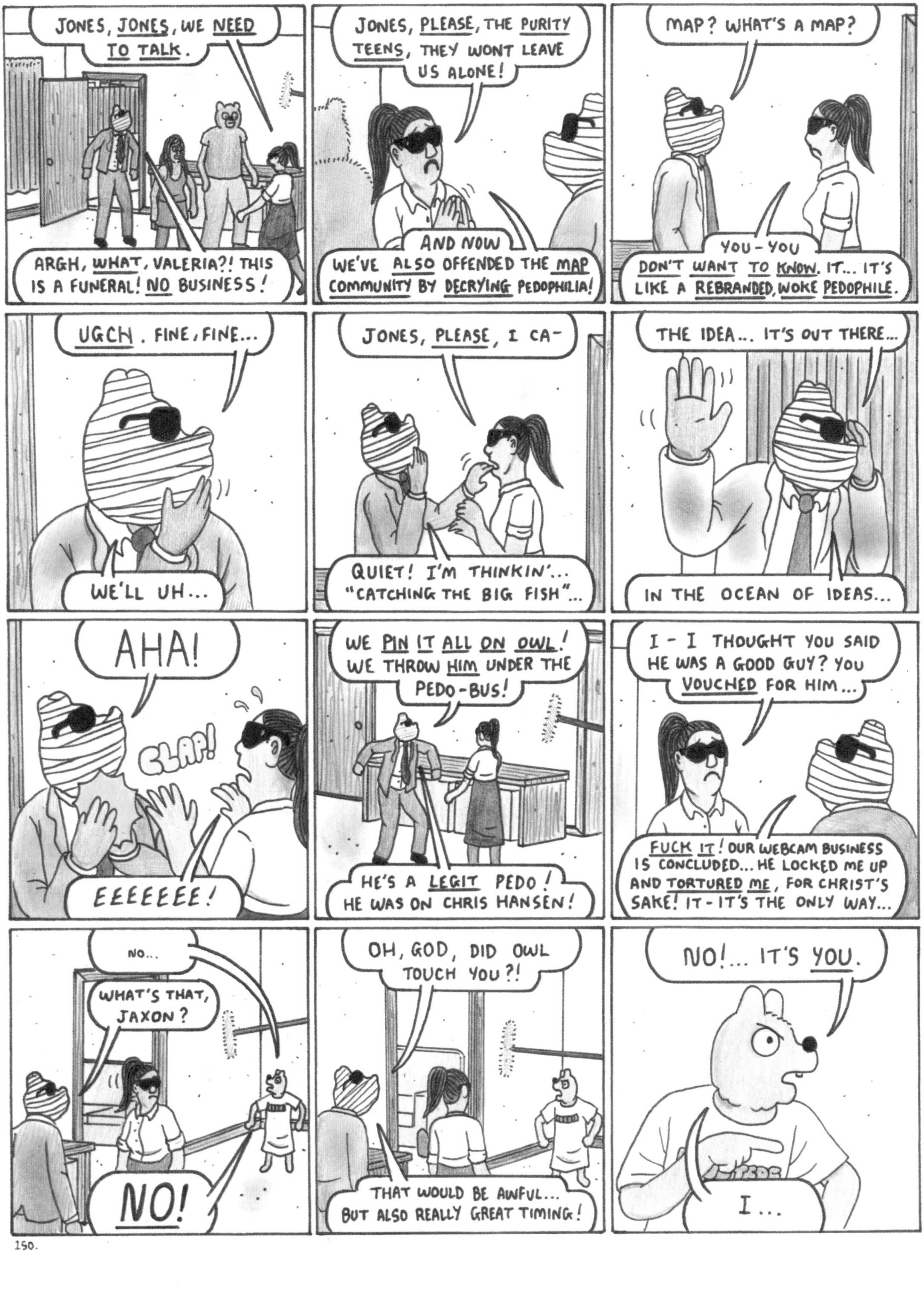
JONES, JONES, WE NEED TO TALK.
ARGH, WHAT, VALERIA?! THIS IS A FUNERAL! NO BUSINESS!
JONES, PLEASE, THE PURITY TEENS, THEY WONT LEAVE US ALONE!
AND NOW
WE'VE ALSO OFFENDED THE MAP COMMUNITY BY DECRYING PEDOPHILIA!
MAP? WHAT'S A MAP?
YOU-YOU
DON'T WANT TO KNOW. IT... IT'S LIKE A REBRANDED, WOKE PEDOPHILE.
UGCH. FINE, FINE...
WE'LL UH...
JONES, PLEASE, I CA-
QUIET! I'M THINKIN'... "CATCHING THE BIG FISH"...
THE IDEA... IT'S OUT THERE...
IN THE OCEAN OF IDEAS...
AHA!
CLAP!
EEEEEEE!
WE PIN IT ALL ON OWL! WE THROW HIM UNDER THE PEDO-BUS!
HE'S A LEGIT PEDO! HE WAS ON CHRIS HANSEN!
I-I THOUGHT YOU SAID HE WAS A GOOD GUY? YOU VOUCHED FOR HIM...
FUCK IT! OUR WEBCAM BUSINESS IS CONCLUDED... HE LOCKED ME UP AND TORTURED ME, FOR CHRIST'S SAKE! IT-IT'S THE ONLY WAY...
NO...
WHAT'S THAT, JAXON?
NO!
OH, GOD, DID OWL TOUCH YOU?!
THAT WOULD BE AWFUL... BUT ALSO REALLY GREAT TIMING!
NO!... IT'S YOU.
I...

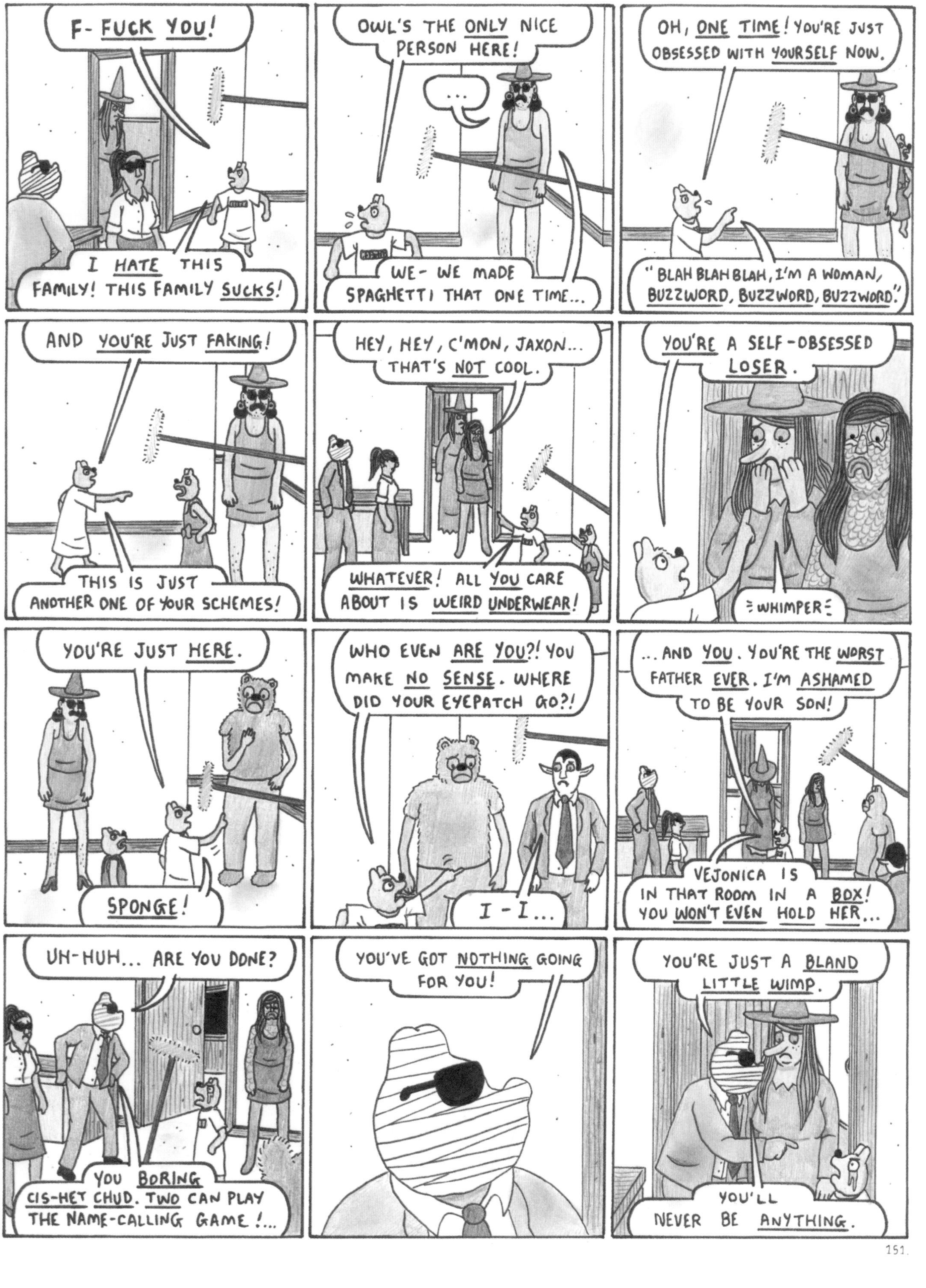
F- FUCK YOU!
I HATE THIS FAMILY! THIS FAMILY SUCKS!
OWL'S THE ONLY NICE PERSON HERE!
...
WE- WE MADE SPAGHETTI THAT ONE TIME...
OH, ONE TIME! YOU'RE JUST OBSESSED WITH YOURSELF NOW.
"BLAH BLAH BLAH, I'M A WOMAN, BUZZWORD, BUZZWORD, BUZZWORD."
AND YOU'RE JUST FAKING!
THIS IS JUST ANOTHER ONE OF YOUR SCHEMES!
HEY, HEY, C'MON, JAXON... THAT'S NOT COOL.
WHATEVER! ALL YOU CARE ABOUT IS WEIRD UNDERWEAR!
YOU'RE A SELF-OBSESSED LOSER.
WHIMPER
YOU'RE JUST HERE.
SPONGE!
WHO EVEN ARE YOU?! YOU MAKE NO SENSE. WHERE DID YOUR EYEPATCH GO?!
I - I...
...AND YOU. YOU'RE THE WORST FATHER EVER. I'M ASHAMED TO BE YOUR SON!
VEJONICA IS IN THAT ROOM IN A BOX! YOU WON'T EVEN HOLD HER...
UH-HUH... ARE YOU DONE?
YOU BORING CIS-HET CHUD. TWO CAN PLAY THE NAME-CALLING GAME!...
YOU'VE GOT NOTHING GOING FOR YOU!
YOU'RE JUST A BLAND LITTLE WIMP.
YOU'LL NEVER BE ANYTHING.

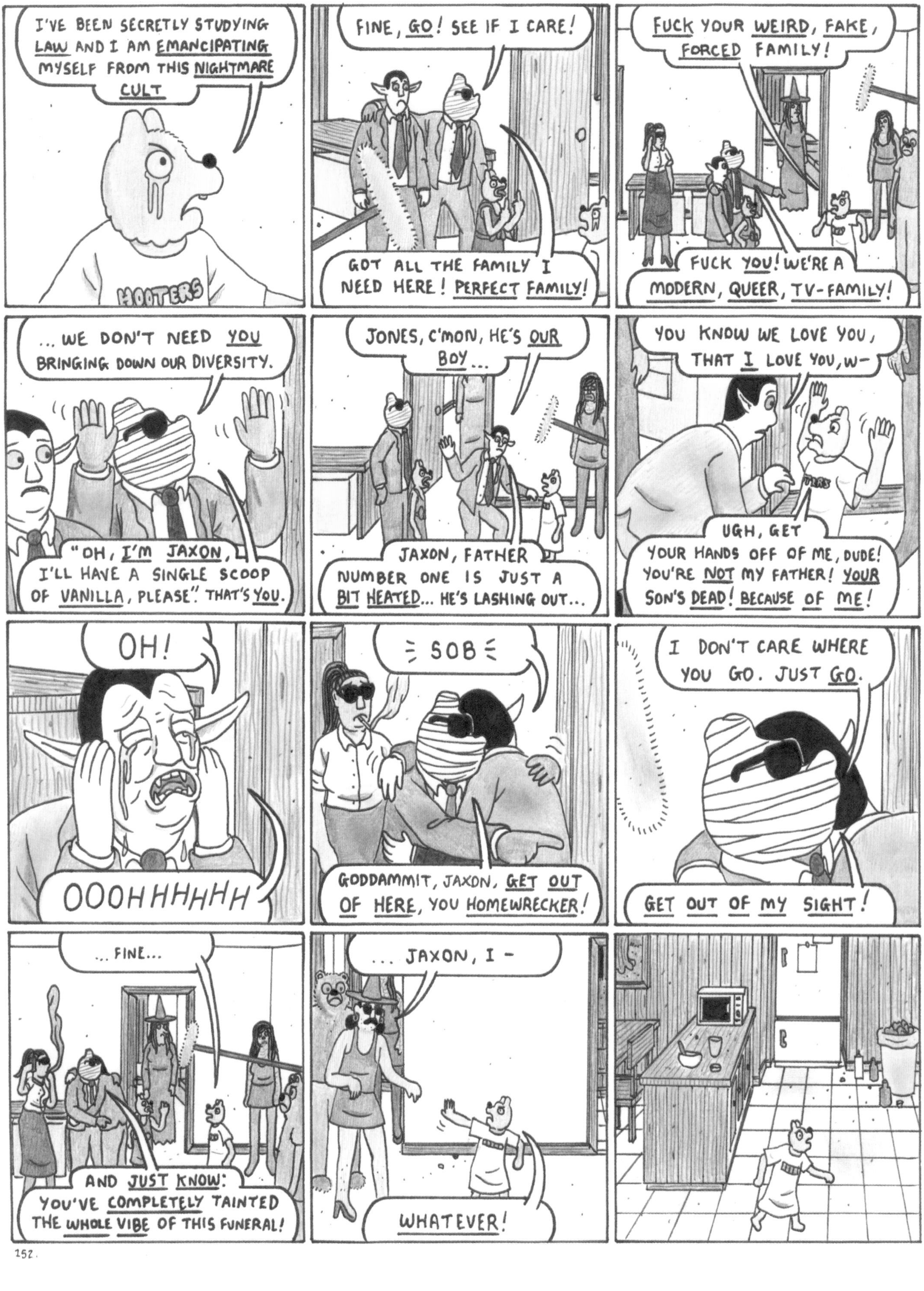
I'VE BEEN SECRETLY STUDYING LAW AND I AM EMANCIPATING MYSELF FROM THIS NIGHTMARE CULT
HOOTERS
FINE, GO! SEE IF I CARE!
GOT ALL THE FAMILY I NEED HERE! PERFECT FAMILY!
FUCK YOUR WEIRD, FAKE, FORCED FAMILY!
FUCK YOU! WE'RE A MODERN, QUEER, TV-FAMILY!
... WE DON'T NEED YOU BRINGING DOWN OUR DIVERSITY.
"OH, I'M JAXON, I'LL HAVE A SINGLE SCOOP OF VANILLA, PLEASE". THAT'S YOU.
JONES, C'MON, HE'S OUR BOY...
JAXON, FATHER NUMBER ONE IS JUST A BIT HEATED... HE'S LASHING OUT...
YOU KNOW WE LOVE YOU, THAT I LOVE YOU, W-
UGH, GET YOUR HANDS OFF OF ME, DUDE! YOU'RE NOT MY FATHER! YOUR SON'S DEAD! BECAUSE OF ME!
OH!
OOOHHHHHH
SOB
GODDAMMIT, JAXON, GET OUT OF HERE, YOU HOMEWRECKER!
I DON'T CARE WHERE YOU GO. JUST GO.
GET OUT OF MY SIGHT!
... FINE...
AND JUST KNOW: YOU'VE COMPLETELY TAINTED THE WHOLE VIBE OF THIS FUNERAL!
... JAXON, I -
WHATEVER!

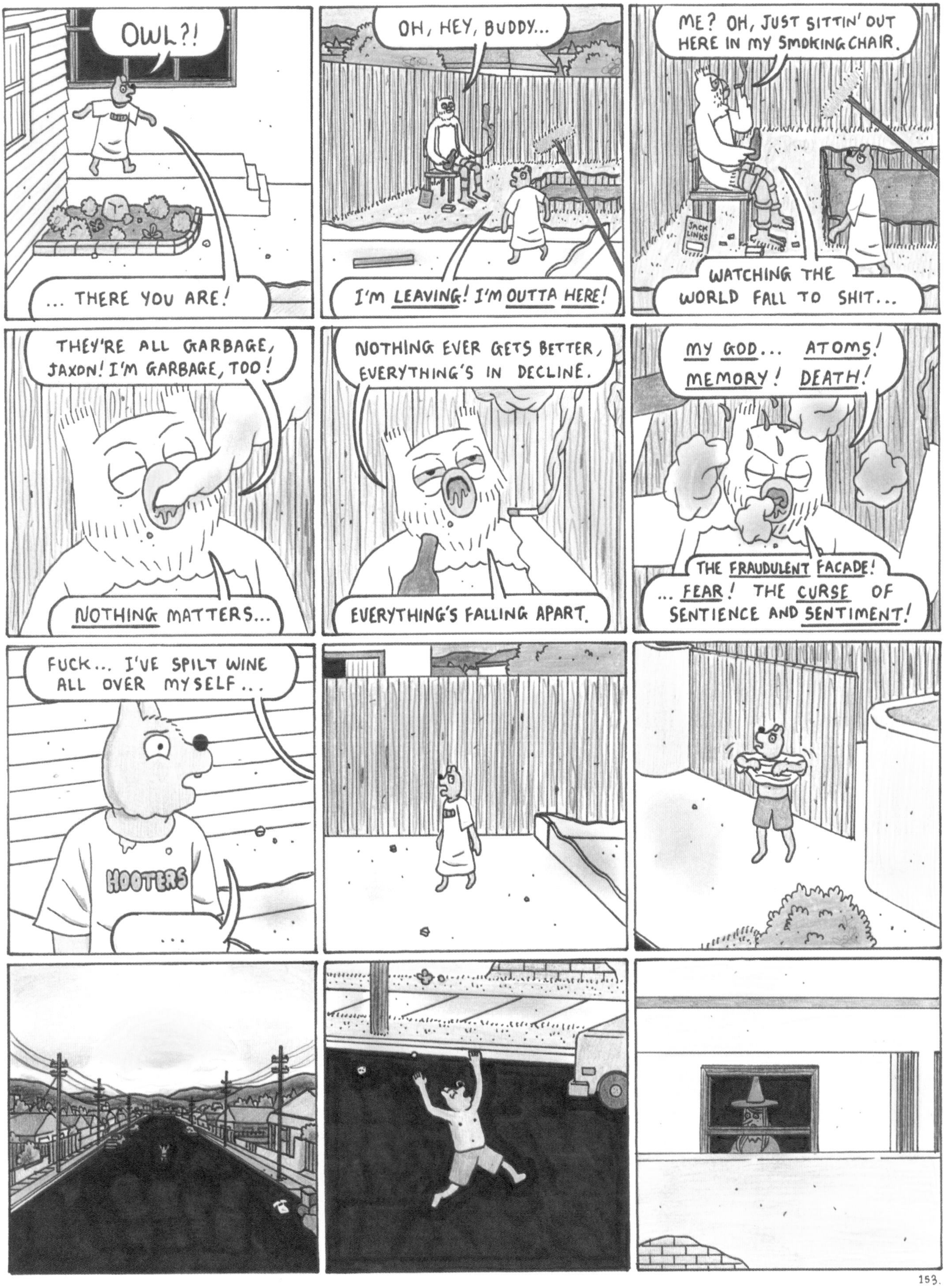
OWL?!
... THERE YOU ARE!
OH, HEY, BUDDY...
I'M LEAVING! I'M OUTTA HERE!
ME? OH, JUST SITTIN' OUT HERE IN MY SMOKING CHAIR.
JACK LINKS
WATCHING THE WORLD FALL TO SHIT...
THEY'RE ALL GARBAGE, JAXON! I'M GARBAGE, TOO!
NOTHING MATTERS...
NOTHING EVER GETS BETTER, EVERYTHING'S IN DECLINE.
EVERYTHING'S FALLING APART.
MY GOD... ATOMS! MEMORY! DEATH!
THE FRAUDULENT FACADE!
... FEAR! THE CURSE OF SENTIENCE AND SENTIMENT!
FUCK... I'VE SPILT WINE ALL OVER MYSELF...
HOOTERS
...

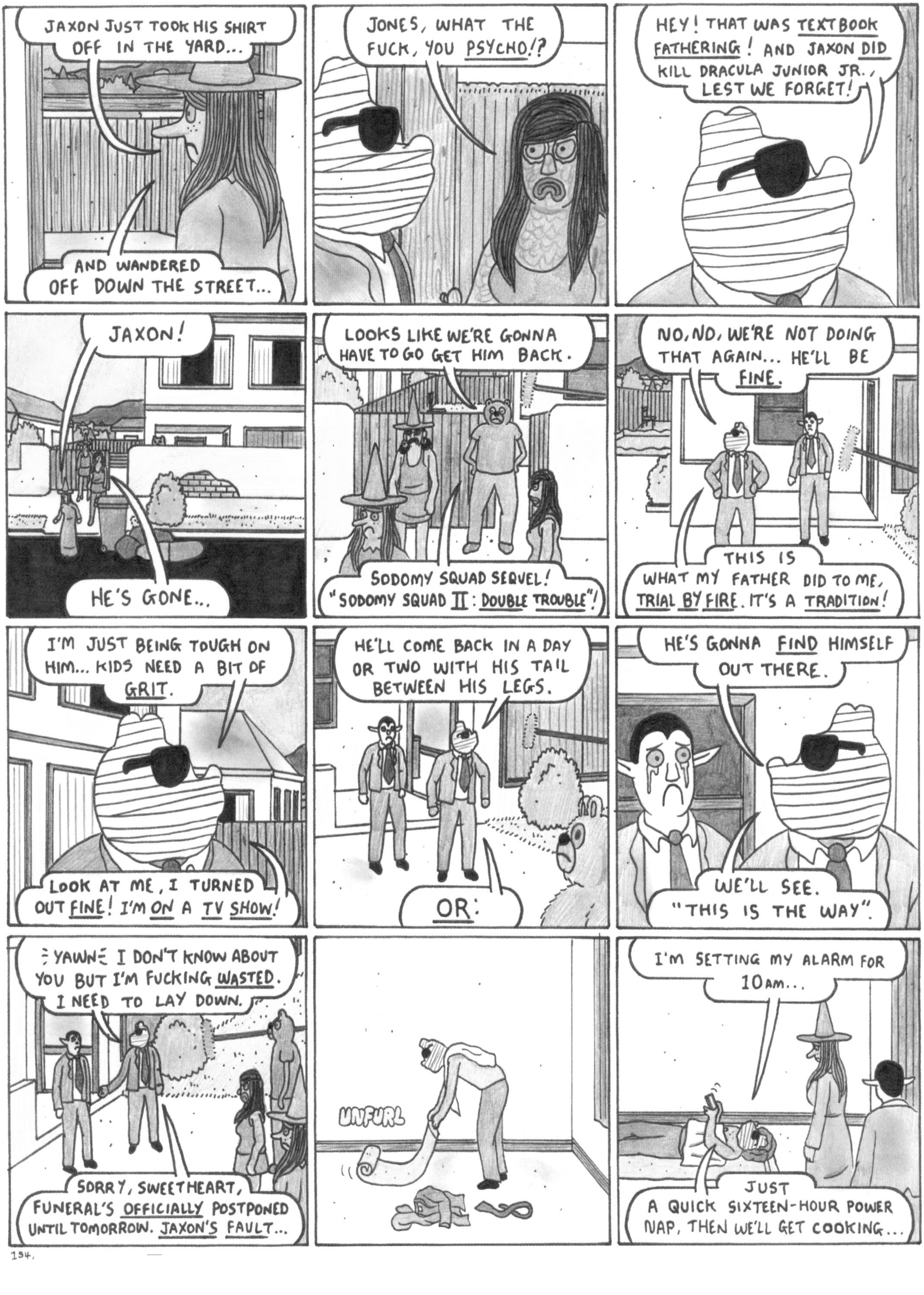
JAXON JUST TOOK HIS SHIRT OFF IN THE YARD...
AND WANDERED OFF DOWN THE STREET...
JONES, WHAT THE FUCK, YOU PSYCHO!?
HEY! THAT WAS TEXTBOOK FATHERING! AND JAXON DID KILL DRACULA JUNIOR JR., LEST WE FORGET!
JAXON!
HE'S GONE...
LOOKS LIKE WE'RE GONNA HAVE TO GO GET HIM BACK.
SODOMY SQUAD SEQUEL! "SODOMY SQUAD II: DOUBLE TROUBLE"!
NO, NO, WE'RE NOT DOING THAT AGAIN... HE'LL BE FINE.
THIS IS WHAT MY FATHER DID TO ME, TRIAL BY FIRE. IT'S A TRADITION!
I'M JUST BEING TOUGH ON HIM... KIDS NEED A BIT OF GRIT.
LOOK AT ME, I TURNED OUT FINE! I'M ON A TV SHOW!
HE'LL COME BACK IN A DAY OR TWO WITH HIS TAIL BETWEEN HIS LEGS.
OR:
HE'S GONNA FIND HIMSELF OUT THERE.
WE'LL SEE. "THIS IS THE WAY".
=YAWN= I DON'T KNOW ABOUT YOU BUT I'M FUCKING WASTED. I NEED TO LAY DOWN.
SORRY, SWEETHEART, FUNERAL'S OFFICIALLY POSTPONED UNTIL TOMORROW. JAXON'S FAULT...
UNFURL
I'M SETTING MY ALARM FOR 10AM...
JUST A QUICK SIXTEEN-HOUR POWER NAP, THEN WE'LL GET COOKING...

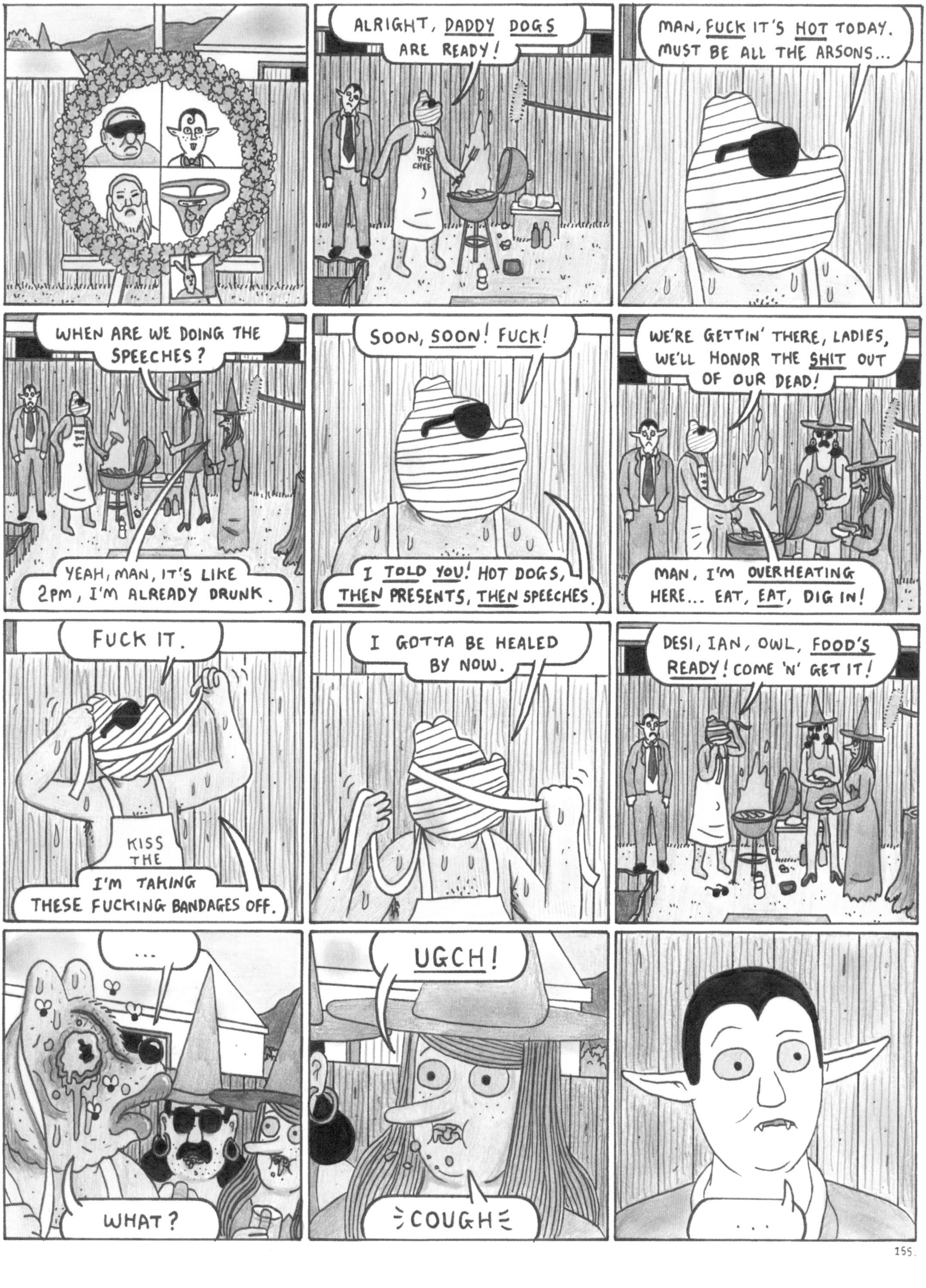
ALRIGHT, DADDY DOGS ARE READY!
MAN, FUCK IT'S HOT TODAY. MUST BE ALL THE ARSONS...
WHEN ARE WE DOING THE SPEECHES?
YEAH, MAN, IT'S LIKE 2PM, I'M ALREADY DRUNK.
SOON, SOON! FUCK!
I TOLD YOU! HOT DOGS, THEN PRESENTS, THEN SPEECHES.
WE'RE GETTIN' THERE, LADIES, WE'LL HONOR THE SHIT OUT OF OUR DEAD!
MAN, I'M OVERHEATING HERE... EAT, EAT, DIG IN!
FUCK IT.
KISS THE
I'M TAKING THESE FUCKING BANDAGES OFF.
I GOTTA BE HEALED BY NOW.
DESI, IAN, OWL, FOOD'S READY! COME 'N' GET IT!
...
WHAT?
UGCH!
COUGH
...

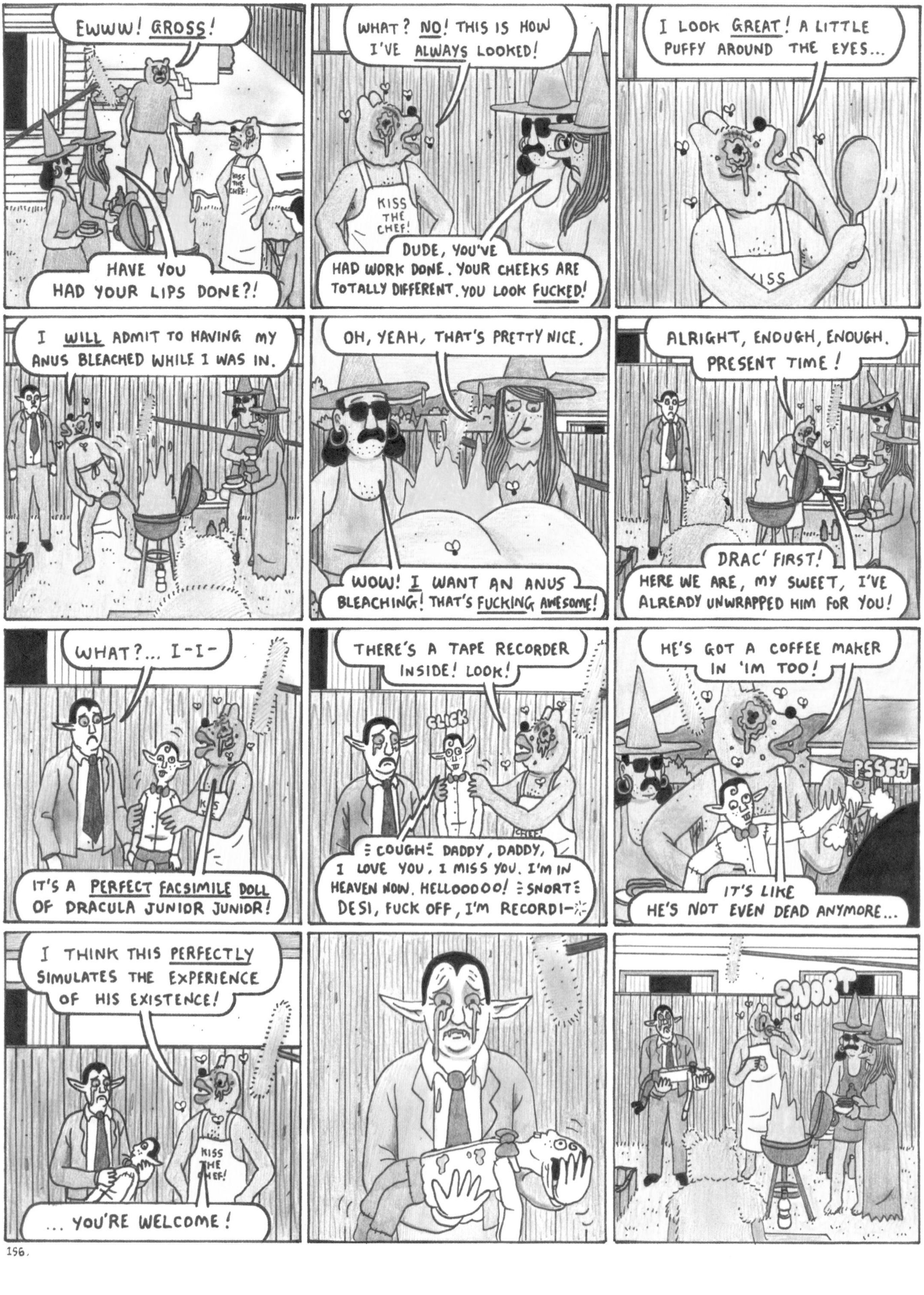
EWWW! GROSS!
HAVE YOU HAD YOUR LIPS DONE?!
KISS THE CHEF!
WHAT? NO! THIS IS HOW I'VE ALWAYS LOOKED!
KISS THE CHEF!
DUDE, YOU'VE HAD WORK DONE. YOUR CHEEKS ARE TOTALLY DIFFERENT. YOU LOOK FUCKED!
I LOOK GREAT! A LITTLE PUFFY AROUND THE EYES...
I WILL ADMIT TO HAVING MY ANUS BLEACHED WHILE I WAS IN.
OH, YEAH, THAT'S PRETTY NICE.
WOW! I WANT AN ANUS BLEACHING! THAT'S FUCKING AWESOME!
ALRIGHT, ENOUGH, ENOUGH. PRESENT TIME!
DRAC' FIRST! HERE WE ARE, MY SWEET, I'VE ALREADY UNWRAPPED HIM FOR YOU!
WHAT?... I-I-
IT'S A PERFECT FACSIMILE DOLL OF DRACULA JUNIOR JUNIOR!
THERE'S A TAPE RECORDER INSIDE! LOOK!
CLICK
COUGH DADDY, DADDY, I LOVE YOU. I MISS YOU. I'M IN HEAVEN NOW. HELLOOOOO! SNORT DESI, FUCK OFF, I'M RECORDI-
HE'S GOT A COFFEE MAKER IN 'IM TOO!
PSSCH
IT'S LIKE HE'S NOT EVEN DEAD ANYMORE...
I THINK THIS PERFECTLY SIMULATES THE EXPERIENCE OF HIS EXISTENCE!
KISS THE CHEF!
... YOU'RE WELCOME!
SNORT

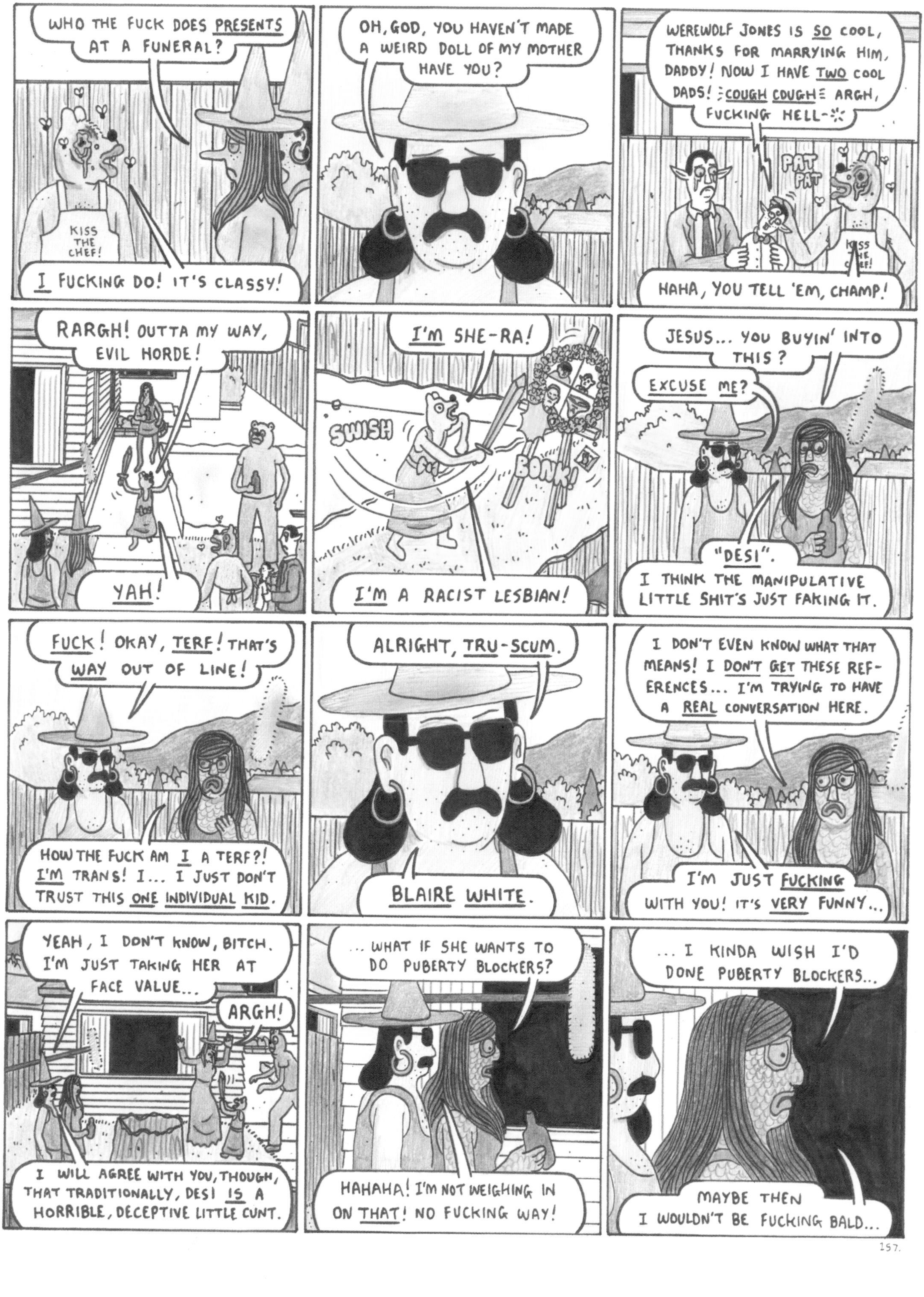
WHO THE FUCK DOES PRESENTS AT A FUNERAL?
KISS THE CHEF!
I FUCKING DO! IT'S CLASSY!
OH, GOD, YOU HAVEN'T MADE A WEIRD DOLL OF MY MOTHER HAVE YOU?
WEREWOLF JONES IS SO COOL, THANKS FOR MARRYING HIM, DADDY! NOW I HAVE TWO COOL DADS! COUGH COUGH ARGH, FUCKING HELL-
PAT PAT
HAHA, YOU TELL 'EM, CHAMP!
RARGH! OUTTA MY WAY, EVIL HORDE!
YAH!
I'M SHE-RA!
SWISH
BONK!
I'M A RACIST LESBIAN!
JESUS... YOU BUYIN' INTO THIS?
EXCUSE ME?
"DESI".
I THINK THE MANIPULATIVE LITTLE SHIT'S JUST FAKING IT.
FUCK! OKAY, TERF! THAT'S WAY OUT OF LINE!
HOW THE FUCK AM I A TERF?! I'M TRANS! I... I JUST DON'T TRUST THIS ONE INDIVIDUAL KID.
ALRIGHT, TRU-SCUM.
BLAIRE WHITE.
I DON'T EVEN KNOW WHAT THAT MEANS! I DON'T GET THESE REFERENCES... I'M TRYING TO HAVE A REAL CONVERSATION HERE.
I'M JUST FUCKING WITH YOU! IT'S VERY FUNNY...
YEAH, I DON'T KNOW, BITCH. I'M JUST TAKING HER AT FACE VALUE...
ARGH!
I WILL AGREE WITH YOU, THOUGH, THAT TRADITIONALLY, DESI IS A HORRIBLE, DECEPTIVE LITTLE CUNT.
...WHAT IF SHE WANTS TO DO PUBERTY BLOCKERS?
HAHAHA! I'M NOT WEIGHING IN ON THAT! NO FUCKING WAY!
...I KINDA WISH I'D DONE PUBERTY BLOCKERS...
MAYBE THEN I WOULDN'T BE FUCKING BALD...

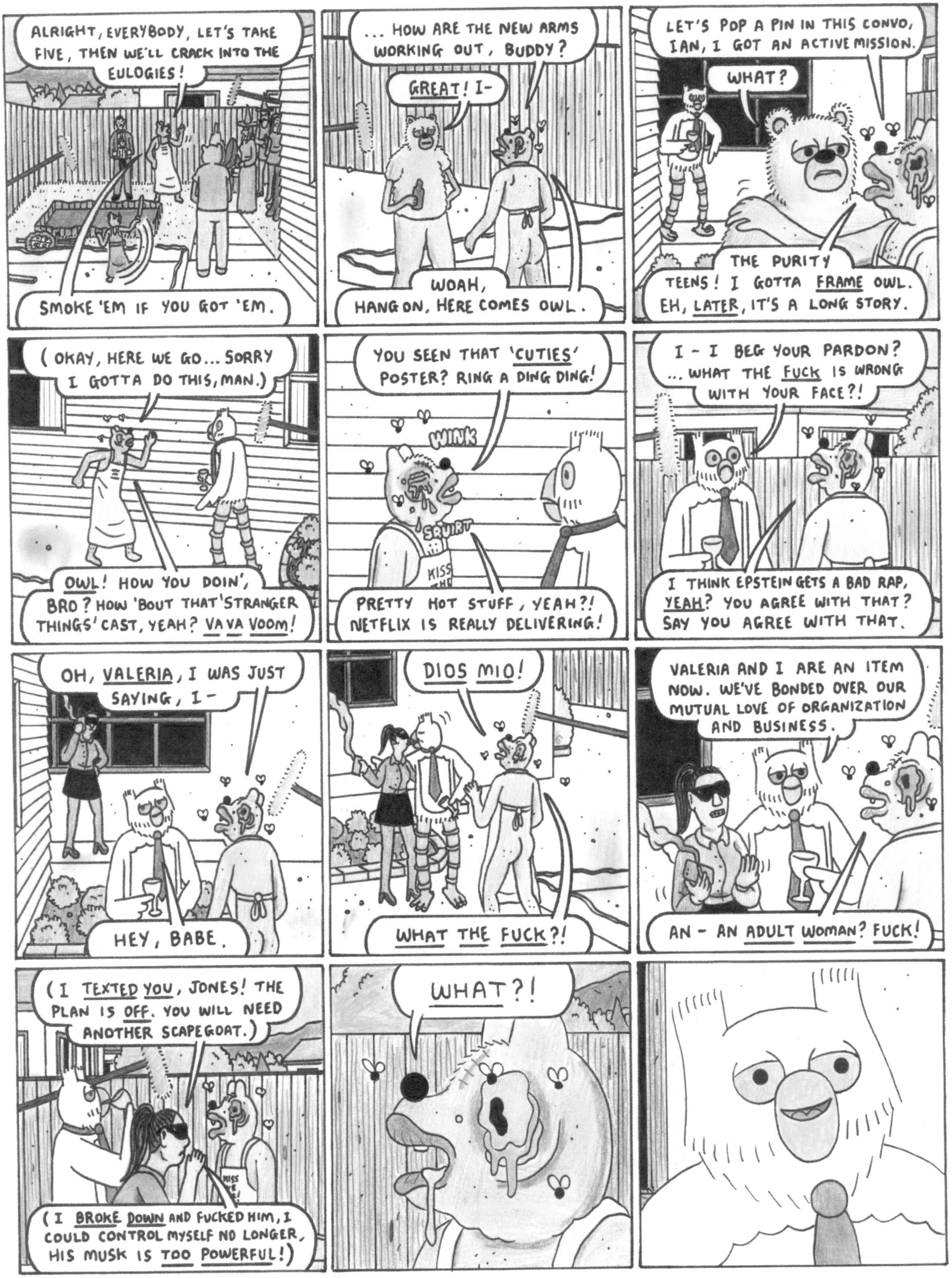
ALRIGHT, EVERYBODY, LET'S TAKE FIVE, THEN WE'LL CRACK INTO THE EULOGIES!
SMOKE 'EM IF YOU GOT 'EM.
... HOW ARE THE NEW ARMS WORKING OUT, BUDDY?
GREAT! I-
WOAH, HANG ON, HERE COMES OWL.
LET'S POP A PIN IN THIS CONVO, IAN, I GOT AN ACTIVE MISSION.
WHAT?
THE PURITY TEENS! I GOTTA FRAME OWL. EH, LATER, IT'S A LONG STORY.
(OKAY, HERE WE GO... SORRY I GOTTA DO THIS, MAN.)
OWL! HOW YOU DOIN', BRO? HOW 'BOUT THAT 'STRANGER THINGS' CAST, YEAH? VA VA VOOM!
YOU SEEN THAT 'CUTIES' POSTER? RING A DING DING!
WINK
SQUIRT
KISS THE
PRETTY HOT STUFF, YEAH?! NETFLIX IS REALLY DELIVERING!
I - I BEG YOUR PARDON? ... WHAT THE FUCK IS WRONG WITH YOUR FACE?!
I THINK EPSTEIN GETS A BAD RAP, YEAH? YOU AGREE WITH THAT? SAY YOU AGREE WITH THAT.
OH, VALERIA, I WAS JUST SAYING, I-
HEY, BABE.
DIOS MIO!
WHAT THE FUCK?!
VALERIA AND I ARE AN ITEM NOW. WE'VE BONDED OVER OUR MUTUAL LOVE OF ORGANIZATION AND BUSINESS.
AN - AN ADULT WOMAN? FUCK!
(I TEXTED YOU, JONES! THE PLAN IS OFF. YOU WILL NEED ANOTHER SCAPEGOAT.)
(I BROKE DOWN AND FUCKED HIM, I COULD CONTROL MYSELF NO LONGER, HIS MUSK IS TOO POWERFUL!)
WHAT?!

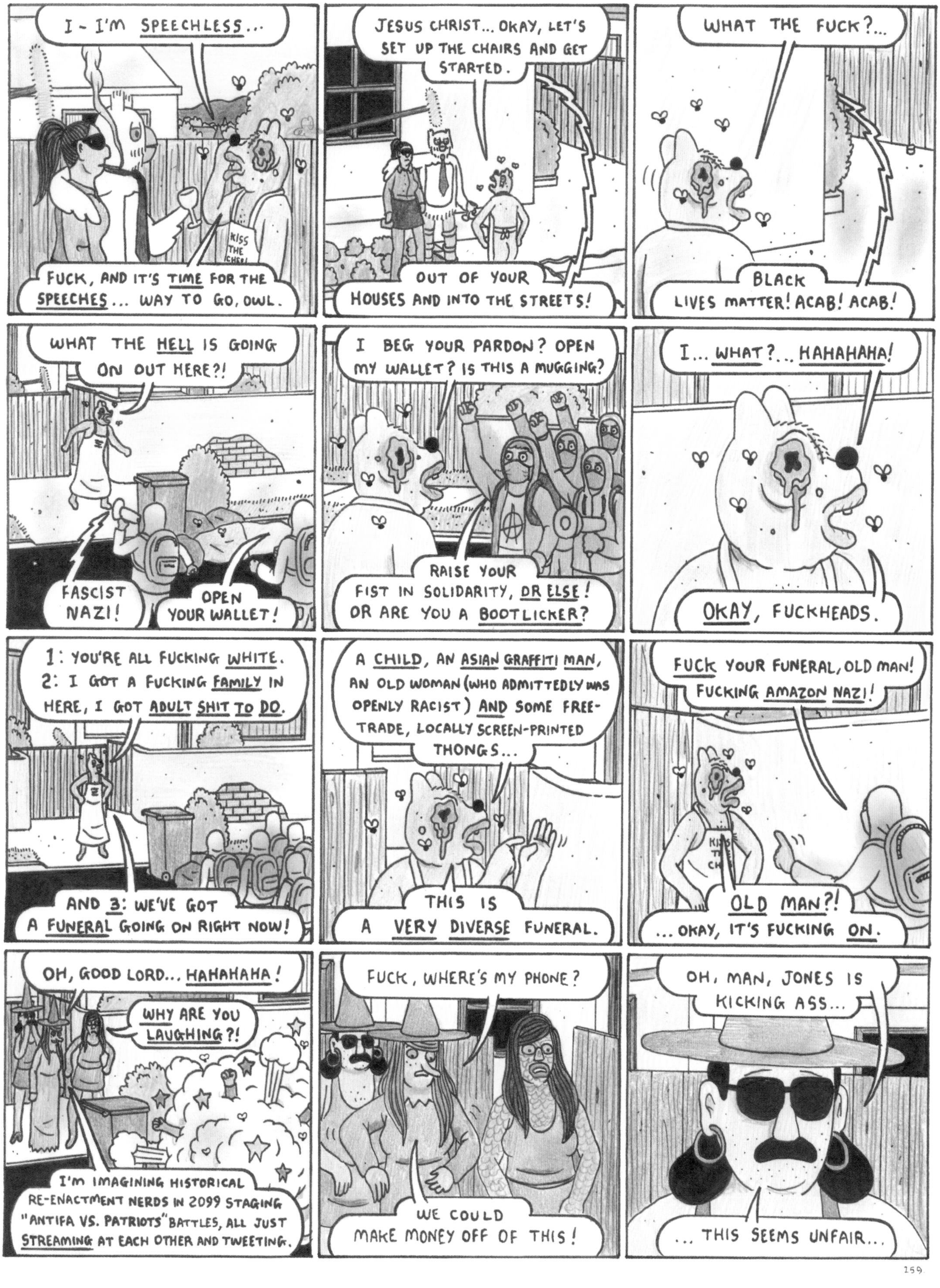
I- I'M SPEECHLESS...
FUCK, AND IT'S TIME FOR THE SPEECHES... WAY TO GO, OWL.
KISS THE CHEF
JESUS CHRIST... OKAY, LET'S SET UP THE CHAIRS AND GET STARTED.
OUT OF YOUR HOUSES AND INTO THE STREETS!
WHAT THE FUCK?...
BLACK LIVES MATTER! ACAB! ACAB!
WHAT THE HELL IS GOING ON OUT HERE?!
FASCIST NAZI!
OPEN YOUR WALLET!
I BEG YOUR PARDON? OPEN MY WALLET? IS THIS A MUGGING?
RAISE YOUR FIST IN SOLIDARITY, OR ELSE! OR ARE YOU A BOOTLICKER?
I... WHAT?... HAHAHAHA!
OKAY, FUCKHEADS.
1: YOU'RE ALL FUCKING WHITE. 2: I GOT A FUCKING FAMILY IN HERE, I GOT ADULT SHIT TO DO.
AND 3: WE'VE GOT A FUNERAL GOING ON RIGHT NOW!
A CHILD, AN ASIAN GRAFFITI MAN, AN OLD WOMAN (WHO ADMITTEDLY WAS OPENLY RACIST) AND SOME FREE-TRADE, LOCALLY SCREEN-PRINTED THONGS...
THIS IS A VERY DIVERSE FUNERAL.
FUCK YOUR FUNERAL, OLD MAN! FUCKING AMAZON NAZI!
OLD MAN?!
... OKAY, IT'S FUCKING ON.
OH, GOOD LORD... HAHAHAHA!
WHY ARE YOU LAUGHING?!
I'M IMAGINING HISTORICAL RE-ENACTMENT NERDS IN 2099 STAGING "ANTIFA VS. PATRIOTS" BATTLES, ALL JUST STREAMING AT EACH OTHER AND TWEETING.
FUCK, WHERE'S MY PHONE?
WE COULD MAKE MONEY OFF OF THIS!
OH, MAN, JONES IS KICKING ASS...
... THIS SEEMS UNFAIR...

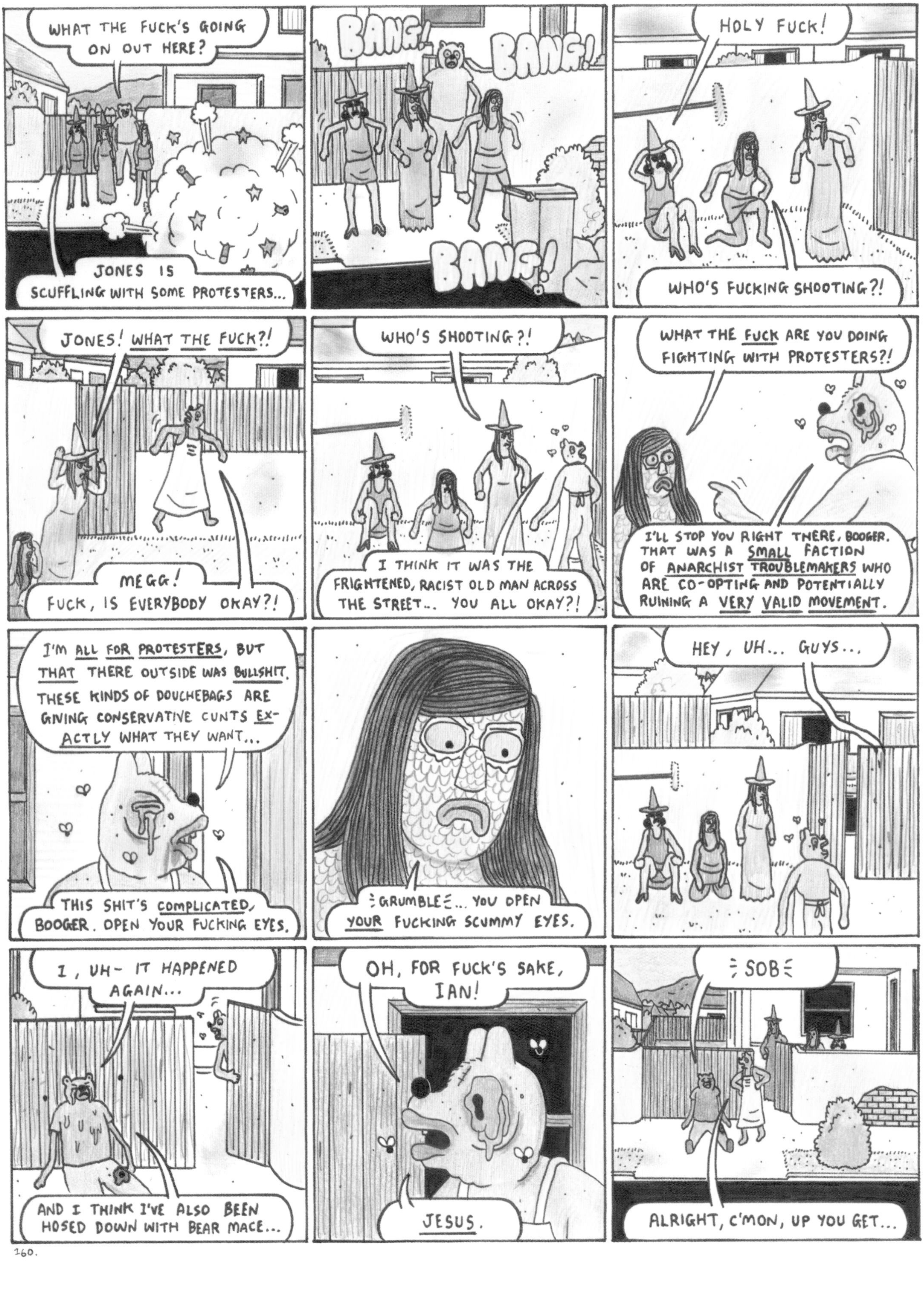
WHAT THE FUCK'S GOING ON OUT HERE?
JONES IS SCUFFLING WITH SOME PROTESTERS...
BANG!
BANG!
BANG!
HOLY FUCK!
WHO'S FUCKING SHOOTING?!
JONES! WHAT THE FUCK?!
MEGG! FUCK, IS EVERYBODY OKAY?!
WHO'S SHOOTING?!
I THINK IT WAS THE FRIGHTENED, RACIST OLD MAN ACROSS THE STREET... YOU ALL OKAY?!
WHAT THE FUCK ARE YOU DOING FIGHTING WITH PROTESTERS?!
I'LL STOP YOU RIGHT THERE, BOOGER. THAT WAS A SMALL FACTION OF ANARCHIST TROUBLEMAKERS WHO ARE CO-OPTING AND POTENTIALLY RUINING A VERY VALID MOVEMENT.
I'M ALL FOR PROTESTERS, BUT THAT THERE OUTSIDE WAS BULLSHIT. THESE KINDS OF DOUCHEBAGS ARE GIVING CONSERVATIVE CUNTS EXACTLY WHAT THEY WANT...
THIS SHIT'S COMPLICATED, BOOGER. OPEN YOUR FUCKING EYES.
GRUMBLE... YOU OPEN YOUR FUCKING SCUMMY EYES.
HEY, UH... GUYS...
I, UH- IT HAPPENED AGAIN...
AND I THINK I'VE ALSO BEEN HOSED DOWN WITH BEAR MACE...
OH, FOR FUCK'S SAKE, IAN!
JESUS.
SOB
ALRIGHT, C'MON, UP YOU GET...

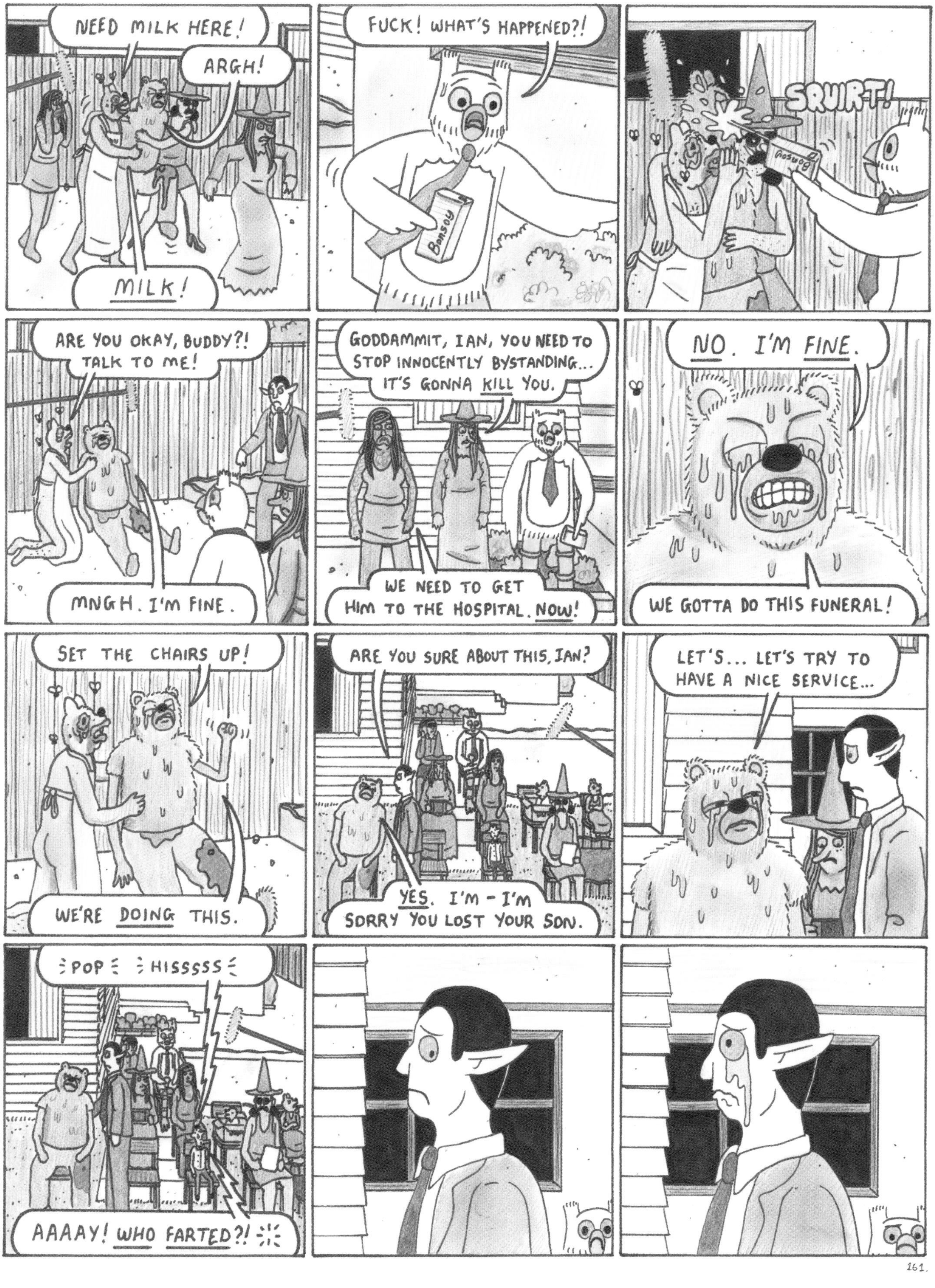
NEED MILK HERE!
ARGH!
MILK!
FUCK! WHAT'S HAPPENED?!
Bonsoy
SQUIRT!
Bonsoy
ARE YOU OKAY, BUDDY?! TALK TO ME!
MNGH. I'M FINE.
GODDAMMIT, IAN, YOU NEED TO STOP INNOCENTLY BYSTANDING... IT'S GONNA KILL YOU.
WE NEED TO GET HIM TO THE HOSPITAL. NOW!
NO. I'M FINE.
WE GOTTA DO THIS FUNERAL!
SET THE CHAIRS UP!
WE'RE DOING THIS.
ARE YOU SURE ABOUT THIS, IAN?
YES. I'M - I'M SORRY YOU LOST YOUR SON.
LET'S... LET'S TRY TO HAVE A NICE SERVICE...
POP HISSSSS
AAAAY! WHO FARTED?!

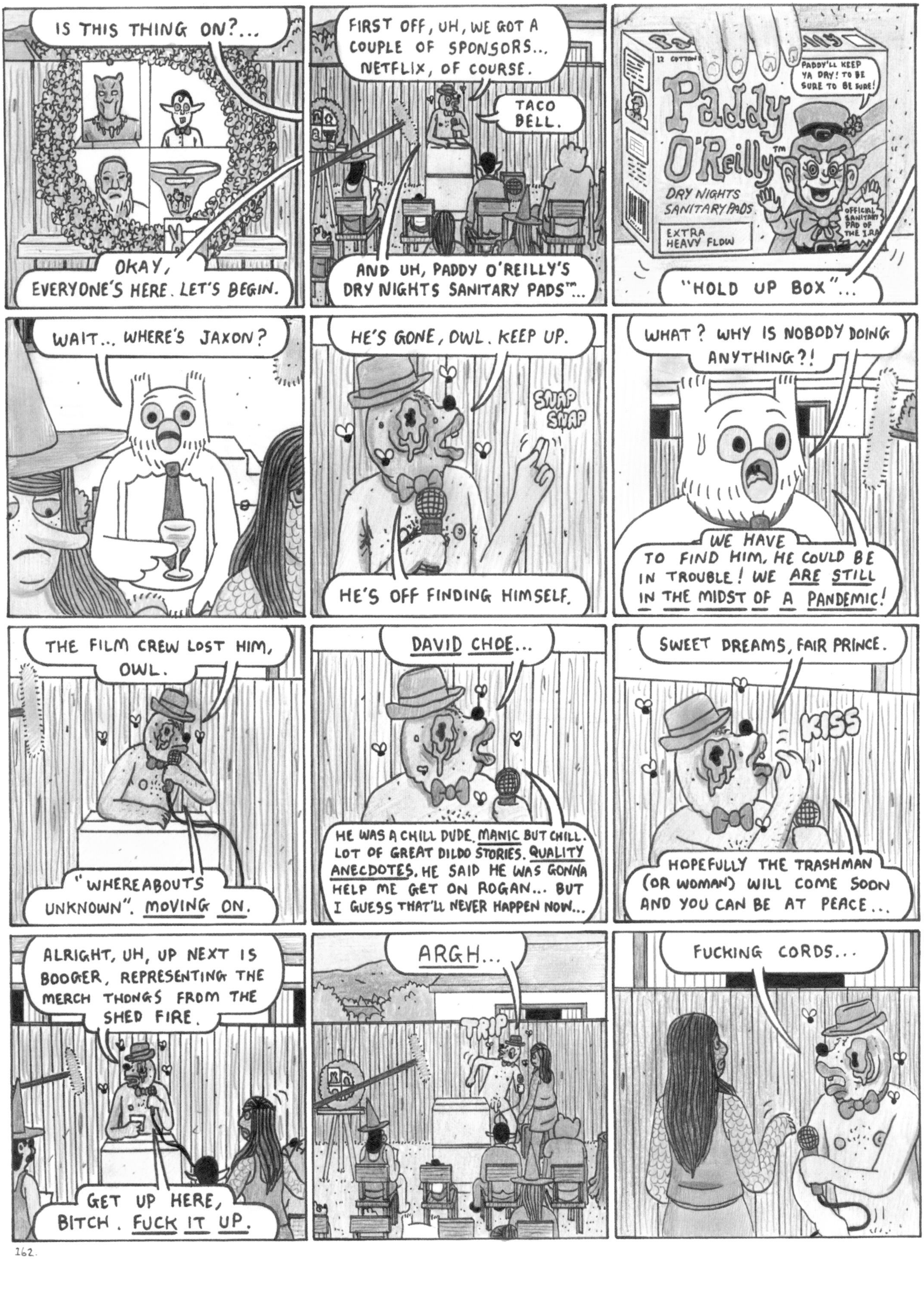
IS THIS THING ON?...
OKAY, EVERYONE'S HERE. LET'S BEGIN.
FIRST OFF, UH, WE GOT A COUPLE OF SPONSORS... NETFLIX, OF COURSE.
TACO BELL.
AND UH, PADDY O'REILLY'S DRY NIGHTS SANITARY PADS™...
PADDY'LL KEEP YA DRY! TO BE SURE TO BE SURE!
Paddy O'Reilly™
DRY NIGHTS SANITARY PADS
EXTRA HEAVY FLOW
OFFICIAL SANITARY PAD OF THE I.R.A.
"HOLD UP BOX"...
WAIT... WHERE'S JAXON?
HE'S GONE, OWL. KEEP UP.
SNAP SNAP
HE'S OFF FINDING HIMSELF.
WHAT? WHY IS NOBODY DOING ANYTHING?!
WE HAVE TO FIND HIM, HE COULD BE IN TROUBLE! WE ARE STILL IN THE MIDST OF A PANDEMIC!
THE FILM CREW LOST HIM, OWL.
"WHEREABOUTS UNKNOWN". MOVING ON.
DAVID CHOE...
HE WAS A CHILL DUDE. MANIC BUT CHILL. LOT OF GREAT DILDO STORIES. QUALITY ANECDOTES. HE SAID HE WAS GONNA HELP ME GET ON ROGAN... BUT I GUESS THAT'LL NEVER HAPPEN NOW...
SWEET DREAMS, FAIR PRINCE.
KISS
HOPEFULLY THE TRASHMAN (OR WOMAN) WILL COME SOON AND YOU CAN BE AT PEACE...
ALRIGHT, UH, UP NEXT IS BOOGER, REPRESENTING THE MERCH THONGS FROM THE SHED FIRE.
GET UP HERE, BITCH. FUCK IT UP.
ARGH...
TRIP
FUCKING CORDS...

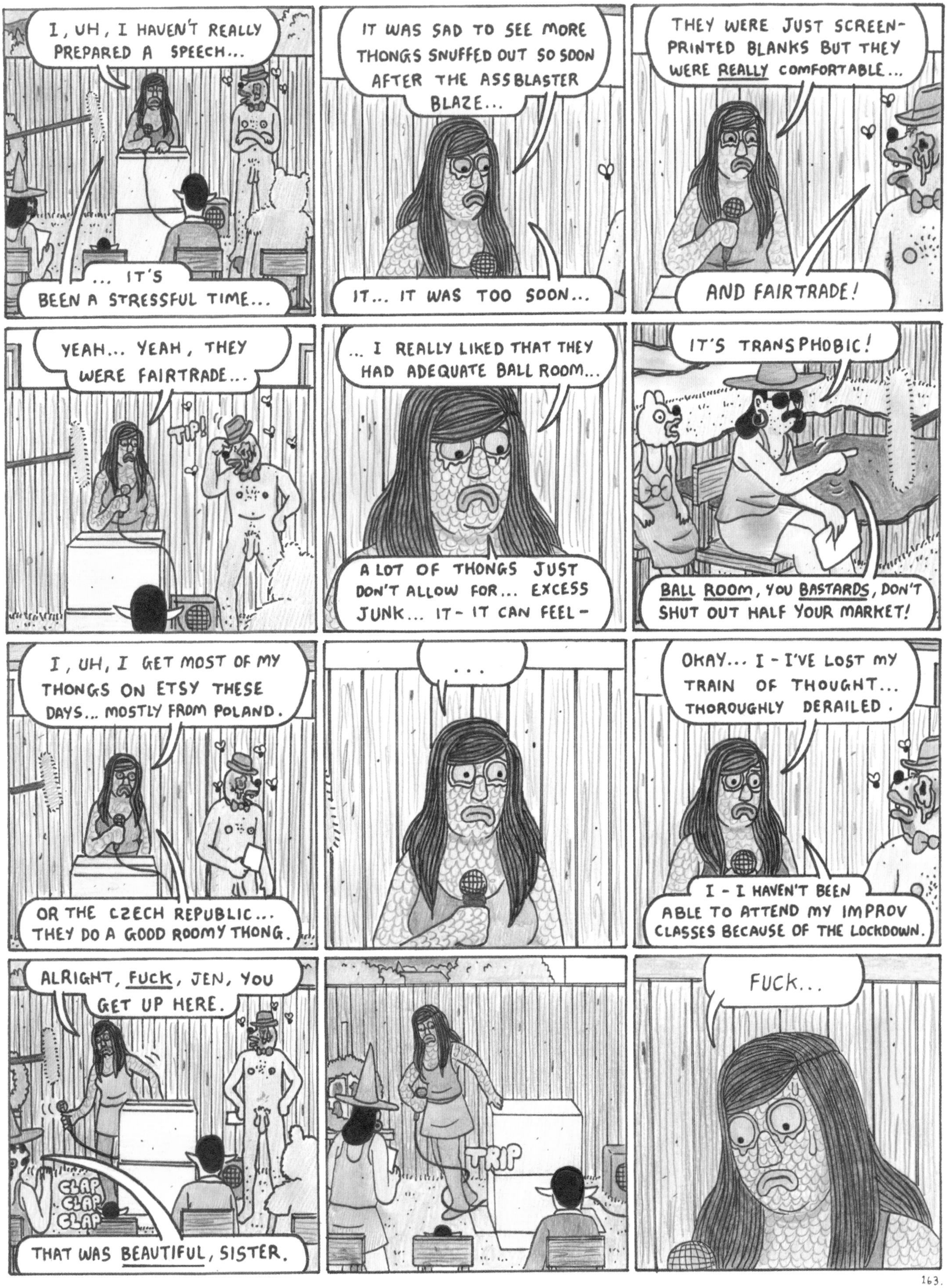

I, UH, I HAVEN'T REALLY PREPARED A SPEECH...
... IT'S BEEN A STRESSFUL TIME...
IT WAS SAD TO SEE MORE THONGS SNUFFED OUT SO SOON AFTER THE ASSBLASTER BLAZE...
IT... IT WAS TOO SOON...
THEY WERE JUST SCREEN-PRINTED BLANKS BUT THEY WERE REALLY COMFORTABLE...
AND FAIRTRADE!
YEAH... YEAH, THEY WERE FAIRTRADE...
TIP!
... I REALLY LIKED THAT THEY HAD ADEQUATE BALL ROOM...
A LOT OF THONGS JUST DON'T ALLOW FOR... EXCESS JUNK... IT- IT CAN FEEL-
IT'S TRANSPHOBIC!
BALL ROOM, YOU BASTARDS, DON'T SHUT OUT HALF YOUR MARKET!
I, UH, I GET MOST OF MY THONGS ON ETSY THESE DAYS... MOSTLY FROM POLAND.
OR THE CZECH REPUBLIC... THEY DO A GOOD ROOMY THONG.
...
OKAY... I - I'VE LOST MY TRAIN OF THOUGHT... THOROUGHLY DERAILED.
I - I HAVEN'T BEEN ABLE TO ATTEND MY IMPROV CLASSES BECAUSE OF THE LOCKDOWN.
ALRIGHT, FUCK, JEN, YOU GET UP HERE.
CLAP CLAP CLAP
THAT WAS BEAUTIFUL, SISTER.
TRIP
FUCK...

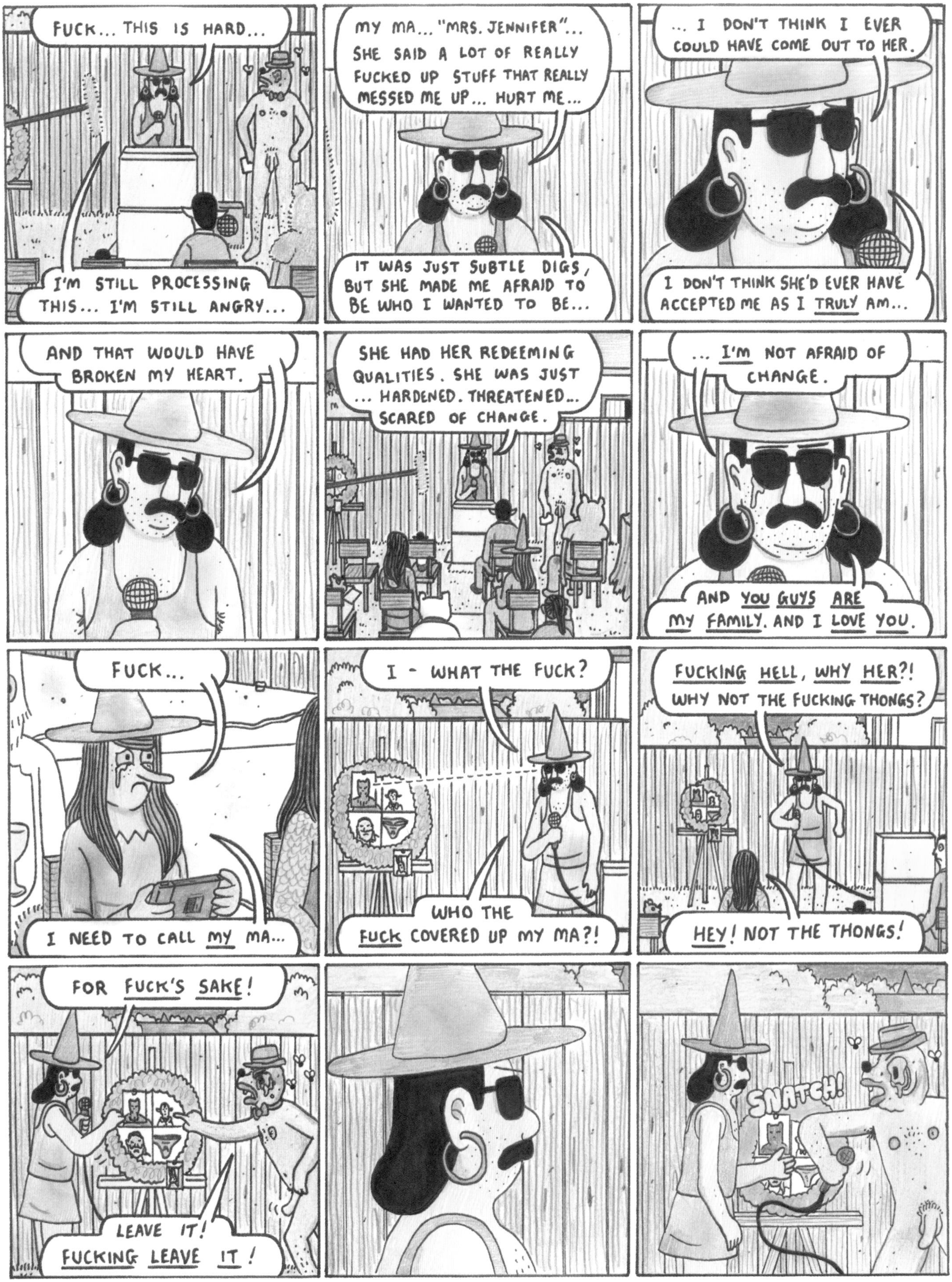
FUCK... THIS IS HARD...
I'M STILL PROCESSING THIS... I'M STILL ANGRY...
MY MA... "MRS. JENNIFER"... SHE SAID A LOT OF REALLY FUCKED UP STUFF THAT REALLY MESSED ME UP... HURT ME...
IT WAS JUST SUBTLE DIGS, BUT SHE MADE ME AFRAID TO BE WHO I WANTED TO BE...
... I DON'T THINK I EVER COULD HAVE COME OUT TO HER.
I DON'T THINK SHE'D EVER HAVE ACCEPTED ME AS I TRULY AM...
AND THAT WOULD HAVE BROKEN MY HEART.
SHE HAD HER REDEEMING QUALITIES. SHE WAS JUST ... HARDENED. THREATENED... SCARED OF CHANGE.
... I'M NOT AFRAID OF CHANGE.
AND YOU GUYS ARE MY FAMILY. AND I LOVE YOU.
FUCK...
I NEED TO CALL MY MA...
I - WHAT THE FUCK?
WHO THE FUCK COVERED UP MY MA?!
FUCKING HELL, WHY HER?! WHY NOT THE FUCKING THONGS?
HEY! NOT THE THONGS!
FOR FUCK'S SAKE!
LEAVE IT! FUCKING LEAVE IT!
SNATCH!

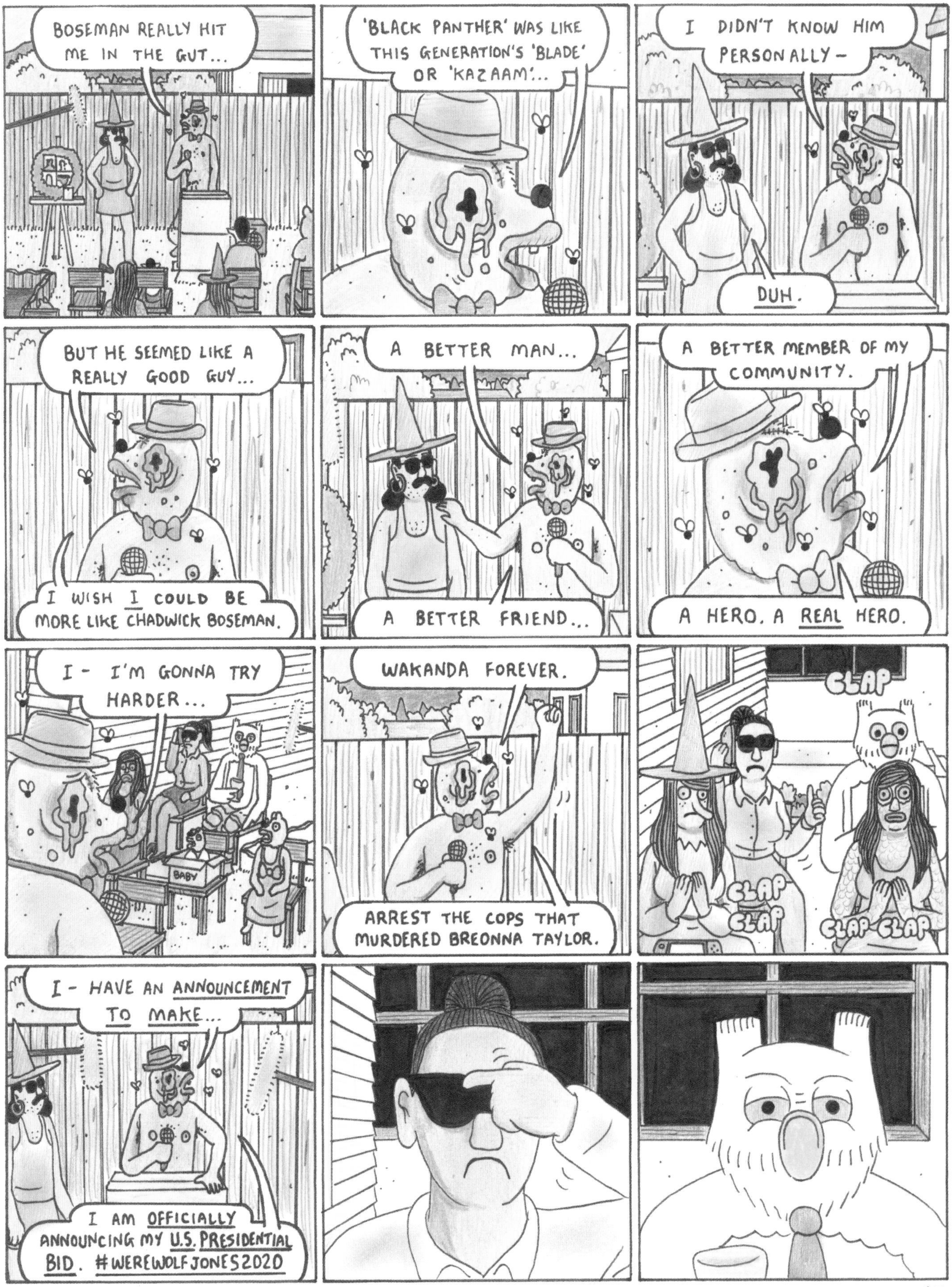
BOSEMAN REALLY HIT ME IN THE GUT...
'BLACK PANTHER' WAS LIKE THIS GENERATION'S 'BLADE' OR 'KAZAAM'...
I DIDN'T KNOW HIM PERSONALLY—
DUH.
BUT HE SEEMED LIKE A REALLY GOOD GUY...
I WISH I COULD BE MORE LIKE CHADWICK BOSEMAN.
A BETTER MAN...
A BETTER FRIEND...
A BETTER MEMBER OF MY COMMUNITY.
A HERO. A REAL HERO.
I- I'M GONNA TRY HARDER...
BABY
WAKANDA FOREVER.
ARREST THE COPS THAT MURDERED BREONNA TAYLOR.
CLAP
CLAP
CLAP
CLAP CLAP
I- HAVE AN ANNOUNCEMENT TO MAKE...
I AM OFFICIALLY ANNOUNCING MY U.S. PRESIDENTIAL BID. #WEREWOLFJONES2020

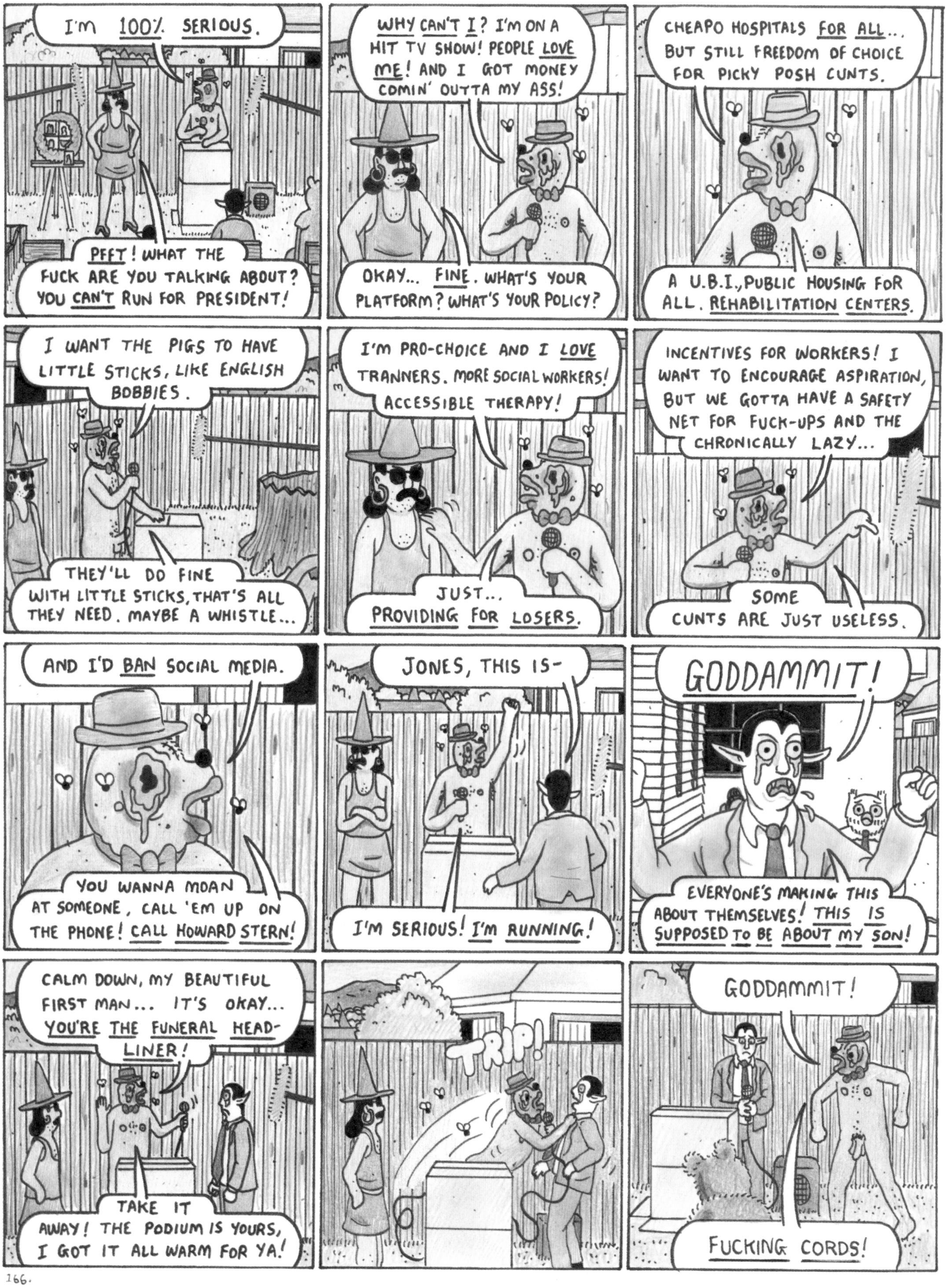
I'M 100% SERIOUS.
PFFT! WHAT THE FUCK ARE YOU TALKING ABOUT? YOU CAN'T RUN FOR PRESIDENT!
WHY CAN'T I? I'M ON A HIT TV SHOW! PEOPLE LOVE ME! AND I GOT MONEY COMIN' OUTTA MY ASS!
OKAY... FINE. WHAT'S YOUR PLATFORM? WHAT'S YOUR POLICY?
CHEAPO HOSPITALS FOR ALL... BUT STILL FREEDOM OF CHOICE FOR PICKY POSH CUNTS.
A U.B.I., PUBLIC HOUSING FOR ALL. REHABILITATION CENTERS.
I WANT THE PIGS TO HAVE LITTLE STICKS, LIKE ENGLISH BOBBIES.
THEY'LL DO FINE WITH LITTLE STICKS, THAT'S ALL THEY NEED. MAYBE A WHISTLE...
I'M PRO-CHOICE AND I LOVE TRANNERS. MORE SOCIAL WORKERS! ACCESSIBLE THERAPY!
JUST... PROVIDING FOR LOSERS.
INCENTIVES FOR WORKERS! I WANT TO ENCOURAGE ASPIRATION, BUT WE GOTTA HAVE A SAFETY NET FOR FUCK-UPS AND THE CHRONICALLY LAZY...
SOME CUNTS ARE JUST USELESS.
AND I'D BAN SOCIAL MEDIA.
YOU WANNA MOAN AT SOMEONE, CALL 'EM UP ON THE PHONE! CALL HOWARD STERN!
JONES, THIS IS-
I'M SERIOUS! I'M RUNNING!
GODDAMMIT!
EVERYONE'S MAKING THIS ABOUT THEMSELVES! THIS IS SUPPOSED TO BE ABOUT MY SON!
CALM DOWN, MY BEAUTIFUL FIRST MAN... IT'S OKAY... YOU'RE THE FUNERAL HEAD-LINER!
TAKE IT AWAY! THE PODIUM IS YOURS, I GOT IT ALL WARM FOR YA!
TRIP!
GODDAMMIT!
FUCKING CORDS!

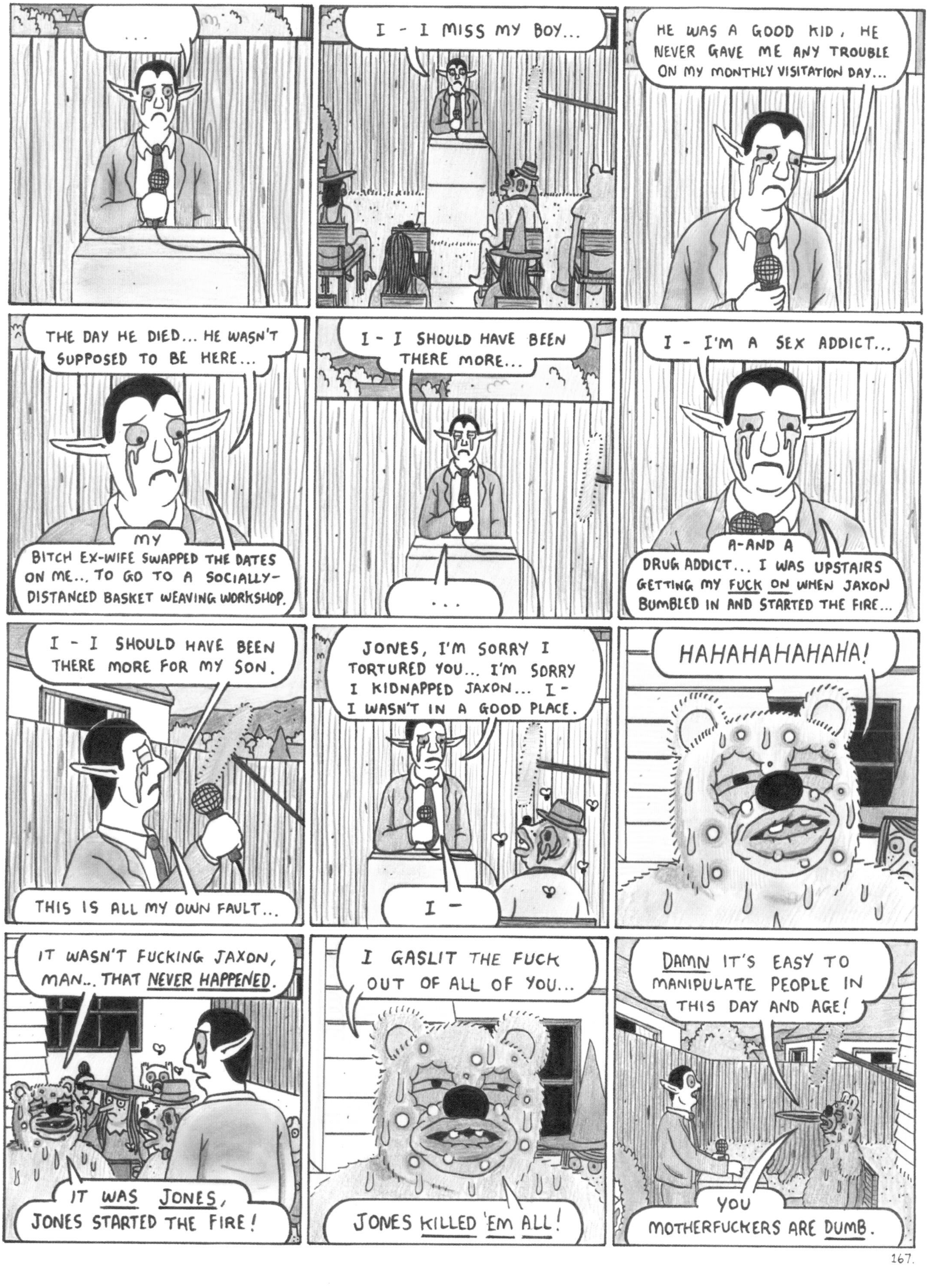
...
I - I MISS MY BOY...
HE WAS A GOOD KID, HE NEVER GAVE ME ANY TROUBLE ON MY MONTHLY VISITATION DAY...
THE DAY HE DIED... HE WASN'T SUPPOSED TO BE HERE...
MY BITCH EX-WIFE SWAPPED THE DATES ON ME... TO GO TO A SOCIALLY-DISTANCED BASKET WEAVING WORKSHOP.
I - I SHOULD HAVE BEEN THERE MORE...
...
I - I'M A SEX ADDICT...
A-AND A DRUG ADDICT... I WAS UPSTAIRS GETTING MY FUCK ON WHEN JAXON BUMBLED IN AND STARTED THE FIRE...
I - I SHOULD HAVE BEEN THERE MORE FOR MY SON.
THIS IS ALL MY OWN FAULT...
JONES, I'M SORRY I TORTURED YOU... I'M SORRY I KIDNAPPED JAXON... I - I WASN'T IN A GOOD PLACE.
I -
HAHAHAHAHAHA!
IT WASN'T FUCKING JAXON, MAN... THAT NEVER HAPPENED.
IT WAS JONES, JONES STARTED THE FIRE!
I GASLIT THE FUCK OUT OF ALL OF YOU...
JONES KILLED 'EM ALL!
DAMN IT'S EASY TO MANIPULATE PEOPLE IN THIS DAY AND AGE!
YOU MOTHERFUCKERS ARE DUMB.

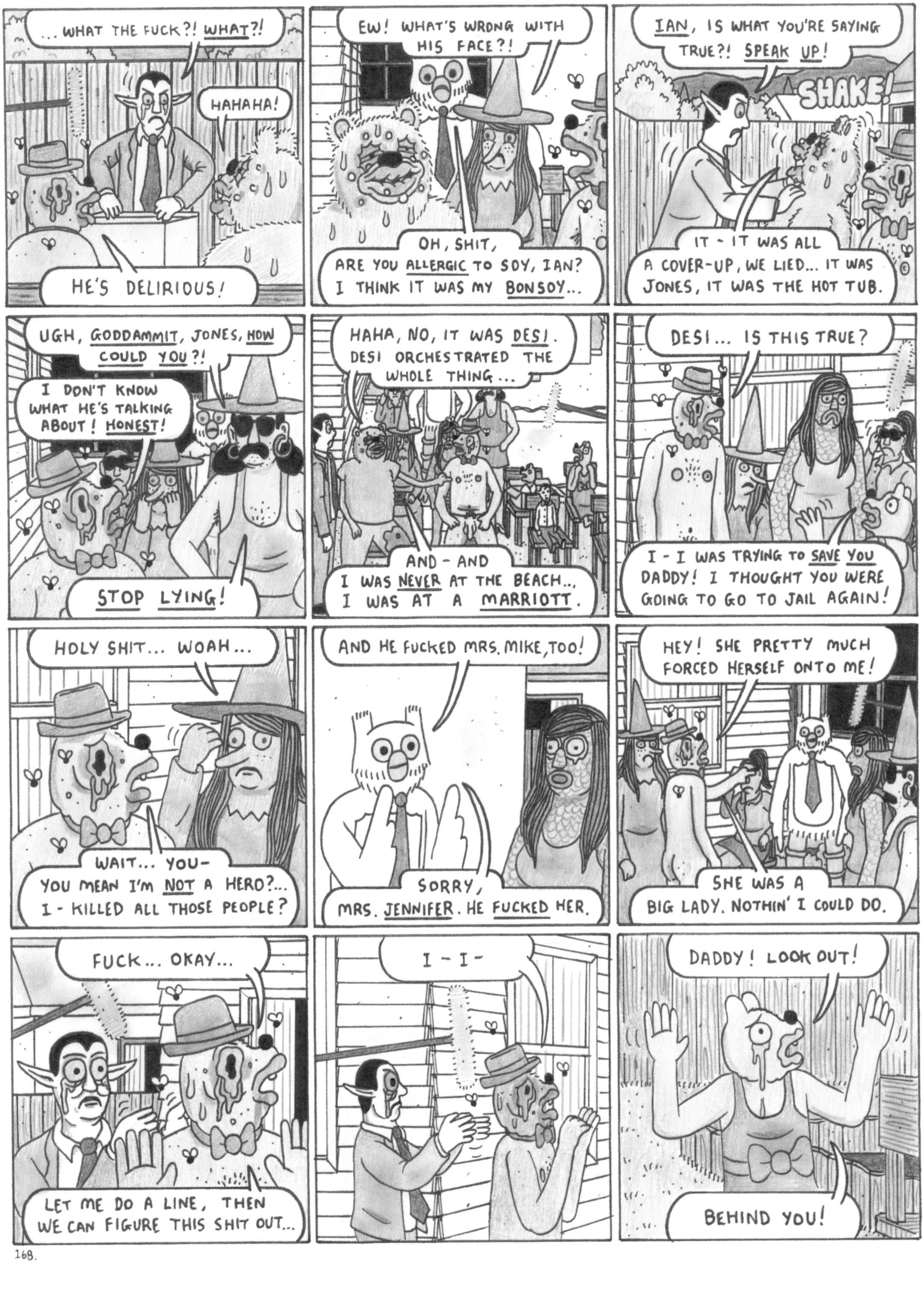

... WHAT THE FUCK?! WHAT?!
HAHAHA!
HE'S DELIRIOUS!
EW! WHAT'S WRONG WITH HIS FACE?!
OH, SHIT, ARE YOU ALLERGIC TO SOY, IAN? I THINK IT WAS MY BONSOY...
IAN, IS WHAT YOU'RE SAYING TRUE?! SPEAK UP!
SHAKE!
IT - IT WAS ALL A COVER-UP, WE LIED... IT WAS JONES, IT WAS THE HOT TUB.
UGH, GODDAMMIT, JONES, HOW COULD YOU?!
I DON'T KNOW WHAT HE'S TALKING ABOUT! HONEST!
STOP LYING!
HAHA, NO, IT WAS DESI. DESI ORCHESTRATED THE WHOLE THING...
AND - AND I WAS NEVER AT THE BEACH... I WAS AT A MARRIOTT.
DESI... IS THIS TRUE?
I - I WAS TRYING TO SAVE YOU DADDY! I THOUGHT YOU WERE GOING TO GO TO JAIL AGAIN!
HOLY SHIT... WOAH...
WAIT... YOU- YOU MEAN I'M NOT A HERO?... I - KILLED ALL THOSE PEOPLE?
AND HE FUCKED MRS. MIKE, TOO!
SORRY, MRS. JENNIFER. HE FUCKED HER.
HEY! SHE PRETTY MUCH FORCED HERSELF ONTO ME!
SHE WAS A BIG LADY. NOTHIN' I COULD DO.
FUCK... OKAY...
LET ME DO A LINE, THEN WE CAN FIGURE THIS SHIT OUT...
I - I-
DADDY! LOOK OUT!
BEHIND YOU!

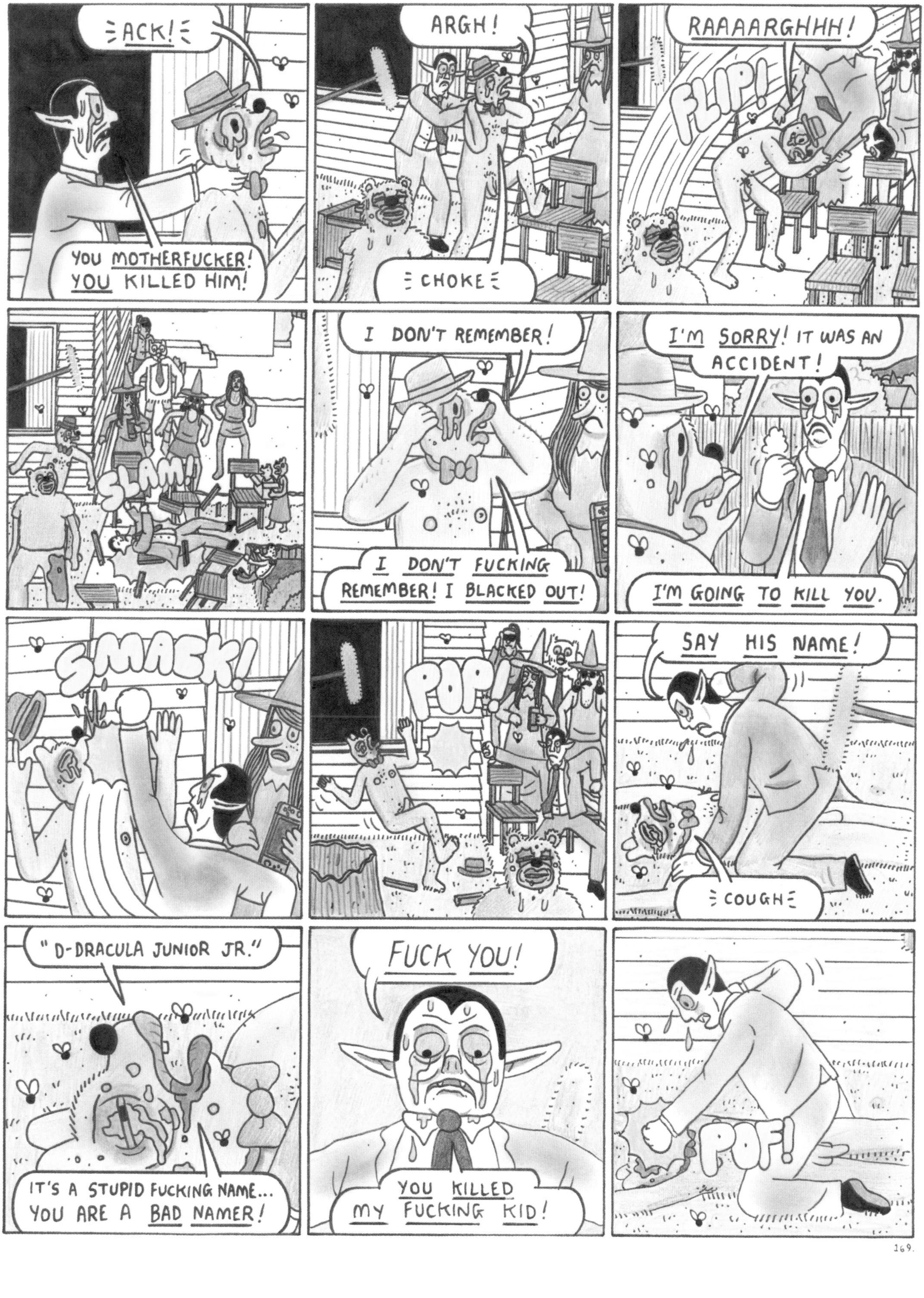
ACK!
YOU MOTHERFUCKER! YOU KILLED HIM!
ARGH!
CHOKE
RAAAARGHHH!
FLIP!
SLAM!
I DON'T REMEMBER!
I DON'T FUCKING REMEMBER! I BLACKED OUT!
I'M SORRY! IT WAS AN ACCIDENT!
I'M GOING TO KILL YOU.
SMACK!
POP!
SAY HIS NAME!
COUGH
"D-DRACULA JUNIOR JR."
IT'S A STUPID FUCKING NAME... YOU ARE A BAD NAMER!
FUCK YOU!
YOU KILLED MY FUCKING KID!
POF!

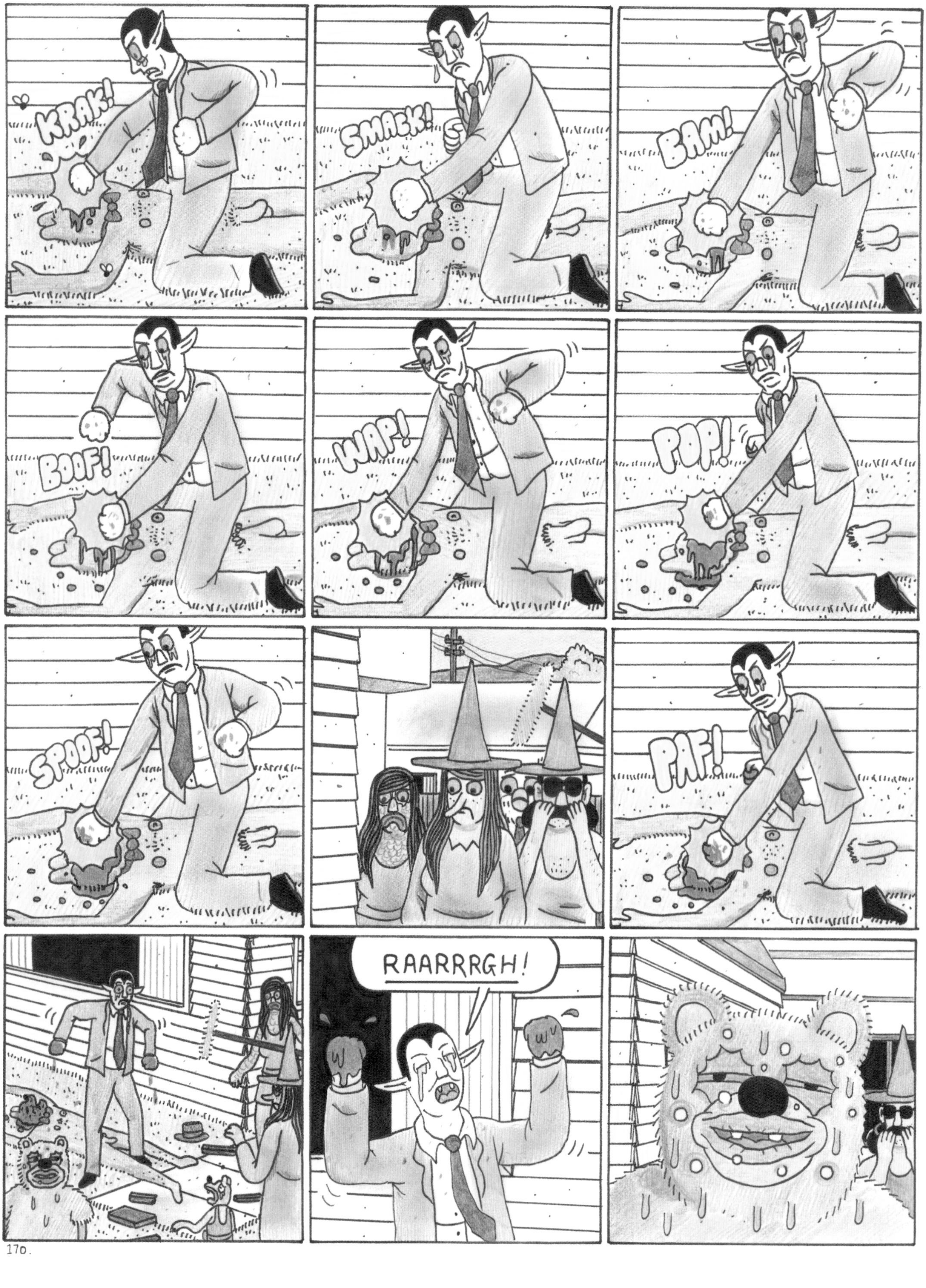
KRAK!
SMACK!
BAM!
BOOF!
WAP!
POP!
SPOOF!
PAF!
RAARRRGH!

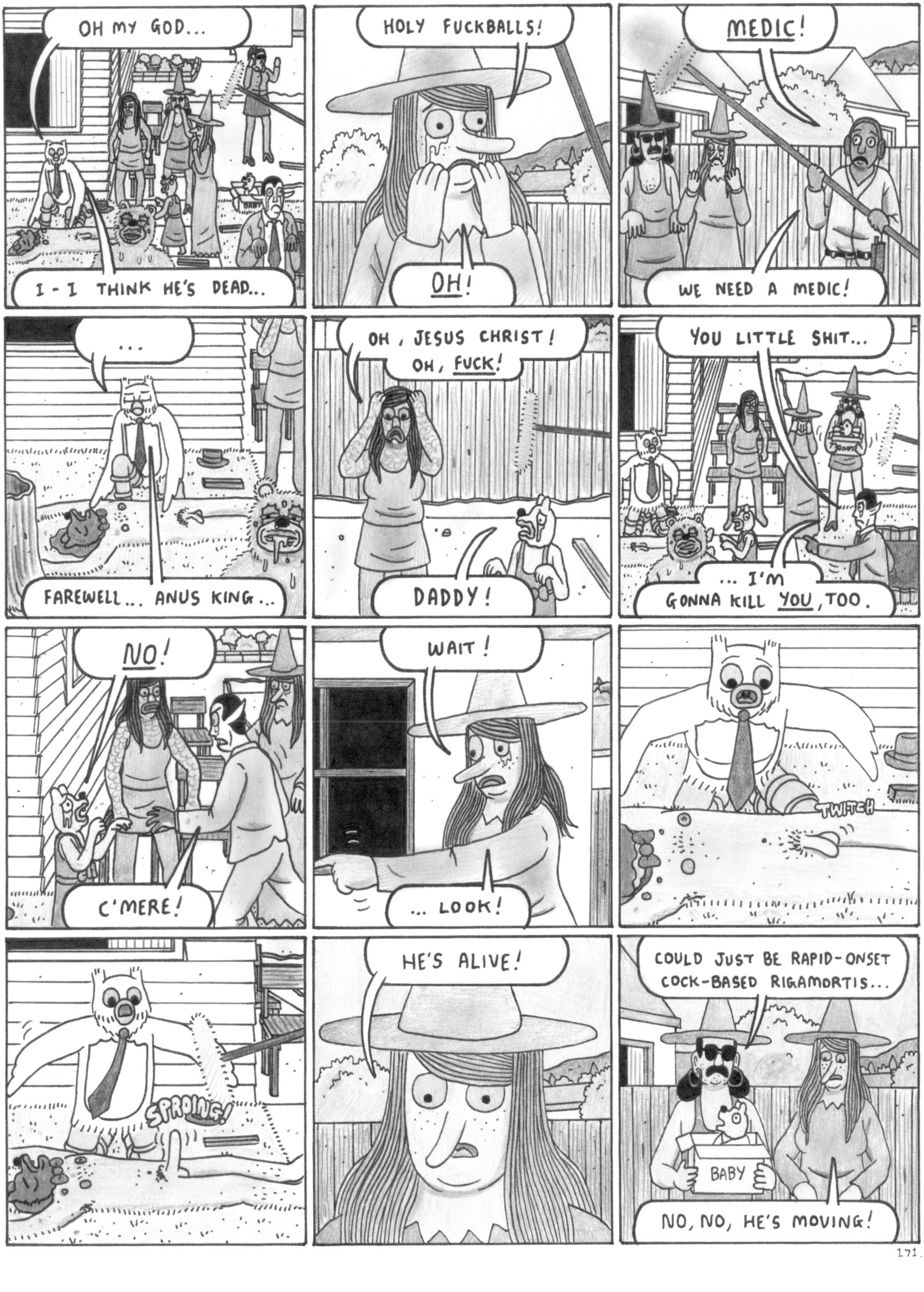
OH MY GOD...
I - I THINK HE'S DEAD...
HOLY FUCKBALLS!
OH!
MEDIC!
WE NEED A MEDIC!
...
FAREWELL... ANUS KING...
OH, JESUS CHRIST! OH, FUCK!
DADDY!
YOU LITTLE SHIT...
... I'M GONNA KILL YOU, TOO.
NO!
C'MERE!
WAIT!
... LOOK!
TWITCH
SPROING!
HE'S ALIVE!
COULD JUST BE RAPID-ONSET COCK-BASED RIGAMORTIS...
BABY
NO, NO, HE'S MOVING!

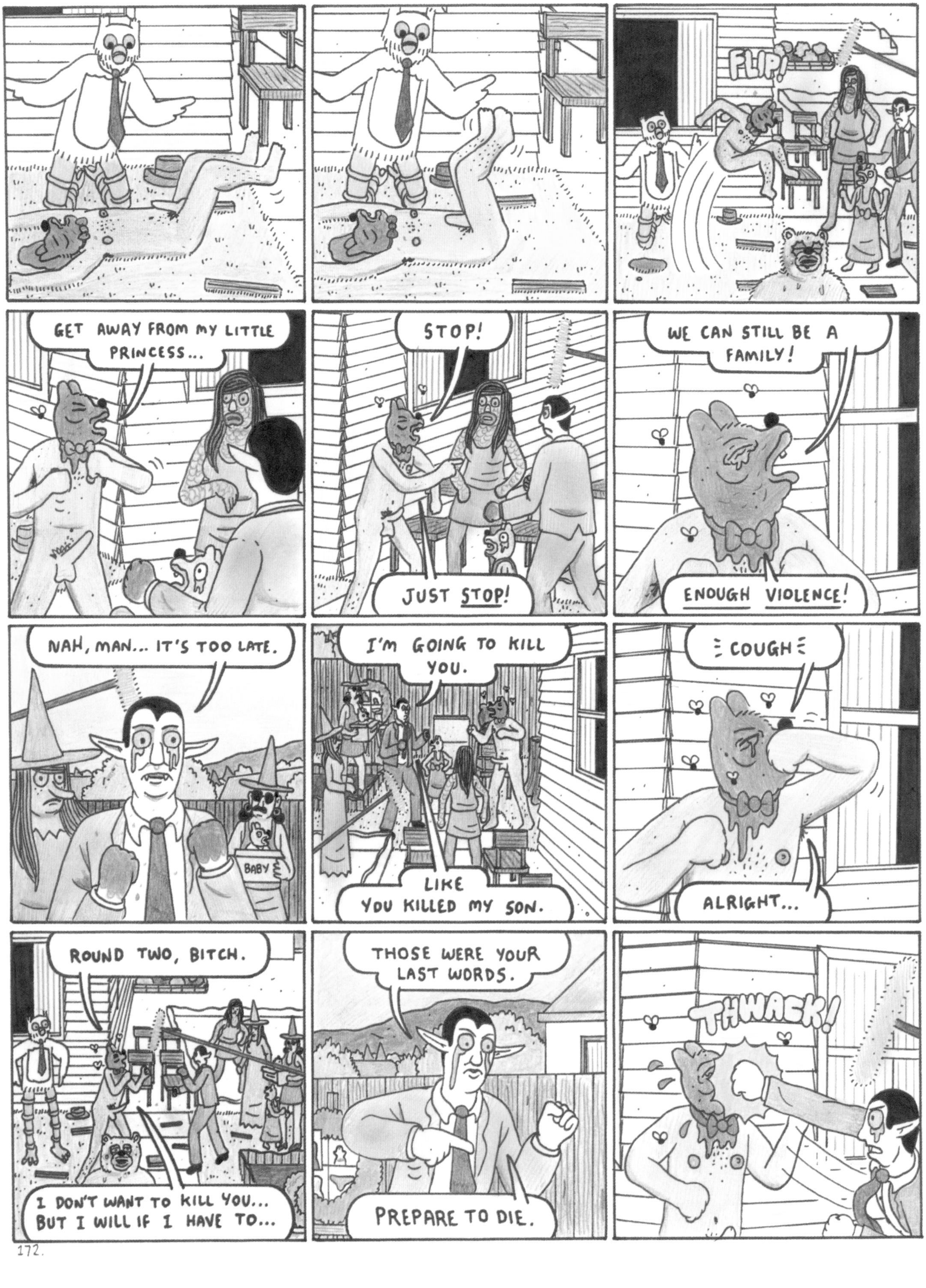
FLIP!
GET AWAY FROM MY LITTLE PRINCESS...
STOP!
JUST STOP!
WE CAN STILL BE A FAMILY!
ENOUGH VIOLENCE!
NAH, MAN... IT'S TOO LATE.
BABY
I'M GOING TO KILL YOU.
LIKE YOU KILLED MY SON.
COUGH
ALRIGHT...
ROUND TWO, BITCH.
I DON'T WANT TO KILL YOU... BUT I WILL IF I HAVE TO...
THOSE WERE YOUR LAST WORDS.
PREPARE TO DIE.
THWACK!

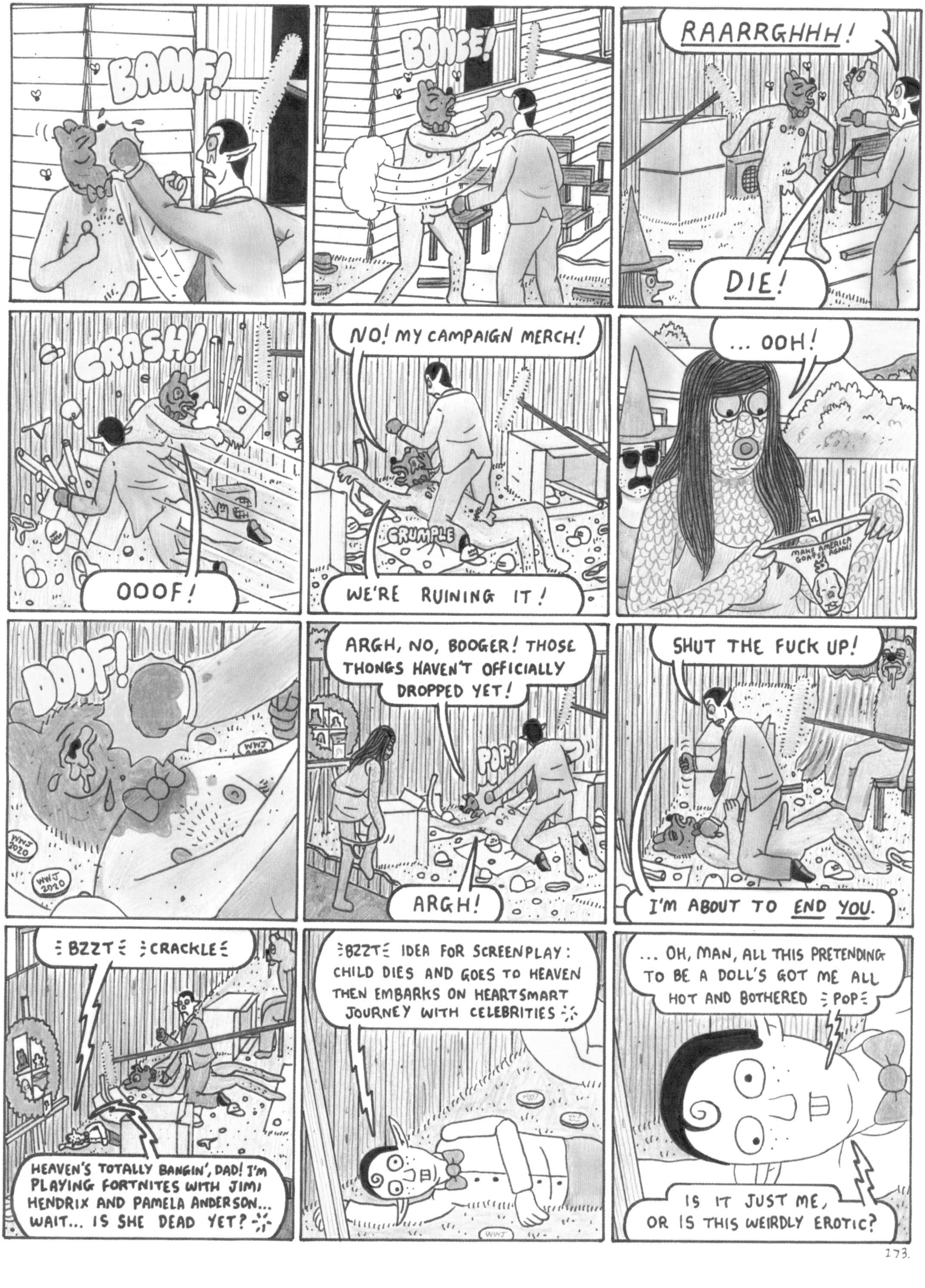
BAMF!
BONCE!
RAARRGHHH!
DIE!
CRASH!
OOOF!
NO! MY CAMPAIGN MERCH!
CRUMPLE
WE'RE RUINING IT!
... OOH!
MAKE AMERICA GOATSE AGAIN!
DOOF!
WWJ 2020
ARGH, NO, BOOGER! THOSE THONGS HAVEN'T OFFICIALLY DROPPED YET!
POP!
ARGH!
SHUT THE FUCK UP!
I'M ABOUT TO END YOU.
BZZT CRACKLE
HEAVEN'S TOTALLY BANGIN', DAD! I'M PLAYING FORTNITES WITH JIMI HENDRIX AND PAMELA ANDERSON... WAIT... IS SHE DEAD YET?
BZZT IDEA FOR SCREENPLAY: CHILD DIES AND GOES TO HEAVEN THEN EMBARKS ON HEARTSMART JOURNEY WITH CELEBRITIES
... OH, MAN, ALL THIS PRETENDING TO BE A DOLL'S GOT ME ALL HOT AND BOTHERED POP
IS IT JUST ME, OR IS THIS WEIRDLY EROTIC?

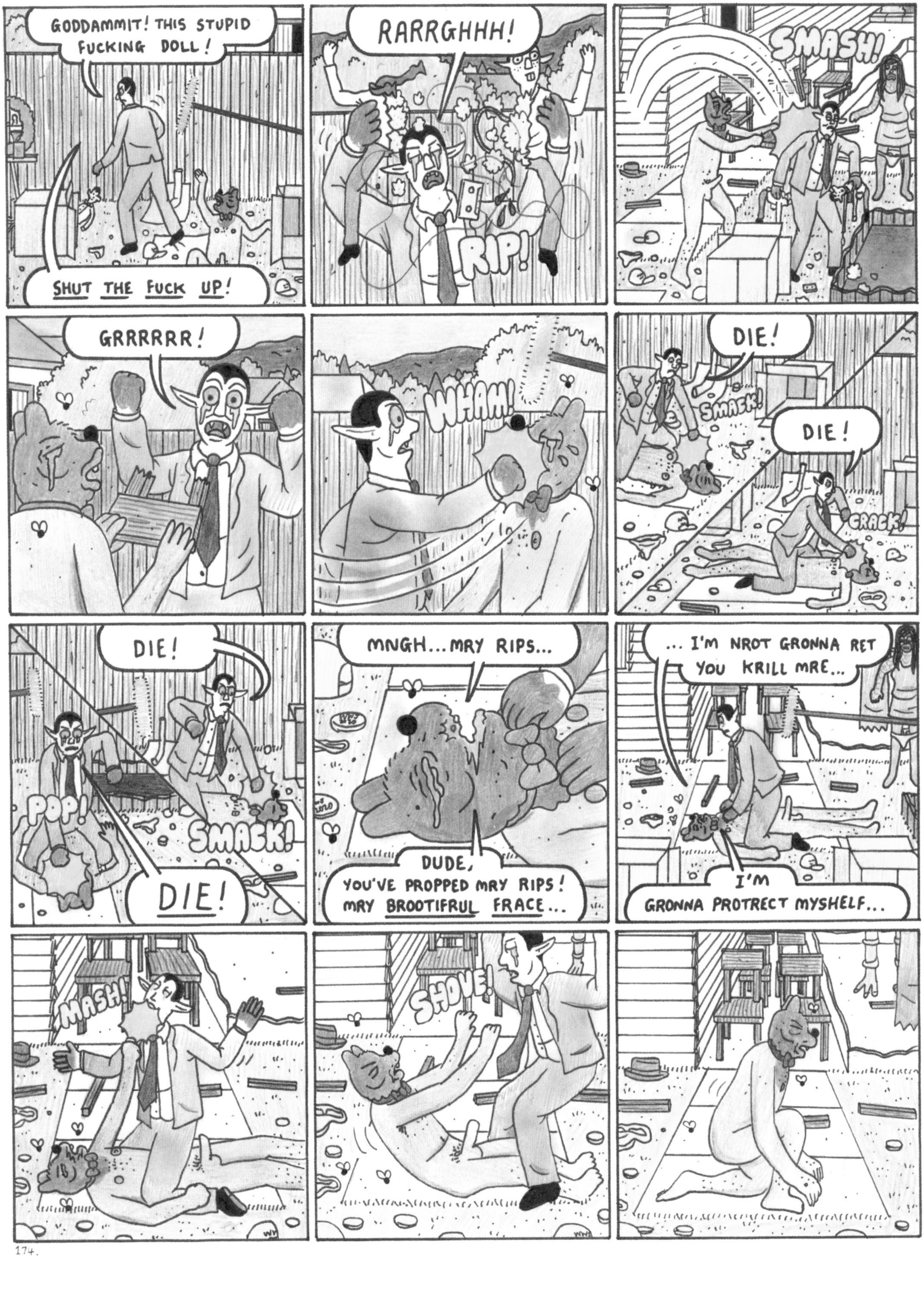
GODDAMMIT! THIS STUPID FUCKING DOLL!
SHUT THE FUCK UP!
RARRGHHH!
RIP!
SMASH!
GRRRRRR!
WHAM!
DIE!
SMACK!
DIE!
CRACK!
DIE!
POP!
SMACK!
DIE!
MNGH... MRY RIPS...
DUDE, YOU'VE PROPPED MRY RIPS! MRY BROOTIFRUL FRACE...
... I'M NROT GRONNA RET YOU KRILL MRE...
I'M GRONNA PROTRECT MYSHELF...
MASH!
SHOVE!

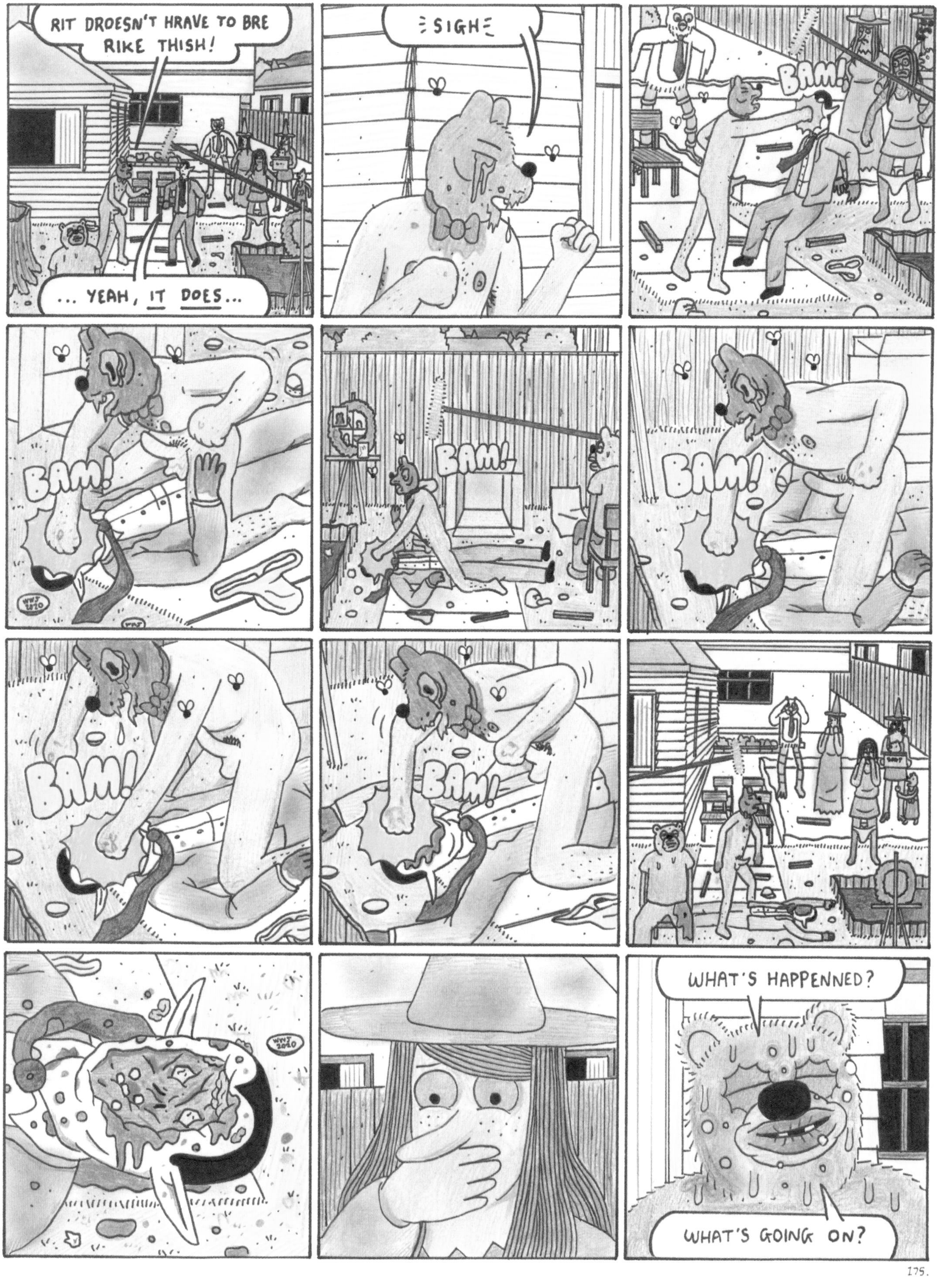
RIT DROESN'T HRAVE TO BRE RIKE THISH!
... YEAH, IT DOES...
SIGH
BAM!
BAM!
BAM!
BAM!
BAM!
BAM!
WHAT'S HAPPENNED?
WHAT'S GOING ON?

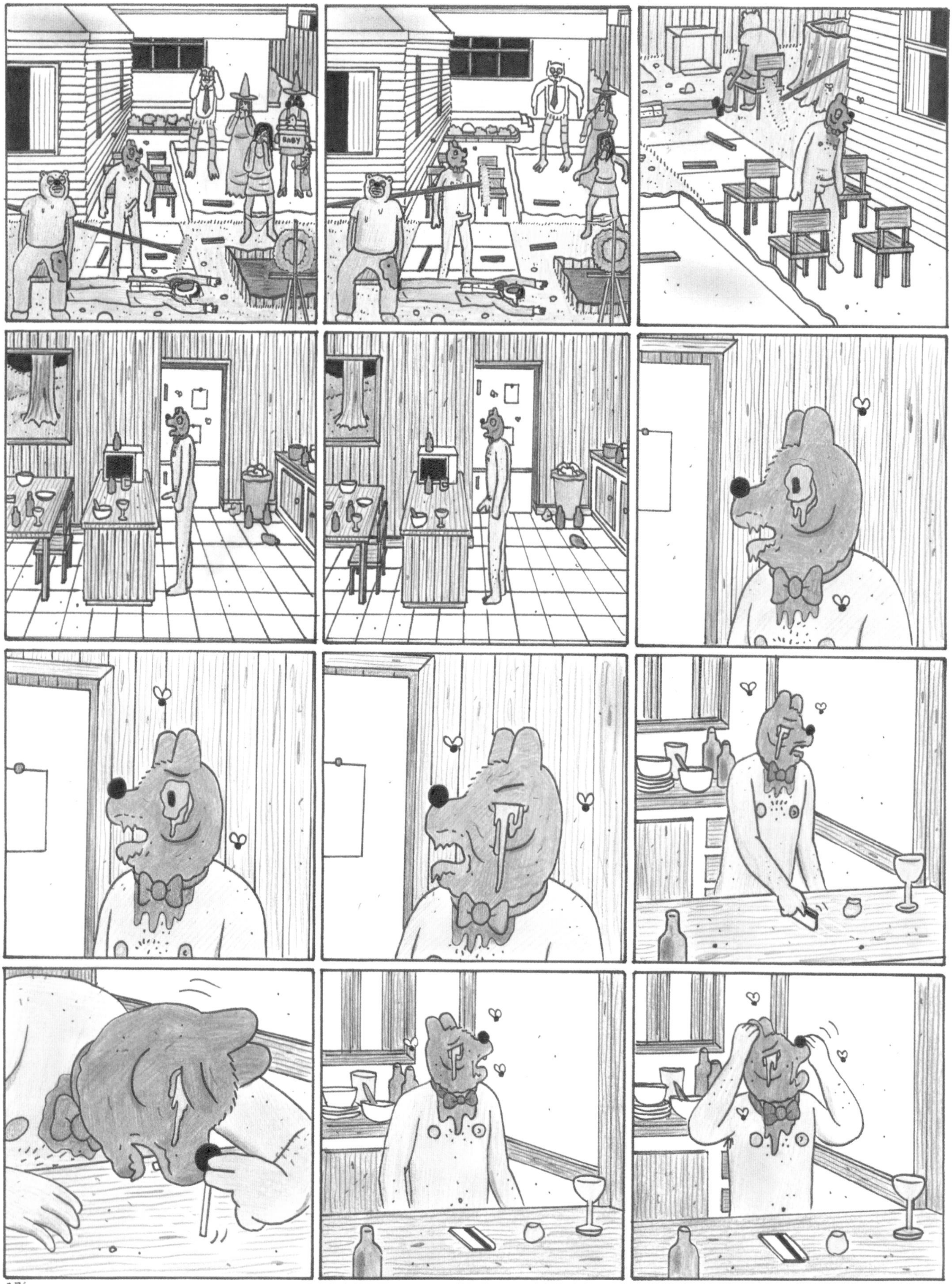
BABY

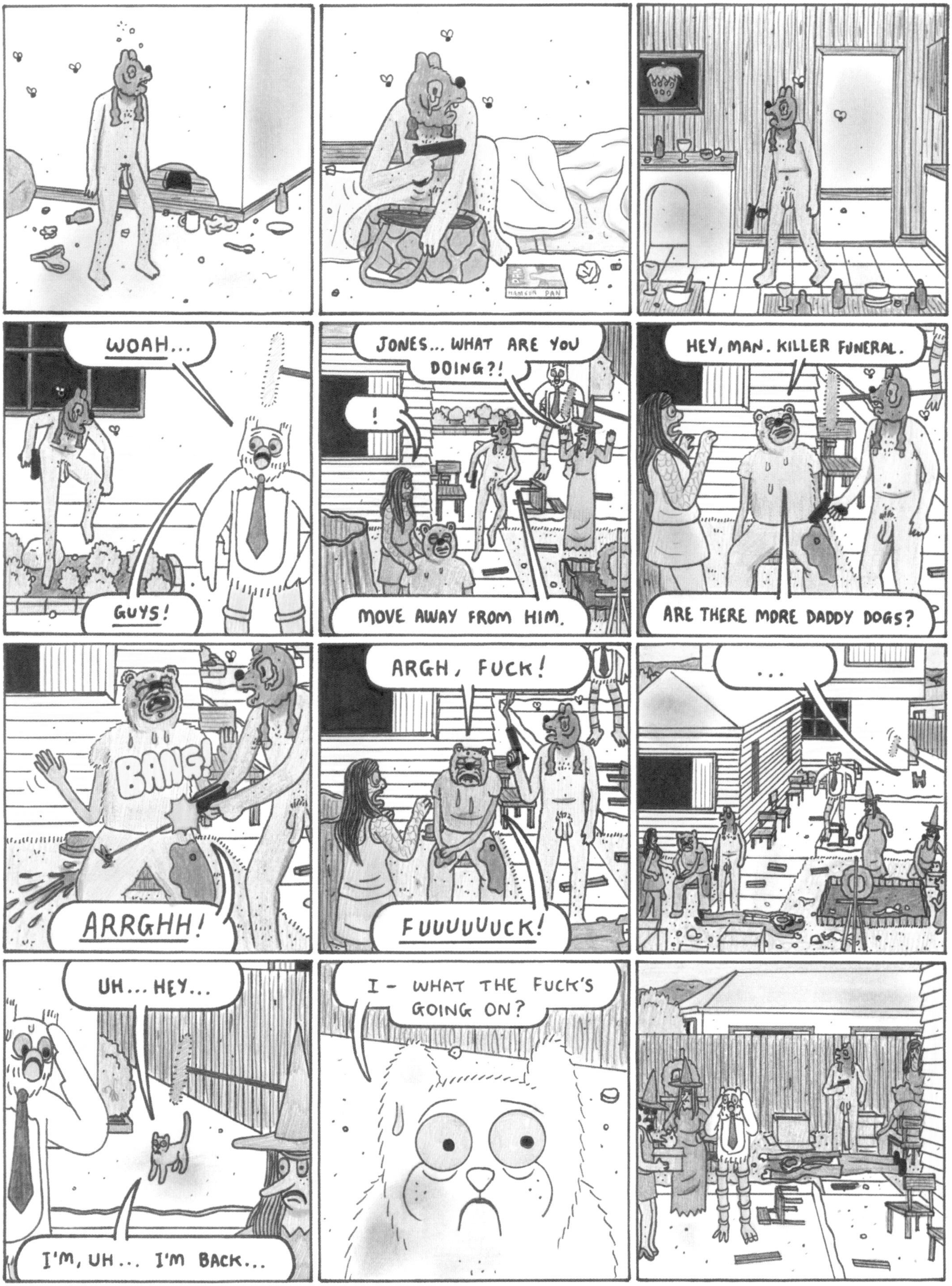

HAMSUN PAN
WOAH...
GUYS!
JONES... WHAT ARE YOU DOING?!
!
MOVE AWAY FROM HIM.
HEY, MAN. KILLER FUNERAL.
ARE THERE MORE DADDY DOGS?
BANG!
ARRGHH!
ARGH, FUCK!
FUUUUUUCK!
...
UH... HEY...
I'M, UH... I'M BACK...
I- WHAT THE FUCK'S GOING ON?

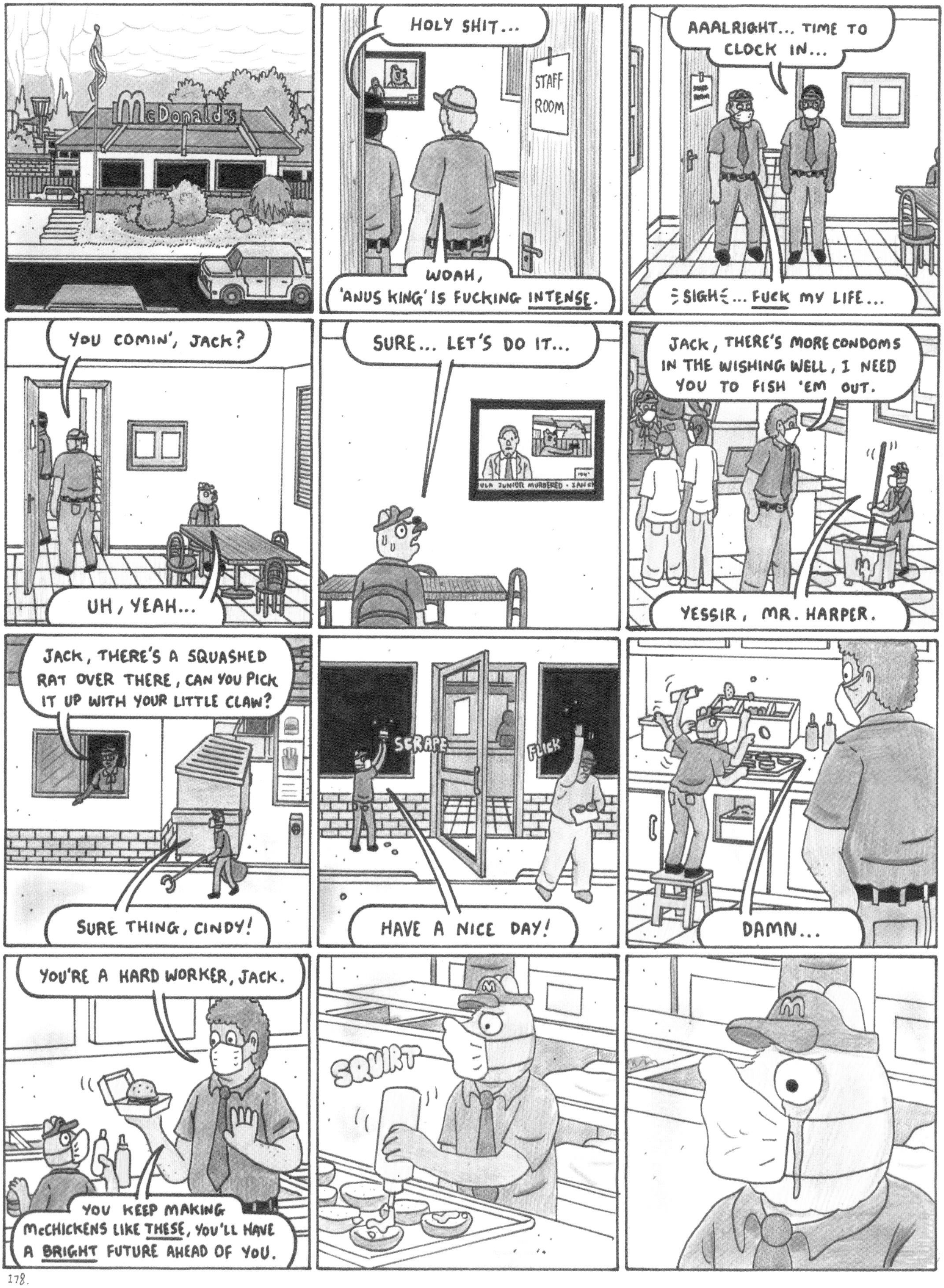
McDonald's
HOLY SHIT...
STAFF ROOM
WOAH, 'ANUS KING' IS FUCKING INTENSE.
AAALRIGHT... TIME TO CLOCK IN...
SIGH... FUCK MY LIFE...
YOU COMIN', JACK?
UH, YEAH...
SURE... LET'S DO IT...
JACK, THERE'S MORE CONDOMS IN THE WISHING WELL, I NEED YOU TO FISH 'EM OUT.
YESSIR, MR. HARPER.
JACK, THERE'S A SQUASHED RAT OVER THERE, CAN YOU PICK IT UP WITH YOUR LITTLE CLAW?
SURE THING, CINDY!
SCRAPE
FLICK
HAVE A NICE DAY!
DAMN...
YOU'RE A HARD WORKER, JACK.
YOU KEEP MAKING McCHICKENS LIKE THESE, YOU'LL HAVE A BRIGHT FUTURE AHEAD OF YOU.
SQUIRT

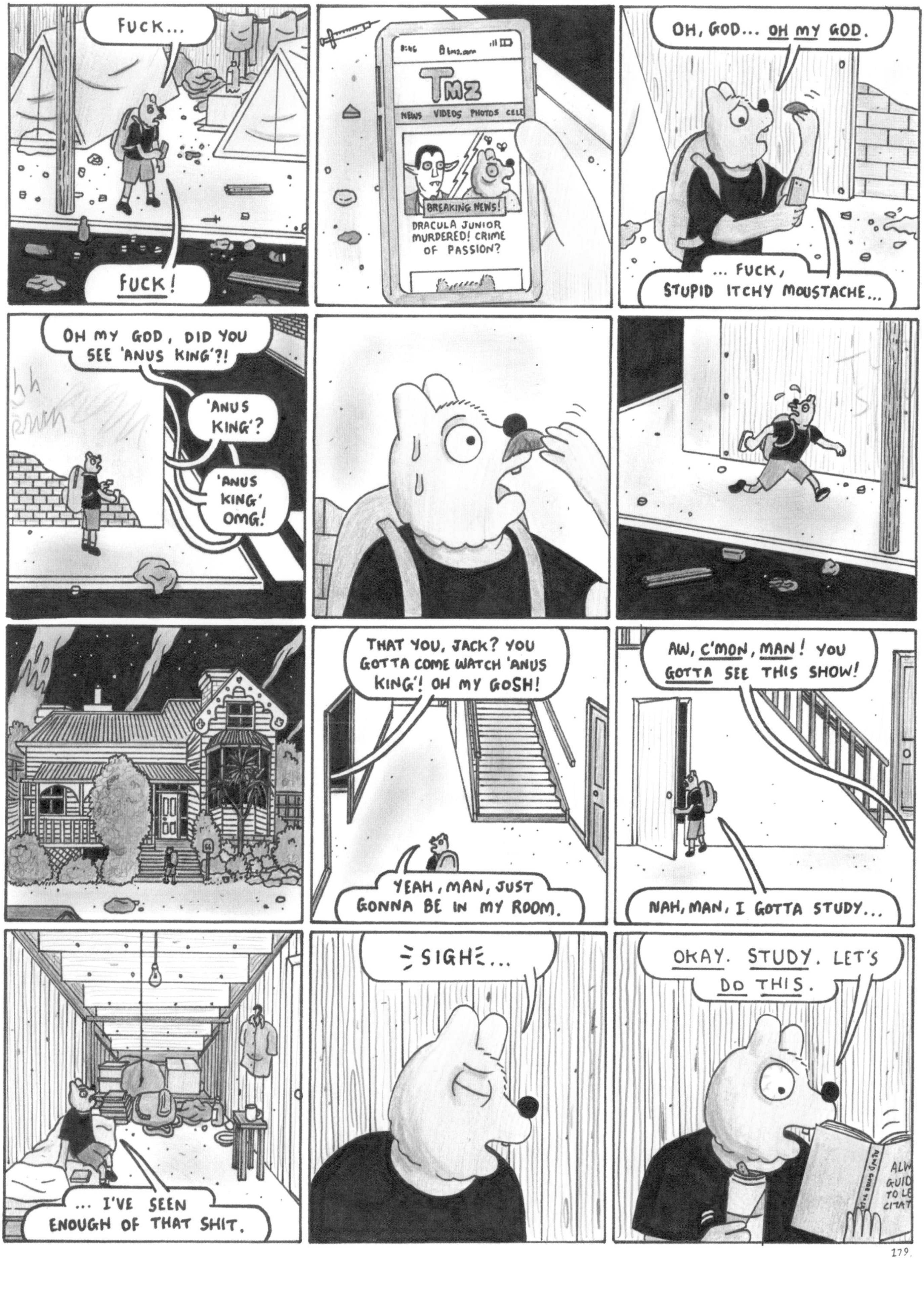

FUCK...
FUCK!
TMZ
NEWS VIDEOS PHOTOS CELE
BREAKING NEWS!
DRACULA JUNIOR MURDERED! CRIME OF PASSION?
OH, GOD... OH MY GOD.
... FUCK, STUPID ITCHY MOUSTACHE...
OH MY GOD, DID YOU SEE 'ANUS KING'?!
'ANUS KING'?
'ANUS KING' OMG!
THAT YOU, JACK? YOU GOTTA COME WATCH 'ANUS KING'! OH MY GOSH!
YEAH, MAN, JUST GONNA BE IN MY ROOM.
AW, C'MON, MAN! YOU GOTTA SEE THIS SHOW!
NAH, MAN, I GOTTA STUDY...
... I'VE SEEN ENOUGH OF THAT SHIT.
SIGH...
OKAY. STUDY. LET'S DO THIS.

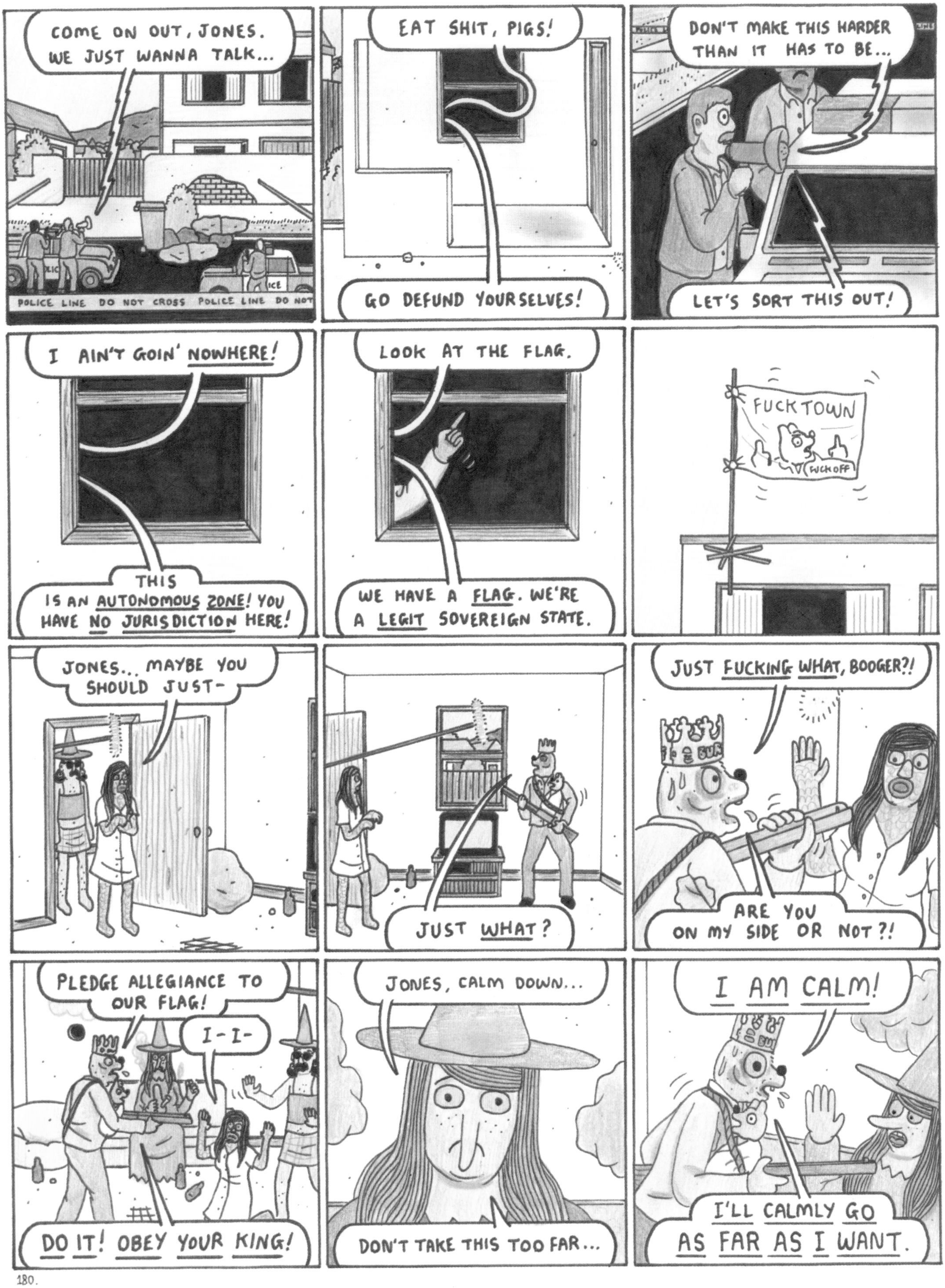
COME ON OUT, JONES. WE JUST WANNA TALK...
POLICE LINE DO NOT CROSS POLICE LINE DO NOT
EAT SHIT, PIGS!
GO DEFUND YOURSELVES!
DON'T MAKE THIS HARDER THAN IT HAS TO BE...
LET'S SORT THIS OUT!
I AIN'T GOIN' NOWHERE!
THIS IS AN AUTONOMOUS ZONE! YOU HAVE NO JURISDICTION HERE!
LOOK AT THE FLAG.
WE HAVE A FLAG. WE'RE A LEGIT SOVEREIGN STATE.
FUCK TOWN
FUCK OFF
JONES... MAYBE YOU SHOULD JUST-
JUST WHAT?
JUST FUCKING WHAT, BOOGER?!
ARE YOU ON MY SIDE OR NOT?!
PLEDGE ALLEGIANCE TO OUR FLAG!
I-I-
DO IT! OBEY YOUR KING!
JONES, CALM DOWN...
DON'T TAKE THIS TOO FAR...
I AM CALM!
I'LL CALMLY GO AS FAR AS I WANT.

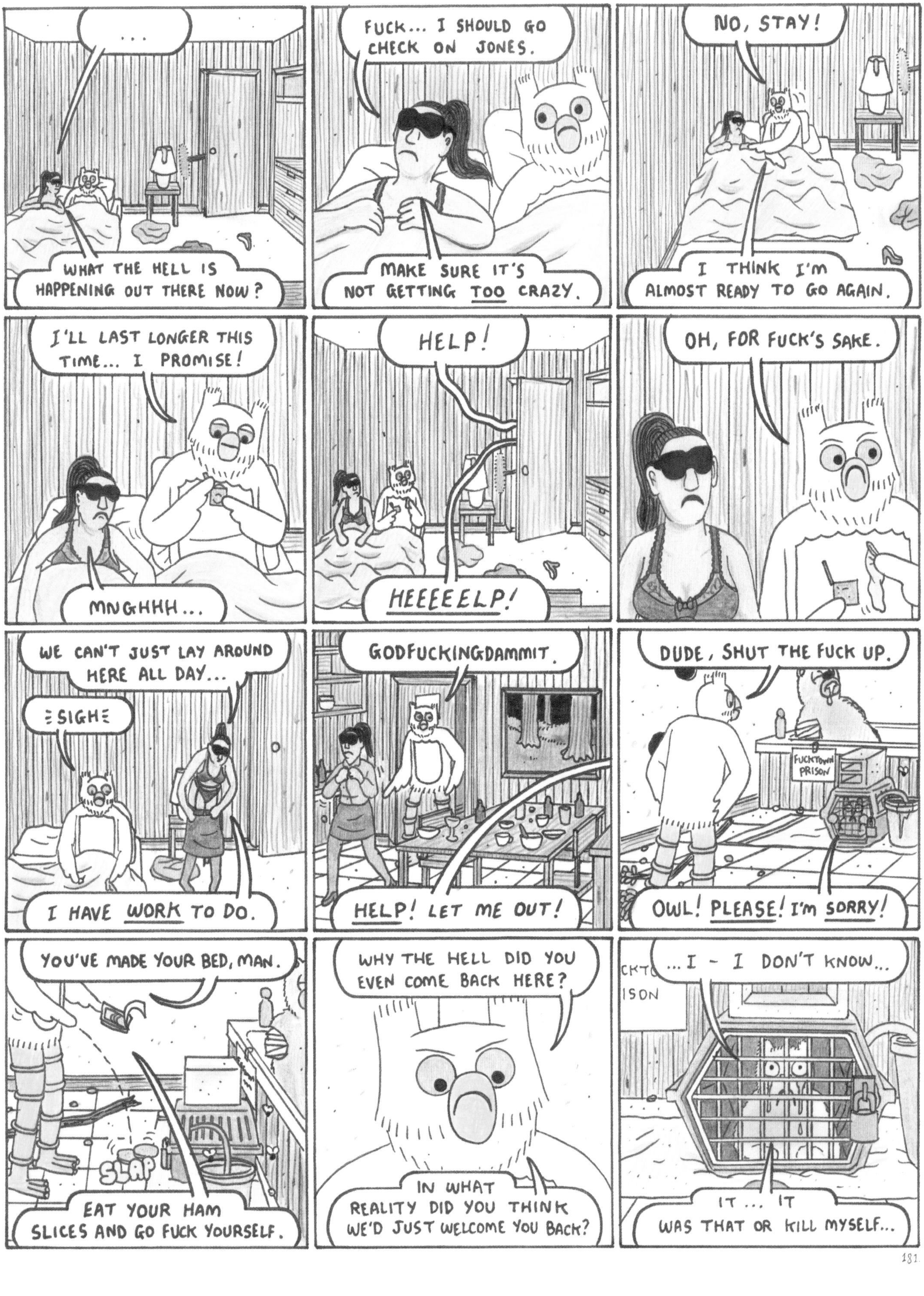
...
WHAT THE HELL IS HAPPENING OUT THERE NOW?
FUCK... I SHOULD GO CHECK ON JONES.
MAKE SURE IT'S NOT GETTING TOO CRAZY.
NO, STAY!
I THINK I'M ALMOST READY TO GO AGAIN.
I'LL LAST LONGER THIS TIME... I PROMISE!
MNGHHH...
HELP!
HEEEEELP!
OH, FOR FUCK'S SAKE.
WE CAN'T JUST LAY AROUND HERE ALL DAY...
SIGH
I HAVE WORK TO DO.
GODFUCKINGDAMMIT.
HELP! LET ME OUT!
DUDE, SHUT THE FUCK UP.
FUCKTOWN PRISON
OWL! PLEASE! I'M SORRY!
YOU'VE MADE YOUR BED, MAN.
SLAP
EAT YOUR HAM SLICES AND GO FUCK YOURSELF.
WHY THE HELL DID YOU EVEN COME BACK HERE?
IN WHAT REALITY DID YOU THINK WE'D JUST WELCOME YOU BACK?
...I - I DON'T KNOW...
IT... IT WAS THAT OR KILL MYSELF...

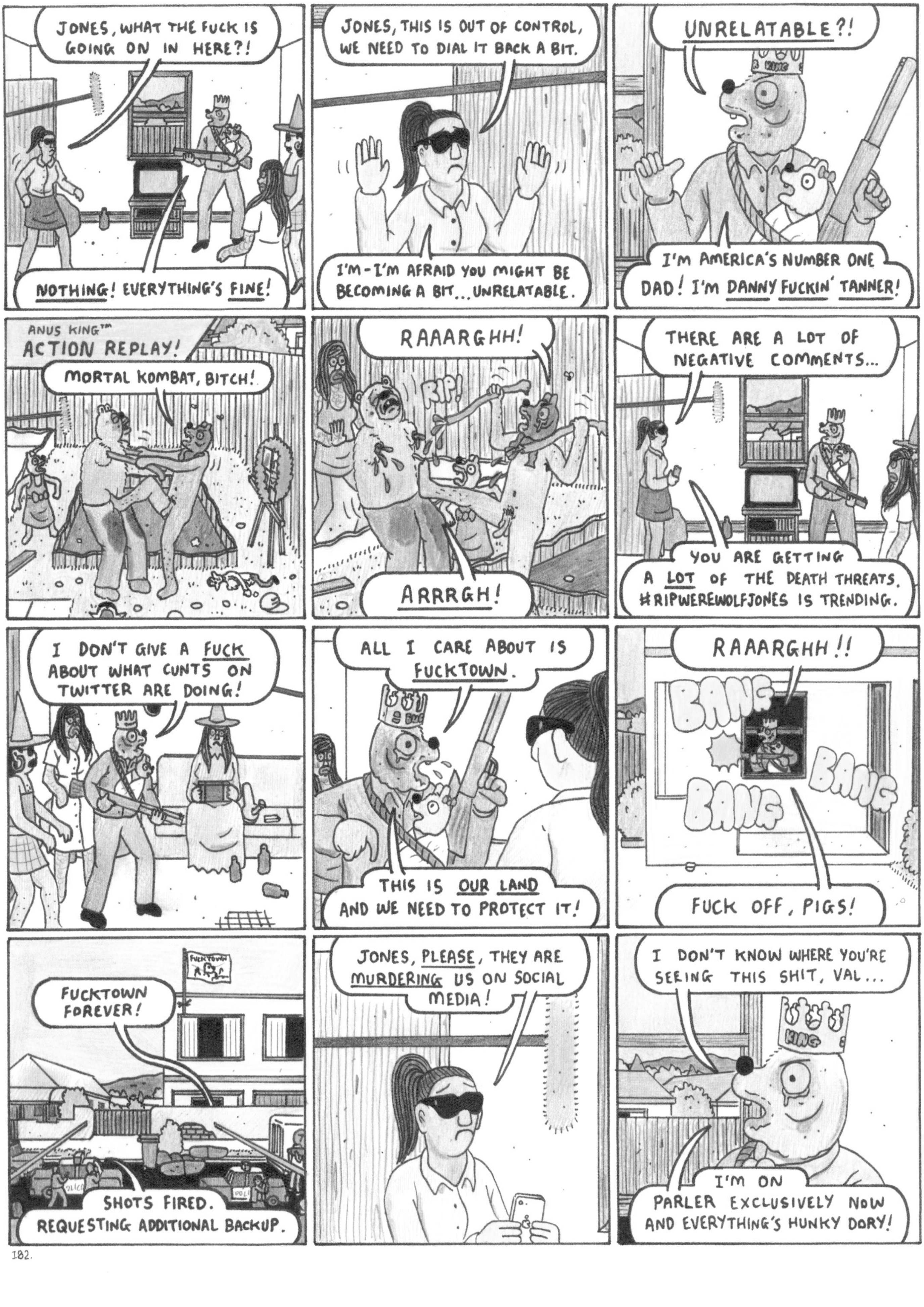
JONES, WHAT THE FUCK IS GOING ON IN HERE?!
NOTHING! EVERYTHING'S FINE!
JONES, THIS IS OUT OF CONTROL, WE NEED TO DIAL IT BACK A BIT.
I'M-I'M AFRAID YOU MIGHT BE BECOMING A BIT... UNRELATABLE.
UNRELATABLE?!
KING
I'M AMERICA'S NUMBER ONE DAD! I'M DANNY FUCKIN' TANNER!
ANUS KING™ ACTION REPLAY!
MORTAL KOMBAT, BITCH!
RAAARGHH!
RIP!
ARRRGH!
THERE ARE A LOT OF NEGATIVE COMMENTS...
YOU ARE GETTING A LOT OF THE DEATH THREATS. #RIPWEREWOLFJONES IS TRENDING.
I DON'T GIVE A FUCK ABOUT WHAT CUNTS ON TWITTER ARE DOING!
ALL I CARE ABOUT IS FUCKTOWN.
THIS IS OUR LAND AND WE NEED TO PROTECT IT!
RAAARGHH!!
BANG
BANG
BANG
FUCK OFF, PIGS!
FUCKTOWN
FUCKTOWN FOREVER!
SHOTS FIRED. REQUESTING ADDITIONAL BACKUP.
JONES, PLEASE, THEY ARE MURDERING US ON SOCIAL MEDIA!
I DON'T KNOW WHERE YOU'RE SEEING THIS SHIT, VAL...
KING
I'M ON PARLER EXCLUSIVELY NOW AND EVERYTHING'S HUNKY DORY!

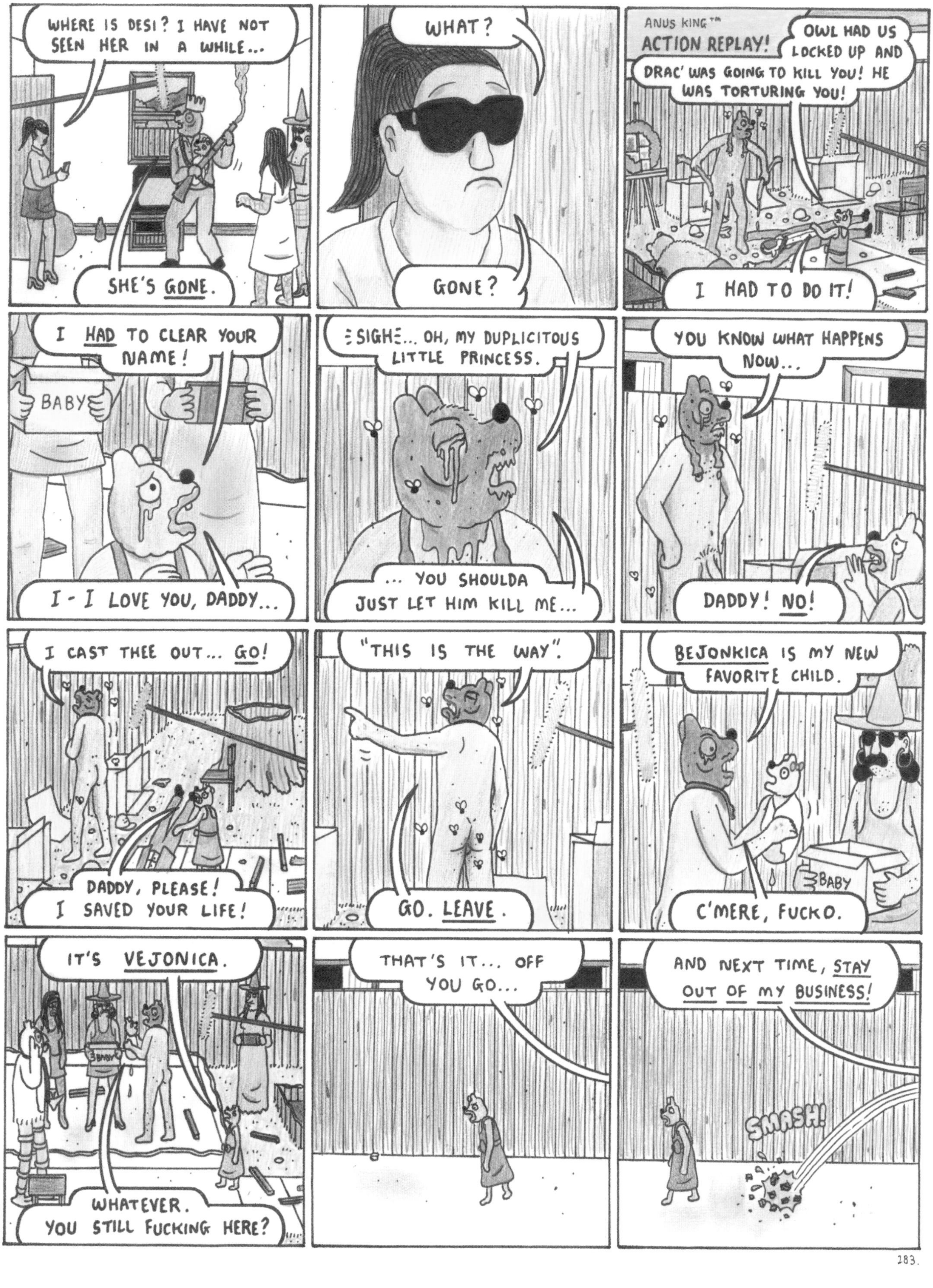
WHERE IS DESI? I HAVE NOT SEEN HER IN A WHILE...
SHE'S GONE.
WHAT?
GONE?
ANUS KING™ ACTION REPLAY!
OWL HAD US LOCKED UP AND
DRAC' WAS GOING TO KILL YOU! HE WAS TORTURING YOU!
I HAD TO DO IT!
I HAD TO CLEAR YOUR NAME!
BABY
I - I LOVE YOU, DADDY...
=SIGH=... OH, MY DUPLICITOUS LITTLE PRINCESS.
... YOU SHOULDA JUST LET HIM KILL ME...
YOU KNOW WHAT HAPPENS NOW...
DADDY! NO!
I CAST THEE OUT... GO!
DADDY, PLEASE! I SAVED YOUR LIFE!
"THIS IS THE WAY".
GO. LEAVE.
BEJONKICA IS MY NEW FAVORITE CHILD.
BABY
C'MERE, FUCKO.
IT'S VEJONICA.
BABY
WHATEVER. YOU STILL FUCKING HERE?
THAT'S IT... OFF YOU GO...
AND NEXT TIME, STAY OUT OF MY BUSINESS!
SMASH!

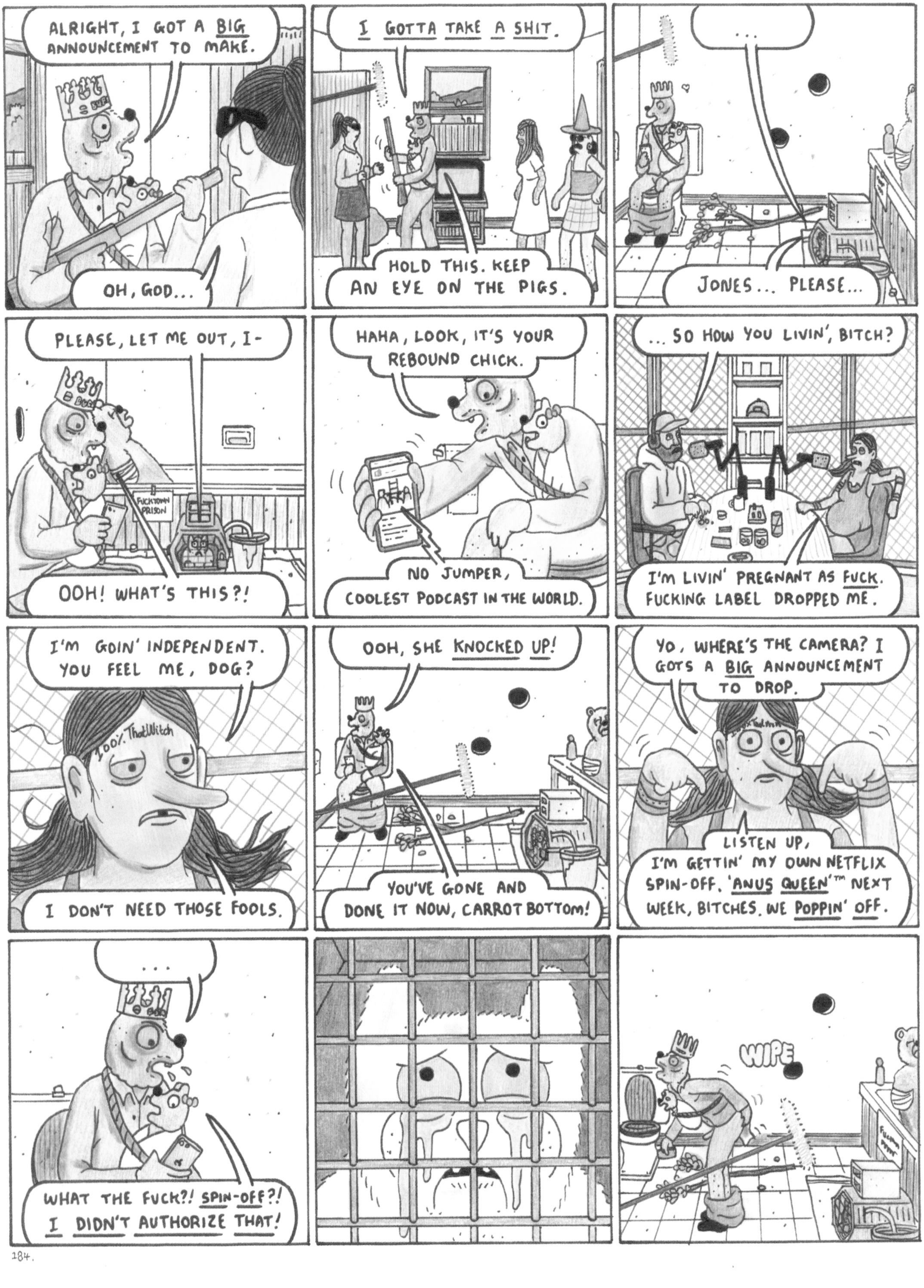
ALRIGHT, I GOT A BIG ANNOUNCEMENT TO MAKE.
OH, GOD...
I GOTTA TAKE A SHIT.
HOLD THIS. KEEP AN EYE ON THE PIGS.
...
JONES... PLEASE...
PLEASE, LET ME OUT, I-
OOH! WHAT'S THIS?!
FUCKTOWN PRISON
HAHA, LOOK, IT'S YOUR REBOUND CHICK.
NO JUMPER, COOLEST PODCAST IN THE WORLD.
...SO HOW YOU LIVIN', BITCH?
I'M LIVIN' PREGNANT AS FUCK. FUCKING LABEL DROPPED ME.
I'M GOIN' INDEPENDENT. YOU FEEL ME, DOG?
100% ThatWitch
I DON'T NEED THOSE FOOLS.
OOH, SHE KNOCKED UP!
YOU'VE GONE AND DONE IT NOW, CARROT BOTTOM!
YO, WHERE'S THE CAMERA? I GOTS A BIG ANNOUNCEMENT TO DROP.
LISTEN UP, I'M GETTIN' MY OWN NETFLIX SPIN-OFF. 'ANUS QUEEN'™ NEXT WEEK, BITCHES. WE POPPIN' OFF.
...
WHAT THE FUCK?! SPIN-OFF?! I DIDN'T AUTHORIZE THAT!
WIPE

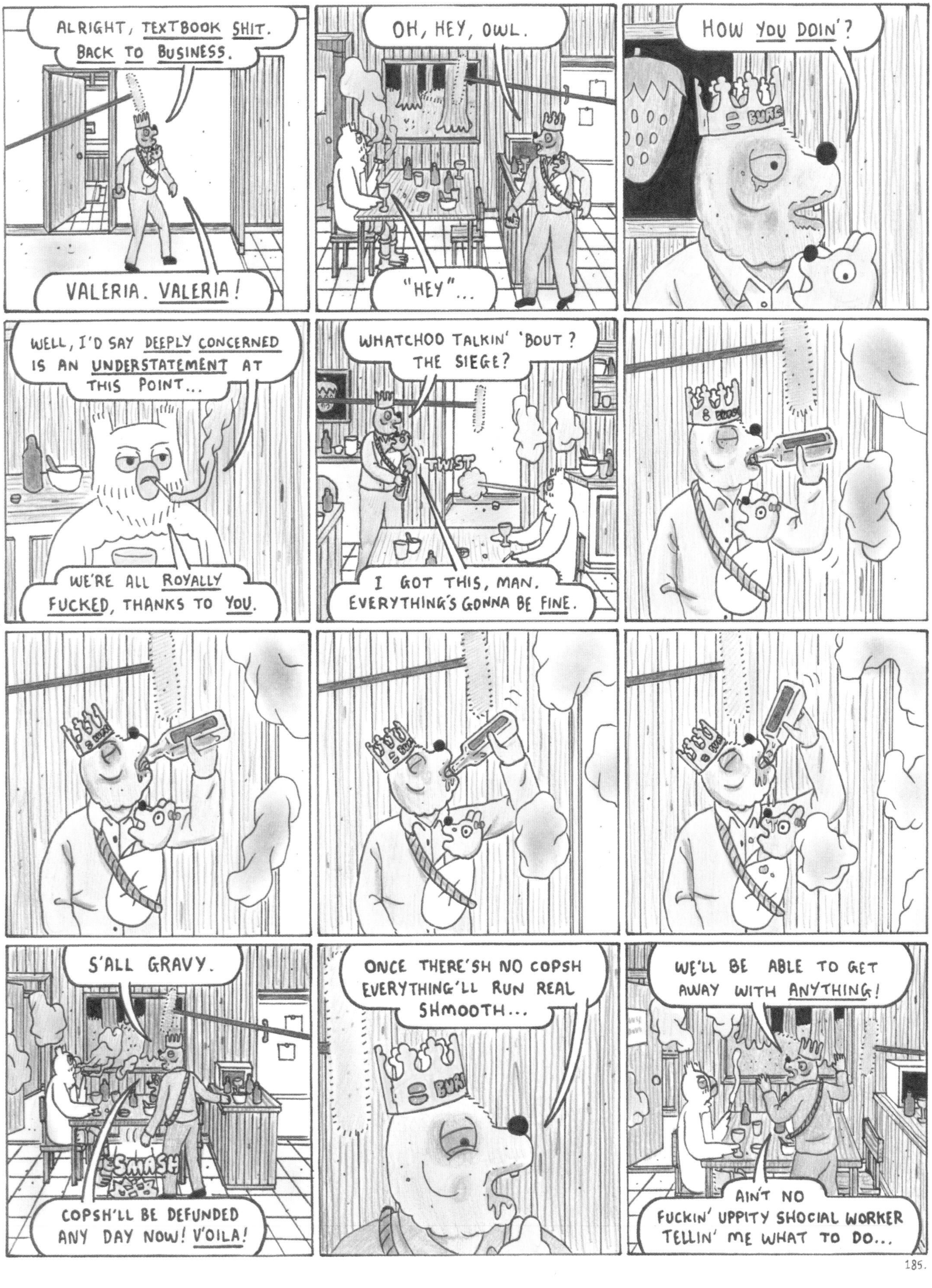
ALRIGHT, TEXTBOOK SHIT. BACK TO BUSINESS.
VALERIA. VALERIA!
OH, HEY, OWL.
"HEY"...
HOW YOU DOIN'?
WELL, I'D SAY DEEPLY CONCERNED IS AN UNDERSTATEMENT AT THIS POINT...
WE'RE ALL ROYALLY FUCKED, THANKS TO YOU.
WHATCHOO TALKIN' 'BOUT? THE SIEGE?
TWIST
I GOT THIS, MAN. EVERYTHING'S GONNA BE FINE.
S'ALL GRAVY.
SMASH
COPSH'LL BE DEFUNDED ANY DAY NOW! V'OILA!
ONCE THERE'SH NO COPSH EVERYTHING'LL RUN REAL SHMOOTH...
WE'LL BE ABLE TO GET AWAY WITH ANYTHING!
AIN'T NO FUCKIN' UPPITY SHOCIAL WORKER TELLIN' ME WHAT TO DO...

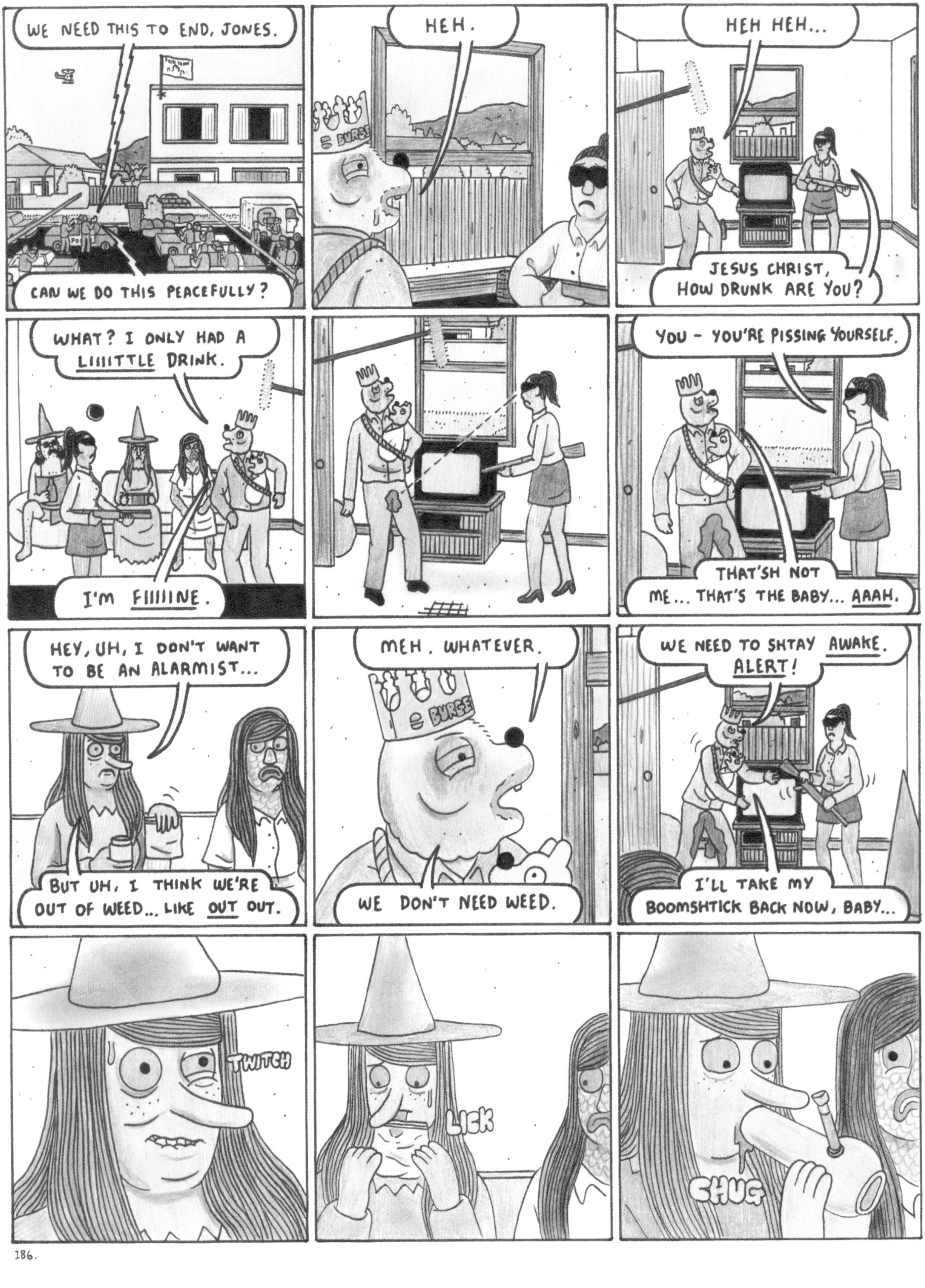
WE NEED THIS TO END, JONES.
CAN WE DO THIS PEACEFULLY?
HEH.
HEH HEH...
JESUS CHRIST, HOW DRUNK ARE YOU?
WHAT? I ONLY HAD A LIIIITTLE DRINK.
I'M FIIIIINE.
YOU - YOU'RE PISSING YOURSELF.
THAT'SH NOT ME... THAT'S THE BABY... AAAH.
HEY, UH, I DON'T WANT TO BE AN ALARMIST...
BUT UH, I THINK WE'RE OUT OF WEED... LIKE OUT OUT.
MEH. WHATEVER.
WE DON'T NEED WEED.
WE NEED TO SHTAY AWAKE. ALERT!
I'LL TAKE MY BOOMSHTICK BACK NOW, BABY...
TWITCH
LICK
CHUG

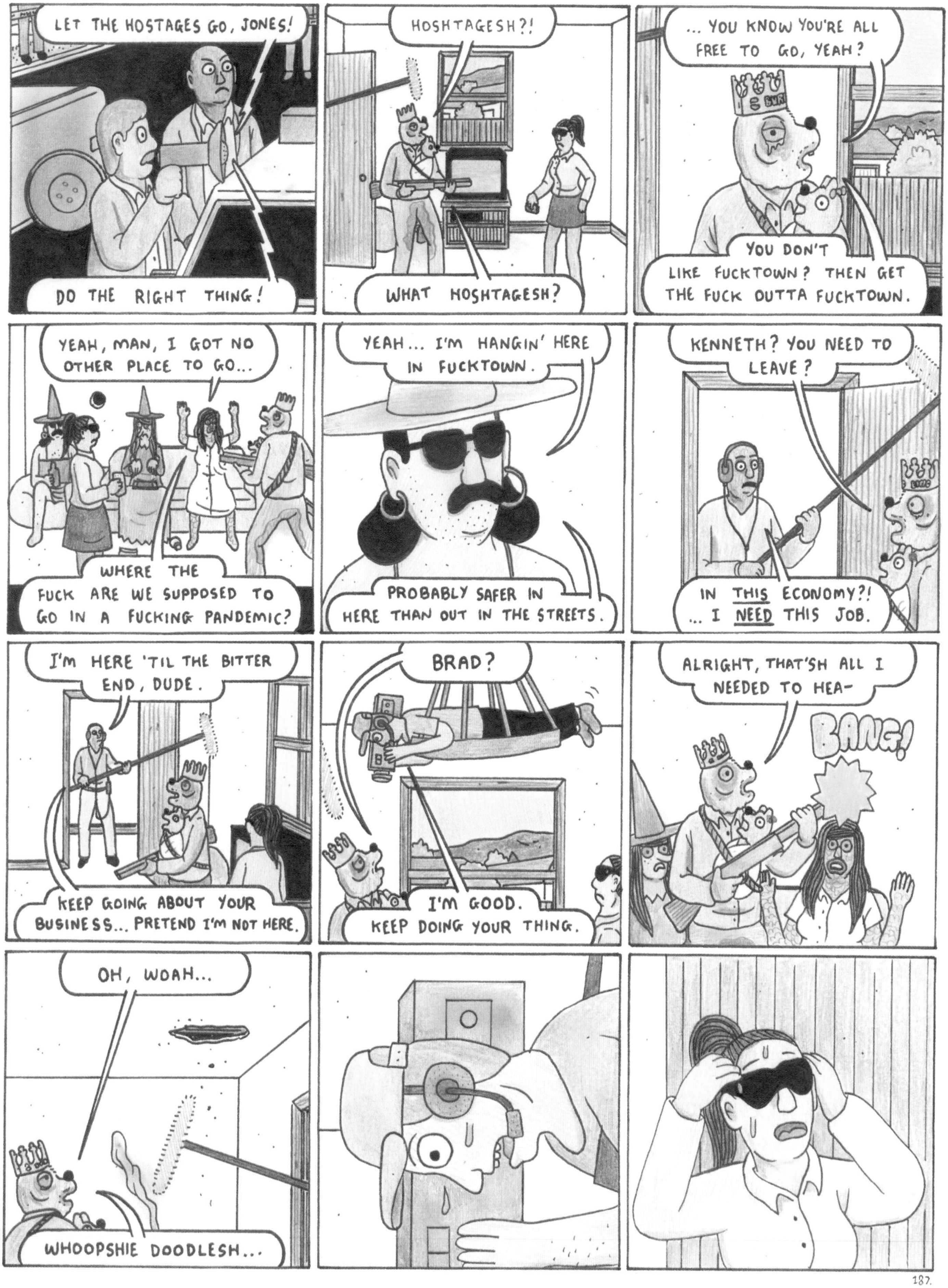
LET THE HOSTAGES GO, JONES!
DO THE RIGHT THING!
HOSHTAGESH?!
WHAT HOSHTAGESH?
... YOU KNOW YOU'RE ALL FREE TO GO, YEAH?
YOU DON'T LIKE FUCKTOWN? THEN GET THE FUCK OUTTA FUCKTOWN.
YEAH, MAN, I GOT NO OTHER PLACE TO GO...
WHERE THE FUCK ARE WE SUPPOSED TO GO IN A FUCKING PANDEMIC?
YEAH... I'M HANGIN' HERE IN FUCKTOWN.
PROBABLY SAFER IN HERE THAN OUT IN THE STREETS.
KENNETH? YOU NEED TO LEAVE?
IN THIS ECONOMY?! ... I NEED THIS JOB.
I'M HERE 'TIL THE BITTER END, DUDE.
KEEP GOING ABOUT YOUR BUSINESS... PRETEND I'M NOT HERE.
BRAD?
I'M GOOD. KEEP DOING YOUR THING.
ALRIGHT, THAT'SH ALL I NEEDED TO HEA-
BANG!
OH, WOAH...
WHOOPSHIE DOODLESH...

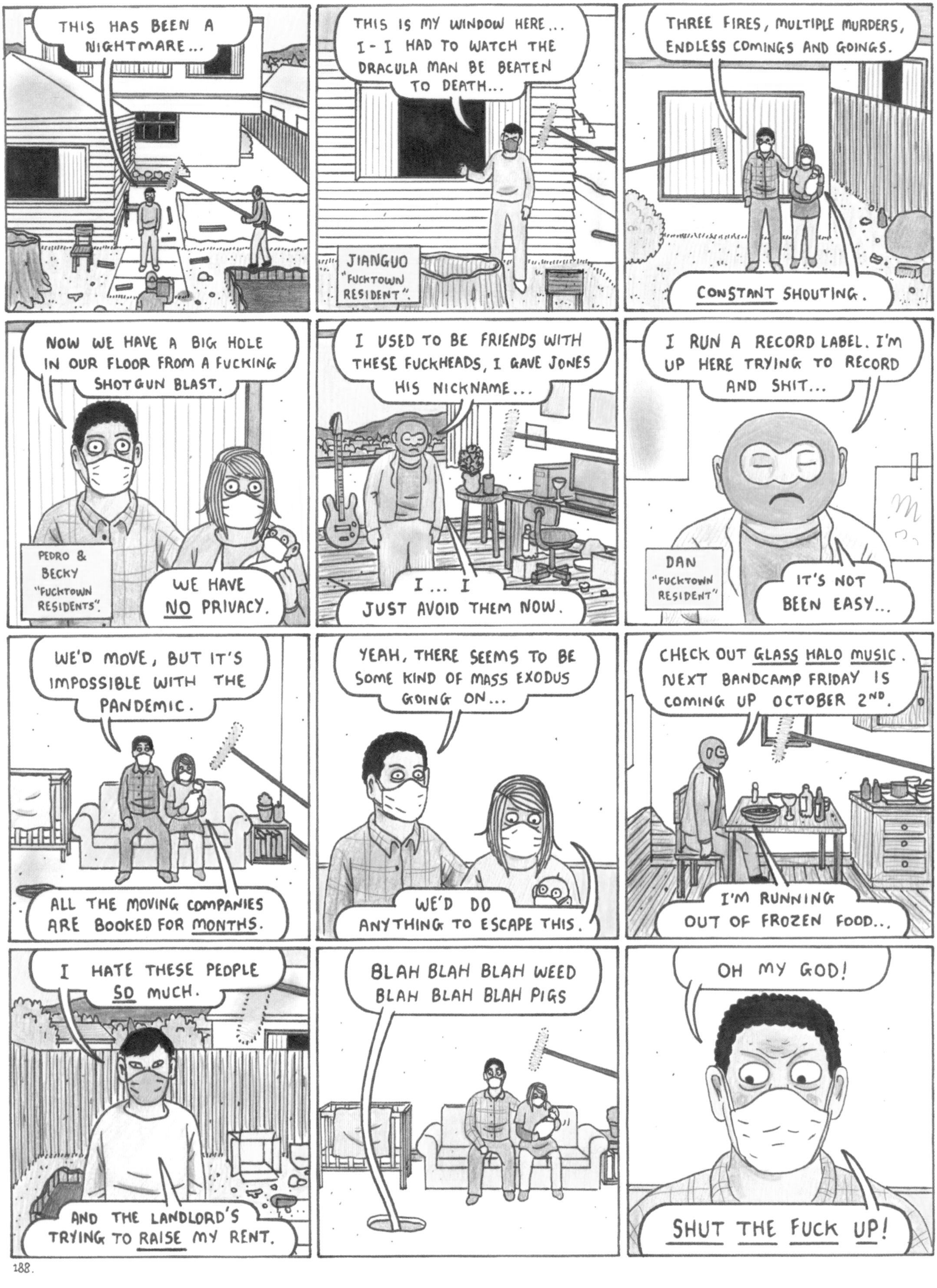
THIS HAS BEEN A NIGHTMARE...
THIS IS MY WINDOW HERE... I- I HAD TO WATCH THE DRACULA MAN BE BEATEN TO DEATH...
JIANGUO "FUCKTOWN RESIDENT".
THREE FIRES, MULTIPLE MURDERS, ENDLESS COMINGS AND GOINGS.
CONSTANT SHOUTING.
NOW WE HAVE A BIG HOLE IN OUR FLOOR FROM A FUCKING SHOTGUN BLAST.
PEDRO & BECKY "FUCKTOWN RESIDENTS".
WE HAVE NO PRIVACY.
I USED TO BE FRIENDS WITH THESE FUCKHEADS, I GAVE JONES HIS NICKNAME...
I... I JUST AVOID THEM NOW.
I RUN A RECORD LABEL. I'M UP HERE TRYING TO RECORD AND SHIT...
DAN "FUCKTOWN RESIDENT"
IT'S NOT BEEN EASY...
WE'D MOVE, BUT IT'S IMPOSSIBLE WITH THE PANDEMIC.
ALL THE MOVING COMPANIES ARE BOOKED FOR MONTHS.
YEAH, THERE SEEMS TO BE SOME KIND OF MASS EXODUS GOING ON...
WE'D DO ANYTHING TO ESCAPE THIS.
CHECK OUT GLASS HALO MUSIC. NEXT BANDCAMP FRIDAY IS COMING UP OCTOBER 2ND.
I'M RUNNING OUT OF FROZEN FOOD...
I HATE THESE PEOPLE SO MUCH.
AND THE LANDLORD'S TRYING TO RAISE MY RENT.
BLAH BLAH BLAH WEED BLAH BLAH BLAH PIGS
OH MY GOD!
SHUT THE FUCK UP!

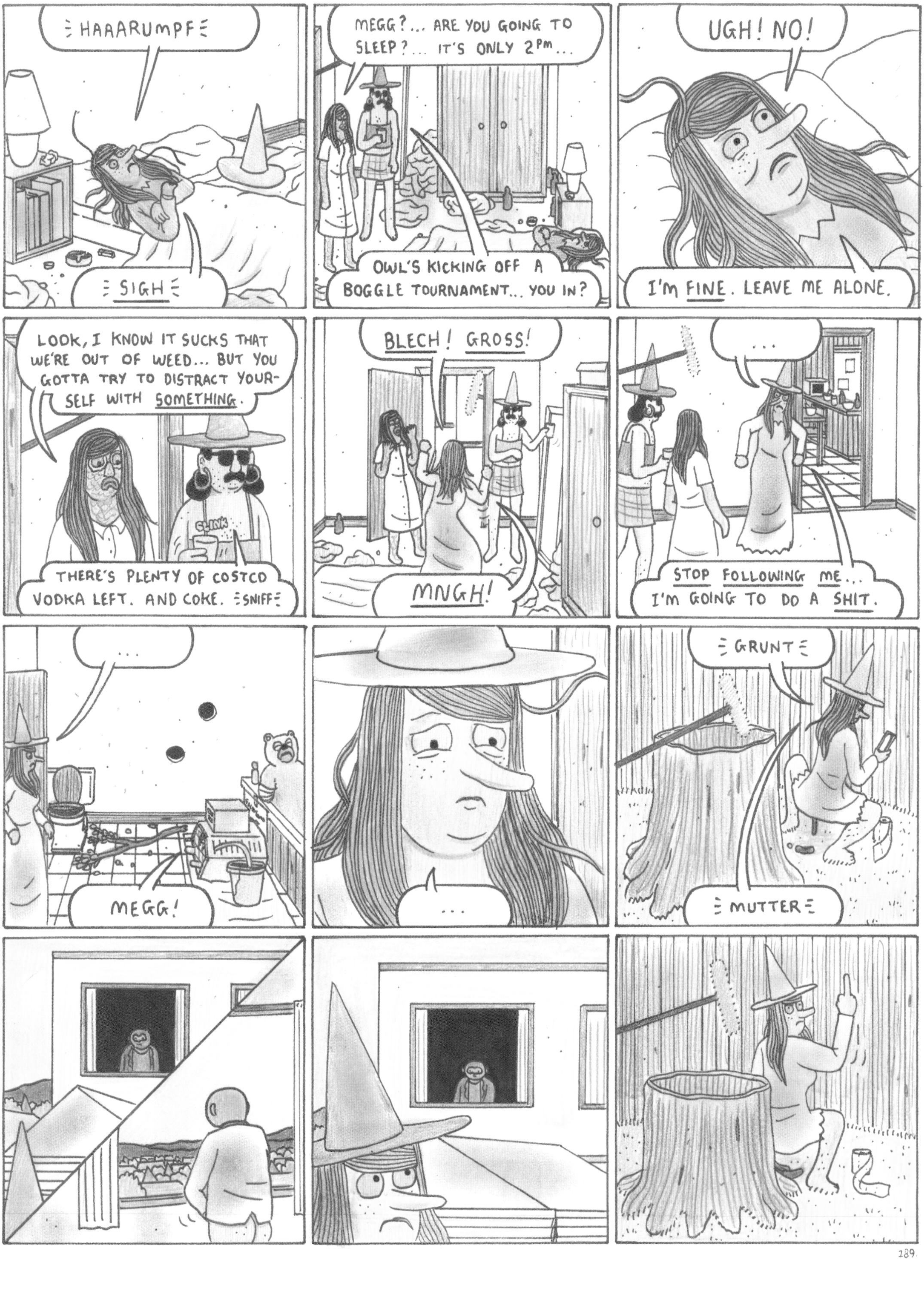
HAAARUMPF
SIGH
MEGG?... ARE YOU GOING TO SLEEP?... IT'S ONLY 2PM...
OWL'S KICKING OFF A BOGGLE TOURNAMENT... YOU IN?
UGH! NO!
I'M FINE. LEAVE ME ALONE.
LOOK, I KNOW IT SUCKS THAT WE'RE OUT OF WEED... BUT YOU GOTTA TRY TO DISTRACT YOURSELF WITH SOMETHING.
CLINK
THERE'S PLENTY OF COSTCO VODKA LEFT. AND COKE. SNIFF
BLECH! GROSS!
MNGH!
...
STOP FOLLOWING ME... I'M GOING TO DO A SHIT.
...
MEGG!
...
GRUNT
MUTTER

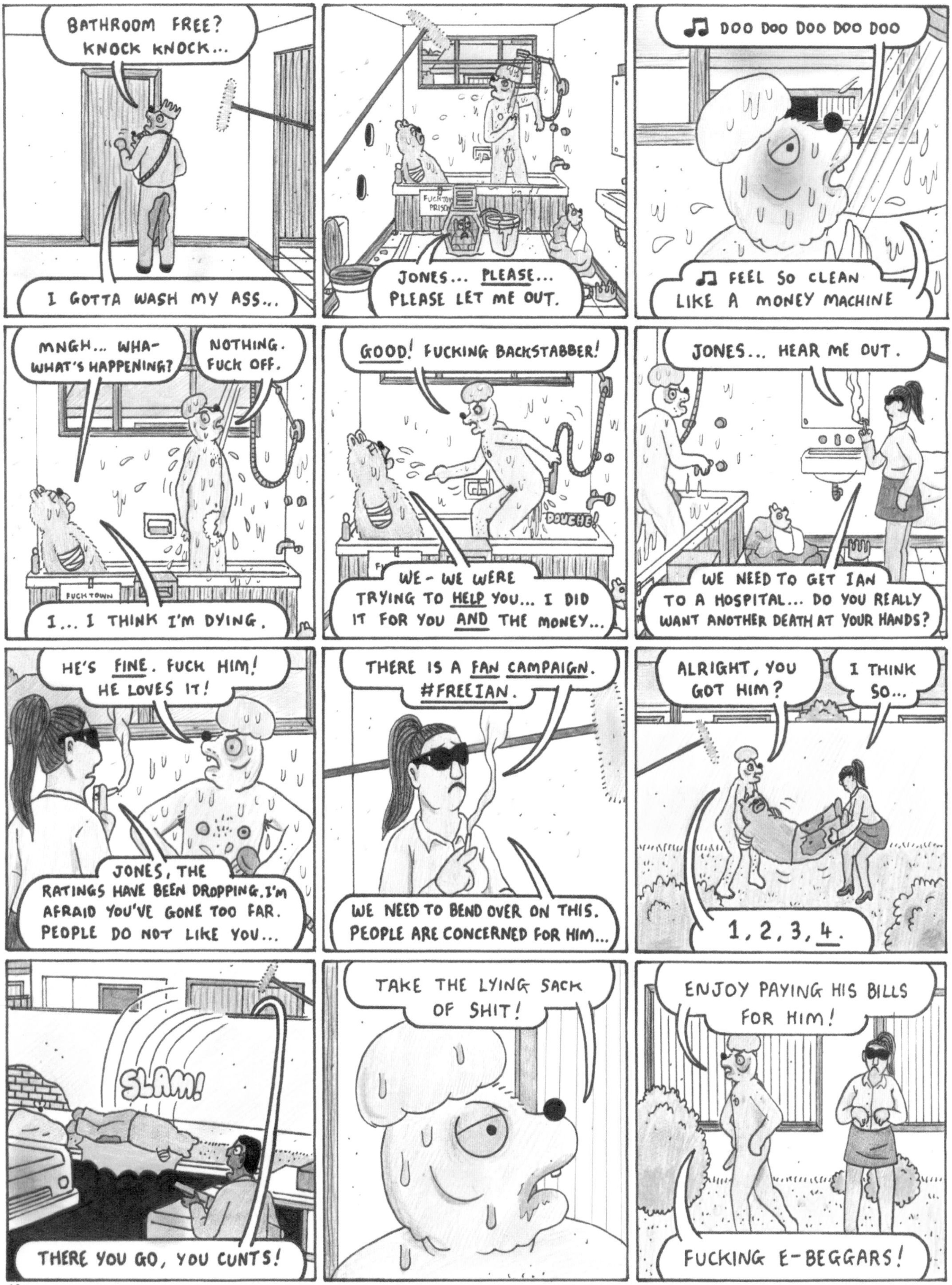
BATHROOM FREE? KNOCK KNOCK...
I GOTTA WASH MY ASS...
FUCKTOWN PRISON
JONES... PLEASE... PLEASE LET ME OUT.
♫ DOO DOO DOO DOO DOO
♫ FEEL SO CLEAN LIKE A MONEY MACHINE
MNGH... WHA- WHAT'S HAPPENING?
NOTHING. FUCK OFF.
FUCKTOWN
I... I THINK I'M DYING.
GOOD! FUCKING BACKSTABBER!
DOUCHE!
WE- WE WERE TRYING TO HELP YOU... I DID IT FOR YOU AND THE MONEY...
JONES... HEAR ME OUT.
WE NEED TO GET IAN TO A HOSPITAL... DO YOU REALLY WANT ANOTHER DEATH AT YOUR HANDS?
HE'S FINE. FUCK HIM! HE LOVES IT!
JONES, THE RATINGS HAVE BEEN DROPPING. I'M AFRAID YOU'VE GONE TOO FAR. PEOPLE DO NOT LIKE YOU...
THERE IS A FAN CAMPAIGN. #FREEIAN.
WE NEED TO BEND OVER ON THIS. PEOPLE ARE CONCERNED FOR HIM...
ALRIGHT, YOU GOT HIM?
I THINK SO...
1, 2, 3, 4.
SLAM!
THERE YOU GO, YOU CUNTS!
TAKE THE LYING SACK OF SHIT!
ENJOY PAYING HIS BILLS FOR HIM!
FUCKING E-BEGGARS!

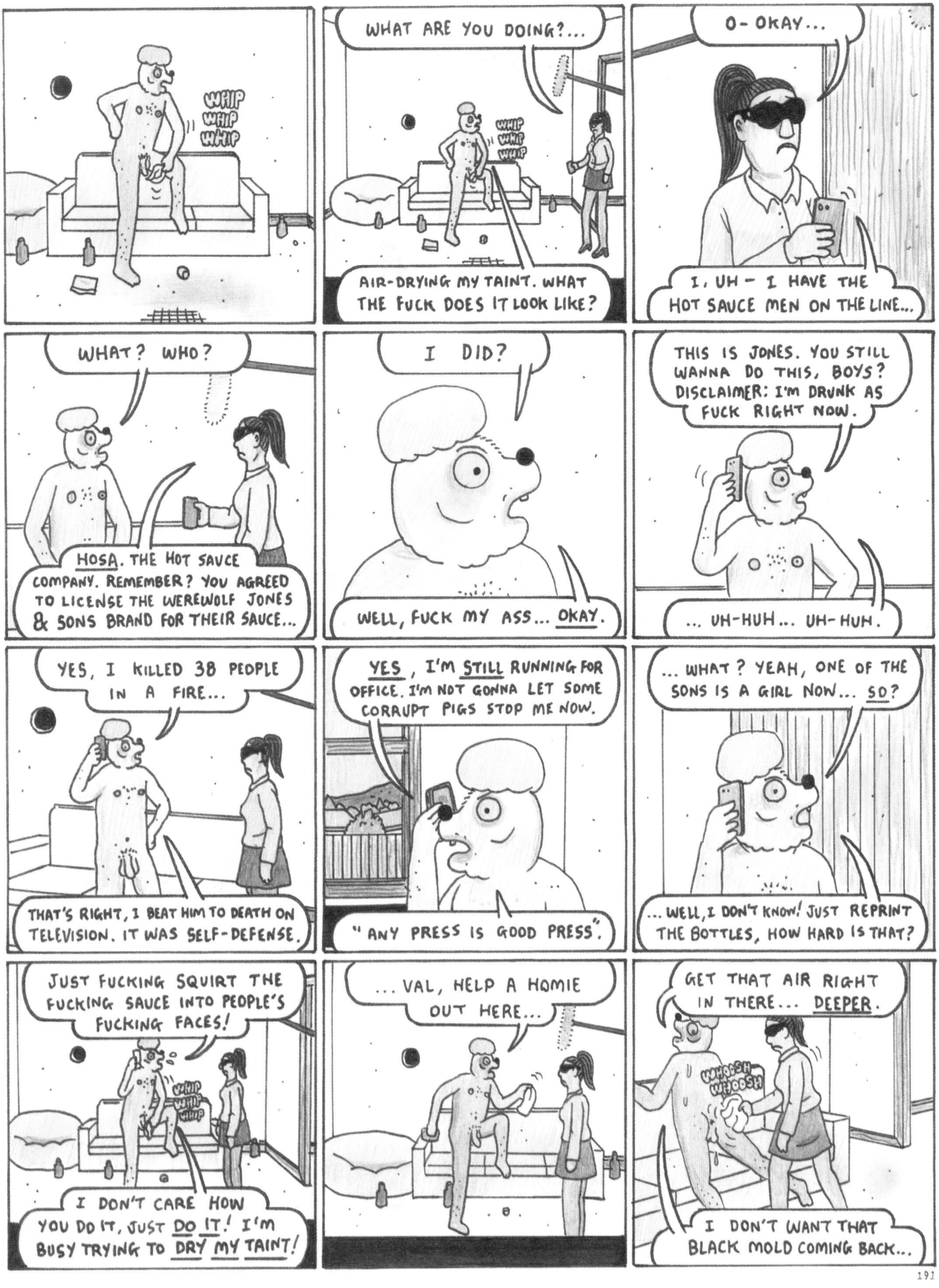
WHIP WHIP WHIP
WHAT ARE YOU DOING?...
WHIP WHIP WHIP
AIR-DRYING MY TAINT. WHAT THE FUCK DOES IT LOOK LIKE?
O-OKAY...
I, UH - I HAVE THE HOT SAUCE MEN ON THE LINE...
WHAT? WHO?
HOSA. THE HOT SAUCE COMPANY. REMEMBER? YOU AGREED TO LICENSE THE WEREWOLF JONES & SONS BRAND FOR THEIR SAUCE...
I DID?
WELL, FUCK MY ASS... OKAY.
THIS IS JONES. YOU STILL WANNA DO THIS, BOYS? DISCLAIMER: I'M DRUNK AS FUCK RIGHT NOW.
... UH-HUH... UH-HUH.
YES, I KILLED 38 PEOPLE IN A FIRE...
THAT'S RIGHT, I BEAT HIM TO DEATH ON TELEVISION. IT WAS SELF-DEFENSE.
YES, I'M STILL RUNNING FOR OFFICE. I'M NOT GONNA LET SOME CORRUPT PIGS STOP ME NOW.
"ANY PRESS IS GOOD PRESS".
... WHAT? YEAH, ONE OF THE SONS IS A GIRL NOW... SO?
... WELL, I DON'T KNOW! JUST REPRINT THE BOTTLES, HOW HARD IS THAT?
JUST FUCKING SQUIRT THE FUCKING SAUCE INTO PEOPLE'S FUCKING FACES!
WHIP WHIP WHIP
I DON'T CARE HOW YOU DO IT, JUST DO IT! I'M BUSY TRYING TO DRY MY TAINT!
... VAL, HELP A HOMIE OUT HERE...
GET THAT AIR RIGHT IN THERE... DEEPER.
WHOOSH-WHOOSH
I DON'T WANT THAT BLACK MOLD COMING BACK...

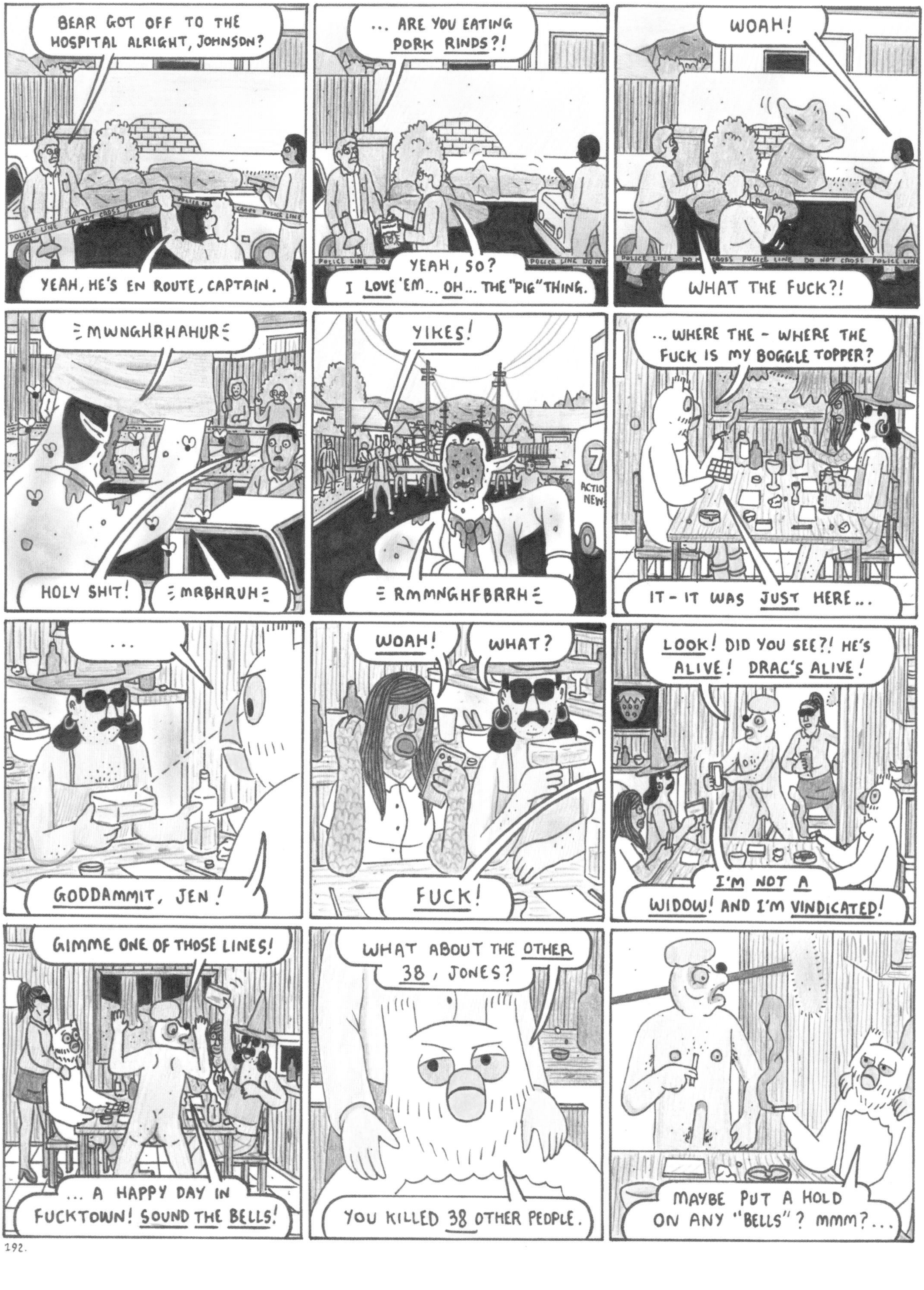
BEAR GOT OFF TO THE HOSPITAL ALRIGHT, JOHNSON?
YEAH, HE'S EN ROUTE, CAPTAIN.
... ARE YOU EATING PORK RINDS?!
YEAH, SO? I LOVE 'EM... OH... THE "PIG" THING.
WOAH!
WHAT THE FUCK?!
MWNGHRHAHUR
HOLY SHIT!
MRBHRUH
YIKES!
RMMNGHFBRRH
... WHERE THE - WHERE THE FUCK IS MY BOGGLE TOPPER?
IT - IT WAS JUST HERE...
...
GODDAMMIT, JEN!
WOAH!
WHAT?
FUCK!
LOOK! DID YOU SEE?! HE'S ALIVE! DRAC'S ALIVE!
I'M NOT A WIDOW! AND I'M VINDICATED!
GIMME ONE OF THOSE LINES!
... A HAPPY DAY IN FUCKTOWN! SOUND THE BELLS!
WHAT ABOUT THE OTHER 38, JONES?
YOU KILLED 38 OTHER PEOPLE.
MAYBE PUT A HOLD ON ANY "BELLS"? MMM?...

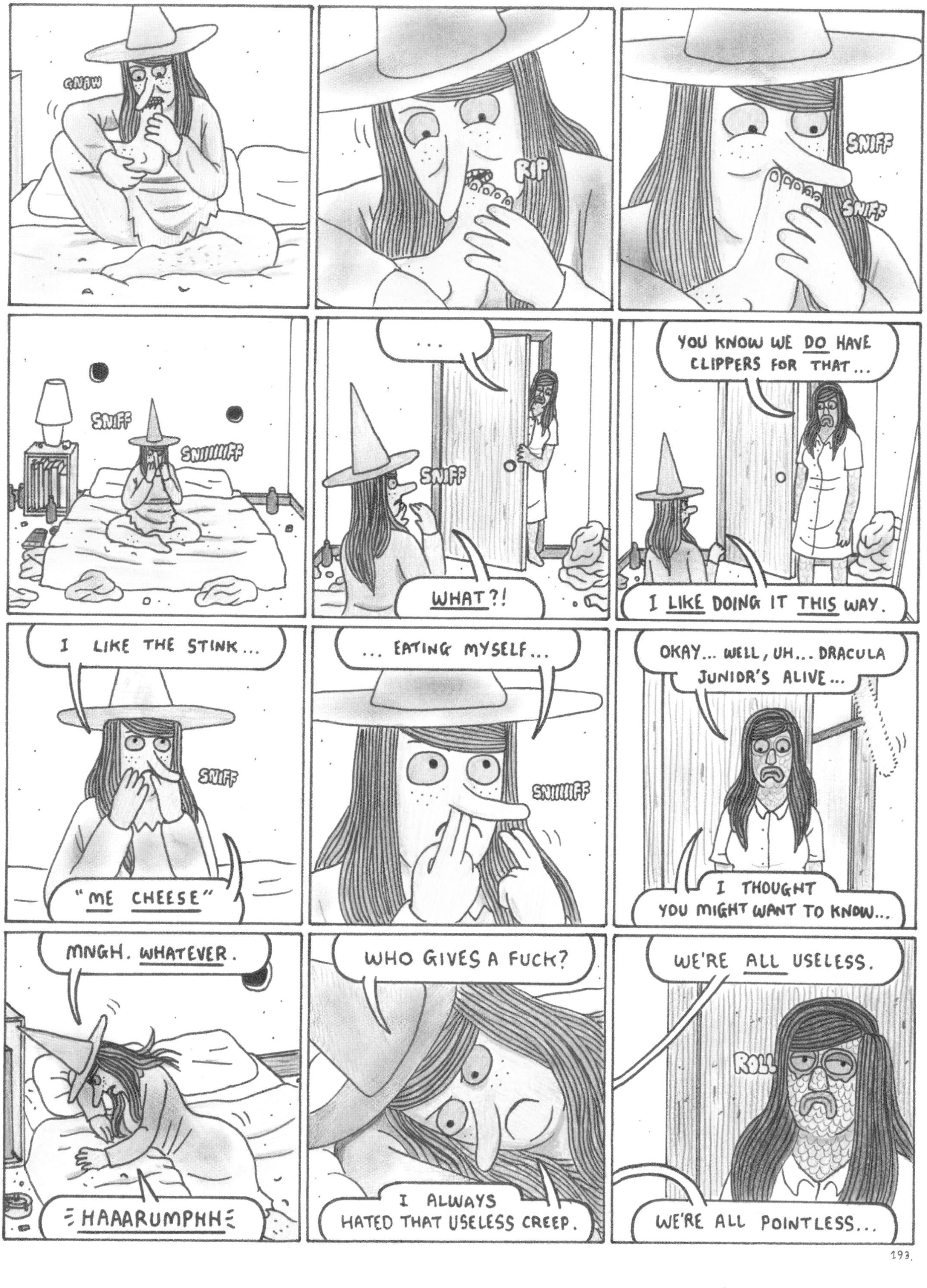
GNAW
RIP
SNIFF
SNIFF
SNIFF
SNIIIIIFF
...
SNIFF
WHAT?!
YOU KNOW WE DO HAVE CLIPPERS FOR THAT...
I LIKE DOING IT THIS WAY.
I LIKE THE STINK...
SNIFF
"ME CHEESE"
... EATING MYSELF...
SNIIIIIFF
OKAY... WELL, UH... DRACULA JUNIOR'S ALIVE...
I THOUGHT YOU MIGHT WANT TO KNOW...
MNGH. WHATEVER.
HAAARUMPHH
WHO GIVES A FUCK?
I ALWAYS HATED THAT USELESS CREEP.
WE'RE ALL USELESS.
ROLL
WE'RE ALL POINTLESS...

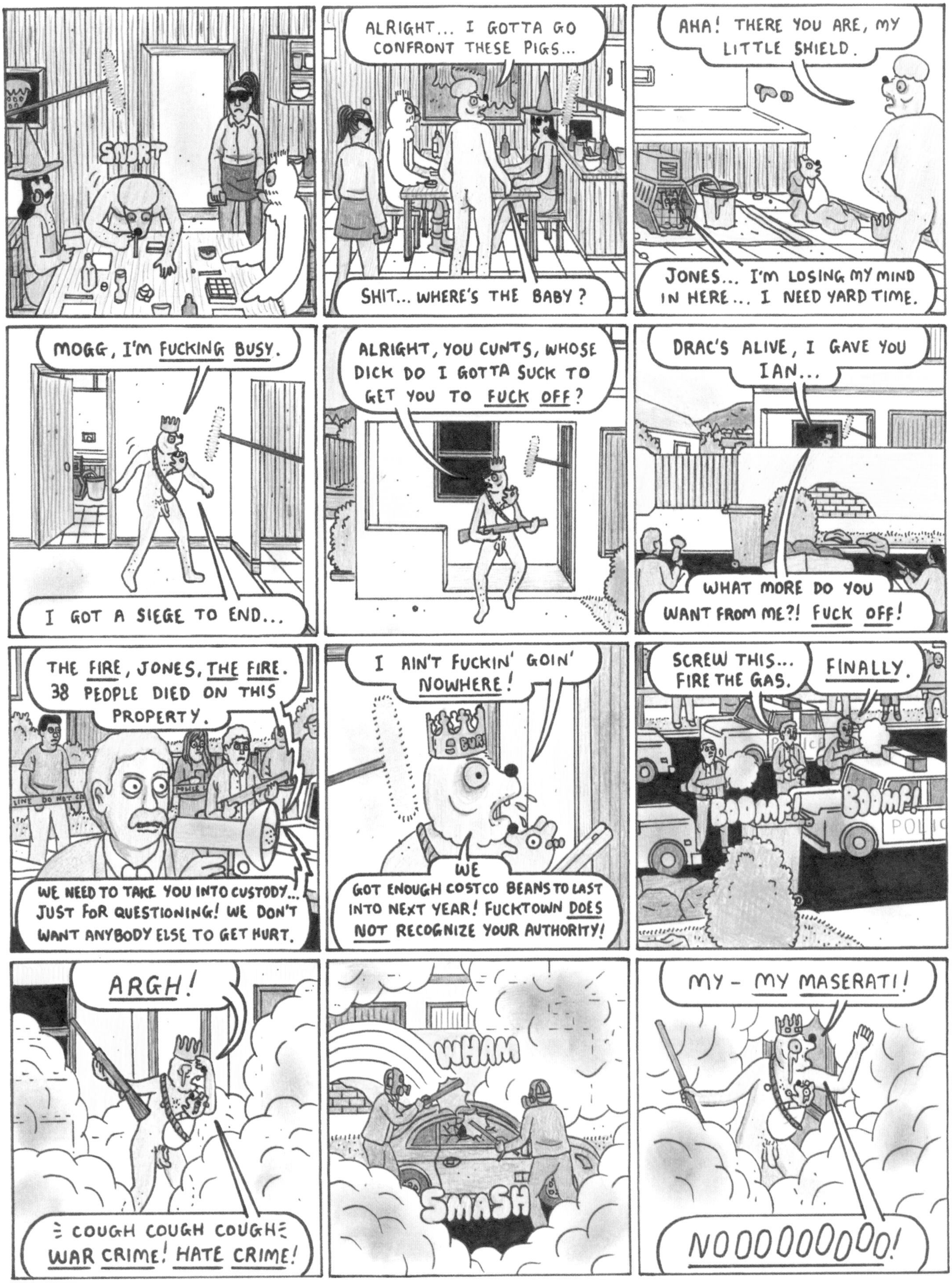
SNORT
ALRIGHT... I GOTTA GO CONFRONT THESE PIGS...
SHIT... WHERE'S THE BABY?
AHA! THERE YOU ARE, MY LITTLE SHIELD.
JONES... I'M LOSING MY MIND IN HERE... I NEED YARD TIME.
MOGG, I'M FUCKING BUSY.
I GOT A SIEGE TO END...
ALRIGHT, YOU CUNTS, WHOSE DICK DO I GOTTA SUCK TO GET YOU TO FUCK OFF?
DRAC'S ALIVE, I GAVE YOU IAN...
WHAT MORE DO YOU WANT FROM ME?! FUCK OFF!
THE FIRE, JONES, THE FIRE. 38 PEOPLE DIED ON THIS PROPERTY.
WE NEED TO TAKE YOU INTO CUSTODY... JUST FOR QUESTIONING! WE DON'T WANT ANYBODY ELSE TO GET HURT.
I AIN'T FUCKIN' GOIN' NOWHERE!
WE GOT ENOUGH COSTCO BEANS TO LAST INTO NEXT YEAR! FUCKTOWN DOES NOT RECOGNIZE YOUR AUTHORITY!
SCREW THIS... FIRE THE GAS.
FINALLY.
BOOMF!
BOOMF!
POLIC
ARGH!
COUGH COUGH COUGH
WAR CRIME! HATE CRIME!
WHAM
SMASH
MY- MY MASERATI!
NOOOOOOOOOO!

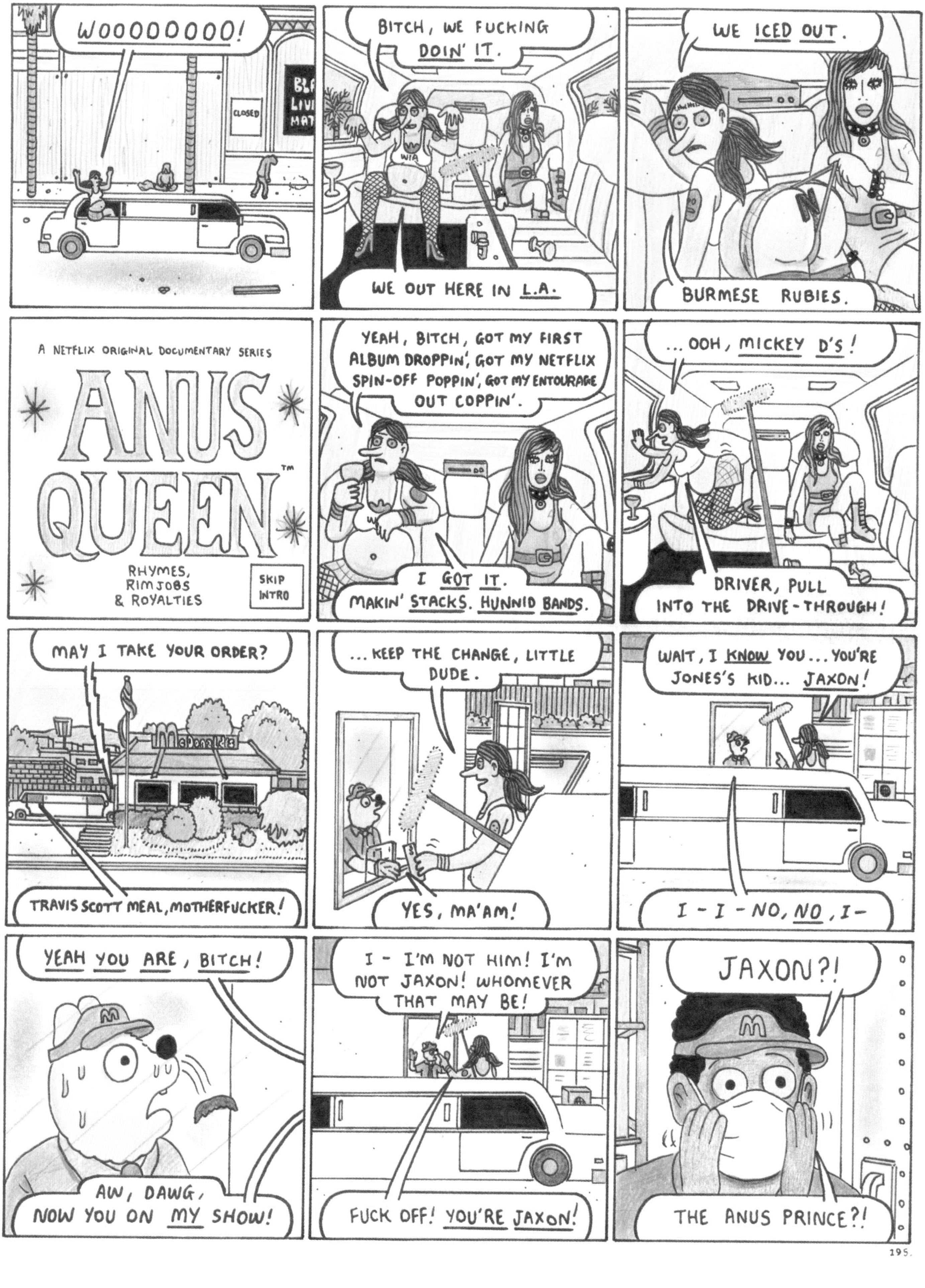
WOOOOOOOO!
CLOSED
BITCH, WE FUCKING DOIN' IT.
WE OUT HERE IN L.A.
WE ICED OUT.
BURMESE RUBIES.
A NETFLIX ORIGINAL DOCUMENTARY SERIES
ANUS QUEEN™
RHYMES, RIMJOBS & ROYALTIES
SKIP INTRO
YEAH, BITCH, GOT MY FIRST ALBUM DROPPIN', GOT MY NETFLIX SPIN-OFF POPPIN', GOT MY ENTOURAGE OUT COPPIN'.
I GOT IT. MAKIN' STACKS. HUNNID BANDS.
... OOH, MICKEY D'S!
DRIVER, PULL INTO THE DRIVE-THROUGH!
MAY I TAKE YOUR ORDER?
TRAVIS SCOTT MEAL, MOTHERFUCKER!
... KEEP THE CHANGE, LITTLE DUDE.
YES, MA'AM!
WAIT, I KNOW YOU... YOU'RE JONES'S KID... JAXON!
I - I - NO, NO, I-
YEAH YOU ARE, BITCH!
AW, DAWG, NOW YOU ON MY SHOW!
I - I'M NOT HIM! I'M NOT JAXON! WHOMEVER THAT MAY BE!
FUCK OFF! YOU'RE JAXON!
JAXON?!
THE ANUS PRINCE?!

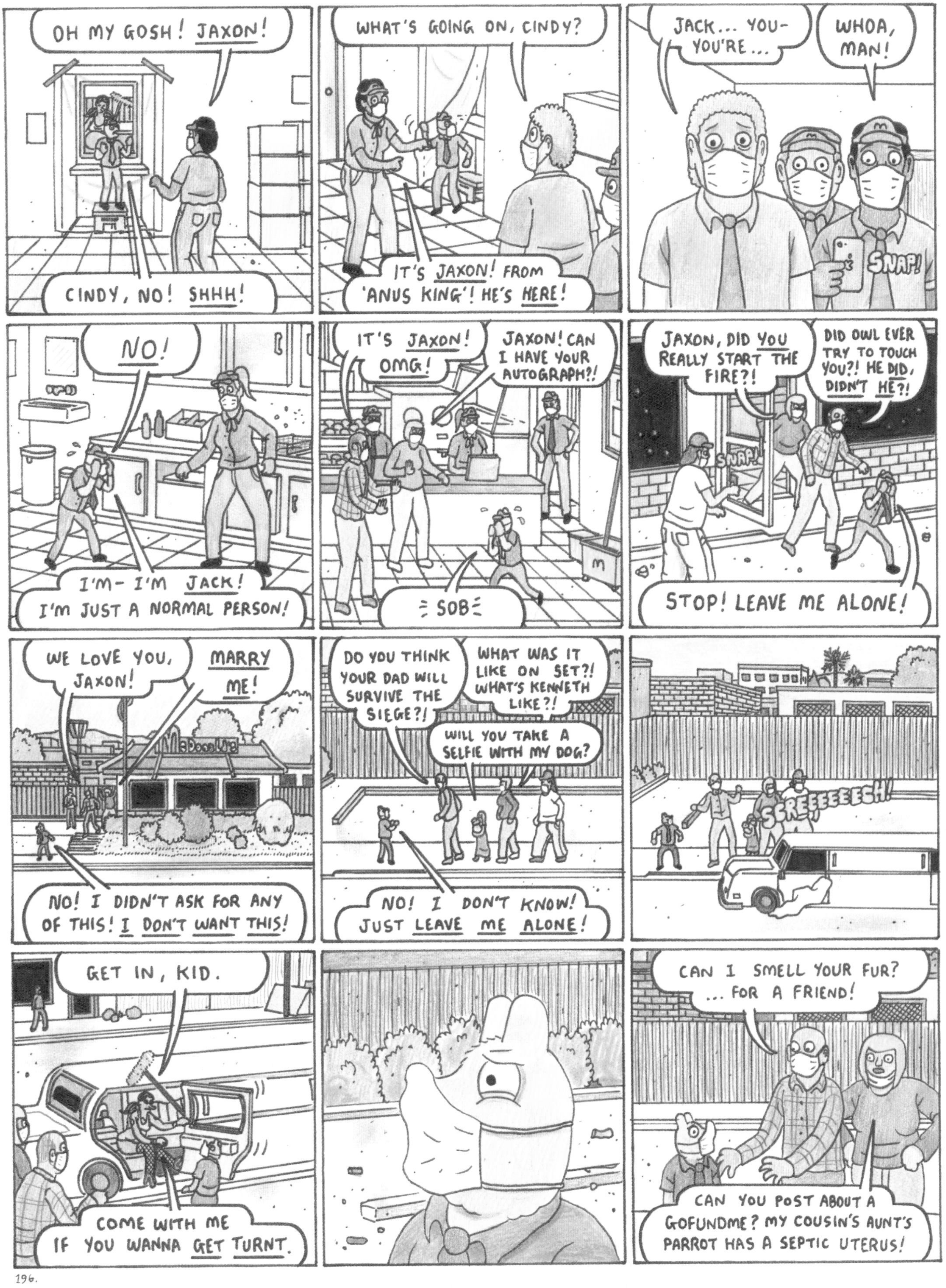
OH MY GOSH! JAXON!
CINDY, NO! SHHH!
WHAT'S GOING ON, CINDY?
IT'S JAXON! FROM 'ANUS KING'! HE'S HERE!
JACK... YOU- YOU'RE...
WHOA, MAN!
SNAP!
NO!
I'M- I'M JACK! I'M JUST A NORMAL PERSON!
IT'S JAXON! OMG!
JAXON! CAN I HAVE YOUR AUTOGRAPH?!
SOB
JAXON, DID YOU REALLY START THE FIRE?!
DID OWL EVER TRY TO TOUCH YOU?! HE DID, DIDN'T HE?!
SNAP!
STOP! LEAVE ME ALONE!
WE LOVE YOU, JAXON!
MARRY ME!
NO! I DIDN'T ASK FOR ANY OF THIS! I DON'T WANT THIS!
DO YOU THINK YOUR DAD WILL SURVIVE THE SIEGE?!
WHAT WAS IT LIKE ON SET?! WHAT'S KENNETH LIKE?!
WILL YOU TAKE A SELFIE WITH MY DOG?
NO! I DON'T KNOW! JUST LEAVE ME ALONE!
SCREEEEEECH!
GET IN, KID.
COME WITH ME IF YOU WANNA GET TURNT.
CAN I SMELL YOUR FUR? ... FOR A FRIEND!
CAN YOU POST ABOUT A GOFUNDME? MY COUSIN'S AUNT'S PARROT HAS A SEPTIC UTERUS!

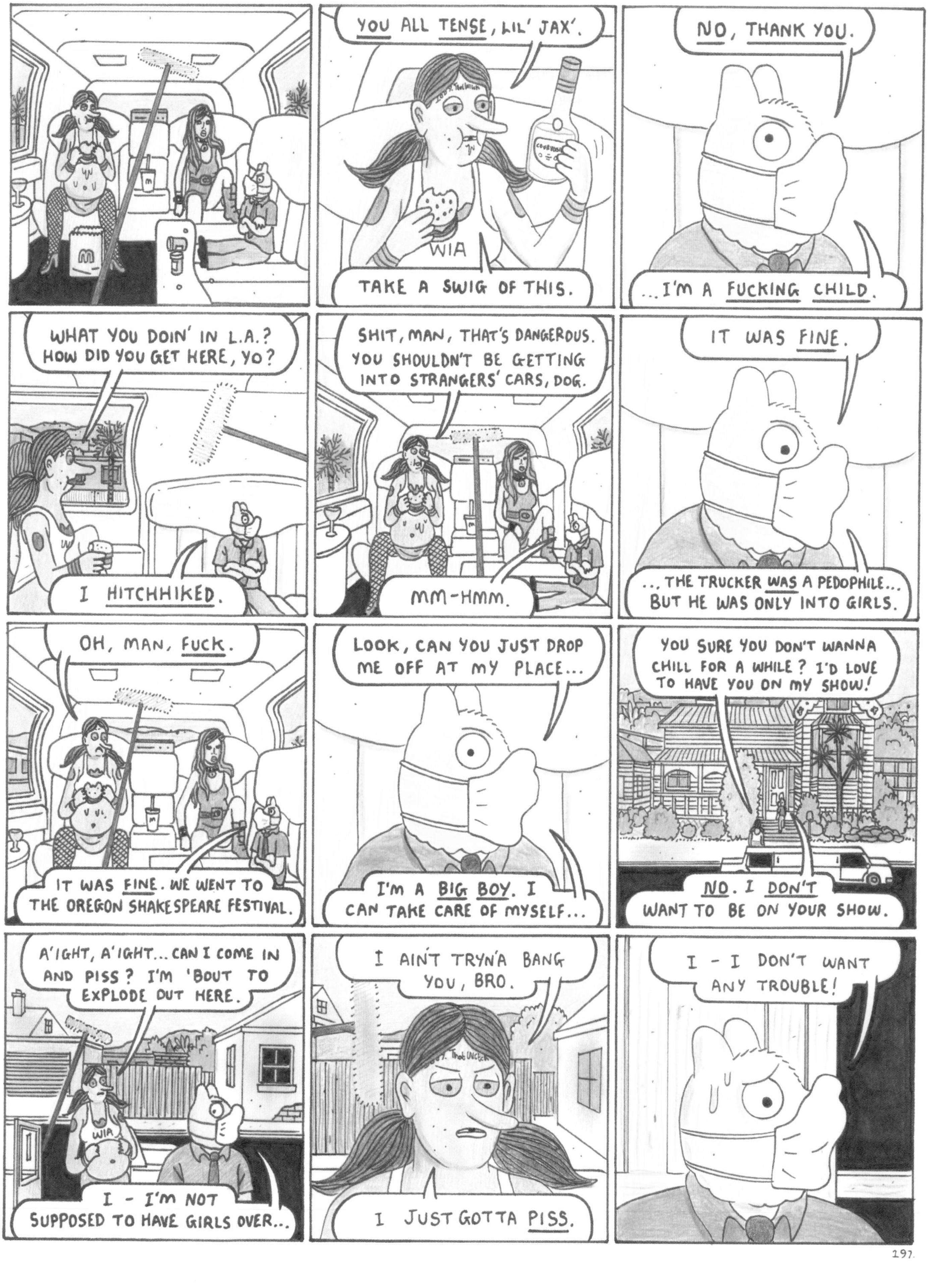
YOU ALL TENSE, LIL' JAX'.
TAKE A SWIG OF THIS.
NO, THANK YOU.
...I'M A FUCKING CHILD.
WHAT YOU DOIN' IN L.A.? HOW DID YOU GET HERE, YO?
I HITCHHIKED.
SHIT, MAN, THAT'S DANGEROUS. YOU SHOULDN'T BE GETTING INTO STRANGERS' CARS, DOG.
MM-HMM.
IT WAS FINE.
..., THE TRUCKER WAS A PEDOPHILE... BUT HE WAS ONLY INTO GIRLS.
OH, MAN, FUCK.
IT WAS FINE. WE WENT TO THE OREGON SHAKESPEARE FESTIVAL.
LOOK, CAN YOU JUST DROP ME OFF AT MY PLACE...
I'M A BIG BOY. I CAN TAKE CARE OF MYSELF...
YOU SURE YOU DON'T WANNA CHILL FOR A WHILE? I'D LOVE TO HAVE YOU ON MY SHOW!
NO. I DON'T WANT TO BE ON YOUR SHOW.
A'IGHT, A'IGHT... CAN I COME IN AND PISS? I'M 'BOUT TO EXPLODE OUT HERE.
I - I'M NOT SUPPOSED TO HAVE GIRLS OVER...
I AIN'T TRYN'A BANG YOU, BRO.
I JUST GOTTA PISS.
I - I DON'T WANT ANY TROUBLE!

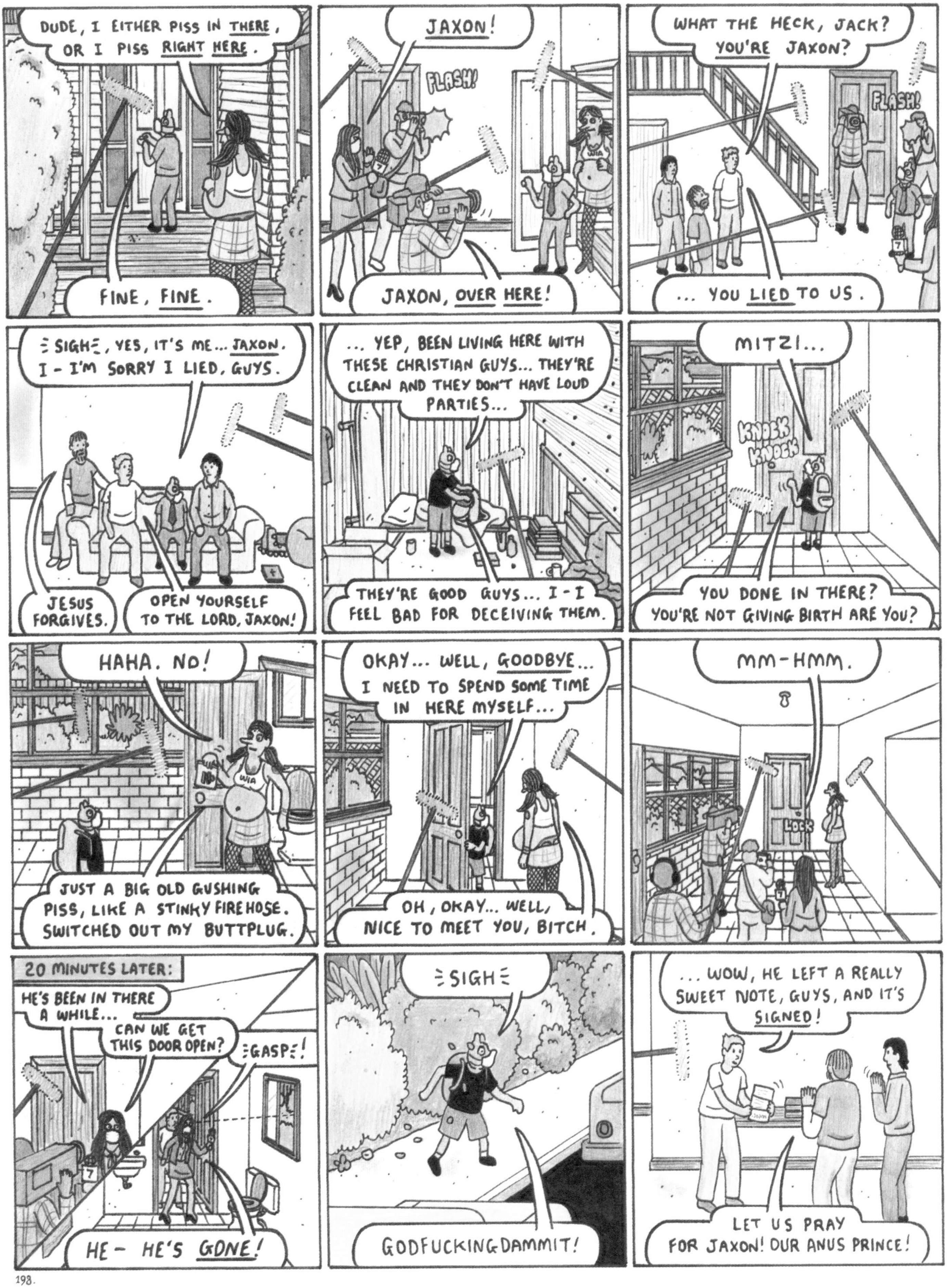
DUDE, I EITHER PISS IN THERE, OR I PISS RIGHT HERE.
FINE, FINE.
JAXON!
FLASH!
JAXON, OVER HERE!
WHAT THE HECK, JACK? YOU'RE JAXON?
FLASH!
... YOU LIED TO US.
SIGH, YES, IT'S ME... JAXON. I - I'M SORRY I LIED, GUYS.
JESUS FORGIVES.
OPEN YOURSELF TO THE LORD, JAXON!
... YEP, BEEN LIVING HERE WITH THESE CHRISTIAN GUYS... THEY'RE CLEAN AND THEY DON'T HAVE LOUD PARTIES...
THEY'RE GOOD GUYS... I-I FEEL BAD FOR DECEIVING THEM.
MITZI...
KNOCK KNOCK
YOU DONE IN THERE? YOU'RE NOT GIVING BIRTH ARE YOU?
HAHA. NO!
JUST A BIG OLD GUSHING PISS, LIKE A STINKY FIREHOSE. SWITCHED OUT MY BUTTPLUG.
OKAY... WELL, GOODBYE... I NEED TO SPEND SOME TIME IN HERE MYSELF...
OH, OKAY... WELL, NICE TO MEET YOU, BITCH.
MM-HMM.
LOCK
20 MINUTES LATER:
HE'S BEEN IN THERE A WHILE...
CAN WE GET THIS DOOR OPEN?
GASP!
HE- HE'S GONE!
SIGH
GODFUCKINGDAMMIT!
... WOW, HE LEFT A REALLY SWEET NOTE, GUYS, AND IT'S SIGNED!
LET US PRAY FOR JAXON! OUR ANUS PRINCE!

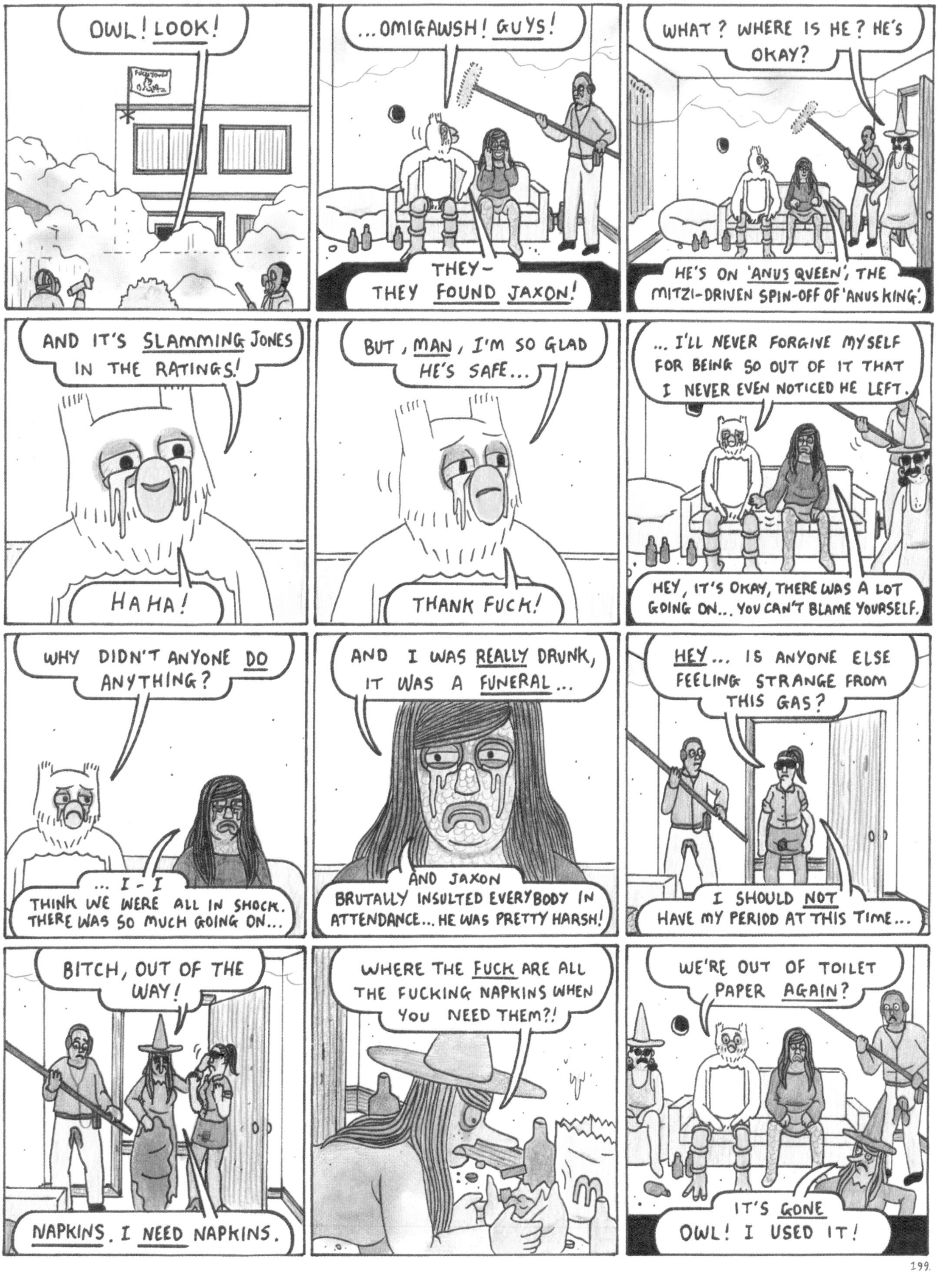
OWL! LOOK!
...OMIGAWSH! GUYS!
THEY- THEY FOUND JAXON!
WHAT? WHERE IS HE? HE'S OKAY?
HE'S ON 'ANUS QUEEN', THE MITZI-DRIVEN SPIN-OFF OF 'ANUS KING'.
AND IT'S SLAMMING JONES IN THE RATINGS!
HA HA!
BUT, MAN, I'M SO GLAD HE'S SAFE...
THANK FUCK!
... I'LL NEVER FORGIVE MYSELF FOR BEING SO OUT OF IT THAT I NEVER EVEN NOTICED HE LEFT.
HEY, IT'S OKAY, THERE WAS A LOT GOING ON... YOU CAN'T BLAME YOURSELF.
WHY DIDN'T ANYONE DO ANYTHING?
... I - I THINK WE WERE ALL IN SHOCK. THERE WAS SO MUCH GOING ON...
AND I WAS REALLY DRUNK, IT WAS A FUNERAL...
AND JAXON BRUTALLY INSULTED EVERYBODY IN ATTENDANCE... HE WAS PRETTY HARSH!
HEY... IS ANYONE ELSE FEELING STRANGE FROM THIS GAS?
I SHOULD NOT HAVE MY PERIOD AT THIS TIME...
BITCH, OUT OF THE WAY!
NAPKINS. I NEED NAPKINS.
WHERE THE FUCK ARE ALL THE FUCKING NAPKINS WHEN YOU NEED THEM?!
WE'RE OUT OF TOILET PAPER AGAIN?
IT'S GONE OWL! I USED IT!

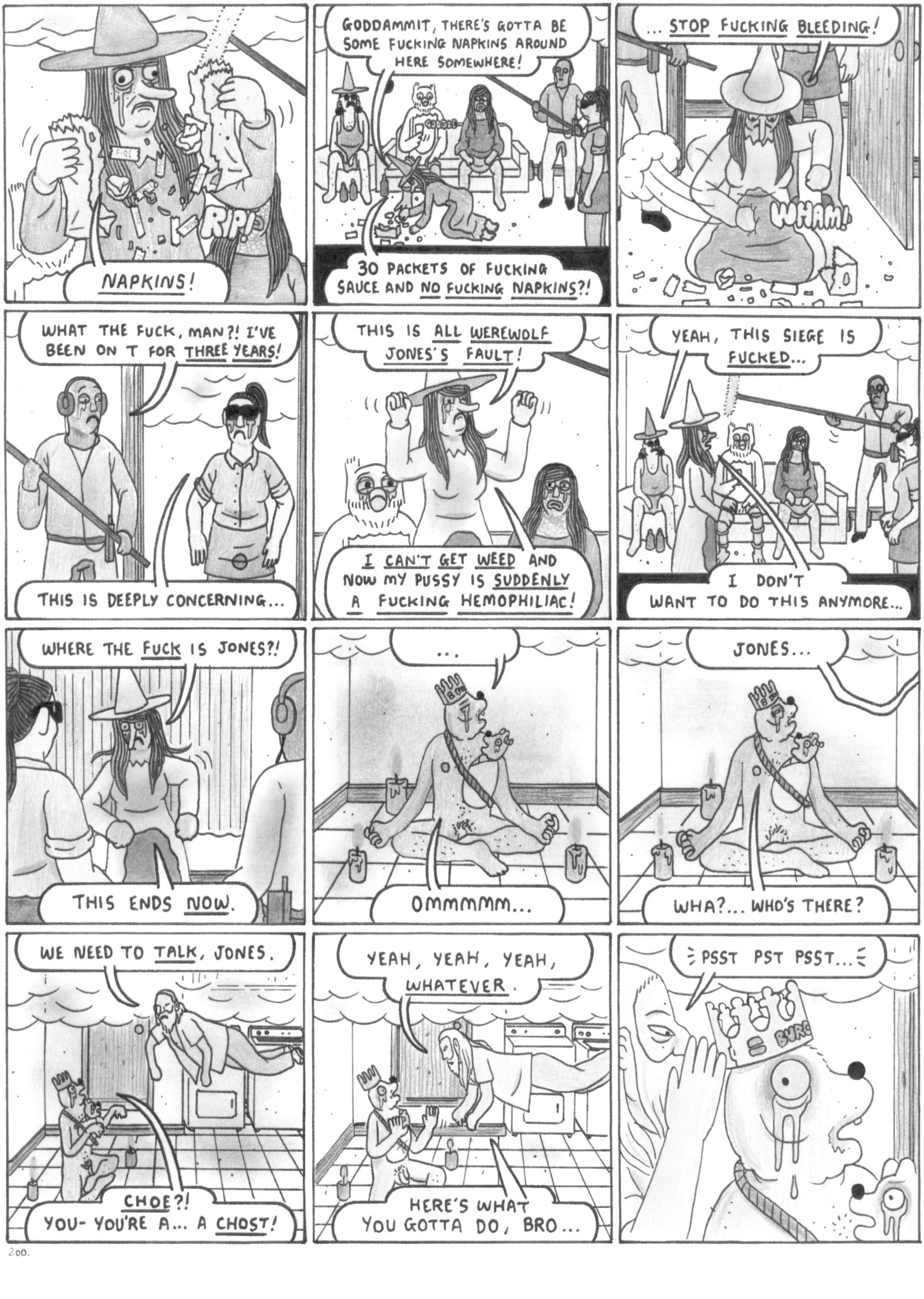
NAPKINS!
RIP!
GODDAMMIT, THERE'S GOTTA BE SOME FUCKING NAPKINS AROUND HERE SOMEWHERE!
30 PACKETS OF FUCKING SAUCE AND NO FUCKING NAPKINS?!
... STOP FUCKING BLEEDING!
WHAM!
WHAT THE FUCK, MAN?! I'VE BEEN ON T FOR THREE YEARS!
THIS IS DEEPLY CONCERNING...
THIS IS ALL WEREWOLF JONES'S FAULT!
I CAN'T GET WEED AND NOW MY PUSSY IS SUDDENLY A FUCKING HEMOPHILIAC!
YEAH, THIS SIEGE IS FUCKED...
I DON'T WANT TO DO THIS ANYMORE...
WHERE THE FUCK IS JONES?!
THIS ENDS NOW.
...
OMMMMM...
JONES...
WHA?... WHO'S THERE?
WE NEED TO TALK, JONES.
CHOE?! YOU- YOU'RE A... A GHOST!
YEAH, YEAH, YEAH, WHATEVER.
HERE'S WHAT YOU GOTTA DO, BRO...
PSST PST PSST...

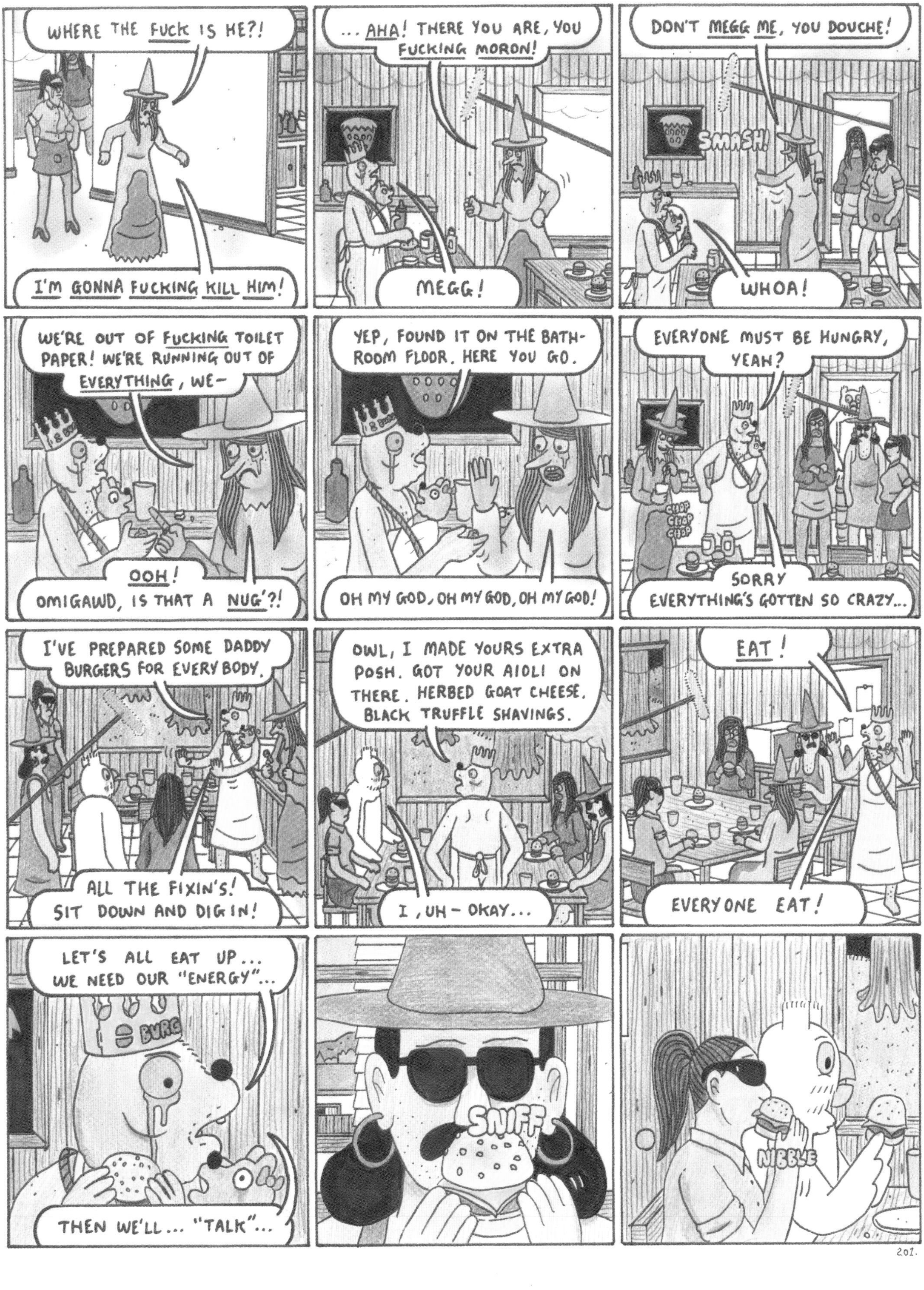
WHERE THE FUCK IS HE?!
I'M GONNA FUCKING KILL HIM!
... AHA! THERE YOU ARE, YOU FUCKING MORON!
MEGG!
DON'T MEGG ME, YOU DOUCHE!
SMASH!
WHOA!
WE'RE OUT OF FUCKING TOILET PAPER! WE'RE RUNNING OUT OF EVERYTHING, WE-
OOH! OMIGAWD, IS THAT A NUG'?!
YEP, FOUND IT ON THE BATH-ROOM FLOOR. HERE YOU GO.
OH MY GOD, OH MY GOD, OH MY GOD!
EVERYONE MUST BE HUNGRY, YEAH?
CHOP CHOP CHOP
SORRY EVERYTHING'S GOTTEN SO CRAZY...
I'VE PREPARED SOME DADDY BURGERS FOR EVERYBODY.
ALL THE FIXIN'S! SIT DOWN AND DIG IN!
OWL, I MADE YOURS EXTRA POSH. GOT YOUR AIOLI ON THERE. HERBED GOAT CHEESE. BLACK TRUFFLE SHAVINGS.
I, UH - OKAY...
EAT!
EVERYONE EAT!
LET'S ALL EAT UP... WE NEED OUR "ENERGY"...
BURG
THEN WE'LL... "TALK"...
SNIFF
NIBBLE

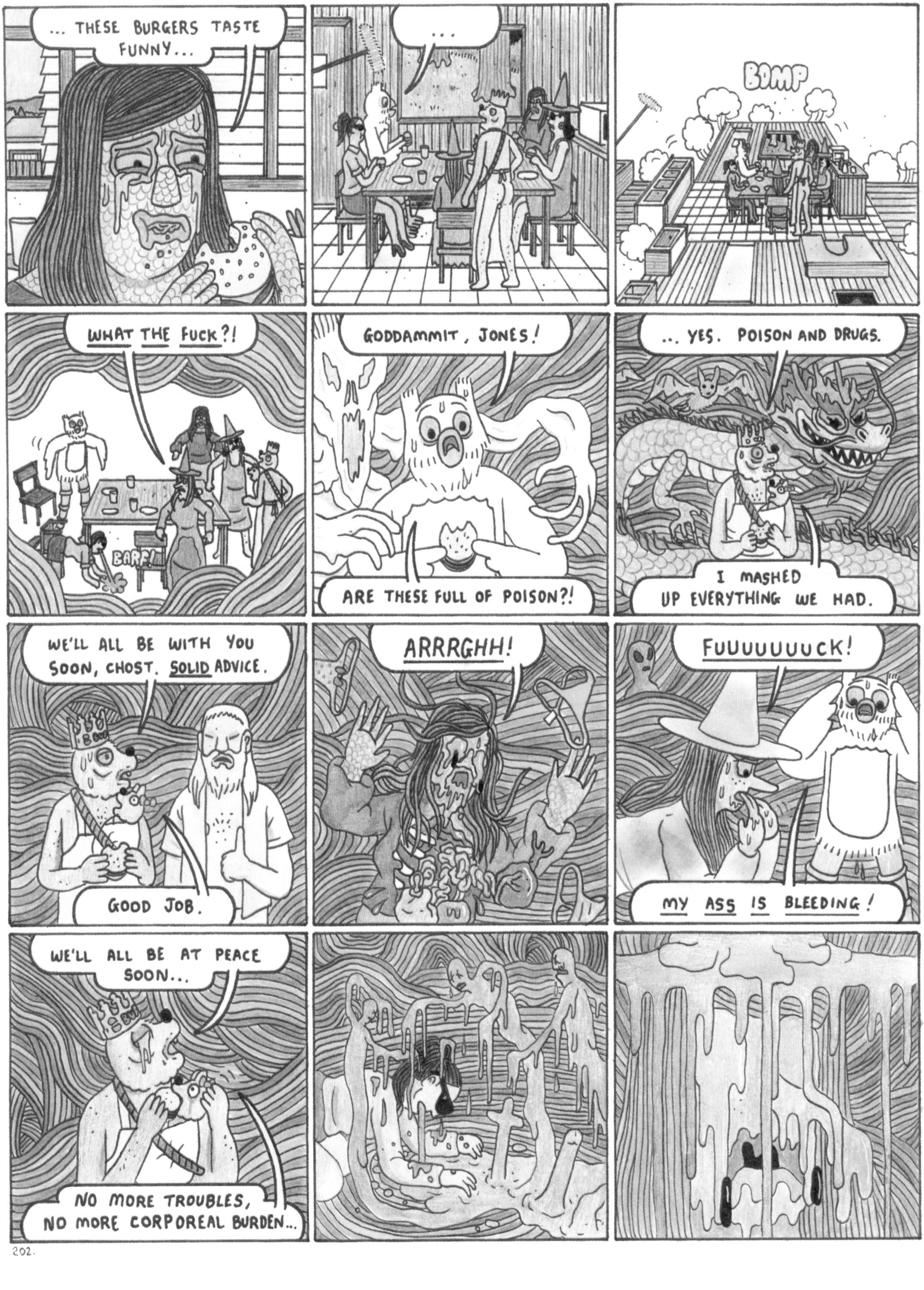

... THESE BURGERS TASTE FUNNY...
...
BOMP
WHAT THE FUCK?!
BARF!
GODDAMMIT, JONES!
ARE THESE FULL OF POISON?!
... YES. POISON AND DRUGS.
I MASHED UP EVERYTHING WE HAD.
WE'LL ALL BE WITH YOU SOON, GHOST. SOLID ADVICE.
GOOD JOB.
ARRRGHH!
FUUUUUUUCK!
MY ASS IS BLEEDING!
WE'LL ALL BE AT PEACE SOON...
NO MORE TROUBLES, NO MORE CORPOREAL BURDEN...

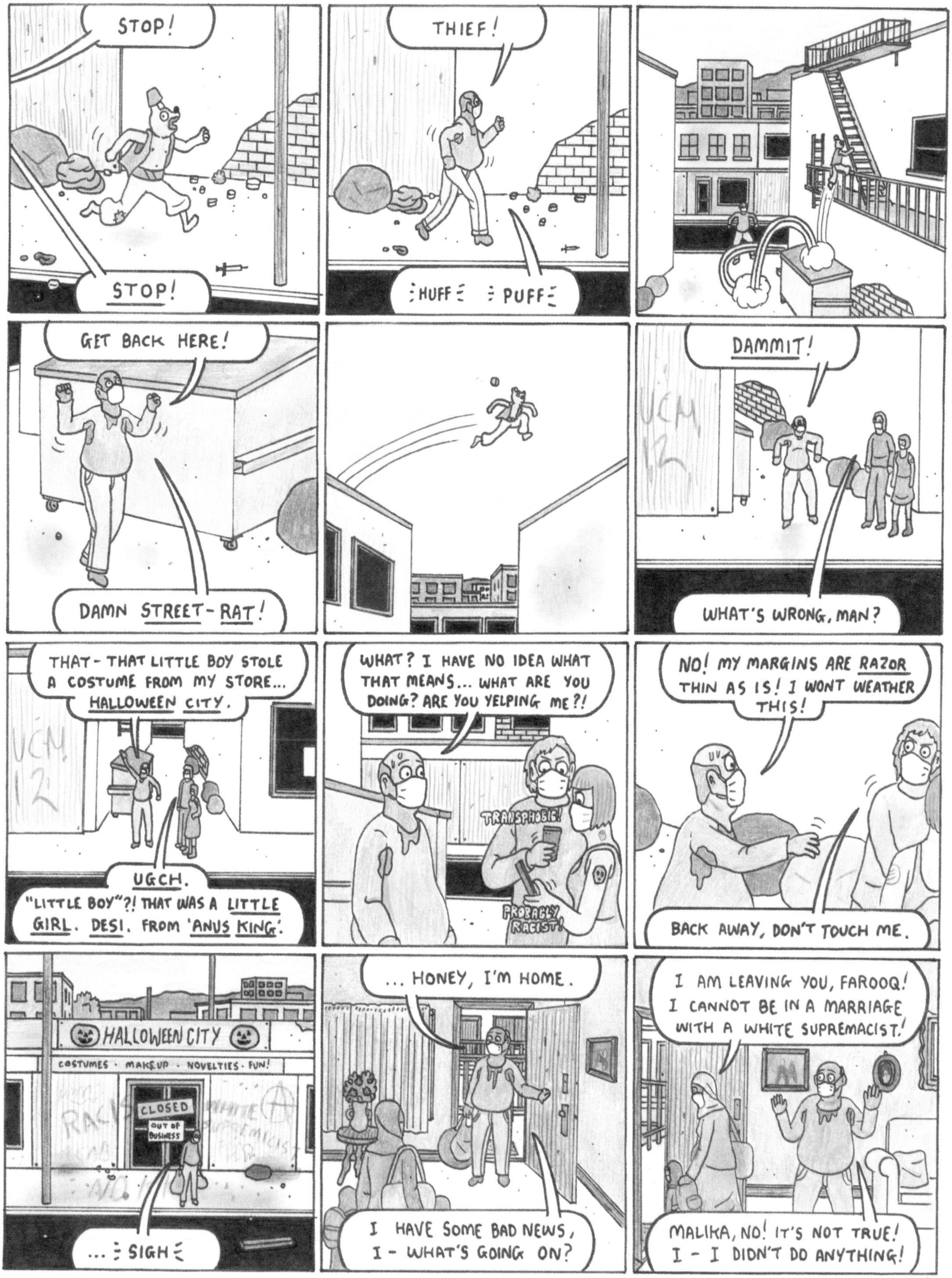
STOP!
STOP!
THIEF!
HUFF PUFF
GET BACK HERE!
DAMN STREET-RAT!
DAMMIT!
WHAT'S WRONG, MAN?
THAT-THAT LITTLE BOY STOLE A COSTUME FROM MY STORE... HALLOWEEN CITY.
UGCH.
"LITTLE BOY"?! THAT WAS A LITTLE GIRL. DESI. FROM 'ANUS KING'.
WHAT? I HAVE NO IDEA WHAT THAT MEANS... WHAT ARE YOU DOING? ARE YOU YELPING ME?!
TRANSPHOBIC!
PROBABLY RACIST!
NO! MY MARGINS ARE RAZOR THIN AS IS! I WONT WEATHER THIS!
BACK AWAY, DON'T TOUCH ME.
HALLOWEEN CITY
COSTUMES · MAKEUP · NOVELTIES · FUN!
CLOSED
OUT OF BUSINESS
... SIGH
... HONEY, I'M HOME.
I HAVE SOME BAD NEWS, I - WHAT'S GOING ON?
I AM LEAVING YOU, FAROOQ! I CANNOT BE IN A MARRIAGE WITH A WHITE SUPREMACIST!
MALIKA, NO! IT'S NOT TRUE! I - I DIDN'T DO ANYTHING!

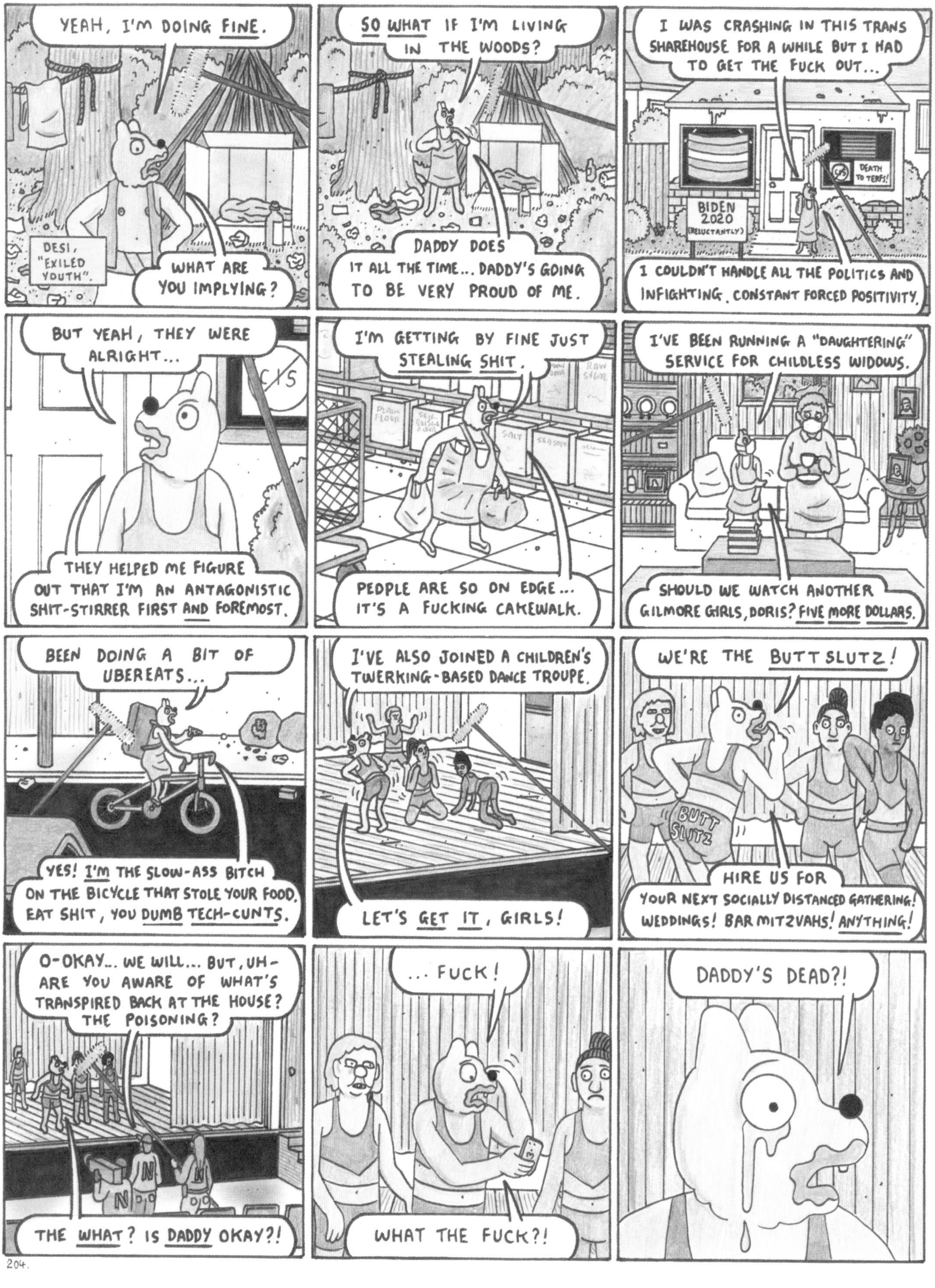
YEAH, I'M DOING FINE.
DESI, "EXILED YOUTH".
WHAT ARE YOU IMPLYING?
SO WHAT IF I'M LIVING IN THE WOODS?
DADDY DOES IT ALL THE TIME... DADDY'S GOING TO BE VERY PROUD OF ME.
I WAS CRASHING IN THIS TRANS SHAREHOUSE FOR A WHILE BUT I HAD TO GET THE FUCK OUT...
BIDEN 2020 (RELUCTANTLY)
DEATH TO TERFS!
I COULDN'T HANDLE ALL THE POLITICS AND INFIGHTING. CONSTANT FORCED POSITIVITY.
BUT YEAH, THEY WERE ALRIGHT...
THEY HELPED ME FIGURE OUT THAT I'M AN ANTAGONISTIC SHIT-STIRRER FIRST AND FOREMOST.
I'M GETTING BY FINE JUST STEALING SHIT.
PEOPLE ARE SO ON EDGE... IT'S A FUCKING CAKEWALK.
I'VE BEEN RUNNING A "DAUGHTERING" SERVICE FOR CHILDLESS WIDOWS.
SHOULD WE WATCH ANOTHER GILMORE GIRLS, DORIS? FIVE MORE DOLLARS.
BEEN DOING A BIT OF UBEREATS...
YES! I'M THE SLOW-ASS BITCH ON THE BICYCLE THAT STOLE YOUR FOOD. EAT SHIT, YOU DUMB TECH-CUNTS.
I'VE ALSO JOINED A CHILDREN'S TWERKING-BASED DANCE TROUPE.
LET'S GET IT, GIRLS!
WE'RE THE BUTTSLUTZ!
BUTT SLUTZ
HIRE US FOR YOUR NEXT SOCIALLY DISTANCED GATHERING! WEDDINGS! BAR MITZVAHS! ANYTHING!
O-OKAY... WE WILL... BUT, UH- ARE YOU AWARE OF WHAT'S TRANSPIRED BACK AT THE HOUSE? THE POISONING?
THE WHAT? IS DADDY OKAY?!
...FUCK!
WHAT THE FUCK?!
DADDY'S DEAD?!

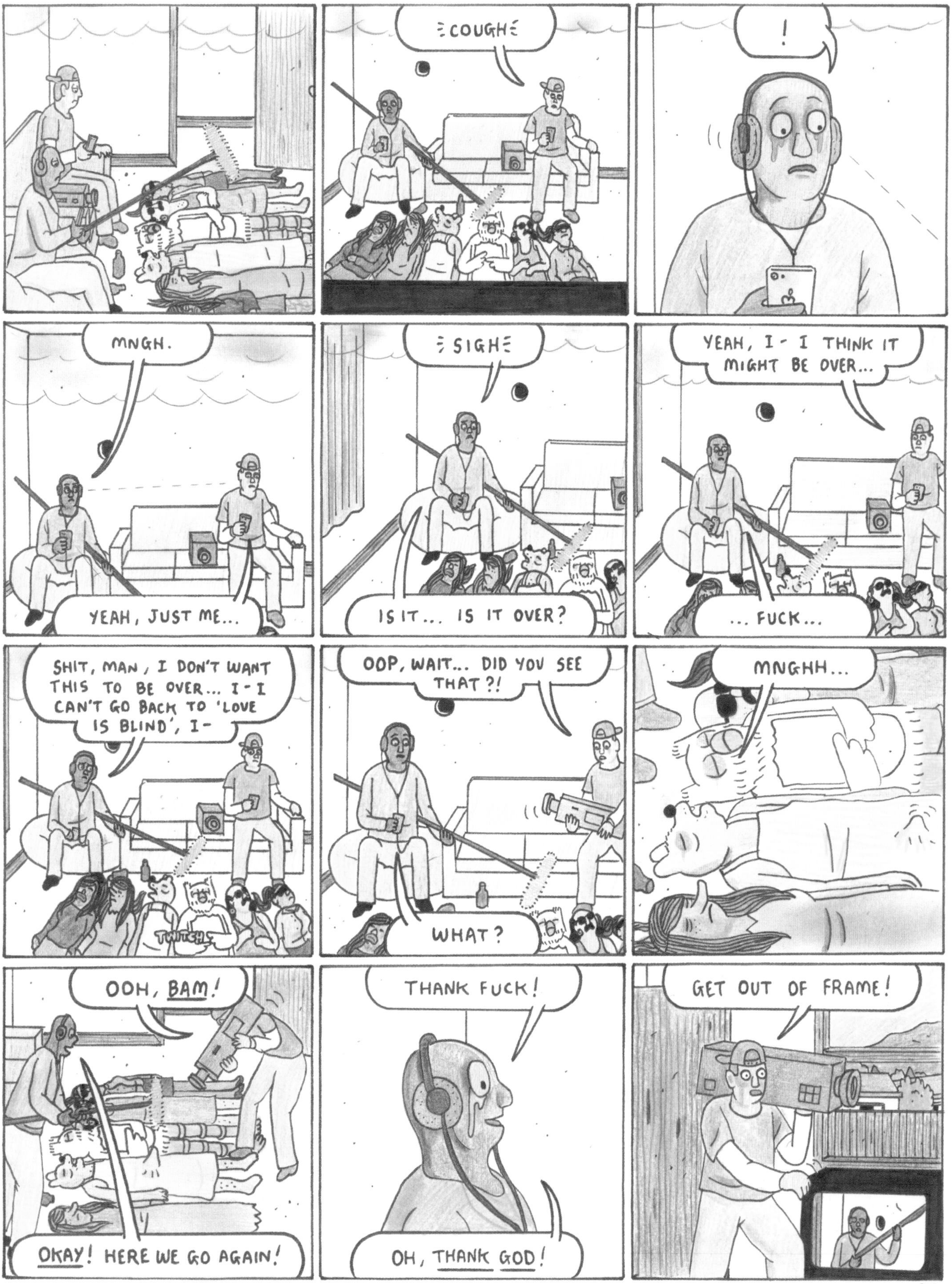
COUGH
!
MNGH.
YEAH, JUST ME...
SIGH
IS IT... IS IT OVER?
YEAH, I- I THINK IT MIGHT BE OVER...
... FUCK...
SHIT, MAN, I DON'T WANT THIS TO BE OVER... I- I CAN'T GO BACK TO 'LOVE IS BLIND', I-
TWITCH
OOP, WAIT... DID YOU SEE THAT?!
WHAT?
MNGHH...
OOH, BAM!
OKAY! HERE WE GO AGAIN!
THANK FUCK!
OH, THANK GOD!
GET OUT OF FRAME!

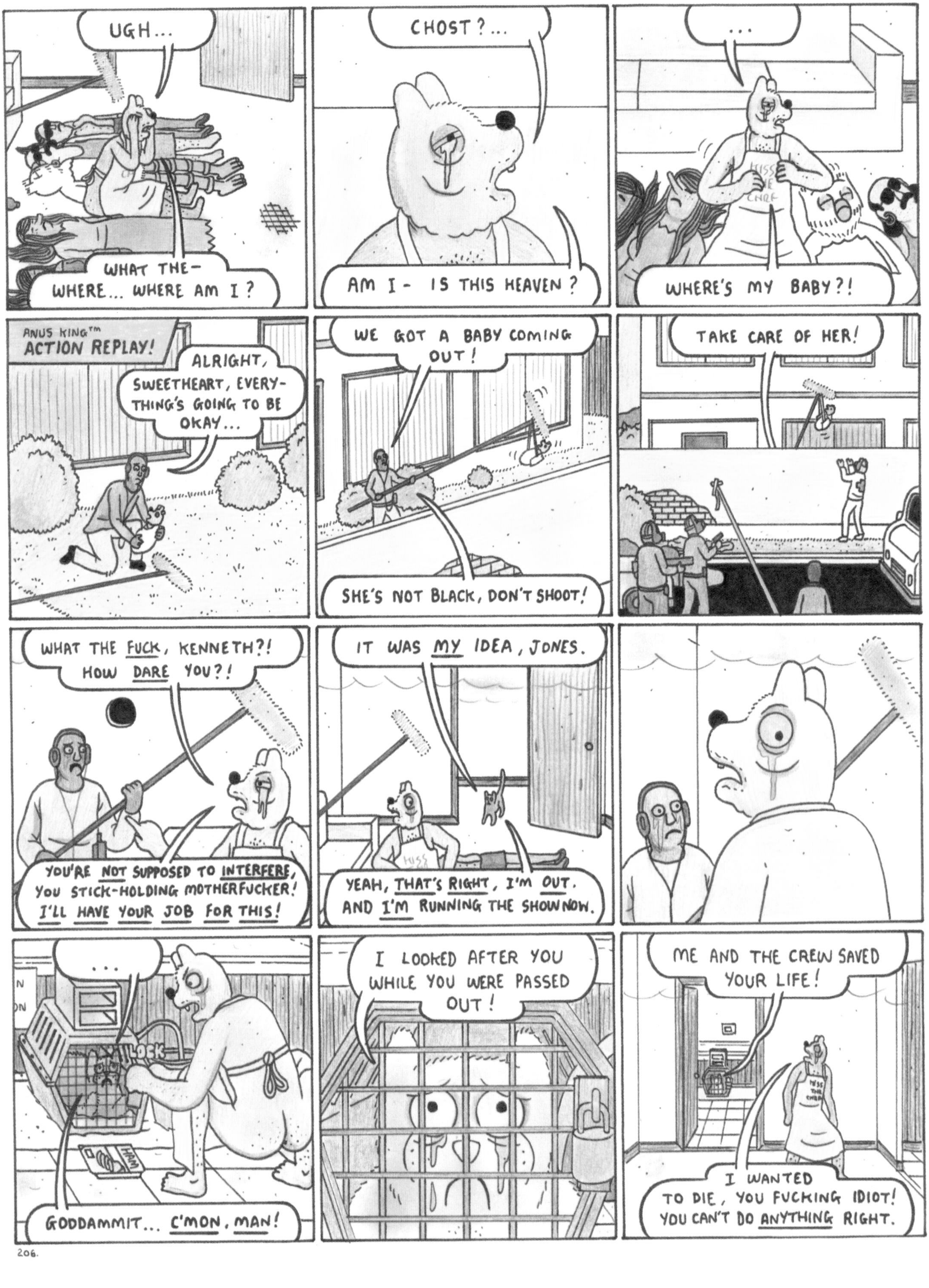
UGH...
WHAT THE— WHERE... WHERE AM I?
GHOST?...
AM I- IS THIS HEAVEN?
...
WHERE'S MY BABY?!
ANUS KING™ ACTION REPLAY!
ALRIGHT, SWEETHEART, EVERYTHING'S GOING TO BE OKAY...
WE GOT A BABY COMING OUT!
SHE'S NOT BLACK, DON'T SHOOT!
TAKE CARE OF HER!
WHAT THE FUCK, KENNETH?! HOW DARE YOU?!
YOU'RE NOT SUPPOSED TO INTERFERE, YOU STICK-HOLDING MOTHERFUCKER! I'LL HAVE YOUR JOB FOR THIS!
IT WAS MY IDEA, JONES.
YEAH, THAT'S RIGHT, I'M OUT. AND I'M RUNNING THE SHOW NOW.
...
LOCK
GODDAMMIT... C'MON, MAN!
I LOOKED AFTER YOU WHILE YOU WERE PASSED OUT!
ME AND THE CREW SAVED YOUR LIFE!
I WANTED TO DIE, YOU FUCKING IDIOT! YOU CAN'T DO ANYTHING RIGHT.

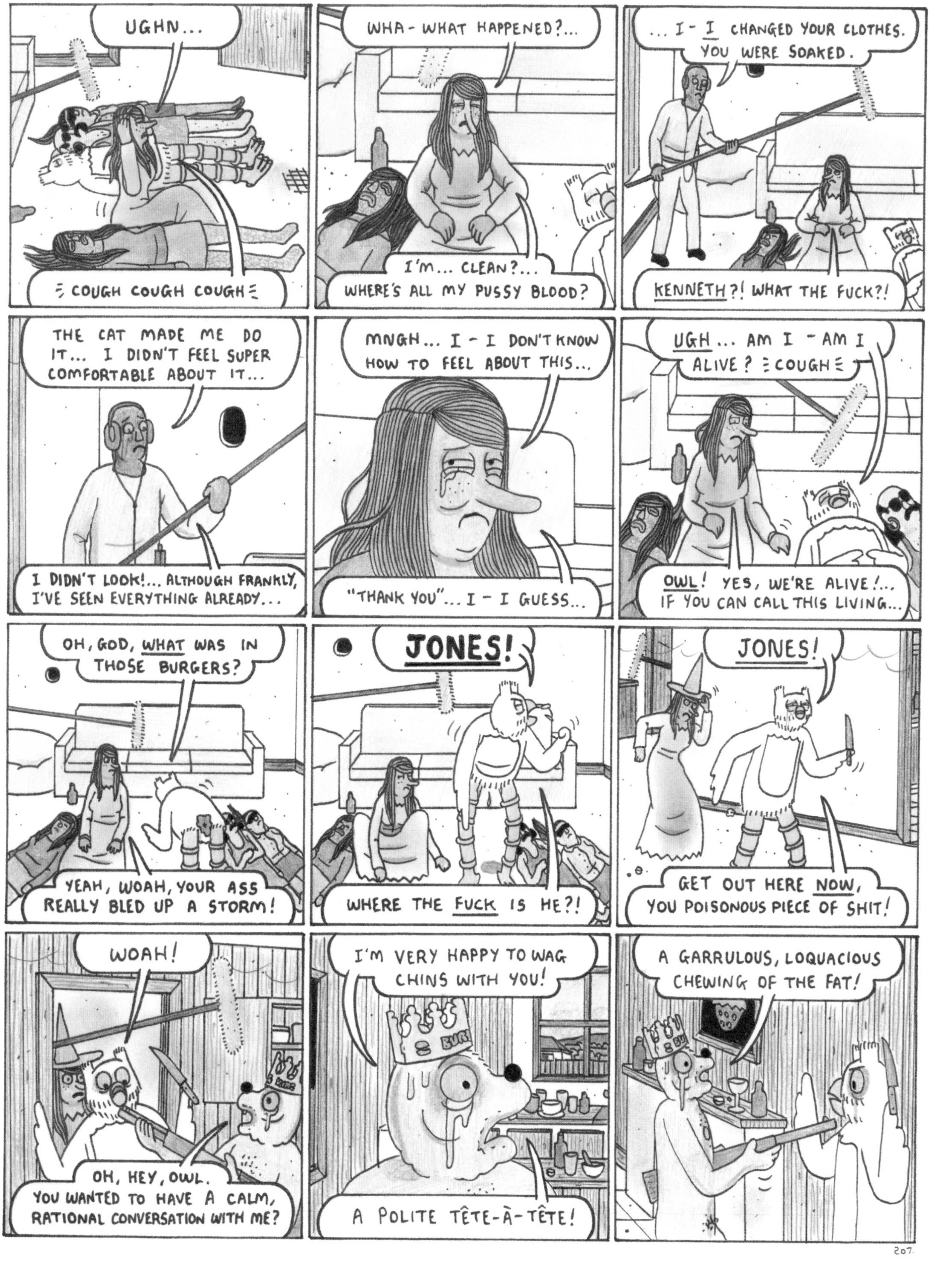

UGHN...
≡COUGH COUGH COUGH≡
WHA-WHAT HAPPENED?...
I'M... CLEAN?...
WHERE'S ALL MY PUSSY BLOOD?
... I- I CHANGED YOUR CLOTHES. YOU WERE SOAKED.
KENNETH?! WHAT THE FUCK?!
THE CAT MADE ME DO IT... I DIDN'T FEEL SUPER COMFORTABLE ABOUT IT...
I DIDN'T LOOK!... ALTHOUGH FRANKLY, I'VE SEEN EVERYTHING ALREADY...
MNGH... I- I DON'T KNOW HOW TO FEEL ABOUT THIS...
"THANK YOU"... I- I GUESS...
UGH... AM I - AM I ALIVE? ≡COUGH≡
OWL! YES, WE'RE ALIVE!... IF YOU CAN CALL THIS LIVING...
OH, GOD, WHAT WAS IN THOSE BURGERS?
YEAH, WOAH, YOUR ASS REALLY BLED UP A STORM!
JONES!
WHERE THE FUCK IS HE?!
JONES!
GET OUT HERE NOW, YOU POISONOUS PIECE OF SHIT!
WOAH!
OH, HEY, OWL. YOU WANTED TO HAVE A CALM, RATIONAL CONVERSATION WITH ME?
I'M VERY HAPPY TO WAG CHINS WITH YOU!
A POLITE TÊTE-À-TÊTE!
A GARRULOUS, LOQUACIOUS CHEWING OF THE FAT!

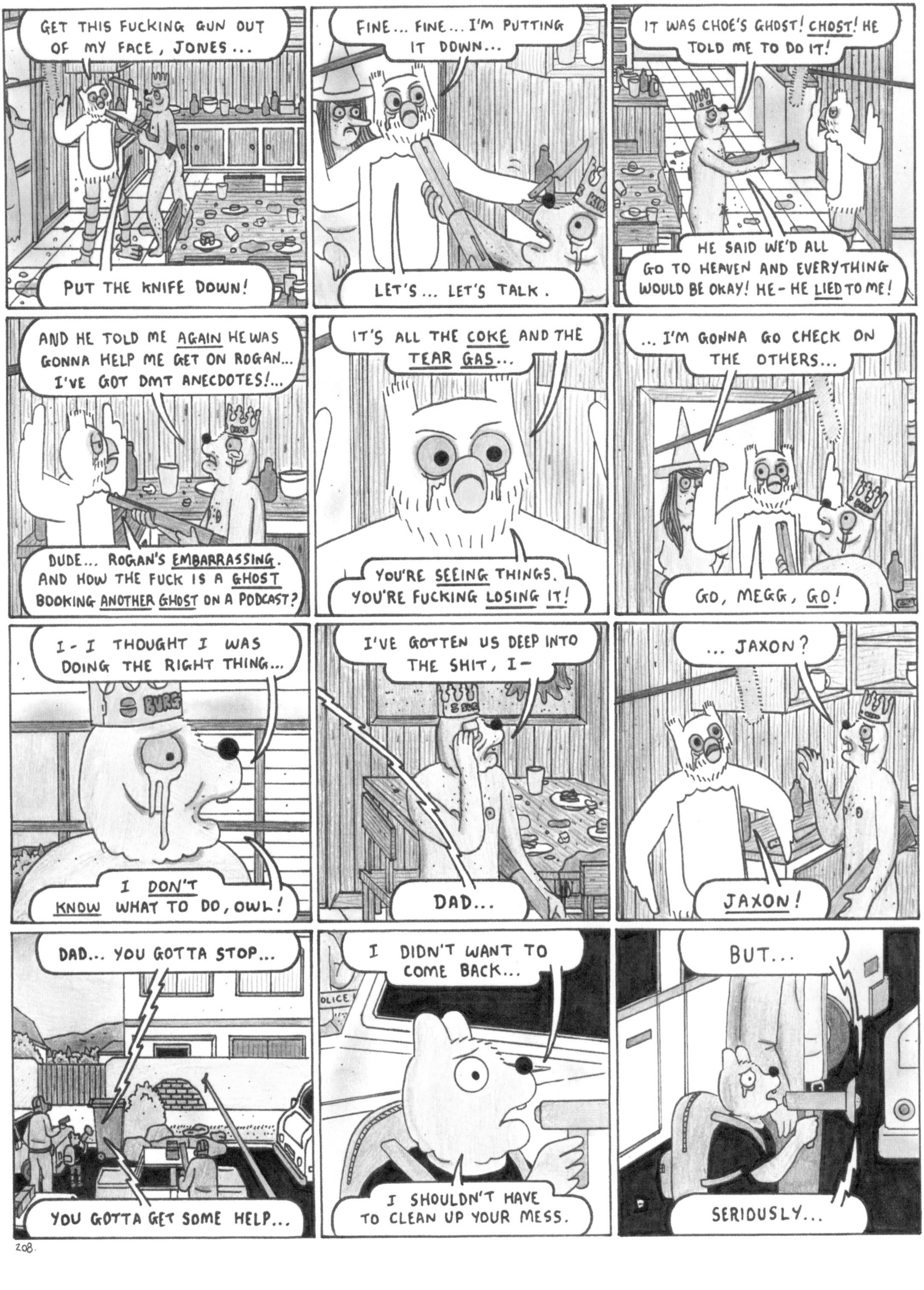
GET THIS FUCKING GUN OUT OF MY FACE, JONES...
PUT THE KNIFE DOWN!
FINE... FINE... I'M PUTTING IT DOWN...
LET'S... LET'S TALK.
IT WAS CHOE'S GHOST! CHOST! HE TOLD ME TO DO IT!
HE SAID WE'D ALL GO TO HEAVEN AND EVERYTHING WOULD BE OKAY! HE - HE LIED TO ME!
AND HE TOLD ME AGAIN HE WAS GONNA HELP ME GET ON ROGAN... I'VE GOT DMT ANECDOTES!...
DUDE... ROGAN'S EMBARRASSING. AND HOW THE FUCK IS A GHOST BOOKING ANOTHER GHOST ON A PODCAST?
IT'S ALL THE COKE AND THE TEAR GAS...
YOU'RE SEEING THINGS. YOU'RE FUCKING LOSING IT!
... I'M GONNA GO CHECK ON THE OTHERS...
GO, MEGG, GO!
I - I THOUGHT I WAS DOING THE RIGHT THING...
I DON'T KNOW WHAT TO DO, OWL!
I'VE GOTTEN US DEEP INTO THE SHIT, I—
DAD...
... JAXON?
JAXON!
DAD... YOU GOTTA STOP...
YOU GOTTA GET SOME HELP...
I DIDN'T WANT TO COME BACK...
I SHOULDN'T HAVE TO CLEAN UP YOUR MESS.
BUT...
SERIOUSLY...

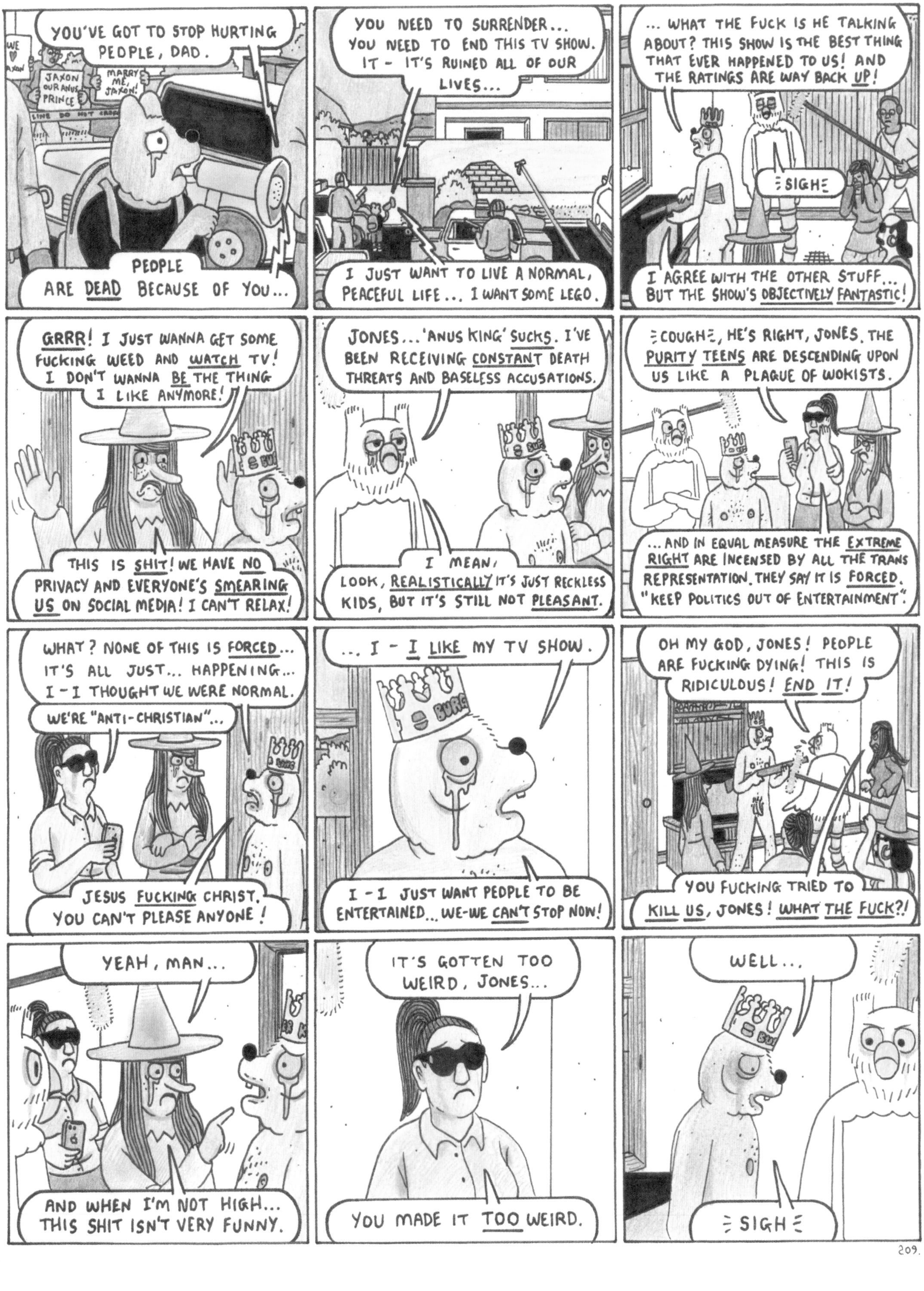
YOU'VE GOT TO STOP HURTING PEOPLE, DAD.
JAXON OUR ANUS PRINCE
MARRY ME, JAXON!
PEOPLE ARE DEAD BECAUSE OF YOU...
YOU NEED TO SURRENDER... YOU NEED TO END THIS TV SHOW. IT - IT'S RUINED ALL OF OUR LIVES...
I JUST WANT TO LIVE A NORMAL, PEACEFUL LIFE... I WANT SOME LEGO.
... WHAT THE FUCK IS HE TALKING ABOUT? THIS SHOW IS THE BEST THING THAT EVER HAPPENED TO US! AND THE RATINGS ARE WAY BACK UP!
SIGH
I AGREE WITH THE OTHER STUFF... BUT THE SHOW'S OBJECTIVELY FANTASTIC!
GRRR! I JUST WANNA GET SOME FUCKING WEED AND WATCH TV! I DON'T WANNA BE THE THING I LIKE ANYMORE!
THIS IS SHIT! WE HAVE NO PRIVACY AND EVERYONE'S SMEARING US ON SOCIAL MEDIA! I CAN'T RELAX!
JONES... 'ANUS KING' SUCKS. I'VE BEEN RECEIVING CONSTANT DEATH THREATS AND BASELESS ACCUSATIONS.
I MEAN, LOOK, REALISTICALLY IT'S JUST RECKLESS KIDS, BUT IT'S STILL NOT PLEASANT.
COUGH, HE'S RIGHT, JONES. THE PURITY TEENS ARE DESCENDING UPON US LIKE A PLAGUE OF WOKISTS.
...AND IN EQUAL MEASURE THE EXTREME RIGHT ARE INCENSED BY ALL THE TRANS REPRESENTATION. THEY SAY IT IS FORCED. "KEEP POLITICS OUT OF ENTERTAINMENT".
WHAT? NONE OF THIS IS FORCED... IT'S ALL JUST... HAPPENING... I - I THOUGHT WE WERE NORMAL.
WE'RE "ANTI-CHRISTIAN"...
JESUS FUCKING CHRIST. YOU CAN'T PLEASE ANYONE!
... I - I LIKE MY TV SHOW.
I - I JUST WANT PEOPLE TO BE ENTERTAINED... WE-WE CAN'T STOP NOW!
OH MY GOD, JONES! PEOPLE ARE FUCKING DYING! THIS IS RIDICULOUS! END IT!
YOU FUCKING TRIED TO KILL US, JONES! WHAT THE FUCK?!
YEAH, MAN...
AND WHEN I'M NOT HIGH... THIS SHIT ISN'T VERY FUNNY.
IT'S GOTTEN TOO WEIRD, JONES...
YOU MADE IT TOO WEIRD.
WELL...
SIGH

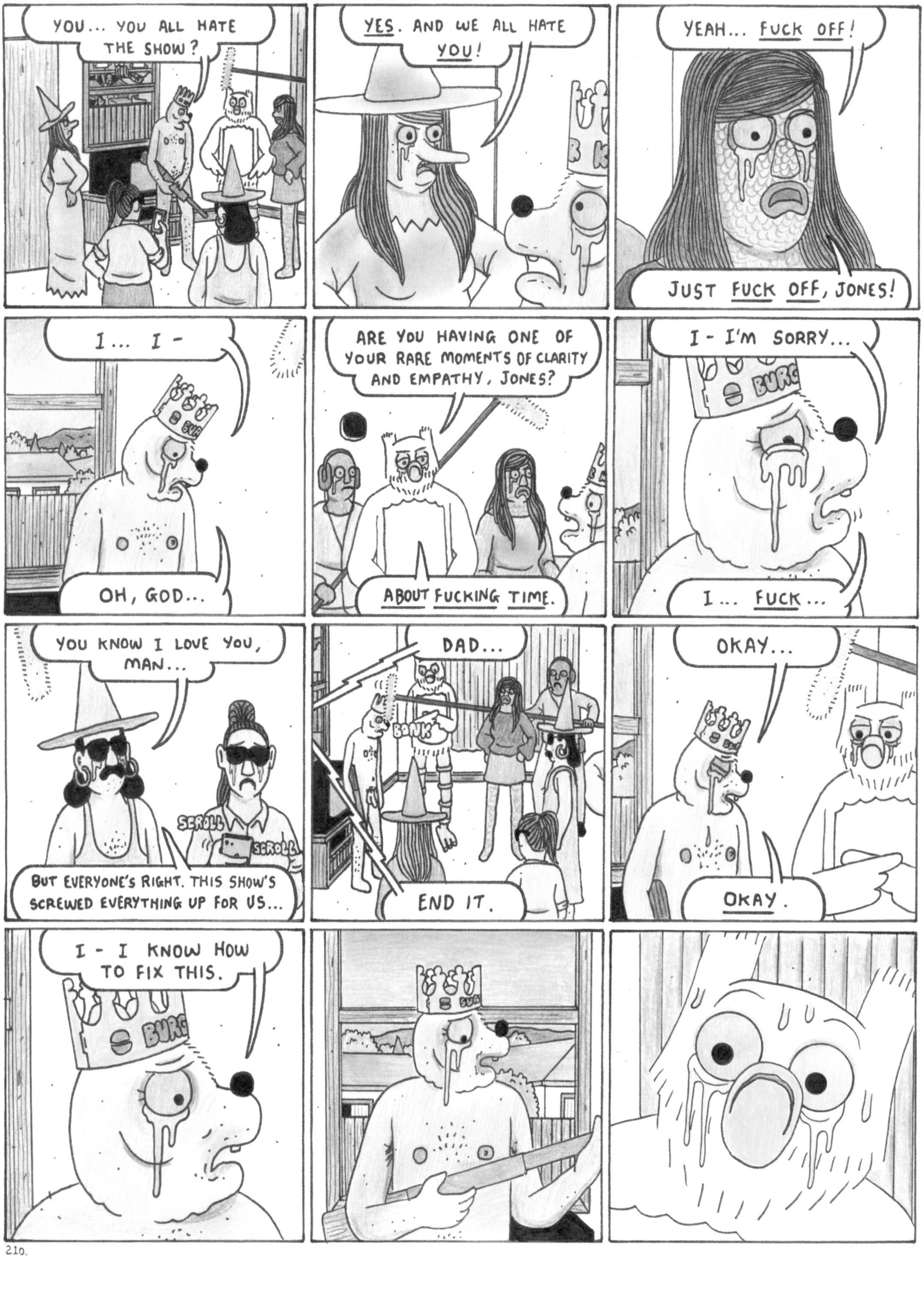
YOU... YOU ALL HATE THE SHOW?
YES. AND WE ALL HATE YOU!
YEAH... FUCK OFF!
JUST FUCK OFF, JONES!
I... I -
OH, GOD...
ARE YOU HAVING ONE OF YOUR RARE MOMENTS OF CLARITY AND EMPATHY, JONES?
ABOUT FUCKING TIME.
I - I'M SORRY...
I... FUCK...
YOU KNOW I LOVE YOU, MAN...
SCROLL
SCROLL
BUT EVERYONE'S RIGHT. THIS SHOW'S SCREWED EVERYTHING UP FOR US...
DAD...
BONK
END IT.
OKAY...
OKAY.
I - I KNOW HOW TO FIX THIS.

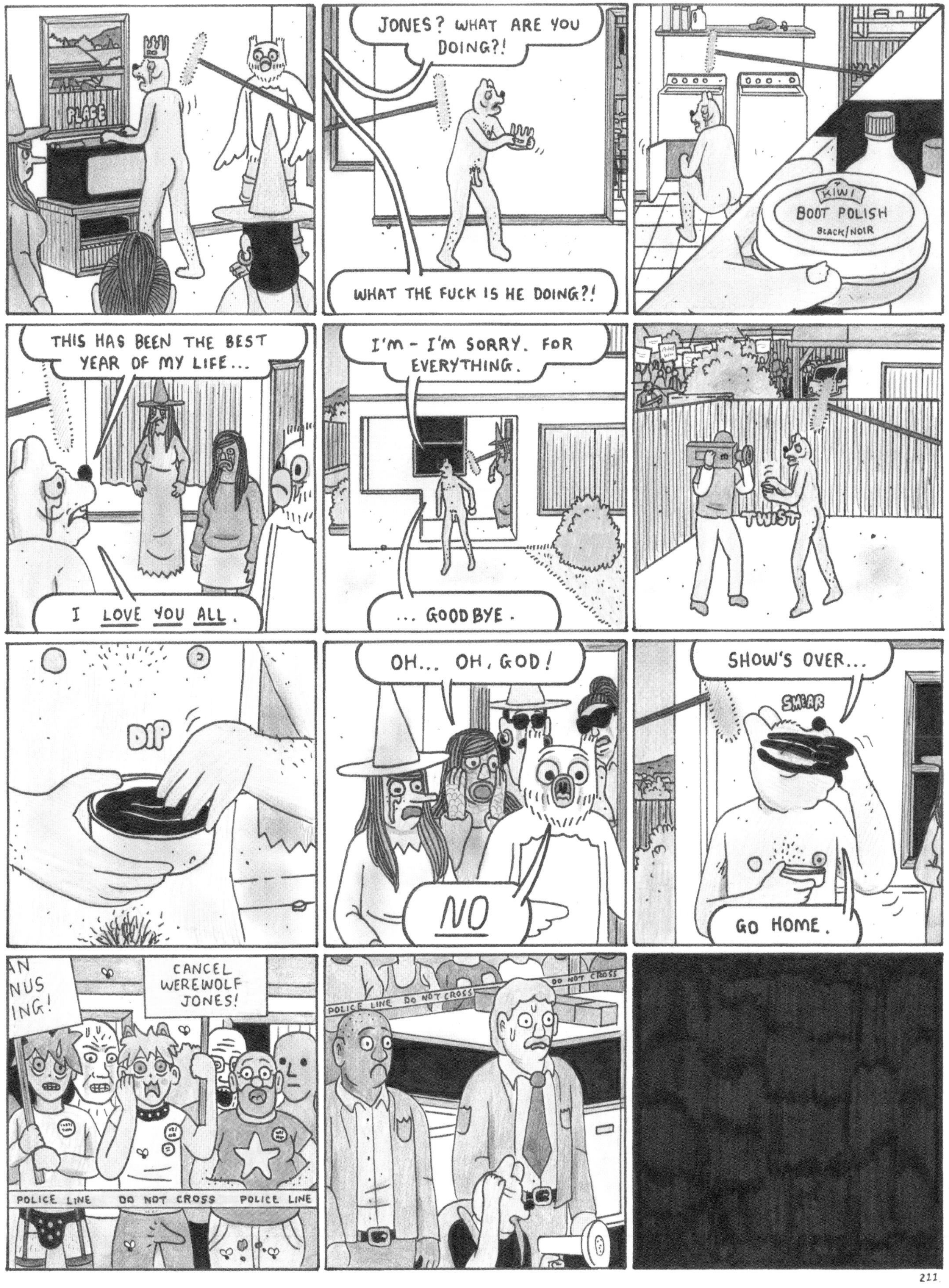
PLACE
JONES? WHAT ARE YOU DOING?!
WHAT THE FUCK IS HE DOING?!
KIWI
BOOT POLISH
BLACK/NOIR
THIS HAS BEEN THE BEST YEAR OF MY LIFE...
I LOVE YOU ALL.
I'M - I'M SORRY. FOR EVERYTHING.
... GOODBYE.
TWIST
DIP
OH... OH, GOD!
NO
SHOW'S OVER...
SMEAR
GO HOME.
CANCEL WEREWOLF JONES!
POLICE LINE DO NOT CROSS POLICE LINE
POLICE LINE DO NOT CROSS
DO NOT CROSS

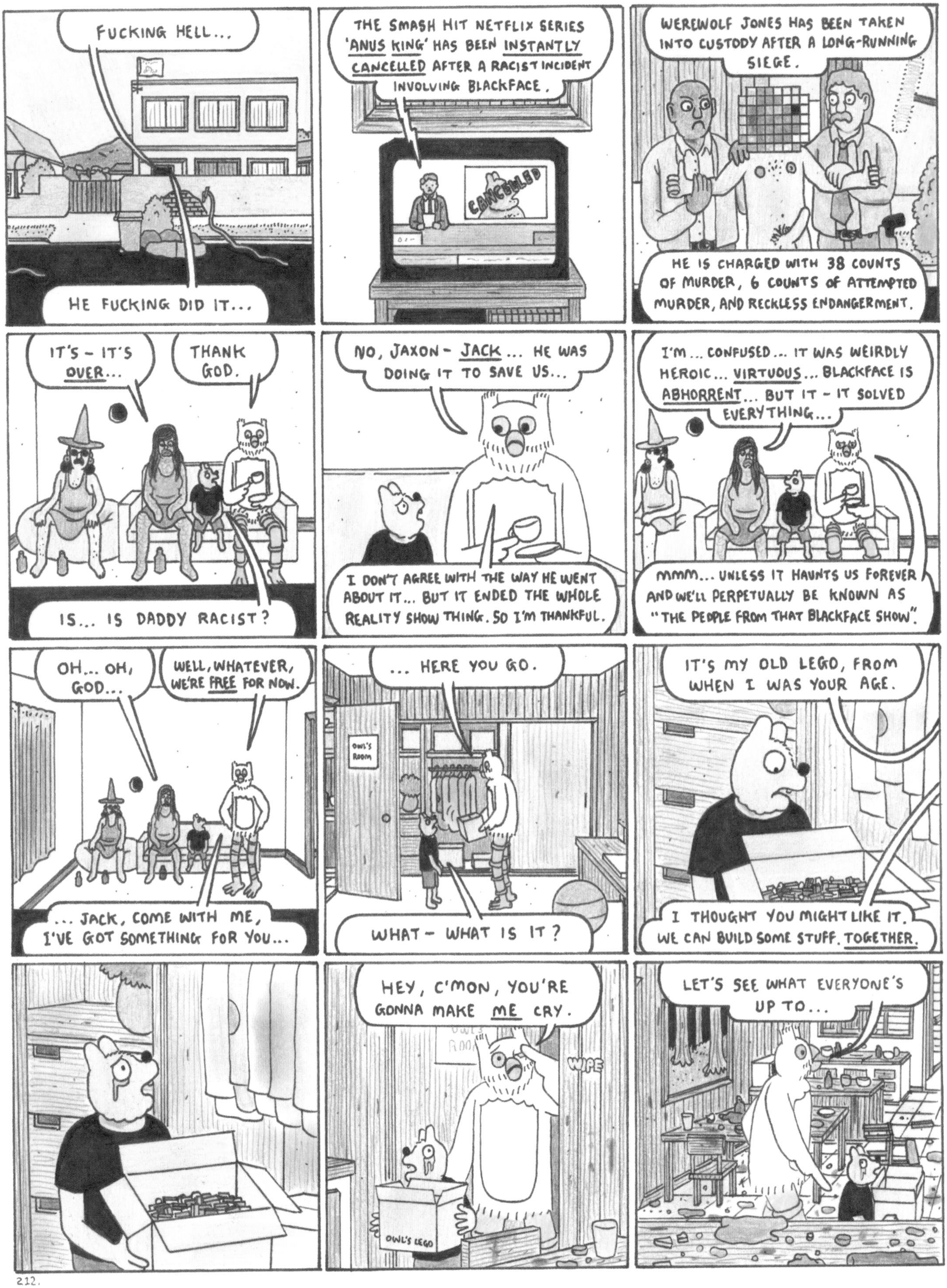
FUCKING HELL...
HE FUCKING DID IT...
THE SMASH HIT NETFLIX SERIES 'ANUS KING' HAS BEEN INSTANTLY CANCELLED AFTER A RACIST INCIDENT INVOLVING BLACKFACE.
CANCELLED
WEREWOLF JONES HAS BEEN TAKEN INTO CUSTODY AFTER A LONG-RUNNING SIEGE.
HE IS CHARGED WITH 38 COUNTS OF MURDER, 6 COUNTS OF ATTEMPTED MURDER, AND RECKLESS ENDANGERMENT.
IT'S - IT'S OVER...
THANK GOD.
IS... IS DADDY RACIST?
NO, JAXON- JACK... HE WAS DOING IT TO SAVE US...
I DON'T AGREE WITH THE WAY HE WENT ABOUT IT... BUT IT ENDED THE WHOLE REALITY SHOW THING. SO I'M THANKFUL.
I'M... CONFUSED... IT WAS WEIRDLY HEROIC... VIRTUOUS... BLACKFACE IS ABHORRENT... BUT IT - IT SOLVED EVERYTHING...
MMM... UNLESS IT HAUNTS US FOREVER AND WE'LL PERPETUALLY BE KNOWN AS "THE PEOPLE FROM THAT BLACKFACE SHOW".
OH... OH, GOD...
WELL, WHATEVER, WE'RE FREE FOR NOW.
... JACK, COME WITH ME, I'VE GOT SOMETHING FOR YOU...
... HERE YOU GO.
OWL'S ROOM
WHAT- WHAT IS IT?
IT'S MY OLD LEGO, FROM WHEN I WAS YOUR AGE.
I THOUGHT YOU MIGHT LIKE IT. WE CAN BUILD SOME STUFF. TOGETHER.
HEY, C'MON, YOU'RE GONNA MAKE ME CRY.
WIPE
OWL'S LEGO
LET'S SEE WHAT EVERYONE'S UP TO...

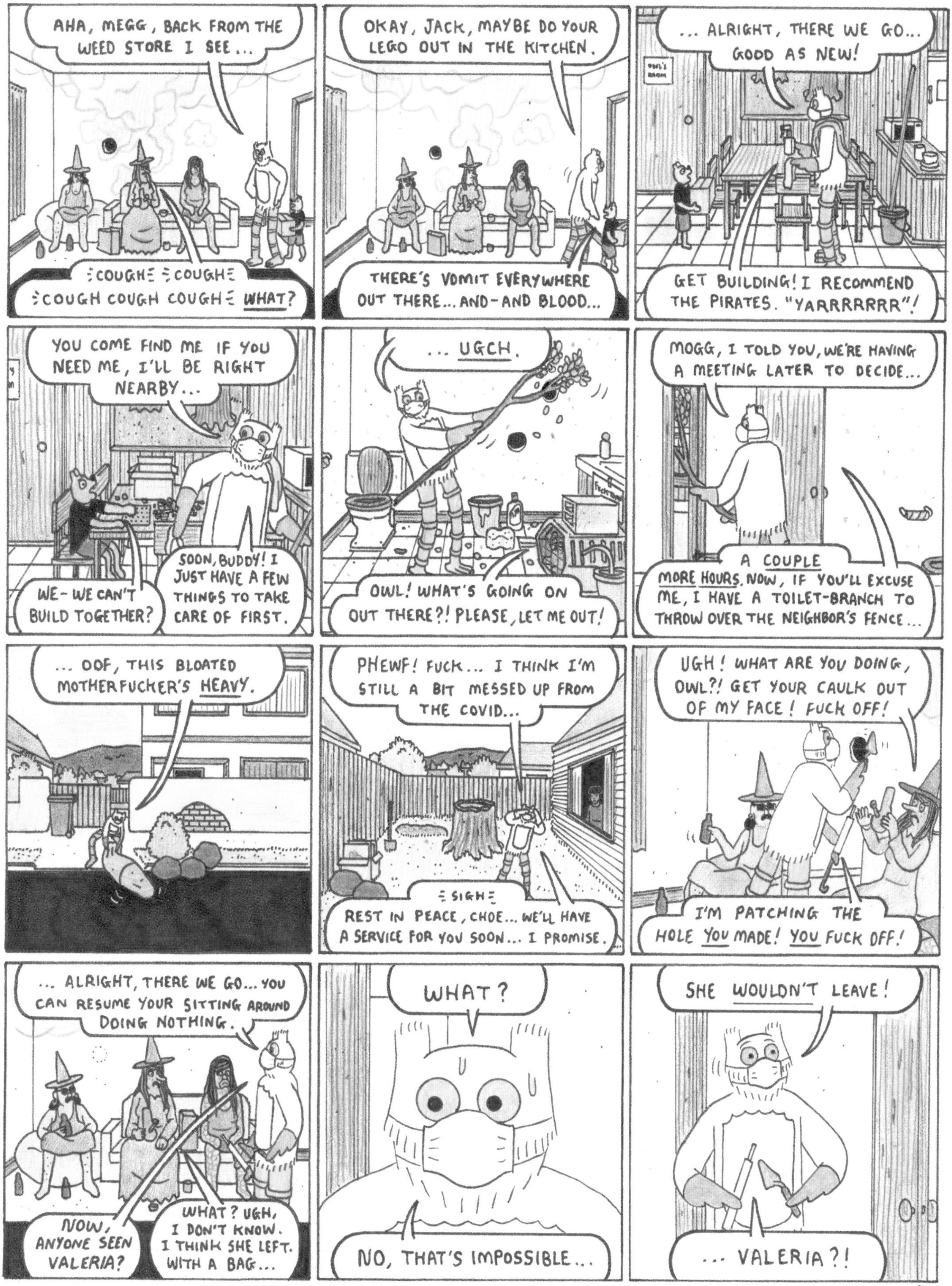
AHA, MEGG, BACK FROM THE WEED STORE I SEE...
COUGH COUGH
COUGH COUGH COUGH WHAT?
OKAY, JACK, MAYBE DO YOUR LEGO OUT IN THE KITCHEN.
THERE'S VOMIT EVERYWHERE OUT THERE... AND-AND BLOOD...
... ALRIGHT, THERE WE GO... GOOD AS NEW!
GET BUILDING! I RECOMMEND THE PIRATES. "YARRRRRRR"!
YOU COME FIND ME IF YOU NEED ME, I'LL BE RIGHT NEARBY...
WE-WE CAN'T BUILD TOGETHER?
SOON, BUDDY! I JUST HAVE A FEW THINGS TO TAKE CARE OF FIRST.
... UGCH.
OWL! WHAT'S GOING ON OUT THERE?! PLEASE, LET ME OUT!
MOGG, I TOLD YOU, WE'RE HAVING A MEETING LATER TO DECIDE...
A COUPLE MORE HOURS. NOW, IF YOU'LL EXCUSE ME, I HAVE A TOILET-BRANCH TO THROW OVER THE NEIGHBOR'S FENCE...
... OOF, THIS BLOATED MOTHERFUCKER'S HEAVY.
PHEWF! FUCK... I THINK I'M STILL A BIT MESSED UP FROM THE COVID...
SIGH
REST IN PEACE, CHOE... WE'LL HAVE A SERVICE FOR YOU SOON... I PROMISE.
UGH! WHAT ARE YOU DOING, OWL?! GET YOUR CAULK OUT OF MY FACE! FUCK OFF!
I'M PATCHING THE HOLE YOU MADE! YOU FUCK OFF!
... ALRIGHT, THERE WE GO... YOU CAN RESUME YOUR SITTING AROUND DOING NOTHING.
NOW, ANYONE SEEN VALERIA?
WHAT? UGH, I DON'T KNOW. I THINK SHE LEFT. WITH A BAG...
WHAT?
NO, THAT'S IMPOSSIBLE...
SHE WOULDN'T LEAVE!
... VALERIA?!

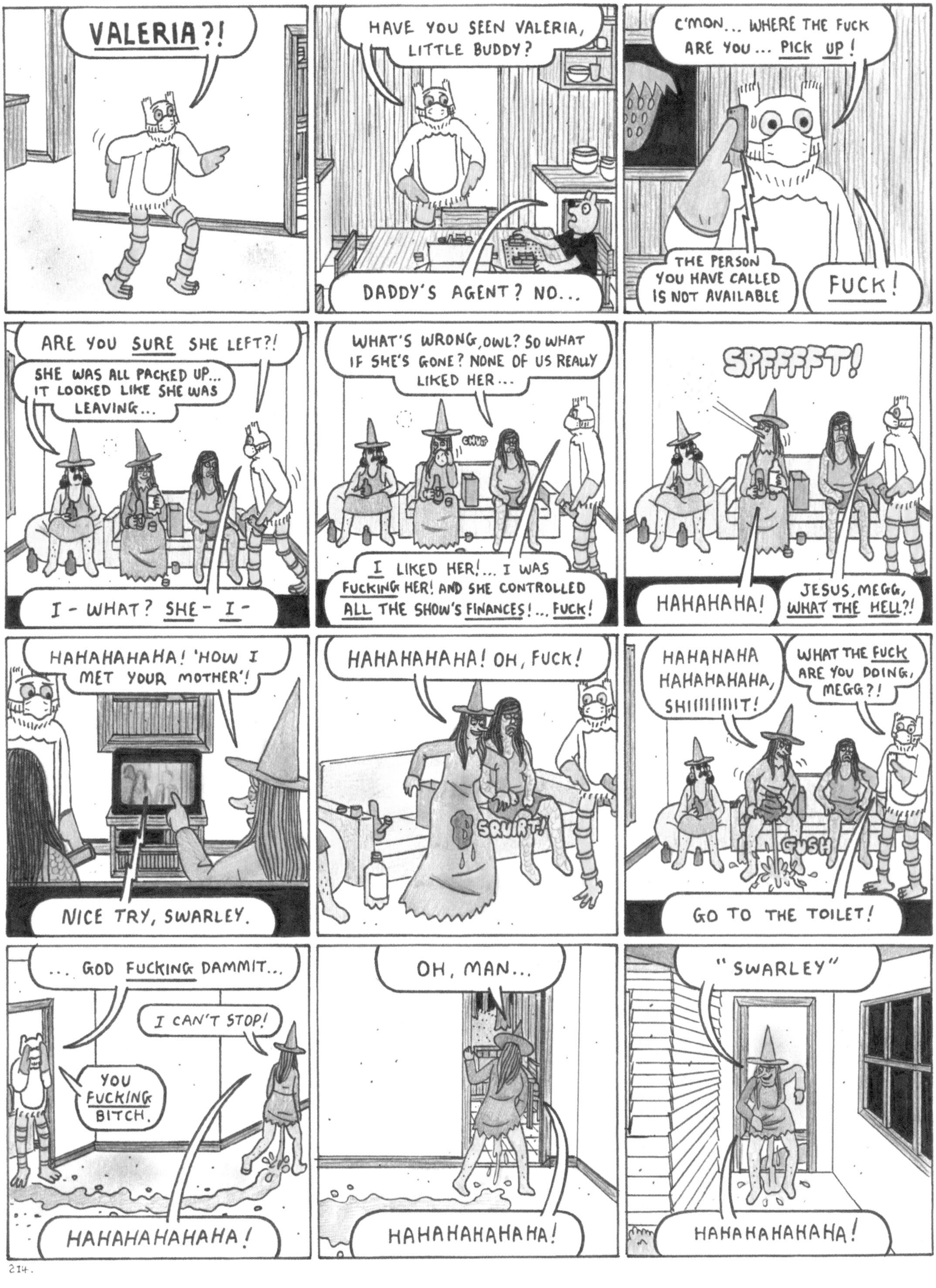
VALERIA?!
HAVE YOU SEEN VALERIA, LITTLE BUDDY?
DADDY'S AGENT? NO...
C'MON... WHERE THE FUCK ARE YOU... PICK UP!
THE PERSON YOU HAVE CALLED IS NOT AVAILABLE
FUCK!
ARE YOU SURE SHE LEFT?!
SHE WAS ALL PACKED UP... IT LOOKED LIKE SHE WAS LEAVING...
I - WHAT? SHE - I -
WHAT'S WRONG, OWL? SO WHAT IF SHE'S GONE? NONE OF US REALLY LIKED HER...
I LIKED HER!... I WAS FUCKING HER! AND SHE CONTROLLED ALL THE SHOW'S FINANCES!... FUCK!
SPFFFFFT!
HAHAHAHA!
JESUS, MEGG, WHAT THE HELL?!
HAHAHAHAHA! 'HOW I MET YOUR MOTHER'!
NICE TRY, SWARLEY.
HAHAHAHAHA! OH, FUCK!
SQUIRT!
HAHAHAHA HAHAHAHAHA, SHIIIIIIIIT!
WHAT THE FUCK ARE YOU DOING, MEGG?!
GUSH
GO TO THE TOILET!
... GOD FUCKING DAMMIT...
I CAN'T STOP!
YOU FUCKING BITCH.
HAHAHAHAHAHA!
OH, MAN...
HAHAHAHAHAHA!
"SWARLEY"
HAHAHAHAHAHA!

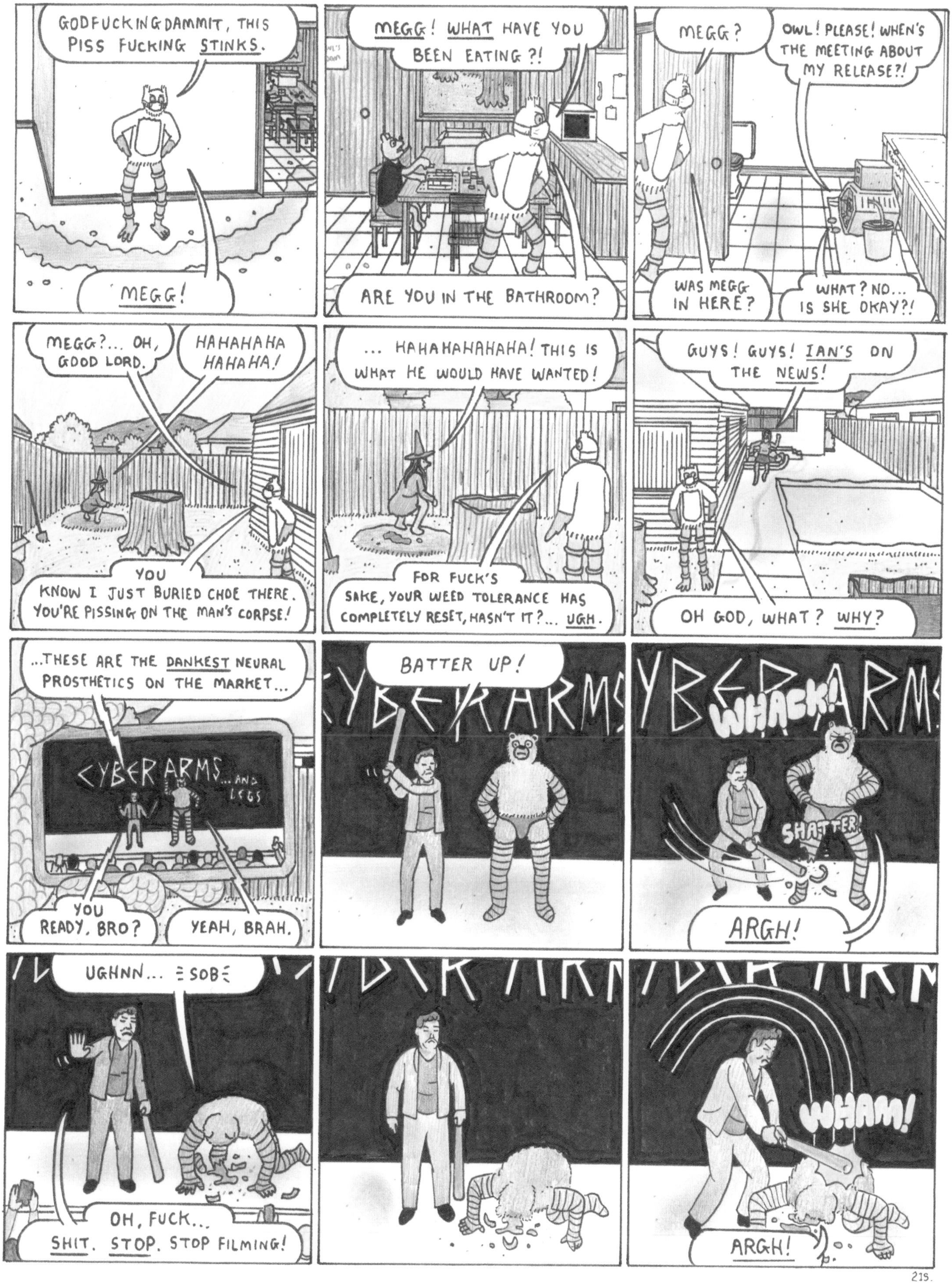
GODFUCKINGDAMMIT, THIS PISS FUCKING STINKS.
MEGG!
MEGG! WHAT HAVE YOU BEEN EATING?!
ARE YOU IN THE BATHROOM?
MEGG?
OWL! PLEASE! WHEN'S THE MEETING ABOUT MY RELEASE?!
WAS MEGG IN HERE?
WHAT? NO... IS SHE OKAY?!
MEGG?... OH, GOOD LORD.
HAHAHAHA HAHAHA!
YOU KNOW I JUST BURIED CHOE THERE. YOU'RE PISSING ON THE MAN'S CORPSE!
... HAHAHAHAHAHA! THIS IS WHAT HE WOULD HAVE WANTED!
FOR FUCK'S SAKE, YOUR WEED TOLERANCE HAS COMPLETELY RESET, HASN'T IT?... UGH.
GUYS! GUYS! IAN'S ON THE NEWS!
OH GOD, WHAT? WHY?
...THESE ARE THE DANKEST NEURAL PROSTHETICS ON THE MARKET...
CYBER ARMS ...AND LEGS
YOU READY, BRO?
YEAH, BRAH.
BATTER UP!
CYBER ARMS
WHACK!
SHATTER!
ARGH!
UGHNN... SOB
OH, FUCK... SHIT. STOP. STOP FILMING!
WHAM!
ARGH!

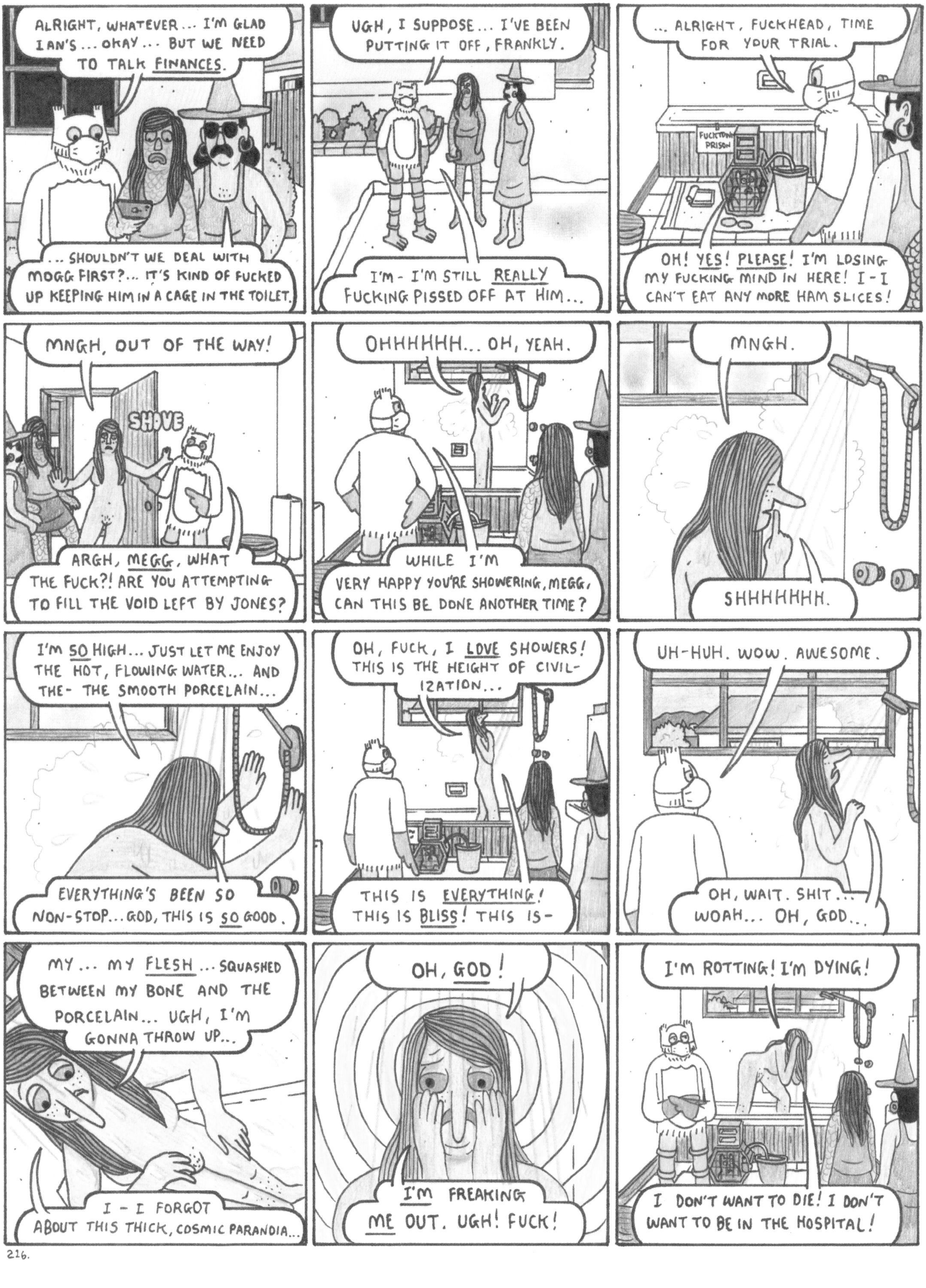
ALRIGHT, WHATEVER... I'M GLAD IAN'S... OKAY... BUT WE NEED TO TALK FINANCES.
...SHOULDN'T WE DEAL WITH MOGG FIRST?... IT'S KIND OF FUCKED UP KEEPING HIM IN A CAGE IN THE TOILET.
UGH, I SUPPOSE... I'VE BEEN PUTTING IT OFF, FRANKLY.
I'M- I'M STILL REALLY FUCKING PISSED OFF AT HIM...
...ALRIGHT, FUCKHEAD, TIME FOR YOUR TRIAL.
FUCKTOWN PRISON
OH! YES! PLEASE! I'M LOSING MY FUCKING MIND IN HERE! I-I CAN'T EAT ANY MORE HAM SLICES!
MNGH, OUT OF THE WAY!
SHOVE
ARGH, MEGG, WHAT THE FUCK?! ARE YOU ATTEMPTING TO FILL THE VOID LEFT BY JONES?
OHHHHHH... OH, YEAH.
WHILE I'M VERY HAPPY YOU'RE SHOWERING, MEGG, CAN THIS BE DONE ANOTHER TIME?
MNGH.
SHHHHHHH.
I'M SO HIGH... JUST LET ME ENJOY THE HOT, FLOWING WATER... AND THE- THE SMOOTH PORCELAIN...
EVERYTHING'S BEEN SO NON-STOP... GOD, THIS IS SO GOOD.
OH, FUCK, I LOVE SHOWERS! THIS IS THE HEIGHT OF CIVIL-IZATION...
THIS IS EVERYTHING! THIS IS BLISS! THIS IS-
UH-HUH. WOW. AWESOME.
OH, WAIT. SHIT... WOAH... OH, GOD...
MY... MY FLESH... SQUASHED BETWEEN MY BONE AND THE PORCELAIN... UGH, I'M GONNA THROW UP...
I-I FORGOT ABOUT THIS THICK, COSMIC PARANOIA...
OH, GOD!
I'M FREAKING ME OUT. UGH! FUCK!
I'M ROTTING! I'M DYING!
I DON'T WANT TO DIE! I DON'T WANT TO BE IN THE HOSPITAL!

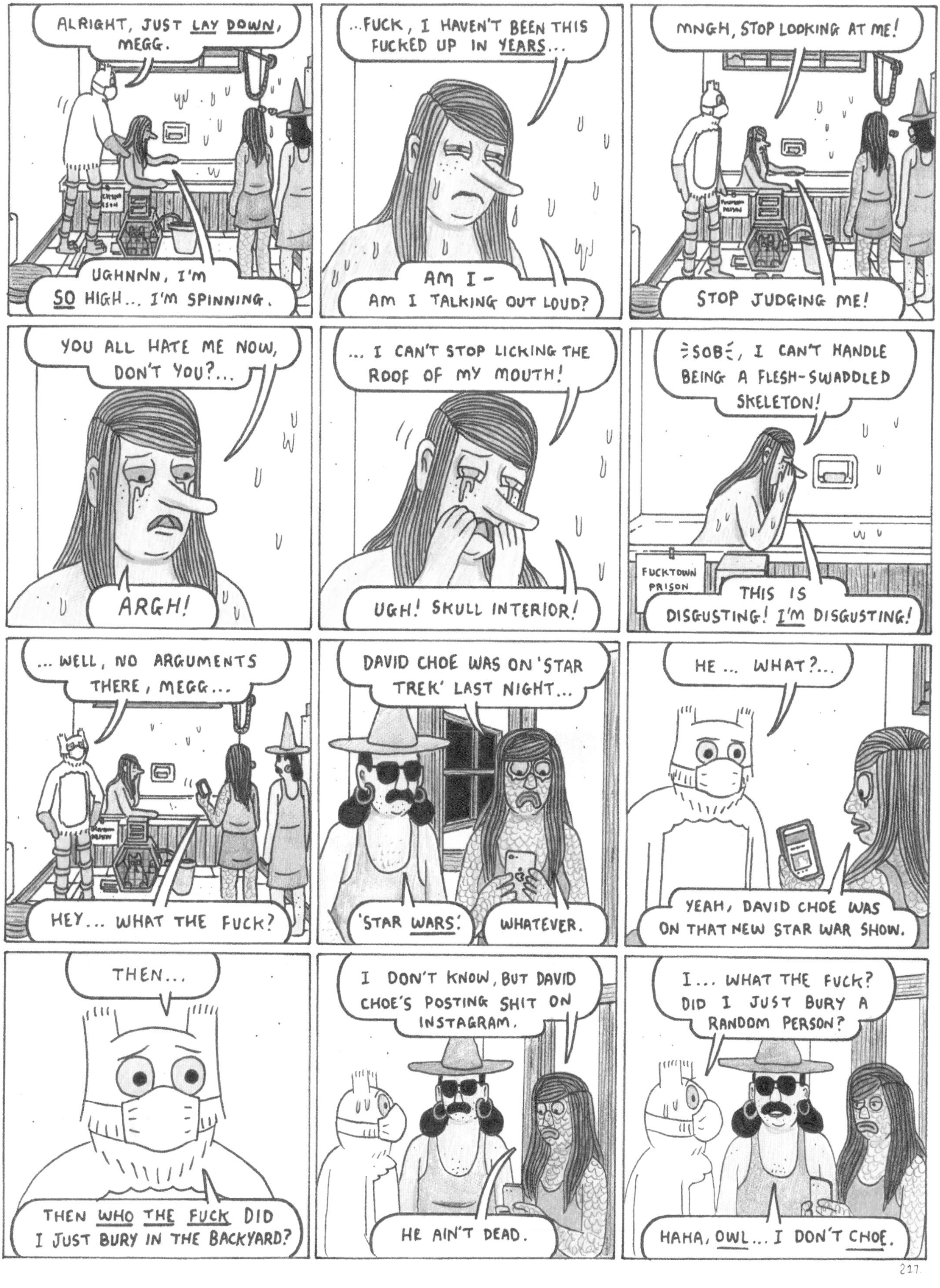
ALRIGHT, JUST LAY DOWN, MEGG.
UGHNNN, I'M SO HIGH... I'M SPINNING.
...FUCK, I HAVEN'T BEEN THIS FUCKED UP IN YEARS...
AM I - AM I TALKING OUT LOUD?
MNGH, STOP LOOKING AT ME!
STOP JUDGING ME!
YOU ALL HATE ME NOW, DON'T YOU?...
ARGH!
... I CAN'T STOP LICKING THE ROOF OF MY MOUTH!
UGH! SKULL INTERIOR!
SOB, I CAN'T HANDLE BEING A FLESH-SWADDLED SKELETON!
FUCKTOWN PRISON
THIS IS DISGUSTING! I'M DISGUSTING!
... WELL, NO ARGUMENTS THERE, MEGG...
HEY... WHAT THE FUCK?
DAVID CHOE WAS ON 'STAR TREK' LAST NIGHT...
'STAR WARS.'
WHATEVER.
HE ... WHAT?...
YEAH, DAVID CHOE WAS ON THAT NEW STAR WAR SHOW.
THEN...
THEN WHO THE FUCK DID I JUST BURY IN THE BACKYARD?
I DON'T KNOW, BUT DAVID CHOE'S POSTING SHIT ON INSTAGRAM.
HE AIN'T DEAD.
I... WHAT THE FUCK? DID I JUST BURY A RANDOM PERSON?
HAHA, OWL... I DON'T CHOE.

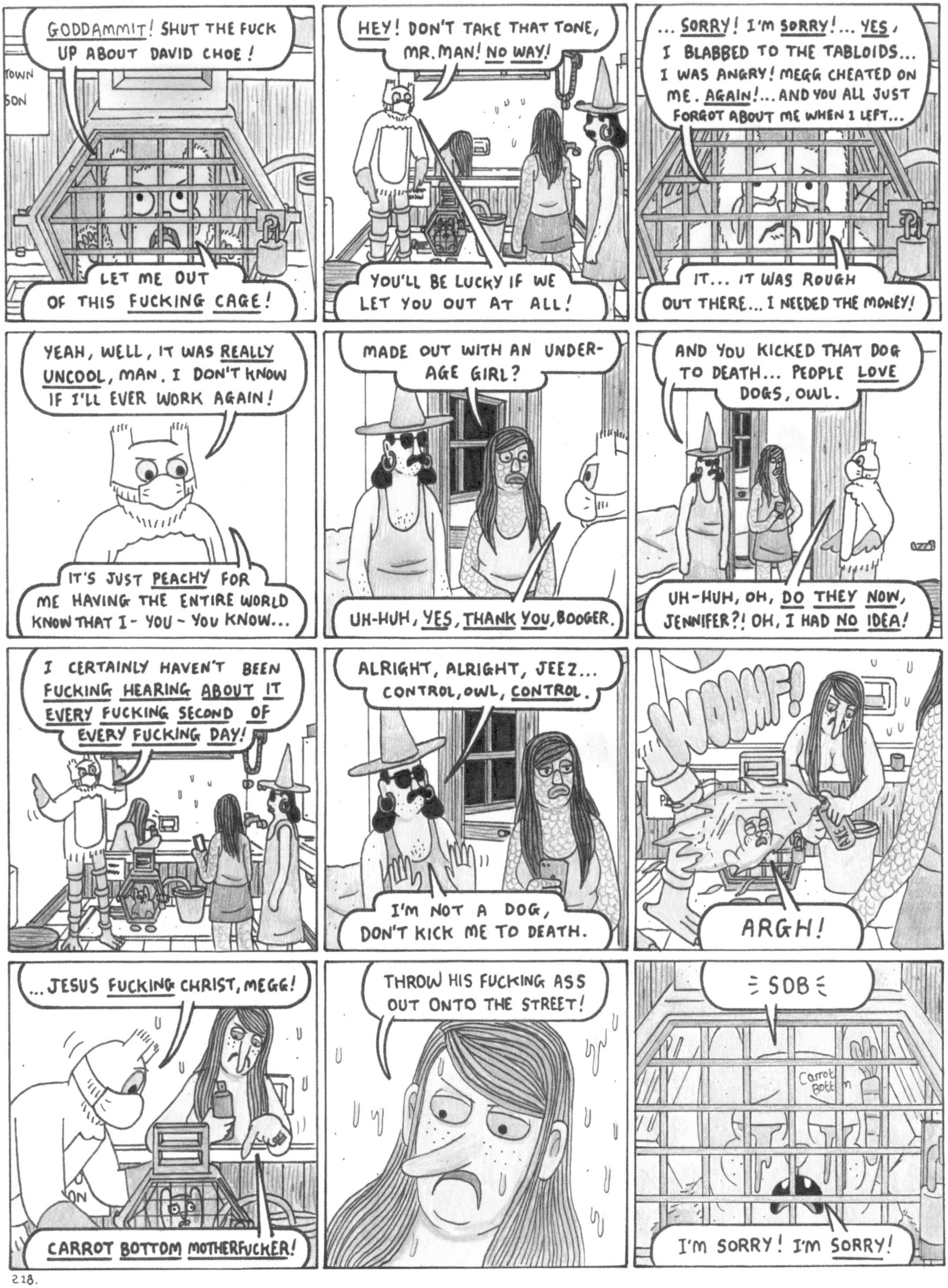
GODDAMMIT! SHUT THE FUCK UP ABOUT DAVID CHOE!
LET ME OUT OF THIS FUCKING CAGE!
HEY! DON'T TAKE THAT TONE, MR. MAN! NO WAY!
YOU'LL BE LUCKY IF WE LET YOU OUT AT ALL!
... SORRY! I'M SORRY!... YES, I BLABBED TO THE TABLOIDS... I WAS ANGRY! MEGG CHEATED ON ME. AGAIN!... AND YOU ALL JUST FORGOT ABOUT ME WHEN I LEFT...
IT... IT WAS ROUGH OUT THERE... I NEEDED THE MONEY!
YEAH, WELL, IT WAS REALLY UNCOOL, MAN. I DON'T KNOW IF I'LL EVER WORK AGAIN!
IT'S JUST PEACHY FOR ME HAVING THE ENTIRE WORLD KNOW THAT I - YOU - YOU KNOW...
MADE OUT WITH AN UNDER-AGE GIRL?
UH-HUH, YES, THANK YOU, BOOGER.
AND YOU KICKED THAT DOG TO DEATH... PEOPLE LOVE DOGS, OWL.
UH-HUH, OH, DO THEY NOW, JENNIFER?! OH, I HAD NO IDEA!
I CERTAINLY HAVEN'T BEEN FUCKING HEARING ABOUT IT EVERY FUCKING SECOND OF EVERY FUCKING DAY!
ALRIGHT, ALRIGHT, JEEZ... CONTROL, OWL, CONTROL.
I'M NOT A DOG, DON'T KICK ME TO DEATH.
WOOMF!
ARGH!
... JESUS FUCKING CHRIST, MEGG!
CARROT BOTTOM MOTHERFUCKER!
THROW HIS FUCKING ASS OUT ONTO THE STREET!
SOB
Carrot Bottom
I'M SORRY! I'M SORRY!

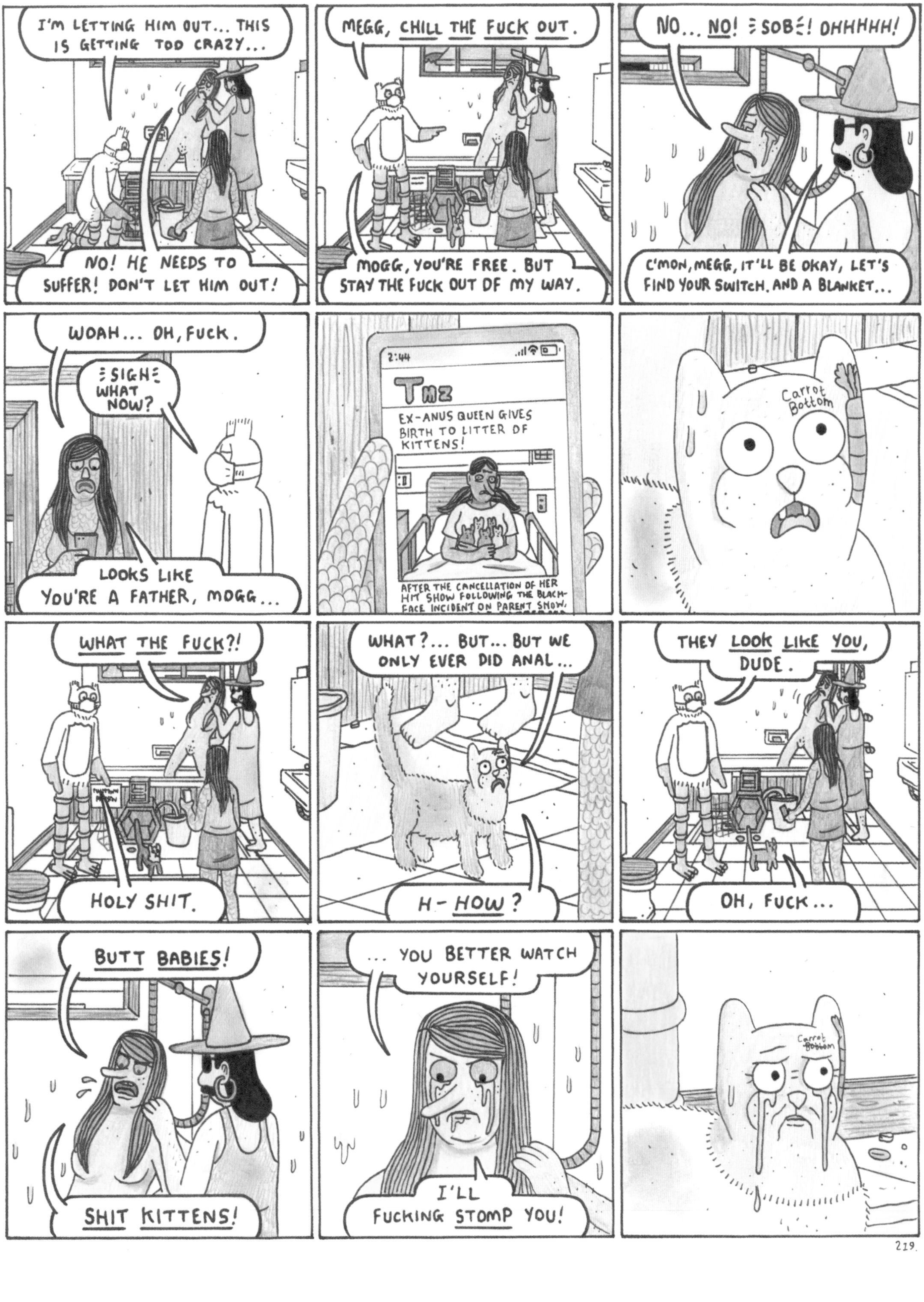
I'M LETTING HIM OUT... THIS IS GETTING TOO CRAZY...
NO! HE NEEDS TO SUFFER! DON'T LET HIM OUT!
MEGG, CHILL THE FUCK OUT.
MOGG, YOU'RE FREE. BUT STAY THE FUCK OUT OF MY WAY.
NO... NO! SOB! OHHHHH!
C'MON, MEGG, IT'LL BE OKAY, LET'S FIND YOUR SWITCH. AND A BLANKET...
WOAH... OH, FUCK.
SIGH WHAT NOW?
LOOKS LIKE YOU'RE A FATHER, MOGG...
2:44
TMZ
EX-ANUS QUEEN GIVES BIRTH TO LITTER OF KITTENS!
AFTER THE CANCELLATION OF HER HIT SHOW FOLLOWING THE BLACKFACE INCIDENT ON PARENT SHOW,
Carrot Bottom
WHAT THE FUCK?!
HOLY SHIT.
WHAT?... BUT... BUT WE ONLY EVER DID ANAL...
H-HOW?
THEY LOOK LIKE YOU, DUDE.
OH, FUCK...
BUTT BABIES!
SHIT KITTENS!
... YOU BETTER WATCH YOURSELF!
I'LL FUCKING STOMP YOU!
Carrot Bottom

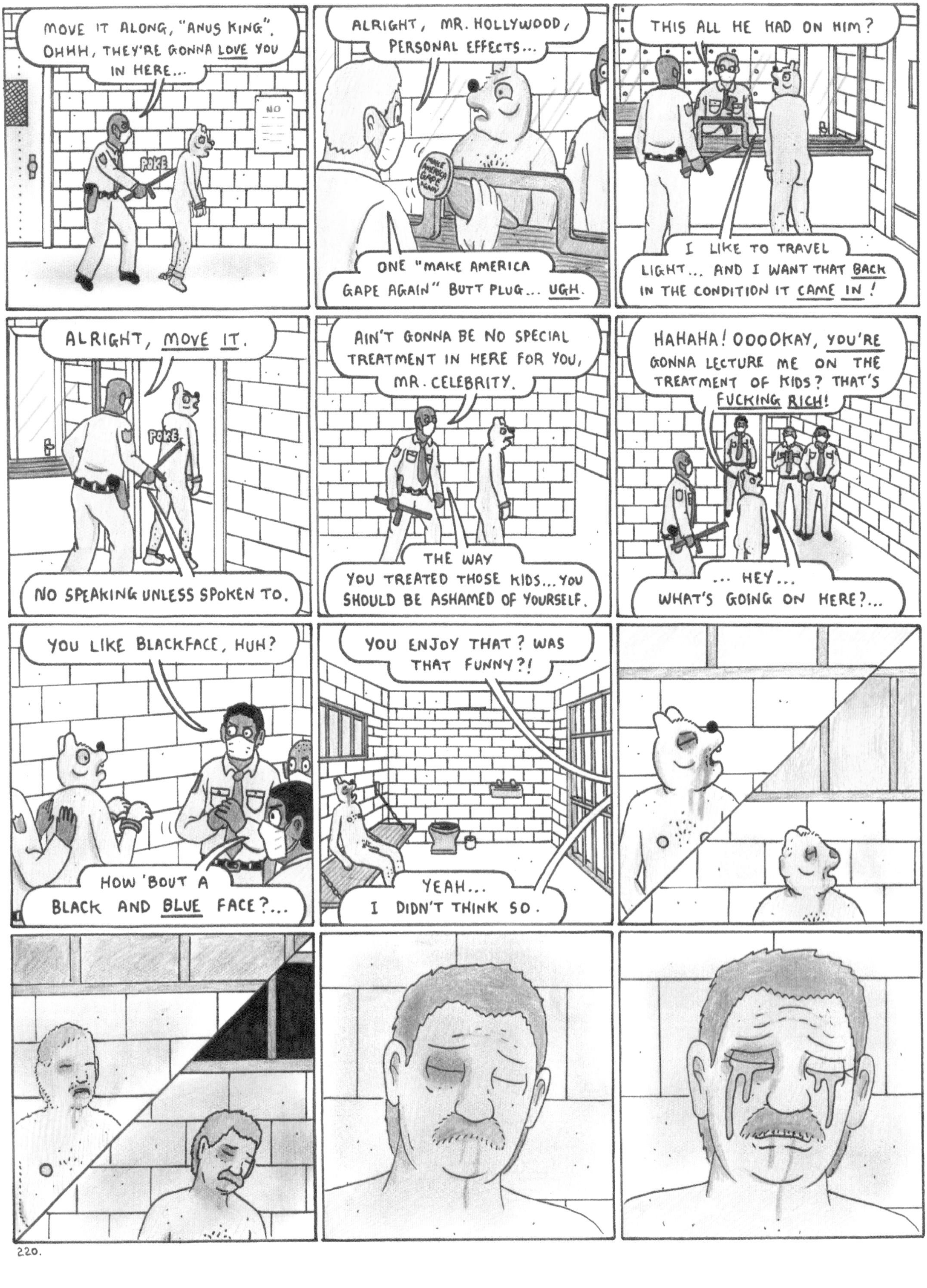
MOVE IT ALONG, "ANUS KING". OHHH, THEY'RE GONNA LOVE YOU IN HERE...
POKE
NO
ALRIGHT, MR. HOLLYWOOD, PERSONAL EFFECTS...
ONE "MAKE AMERICA GAPE AGAIN" BUTT PLUG... UGH.
THIS ALL HE HAD ON HIM?
I LIKE TO TRAVEL LIGHT... AND I WANT THAT BACK IN THE CONDITION IT CAME IN!
ALRIGHT, MOVE IT.
POKE
NO SPEAKING UNLESS SPOKEN TO.
AIN'T GONNA BE NO SPECIAL TREATMENT IN HERE FOR YOU, MR. CELEBRITY.
THE WAY YOU TREATED THOSE KIDS... YOU SHOULD BE ASHAMED OF YOURSELF.
HAHAHA! OOOOKAY, YOU'RE GONNA LECTURE ME ON THE TREATMENT OF KIDS? THAT'S FUCKING RICH!
... HEY... WHAT'S GOING ON HERE?...
YOU LIKE BLACKFACE, HUH?
HOW 'BOUT A BLACK AND BLUE FACE?...
YOU ENJOY THAT? WAS THAT FUNNY?!
YEAH... I DIDN'T THINK SO.

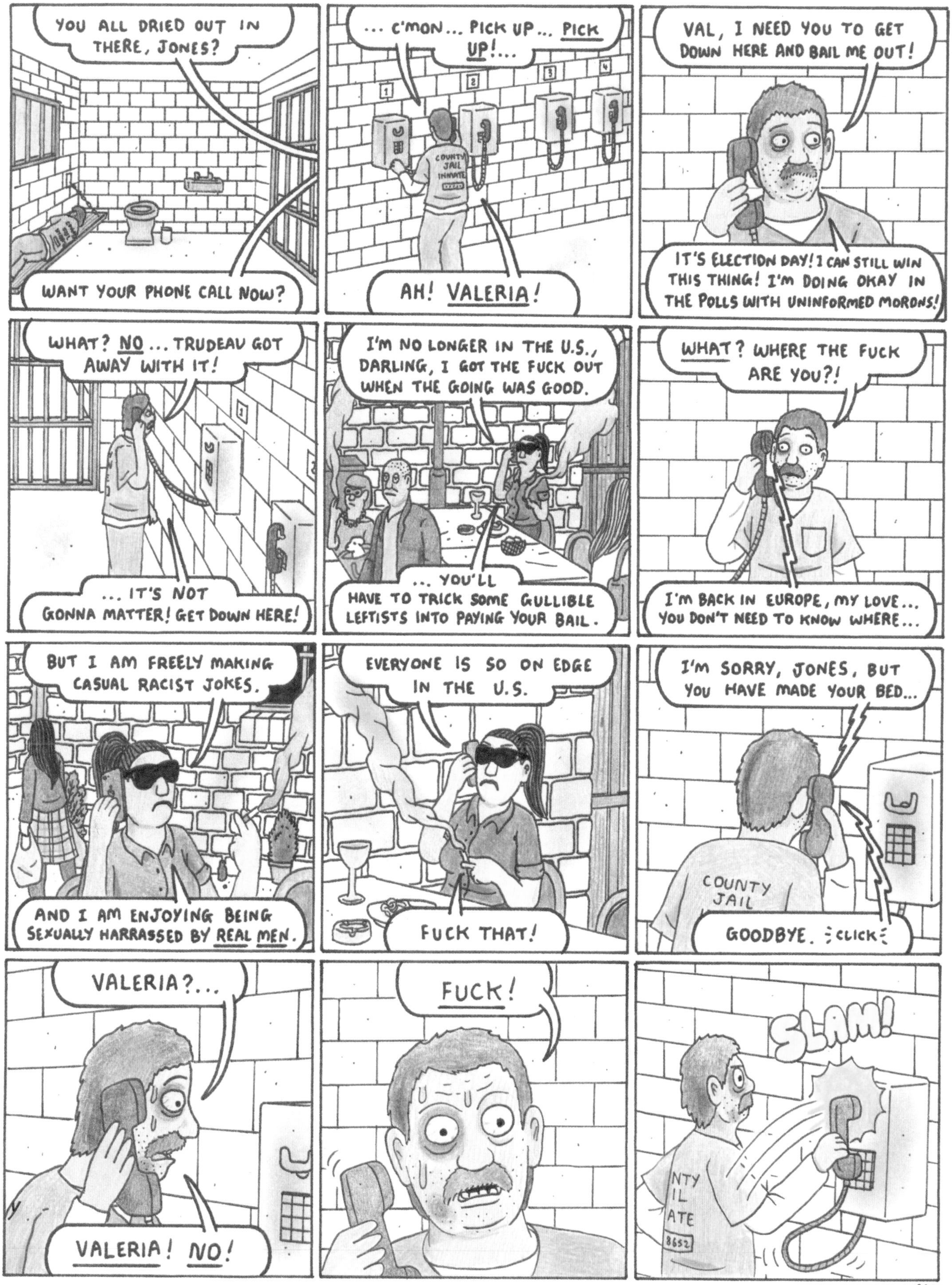
YOU ALL DRIED OUT IN THERE, JONES?
WANT YOUR PHONE CALL NOW?
... C'MON... PICK UP... PICK UP!...
AH! VALERIA!
VAL, I NEED YOU TO GET DOWN HERE AND BAIL ME OUT!
IT'S ELECTION DAY! I CAN STILL WIN THIS THING! I'M DOING OKAY IN THE POLLS WITH UNINFORMED MORONS!
WHAT? NO... TRUDEAU GOT AWAY WITH IT!
... IT'S NOT GONNA MATTER! GET DOWN HERE!
I'M NO LONGER IN THE U.S., DARLING, I GOT THE FUCK OUT WHEN THE GOING WAS GOOD.
... YOU'LL HAVE TO TRICK SOME GULLIBLE LEFTISTS INTO PAYING YOUR BAIL.
WHAT? WHERE THE FUCK ARE YOU?!
I'M BACK IN EUROPE, MY LOVE... YOU DON'T NEED TO KNOW WHERE...
BUT I AM FREELY MAKING CASUAL RACIST JOKES.
AND I AM ENJOYING BEING SEXUALLY HARRASSED BY REAL MEN.
EVERYONE IS SO ON EDGE IN THE U.S.
FUCK THAT!
I'M SORRY, JONES, BUT YOU HAVE MADE YOUR BED...
COUNTY JAIL
GOODBYE. CLICK
VALERIA?...
VALERIA! NO!
FUCK!
SLAM!

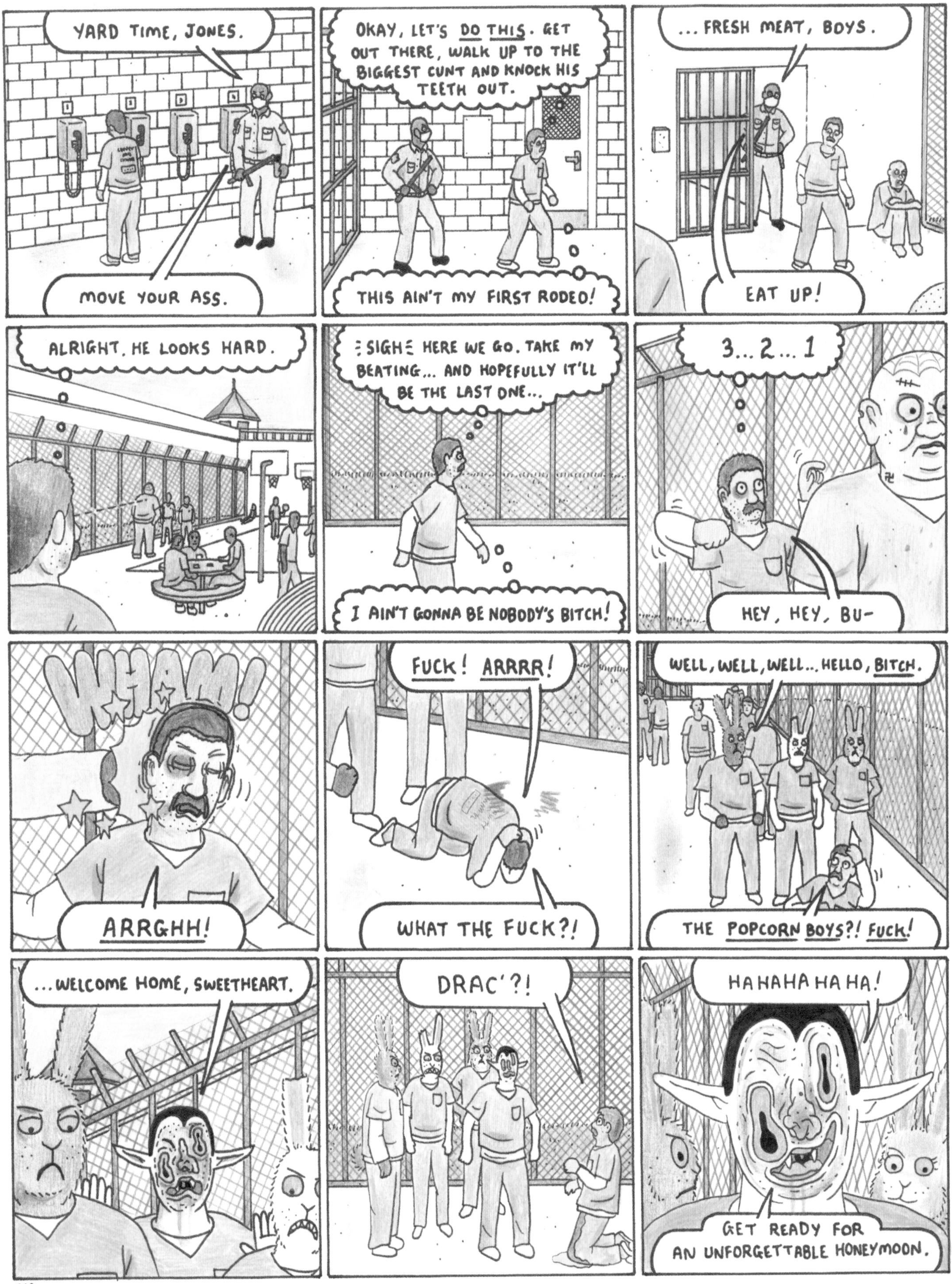
YARD TIME, JONES.
MOVE YOUR ASS.
OKAY, LET'S DO THIS. GET OUT THERE, WALK UP TO THE BIGGEST CUNT AND KNOCK HIS TEETH OUT.
THIS AIN'T MY FIRST RODEO!
... FRESH MEAT, BOYS.
EAT UP!
ALRIGHT. HE LOOKS HARD.
SIGH HERE WE GO. TAKE MY BEATING... AND HOPEFULLY IT'LL BE THE LAST ONE...
I AIN'T GONNA BE NOBODY'S BITCH!
3... 2... 1
HEY, HEY, BU-
WHAM!
ARRGHH!
FUCK! ARRRR!
WHAT THE FUCK?!
WELL, WELL, WELL... HELLO, BITCH.
THE POPCORN BOYS?! FUCK!
... WELCOME HOME, SWEETHEART.
DRAC'?!
HA HAHA HA HA!
GET READY FOR AN UNFORGETTABLE HONEYMOON.

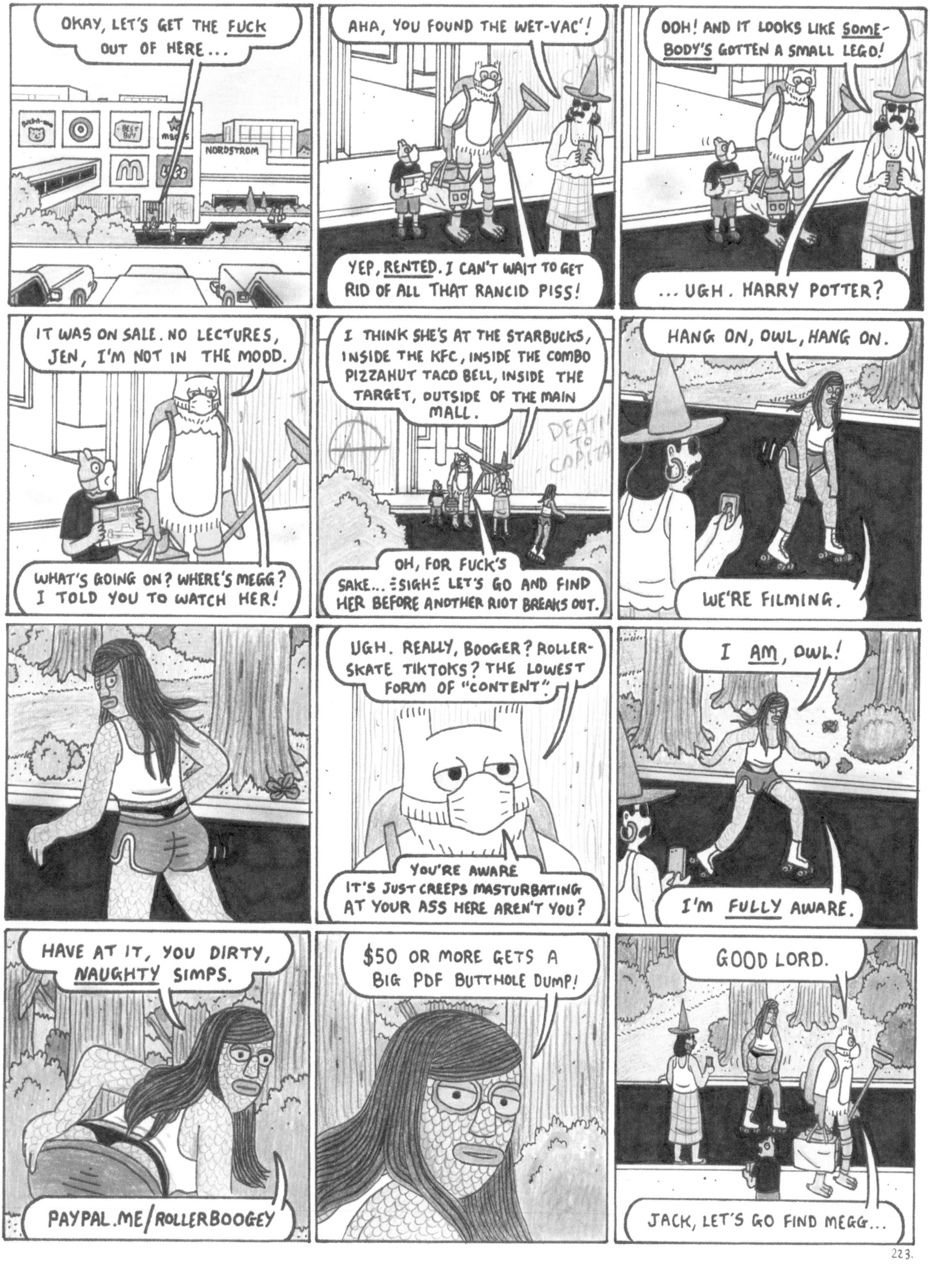

OKAY, LET'S GET THE FUCK OUT OF HERE...
BEST BUY
NORDSTROM
AHA, YOU FOUND THE WET-VAC'!
YEP, RENTED. I CAN'T WAIT TO GET RID OF ALL THAT RANCID PISS!
OOH! AND IT LOOKS LIKE SOMEBODY'S GOTTEN A SMALL LEGO!
... UGH. HARRY POTTER?
IT WAS ON SALE. NO LECTURES, JEN, I'M NOT IN THE MOOD.
WHAT'S GOING ON? WHERE'S MEGG? I TOLD YOU TO WATCH HER!
I THINK SHE'S AT THE STARBUCKS, INSIDE THE KFC, INSIDE THE COMBO PIZZAHUT TACO BELL, INSIDE THE TARGET, OUTSIDE OF THE MAIN MALL.
DEATH TO CAPITA
OH, FOR FUCK'S SAKE... ≡SIGH≡ LET'S GO AND FIND HER BEFORE ANOTHER RIOT BREAKS OUT.
HANG ON, OWL, HANG ON.
WE'RE FILMING.
UGH. REALLY, BOOGER? ROLLER-SKATE TIKTOKS? THE LOWEST FORM OF "CONTENT".
YOU'RE AWARE IT'S JUST CREEPS MASTURBATING AT YOUR ASS HERE AREN'T YOU?
I AM, OWL!
I'M FULLY AWARE.
HAVE AT IT, YOU DIRTY, NAUGHTY SIMPS.
PAYPAL.ME/ROLLERBOOGEY
$50 OR MORE GETS A BIG PDF BUTTHOLE DUMP!
GOOD LORD.
JACK, LET'S GO FIND MEGG...

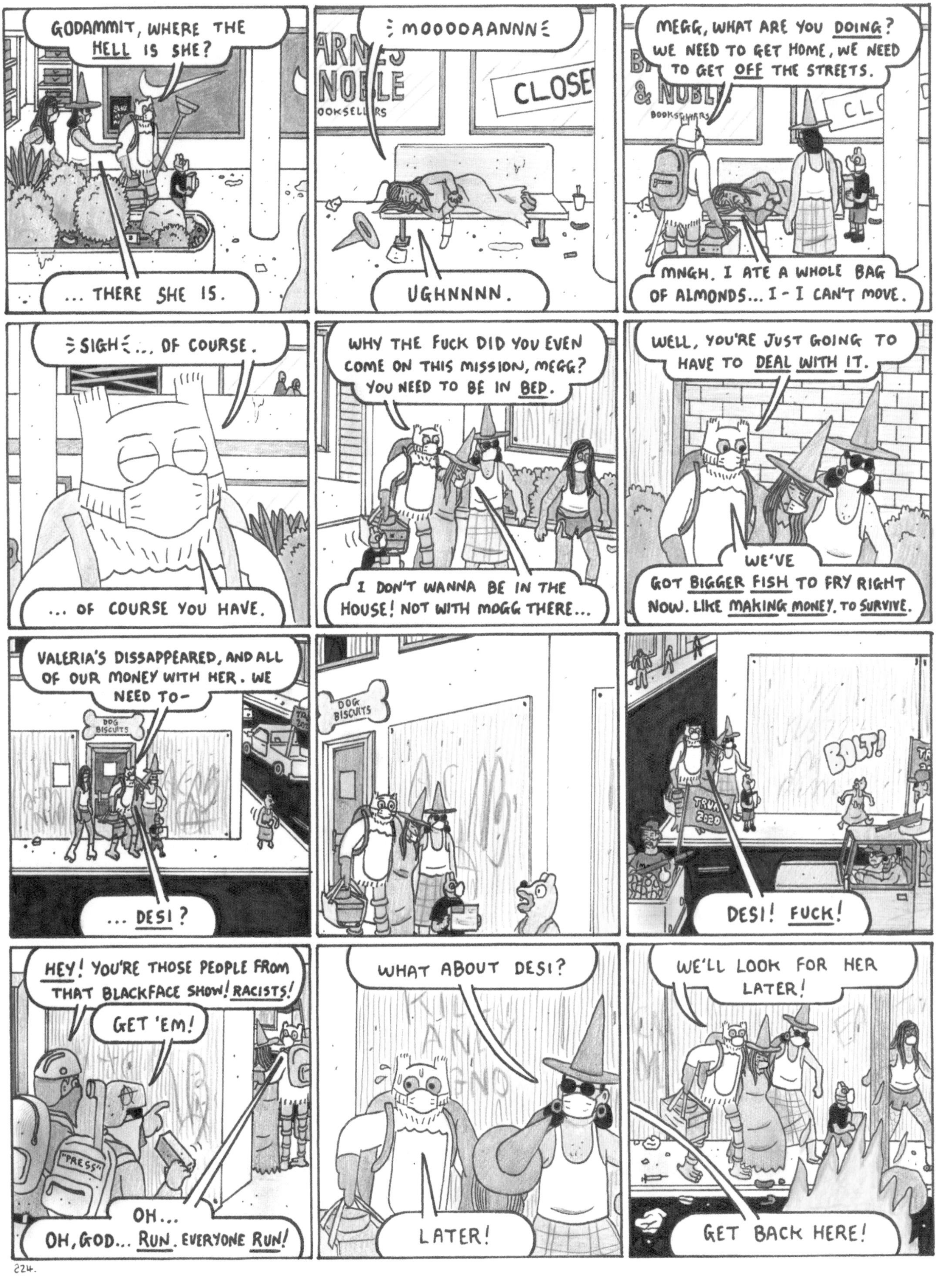
GODAMMIT, WHERE THE HELL IS SHE?
... THERE SHE IS.
≡ MOOOOAANNN ≡
CLOSED
UGHNNNN.
MEGG, WHAT ARE YOU DOING? WE NEED TO GET HOME, WE NEED TO GET OFF THE STREETS.
MNGH. I ATE A WHOLE BAG OF ALMONDS... I - I CAN'T MOVE.
≡ SIGH ≡ ... OF COURSE.
... OF COURSE YOU HAVE.
WHY THE FUCK DID YOU EVEN COME ON THIS MISSION, MEGG? YOU NEED TO BE IN BED.
I DON'T WANNA BE IN THE HOUSE! NOT WITH MOGG THERE...
WELL, YOU'RE JUST GOING TO HAVE TO DEAL WITH IT.
WE'VE GOT BIGGER FISH TO FRY RIGHT NOW. LIKE MAKING MONEY. TO SURVIVE.
VALERIA'S DISSAPPEARED, AND ALL OF OUR MONEY WITH HER. WE NEED TO-
DOG BISCUITS
... DESI?
DOG BISCUITS
BOLT!
TRUMP 2020
DESI! FUCK!
HEY! YOU'RE THOSE PEOPLE FROM THAT BLACKFACE SHOW! RACISTS!
GET 'EM!
"PRESS"
OH...
OH, GOD... RUN. EVERYONE RUN!
WHAT ABOUT DESI?
LATER!
WE'LL LOOK FOR HER LATER!
GET BACK HERE!

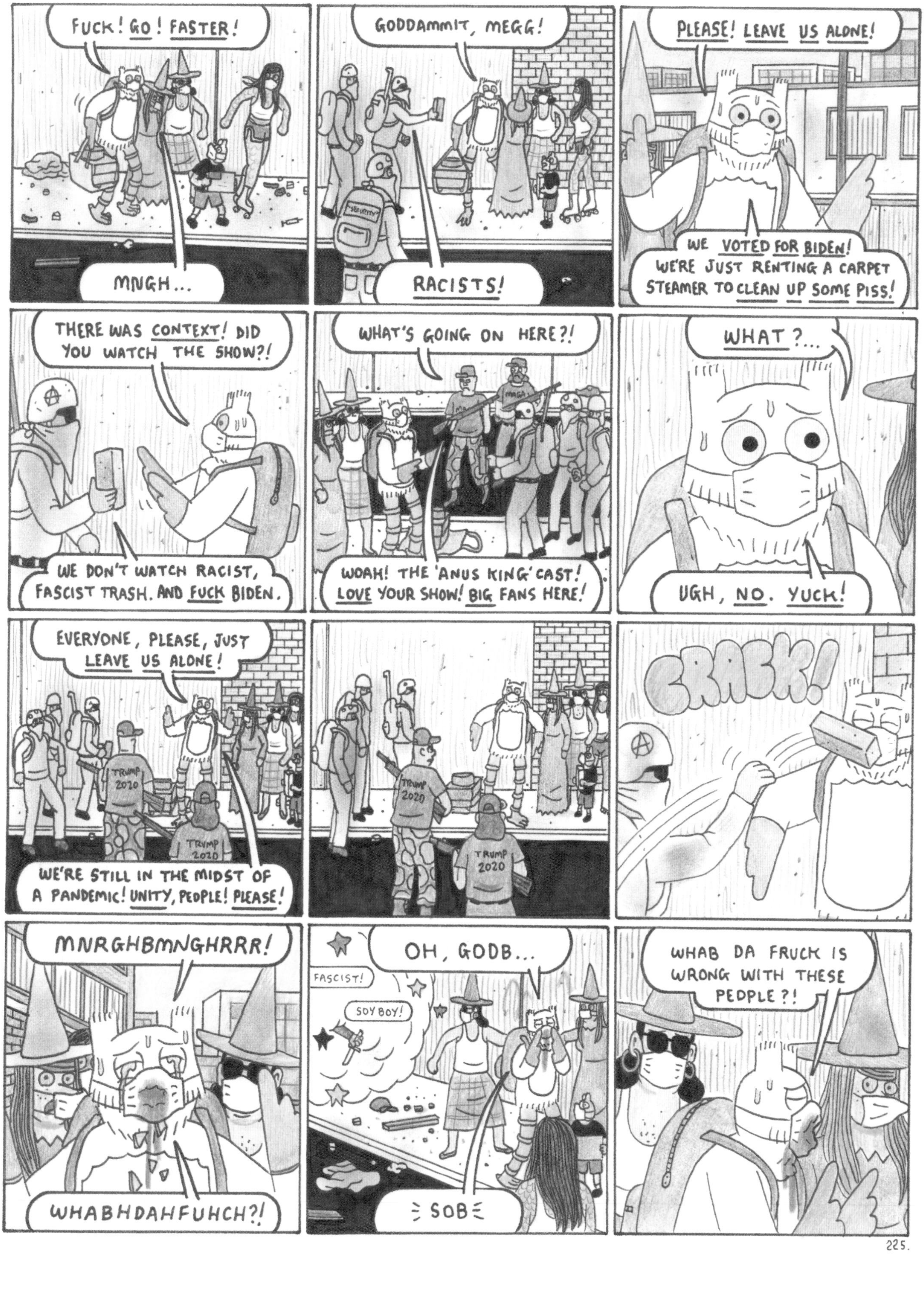
FUCK! GO! FASTER!
MNGH...
GODDAMMIT, MEGG!
"SECURITY"
RACISTS!
PLEASE! LEAVE US ALONE!
WE VOTED FOR BIDEN! WE'RE JUST RENTING A CARPET STEAMER TO CLEAN UP SOME PISS!
THERE WAS CONTEXT! DID YOU WATCH THE SHOW?!
WE DON'T WATCH RACIST, FASCIST TRASH. AND FUCK BIDEN.
WHAT'S GOING ON HERE?!
MAGA
WOAH! THE 'ANUS KING' CAST! LOVE YOUR SHOW! BIG FANS HERE!
WHAT?...
UGH, NO. YUCK!
EVERYONE, PLEASE, JUST LEAVE US ALONE!
TRUMP 2020
TRUMP 2020
WE'RE STILL IN THE MIDST OF A PANDEMIC! UNITY, PEOPLE! PLEASE!
TRUMP 2020
TRUMP 2020
CRACK!
MNRGHBMNGHRRR!
WHABHDAHFUHCH?!
OH, GODB...
FASCIST!
SOY BOY!
SOB
WHAB DA FRUCK IS WRONG WITH THESE PEOPLE?!

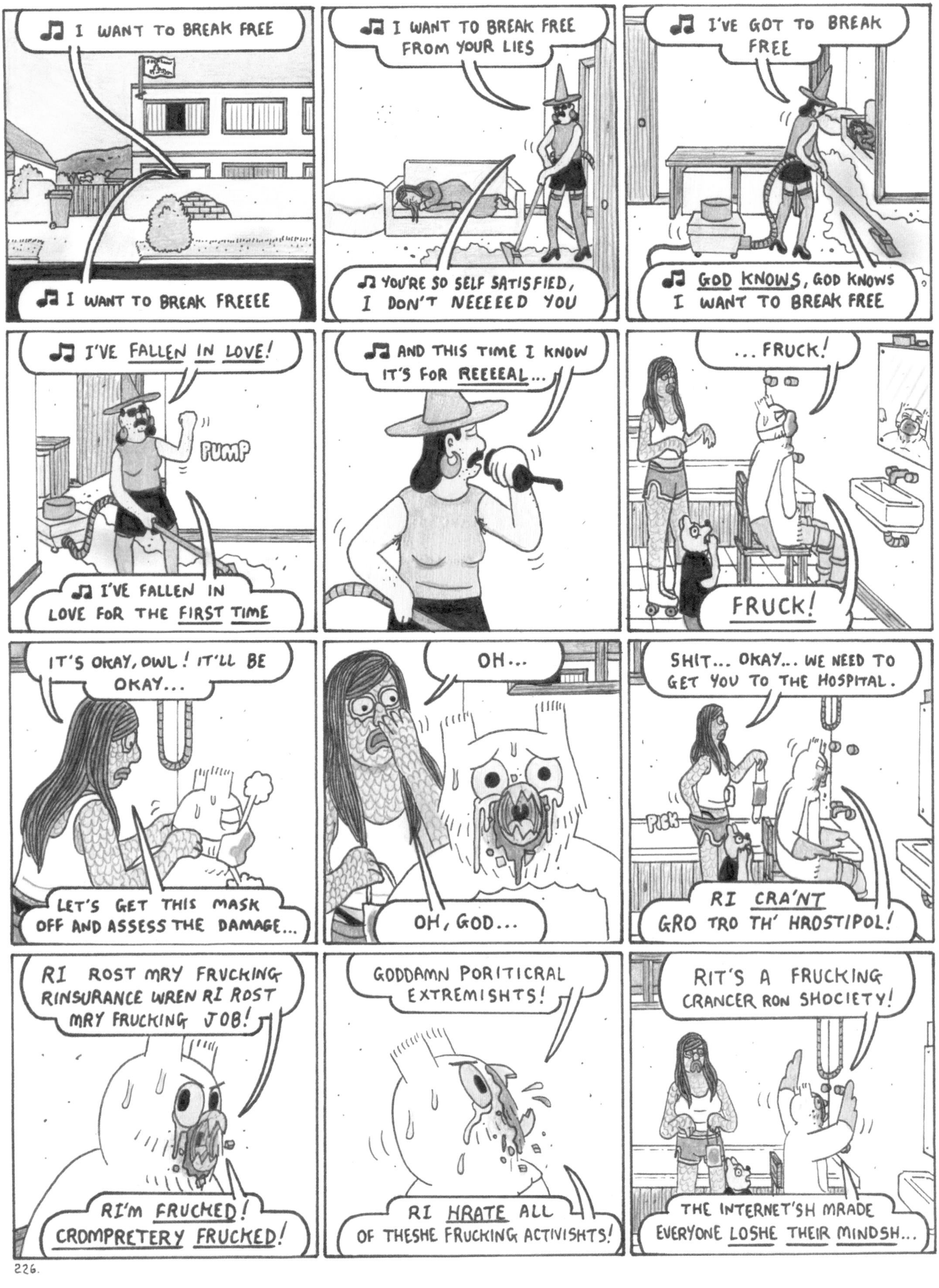
♫ I WANT TO BREAK FREE
♫ I WANT TO BREAK FREEEE
♫ I WANT TO BREAK FREE FROM YOUR LIES
♫ YOU'RE SO SELF SATISFIED, I DON'T NEEEEED YOU
♫ I'VE GOT TO BREAK FREE
♫ GOD KNOWS, GOD KNOWS I WANT TO BREAK FREE
♫ I'VE FALLEN IN LOVE!
PUMP
♫ I'VE FALLEN IN LOVE FOR THE FIRST TIME
♫ AND THIS TIME I KNOW IT'S FOR REEEEAL...
...FRUCK!
FRUCK!
IT'S OKAY, OWL! IT'LL BE OKAY...
LET'S GET THIS MASK OFF AND ASSESS THE DAMAGE...
OH...
OH, GOD...
SHIT... OKAY... WE NEED TO GET YOU TO THE HOSPITAL.
PICK
RI CRA'NT GRO TRO TH' HROSTIPOL!
RI ROST MRY FRUCKING RINSURANCE WREN RI ROST MRY FRUCKING JOB!
RI'M FRUCKED! CROMPRETERY FRUCKED!
GODDAMN PORITICRAL EXTREMISHTS!
RI HRATE ALL OF THESHE FRUCKING ACTIVISHTS!
RIT'S A FRUCKING CRANCER RON SHOCIETY!
THE INTERNET'SH MRADE EVERYONE LOSHE THEIR MINDSH...

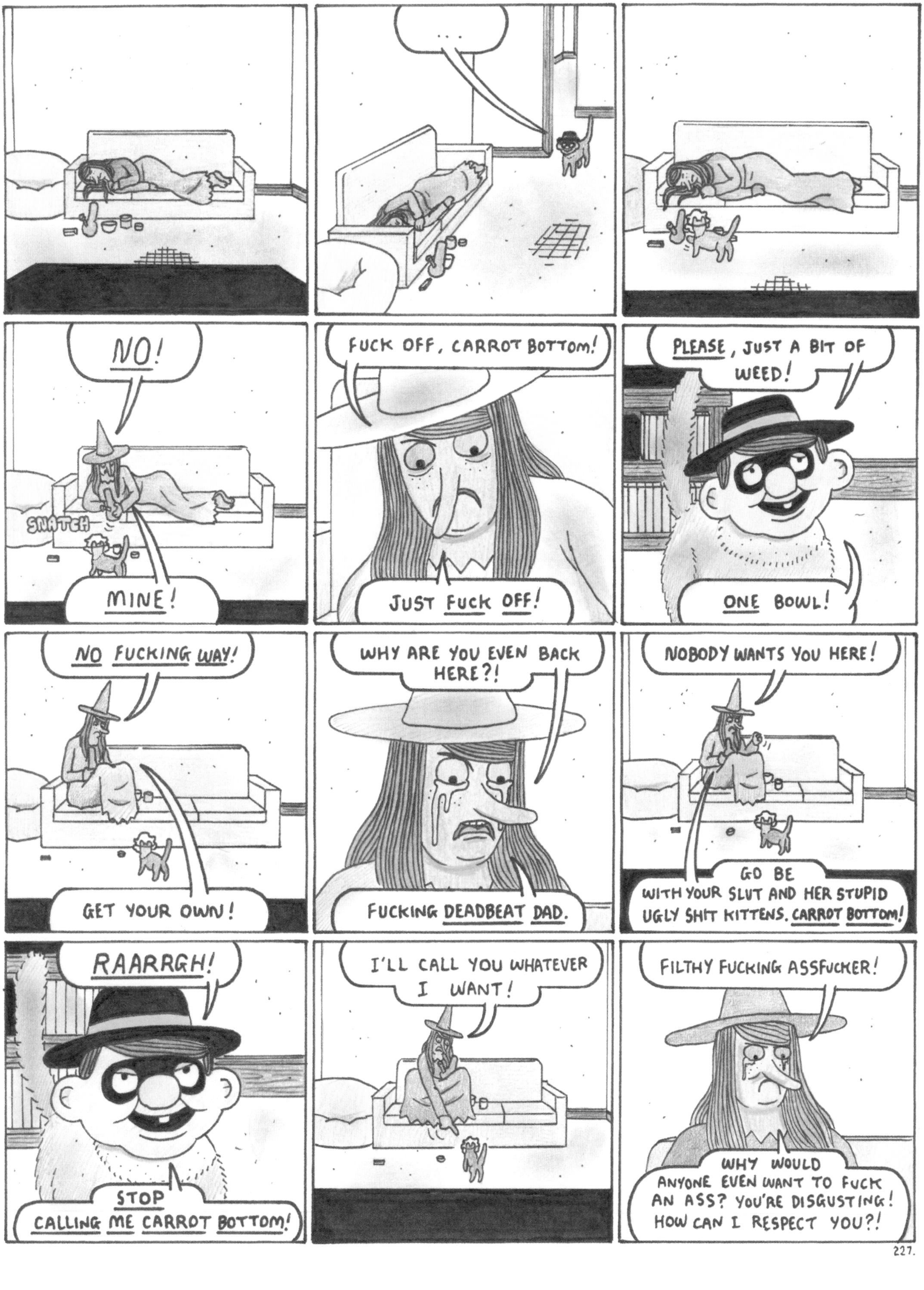
...
NO!
SNATCH
MINE!
FUCK OFF, CARROT BOTTOM!
JUST FUCK OFF!
PLEASE, JUST A BIT OF WEED!
ONE BOWL!
NO FUCKING WAY!
GET YOUR OWN!
WHY ARE YOU EVEN BACK HERE?!
FUCKING DEADBEAT DAD.
NOBODY WANTS YOU HERE!
GO BE WITH YOUR SLUT AND HER STUPID UGLY SHIT KITTENS. CARROT BOTTOM!
RAARRGH!
STOP CALLING ME CARROT BOTTOM!
I'LL CALL YOU WHATEVER I WANT!
FILTHY FUCKING ASSFUCKER!
WHY WOULD ANYONE EVEN WANT TO FUCK AN ASS? YOU'RE DISGUSTING! HOW CAN I RESPECT YOU?!

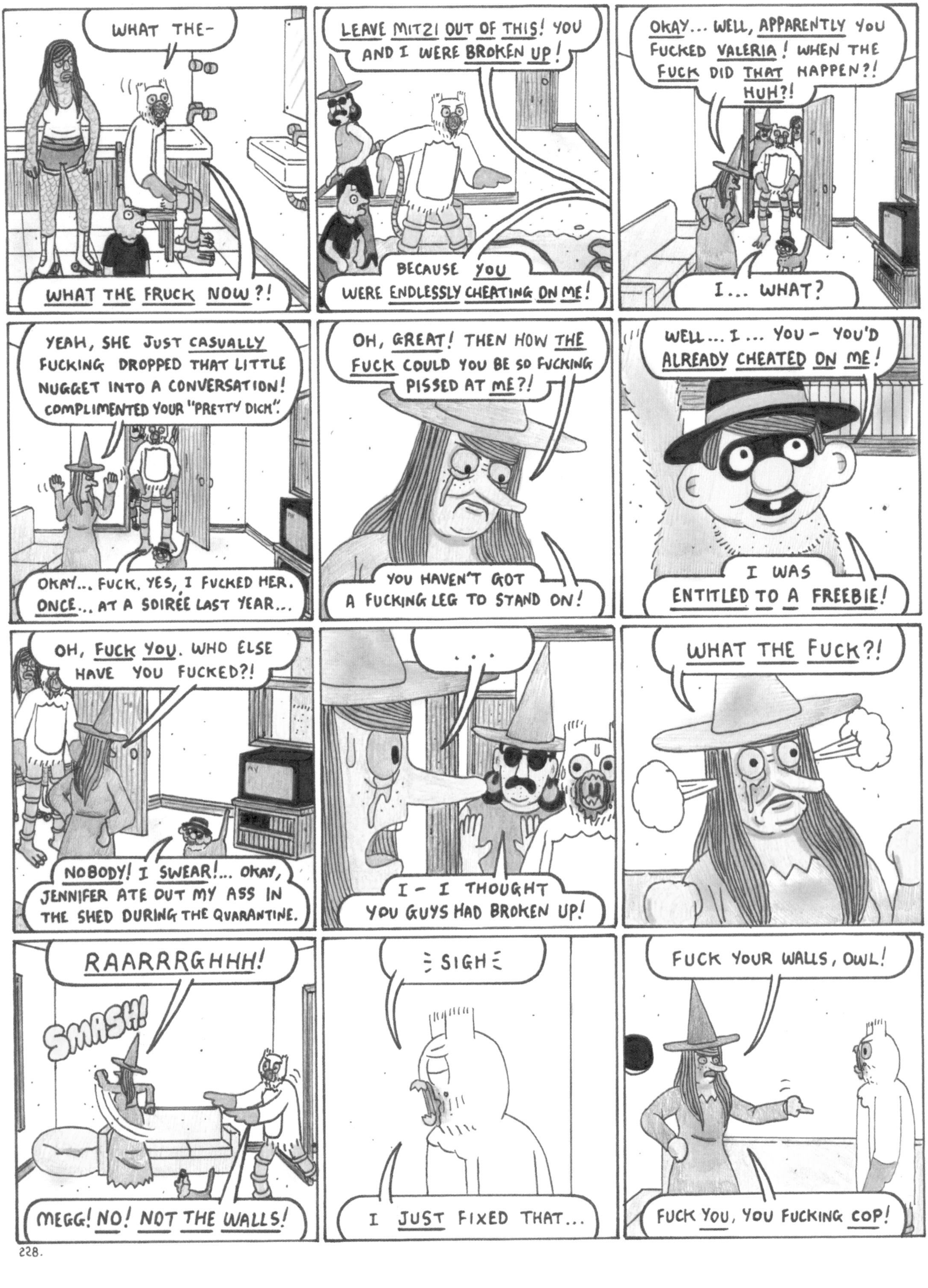
WHAT THE-
WHAT THE FRUCK NOW?!
LEAVE MITZI OUT OF THIS! YOU AND I WERE BROKEN UP!
BECAUSE YOU WERE ENDLESSLY CHEATING ON ME!
OKAY... WELL, APPARENTLY YOU FUCKED VALERIA! WHEN THE FUCK DID THAT HAPPEN?! HUH?!
I... WHAT?
YEAH, SHE JUST CASUALLY FUCKING DROPPED THAT LITTLE NUGGET INTO A CONVERSATION! COMPLIMENTED YOUR "PRETTY DICK".
OKAY... FUCK. YES, I FUCKED HER. ONCE... AT A SOIRÉE LAST YEAR...
OH, GREAT! THEN HOW THE FUCK COULD YOU BE SO FUCKING PISSED AT ME?!
YOU HAVEN'T GOT A FUCKING LEG TO STAND ON!
WELL... I... YOU- YOU'D ALREADY CHEATED ON ME!
I WAS ENTITLED TO A FREEBIE!
OH, FUCK YOU. WHO ELSE HAVE YOU FUCKED?!
NOBODY! I SWEAR!... OKAY, JENNIFER ATE OUT MY ASS IN THE SHED DURING THE QUARANTINE.
. . .
I - I THOUGHT YOU GUYS HAD BROKEN UP!
WHAT THE FUCK?!
RAAARRRGHHH!
SMASH!
MEGG! NO! NOT THE WALLS!
SIGH
I JUST FIXED THAT...
FUCK YOUR WALLS, OWL!
FUCK YOU, YOU FUCKING COP!

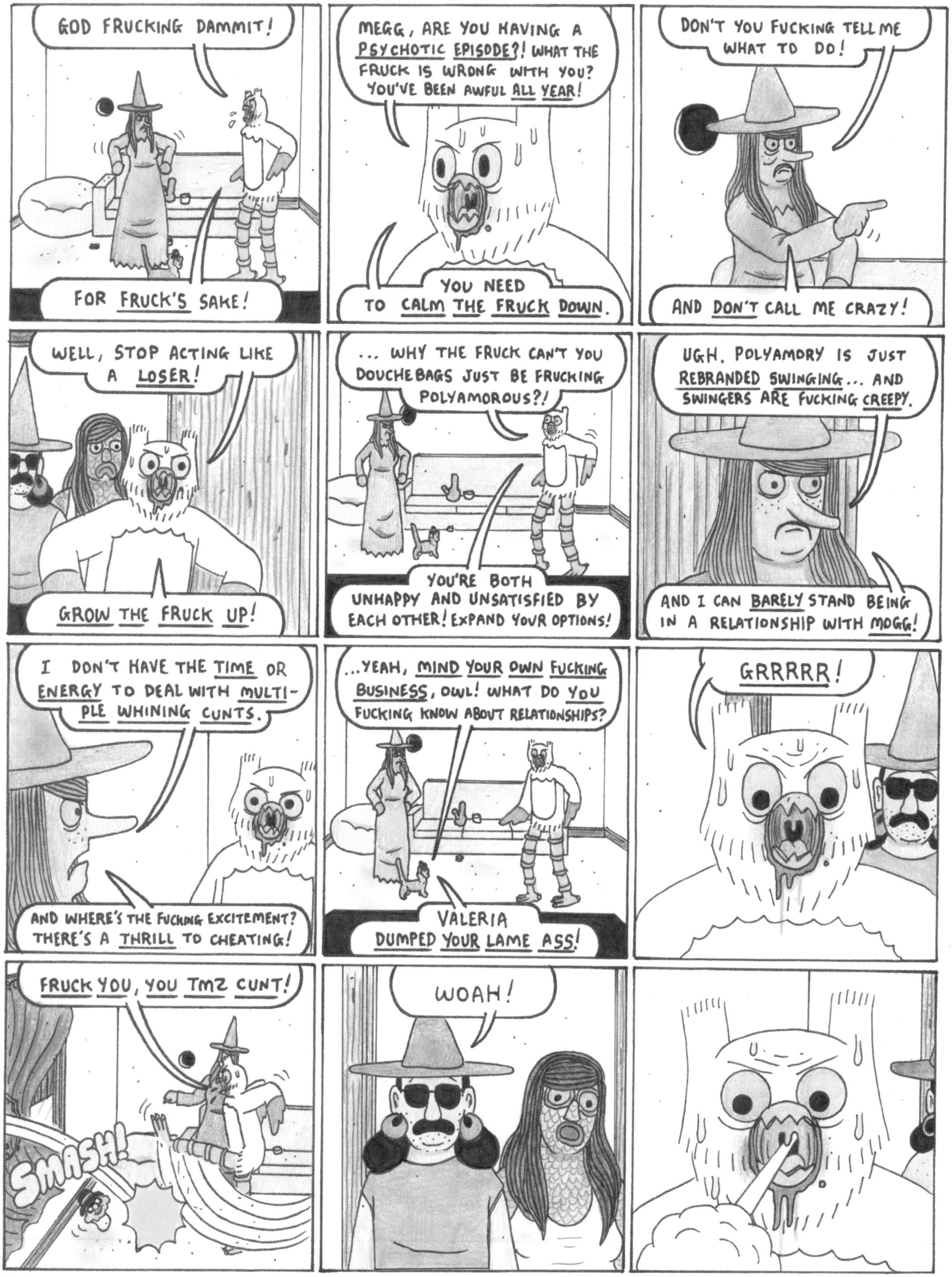
GOD FRUCKING DAMMIT!
FOR FRUCK'S SAKE!
MEGG, ARE YOU HAVING A PSYCHOTIC EPISODE?! WHAT THE FRUCK IS WRONG WITH YOU? YOU'VE BEEN AWFUL ALL YEAR!
YOU NEED TO CALM THE FRUCK DOWN.
DON'T YOU FUCKING TELL ME WHAT TO DO!
AND DON'T CALL ME CRAZY!
WELL, STOP ACTING LIKE A LOSER!
GROW THE FRUCK UP!
... WHY THE FRUCK CAN'T YOU DOUCHEBAGS JUST BE FRUCKING POLYAMOROUS?!
YOU'RE BOTH UNHAPPY AND UNSATISFIED BY EACH OTHER! EXPAND YOUR OPTIONS!
UGH. POLYAMORY IS JUST REBRANDED SWINGING... AND SWINGERS ARE FUCKING CREEPY.
AND I CAN BARELY STAND BEING IN A RELATIONSHIP WITH MOGG!
I DON'T HAVE THE TIME OR ENERGY TO DEAL WITH MULTI-PLE WHINING CUNTS.
AND WHERE'S THE FUCKING EXCITEMENT? THERE'S A THRILL TO CHEATING!
...YEAH, MIND YOUR OWN FUCKING BUSINESS, OWL! WHAT DO YOU FUCKING KNOW ABOUT RELATIONSHIPS?
VALERIA DUMPED YOUR LAME ASS!
GRRRRR!
FRUCK YOU, YOU TMZ CUNT!
SMASH!
WOAH!

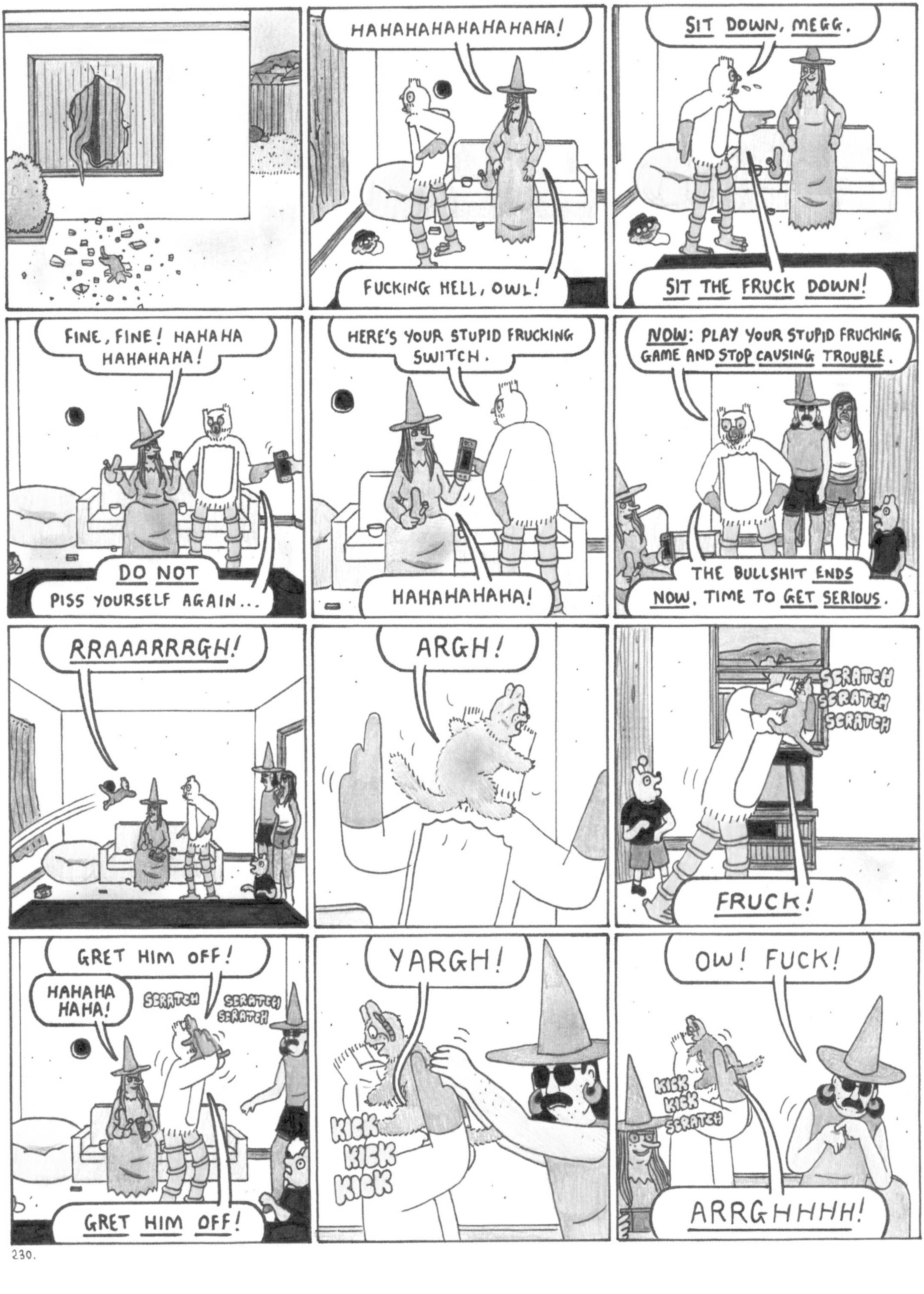
HAHAHAHAHAHAHAHA!
FUCKING HELL, OWL!
SIT DOWN, MEGG.
SIT THE FRUCK DOWN!
FINE, FINE! HAHAHA HAHAHAHA!
DO NOT PISS YOURSELF AGAIN...
HERE'S YOUR STUPID FRUCKING SWITCH.
HAHAHAHAHA!
NOW: PLAY YOUR STUPID FRUCKING GAME AND STOP CAUSING TROUBLE.
THE BULLSHIT ENDS NOW. TIME TO GET SERIOUS.
RRAAARRRGH!
ARGH!
SCRATCH SCRATCH SCRATCH
FRUCK!
GRET HIM OFF!
HAHAHA HAHA!
SCRATCH
SCRATCH SCRATCH
GRET HIM OFF!
YARGH!
KICK KICK KICK
OW! FUCK!
KICK KICK SCRATCH
ARRGHHHH!

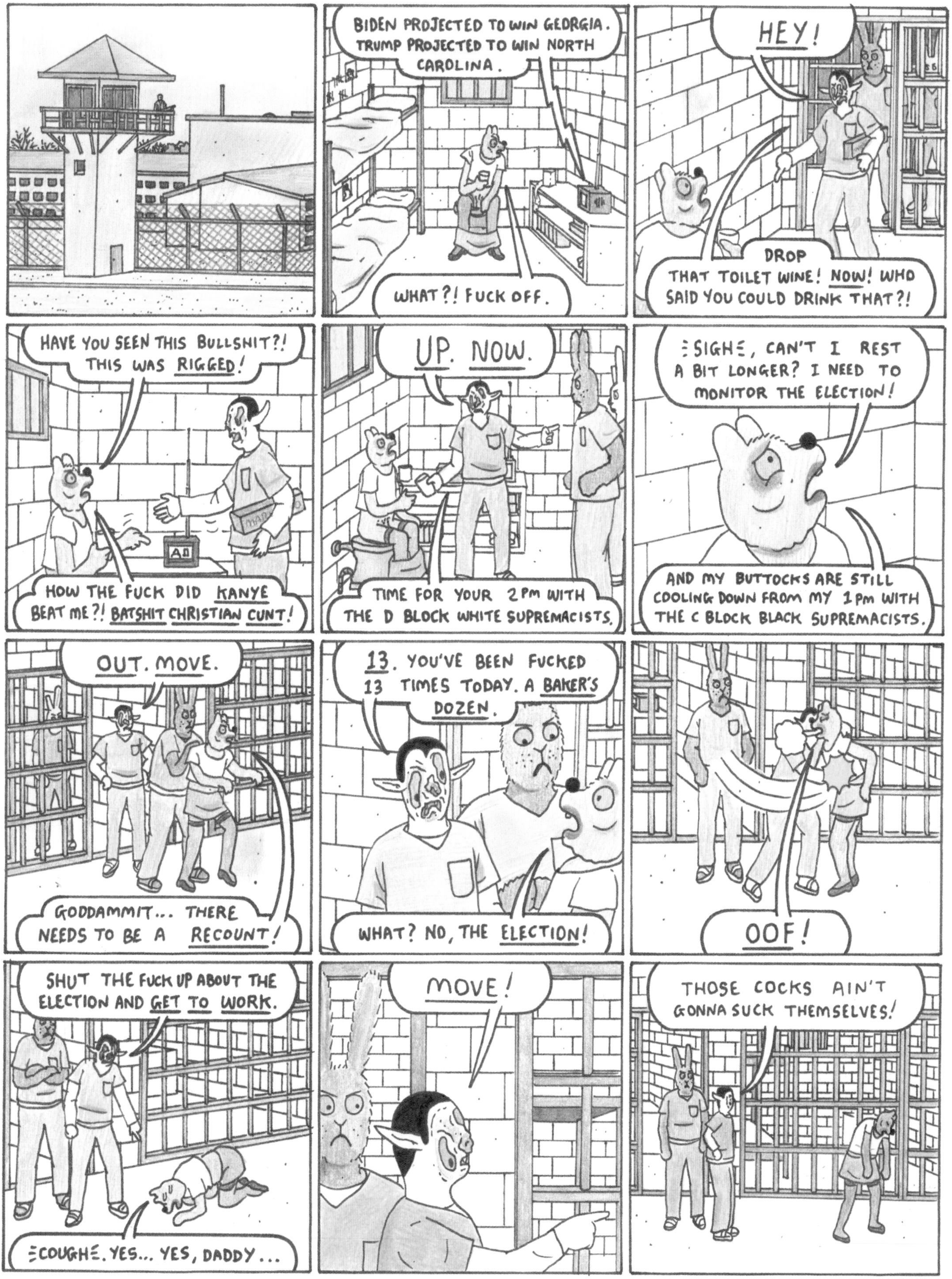
BIDEN PROJECTED TO WIN GEORGIA. TRUMP PROJECTED TO WIN NORTH CAROLINA.
WHAT?! FUCK OFF.
HEY!
DROP THAT TOILET WINE! NOW! WHO SAID YOU COULD DRINK THAT?!
HAVE YOU SEEN THIS BULLSHIT?! THIS WAS RIGGED!
HOW THE FUCK DID KANYE BEAT ME?! BATSHIT CHRISTIAN CUNT!
UP. NOW.
TIME FOR YOUR 2PM WITH THE D BLOCK WHITE SUPREMACISTS.
≡SIGH≡, CAN'T I REST A BIT LONGER? I NEED TO MONITOR THE ELECTION!
AND MY BUTTOCKS ARE STILL COOLING DOWN FROM MY 1PM WITH THE C BLOCK BLACK SUPREMACISTS.
OUT. MOVE.
GODDAMMIT... THERE NEEDS TO BE A RECOUNT!
13. YOU'VE BEEN FUCKED 13 TIMES TODAY. A BAKER'S DOZEN.
WHAT? NO, THE ELECTION!
OOF!
SHUT THE FUCK UP ABOUT THE ELECTION AND GET TO WORK.
≡COUGH≡. YES... YES, DADDY...
MOVE!
THOSE COCKS AIN'T GONNA SUCK THEMSELVES!

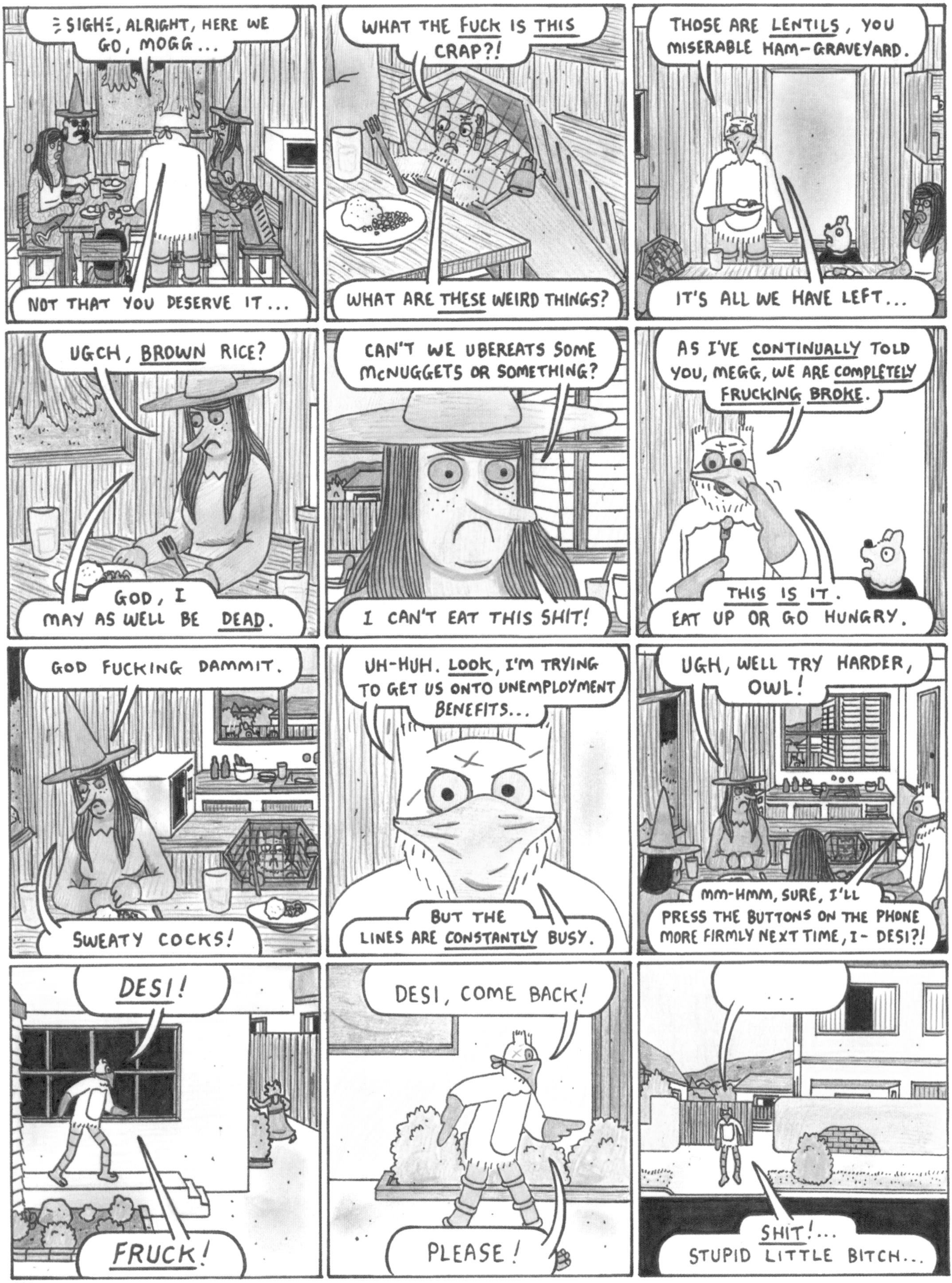

=SIGH=, ALRIGHT, HERE WE GO, MOGG...
NOT THAT YOU DESERVE IT...
WHAT THE FUCK IS THIS CRAP?!
WHAT ARE THESE WEIRD THINGS?
THOSE ARE LENTILS, YOU MISERABLE HAM-GRAVEYARD.
IT'S ALL WE HAVE LEFT...
UGCH, BROWN RICE?
GOD, I MAY AS WELL BE DEAD.
CAN'T WE UBEREATS SOME McNUGGETS OR SOMETHING?
I CAN'T EAT THIS SHIT!
AS I'VE CONTINUALLY TOLD YOU, MEGG, WE ARE COMPLETELY FRUCKING BROKE.
THIS IS IT. EAT UP OR GO HUNGRY.
GOD FUCKING DAMMIT.
SWEATY COCKS!
UH-HUH. LOOK, I'M TRYING TO GET US ONTO UNEMPLOYMENT BENEFITS...
BUT THE LINES ARE CONSTANTLY BUSY.
UGH, WELL TRY HARDER, OWL!
MM-HMM, SURE, I'LL PRESS THE BUTTONS ON THE PHONE MORE FIRMLY NEXT TIME, I- DESI?!
DESI!
FRUCK!
DESI, COME BACK!
PLEASE!
...
SHIT!... STUPID LITTLE BITCH...

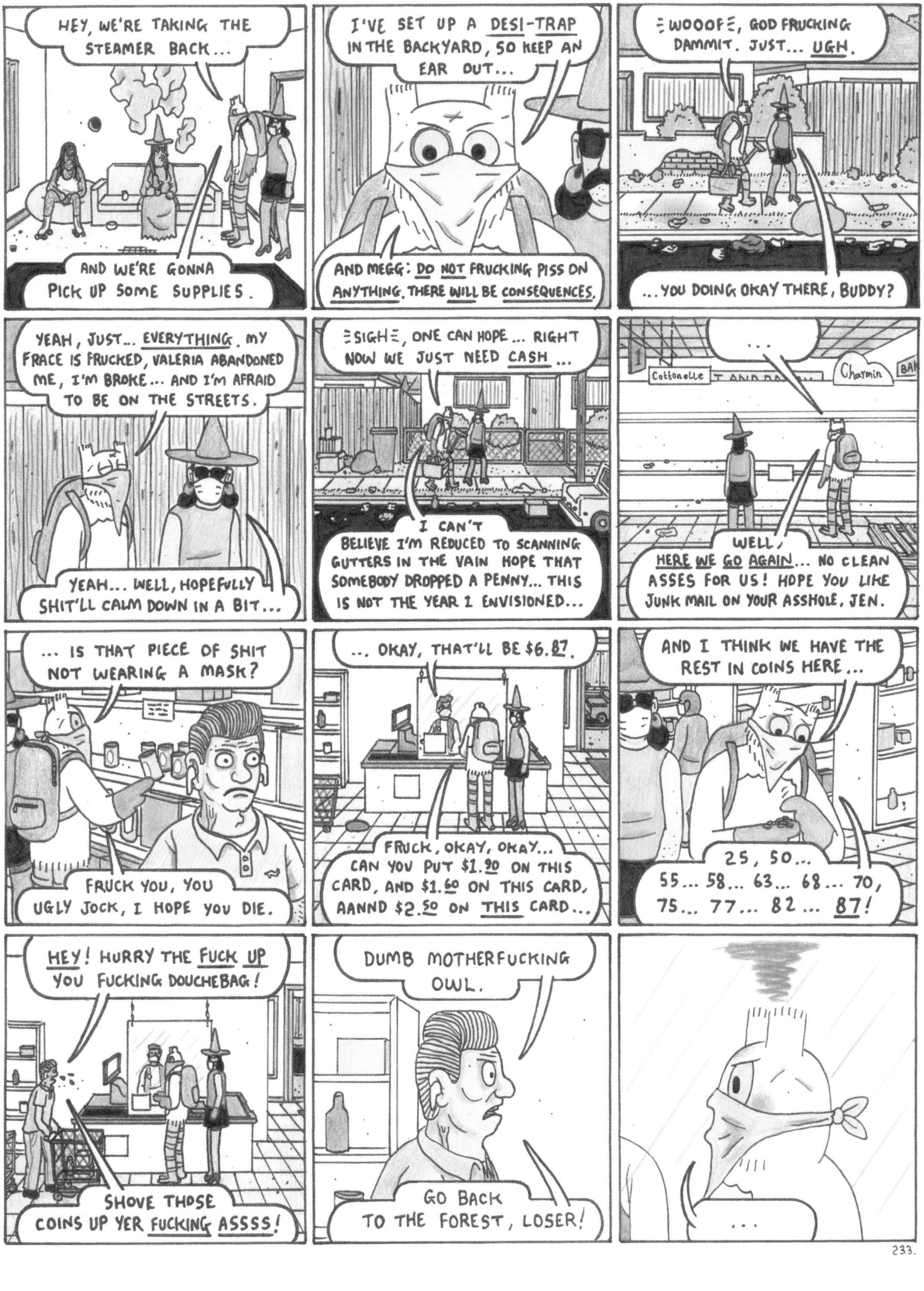
HEY, WE'RE TAKING THE STEAMER BACK...
AND WE'RE GONNA PICK UP SOME SUPPLIES.
I'VE SET UP A DESI-TRAP IN THE BACKYARD, SO KEEP AN EAR OUT...
AND MEGG: DO NOT FRUCKING PISS ON ANYTHING. THERE WILL BE CONSEQUENCES.
≡WOOOF≡, GOD FRUCKING DAMMIT. JUST... UGH.
...YOU DOING OKAY THERE, BUDDY?
YEAH, JUST... EVERYTHING. MY FRACE IS FRUCKED, VALERIA ABANDONED ME, I'M BROKE... AND I'M AFRAID TO BE ON THE STREETS.
YEAH... WELL, HOPEFULLY SHIT'LL CALM DOWN IN A BIT...
≡SIGH≡, ONE CAN HOPE... RIGHT NOW WE JUST NEED CASH...
I CAN'T BELIEVE I'M REDUCED TO SCANNING GUTTERS IN THE VAIN HOPE THAT SOMEBODY DROPPED A PENNY... THIS IS NOT THE YEAR I ENVISIONED...
Cottonelle
Charmin
...
WELL, HERE WE GO AGAIN... NO CLEAN ASSES FOR US! HOPE YOU LIKE JUNK MAIL ON YOUR ASSHOLE, JEN.
... IS THAT PIECE OF SHIT NOT WEARING A MASK?
FRUCK YOU, YOU UGLY JOCK, I HOPE YOU DIE.
... OKAY, THAT'LL BE $6.87.
FRUCK, OKAY, OKAY... CAN YOU PUT $1.90 ON THIS CARD, AND $1.60 ON THIS CARD, AANND $2.50 ON THIS CARD...
AND I THINK WE HAVE THE REST IN COINS HERE...
25, 50... 55... 58... 63... 68... 70, 75... 77... 82... 87!
HEY! HURRY THE FUCK UP YOU FUCKING DOUCHEBAG!
SHOVE THOSE COINS UP YER FUCKING ASSSS!
DUMB MOTHERFUCKING OWL.
GO BACK TO THE FOREST, LOSER!
...

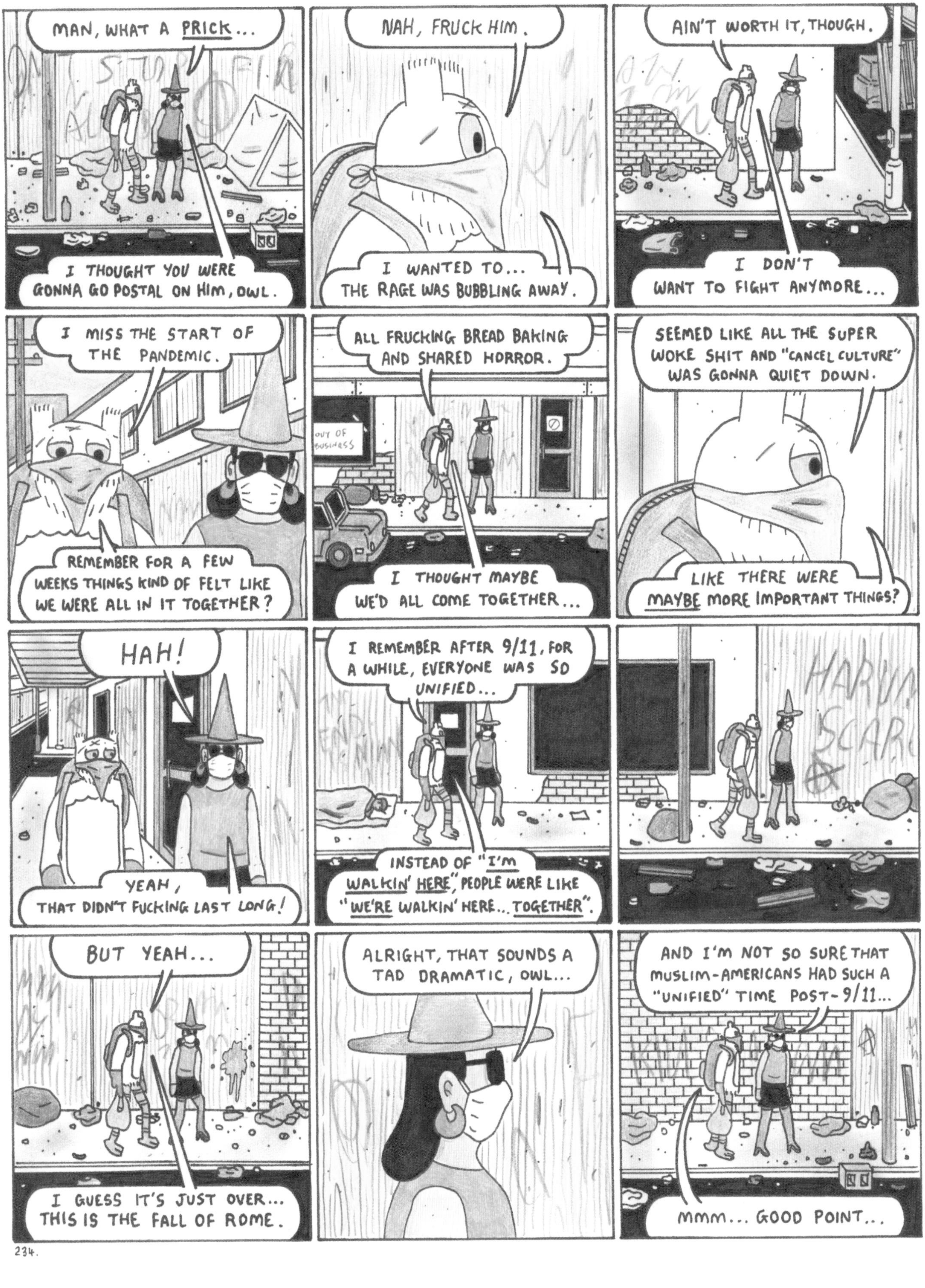
MAN, WHAT A PRICK...
I THOUGHT YOU WERE GONNA GO POSTAL ON HIM, OWL.
NAH, FRUCK HIM.
I WANTED TO... THE RAGE WAS BUBBLING AWAY.
AIN'T WORTH IT, THOUGH.
I DON'T WANT TO FIGHT ANYMORE...
I MISS THE START OF THE PANDEMIC.
REMEMBER FOR A FEW WEEKS THINGS KIND OF FELT LIKE WE WERE ALL IN IT TOGETHER?
ALL FRUCKING BREAD BAKING AND SHARED HORROR.
OUT OF BUSINESS
I THOUGHT MAYBE WE'D ALL COME TOGETHER...
SEEMED LIKE ALL THE SUPER WOKE SHIT AND "CANCEL CULTURE" WAS GONNA QUIET DOWN.
LIKE THERE WERE MAYBE MORE IMPORTANT THINGS?
HAH!
YEAH, THAT DIDN'T FUCKING LAST LONG!
I REMEMBER AFTER 9/11, FOR A WHILE, EVERYONE WAS SO UNIFIED...
INSTEAD OF "I'M WALKIN' HERE", PEOPLE WERE LIKE "WE'RE WALKIN' HERE... TOGETHER".
BUT YEAH...
I GUESS IT'S JUST OVER... THIS IS THE FALL OF ROME.
ALRIGHT, THAT SOUNDS A TAD DRAMATIC, OWL...
AND I'M NOT SO SURE THAT MUSLIM-AMERICANS HAD SUCH A "UNIFIED" TIME POST-9/11...
MMM... GOOD POINT...

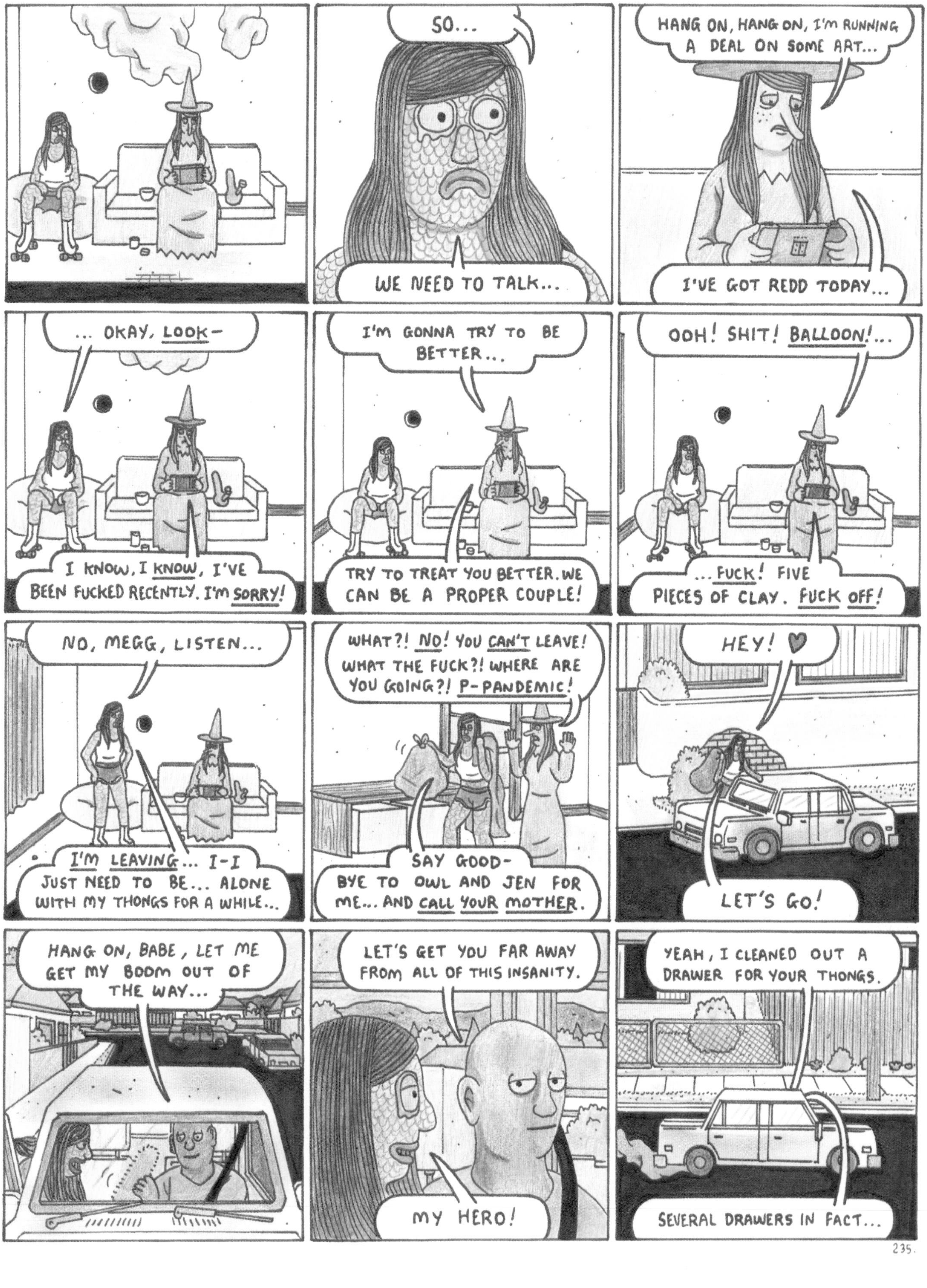
SO...
WE NEED TO TALK...
HANG ON, HANG ON, I'M RUNNING A DEAL ON SOME ART...
I'VE GOT REDD TODAY...
... OKAY, LOOK-
I KNOW, I KNOW, I'VE BEEN FUCKED RECENTLY. I'M SORRY!
I'M GONNA TRY TO BE BETTER...
TRY TO TREAT YOU BETTER. WE CAN BE A PROPER COUPLE!
OOH! SHIT! BALLOON!...
...FUCK! FIVE PIECES OF CLAY. FUCK OFF!
NO, MEGG, LISTEN...
I'M LEAVING... I-I JUST NEED TO BE... ALONE WITH MY THONGS FOR A WHILE...
WHAT?! NO! YOU CAN'T LEAVE! WHAT THE FUCK?! WHERE ARE YOU GOING?! P-PANDEMIC!
SAY GOOD-BYE TO OWL AND JEN FOR ME... AND CALL YOUR MOTHER.
HEY! ♥
LET'S GO!
HANG ON, BABE, LET ME GET MY BOOM OUT OF THE WAY...
LET'S GET YOU FAR AWAY FROM ALL OF THIS INSANITY.
MY HERO!
YEAH, I CLEANED OUT A DRAWER FOR YOUR THONGS.
SEVERAL DRAWERS IN FACT...

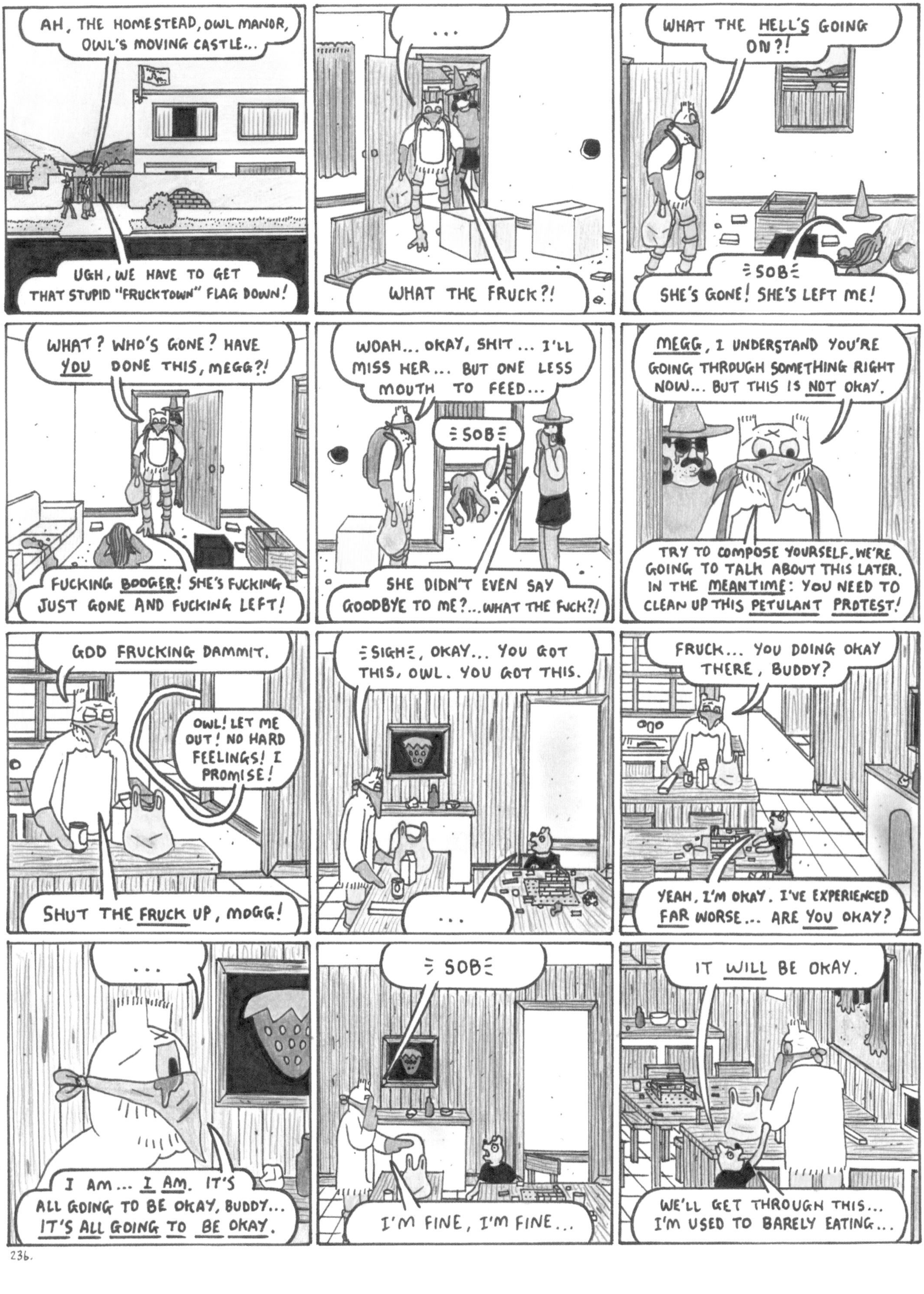
AH, THE HOMESTEAD, OWL MANOR, OWL'S MOVING CASTLE...
UGH, WE HAVE TO GET THAT STUPID "FRUCKTOWN" FLAG DOWN!
...
WHAT THE FRUCK?!
WHAT THE HELL'S GOING ON?!
SOB
SHE'S GONE! SHE'S LEFT ME!
WHAT? WHO'S GONE? HAVE YOU DONE THIS, MEGG?!
FUCKING BOOGER! SHE'S FUCKING JUST GONE AND FUCKING LEFT!
WOAH... OKAY, SHIT... I'LL MISS HER... BUT ONE LESS MOUTH TO FEED...
SOB
SHE DIDN'T EVEN SAY GOODBYE TO ME?...WHAT THE FUCK?!
MEGG, I UNDERSTAND YOU'RE GOING THROUGH SOMETHING RIGHT NOW... BUT THIS IS NOT OKAY.
TRY TO COMPOSE YOURSELF, WE'RE GOING TO TALK ABOUT THIS LATER. IN THE MEANTIME: YOU NEED TO CLEAN UP THIS PETULANT PROTEST!
GOD FRUCKING DAMMIT.
OWL! LET ME OUT! NO HARD FEELINGS! I PROMISE!
SHUT THE FRUCK UP, MOGG!
SIGH, OKAY... YOU GOT THIS, OWL. YOU GOT THIS.
...
FRUCK... YOU DOING OKAY THERE, BUDDY?
YEAH, I'M OKAY. I'VE EXPERIENCED FAR WORSE... ARE YOU OKAY?
...
I AM... I AM. IT'S ALL GOING TO BE OKAY, BUDDY... IT'S ALL GOING TO BE OKAY.
SOB
I'M FINE, I'M FINE...
IT WILL BE OKAY.
WE'LL GET THROUGH THIS... I'M USED TO BARELY EATING...

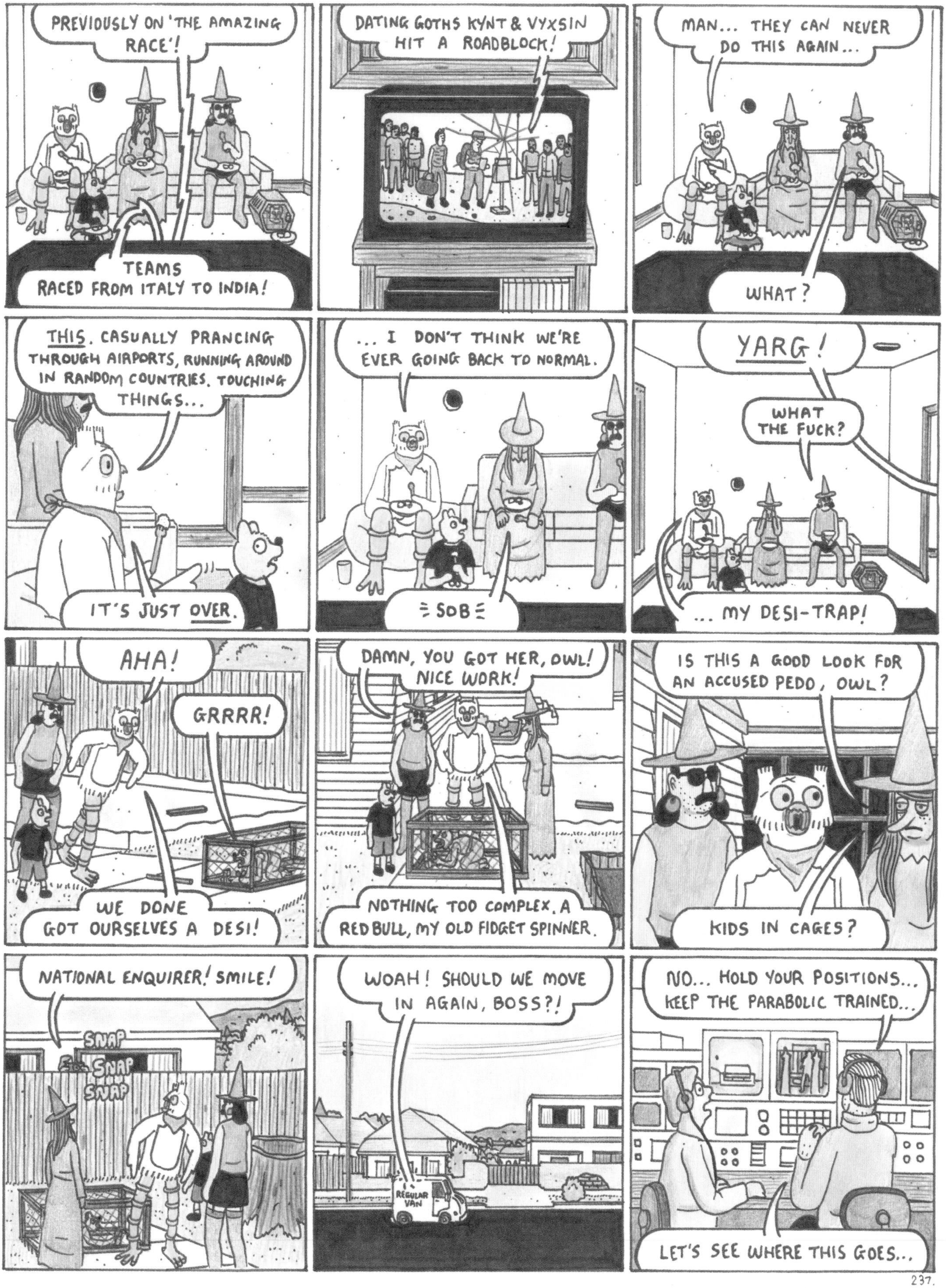

PREVIOUSLY ON 'THE AMAZING RACE'!
TEAMS RACED FROM ITALY TO INDIA!
DATING GOTHS KYNT & VYXSIN HIT A ROADBLOCK!
MAN... THEY CAN NEVER DO THIS AGAIN...
WHAT?
THIS. CASUALLY PRANCING THROUGH AIRPORTS, RUNNING AROUND IN RANDOM COUNTRIES. TOUCHING THINGS...
IT'S JUST OVER.
... I DON'T THINK WE'RE EVER GOING BACK TO NORMAL.
SOB
YARG!
WHAT THE FUCK?
... MY DESI-TRAP!
AHA!
GRRRR!
WE DONE GOT OURSELVES A DESI!
DAMN, YOU GOT HER, OWL! NICE WORK!
NOTHING TOO COMPLEX. A RED BULL, MY OLD FIDGET SPINNER.
IS THIS A GOOD LOOK FOR AN ACCUSED PEDO, OWL?
KIDS IN CAGES?
NATIONAL ENQUIRER! SMILE!
SNAP
SNAP
SNAP
WOAH! SHOULD WE MOVE IN AGAIN, BOSS?!
REGULAR VAN
NO... HOLD YOUR POSITIONS... KEEP THE PARABOLIC TRAINED...
LET'S SEE WHERE THIS GOES...

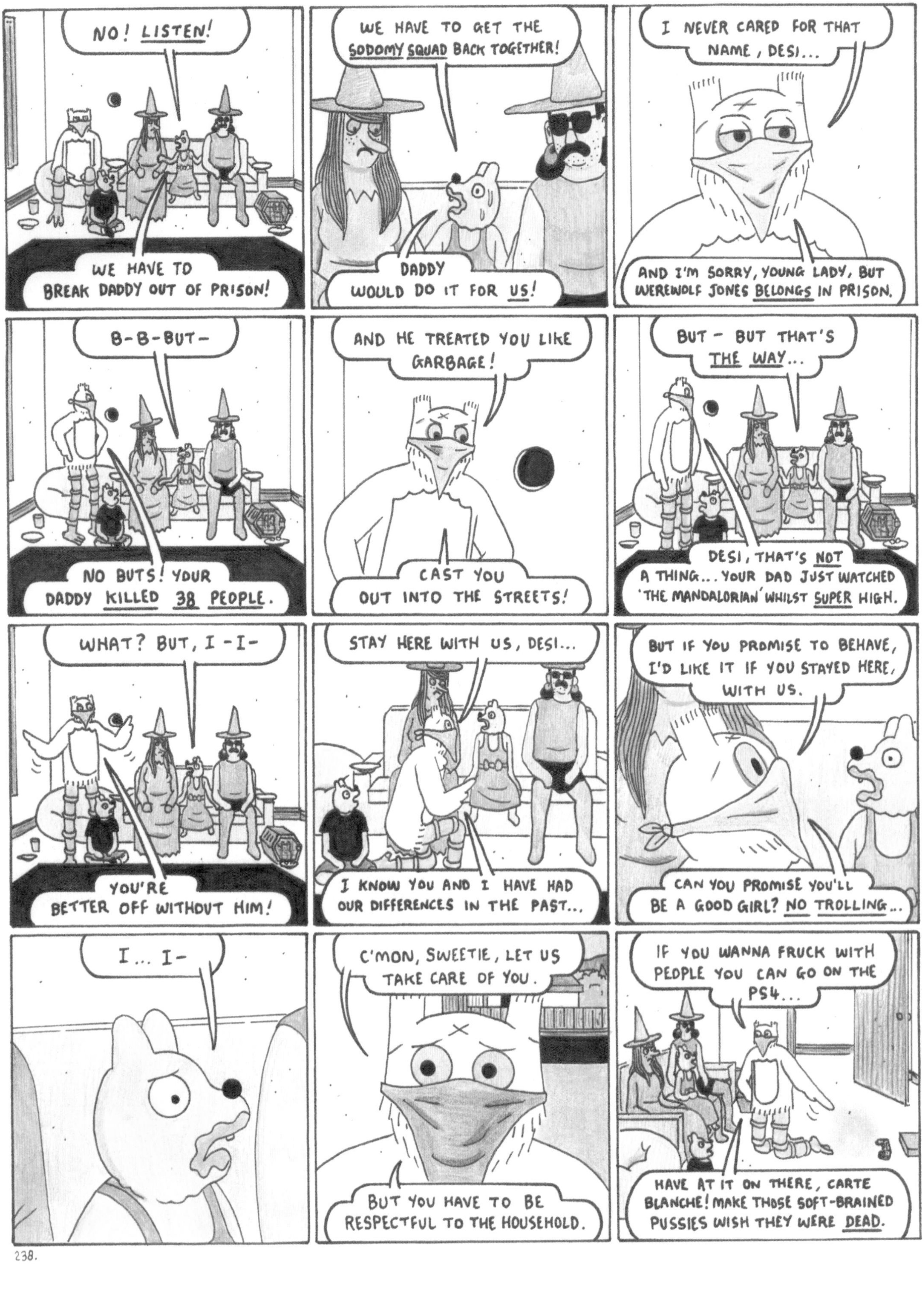
NO! LISTEN!
WE HAVE TO BREAK DADDY OUT OF PRISON!
WE HAVE TO GET THE SODOMY SQUAD BACK TOGETHER!
DADDY WOULD DO IT FOR US!
I NEVER CARED FOR THAT NAME, DESI...
AND I'M SORRY, YOUNG LADY, BUT WEREWOLF JONES BELONGS IN PRISON.
B-B-BUT-
NO BUTS! YOUR DADDY KILLED 38 PEOPLE.
AND HE TREATED YOU LIKE GARBAGE!
CAST YOU OUT INTO THE STREETS!
BUT - BUT THAT'S THE WAY...
DESI, THAT'S NOT A THING... YOUR DAD JUST WATCHED 'THE MANDALORIAN' WHILST SUPER HIGH.
WHAT? BUT, I-I-
YOU'RE BETTER OFF WITHOUT HIM!
STAY HERE WITH US, DESI...
I KNOW YOU AND I HAVE HAD OUR DIFFERENCES IN THE PAST...
BUT IF YOU PROMISE TO BEHAVE, I'D LIKE IT IF YOU STAYED HERE, WITH US.
CAN YOU PROMISE YOU'LL BE A GOOD GIRL? NO TROLLING...
I... I-
C'MON, SWEETIE, LET US TAKE CARE OF YOU.
BUT YOU HAVE TO BE RESPECTFUL TO THE HOUSEHOLD.
IF YOU WANNA FRUCK WITH PEOPLE YOU CAN GO ON THE PS4...
HAVE AT IT ON THERE, CARTE BLANCHE! MAKE THOSE SOFT-BRAINED PUSSIES WISH THEY WERE DEAD.

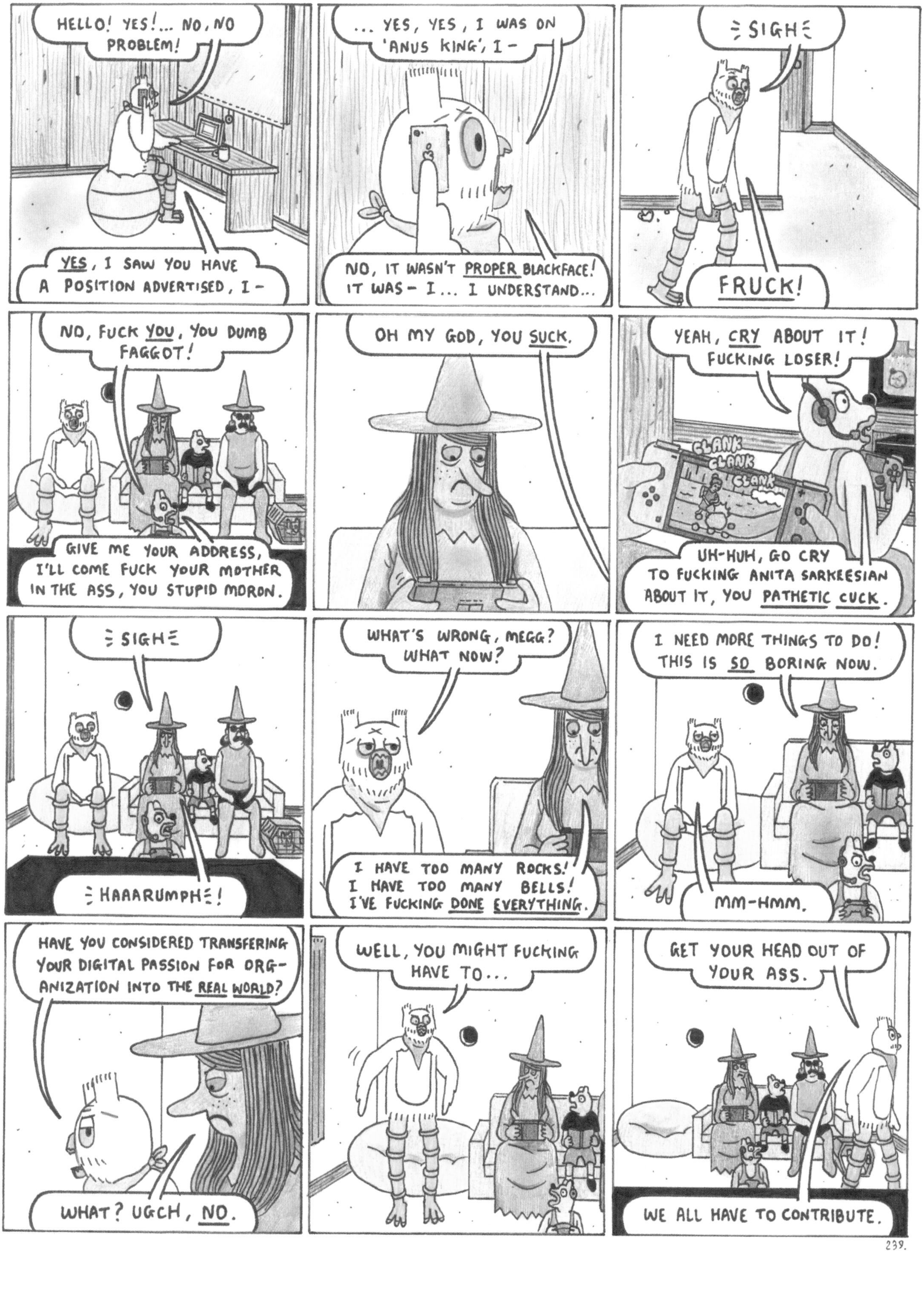

HELLO! YES!... NO, NO PROBLEM!
YES, I SAW YOU HAVE A POSITION ADVERTISED, I-
... YES, YES, I WAS ON 'ANUS KING', I-
NO, IT WASN'T PROPER BLACKFACE! IT WAS- I... I UNDERSTAND...
SIGH
FRUCK!
NO, FUCK YOU, YOU DUMB FAGGOT!
GIVE ME YOUR ADDRESS, I'LL COME FUCK YOUR MOTHER IN THE ASS, YOU STUPID MORON.
OH MY GOD, YOU SUCK.
YEAH, CRY ABOUT IT! FUCKING LOSER!
CLANK
CLANK
CLANK
UH-HUH, GO CRY TO FUCKING ANITA SARKEESIAN ABOUT IT, YOU PATHETIC CUCK.
SIGH
HAAARUMPH!
WHAT'S WRONG, MEGG? WHAT NOW?
I HAVE TOO MANY ROCKS! I HAVE TOO MANY BELLS! I'VE FUCKING DONE EVERYTHING.
I NEED MORE THINGS TO DO! THIS IS SO BORING NOW.
MM-HMM.
HAVE YOU CONSIDERED TRANSFERING YOUR DIGITAL PASSION FOR ORGANIZATION INTO THE REAL WORLD?
WHAT? UGCH, NO.
WELL, YOU MIGHT FUCKING HAVE TO...
GET YOUR HEAD OUT OF YOUR ASS.
WE ALL HAVE TO CONTRIBUTE.

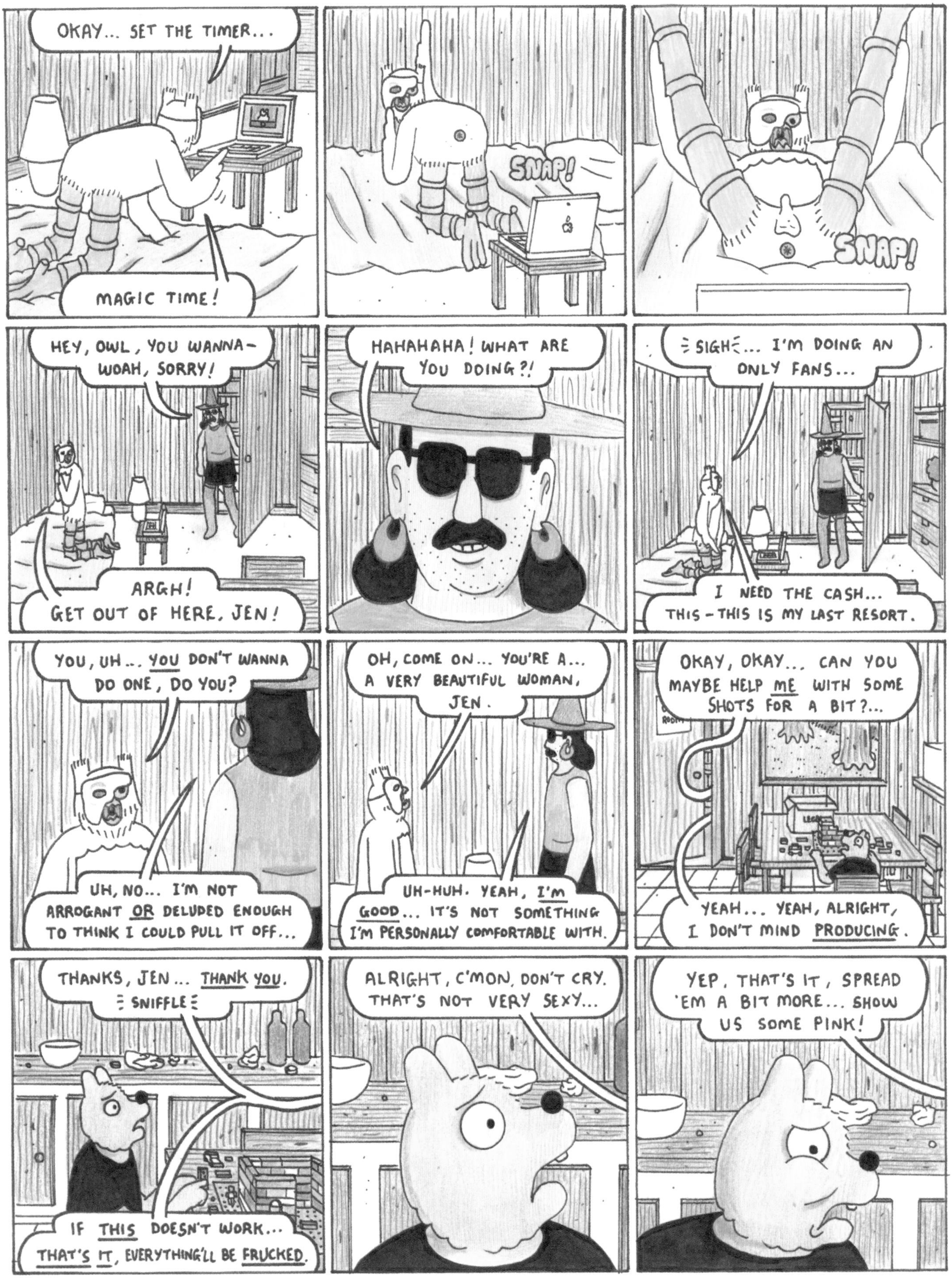
OKAY... SET THE TIMER...
MAGIC TIME!
SNAP!
SNAP!
HEY, OWL, YOU WANNA- WOAH, SORRY!
ARGH! GET OUT OF HERE, JEN!
HAHAHAHA! WHAT ARE YOU DOING?!
SIGH... I'M DOING AN ONLY FANS...
I NEED THE CASH... THIS - THIS IS MY LAST RESORT.
YOU, UH... YOU DON'T WANNA DO ONE, DO YOU?
UH, NO... I'M NOT ARROGANT OR DELUDED ENOUGH TO THINK I COULD PULL IT OFF...
OH, COME ON... YOU'RE A... A VERY BEAUTIFUL WOMAN, JEN.
UH-HUH. YEAH, I'M GOOD... IT'S NOT SOMETHING I'M PERSONALLY COMFORTABLE WITH.
OKAY, OKAY... CAN YOU MAYBE HELP ME WITH SOME SHOTS FOR A BIT?...
YEAH... YEAH, ALRIGHT, I DON'T MIND PRODUCING.
THANKS, JEN... THANK YOU. SNIFFLE
IF THIS DOESN'T WORK... THAT'S IT, EVERYTHING'LL BE FRUCKED.
ALRIGHT, C'MON, DON'T CRY. THAT'S NOT VERY SEXY...
YEP, THAT'S IT, SPREAD 'EM A BIT MORE... SHOW US SOME PINK!

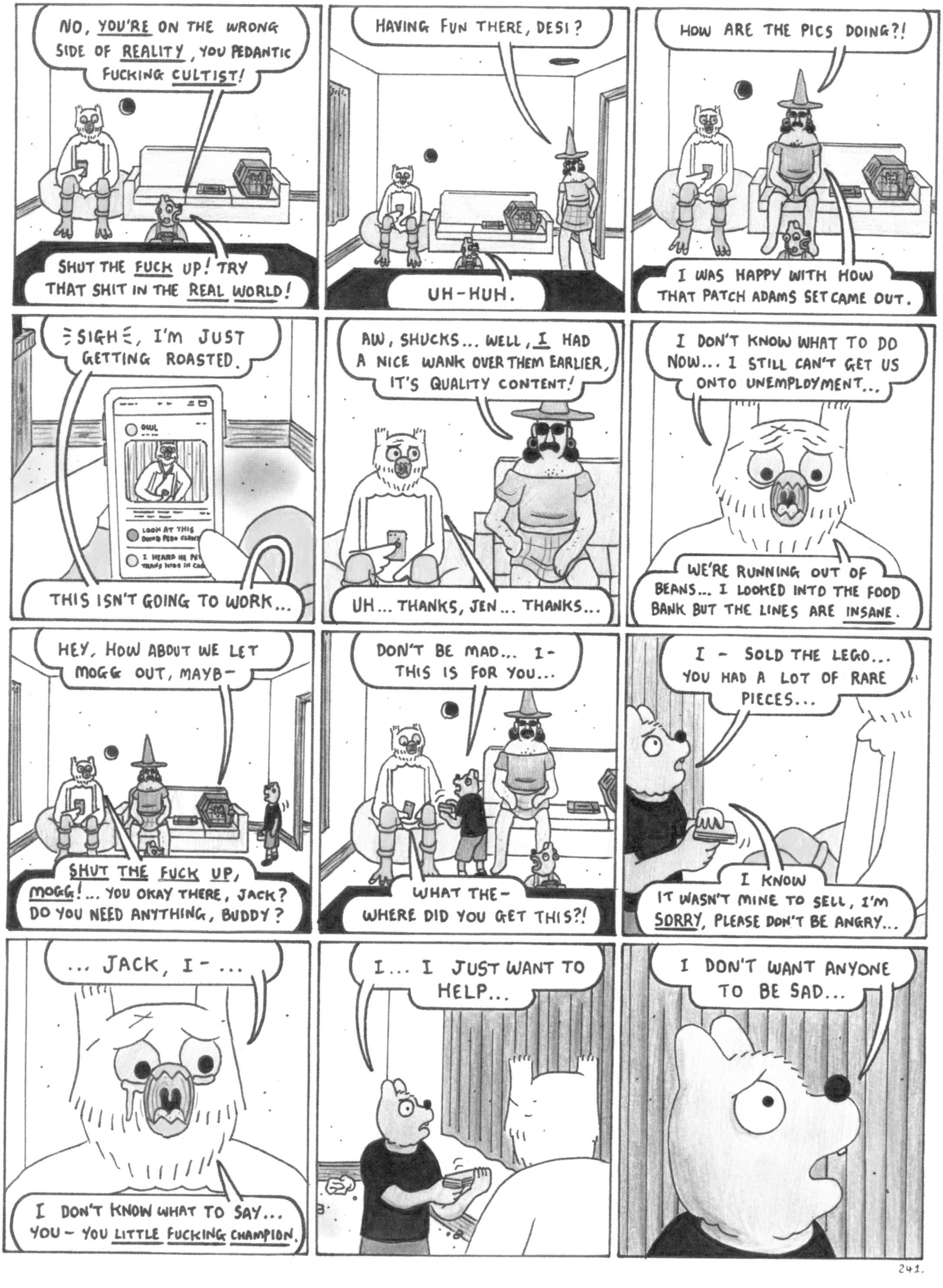
NO, YOU'RE ON THE WRONG SIDE OF REALITY, YOU PEDANTIC FUCKING CULTIST!
SHUT THE FUCK UP! TRY THAT SHIT IN THE REAL WORLD!
HAVING FUN THERE, DESI?
UH-HUH.
HOW ARE THE PICS DOING?!
I WAS HAPPY WITH HOW THAT PATCH ADAMS SET CAME OUT.
≡SIGH≡, I'M JUST GETTING ROASTED.
OWL
LOOK AT THIS DUMB PEDO CLOWN
THIS ISN'T GOING TO WORK...
AW, SHUCKS... WELL, I HAD A NICE WANK OVER THEM EARLIER, IT'S QUALITY CONTENT!
UH... THANKS, JEN... THANKS...
I DON'T KNOW WHAT TO DO NOW... I STILL CAN'T GET US ONTO UNEMPLOYMENT...
WE'RE RUNNING OUT OF BEANS... I LOOKED INTO THE FOOD BANK BUT THE LINES ARE INSANE.
HEY, HOW ABOUT WE LET MOGG OUT, MAYB-
SHUT THE FUCK UP, MOGG!... YOU OKAY THERE, JACK? DO YOU NEED ANYTHING, BUDDY?
DON'T BE MAD... I- THIS IS FOR YOU...
WHAT THE- WHERE DID YOU GET THIS?!
I - SOLD THE LEGO... YOU HAD A LOT OF RARE PIECES...
I KNOW IT WASN'T MINE TO SELL, I'M SORRY, PLEASE DON'T BE ANGRY...
... JACK, I- ...
I DON'T KNOW WHAT TO SAY... YOU - YOU LITTLE FUCKING CHAMPION.
I... I JUST WANT TO HELP...
I DON'T WANT ANYONE TO BE SAD...

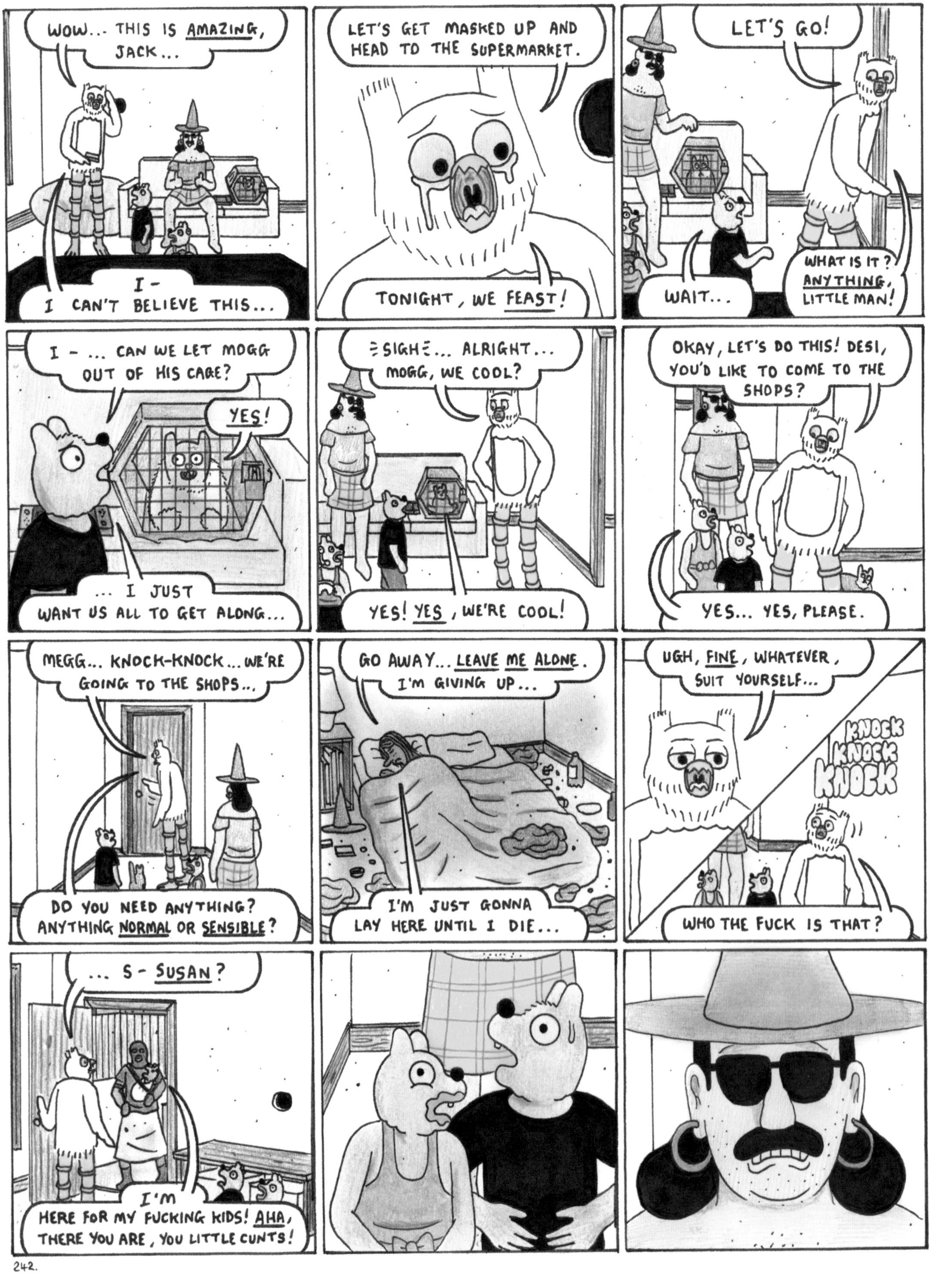
WOW... THIS IS AMAZING, JACK...
I - I CAN'T BELIEVE THIS...
LET'S GET MASKED UP AND HEAD TO THE SUPERMARKET.
TONIGHT, WE FEAST!
LET'S GO!
WAIT...
WHAT IS IT? ANYTHING, LITTLE MAN!
I - ... CAN WE LET MOGG OUT OF HIS CAGE?
YES!
... I JUST WANT US ALL TO GET ALONG...
=SIGH=... ALRIGHT... MOGG, WE COOL?
YES! YES, WE'RE COOL!
OKAY, LET'S DO THIS! DESI, YOU'D LIKE TO COME TO THE SHOPS?
YES... YES, PLEASE.
MEGG... KNOCK-KNOCK... WE'RE GOING TO THE SHOPS...
DO YOU NEED ANYTHING? ANYTHING NORMAL OR SENSIBLE?
GO AWAY... LEAVE ME ALONE. I'M GIVING UP...
I'M JUST GONNA LAY HERE UNTIL I DIE...
UGH, FINE, WHATEVER, SUIT YOURSELF...
KNOCK KNOCK KNOCK
WHO THE FUCK IS THAT?
... S- SUSAN?
I'M HERE FOR MY FUCKING KIDS! AHA, THERE YOU ARE, YOU LITTLE CUNTS!

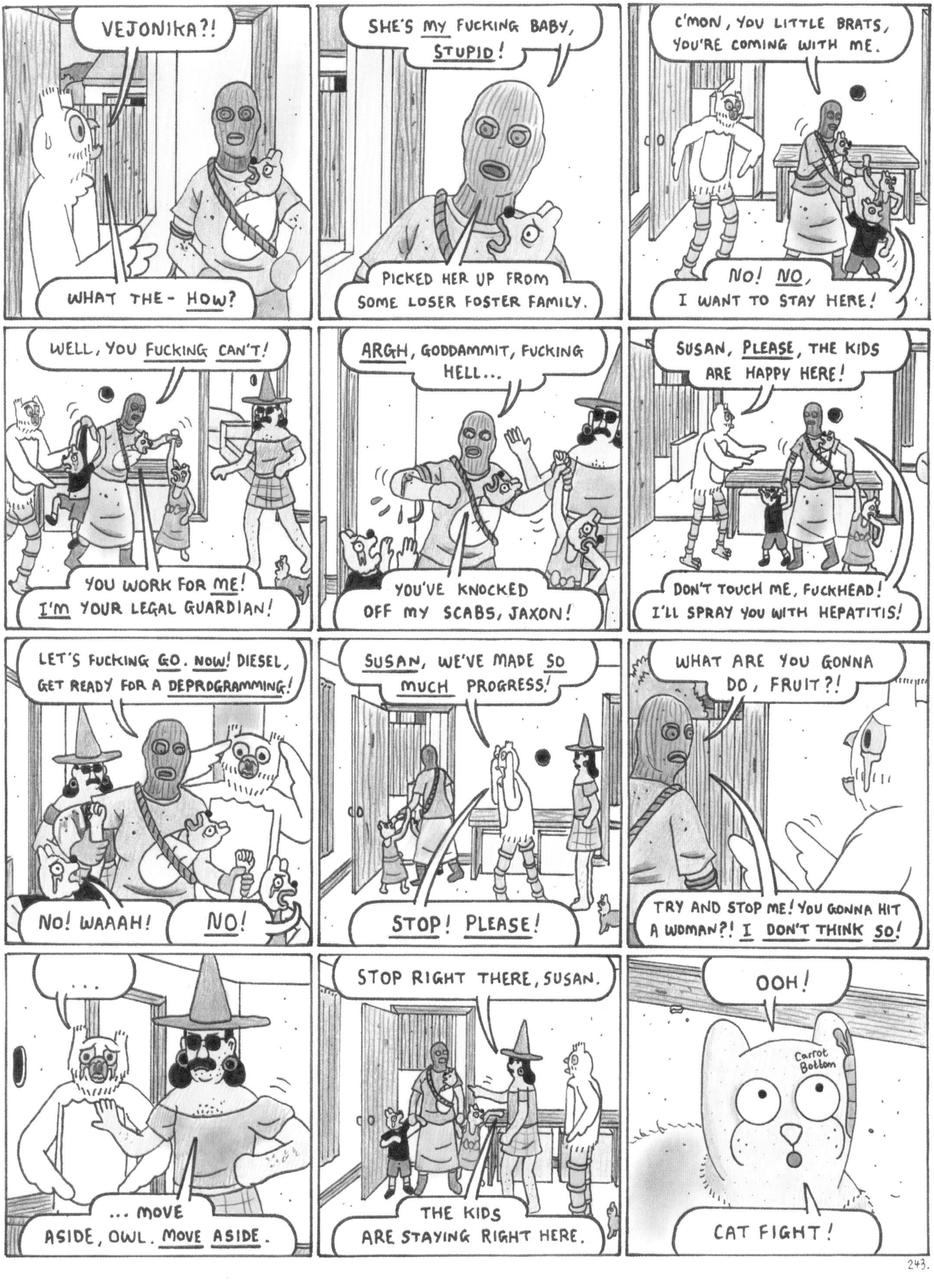
VEJONIKA?!
WHAT THE- HOW?
SHE'S MY FUCKING BABY, STUPID!
PICKED HER UP FROM SOME LOSER FOSTER FAMILY.
C'MON, YOU LITTLE BRATS, YOU'RE COMING WITH ME.
NO! NO, I WANT TO STAY HERE!
WELL, YOU FUCKING CAN'T!
YOU WORK FOR ME! I'M YOUR LEGAL GUARDIAN!
ARGH, GODDAMMIT, FUCKING HELL...
YOU'VE KNOCKED OFF MY SCABS, JAXON!
SUSAN, PLEASE, THE KIDS ARE HAPPY HERE!
DON'T TOUCH ME, FUCKHEAD! I'LL SPRAY YOU WITH HEPATITIS!
LET'S FUCKING GO. NOW! DIESEL, GET READY FOR A DEPROGRAMMING!
NO! WAAAH!
NO!
SUSAN, WE'VE MADE SO MUCH PROGRESS!
STOP! PLEASE!
WHAT ARE YOU GONNA DO, FRUIT?!
TRY AND STOP ME! YOU GONNA HIT A WOMAN?! I DON'T THINK SO!
...
... MOVE ASIDE, OWL. MOVE ASIDE.
STOP RIGHT THERE, SUSAN.
THE KIDS ARE STAYING RIGHT HERE.
OOH!
Carrot Bottom
CAT FIGHT!

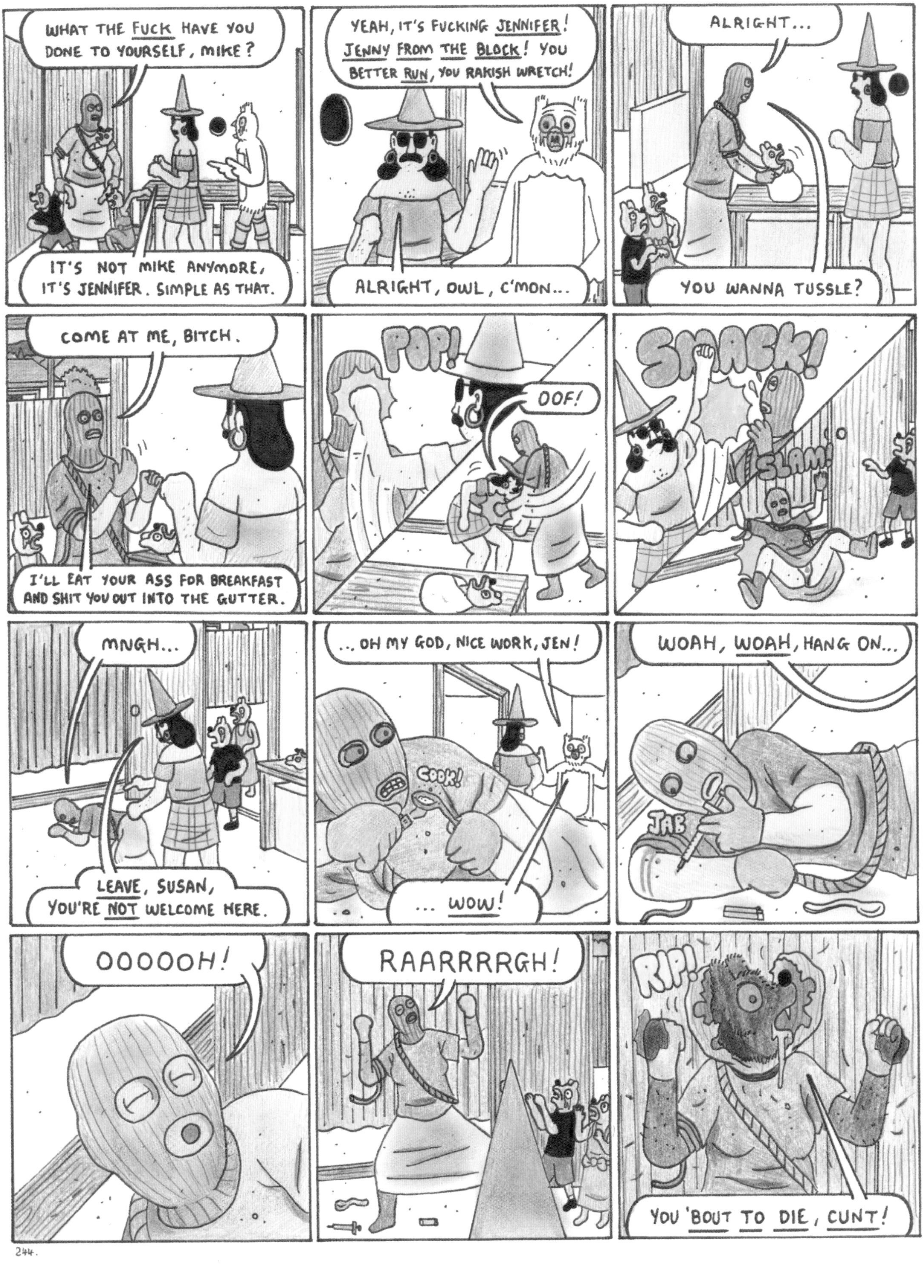
WHAT THE FUCK HAVE YOU DONE TO YOURSELF, MIKE?
IT'S NOT MIKE ANYMORE, IT'S JENNIFER. SIMPLE AS THAT.
YEAH, IT'S FUCKING JENNIFER! JENNY FROM THE BLOCK! YOU BETTER RUN, YOU RAKISH WRETCH!
ALRIGHT, OWL, C'MON...
ALRIGHT...
YOU WANNA TUSSLE?
COME AT ME, BITCH.
I'LL EAT YOUR ASS FOR BREAKFAST AND SHIT YOU OUT INTO THE GUTTER.
POP!
OOF!
SMACK!
SLAM!
MNGH...
LEAVE, SUSAN, YOU'RE NOT WELCOME HERE.
... OH MY GOD, NICE WORK, JEN!
COOK!
... WOW!
WOAH, WOAH, HANG ON...
JAB
OOOOOH!
RAARRRRGH!
RIP!
YOU 'BOUT TO DIE, CUNT!

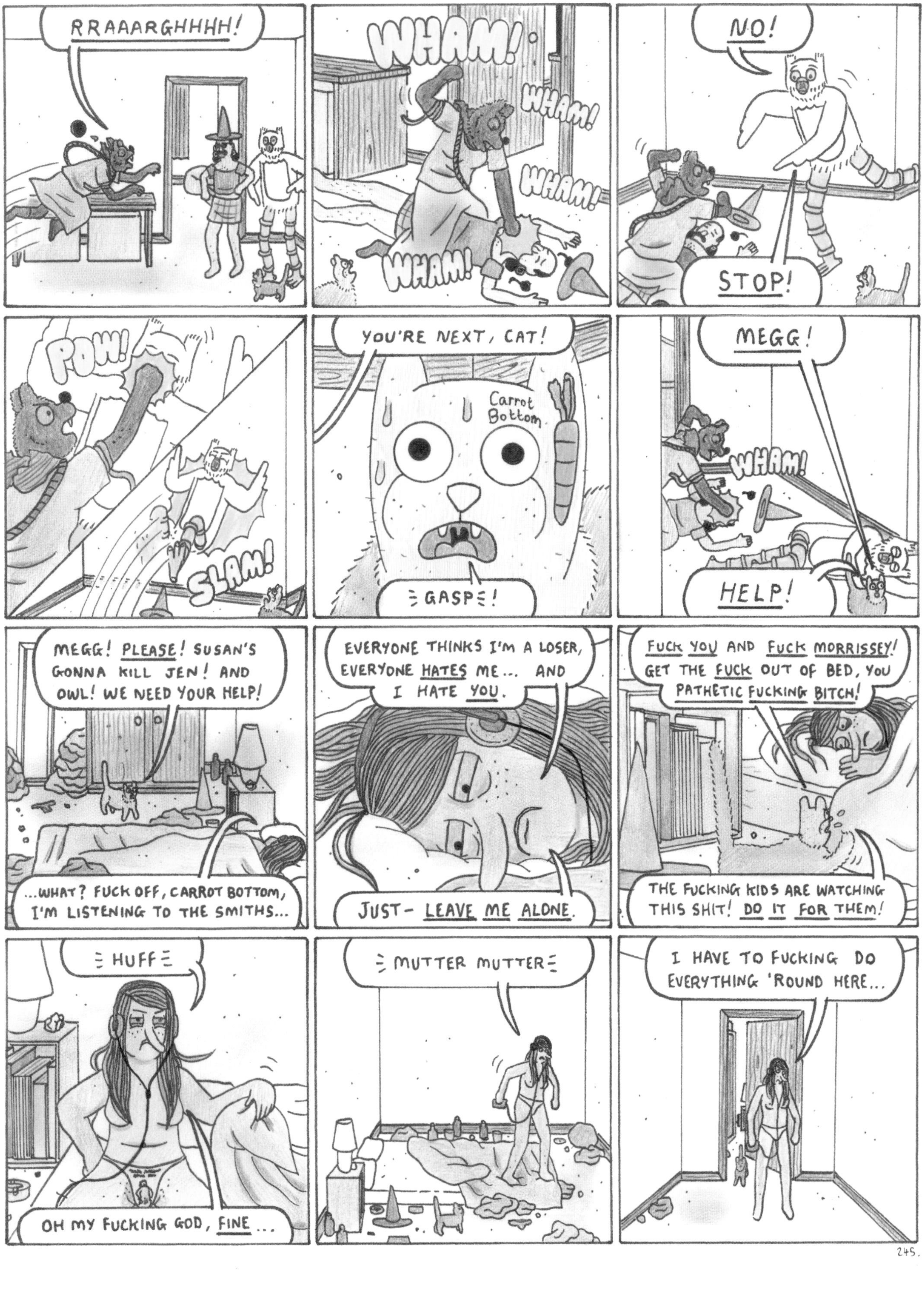
RRAAARGHHHH!
WHAM!
WHAM!
WHAM!
WHAM!
NO!
STOP!
POW!
SLAM!
YOU'RE NEXT, CAT!
Carrot Bottom
GASP!
MEGG!
WHAM!
HELP!
MEGG! PLEASE! SUSAN'S GONNA KILL JEN! AND OWL! WE NEED YOUR HELP!
...WHAT? FUCK OFF, CARROT BOTTOM, I'M LISTENING TO THE SMITHS...
EVERYONE THINKS I'M A LOSER, EVERYONE HATES ME... AND I HATE YOU.
JUST- LEAVE ME ALONE.
FUCK YOU AND FUCK MORRISSEY! GET THE FUCK OUT OF BED, YOU PATHETIC FUCKING BITCH!
THE FUCKING KIDS ARE WATCHING THIS SHIT! DO IT FOR THEM!
HUFF
OH MY FUCKING GOD, FINE...
MUTTER MUTTER
I HAVE TO FUCKING DO EVERYTHING 'ROUND HERE...

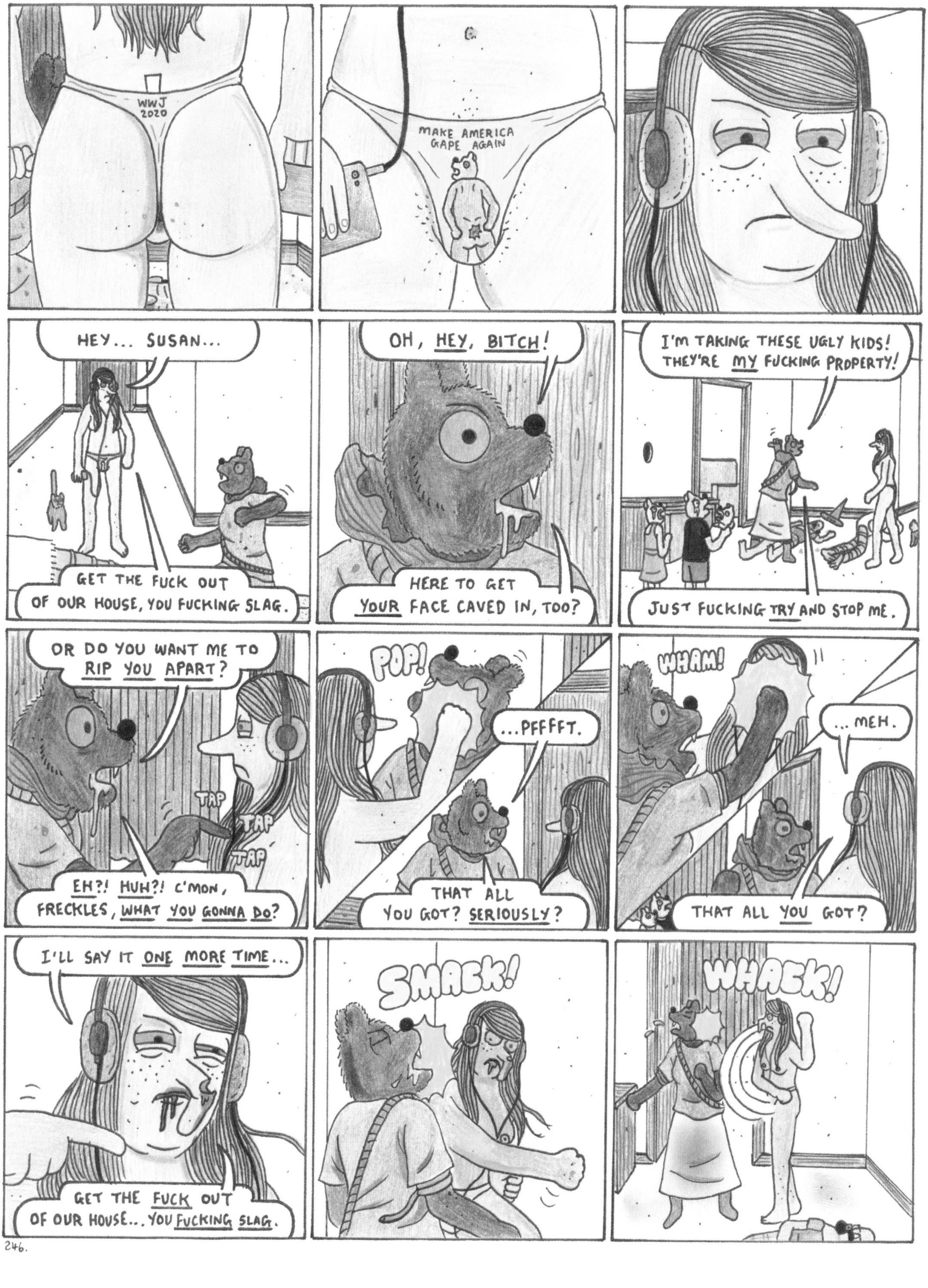
WWJ 2020
MAKE AMERICA GAPE AGAIN
HEY... SUSAN...
GET THE FUCK OUT OF OUR HOUSE, YOU FUCKING SLAG.
OH, HEY, BITCH!
HERE TO GET YOUR FACE CAVED IN, TOO?
I'M TAKING THESE UGLY KIDS! THEY'RE MY FUCKING PROPERTY!
JUST FUCKING TRY AND STOP ME.
OR DO YOU WANT ME TO RIP YOU APART?
TAP
TAP
TAP
EH?! HUH?! C'MON, FRECKLES, WHAT YOU GONNA DO?
POP!
...PFFFFT.
THAT ALL YOU GOT? SERIOUSLY?
WHAM!
...MEH.
THAT ALL YOU GOT?
I'LL SAY IT ONE MORE TIME...
GET THE FUCK OUT OF OUR HOUSE... YOU FUCKING SLAG.
SMACK!
WHACK!

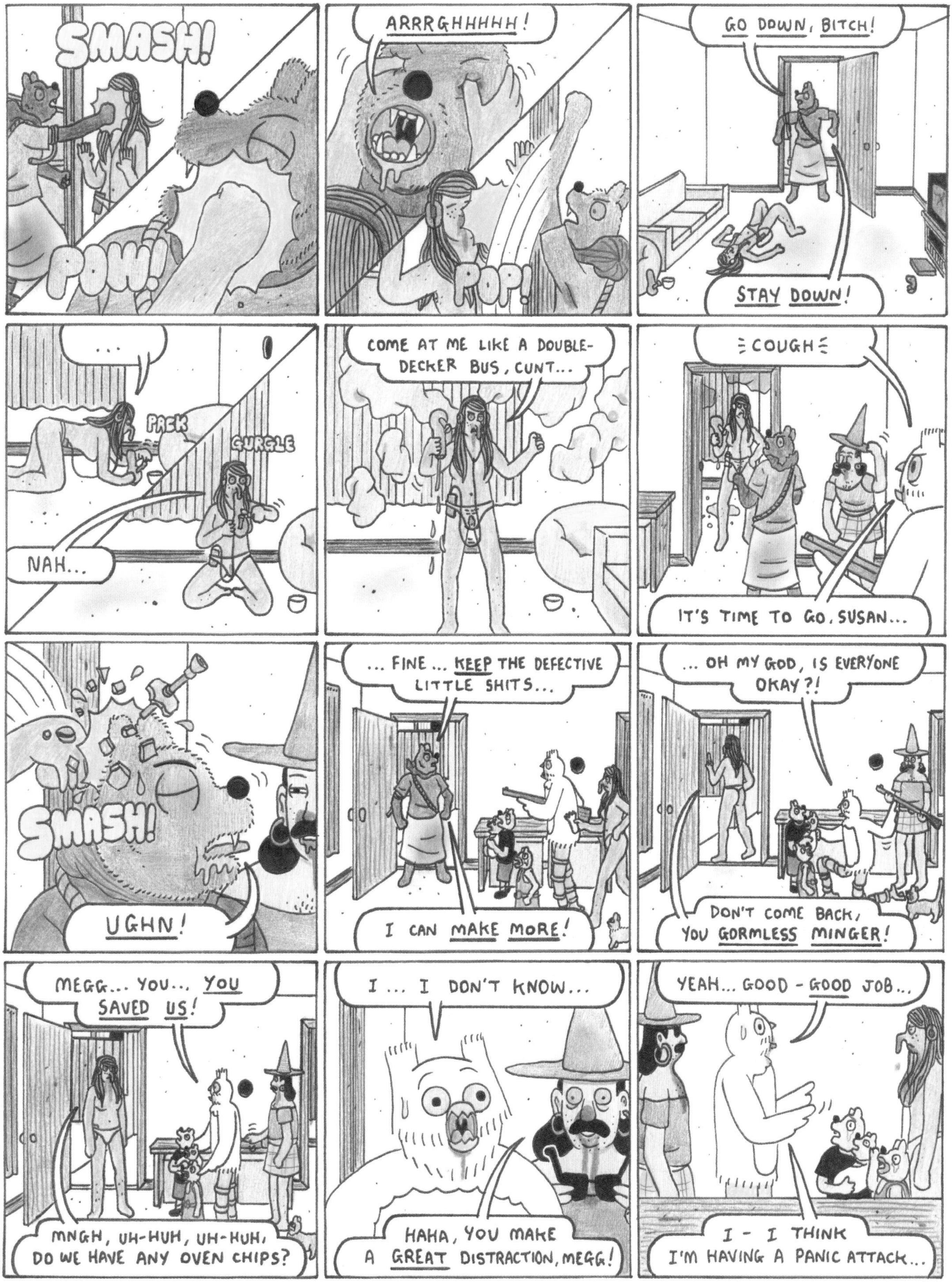
SMASH!
POW!
ARRRGHHHHH!
POP!
GO DOWN, BITCH!
STAY DOWN!
...
PACK
GURGLE
NAH...
COME AT ME LIKE A DOUBLE-DECKER BUS, CUNT...
COUGH
IT'S TIME TO GO, SUSAN...
SMASH!
UGHN!
... FINE ... KEEP THE DEFECTIVE LITTLE SHITS...
I CAN MAKE MORE!
... OH MY GOD, IS EVERYONE OKAY?!
DON'T COME BACK, YOU GORMLESS MINGER!
MEGG... YOU... YOU SAVED US!
MNGH, UH-HUH, UH-HUH, DO WE HAVE ANY OVEN CHIPS?
I ... I DON'T KNOW...
HAHA, YOU MAKE A GREAT DISTRACTION, MEGG!
YEAH... GOOD - GOOD JOB...
I - I THINK I'M HAVING A PANIC ATTACK...

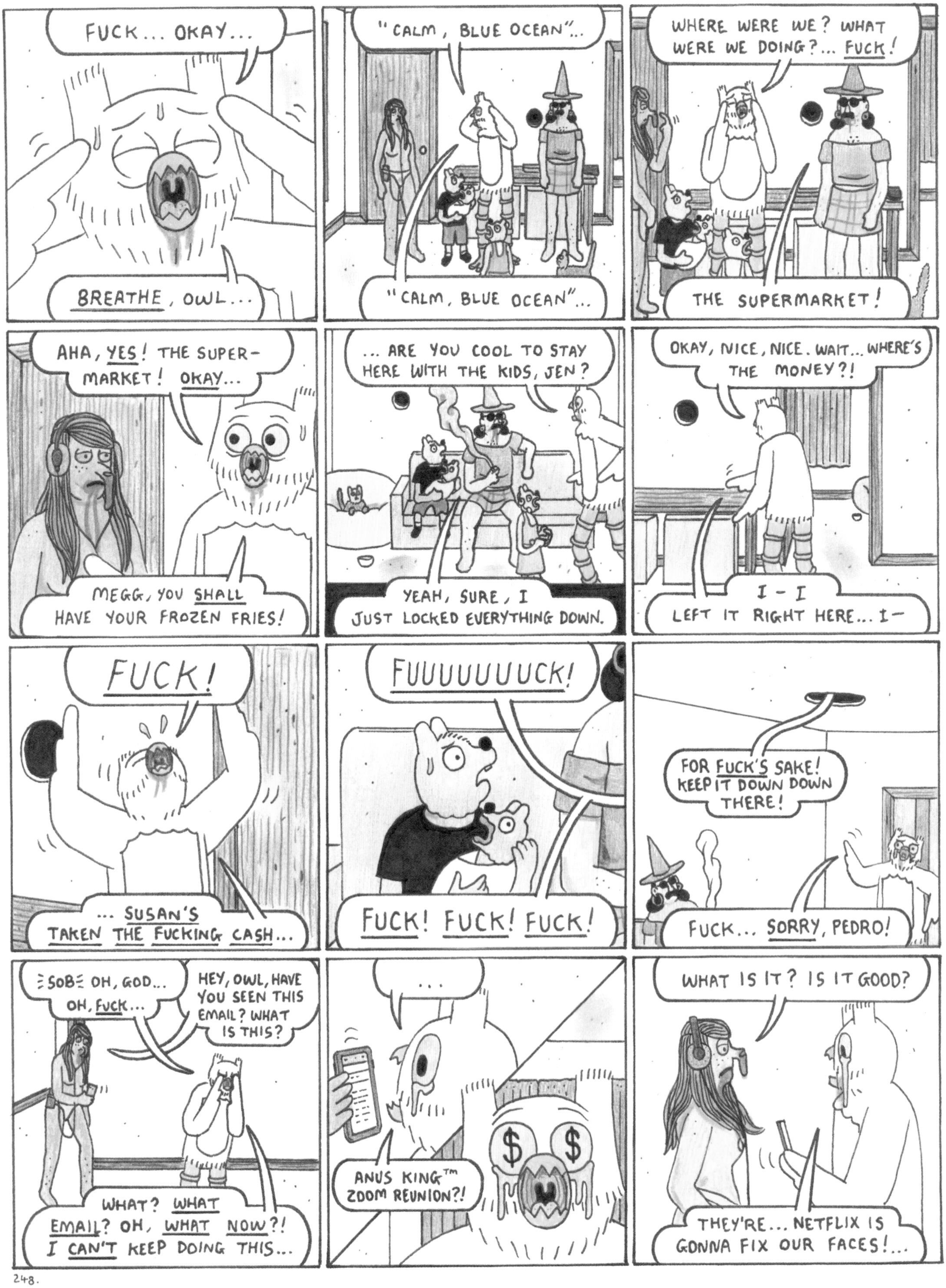
FUCK... OKAY...
BREATHE, OWL...
"CALM, BLUE OCEAN"...
"CALM, BLUE OCEAN"...
WHERE WERE WE? WHAT WERE WE DOING?... FUCK!
THE SUPERMARKET!
AHA, YES! THE SUPER-MARKET! OKAY...
MEGG, YOU SHALL HAVE YOUR FROZEN FRIES!
... ARE YOU COOL TO STAY HERE WITH THE KIDS, JEN?
YEAH, SURE, I JUST LOCKED EVERYTHING DOWN.
OKAY, NICE, NICE. WAIT... WHERE'S THE MONEY?!
I - I LEFT IT RIGHT HERE... I-
FUCK!
... SUSAN'S TAKEN THE FUCKING CASH...
FUUUUUUUCK!
FUCK! FUCK! FUCK!
FOR FUCK'S SAKE! KEEP IT DOWN DOWN THERE!
FUCK... SORRY, PEDRO!
≡SOB≡ OH, GOD... OH, FUCK...
HEY, OWL, HAVE YOU SEEN THIS EMAIL? WHAT IS THIS?
WHAT? WHAT EMAIL? OH, WHAT NOW?! I CAN'T KEEP DOING THIS...
...
ANUS KING™ ZOOM REUNION?!
WHAT IS IT? IS IT GOOD?
THEY'RE... NETFLIX IS GONNA FIX OUR FACES!...

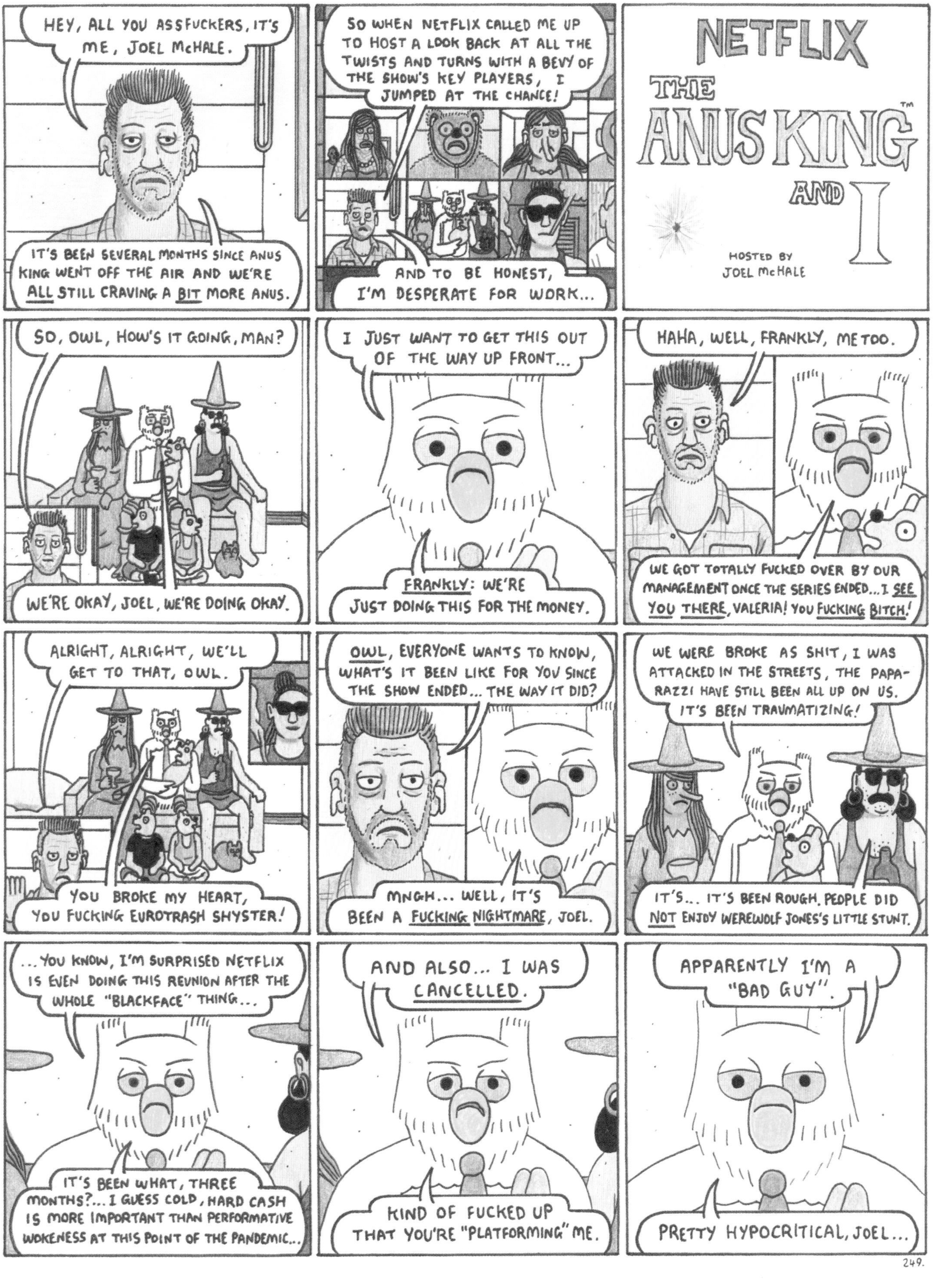
HEY, ALL YOU ASSFUCKERS, IT'S ME, JOEL McHALE.
IT'S BEEN SEVERAL MONTHS SINCE ANUS KING WENT OFF THE AIR AND WE'RE ALL STILL CRAVING A BIT MORE ANUS.
SO WHEN NETFLIX CALLED ME UP TO HOST A LOOK BACK AT ALL THE TWISTS AND TURNS WITH A BEVY OF THE SHOW'S KEY PLAYERS, I JUMPED AT THE CHANCE!
AND TO BE HONEST, I'M DESPERATE FOR WORK...
NETFLIX
THE ANUS KING AND I
TM
HOSTED BY JOEL McHALE
SO, OWL, HOW'S IT GOING, MAN?
WE'RE OKAY, JOEL, WE'RE DOING OKAY.
I JUST WANT TO GET THIS OUT OF THE WAY UP FRONT...
FRANKLY: WE'RE JUST DOING THIS FOR THE MONEY.
HAHA, WELL, FRANKLY, ME TOO.
WE GOT TOTALLY FUCKED OVER BY OUR MANAGEMENT ONCE THE SERIES ENDED... I SEE YOU THERE, VALERIA! YOU FUCKING BITCH!
ALRIGHT, ALRIGHT, WE'LL GET TO THAT, OWL.
YOU BROKE MY HEART, YOU FUCKING EUROTRASH SHYSTER!
OWL, EVERYONE WANTS TO KNOW, WHAT'S IT BEEN LIKE FOR YOU SINCE THE SHOW ENDED... THE WAY IT DID?
MNGH... WELL, IT'S BEEN A FUCKING NIGHTMARE, JOEL.
WE WERE BROKE AS SHIT, I WAS ATTACKED IN THE STREETS, THE PAPARAZZI HAVE STILL BEEN ALL UP ON US. IT'S BEEN TRAUMATIZING!
IT'S... IT'S BEEN ROUGH. PEOPLE DID NOT ENJOY WEREWOLF JONES'S LITTLE STUNT.
...YOU KNOW, I'M SURPRISED NETFLIX IS EVEN DOING THIS REUNION AFTER THE WHOLE "BLACKFACE" THING...
IT'S BEEN WHAT, THREE MONTHS?... I GUESS COLD, HARD CASH IS MORE IMPORTANT THAN PERFORMATIVE WOKENESS AT THIS POINT OF THE PANDEMIC...
AND ALSO... I WAS CANCELLED.
KIND OF FUCKED UP THAT YOU'RE "PLATFORMING" ME.
APPARENTLY I'M A "BAD GUY".
PRETTY HYPOCRITICAL, JOEL...

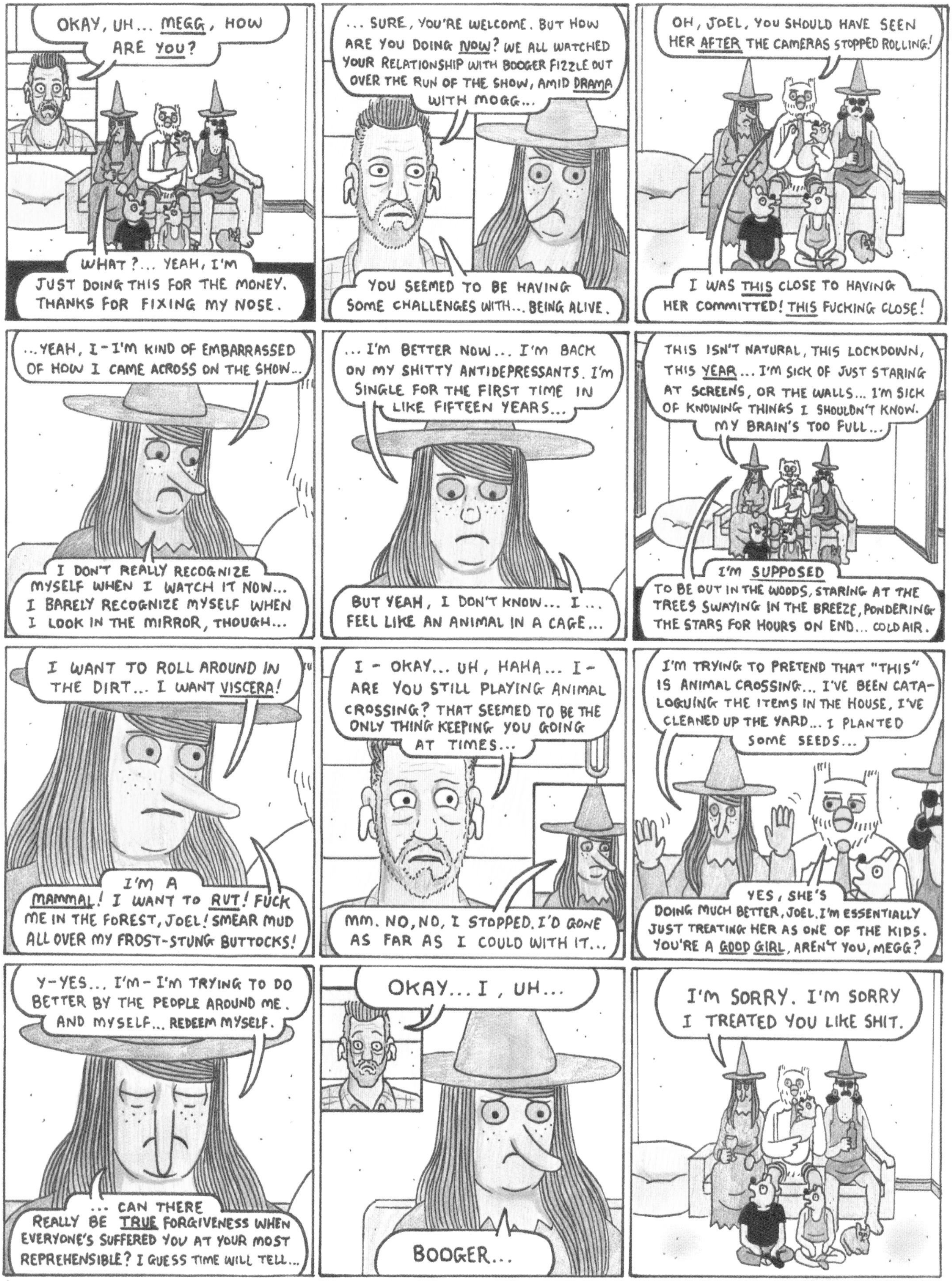
OKAY, UH... MEGG, HOW ARE YOU?
WHAT?... YEAH, I'M JUST DOING THIS FOR THE MONEY. THANKS FOR FIXING MY NOSE.
... SURE, YOU'RE WELCOME. BUT HOW ARE YOU DOING NOW? WE ALL WATCHED YOUR RELATIONSHIP WITH BOOGER FIZZLE OUT OVER THE RUN OF THE SHOW, AMID DRAMA WITH MOGG...
YOU SEEMED TO BE HAVING SOME CHALLENGES WITH... BEING ALIVE.
OH, JOEL, YOU SHOULD HAVE SEEN HER AFTER THE CAMERAS STOPPED ROLLING!
I WAS THIS CLOSE TO HAVING HER COMMITTED! THIS FUCKING CLOSE!
...YEAH, I-I'M KIND OF EMBARRASSED OF HOW I CAME ACROSS ON THE SHOW...
I DON'T REALLY RECOGNIZE MYSELF WHEN I WATCH IT NOW... I BARELY RECOGNIZE MYSELF WHEN I LOOK IN THE MIRROR, THOUGH...
... I'M BETTER NOW... I'M BACK ON MY SHITTY ANTIDEPRESSANTS. I'M SINGLE FOR THE FIRST TIME IN LIKE FIFTEEN YEARS...
BUT YEAH, I DON'T KNOW... I... FEEL LIKE AN ANIMAL IN A CAGE...
THIS ISN'T NATURAL, THIS LOCKDOWN, THIS YEAR... I'M SICK OF JUST STARING AT SCREENS, OR THE WALLS... I'M SICK OF KNOWING THINGS I SHOULDN'T KNOW. MY BRAIN'S TOO FULL...
I'M SUPPOSED TO BE OUT IN THE WOODS, STARING AT THE TREES SWAYING IN THE BREEZE, PONDERING THE STARS FOR HOURS ON END... COLD AIR.
I WANT TO ROLL AROUND IN THE DIRT... I WANT VISCERA!
I'M A MAMMAL! I WANT TO RUT! FUCK ME IN THE FOREST, JOEL! SMEAR MUD ALL OVER MY FROST-STUNG BUTTOCKS!
I - OKAY... UH, HAHA... I - ARE YOU STILL PLAYING ANIMAL CROSSING? THAT SEEMED TO BE THE ONLY THING KEEPING YOU GOING AT TIMES...
MM. NO, NO, I STOPPED. I'D GONE AS FAR AS I COULD WITH IT...
I'M TRYING TO PRETEND THAT "THIS" IS ANIMAL CROSSING... I'VE BEEN CATALOGUING THE ITEMS IN THE HOUSE, I'VE CLEANED UP THE YARD... I PLANTED SOME SEEDS...
YES, SHE'S DOING MUCH BETTER, JOEL. I'M ESSENTIALLY JUST TREATING HER AS ONE OF THE KIDS. YOU'RE A GOOD GIRL, AREN'T YOU, MEGG?
Y-YES... I'M- I'M TRYING TO DO BETTER BY THE PEOPLE AROUND ME. AND MYSELF... REDEEM MYSELF.
... CAN THERE REALLY BE TRUE FORGIVENESS WHEN EVERYONE'S SUFFERED YOU AT YOUR MOST REPREHENSIBLE? I GUESS TIME WILL TELL...
OKAY... I, UH...
BOOGER...
I'M SORRY. I'M SORRY I TREATED YOU LIKE SHIT.

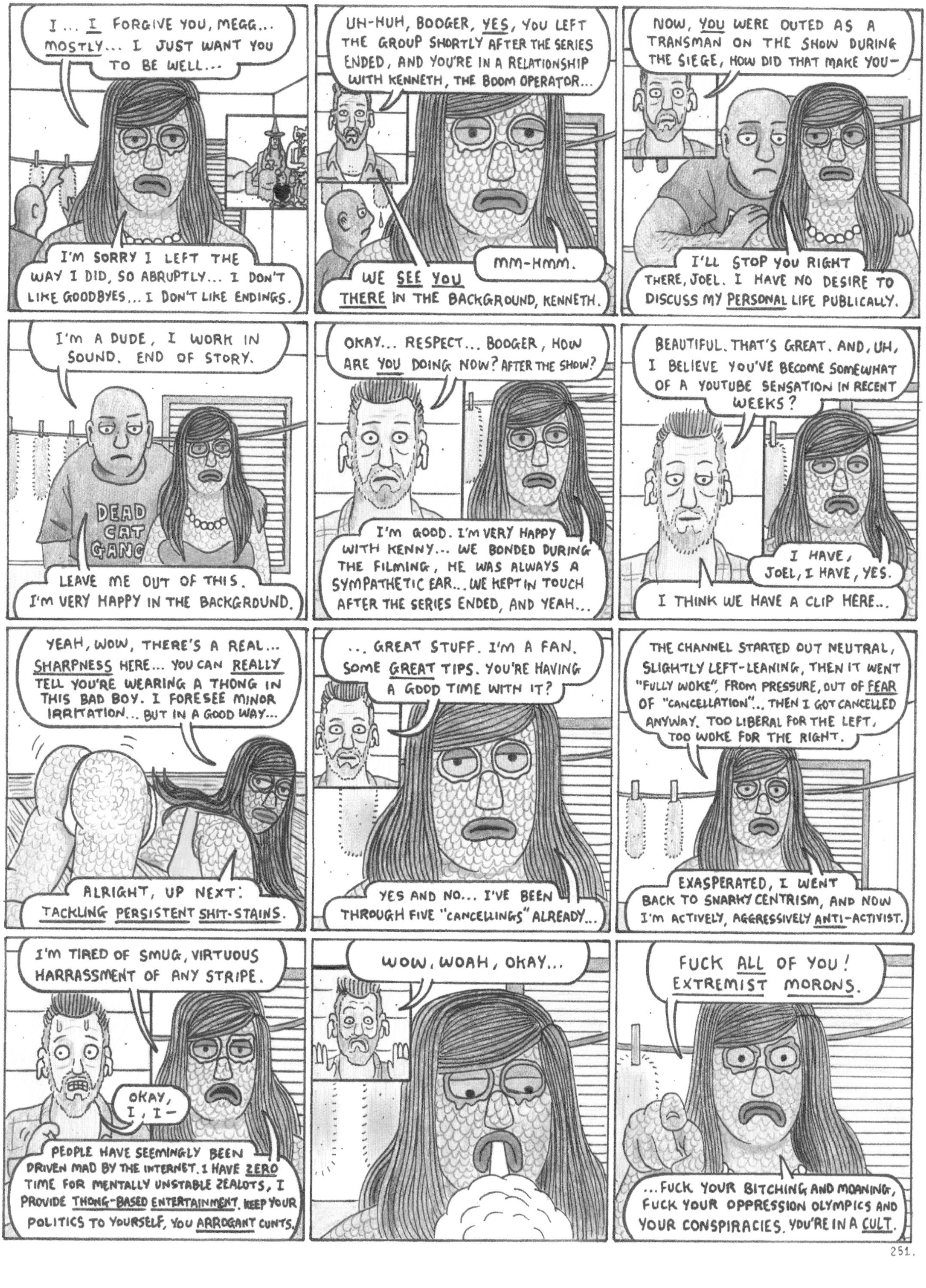
I... I FORGIVE YOU, MEGG... MOSTLY... I JUST WANT YOU TO BE WELL...
I'M SORRY I LEFT THE WAY I DID, SO ABRUPTLY... I DON'T LIKE GOODBYES... I DON'T LIKE ENDINGS.
UH-HUH, BOOGER, YES, YOU LEFT THE GROUP SHORTLY AFTER THE SERIES ENDED, AND YOU'RE IN A RELATIONSHIP WITH KENNETH, THE BOOM OPERATOR...
MM-HMM.
WE SEE YOU THERE IN THE BACKGROUND, KENNETH.
NOW, YOU WERE OUTED AS A TRANSMAN ON THE SHOW DURING THE SIEGE, HOW DID THAT MAKE YOU—
I'LL STOP YOU RIGHT THERE, JOEL. I HAVE NO DESIRE TO DISCUSS MY PERSONAL LIFE PUBLICALLY.
I'M A DUDE, I WORK IN SOUND. END OF STORY.
DEAD CAT GANG
LEAVE ME OUT OF THIS. I'M VERY HAPPY IN THE BACKGROUND.
OKAY... RESPECT... BOOGER, HOW ARE YOU DOING NOW? AFTER THE SHOW?
I'M GOOD. I'M VERY HAPPY WITH KENNY... WE BONDED DURING THE FILMING, HE WAS ALWAYS A SYMPATHETIC EAR... WE KEPT IN TOUCH AFTER THE SERIES ENDED, AND YEAH...
BEAUTIFUL. THAT'S GREAT. AND, UH, I BELIEVE YOU'VE BECOME SOMEWHAT OF A YOUTUBE SENSATION IN RECENT WEEKS?
I HAVE, JOEL, I HAVE, YES.
I THINK WE HAVE A CLIP HERE...
YEAH, WOW, THERE'S A REAL... SHARPNESS HERE... YOU CAN REALLY TELL YOU'RE WEARING A THONG IN THIS BAD BOY. I FORESEE MINOR IRRITATION... BUT IN A GOOD WAY...
ALRIGHT, UP NEXT: TACKLING PERSISTENT SHIT-STAINS.
... GREAT STUFF. I'M A FAN. SOME GREAT TIPS. YOU'RE HAVING A GOOD TIME WITH IT?
YES AND NO... I'VE BEEN THROUGH FIVE "CANCELLINGS" ALREADY...
THE CHANNEL STARTED OUT NEUTRAL, SLIGHTLY LEFT-LEANING, THEN IT WENT "FULLY WOKE", FROM PRESSURE, OUT OF FEAR OF "CANCELLATION"... THEN I GOT CANCELLED ANYWAY. TOO LIBERAL FOR THE LEFT, TOO WOKE FOR THE RIGHT.
EXASPERATED, I WENT BACK TO SNARKY CENTRISM, AND NOW I'M ACTIVELY, AGGRESSIVELY ANTI-ACTIVIST.
I'M TIRED OF SMUG, VIRTUOUS HARRASSMENT OF ANY STRIPE.
OKAY, I, I—
PEOPLE HAVE SEEMINGLY BEEN DRIVEN MAD BY THE INTERNET. I HAVE ZERO TIME FOR MENTALLY UNSTABLE ZEALOTS, I PROVIDE THONG-BASED ENTERTAINMENT. KEEP YOUR POLITICS TO YOURSELF, YOU ARROGANT CUNTS.
WOW, WOAH, OKAY...
FUCK ALL OF YOU! EXTREMIST MORONS.
...FUCK YOUR BITCHING AND MOANING, FUCK YOUR OPPRESSION OLYMPICS AND YOUR CONSPIRACIES. YOU'RE IN A CULT.

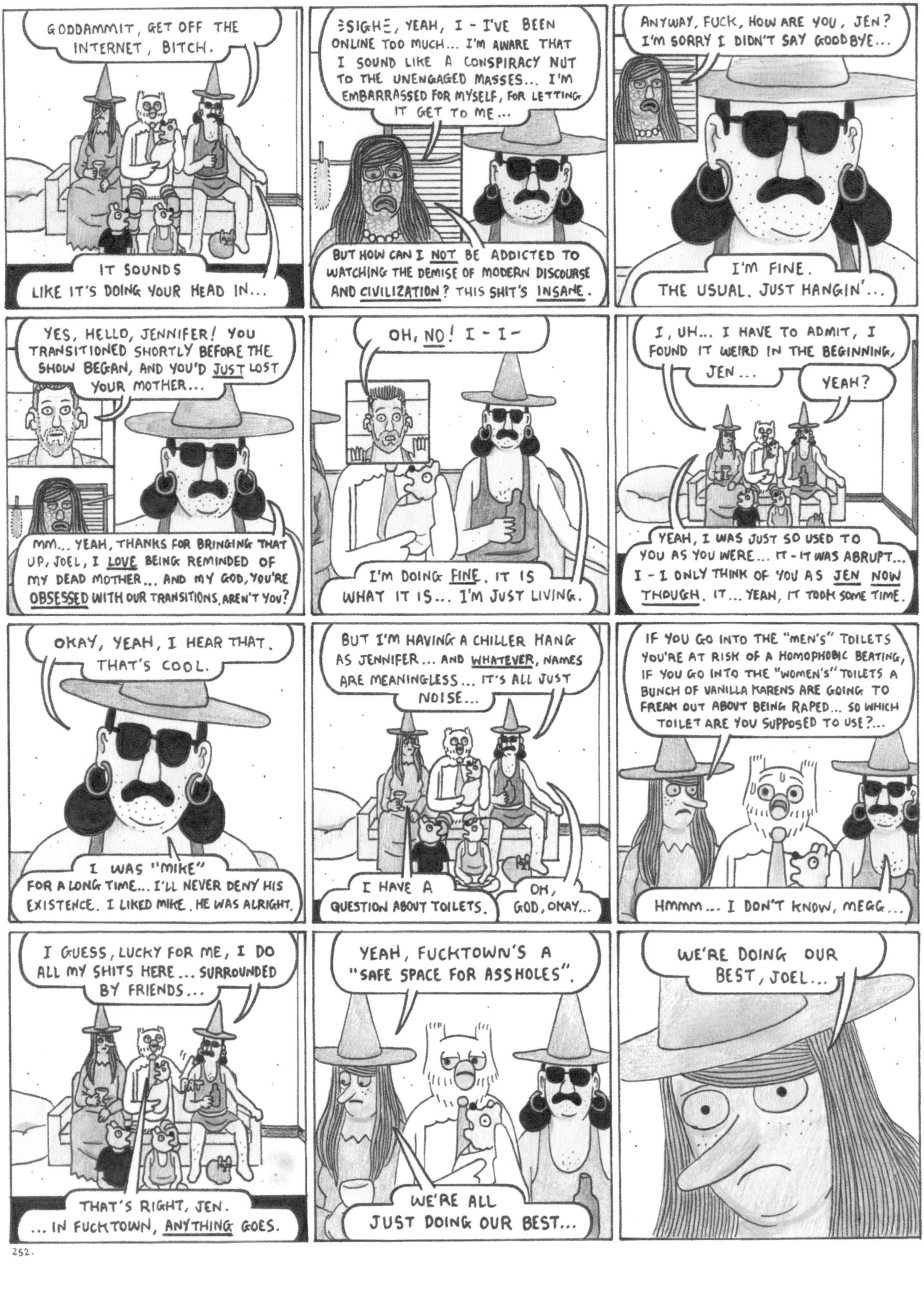
GODDAMMIT, GET OFF THE INTERNET, BITCH.
IT SOUNDS LIKE IT'S DOING YOUR HEAD IN...
SIGH, YEAH, I - I'VE BEEN ONLINE TOO MUCH... I'M AWARE THAT I SOUND LIKE A CONSPIRACY NUT TO THE UNENGAGED MASSES... I'M EMBARRASSED FOR MYSELF, FOR LETTING IT GET TO ME...
BUT HOW CAN I NOT BE ADDICTED TO WATCHING THE DEMISE OF MODERN DISCOURSE AND CIVILIZATION? THIS SHIT'S INSANE.
ANYWAY, FUCK, HOW ARE YOU, JEN? I'M SORRY I DIDN'T SAY GOODBYE...
I'M FINE. THE USUAL. JUST HANGIN'...
YES, HELLO, JENNIFER! YOU TRANSITIONED SHORTLY BEFORE THE SHOW BEGAN, AND YOU'D JUST LOST YOUR MOTHER...
MM... YEAH, THANKS FOR BRINGING THAT UP, JOEL, I LOVE BEING REMINDED OF MY DEAD MOTHER... AND MY GOD, YOU'RE OBSESSED WITH OUR TRANSITIONS, AREN'T YOU?
OH, NO! I - I-
I'M DOING FINE. IT IS WHAT IT IS... I'M JUST LIVING.
I, UH... I HAVE TO ADMIT, I FOUND IT WEIRD IN THE BEGINNING, JEN...
YEAH?
YEAH, I WAS JUST SO USED TO YOU AS YOU WERE... IT - IT WAS ABRUPT... I - I ONLY THINK OF YOU AS JEN NOW THOUGH. IT... YEAH, IT TOOK SOME TIME.
OKAY, YEAH, I HEAR THAT. THAT'S COOL.
I WAS "MIKE" FOR A LONG TIME... I'LL NEVER DENY HIS EXISTENCE. I LIKED MIKE. HE WAS ALRIGHT.
BUT I'M HAVING A CHILLER HANG AS JENNIFER... AND WHATEVER, NAMES ARE MEANINGLESS... IT'S ALL JUST NOISE...
I HAVE A QUESTION ABOUT TOILETS.
OH, GOD, OKAY...
IF YOU GO INTO THE "MEN'S" TOILETS YOU'RE AT RISK OF A HOMOPHOBIC BEATING, IF YOU GO INTO THE "WOMEN'S" TOILETS A BUNCH OF VANILLA KARENS ARE GOING TO FREAK OUT ABOUT BEING RAPED... SO WHICH TOILET ARE YOU SUPPOSED TO USE?...
HMMM... I DON'T KNOW, MEGG...
I GUESS, LUCKY FOR ME, I DO ALL MY SHITS HERE... SURROUNDED BY FRIENDS...
THAT'S RIGHT, JEN. ... IN FUCKTOWN, ANYTHING GOES.
YEAH, FUCKTOWN'S A "SAFE SPACE FOR ASSHOLES".
WE'RE ALL JUST DOING OUR BEST...
WE'RE DOING OUR BEST, JOEL...

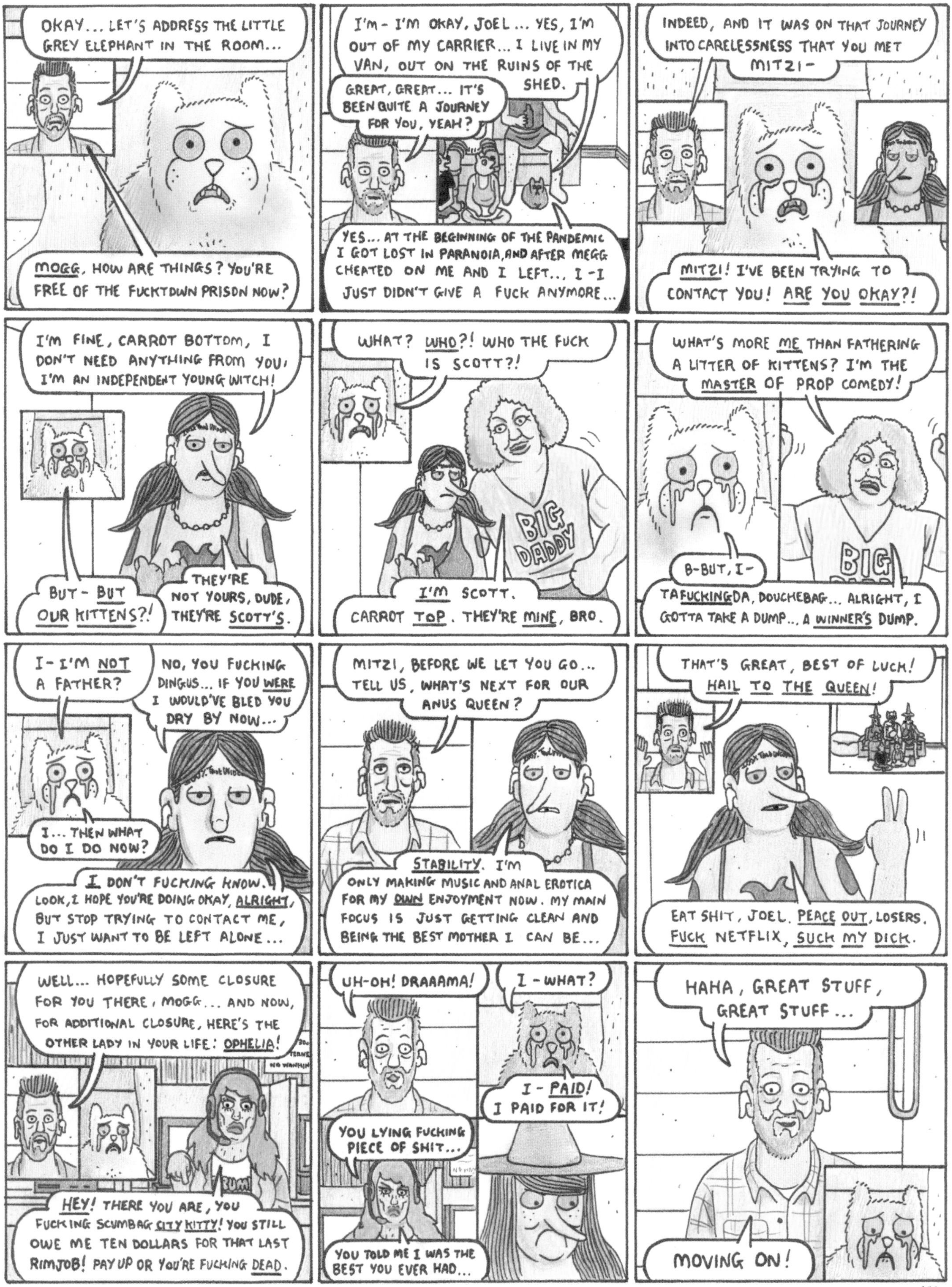
OKAY... LET'S ADDRESS THE LITTLE GREY ELEPHANT IN THE ROOM...
MOGG, HOW ARE THINGS? YOU'RE FREE OF THE FUCKTOWN PRISON NOW?
I'M- I'M OKAY, JOEL... YES, I'M OUT OF MY CARRIER... I LIVE IN MY VAN, OUT ON THE RUINS OF THE SHED.
GREAT, GREAT... IT'S BEEN QUITE A JOURNEY FOR YOU, YEAH?
YES... AT THE BEGINNING OF THE PANDEMIC I GOT LOST IN PARANOIA, AND AFTER MEGG CHEATED ON ME AND I LEFT... I-I JUST DIDN'T GIVE A FUCK ANYMORE...
INDEED, AND IT WAS ON THAT JOURNEY INTO CARELESSNESS THAT YOU MET MITZI-
MITZI! I'VE BEEN TRYING TO CONTACT YOU! ARE YOU OKAY?!
I'M FINE, CARROT BOTTOM, I DON'T NEED ANYTHING FROM YOU, I'M AN INDEPENDENT YOUNG WITCH!
BUT- BUT OUR KITTENS?!
THEY'RE NOT YOURS, DUDE, THEY'RE SCOTT'S.
WHAT? WHO?! WHO THE FUCK IS SCOTT?!
BIG DADDY
I'M SCOTT. CARROT TOP. THEY'RE MINE, BRO.
WHAT'S MORE ME THAN FATHERING A LITTER OF KITTENS? I'M THE MASTER OF PROP COMEDY!
B-BUT, I-
TAFUCKINGDA, DOUCHEBAG... ALRIGHT, I GOTTA TAKE A DUMP... A WINNER'S DUMP.
I- I'M NOT A FATHER?
NO, YOU FUCKING DINGUS... IF YOU WERE I WOULD'VE BLED YOU DRY BY NOW...
I... THEN WHAT DO I DO NOW?
I DON'T FUCKING KNOW. LOOK, I HOPE YOU'RE DOING OKAY, ALRIGHT, BUT STOP TRYING TO CONTACT ME, I JUST WANT TO BE LEFT ALONE...
MITZI, BEFORE WE LET YOU GO... TELL US, WHAT'S NEXT FOR OUR ANUS QUEEN?
STABILITY. I'M ONLY MAKING MUSIC AND ANAL EROTICA FOR MY OWN ENJOYMENT NOW. MY MAIN FOCUS IS JUST GETTING CLEAN AND BEING THE BEST MOTHER I CAN BE...
THAT'S GREAT, BEST OF LUCK! HAIL TO THE QUEEN!
EAT SHIT, JOEL. PEACE OUT, LOSERS. FUCK NETFLIX, SUCK MY DICK.
WELL... HOPEFULLY SOME CLOSURE FOR YOU THERE, MOGG... AND NOW, FOR ADDITIONAL CLOSURE, HERE'S THE OTHER LADY IN YOUR LIFE: OPHELIA!
HEY! THERE YOU ARE, YOU FUCKING SCUMBAG CITY KITTY! YOU STILL OWE ME TEN DOLLARS FOR THAT LAST RIMJOB! PAY UP OR YOU'RE FUCKING DEAD.
UH-OH! DRAAAMA!
I-WHAT?
I-PAID! I PAID FOR IT!
YOU LYING FUCKING PIECE OF SHIT...
YOU TOLD ME I WAS THE BEST YOU EVER HAD...
HAHA, GREAT STUFF, GREAT STUFF...
MOVING ON!

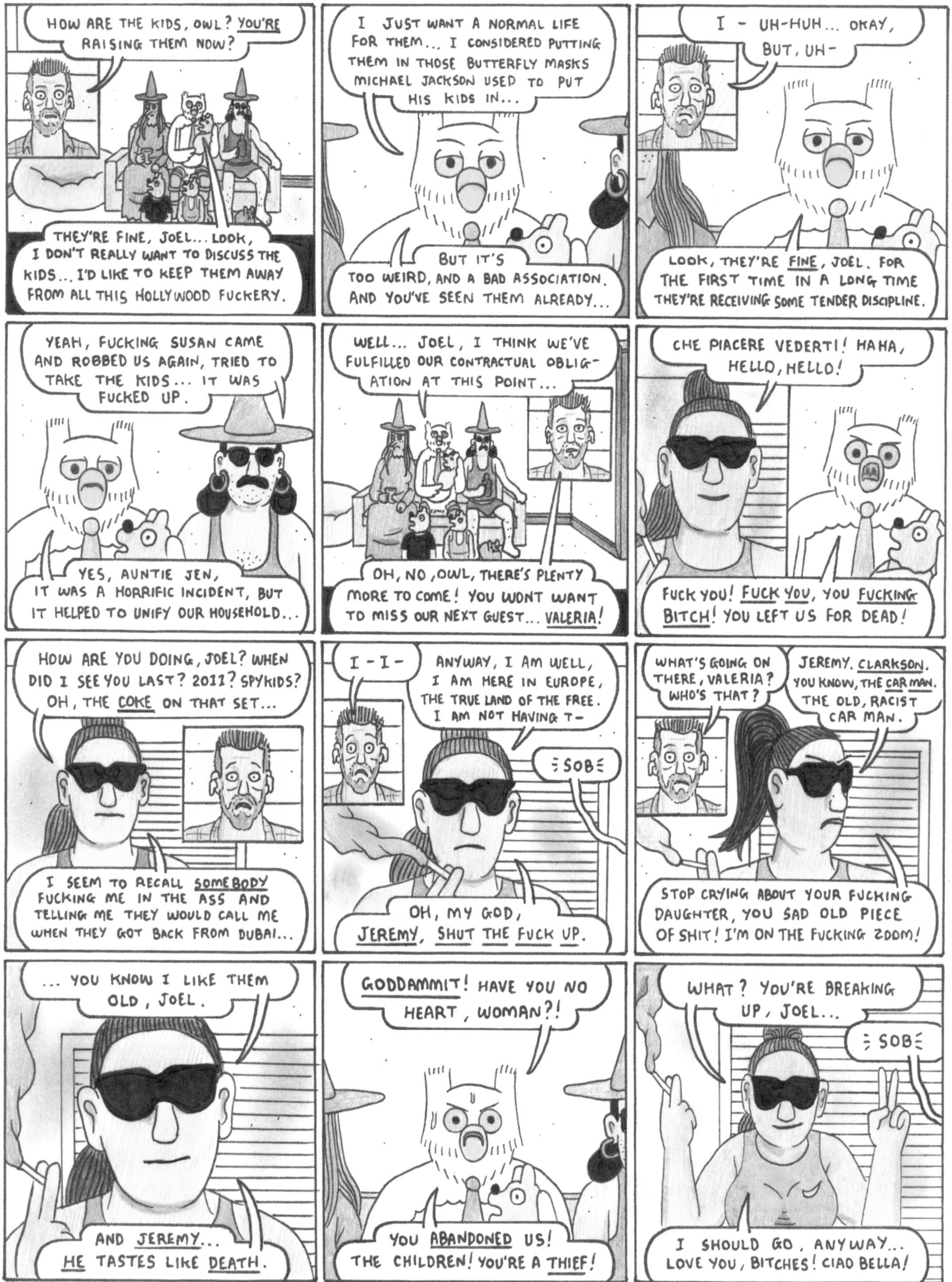
HOW ARE THE KIDS, OWL? YOU'RE RAISING THEM NOW?
THEY'RE FINE, JOEL... LOOK, I DON'T REALLY WANT TO DISCUSS THE KIDS... I'D LIKE TO KEEP THEM AWAY FROM ALL THIS HOLLYWOOD FUCKERY.
I JUST WANT A NORMAL LIFE FOR THEM... I CONSIDERED PUTTING THEM IN THOSE BUTTERFLY MASKS MICHAEL JACKSON USED TO PUT HIS KIDS IN...
BUT IT'S TOO WEIRD, AND A BAD ASSOCIATION. AND YOU'VE SEEN THEM ALREADY...
I - UH-HUH... OKAY, BUT, UH-
LOOK, THEY'RE FINE, JOEL. FOR THE FIRST TIME IN A LONG TIME THEY'RE RECEIVING SOME TENDER DISCIPLINE.
YEAH, FUCKING SUSAN CAME AND ROBBED US AGAIN, TRIED TO TAKE THE KIDS... IT WAS FUCKED UP.
YES, AUNTIE JEN, IT WAS A HORRIFIC INCIDENT, BUT IT HELPED TO UNIFY OUR HOUSEHOLD...
WELL... JOEL, I THINK WE'VE FULFILLED OUR CONTRACTUAL OBLIG-ATION AT THIS POINT...
OH, NO, OWL, THERE'S PLENTY MORE TO COME! YOU WONT WANT TO MISS OUR NEXT GUEST... VALERIA!
CHE PIACERE VEDERTI! HAHA, HELLO, HELLO!
FUCK YOU! FUCK YOU, YOU FUCKING BITCH! YOU LEFT US FOR DEAD!
HOW ARE YOU DOING, JOEL? WHEN DID I SEE YOU LAST? 2011? SPYKIDS? OH, THE COKE ON THAT SET...
I SEEM TO RECALL SOMEBODY FUCKING ME IN THE ASS AND TELLING ME THEY WOULD CALL ME WHEN THEY GOT BACK FROM DUBAI...
I - I -
ANYWAY, I AM WELL, I AM HERE IN EUROPE, THE TRUE LAND OF THE FREE. I AM NOT HAVING T-
SOB
OH, MY GOD, JEREMY, SHUT THE FUCK UP.
WHAT'S GOING ON THERE, VALERIA? WHO'S THAT?
JEREMY. CLARKSON. YOU KNOW, THE CAR MAN. THE OLD, RACIST CAR MAN.
STOP CRYING ABOUT YOUR FUCKING DAUGHTER, YOU SAD OLD PIECE OF SHIT! I'M ON THE FUCKING ZOOM!
... YOU KNOW I LIKE THEM OLD, JOEL.
AND JEREMY... HE TASTES LIKE DEATH.
GODDAMMIT! HAVE YOU NO HEART, WOMAN?!
YOU ABANDONED US! THE CHILDREN! YOU'RE A THIEF!
WHAT? YOU'RE BREAKING UP, JOEL...
SOB
I SHOULD GO, ANYWAY... LOVE YOU, BITCHES! CIAO BELLA!

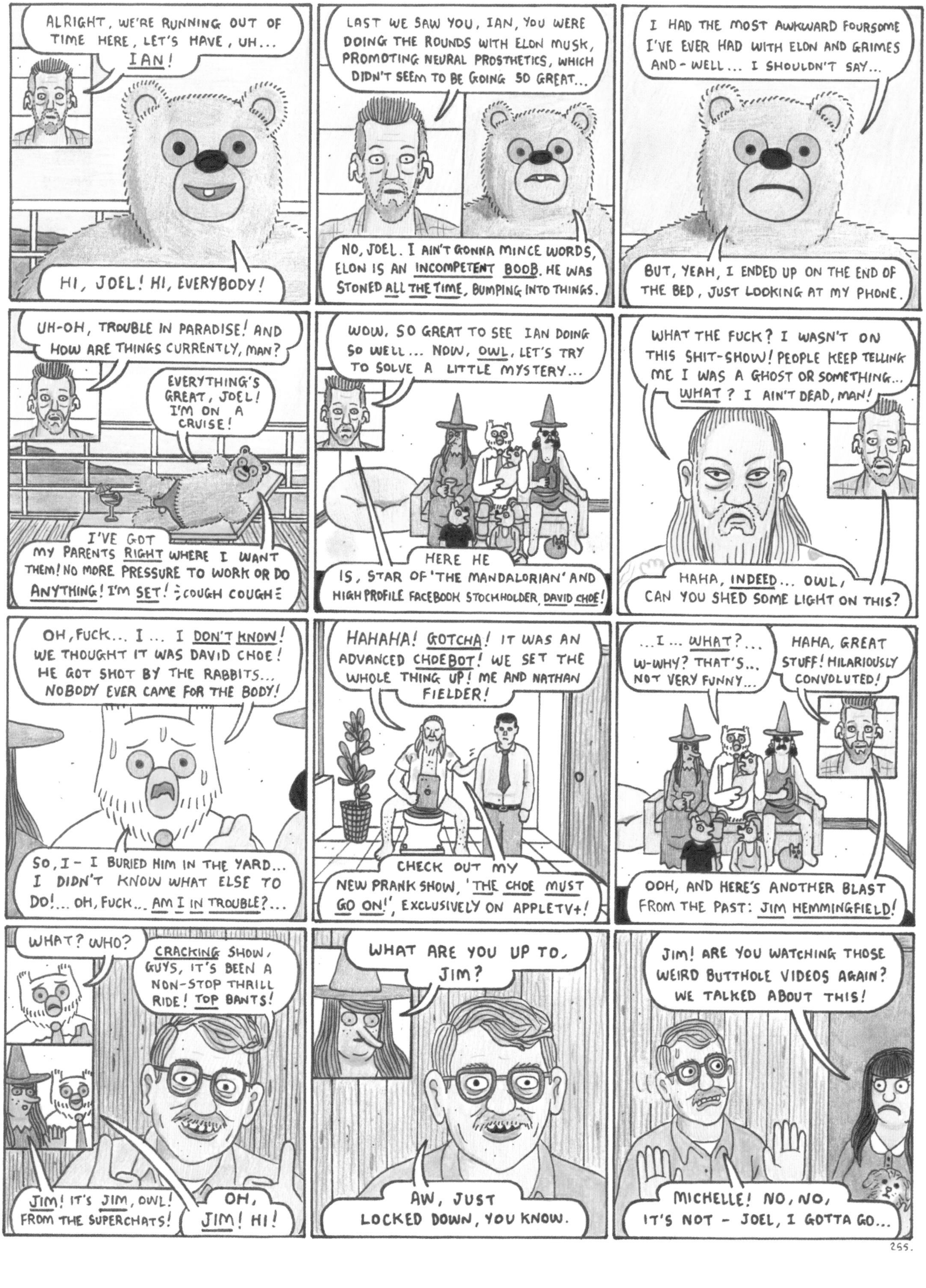
ALRIGHT, WE'RE RUNNING OUT OF TIME HERE, LET'S HAVE, UH... IAN!
HI, JOEL! HI, EVERYBODY!
LAST WE SAW YOU, IAN, YOU WERE DOING THE ROUNDS WITH ELON MUSK, PROMOTING NEURAL PROSTHETICS, WHICH DIDN'T SEEM TO BE GOING SO GREAT...
NO, JOEL. I AIN'T GONNA MINCE WORDS, ELON IS AN INCOMPETENT BOOB. HE WAS STONED ALL THE TIME, BUMPING INTO THINGS.
I HAD THE MOST AWKWARD FOURSOME I'VE EVER HAD WITH ELON AND GRIMES AND - WELL... I SHOULDN'T SAY...
BUT, YEAH, I ENDED UP ON THE END OF THE BED, JUST LOOKING AT MY PHONE.
UH-OH, TROUBLE IN PARADISE! AND HOW ARE THINGS CURRENTLY, MAN?
EVERYTHING'S GREAT, JOEL! I'M ON A CRUISE!
I'VE GOT MY PARENTS RIGHT WHERE I WANT THEM! NO MORE PRESSURE TO WORK OR DO ANYTHING! I'M SET! COUGH COUGH
WOW, SO GREAT TO SEE IAN DOING SO WELL... NOW, OWL, LET'S TRY TO SOLVE A LITTLE MYSTERY...
HERE HE IS, STAR OF 'THE MANDALORIAN' AND HIGH PROFILE FACEBOOK STOCKHOLDER, DAVID CHOE!
WHAT THE FUCK? I WASN'T ON THIS SHIT-SHOW! PEOPLE KEEP TELLING ME I WAS A GHOST OR SOMETHING... WHAT? I AIN'T DEAD, MAN!
HAHA, INDEED... OWL, CAN YOU SHED SOME LIGHT ON THIS?
OH, FUCK... I... I DON'T KNOW! WE THOUGHT IT WAS DAVID CHOE! HE GOT SHOT BY THE RABBITS... NOBODY EVER CAME FOR THE BODY!
SO, I- I BURIED HIM IN THE YARD... I DIDN'T KNOW WHAT ELSE TO DO!... OH, FUCK... AM I IN TROUBLE?...
HAHAHA! GOTCHA! IT WAS AN ADVANCED CHOEBOT! WE SET THE WHOLE THING UP! ME AND NATHAN FIELDER!
CHECK OUT MY NEW PRANK SHOW, 'THE CHOE MUST GO ON!', EXCLUSIVELY ON APPLETV+!
...I... WHAT?... W-WHY? THAT'S... NOT VERY FUNNY...
HAHA, GREAT STUFF! HILARIOUSLY CONVOLUTED!
OOH, AND HERE'S ANOTHER BLAST FROM THE PAST: JIM HEMMINGFIELD!
WHAT? WHO?
CRACKING SHOW, GUYS, IT'S BEEN A NON-STOP THRILL RIDE! TOP BANTS!
JIM! IT'S JIM, OWL! FROM THE SUPERCHATS!
OH, JIM! HI!
WHAT ARE YOU UP TO, JIM?
AW, JUST LOCKED DOWN, YOU KNOW.
JIM! ARE YOU WATCHING THOSE WEIRD BUTTHOLE VIDEOS AGAIN? WE TALKED ABOUT THIS!
MICHELLE! NO, NO, IT'S NOT - JOEL, I GOTTA GO...

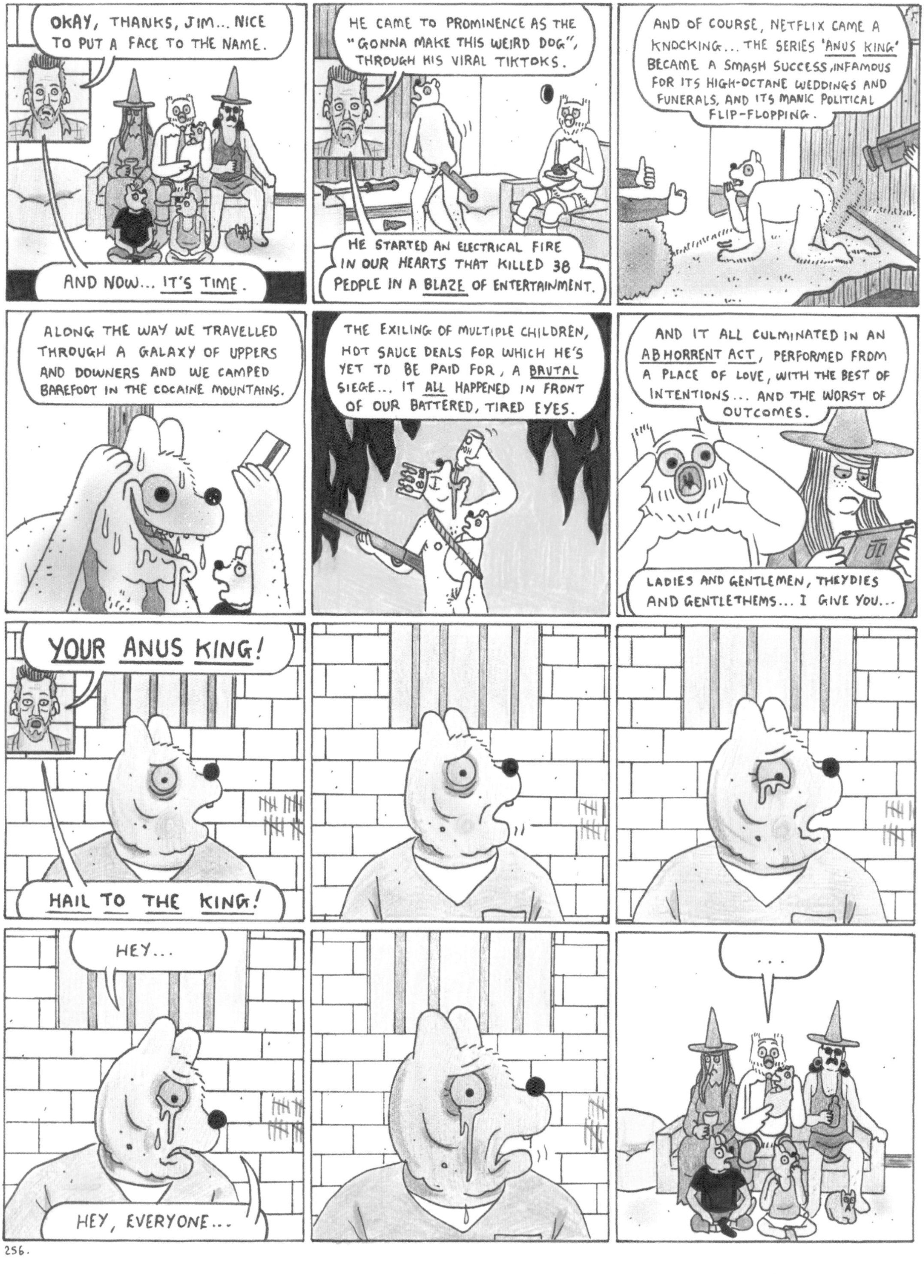
OKAY, THANKS, JIM... NICE TO PUT A FACE TO THE NAME.
AND NOW... IT'S TIME.
HE CAME TO PROMINENCE AS THE "GONNA MAKE THIS WEIRD DOG", THROUGH HIS VIRAL TIKTOKS.
HE STARTED AN ELECTRICAL FIRE IN OUR HEARTS THAT KILLED 38 PEOPLE IN A BLAZE OF ENTERTAINMENT.
AND OF COURSE, NETFLIX CAME A KNOCKING... THE SERIES 'ANUS KING' BECAME A SMASH SUCCESS, INFAMOUS FOR ITS HIGH-OCTANE WEDDINGS AND FUNERALS, AND ITS MANIC POLITICAL FLIP-FLOPPING.
ALONG THE WAY WE TRAVELLED THROUGH A GALAXY OF UPPERS AND DOWNERS AND WE CAMPED BAREFOOT IN THE COCAINE MOUNTAINS.
THE EXILING OF MULTIPLE CHILDREN, HOT SAUCE DEALS FOR WHICH HE'S YET TO BE PAID FOR, A BRUTAL SIEGE... IT ALL HAPPENED IN FRONT OF OUR BATTERED, TIRED EYES.
AND IT ALL CULMINATED IN AN ABHORRENT ACT, PERFORMED FROM A PLACE OF LOVE, WITH THE BEST OF INTENTIONS... AND THE WORST OF OUTCOMES.
LADIES AND GENTLEMEN, THEYDIES AND GENTLETHEMS... I GIVE YOU...
YOUR ANUS KING!
HAIL TO THE KING!
HEY...
HEY, EVERYONE...
...

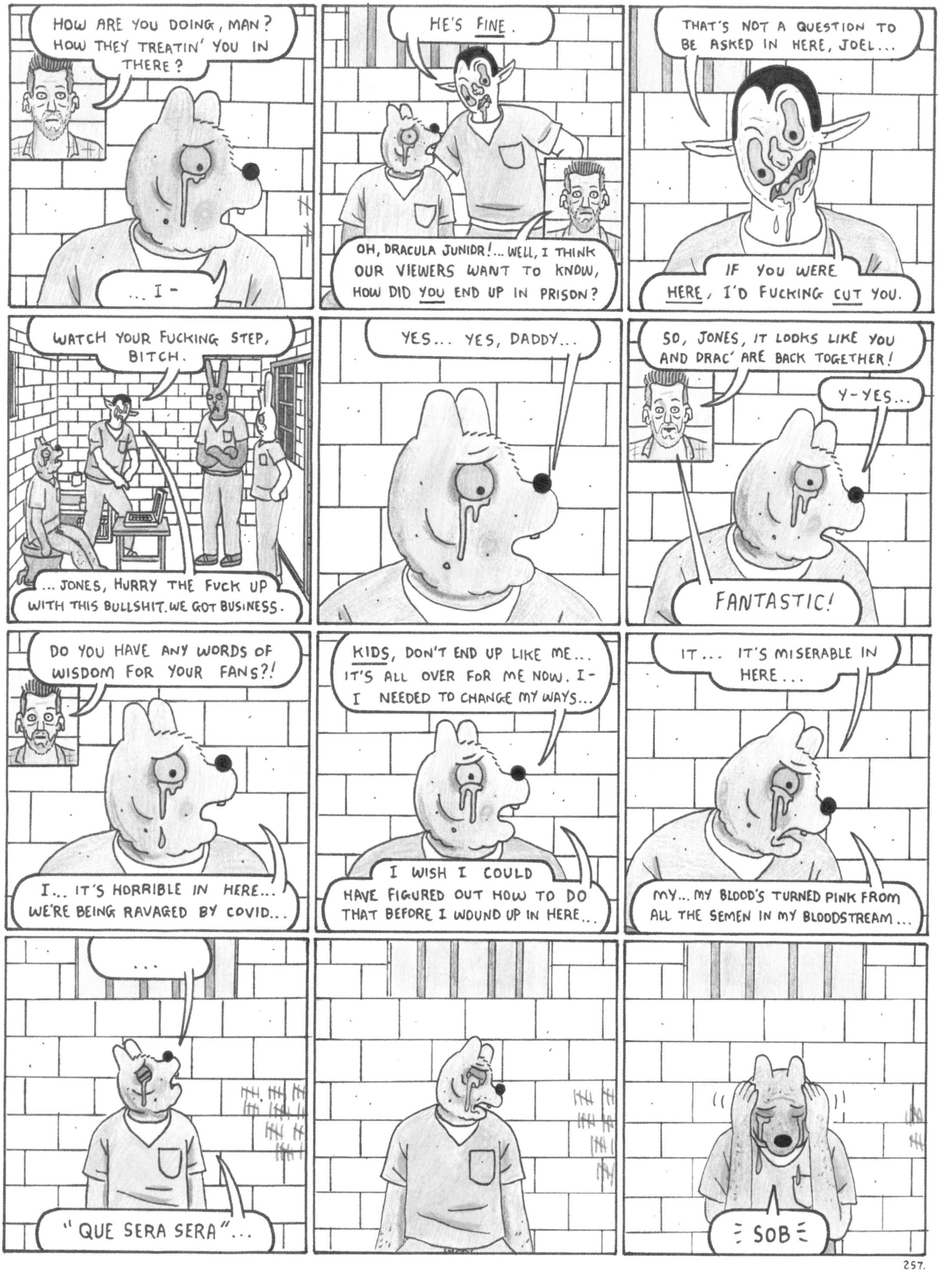
HOW ARE YOU DOING, MAN? HOW THEY TREATIN' YOU IN THERE?
... I -
HE'S FINE.
OH, DRACULA JUNIOR!... WELL, I THINK OUR VIEWERS WANT TO KNOW, HOW DID YOU END UP IN PRISON?
THAT'S NOT A QUESTION TO BE ASKED IN HERE, JOEL...
IF YOU WERE HERE, I'D FUCKING CUT YOU.
WATCH YOUR FUCKING STEP, BITCH.
... JONES, HURRY THE FUCK UP WITH THIS BULLSHIT. WE GOT BUSINESS.
YES... YES, DADDY...
SO, JONES, IT LOOKS LIKE YOU AND DRAC' ARE BACK TOGETHER!
Y-YES...
FANTASTIC!
DO YOU HAVE ANY WORDS OF WISDOM FOR YOUR FANS?!
I... IT'S HORRIBLE IN HERE... WE'RE BEING RAVAGED BY COVID...
KIDS, DON'T END UP LIKE ME... IT'S ALL OVER FOR ME NOW. I- I NEEDED TO CHANGE MY WAYS...
I WISH I COULD HAVE FIGURED OUT HOW TO DO THAT BEFORE I WOUND UP IN HERE...
IT... IT'S MISERABLE IN HERE...
MY... MY BLOOD'S TURNED PINK FROM ALL THE SEMEN IN MY BLOODSTREAM...
...
"QUE SERA SERA"...
SOB

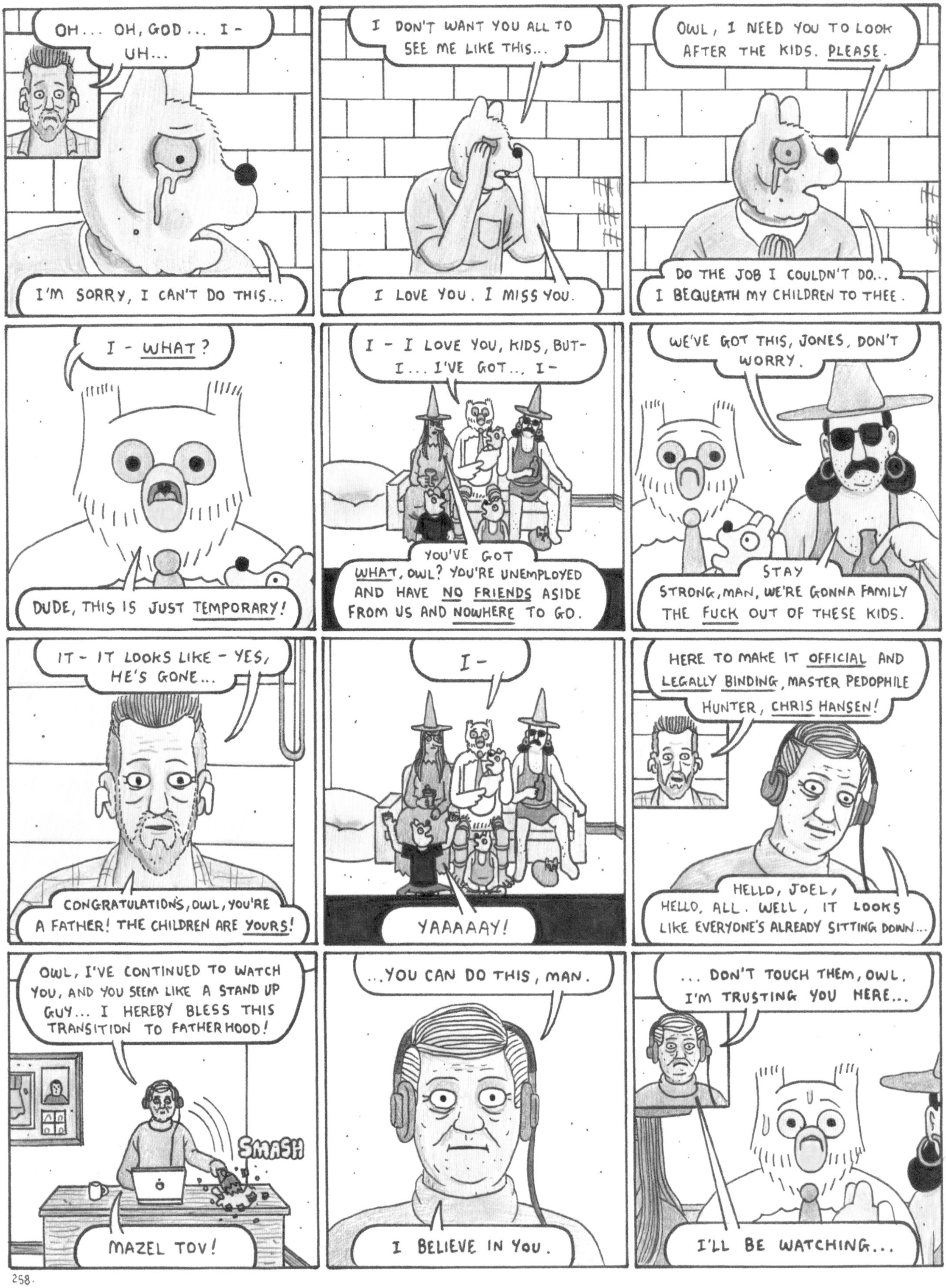
OH... OH, GOD... I - UH...
I'M SORRY, I CAN'T DO THIS...
I DON'T WANT YOU ALL TO SEE ME LIKE THIS...
I LOVE YOU. I MISS YOU.
OWL, I NEED YOU TO LOOK AFTER THE KIDS. PLEASE.
DO THE JOB I COULDN'T DO... I BEQUEATH MY CHILDREN TO THEE.
I - WHAT?
DUDE, THIS IS JUST TEMPORARY!
I - I LOVE YOU, KIDS, BUT- I... I'VE GOT... I-
YOU'VE GOT WHAT, OWL? YOU'RE UNEMPLOYED AND HAVE NO FRIENDS ASIDE FROM US AND NOWHERE TO GO.
WE'VE GOT THIS, JONES, DON'T WORRY.
STAY STRONG, MAN, WE'RE GONNA FAMILY THE FUCK OUT OF THESE KIDS.
IT - IT LOOKS LIKE - YES, HE'S GONE...
CONGRATULATIONS, OWL, YOU'RE A FATHER! THE CHILDREN ARE YOURS!
I-
YAAAAAY!
HERE TO MAKE IT OFFICIAL AND LEGALLY BINDING, MASTER PEDOPHILE HUNTER, CHRIS HANSEN!
HELLO, JOEL, HELLO, ALL. WELL, IT LOOKS LIKE EVERYONE'S ALREADY SITTING DOWN...
OWL, I'VE CONTINUED TO WATCH YOU, AND YOU SEEM LIKE A STAND UP GUY... I HEREBY BLESS THIS TRANSITION TO FATHERHOOD!
SMASH
MAZEL TOV!
...YOU CAN DO THIS, MAN.
I BELIEVE IN YOU.
... DON'T TOUCH THEM, OWL. I'M TRUSTING YOU HERE...
I'LL BE WATCHING...

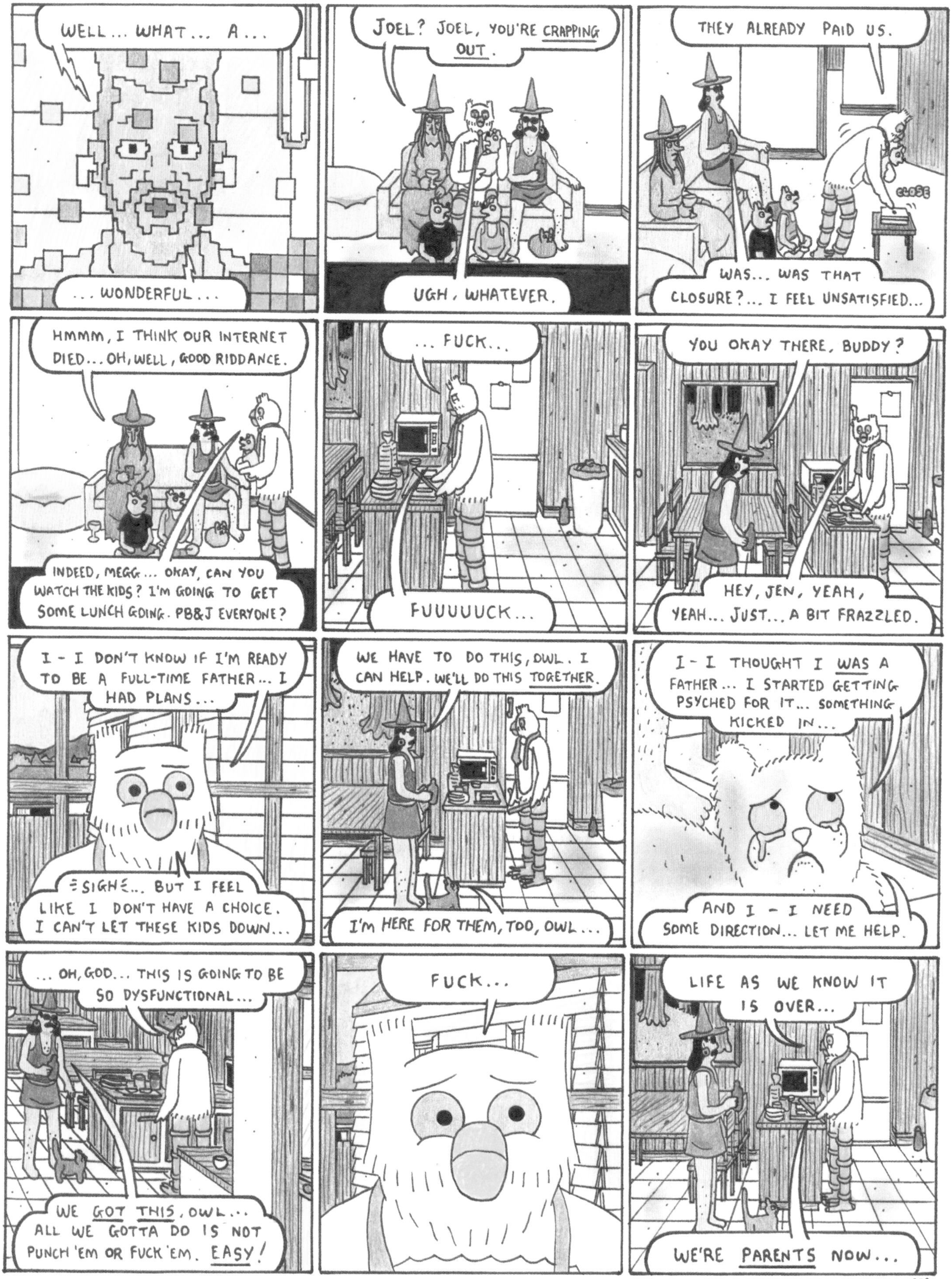
WELL... WHAT... A...
...WONDERFUL...
JOEL? JOEL, YOU'RE CRAPPING OUT.
UGH, WHATEVER.
THEY ALREADY PAID US.
CLOSE
WAS... WAS THAT CLOSURE?... I FEEL UNSATISFIED...
HMMM, I THINK OUR INTERNET DIED... OH, WELL, GOOD RIDDANCE.
INDEED, MEGG... OKAY, CAN YOU WATCH THE KIDS? I'M GOING TO GET SOME LUNCH GOING. PB&J EVERYONE?
...FUCK...
FUUUUUCK...
YOU OKAY THERE, BUDDY?
HEY, JEN, YEAH, YEAH... JUST... A BIT FRAZZLED.
I - I DON'T KNOW IF I'M READY TO BE A FULL-TIME FATHER... I HAD PLANS...
≡SIGH≡... BUT I FEEL LIKE I DON'T HAVE A CHOICE. I CAN'T LET THESE KIDS DOWN...
WE HAVE TO DO THIS, OWL. I CAN HELP. WE'LL DO THIS TOGETHER.
I'M HERE FOR THEM, TOO, OWL...
I - I THOUGHT I WAS A FATHER... I STARTED GETTING PSYCHED FOR IT... SOMETHING KICKED IN...
AND I - I NEED SOME DIRECTION... LET ME HELP.
...OH, GOD... THIS IS GOING TO BE SO DYSFUNCTIONAL...
WE GOT THIS, OWL... ALL WE GOTTA DO IS NOT PUNCH 'EM OR FUCK 'EM. EASY!
FUCK...
LIFE AS WE KNOW IT IS OVER...
WE'RE PARENTS NOW...

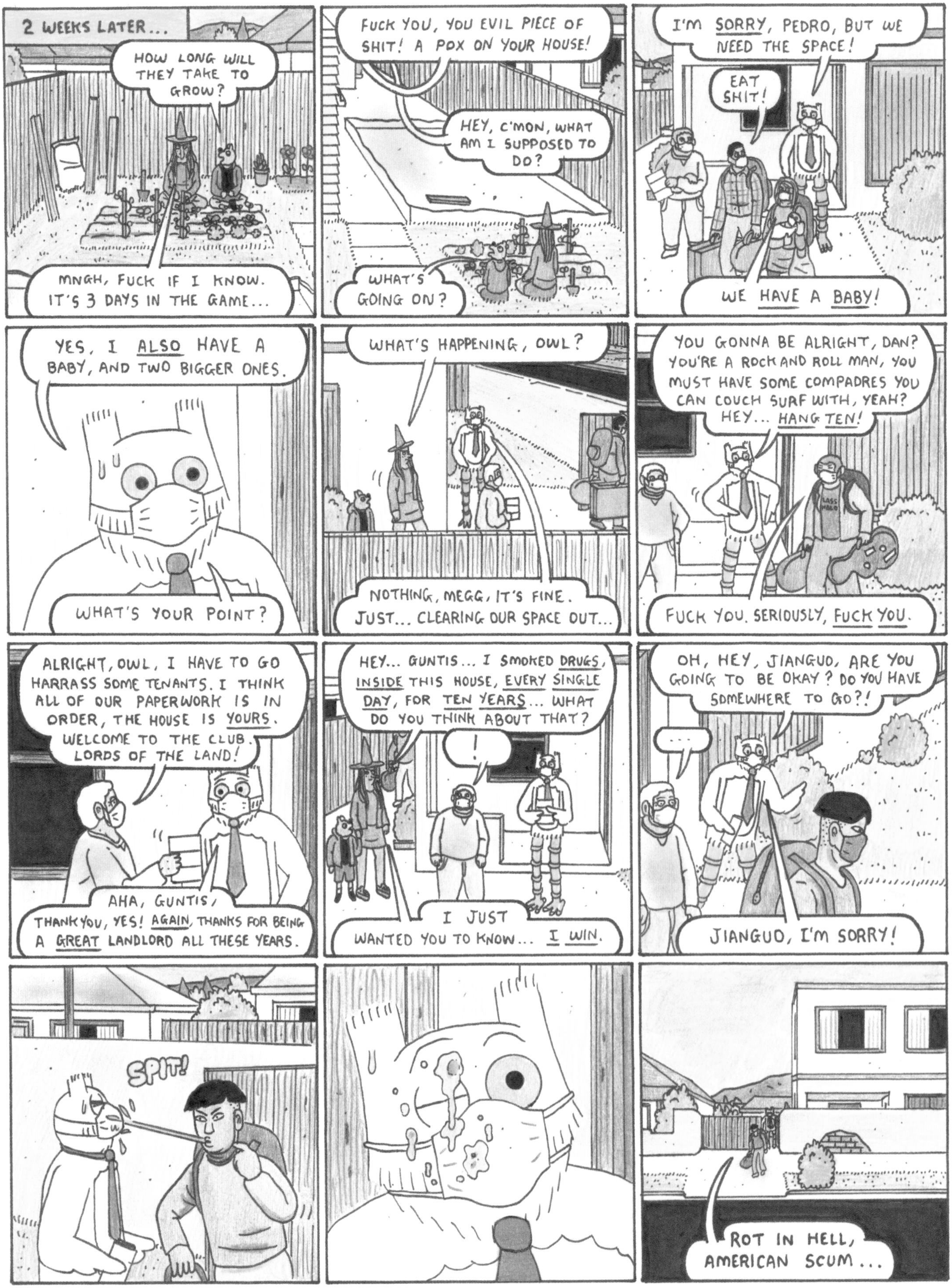
2 WEEKS LATER...
HOW LONG WILL THEY TAKE TO GROW?
MNGH, FUCK IF I KNOW. IT'S 3 DAYS IN THE GAME...
FUCK YOU, YOU EVIL PIECE OF SHIT! A POX ON YOUR HOUSE!
HEY, C'MON, WHAT AM I SUPPOSED TO DO?
WHAT'S GOING ON?
I'M SORRY, PEDRO, BUT WE NEED THE SPACE!
EAT SHIT!
WE HAVE A BABY!
YES, I ALSO HAVE A BABY, AND TWO BIGGER ONES.
WHAT'S YOUR POINT?
WHAT'S HAPPENING, OWL?
NOTHING, MEGG, IT'S FINE. JUST... CLEARING OUR SPACE OUT...
YOU GONNA BE ALRIGHT, DAN? YOU'RE A ROCK AND ROLL MAN, YOU MUST HAVE SOME COMPADRES YOU CAN COUCH SURF WITH, YEAH? HEY... HANG TEN!
FUCK YOU. SERIOUSLY, FUCK YOU.
ALRIGHT, OWL, I HAVE TO GO HARRASS SOME TENANTS. I THINK ALL OF OUR PAPERWORK IS IN ORDER, THE HOUSE IS YOURS. WELCOME TO THE CLUB. LORDS OF THE LAND!
AHA, GUNTIS, THANK YOU, YES! AGAIN, THANKS FOR BEING A GREAT LANDLORD ALL THESE YEARS.
HEY... GUNTIS... I SMOKED DRUGS, INSIDE THIS HOUSE, EVERY SINGLE DAY, FOR TEN YEARS... WHAT DO YOU THINK ABOUT THAT?
!
I JUST WANTED YOU TO KNOW... I WIN.
OH, HEY, JIANGUO, ARE YOU GOING TO BE OKAY? DO YOU HAVE SOMEWHERE TO GO?!
...
JIANGUO, I'M SORRY!
SPIT!
ROT IN HELL, AMERICAN SCUM...

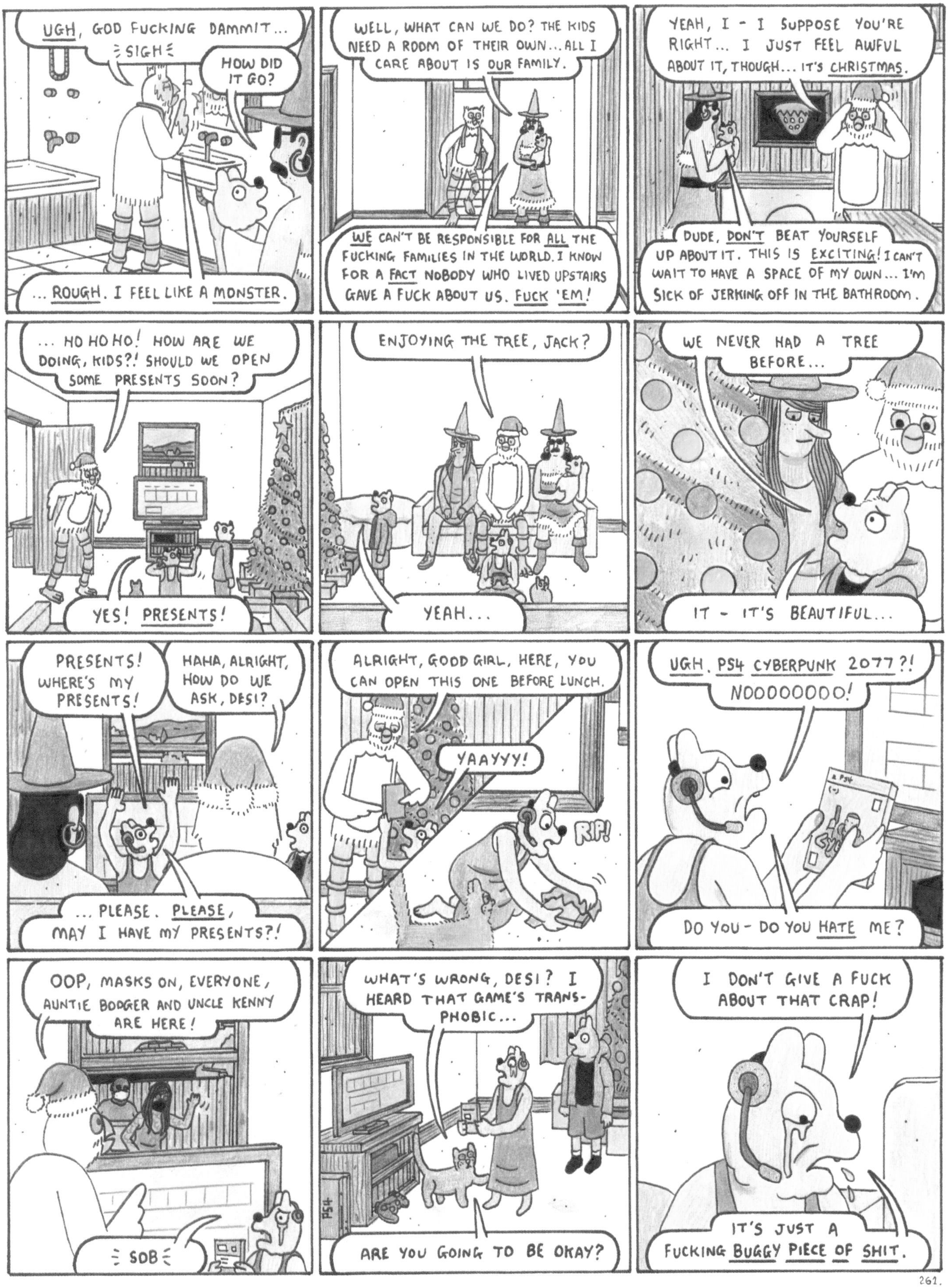
UGH, GOD FUCKING DAMMIT...
SIGH
HOW DID IT GO?
... ROUGH. I FEEL LIKE A MONSTER.
WELL, WHAT CAN WE DO? THE KIDS NEED A ROOM OF THEIR OWN... ALL I CARE ABOUT IS OUR FAMILY.
WE CAN'T BE RESPONSIBLE FOR ALL THE FUCKING FAMILIES IN THE WORLD. I KNOW FOR A FACT NOBODY WHO LIVED UPSTAIRS GAVE A FUCK ABOUT US. FUCK 'EM!
YEAH, I - I SUPPOSE YOU'RE RIGHT... I JUST FEEL AWFUL ABOUT IT, THOUGH... IT'S CHRISTMAS.
DUDE, DON'T BEAT YOURSELF UP ABOUT IT. THIS IS EXCITING! I CAN'T WAIT TO HAVE A SPACE OF MY OWN... I'M SICK OF JERKING OFF IN THE BATHROOM.
... HO HO HO! HOW ARE WE DOING, KIDS?! SHOULD WE OPEN SOME PRESENTS SOON?
YES! PRESENTS!
ENJOYING THE TREE, JACK?
YEAH...
WE NEVER HAD A TREE BEFORE...
IT - IT'S BEAUTIFUL...
PRESENTS! WHERE'S MY PRESENTS!
HAHA, ALRIGHT, HOW DO WE ASK, DESI?
... PLEASE. PLEASE, MAY I HAVE MY PRESENTS?!
ALRIGHT, GOOD GIRL, HERE, YOU CAN OPEN THIS ONE BEFORE LUNCH.
YAAYYY!
RIP!
UGH. PS4 CYBERPUNK 2077?! NOOOOOOOO!
DO YOU - DO YOU HATE ME?
OOP, MASKS ON, EVERYONE, AUNTIE BODGER AND UNCLE KENNY ARE HERE!
SOB
WHAT'S WRONG, DESI? I HEARD THAT GAME'S TRANS-PHOBIC...
ARE YOU GOING TO BE OKAY?
I DON'T GIVE A FUCK ABOUT THAT CRAP!
IT'S JUST A FUCKING BUGGY PIECE OF SHIT.

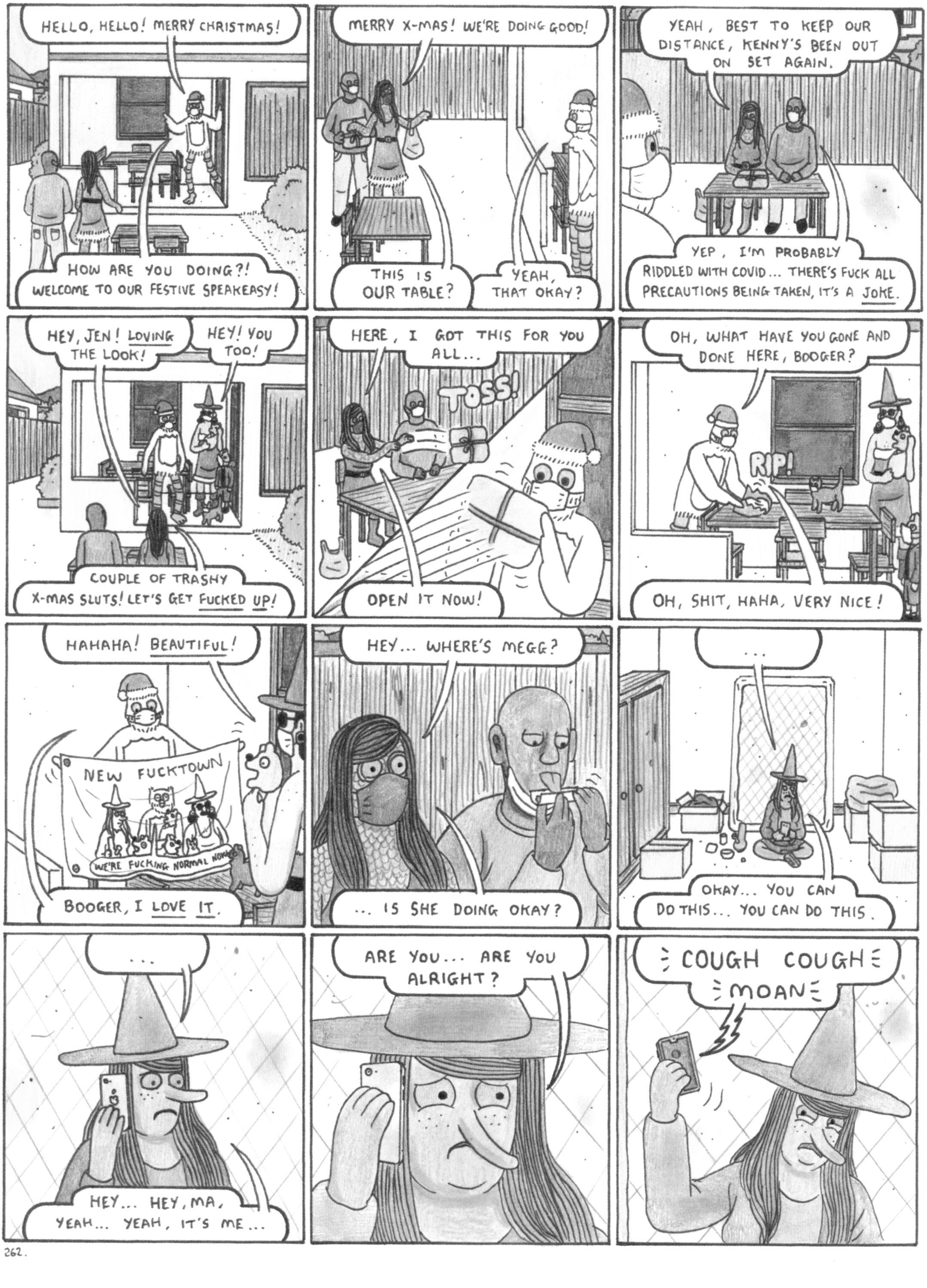
HELLO, HELLO! MERRY CHRISTMAS!
HOW ARE YOU DOING?! WELCOME TO OUR FESTIVE SPEAKEASY!
MERRY X-MAS! WE'RE DOING GOOD!
THIS IS OUR TABLE?
YEAH, THAT OKAY?
YEAH, BEST TO KEEP OUR DISTANCE, KENNY'S BEEN OUT ON SET AGAIN.
YEP, I'M PROBABLY RIDDLED WITH COVID... THERE'S FUCK ALL PRECAUTIONS BEING TAKEN, IT'S A JOKE.
HEY, JEN! LOVING THE LOOK!
HEY! YOU TOO!
COUPLE OF TRASHY X-MAS SLUTS! LET'S GET FUCKED UP!
HERE, I GOT THIS FOR YOU ALL...
TOSS!
OPEN IT NOW!
OH, WHAT HAVE YOU GONE AND DONE HERE, BOOGER?
RIP!
OH, SHIT, HAHA, VERY NICE!
HAHAHA! BEAUTIFUL!
NEW FUCKTOWN
WE'RE FUCKING NORMAL NOW
BOOGER, I LOVE IT.
HEY... WHERE'S MEGG?
... IS SHE DOING OKAY?
...
OKAY... YOU CAN DO THIS... YOU CAN DO THIS.
...
HEY... HEY, MA, YEAH... YEAH, IT'S ME...
ARE YOU... ARE YOU ALRIGHT?
COUGH COUGH
MOAN

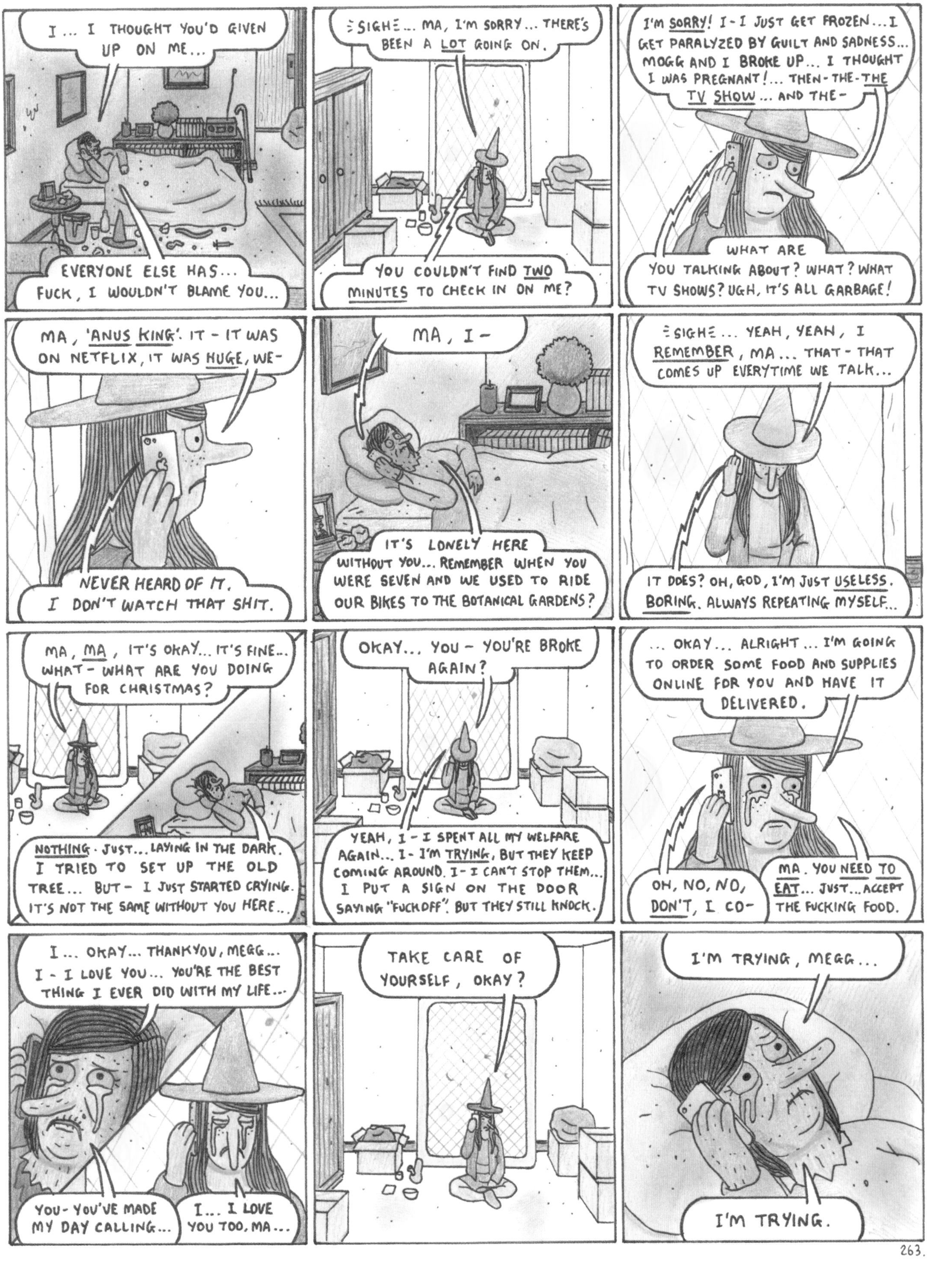
I... I THOUGHT YOU'D GIVEN UP ON ME...
EVERYONE ELSE HAS... FUCK, I WOULDN'T BLAME YOU...
≡SIGH≡... MA, I'M SORRY... THERE'S BEEN A LOT GOING ON.
YOU COULDN'T FIND TWO MINUTES TO CHECK IN ON ME?
I'M SORRY! I-I JUST GET FROZEN... I GET PARALYZED BY GUILT AND SADNESS... MOGG AND I BROKE UP... I THOUGHT I WAS PREGNANT!... THEN-THE-THE TV SHOW... AND THE-
WHAT ARE YOU TALKING ABOUT? WHAT? WHAT TV SHOWS? UGH, IT'S ALL GARBAGE!
MA, 'ANUS KING'. IT-IT WAS ON NETFLIX, IT WAS HUGE, WE-
NEVER HEARD OF IT. I DON'T WATCH THAT SHIT.
MA, I-
IT'S LONELY HERE WITHOUT YOU... REMEMBER WHEN YOU WERE SEVEN AND WE USED TO RIDE OUR BIKES TO THE BOTANICAL GARDENS?
≡SIGH≡... YEAH, YEAH, I REMEMBER, MA... THAT-THAT COMES UP EVERYTIME WE TALK...
IT DOES? OH, GOD, I'M JUST USELESS. BORING. ALWAYS REPEATING MYSELF...
MA, MA, IT'S OKAY... IT'S FINE... WHAT-WHAT ARE YOU DOING FOR CHRISTMAS?
NOTHING. JUST... LAYING IN THE DARK. I TRIED TO SET UP THE OLD TREE... BUT- I JUST STARTED CRYING. IT'S NOT THE SAME WITHOUT YOU HERE...
OKAY... YOU-YOU'RE BROKE AGAIN?
YEAH, I-I SPENT ALL MY WELFARE AGAIN... I-I'M TRYING, BUT THEY KEEP COMING AROUND. I-I CAN'T STOP THEM... I PUT A SIGN ON THE DOOR SAYING "FUCK OFF". BUT THEY STILL KNOCK.
... OKAY... ALRIGHT... I'M GOING TO ORDER SOME FOOD AND SUPPLIES ONLINE FOR YOU AND HAVE IT DELIVERED.
OH, NO, NO, DON'T, I CO-
MA. YOU NEED TO EAT... JUST... ACCEPT THE FUCKING FOOD.
I... OKAY... THANKYOU, MEGG... I-I LOVE YOU... YOU'RE THE BEST THING I EVER DID WITH MY LIFE...
YOU-YOU'VE MADE MY DAY CALLING...
I... I LOVE YOU TOO, MA...
TAKE CARE OF YOURSELF, OKAY?
I'M TRYING, MEGG...
I'M TRYING.

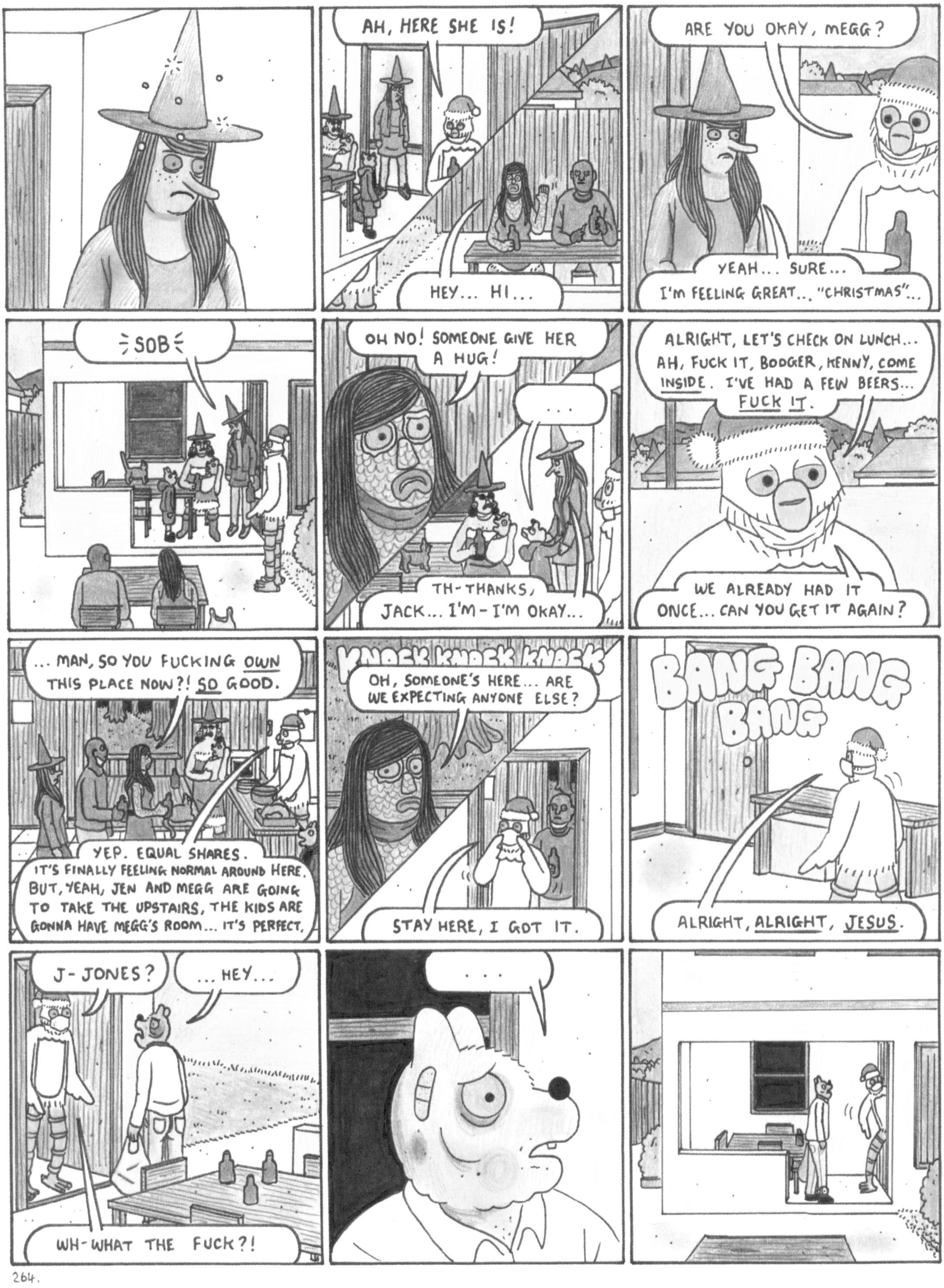
AH, HERE SHE IS!
HEY... HI...
ARE YOU OKAY, MEGG?
YEAH... SURE...
I'M FEELING GREAT... "CHRISTMAS"...
SOB
OH NO! SOMEONE GIVE HER A HUG!
...
TH-THANKS, JACK... I'M - I'M OKAY...
ALRIGHT, LET'S CHECK ON LUNCH... AH, FUCK IT, BODGER, KENNY, COME INSIDE. I'VE HAD A FEW BEERS... FUCK IT.
WE ALREADY HAD IT ONCE... CAN YOU GET IT AGAIN?
... MAN, SO YOU FUCKING OWN THIS PLACE NOW?! SO GOOD.
YEP. EQUAL SHARES.
IT'S FINALLY FEELING NORMAL AROUND HERE. BUT, YEAH, JEN AND MEGG ARE GOING TO TAKE THE UPSTAIRS, THE KIDS ARE GONNA HAVE MEGG'S ROOM... IT'S PERFECT.
KNOCK KNOCK KNOCK
OH, SOMEONE'S HERE... ARE WE EXPECTING ANYONE ELSE?
STAY HERE, I GOT IT.
BANG BANG BANG
ALRIGHT, ALRIGHT, JESUS.
J-JONES?
... HEY...
WH-WHAT THE FUCK?!
...

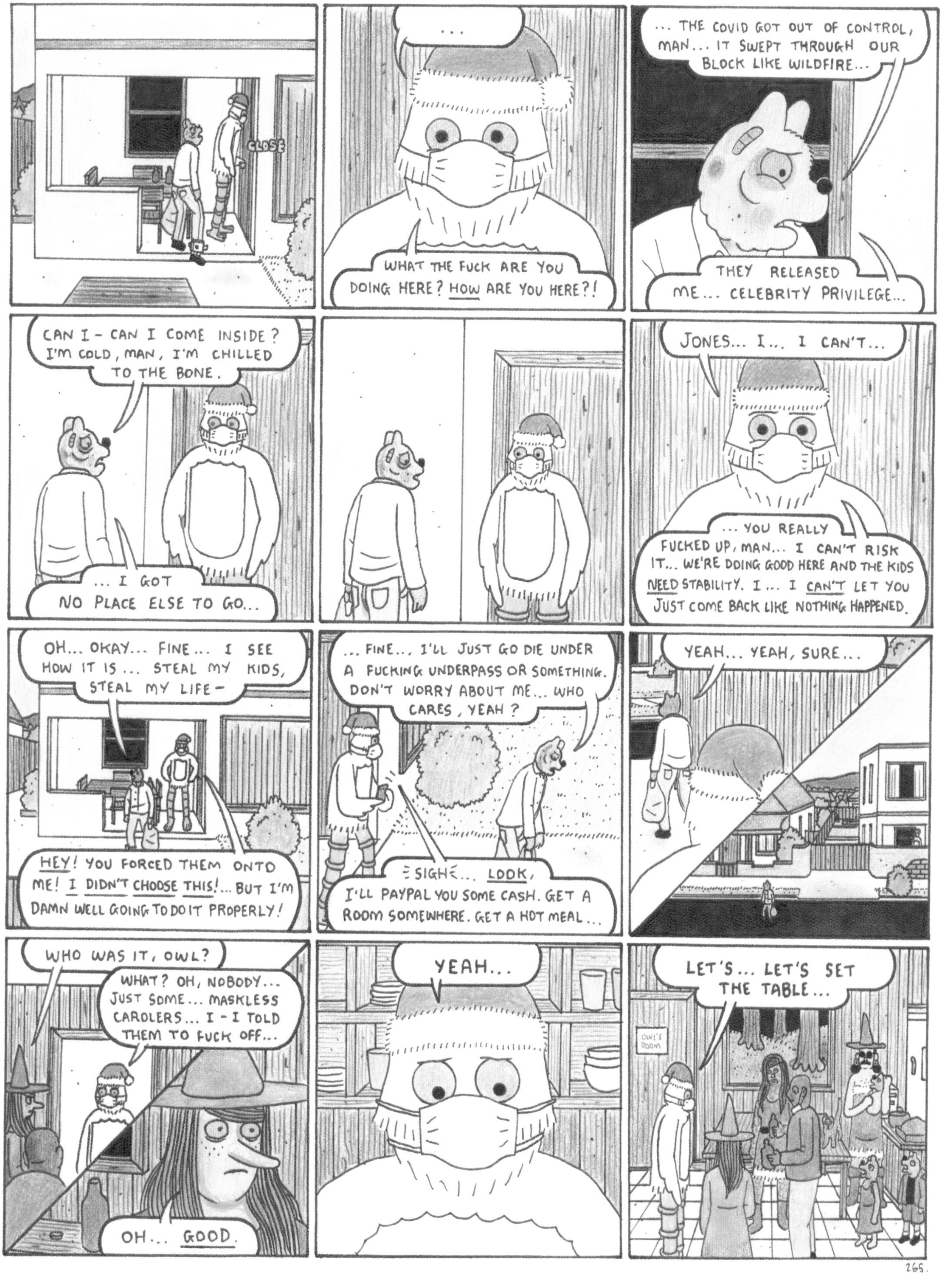
CLOSE
...
WHAT THE FUCK ARE YOU DOING HERE? HOW ARE YOU HERE?!
... THE COVID GOT OUT OF CONTROL, MAN... IT SWEPT THROUGH OUR BLOCK LIKE WILDFIRE...
THEY RELEASED ME... CELEBRITY PRIVILEGE...
CAN I - CAN I COME INSIDE? I'M COLD, MAN, I'M CHILLED TO THE BONE.
... I GOT NO PLACE ELSE TO GO...
JONES... I... I CAN'T...
... YOU REALLY FUCKED UP, MAN... I CAN'T RISK IT... WE'RE DOING GOOD HERE AND THE KIDS NEED STABILITY. I... I CAN'T LET YOU JUST COME BACK LIKE NOTHING HAPPENED.
OH... OKAY... FINE... I SEE HOW IT IS... STEAL MY KIDS, STEAL MY LIFE-
HEY! YOU FORCED THEM ONTO ME! I DIDN'T CHOOSE THIS!... BUT I'M DAMN WELL GOING TO DO IT PROPERLY!
... FINE... I'LL JUST GO DIE UNDER A FUCKING UNDERPASS OR SOMETHING. DON'T WORRY ABOUT ME... WHO CARES, YEAH?
≡SIGH≡... LOOK, I'LL PAYPAL YOU SOME CASH. GET A ROOM SOMEWHERE. GET A HOT MEAL...
YEAH... YEAH, SURE...
WHO WAS IT, OWL?
WHAT? OH, NOBODY... JUST SOME... MASKLESS CAROLERS... I - I TOLD THEM TO FUCK OFF...
OH... GOOD.
YEAH...
LET'S... LET'S SET THE TABLE...
OWL'S ROOM

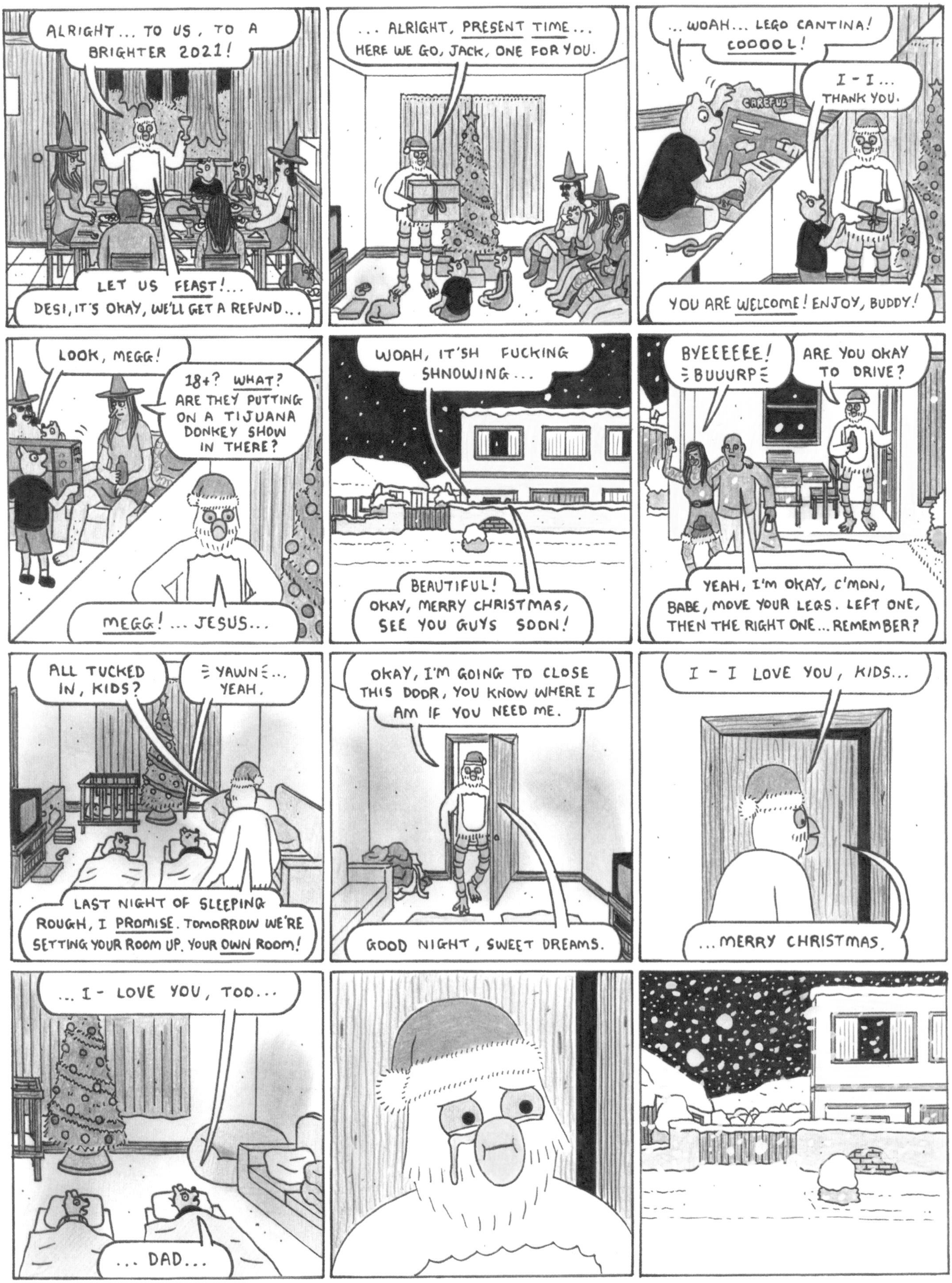
ALRIGHT... TO US, TO A BRIGHTER 2021!
LET US FEAST!...
DESI, IT'S OKAY, WE'LL GET A REFUND...
... ALRIGHT, PRESENT TIME...
HERE WE GO, JACK, ONE FOR YOU.
... WOAH... LEGO CANTINA! COOOOL!
CAREFUL
I - I... THANK YOU.
YOU ARE WELCOME! ENJOY, BUDDY!
LOOK, MEGG!
18+? WHAT? ARE THEY PUTTING ON A TIJUANA DONKEY SHOW IN THERE?
MEGG! ... JESUS...
WOAH, IT'SH FUCKING SHNOWING...
BEAUTIFUL! OKAY, MERRY CHRISTMAS, SEE YOU GUYS SOON!
BYEEEEEE! BUUURP
ARE YOU OKAY TO DRIVE?
YEAH, I'M OKAY, C'MON, BABE, MOVE YOUR LEGS. LEFT ONE, THEN THE RIGHT ONE... REMEMBER?
ALL TUCKED IN, KIDS?
YAWN... YEAH.
LAST NIGHT OF SLEEPING ROUGH, I PROMISE. TOMORROW WE'RE SETTING YOUR ROOM UP. YOUR OWN ROOM!
OKAY, I'M GOING TO CLOSE THIS DOOR, YOU KNOW WHERE I AM IF YOU NEED ME.
GOOD NIGHT, SWEET DREAMS.
I - I LOVE YOU, KIDS...
... MERRY CHRISTMAS.
... I - LOVE YOU, TOO...
... DAD...

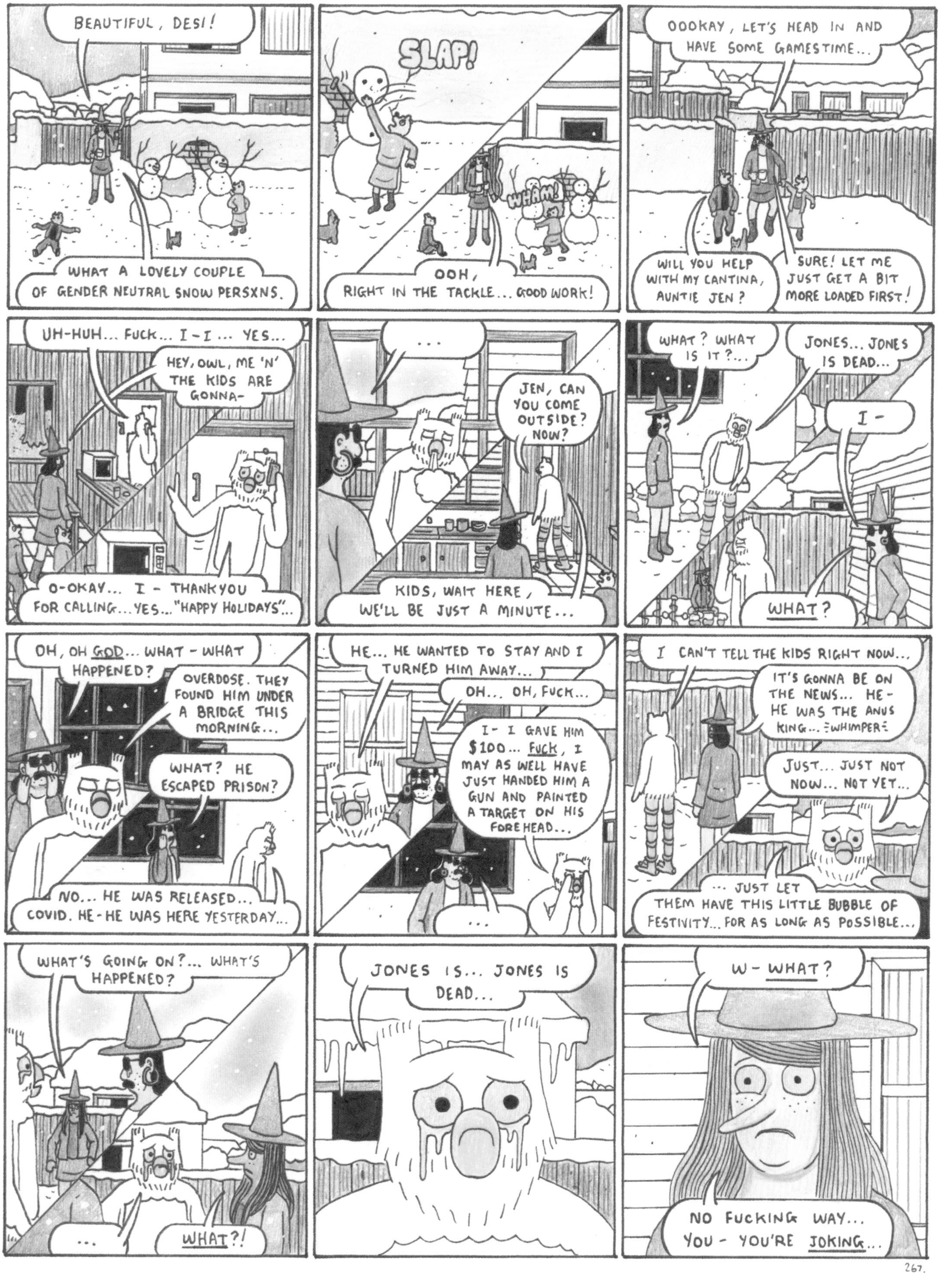
BEAUTIFUL, DESI!
WHAT A LOVELY COUPLE OF GENDER NEUTRAL SNOW PERSXNS.
SLAP!
WHAM!
OOH, RIGHT IN THE TACKLE... GOOD WORK!
OOOKAY, LET'S HEAD IN AND HAVE SOME GAMESTIME...
WILL YOU HELP WITH MY CANTINA, AUNTIE JEN?
SURE! LET ME JUST GET A BIT MORE LOADED FIRST!
UH-HUH... FUCK... I-I... YES...
HEY, OWL, ME 'N' THE KIDS ARE GONNA-
O-OKAY... I - THANKYOU FOR CALLING... YES... "HAPPY HOLIDAYS"...
...
JEN, CAN YOU COME OUTSIDE? NOW?
KIDS, WAIT HERE, WE'LL BE JUST A MINUTE...
WHAT? WHAT IS IT?...
JONES... JONES IS DEAD...
I-
WHAT?
OH, OH GOD... WHAT-WHAT HAPPENED?
OVERDOSE. THEY FOUND HIM UNDER A BRIDGE THIS MORNING...
WHAT? HE ESCAPED PRISON?
NO... HE WAS RELEASED... COVID. HE-HE WAS HERE YESTERDAY...
HE... HE WANTED TO STAY AND I TURNED HIM AWAY...
OH... OH, FUCK...
I- I GAVE HIM $100... FUCK, I MAY AS WELL HAVE JUST HANDED HIM A GUN AND PAINTED A TARGET ON HIS FOREHEAD...
...
I CAN'T TELL THE KIDS RIGHT NOW...
IT'S GONNA BE ON THE NEWS... HE-HE WAS THE ANUS KING... WHIMPER
JUST... JUST NOT NOW... NOT YET...
...JUST LET THEM HAVE THIS LITTLE BUBBLE OF FESTIVITY... FOR AS LONG AS POSSIBLE...
WHAT'S GOING ON?... WHAT'S HAPPENED?
...
WHAT?!
JONES IS... JONES IS DEAD...
W-WHAT?
NO FUCKING WAY... YOU-YOU'RE JOKING...

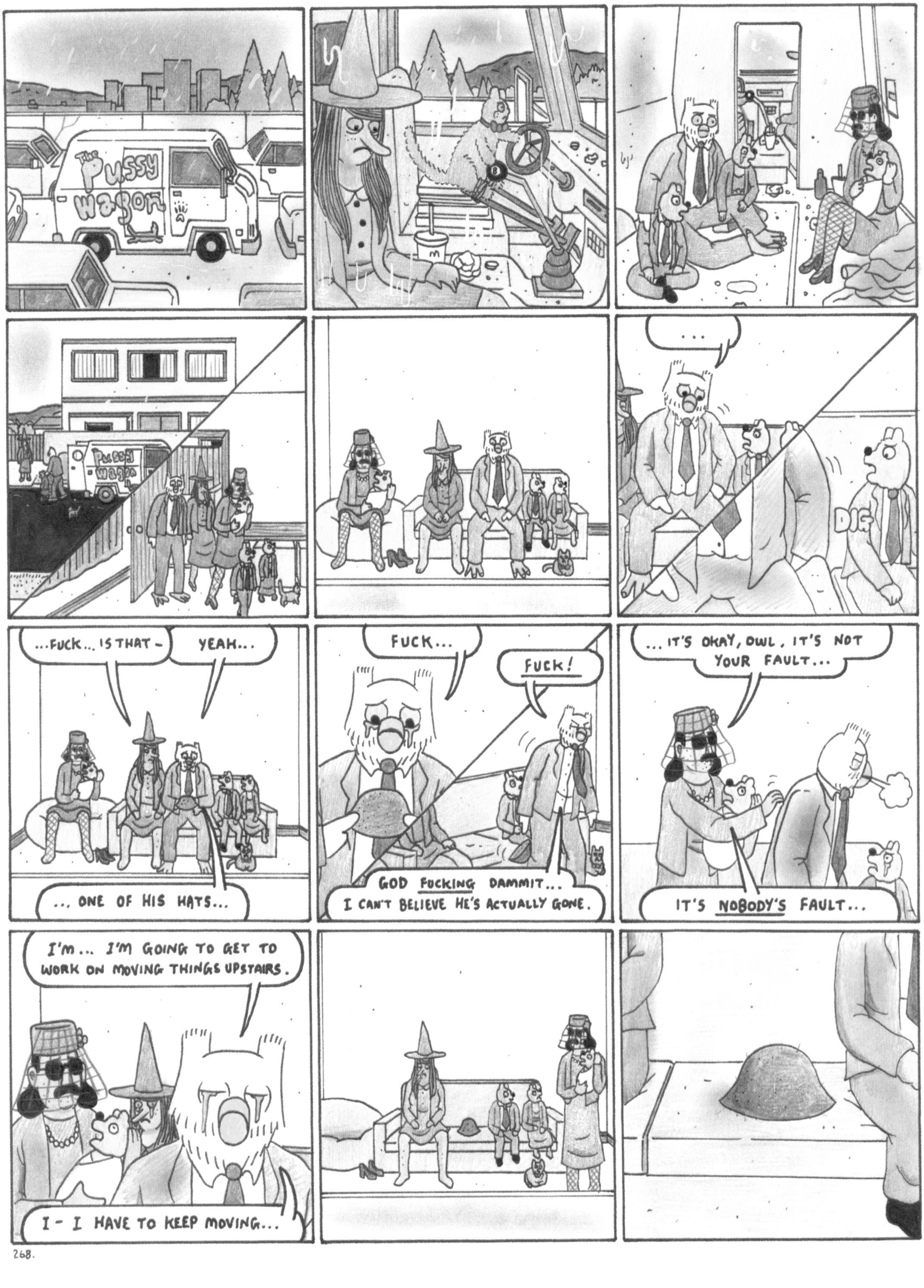

The Pussy Wagon
...
DIG
...FUCK... IS THAT –
YEAH...
..., ONE OF HIS HATS...
FUCK...
FUCK!
GOD FUCKING DAMMIT...
I CAN'T BELIEVE HE'S ACTUALLY GONE.
... IT'S OKAY, OWL, IT'S NOT YOUR FAULT...
IT'S NOBODY'S FAULT...
I'M... I'M GOING TO GET TO WORK ON MOVING THINGS UPSTAIRS.
I – I HAVE TO KEEP MOVING...

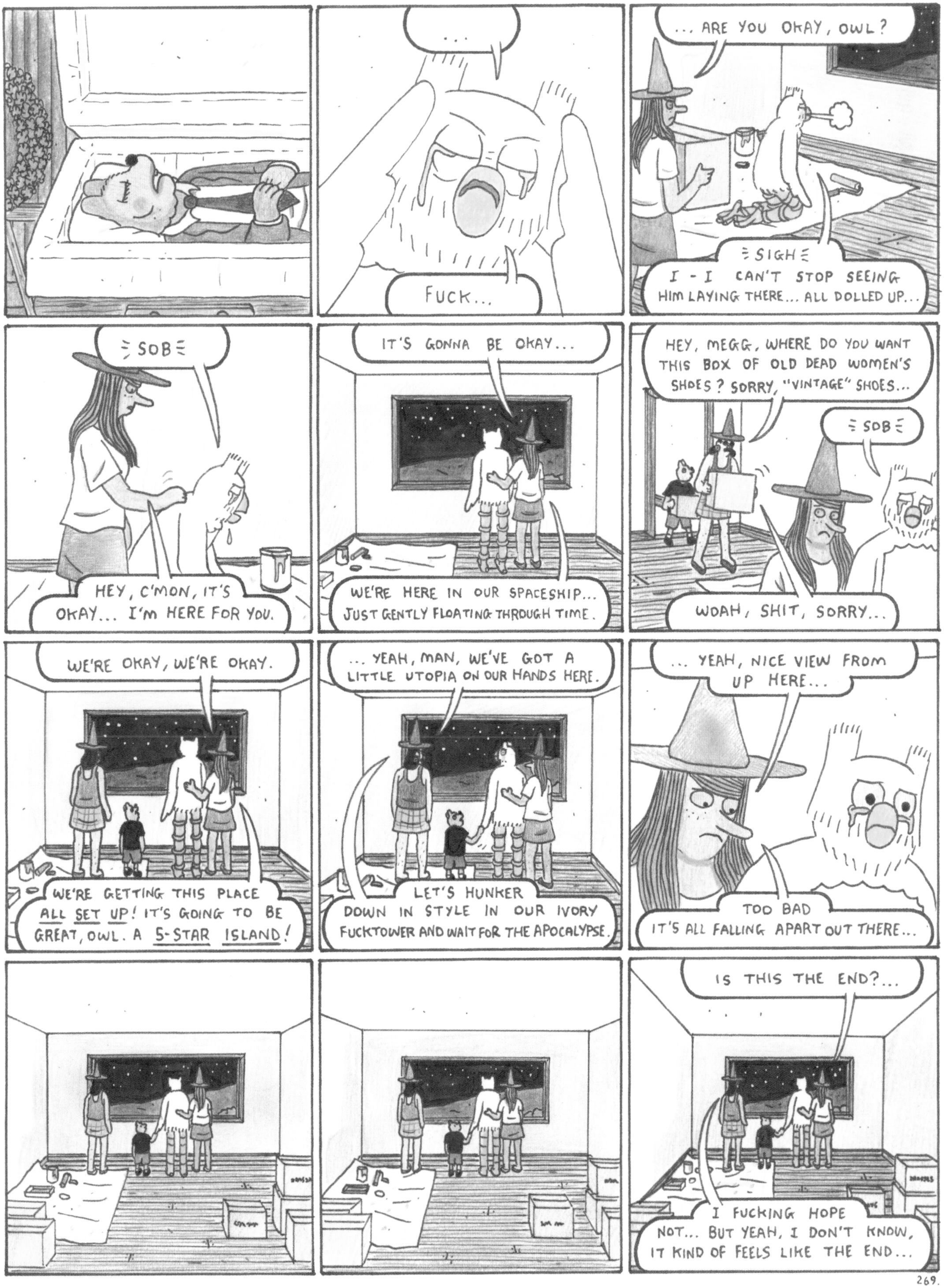
...
FUCK...
..., ARE YOU OKAY, OWL?
SIGH
I - I CAN'T STOP SEEING HIM LAYING THERE... ALL DOLLED UP...
SOB
HEY, C'MON, IT'S OKAY... I'M HERE FOR YOU.
IT'S GONNA BE OKAY...
WE'RE HERE IN OUR SPACESHIP... JUST GENTLY FLOATING THROUGH TIME.
HEY, MEGG, WHERE DO YOU WANT THIS BOX OF OLD DEAD WOMEN'S SHOES? SORRY, "VINTAGE" SHOES...
SOB
WOAH, SHIT, SORRY...
WE'RE OKAY, WE'RE OKAY.
WE'RE GETTING THIS PLACE ALL SET UP! IT'S GOING TO BE GREAT, OWL. A 5-STAR ISLAND!
... YEAH, MAN, WE'VE GOT A LITTLE UTOPIA ON OUR HANDS HERE.
LET'S HUNKER DOWN IN STYLE IN OUR IVORY FUCKTOWER AND WAIT FOR THE APOCALYPSE.
... YEAH, NICE VIEW FROM UP HERE...
TOO BAD IT'S ALL FALLING APART OUT THERE...
IS THIS THE END?...
I FUCKING HOPE NOT... BUT YEAH, I DON'T KNOW, IT KIND OF FEELS LIKE THE END...

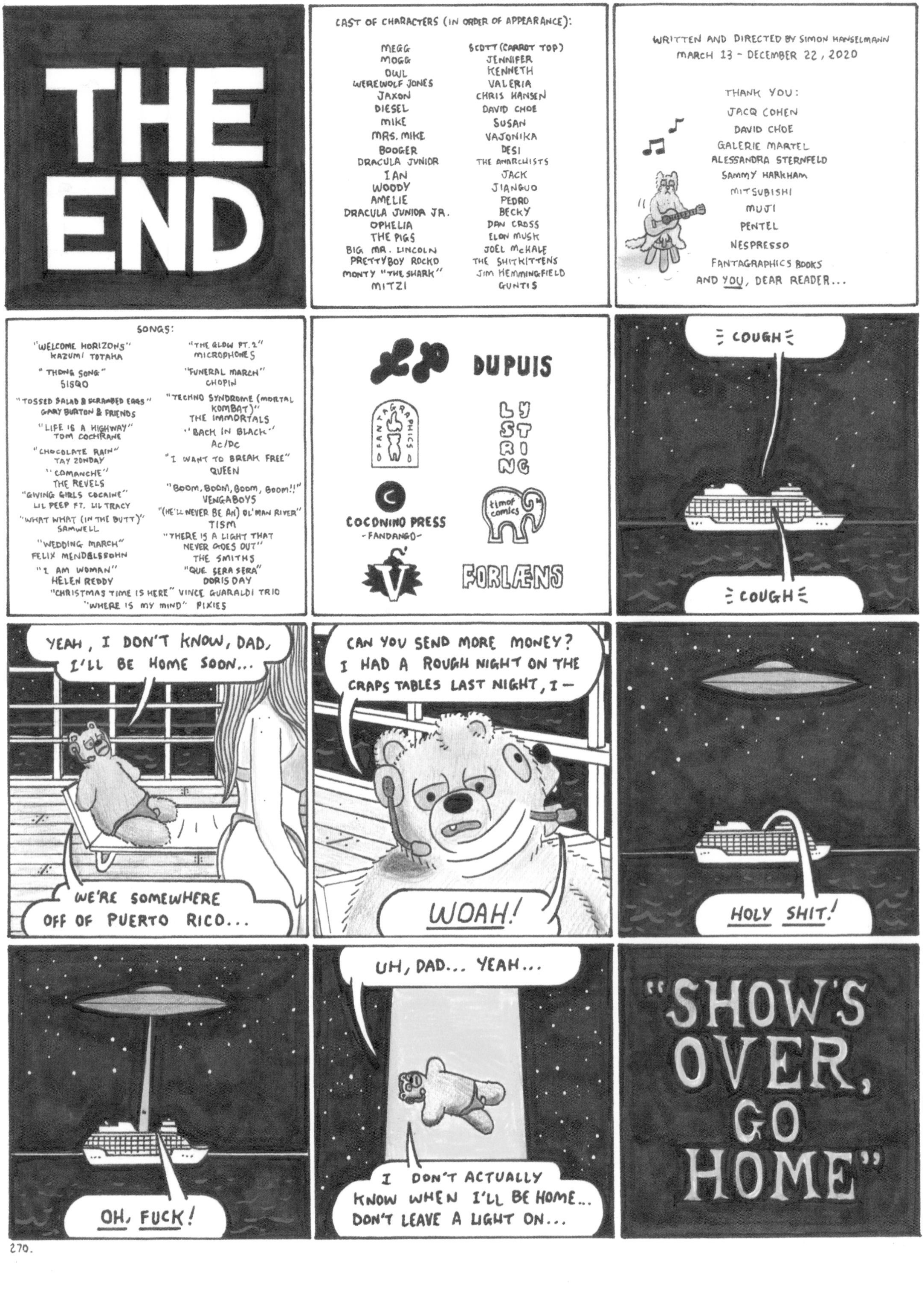

THE END
CAST OF CHARACTERS (IN ORDER OF APPEARANCE):
MEGG
MOGG
OWL
WEREWOLF JONES
JAXON
DIESEL
MIKE
MRS. MIKE
BOOGER
DRACULA JUNIOR
IAN
WOODY
AMELIE
DRACULA JUNIOR JR.
OPHELIA
THE PIGS
BIG MR. LINCOLN
PRETTYBOY ROCKO
MONTY "THE SHARK"
MITZI
SCOTT (CARROT TOP)
JENNIFER
KENNETH
VALERIA
CHRIS HANSEN
DAVID CHOE
SUSAN
VAJONIKA
DESI
THE ANARCHISTS
JACK
JIANGUO
PEDRO
BECKY
DAN CROSS
ELON MUSK
JOEL McHALE
THE SHITKITTENS
JIM HEMMINGFIELD
GUNTIS
WRITTEN AND DIRECTED BY SIMON HANSELMANN
MARCH 13 - DECEMBER 22, 2020
THANK YOU:
JACQ COHEN
DAVID CHOE
GALERIE MARTEL
ALESSANDRA STERNFELD
SAMMY HARKHAM
MITSUBISHI
MUJI
PENTEL
NESPRESSO
FANTAGRAPHICS BOOKS
AND YOU, DEAR READER...
SONGS:
"WELCOME HORIZONS" KAZUMI TOTAKA
"THONG SONG" SISQO
"TOSSED SALAD & SCRAMBLED EGGS" GARY BURTON & FRIENDS
"LIFE IS A HIGHWAY" TOM COCHRANE
"CHOCOLATE RAIN" TAY ZONDAY
"COMANCHE" THE REVELS
"GIVING GIRLS COCAINE" LIL PEEP FT. LIL TRACY
"WHAT WHAT (IN THE BUTT)" SAMWELL
"WEDDING MARCH" FELIX MENDELSSOHN
"I AM WOMAN" HELEN REDDY
"THE GLOW PT. 2" MICROPHONES
"FUNERAL MARCH" CHOPIN
"TECHNO SYNDROME (MORTAL KOMBAT)" THE IMMORTALS
"BACK IN BLACK" AC/DC
"I WANT TO BREAK FREE" QUEEN
"BOOM, BOOM, BOOM, BOOM!!" VENGABOYS
"(HE'LL NEVER BE AN) OL' MAN RIVER" TISM
"THERE IS A LIGHT THAT NEVER GOES OUT" THE SMITHS
"QUE SERA SERA" DORIS DAY
"CHRISTMAS TIME IS HERE" VINCE GUARALDI TRIO
"WHERE IS MY MIND" PIXIES
DUPUIS
FANTAGRAPHICS
LYSTRING
COCONINO PRESS -FANDANGO-
timof comics
FORLÆNS
COUGH
COUGH
YEAH, I DON'T KNOW, DAD, I'LL BE HOME SOON...
WE'RE SOMEWHERE OFF OF PUERTO RICO...
CAN YOU SEND MORE MONEY? I HAD A ROUGH NIGHT ON THE CRAPS TABLES LAST NIGHT, I—
WOAH!
HOLY SHIT!
OH, FUCK!
UH, DAD... YEAH...
I DON'T ACTUALLY KNOW WHEN I'LL BE HOME... DON'T LEAVE A LIGHT ON...
"SHOW'S OVER, GO HOME"

BONUS FEATURE:

"DIRECTOR'S COMMENTARY"

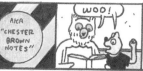

AKA "CHESTER BROWN NOTES"

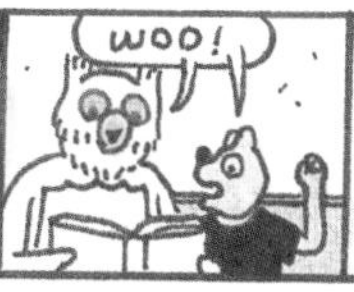
WOO!

CASUAL READERS: YOU MAY CLOSE THE BOOK NOW... THIS IS EXCLUSIVELY FOR HORRIBLE NERDS AND YOUNG ASPIRANTS.

≡COUGH≡ ≡COUGH≡, MNGH... ALRIGHT. HELLO, YES, IT'S ME, SIMON HANSELMANN, WORLD FAMOUS CARTOONIST. ANGOULEME AWARD WINNER, EISNER NOMINEE, NEW YORK TIMES BESTSELLER, ETC. GET READY FOR A DEEP DIVE INTO THE SCINTILLATING WORLD OF ALTERNATIVE COMICS AND LIFE IN GENERAL. I AM OFTEN ASKED IF I AM THE MOST SUCCESSFUL ALTERNATIVE CARTOONIST OF MY GENERATION... AND MY ANSWER IS MOST OFTEN "YES". MY CREATIVE OUTPUT IS TRANSLATED INTO 14 LANGUAGES AND I'VE TRAVELLED THE GLOBE FROM RUSSIA TO COLUMBIA, SPAIN TO NORWAY, I'VE BEEN EVERYWHERE. PEOPLE GOOGLE "SIMON HANSELMANN NET WORTH"... THAT'S HOW YOU KNOW YOU'VE MADE IT. AT THE BEGINNING OF 2020 I HAD JUST WRAPPED UP THE PRODUCTION OF 'SEEDS & STEMS', A BOOK COLLECTION OF THE VARIOUS ZINES I HAD PUBLISHED IN RECENT YEARS... 2019 HAD BEEN A GOOD YEAR, I MOUNTED AN AMBITIOUS MUSEUM INSTALLATION AT THE PRESTIGIOUS BELLEVUE ARTS MUSEUM HERE IN WASHINGTON, I'D RELEASED THE DRAMATIC MEGG AND MOGG VOLUME 'BAD GATEWAY', I'D TRAVELLED TO THE MADRID BOOK FAIR, LUCCA COMICS AND GAMES, SAN DIEGO COMIC CON AND NUMEROUS OTHER HIGH-PROFILE INDUSTRY TRADE SHOWS. 2020 WAS SET TO BE ANOTHER BANGER! MY PLAN WAS TO PRODUCE 'MEGG'S COVEN', THE NEXT MAJOR MEGG AND MOGG BOOK, FOLLOWING ON FROM 'BAD GATEWAY', I HAD BEEN CAREFULLY WORKING MY WAY UP TO THIS PROJECT SINCE 2012. I ALSO HAD A LOT OF TRAVEL PLANNED. A RESIDENCY AT A 5-STAR HOTEL FOR THE SWISS FUMETTO FESTIVAL, A LEISURE TRIP TO MAJORCA WITH MY SPANISH PUBLISHER, AN EXHIBITION IN IRELAND, A RETURN TO TUSCANY... IT WAS GOING TO BE FANTASTIC... PARTYING WITH ALL OF MY INTERNATIONAL FRIENDS AND COLLEAGUES, FINE DINING, INEBRIATED ADVENTURES, EXOTIC TREATS... MY FIRST ORDER OF BUSINESS THOUGH, WAS TO MAKE A FRESH ZINE FOR THE NEW YEAR. A HEALTHY PORTION OF MY YEARLY INCOME COMES FROM MY SELF-PUBLISHED ZINES. I PRINT THEM MYSELF LOCALLY AND SELL THEM THROUGH THE INTERNET, DIRECT TO CONSUMER, IT'S A FANTASTIC GRIFT. AS I WAS COMING OUT OF THE ARTISTIC-TRANCE REQUIRED TO PRODUCE SUCH QUALITY WORK IN SUCH A SHORT FRAME OF TIME, I BEGAN TO NOTICE SOME TROUBLING NEWS... SOME KIND OF VIRUS WAS CIRCULATING... SURELY IT WOULDN'T AFFECT ANY OF MY PLANS, I THOUGHT. HOW WRONG I WAS. EVERYTHING WAS ABOUT TO CHANGE... I WAS ONTO THIS CORONA SHIT WEEKS BEFORE MY PEERS. I KEPT TELLING PEOPLE IN EARLY FEBRUARY, WE'RE GOING TO SEE TRAVEL BANS, BORDER SHUTDOWNS. PEOPLE LAUGHED IN MY FACE, I WAS CALLED A "CONSPIRACY NUT" AND AN "INTERNET FUCKHEAD". I'M NOT A FUCKHEAD THOUGH, I HAD SEEN THE WRITING ON THE WALLS AND I BEGAN CANCELLING ALL OF MY UPCOMING TRAVEL, MUCH TO THE DISMAY OF MY LITERARY AGENT AND FESTIVAL ORGANIZERS. "FUCK YOU", I SAID, "JUST YOU WAIT", AND SLOWLY BUT SURELY THE TRAVEL BANS CAME TO PASS. NO FUCKING WAY WAS I GETTING STRANDED IN SOME EUROPEAN SHITHOLE, APART FROM MY BELOVED WIFE, FOR SOME BULLSHIT COMICS EVENT... SLOWLY EVERYBODY CAUGHT UP TO WHAT I'D BEEN SAYING FOR WEEKS. "YOU WERE 100% RIGHT, SIMON", THEY SHEEPISHLY CONFESSED. BUT WHAT TO DO NOW? I WAS CONFINED TO MY QUARTERS, MY LOCAL PRINTER HAD SHUT DOWN, THE POSTAL SYSTEM WAS OVERWHELMED. ZINES WERE NO LONGER A VIABLE MEAL-TICKET. HOW BEST TO GET MY RIBALD CONTENT OUT TO THE HUNGRY MASSES? IT WAS FINALLY TIME FOR ME TO DO A "WEBCOMIC". I HAD RESISTED DOING SUCH A REPULSIVE THING FOR MANY YEARS. PREVIOUSLY I HAD SERIALIZED WORK ON VICE.COM, WHICH I HAD NOT ENJOYED, THEY OFTEN DID NOT PAY ME ON TIME AND I DID NOT ENJOY BEING AFFILIATED WITH SUCH A POLARIZING OUTFIT. EVERYONE HATES VICE. ALSO, IN GENERAL, I DETEST WEBCOMICS AS A WHOLE, UGLY AESTHETICALLY BANKRUPT GARBAGE. I'VE NEVER WANTED TO BE TARRED WITH THAT SHITTY BRUSH... BUT NOW WAS THE TIME... PEOPLE ALL OVER THE GLOBE WERE TRAPPED IN THEIR HOVELS AND DESPERATE FOR DISTRACTION FROM THE NIGHTMARISH SITUATION WE ALL SIMULTANEOUSLY FOUND OURSELVES IN TOGETHER. I WAS IN A GOOD POSITION TO PUMP OUT FREE, EASILY ACCESSIBLE ENTERTAINMENT FOR THE UNWASHED MASSES. I'D HAD A GOOD FEW YEARS AND MY RENT WAS PAID UP FOR THE YEAR, I DECIDED TO SELFLESSLY DEDICATE MYSELF TO BECOMING "THE PEOPLE'S POET", I WOULD PERFORM A ONE-MAN U.S.O. SHOW, QUALITY WARTIME ENTERTAINMENT FOR THE TROOPS. NO GRUBBY DONATE BUTTONS OR PATREON BULLSHIT, JUST FREE SHIT, EVERYDAY, NO CATCHES. YOU'RE WELCOME! TAKE A LOAD OFF, I WORK FOR YOU. ENJOY! INITIALLY I FIGURED THIS "PANDEMIC WEBCOMIC" WOULD RUN FOR ABOUT A MONTH, SURELY BY THEN EVERYTHING WOULD HAVE CALMED DOWN AND I WOULD GET BACK TO WORK ON 'MEGG'S COVEN', I WOULD MAKE A LITTLE ZINE OF THE WEBCOMIC WHEN THE SITUATION ALLOWED... AS YOU MAY BE ABLE TO TELL BY THE WEIGHT OF THIS VOLUME, THINGS INDEED DID NOT CALM DOWN... AS I WRITE THIS ON JANUARY 26TH, 2021, THINGS ARE MORE FUCKED THAN EVER. MASS DESTRUCTION IN THE NETHERLANDS, MUTANT STRAINS IN THE U.K., SHITTY VACCINE ROLLOUTS, MENTAL ILLNESS POPPIN' OFF, A RAPIDLY ESCALATING ONLINE CULTURE WAR... I KINDA WISH I HADN'T HAD TO STOP PRODUCING CRISIS ZONE TO MEET A BOOK DEADLINE, I FEEL LIKE I COULD HAVE KEPT IT GOING FOREVER IF I HAD CHOSEN SO... BUT I HAD TO STOP, I CAN'T JUST GIVE OUT FREE CONTENT FOREVER, IT HAS TO BE MONETIZED, I HAVE TO RELEASE ANOTHER BOOK. I GUESS I COULD DO A FUCKING PATREON BUT I'M OLD FASHIONED, I LIKE TO SELL PHYSICAL PRODUCTS. TO ME, IT FEELS MORE HONEST, IT'S REAL, NOT JUST SOME FUCKING WORTHLESS PIXELS ON A SCREEN. SO, HERE YOU HOLD THE BOOK OF CRISIS ZONE... A YEAR OF MY LIFE, OF ALL OF OUR LIVES, A SNAPSHOT OF A VERY FUCKED UP YEAR, A TIME CAPSULE. I'M HOPING THIS WILL BE REQUIRED READING IN SCHOOLS IN THE COMING YEARS. AND CAN I EXPECT A NOBEL PRIZE THIS YEAR? MANY HAVE SUGGESTED THAT I REASONABLY COULD, AND WHO AM I TO TELL THEM NO? BUT FOR NOW, LET'S JUMP INTO THIS COMMENTARY, LET'S REFLECT, TOGETHER, ON WHAT THE FUCK THIS WHOLE "CRISIS ZONE" THING WAS AND IS!... A NOTE ON THE TITLE: IN THE PAST I HAD PRODUCED A SERIES ENTITLED "TRUTH ZONE", IN WHICH MEGG, MOGG AND THE REST OF THE GANG PLAY THE PART OF COMICS CREATORS AND CRITICS, IT EXISTS SEPARATELY FROM THE MAIN MEGG AND MOGG CANON. I DECIDED TO APPLY THE SAME BASIC IDEA HERE, IT'S THE CHARACTERS WE ALL KNOW AND LOVE, JUST IN A DIFFERENT SETTING. INSTEAD OF "COMICS PRODUCTION" AND "PATHETIC INFIGHTING AT GLORIFIED FLEA MARKETS" WE WOULD EXPLORE GLOBAL LOCKDOWNS AND INTERNET DISCOURSE. "CRISIS ZONE". A FEW WEEKS AFTER DECIDING UPON THIS TITLE, I RECALLED THAT THE CARTOONIST BEN MARCUS HAD ALREADY PRODUCED A COMIC ENTITLED "CRISIS ZONE". I'VE MET BEN MARCUS AND HE'S A NICE GUY, SO I FELT BAD ABOUT THIS... UPON GOOGLING THE TITLE HOWEVER, I FOUND THAT 'CRISIS ZONE' IS ALSO A 1999 VIDEO GAME BY NAMCO. SO FUCK IT, ALL BETS ARE OFF. EAT SHIT, BEN MARCUS. OKAY, WITHOUT FURTHER ADO, LET'S JUMP INTO THIS COMMENTARY...

PAGE 1. THIS OPENING SPLASH/TITLE PAGE WAS PRODUCED SOMETIME IN APRIL OR MAY, WHEN THE PROJECT WAS STILL INTENDED TO SIMPLY BE A SELF-PUBLISHED ZINE, BEFORE IT GOT OUT OF HAND AND I REALIZED I WOULD NOT PHYSICALLY BE ABLE TO STOP MAKING DAILY POSTS... I QUICKLY BECAME ADDICTED TO THE RUSH OF POSTING DAILY CONTENT FOR A GROWING AUDIENCE... I WOULD SAY IT WAS AROUND AUGUST WHEN I LOCKED THE PROJECT IN FOR PUBLICATION WITH MY VARIOUS PUBLISHERS AROUND THE WORLD. THAT GAVE ME A DEADLINE AND A CUT-OFF POINT...

MARCH 13TH, EPISODE 1. GOING INTO THIS THING I HAD NO GRAND PLAN, I JUST DECIDED TO JUMP IN AND SEE WHERE IT WENT... INSTAGRAM HAS A LIMIT OF TEN FRAMES PER POST, SO I WOULD HAVE TO WORK UNDER THESE STRICT CONDITIONS, WHICH WAS FINE BY ME, WITHOUT THIS LIMIT IT WOULD HAVE BEEN TOO EASY TO DO 11, 12 OR 20 PANELS A DAY. IT WAS GREAT TO HAVE THAT MANAGABLE, DAILY CAP. MY FAVOURITE PAGE LAYOUT IS THE 12-GRID, SO MY PLAN WAS TO SCRIPT TWO ADDITIONAL "SECRET" PANELS PER EPISODE, WHICH WOULD BE AN EXCLUSIVE TREAT FOR FUTURE PHYSICAL PRODUCT PURCHASEES. FOR SOME REASON THIS FIRST INSTALLMENT WAS ONLY EIGHT PANELS, LATER IN THE RUN I WOULD BE <u>DESPERATE</u> FOR EXTRA STORYTELLING SPACE AND WOULD RESORT TO SPLIT TRIANGULAR PANELS AND WOULD CRAM IN MORE DIALOGUE THAN I WOULD LIKE UNDER REGULAR CIRCUMSTANCES... 'ANIMAL CROSSING' IS A LIFE-SIMULATION VIDEOGAME PRODUCED BY NINTENDO. I HAVE PLAYED EVERY ITERATION OF THIS SERIES SINCE 2003. I WAS VERY EXCITED FOR THE RELEASE OF 'ANIMAL CROSSING NEW HORIZONS' IN MARCH, 2020. I CONFESS TO SELFISHLY WORRYING ABOUT THE STATUS OF MY PREORDER AT THE OUTSET OF THE PANDEMIC... ANIMAL CROSSING IS THE PERFECT LOCKDOWN TIME-WASTER. THE QUARANTINE WAS <u>PERFECT</u> TIMING FOR ANIMAL CROSSING AND NINTENDO WENT ON TO SHIFT 26 MILLION UNITS DURING 2020.

3. THE SANITIZER PANIC BEGINS! EVERYONE BEGAN SPRAYING CHEMICALS ALL OVER EVERY AVAILABLE SURFACE. TOILET PAPER PANIC-BUYING DOMINATED THE NEWS. LUCKILY FOR MY WIFE AND I WE ALWAYS KEEP A HEFTY STOCK OF TOILET TISSUE ON HAND UNDER NORMAL CIRCUMSTANCES, WE HAD PILES OF THE STUFF AND WERE WIPING WITH RECKLESS ABANDON. I FELT SORRY FOR ALL THE POOR BASTARDS OUT THERE REDUCED TO DOUCHING THEMSELVES IN THE SHOWER. I RECALL HAVING TO SOMETIMES USE NEWSPAPER AS A CHILD, OR GLOSSY JUNK MAIL... I REFUSE TO EVER BE CAUGHT TISSUELESS AGAIN... WEREWOLF JONES USING HIS FELT HATS AS A MASK HERE WAS A LATE ADDITION TO THE SCRIPT AND I'M GLAD THAT MADE IT IN. FOR THOSE NEW TO THE MEGG AND MOGG WORLD, JONES HAS A LONG HISTORY OF FELT PRODUCTION AS SEEN IN THE CLASSIC EPISODES "FELT HATS" AND "QATAR FELT HAT EXPO". HIS OBSESSION WITH FELT HATS WAS BASED ON AN EX-BANDMATE OF MINE WHO WAS KICKED OUT OF OUR BAND FOR NOT FOCUSING AT PRACTICES AND INSTEAD FOCUSING ON HIS RATTY FELT HATS...

4. NOT REALLY MUCH TO SAY HERE. "SOCIAL DISTANCING" ENTERED THE PUBLIC LEXICON IN FULL FORCE. WEREWOLF JONES BEGINS HIS REIGN OF TERROR UPON THE HOUSE. OWL IS OUR CLASSIC STRAIGHT-MAN, WHILST JONES IS OUR CHAOTIC, UNRESTRAINED ID. OVER THE PAST DECADE OF PRODUCING THE MEGG AND MOGG SERIES, OWL AND JONES HAVE BECOME MY FAVORITE CHARACTERS TO WRITE AND THEY DEFINITELY BECAME THE MAIN CHARACTERS OF THIS SAGA.

5. HERE WE FIND MEGG ATTEMPTING TO INNOCENTLY LOSE HERSELF IN FANTASY BY WATCHING A POSITIVE, UPBEAT PIECE OF FLUFFY ENTERTAINMENT IN 'RUPAUL'S DRAG RACE', A DRAG-BASED REALITY SHOW. MOGG'S OBSESSION WITH FOLLOWING UP-TO-THE-SECOND NEWS BEGINS. DIESEL CALLS MEGG A "BOOMER" UPON HER SUGGESTION THAT THEY WATCH 'THE SIMPSONS' TOGETHER... DO KIDS WATCH 'THE SIMPSONS' THESE DAYS? I HIGHLY DOUBT IT. I USED TO SAY THAT MY WORK WAS INFLUENCED BY 'THE SIMPSONS' BUT I TRY TO AVOID THAT THESE DAYS, THE SHOW IS TWO DECADES REMOVED FROM ITS HEYDAY. TO TELL YOUNG PEOPLE THAT YOU ARE INFLUENCED BY 'THE SIMPSONS' IN THIS DAY AND AGE IS POTENTIALLY VERY EMBARRASSING.

6. THIS EPISODE DID NOT APPEAR IN THE INSTAGRAM RUN. IN THE COMMENTS FOR THE PREVIOUS EPISODE NUMEROUS PEOPLE GLEEFULLY NOTED THAT RUPAUL ENGAGES IN "FRACKING" ON HIS WYOMING RANCH. I WROTE THIS EPISODE IN RESPONSE, WITH OWL HASSLING MEGG ABOUT THE FRACKING AND HER FRUSTRATEDLY TELLING HIM TO FUCK OFF. WHY CAN'T SHE JUST ENJOY HER ESCAPIST ENTERTAINMENT? I ALSO FIND RUPAUL BEING REGULARLY ACCUSED OF TRANSPHOBIA FUCKING HILARIOUS. MY WIFE MADE ME PARANOID, TOLD ME I SHOULDN'T ANTAGONIZE PEOPLE IN THE COMMENTS, SHOULDN'T START SHIT... I PUT THE SCRIPT ASIDE AND FIGURED I'D DRAW IT LATER AND PUT IT IN THE BOOK... "TOO HOT FOR INSTAGRAM"... LATER IN THE RUN I WOULD START TO IGNORE MY WIFE'S SENSIBLE CONCERNS AND BAIT THE FUCK OUT OF THE COMMENTERS.

7. HERE WE HAVE MRS. MIKE, MIKE'S MOTHER, WHO HAD MADE HER FIRST APPEARANCE IN THE MAIN CANON JUST A FEW MONTHS EARLIER IN THE 'MEGAHEX WINTER TRAUMA ANNUAL' ZINE (REPRINTED IN SEEDS & STEMS). I RECALL THAT JESSICA CIOCCI OF THE ART COLLECTIVE PAPER RAD TOOK ISSUE WITH THIS EPISODE IN THE COMMENTS. IN RECENT YEARS SHE HAD BECOME AN OUTSPOKEN RIGHT WINGER AND GUN RIGHTS ADVOCATE. I WAS NEVER QUITE CERTAIN IF IT WAS SOME KIND OF "PERFORMANCE" OR IF SHE WAS SERIOUS... I LIKE HER ART, I LIKED PAPER RAD, I'D HAD JESSICA AS A GUEST ARTIST IN THE 'WEREWOLF JONES AND SONS' ZINE SERIES (A PAID GIG FOR HER). ANYWAY, IT WAS CONFUSING. SHE STARTED GOING OFF IN THE COMMENTS ABOUT WAFFLE HOUSES AND TELLING ME I WAS AUSTRALIAN AND THAT I DIDN'T KNOW WHAT I WAS TALKING ABOUT. I POLITELY INFORMED HER THAT I CURRENTLY LIVED IN SEATTLE AND THAT I HAD INDEED ACTUALLY BEEN INSIDE A WAFFLE HOUSE ONCE. OTHER COMMENTERS BEGAN ROASTING HER AND SHE THEN DELETED HER ACCOUNT. I WAS SADDENED BY THIS. A FEW MONTHS EARLIER HER DOG HAD PASSED AND I WAS ONE OF THE ONLY PEOPLE TO REACH OUT WITH MY CONDOLENCES... I MISS HER WEIRD ACCOUNTS, HER ENDLESS REPETITIVE POSTING OF POINTLESS SHIT, HER HARRASSMENT OF FRIENDS OF MINE WHO POSTED PRO-BERNIE SANDERS MATERIAL, SHE WAS AN ENTERTAINING CHARACTER! I HOPE SHE IS DOING OKAY... I RECALL MY TREK TO HER 2013 EXHIBITION AT TOMATO HOUSE IN NYC, STILL GOT THE FLYER HANGING ON MY STUDIO WALL... I'LL NEVER FORGET WHEN THE 'COLLECTED ZINES OF PAPER RAD' BOOK CAME OUT AND JESSICA POSTED PICTURES OF HERSELF BURNING THEM AND ACCUSED A BUNCH OF ARTIST PEOPLE OF BEING RAPISTS, THEN POSTED A BUNCH OF SCREENCAPS OF HER BROTHER'S TEXTS ASKING HER WHAT THE FUCK SHE WAS DOING... SHE WAS A REAL ONE!

8. BOOGER ARRIVES WITH HER BAGS OF THONGS, THREE BAGS FULL. "ONE FOR THE MASTER, ONE FOR THE DAME, AND ONE FOR THE LITTLE BOY WHO LIVES DOWN THE LANE"... WE ARE ONE WEEK INTO THE PROJECT. I AM GETTING A RHYTHM GOING. I AWAKE AND DRINK A COFFEE AND SMOKE A CIGARETTE AND THEN JUST SIT STRAIGHT DOWN AND GET WRITING. I HAD A BIG SHEET OF PAPER WITH LOTS OF RANDOM LITTLE IDEAS AND POTENTIAL THEMES. USUALLY I COULD KNOCK OFF A PAGE BY AROUND 5 OR 6 IN THE EVENING IF I HUSTLED AND COULD MAINTAIN FOCUS THROUGHOUT THE DAY. I HAD NOWHERE TO GO, SO THIS WASN'T TOO DIFFICULT. I LOVE HARD WORK, I LOVE HAVING A DEEP PROJECT TO FOCUS ON, I GO OFF INTO ANOTHER WORLD. I HIGHLY RECOMMEND IT...

9. I AM TERRIFIED OF MY TOILET CLOGGING AND BECOMING NON-OPERATIONAL. THE TOILET IS TRULY THE FINEST INVENTION IN MODERN HISTORY. THEY ARE UTTERLY MAGICAL. I FEEL LIKE A MAGICIAN EVERYTIME I TAKE A SHIT, WITH THE PRESS OF A BUTTON, I MAKE MY SHAME "DISSAPPEAR"... CAN YOU IMAGINE HAVING TO DEAL WITH A CHAMBER POT? I GUESS YOU'D GET USED TO THE RANCID STENCH OF FESTERING FECES AND IT WOULD JUST BE NORMAL... I MUCH PREFER LIVING IN A WORLD WHERE I DON'T HAVE TO CONSTANTLY INHALE FECAL STINK... WE REALLY ARE AT A GREAT POINT IN HISTORY. MAGIC TOILETS AND VIDEO GAMES. I AM VERY THANKFUL...

10. "DUDE, IT'S MY I.B.S., _I'M_ THE _VICTIM_." CRACKS ME UP EVERYTIME I READ IT ... MY WIFE WILL OFTEN COME INTO MY STUDIO TO INQUIRE AS TO WHAT I WAS LAUGHING AT AND IT IS MOST OFTEN MY OWN JOKES... I'M GENERALLY JUST TRYING AMUSE MYSELF WITH THIS SHIT, IF OTHER PEOPLE ARE ALSO AMUSED, GREAT. I'M CERTAINLY NOT TRYING TO PANDER TO ANY CERTAIN DEMOGRAPHIC ... IF I WAS, IT WOULD BE TO "NORMAL PEOPLE WHO ARE NOT FUCKHEADS WHO ENJOY BEING ENTERTAINED", A VERY NICHE MARKET IN THIS DAY AND AGE.

11. THERE WAS A BREAK HERE. THE PREVIOUS EPISODE RAN ON MARCH 20TH, THIS ONE APPEARED ON MARCH 23RD. THE REASON? ANIMAL CROSSING. MY PHYSICAL PREORDER WAS INDEED DELAYED IN REAL LIFE, IT WAS PROMPTLY CANCELLED AND REPLACED WITH A MORE TIMELY DIGITAL PURCHASE (BEGRUDGINGLY). I SUNK 40 OR SO HOURS THAT WEEKEND... DIDN'T EVEN BOTHER GETTING OUT OF BED FOR TWO WHOLE DAYS. IT WAS A GREAT TIME. MY WIFE IS NOT A GAMER BUT KNOWING THAT SHE WOULD REQUIRE ADDITIONAL ENTERTAINMENT TO BUSY HER MIND DURING OUR QUARANTINE, I HAD FORCED A YELLOW NINTENDO SWITCH LITE UPON HER. SHE WAS NOT HAPPY ABOUT THIS. THE ANALOGUE JOYSTICK AND COMPLICATED ARRAY OF BUTTONS DISGUSTED HER. ONCE AGAIN THOUGH, I WAS RIGHT AND SHE WAS WRONG. SHE WAS INSTANTLY HOOKED ON THE ANIMAL CROSSING GRIND AND SIDE BY SIDE WE LAY, STINKING, WITH EMPTY STOMACHS, PARADING DIGITALLY THROUGH MULTIPLE HEMISPHERES, STOCKPILING RESOURCES AND RAVAGING THE LAND. IT WAS A LOVELY THING TO EXPERIENCE TOGETHER... ALL THE WHILE THOUGH, THE GUILT WAS THERE, GNAWING AT MY ENJOYMENT OF THIS CHILD'S VIDEO GAME. "GET BACK TO WORK, YOU PATHETIC CUNT", "THE PEOPLE NEED ENTERTAINMENT!", SO IT WAS BACK TO THE GRIND. THIS WAS A VERY DIFFICULT PAGE TO DRAW, I DESPERATELY JUST WANTED TO BE LAYING IN A DARK ROOM, ENSCONCED IN ANIMAL CROSSING, BUT I FORCED MYSELF TO BATTLE THROUGH IT... THE BOYS HAVE BEGUN WORK ON THEIR TREEHOUSE, WHICH LATER BECOMES A MAJOR PLOT POINT ...

12. A TRIP TO THE SUPERMARKET... IN MARCH 2020 THAT WAS ALL I LEFT THE HOUSE FOR (AND CONTINUES TO BE IN 2021), I RECALL BEING TERRIFIED BY THE HALF-EMPTY SHELVES. THERE WAS NO WATER, NO SANITIZER, NO TOILET PAPER, NO BEANS. WE HAVE 7 RESCUE RABBITS THAT LIVE IN OUR BASEMENT AND I WAS VERY WORRIED ABOUT NOT BEING ABLE TO PROCURE THEIR FRESH PRODUCE. WE WENT NUTS AND DRIED A BULK AMOUNT OF PARSLEY AND CILANTRO USING OUR PROFESSIONAL-GRADE EXCALIBUR FOOD DEHYDRATOR. LUCKILY THE SUPPLY LINES STAYED FREE AND FLOWING AND THE RABBITS HAD AMPLE FRESH PRODUCE. ONE OF THE RABBITS HAS A MEDICAL CONDITION THAT REQUIRES HIM TO EXCLUSIVELY EAT DRIED PRODUCE, SO ALL THE DRY SHIT DIDN'T GO TO WASTE... OWL HOLDS UP A COPY OF LENA DUNHAM'S AUTOBIOGRAPHY, 'NOT THAT KIND OF GIRL', WHICH HE INTENDS TO USE FOR TOILET PAPER. I THINK THIS REFERENCE IS THERE BECAUSE THAT WEEK DUNHAM ANNOUNCED SOME KIND OF SERIALIZED PANDEMIC SHORT STORY THING, HER VERSION OF CRISIS ZONE, I SUPPOSE... I DID NOT READ IT. I'D IMAGINE IT WAS SHIT. I ACTUALLY RATHER ENJOY THE SHOW 'GIRLS', BUT WHAT LENA DUNHAM DID TO JULIA DAVIS'S 'CAMPING' IN ITS AMERICAN ADAPTATION CANNOT BE FORGIVEN. I USED TO HARBOR SOME RESPECT FOR DUNHAM BUT NONE EXISTS CURRENTLY. JULIA DAVIS IS A BRILLIANT BRITISH WRITER AND HER PRODUCTIONS ARE SOME OF MY FAVORITE TELEVISION COMEDY EVER. CHECK OUT 'NIGHTYNIGHT' (BBC) OR 'SALLY 4 EVER' (HBO) OR 'CAMPING' (SKY), BRILLIANT, _DARK_ COMEDY. THE AMERICAN ADAPTATION OF 'CAMPING' WAS AN UTTER EMBARRASSMENT, A STINKING TURD. LENA DUNHAM DESERVES TO BE SHOT FOR WHAT SHE DID TO THAT MATERIAL.

13. HERE WE FIND MOGG FALLING VICTIM TO THE NEWS CYCLE AND PARANOIA, WASHING HIS PAWS AND FACE UNTIL THEY ARE CRACKED AND RAW, WATCHING DOUCHEY YOUTUBE CONSPIRACY CONTENT. HERE HE IS WATCHING TIMOTHY POOL, AN EX-VICE "INDEPENDENT JOURNALIST" WHO MOANS ON ABOUT POLITICS ON A YOUTUBE CHANNEL WITH HIS RAGTAG GROUP OF UNATTRACTIVE, CRACKPOT BUDDIES. I FIND HIM VERY AMUSING, ESPECIALLY HIS PEDDLING OF BOMB SHELTER DRIED FOOD BUCKETS AND HOW HE NEVER SHUTS UP ABOUT DRIVING OFF INTO THE WOODS IN HIS VAN.

14. HERE WE FIND MEGG DEEP INTO HER ANIMAL CROSSING DIVE, REALITY AND THE GAME PERVERSELY BLENDING TOGETHER, MUCH AS IT DID FOR ME IN REAL LIFE. OWL HAS BECOME 'BLATHERS', WHO IS AN OWL THAT RUNS THE MUSEUM IN ANIMAL CROSSING, YOU DONATE FISH AND FOSSILS AND ART TO HIM AND HE REWARDS YOU WITH ENDLESS BABBLE ABOUT THE SHIT YOU'RE GIVING HIM. HE AND OWL WOULD PROBABLY GET ALONG.

15. I WAS SURPRISED THAT THIS EPISODE WASN'T FLAGGED FOR CONTENT BY INSTAGRAM... I DIDN'T THINK THEY'D ALLOW A GRAPHIC, CLOSE-UP ANAL FINGERING. I'VE SEEN LESS OFFENSIVE MATERIAL BE TAKEN DOWN, BUT YEAH, I DON'T KNOW, IT'S STILL UP THERE... AT NO POINT WAS I CHALLENGED ON ANY OF THE CONTENT OF CRISIS ZONE BY INSTAGRAM AND I'D IMAGINE AT LEAST A FEW PRUDISH CUNTS MUST HAVE BEEN SNITCHING TO DADDY... WELL, WHATEVER, THANKS, INSTAGRAM. THANKS FOR BEING COOL ABOUT BUTTHOLE FINGERING AND WEREWOLF COCK. MORE ANIMAL CROSSING REFERENCES HERE, DIESEL AND JAXON AS 'TIMMY & TOMMY NOOK', JONES AS 'TOM NOOK', WE ALSO SEE IAN AS 'GRIZZLY' AND AN UNKNOWN CHARACTER (DRACULA JUNIOR) AS 'HARV', THE CREEPY PHOTOGRAPHY DOG. "DADDY BURGERS" IS WHAT MY FRIEND KARL'S FATHER WOULD CALL HIS HOME-MADE HAMBURGERS. THIS IS A CLASSIC TASMANIAN, HOBART NOISE SCENE IN-JOKE. I USED TO WEAR A RED T-SHIRT WITH DADDY BURGERS SCRAWLED ON IT WITH A SHARPIE, CIRCA 2005... "KIDS, YOUR DADDY BURGERS ARE READY". _CLASSIC_. R.I.P. KARL VON BAMBERGER.

16. "BARE ANUSES ON THE CUSHIONS". THIS IS AUTOBIOGRAPHY. MY WIFE HAD HER HIPPY FRIEND STAYING AT OUR HOUSE THE YEAR PREVIOUS AND SHE'S ONE OF THOSE "EARTH MOTHER" TYPES AND DOESN'T WANT HER KIDS BEING KEPT DOWN BY SUCH OPPRESSIONS AS WEARING CLOTHING. WE HAD TO WASH ALL THE CUSHION COVERS AFTER THEY'D LEFT, ONE OF THE KIDS HAD AN INFECTED PENIS (?!) AND I WAS _NOT_ HAPPY ABOUT ITS PROXIMITY TO OUR CUSHIONS.

17. OWL STARTS TAKING CHARGE. NO MORE BULLSHIT. FIRST APPEARANCE OF OWL'S "TALKING KNIFE". DRACULA JUNIOR AND IAN ARE CHASED AWAY IN PANEL 3 WHERE WE ALSO SEE 'WOODY' THE RABBIT. THIS IS TECHNICALLY WOODY'S 2ND APPEARANCE IN THE MEGG AND MOGG MULTIVERSE, HIS FIRST BEING IN A BACKUP STRIP IN THE ZINE 'KNIFE CRIME'. HE IS BASED ON A REAL LIFE RABBIT OF MINE ALSO NAMED WOODY. HE WAS MY BEST FRIEND UNTIL HE PASSED AWAY IN 2017... IT BROKE MY HEART AND IS STILL PAINFUL TO THIS DAY...

PAGE	
18-19.	OWL HAS CONTRACTED COVID. I THINK I MAY HAVE HAD COVID AT SOME POINT IN FEBRUARY, BUT I'M NOT SURE... I HAD A FEW DAYS WHERE I FELT ABSOLUTELY FUCKED AND SUPER DIZZY AND FOUND IT DIFFICULT TO GET OUT OF BED. IT MAY HAVE JUST BEEN A BAD HANGOVER... GARY GROTH (FANTAGRAPHICS HEAD HONCHO) DEFINITELY HAD IT AROUND THE TIME OF THESE EPISODES. HE REPORTED FEELING "A BIT FUNNY" AND CUT HIMSELF OFF FROM POLITE SOCIETY...
20-22.	MIKE RETURNS AND REVEALS MRS. MIKE HAS PASSED AWAY AFTER A GUNFIGHT AT THE WAFFLE HOUSE. SHE DIED DOING WHAT SHE LOVED... THIS IS THE FIRST MAJOR DEATH OF THE SERIES AND PROMPTS A GRATUITOUS HALLWAY SODOMIZING THAT I THOUGHT WOULD PERHAPS BE CENSORED BY INSTAGRAM, BUT AGAIN, NO. INSTAGRAM SEEMINGLY LOVES HALLWAY BUTT-STUFF. I GUESS THIS KIND OF SHIT IS ALLOWED, AS LONG AS NO FEMALE NIPPLES APPEAR.
23.	DUE TO THE LOCKDOWNS, WEREWOLF JONES'S OUTDOOR HAT SALES MUST BE PUT ON HOLD, HE IS FORCED TO RETURN TO HIS INDEPENDENT ONLINE SEX WORK. THIS SETS IN MOTION THE ENTIRE "ANUS KING" NETFLIX THING. I WOULD IMAGINE A LOT OF PEOPLE PROBABLY RESORTED TO "CAMMING" LAST YEAR. I HOPE THEY ALL GOT A NETFLIX SERIES.
24-25	MMM, PILLS. GOOD OLD PILLS. THAT'LL CHASE THE BLUES AWAY. I LIKE THIS SCENE OF OWL AND MOGG TALKING ABOUT DATING DURING WHAT WAS GOING ON. I'M SO FUCKING GLAD I'M IN A HAPPY MARRIAGE AND I DON'T HAVE TO DEAL WITH ANY OF THAT SHIT. GOD, IT MUST BE AWFUL. POOR, LONELY MOTHERFUCKERS. A WORLD OF INCELS.
26.	THE FIRST MENTION HERE OF "JIM HEMMINGFIELD", WHO IS WEREWOLF JONES'S #1 FAN. JIM IS ALSO MENTIONED IN THE MAIN SERIES OF BOOKS, WHEREIN HE IS WEREWOLF JONES'S FIRST ETSY CUSTOMER. JIM IS A REAL, LIVING HUMAN PERSON. HE IS BRITISH AND A PART OF 'BREAKDOWN PRESS', A QUALITY PUBLISHER OF ALTERNATIVE COMICS. ONCE, WHILE I WAS ON TOUR, I STAYED AT JIM AND HIS WIFE MICHELLE'S APARTMENT, THE OTHER OPTION WAS JOE KESSLER'S DISGUSTING BACHELOR SHAREHOUSE WHERE AT A PARTY THE PREVIOUS NIGHT, THE TOILET DOOR HAD BEEN RIPPED OFF OF ITS HINGES. JIM AND MICHELLE WERE LIFESAVERS. THEY HAVE A VERY LOVELY, CLEAN APARTMENT, WITH A FUNCTIONAL BATHROOM. JIM AND MICHELLE ARE TWO OF THE LOVLIEST PEOPLE I KNOW. MY APOLOGIES TO BOTH OF THEM.
27.	HERE WE FIND MEGG CALLING TO CHECK IN ON HER MOTHER. THIS IS BASICALLY RIPPED FROM REAL LIFE. I WAS VERY CONCERNED THAT MY MOTHER WOULD CATCH THE VIRUS AND IT WOULD TAKE HER OUT, SHE IS CONSTANTLY PUNISHING HER BODY WITH VARIED ASSORTMENTS OF CLASS A SUBSTANCES. SHE CONSTANTLY FORCES UPON ME A BARRAGE OF SQUALID ANECDOTES ABOUT DEALS GONE WRONG AND HER CREEPY, LOW-CLASS "ASSOCIATES" TREATING HER LIKE DIRT. IT CAN BE UTTERLY HEARTBREAKING AT TIMES, SOMETIMES AFTER A PARTICULARLY BAD CALL I CAN FALL INTO A DEEP DEPRESSION... I DON'T KNOW HOW TO HELP HER..."THE ADDICTION IS POWERFUL IN THIS ONE"...
28.	BLINDED BY HER ANXIETY AND FRUSTRATION, MEGG SEEKS SEXUAL ESCAPE/RELIEF FROM BOOGER. IN THE MAIN CANON, MEGG AND BOOGER ARE OFTEN FOOLING AROUND BEHIND MOGG'S BACK AND THAT CONTINUES HERE IN THIS CORNER OF THE MULTIVERSE. I RECALL A FEW OF MY MORE SENSITIVE AUDIENCE MEMBERS BEING UPSET BY THIS EPISODE. "RAPE!", THEY CRIED. YEAH, BASICALLY, BUT ALSO... IT'S COMPLICATED... ISN'T IT? WHEN I WROTE THIS EPISODE I KNEW THAT I WANTED MEGG TO HAVE A PREGNANCY SCARE AND I WANTED IT TO BE AS MESSY AS POSSIBLE, I WANTED TO LEAN INTO TELENOVELLA STYLE CLIFFHANGERS AND HEAVY RELATIONSHIP DRAMA/TRAUMA... A HORSE MACKERAL IS THE WORST FISH IN ANIMAL CROSSING. I THINK THEY RUN AROUND 120 BELLS. SEA BASS ARE BETTER.
29, 30.	PREDICTABLY, THERE WAS A LOT OF ANTI-ASIAN RACISM GOING AROUND DURING THE BEGINNING OF ALL THIS SHIT. THE LAST TIME I DINED OUT BEFORE LOCKING DOWN WAS AT A SHITTY KOREAN BBQ WITH MY BUDDY, TONY ONG. HE, AN ASIAN MAN, CONGRATULATED ME ON MY OBVIOUS LACK OF RACISM, DUE TO MY DINING OUT AT A VERY SKETCHY KOREAN BBQ. TERRIBLE MEAT QUALITY. A REAL STINK-HOUSE. AS THE PANDEMIC HAS CONTINUED, I MYSELF HAVE CONTINUED TO SUPPORT LOCAL RESTAURANTS THAT OFFER CURBSIDE PICK-UP, INCLUDING SEVERAL ASIAN-THEMED BUSINESSES. #OFFICIALLYNOTRACIST. PAGE 30 HERE ELICITED YET MORE UNREQUESTED WHINING FROM THE MORE "PROGRESSIVE" SEGMENT OF MY READERSHIP. HOW DARE I MAKE LIGHT OF THE ARROGANCE OF CHILDREN? HOW DARE I? AND HOW DARE I PORTRAY BOOGER AS A FREE-THINKING INDIVIDUAL WHO DOES NOT SEE THEMSELF AS A VICTIM? I AM HISTORY'S GREATEST MONSTER.
31-33.	THINGS START TO HEAT UP WITH THE INTRODUCTION OF JONES'S PREMIUM PETROLEUM-FUELED "ASSBLASTER" MACHINES. I HAD TO KEEP UPPING THE ANTE... THIS WAS APRIL 13TH, NOBODY GAVE A FUCK ABOUT BIDEN, EVERY- ONE WAS STILL JUST WET FOR BERNIE. IT SEEMED THE ONLY DEMOGRAPHIC WITH ANY ENTHUSIASM FOR BIDEN WAS OLD WHITE WOMEN WHO WANTED A RETURN TO "NORMALCY"... I REALLY DIDN'T THINK BIDEN WOULD BEAT TRUMP, THERE WAS SUCH A LACK OF ENTHUSIASM FROM BASICALLY EVERYBODY FOR HIM. HERE WE ARE NOW IN 2021 THOUGH, THE OLD FUCKER DID IT. UPON RETURNING HOME, MEGG, MOGG AND BOOGER DISCOVER THAT THE HOUSE IS ON FIRE. THE FIRST OF MANY FIRES...
34, 35.	HERE WE HAVE THE ESTABLISHMENT OF THE "QUARANTINE SHED" AFTER OWL'S CLOACA EXPLODES ALL OVER THE LIVING ROOM. "THIS IS SERIOUS NOW". I THINK EVERYBODY REALLY FELT BOOGER'S LOSS HERE. YOU WORK SO HARD TO BUILD SOMETHING... TO HAVE IT ALL TORN AWAY. DEVASTATING. IF YOU TAKE CARE OF YOUR DELICATES AND ONLY WASH THEM ON A GENTLE CYCLE AND AIR DRY THEM, THEY CAN INDEED LAST DECADES. #NEVERFORGET.
36, 37.	IT WAS FUN DRAWING THIS FRASIER SEQUENCE. LATER IN THE BOOK WHEN EVERYBODY IS IN THE QUARANTINE SHED I CONSIDERED DOING A 'FRIENDS' HALLUCINATION IN A SIMILAR VEIN, BUT IT WAS NIXED. I THINK MY WIFE WAS DEAD AGAINST IT... BLAME HER. SHE WAS ACTUALLY FANTASTIC THROUGHOUT THIS WHOLE PROCESS. I'D TALK THROUGH IDEAS WITH HER, SHE'D ATTEMPT TO STEER ME IN SENSIBLE DIRECTIONS. SHE WAS AN INVALUABLE ADDITION TO THE LONELY WRITER'S ROOM... HERE COMES MOGG AGAIN, AND HE HAS COMPLETELY MORPHED INTO TIM POOL, A SAD, PARANOID MAN THAT IS TOO OLD TO BE SKATEBOARDING AND IS LOSING HIS SHIT FROM MAINLINING THE NEWS.
38.	I THINK JONES'S OFF-PANEL LOCKING OF MIKE IN THE SHED WAS JUST ME BEING OVERWHELMED BY THE AMOUNT OF CHARACTERS I WAS JUGGLING, I NEEDED TO GET SOMEONE OUT OF THE WAY AND MIKE WAS JUST SITTING AROUND CRYING ANYWAY... IT MADE ENOUGH SENSE... JONES RECITES A POEM BY THOMAS HARDY.

39-41.	DIESEL RUNS A SMART BUSINESS. HE DOESN'T GIVE A FUCK WHO HIS CUSTOMERS ARE, HE JUST PROVIDES A QUALITY SERVICE AND ACCEPTS CURRENCY IN EXCHANGE, AS CRAZY AS THAT SOUNDS. FIRST APPEARANCE OF DRACULA JUNIOR JR. I JUST THOUGHT IT WAS FUNNY THAT DRACULA JUNIOR WOULD HAVE A KID CALLED DRACULA JUNIOR JR... AND HERE COMES JONES'S HOT TUB IN THE MAIL AND WE PREPARE OURSELVES FOR THE FIRST MAJOR DISASTER OF CRISIS ZONE'S RUN...
42-45.	WEREWOLF JONES REFERENCES THE 2010 FILM 'HOT TUB TIME MACHINE' AS HE FRUSTRATEDLY BEATS THE SHIT OUT OF HIS COVID-TUB IN A FUTILE ATTEMPT TO RETURN TO A SIMPLER TIME. I HAD BEEN HOLDING ONTO THE PHRASE "WEREWOLF JONESTOWN MASSACRE' FOR MANY, MANY YEARS AND I WAS VERY HAPPY TO FINALLY BE ABLE TO DEPLOY IT. WEREWOLF JONES CLAIMS HE IS PLAYING 'BEAT SABER' ON HIS VR SET-UP BUT HE IS CLEARLY PLAYING 'ANGRY BIRDS VR'...
46-48.	JAXON TRIES TO KILL HIMSELF. FOR REAL. HE'S HAD ENOUGH OF LIFE AND HIS FATHER'S ANTICS. I CONTINUE TO HEAR VERY DEPRESSING STATISTICS ABOUT THE RATES OF SUICIDES DURING THIS LOCKDOWN ERA... I GENERALLY HATE LEAVING THE HOUSE SO I ACTUALLY FUCKING <u>LOVE</u> BEING LOCKED DOWN. I LIKE THAT NO CUNTS CAN COME OVER TO THE HOUSE, JUST LOTS OF TIME TO HEAVILY FOCUS ON MY PROJECTS AND SPACE OUT STARING AT THE WALLS. IT'S BLISS... OWL TAKES FLIGHT. OF COURSE OWL CAN FLY, "HE'S A BIG DUMB BIRD". THIS IS OFFICIALLY THE FIRST TIME WE SEE OWL FLY, THERE IS A SCENE OF HIM FLYING AT THE END OF 'MEGAHEX' BUT THAT IS MERELY A VISUAL REPRESENTATION OF THE FREEDOM HE FEELS UPON REMOVING HIMSELF FROM THE ABUSIVE FRIENDSHIP HE HAS ALLOWED HIMSELF TO BE IN FOR MOST OF HIS ADULT LIFE... I PLANNED TO REVEAL OWL'S FLIGHT ABILITY IN THE MAIN CANON'S FUTURE BUT HAVE BLOWN MY LOAD HERE...
49-53.	OWL HAS TAKEN FULL CONTROL OF THE HOUSE. NO MORE SHENANIGANS. EVERYTHING SHOULD RUN SMOOTHLY NOW. THE END. NARRATOR: "IT WAS NOT THE END". SANGFROID MEANS COMPOSURE, OR COOLNESS. OWL IS A PRETENTIOUS TWAT WHO IS TOO ARROGANT TO REALIZE THAT NOBODY AROUND HIM CAN UNDERSTAND A WORD HE'S SAYING... JONES DEFINITELY DESERVES TO BE LOCKED UP HERE, IN MY OPINION, HE HAS LITERALLY CAUSED A FIRE THAT TOOK 38 LIVES. OWL IS WELL WITHIN HIS RIGHTS TO FORCE JONES TO STRIP AT KNIFEPOINT AND HOSE HIM DOWN WITH LOW QUALITY, ICE COLD WATER... HERE WE SEE MIKE ENJOYING SOME HARRY POTTER. IN THE MAIN CANON MIKE IS ALREADY A HUGE POTTER-HEAD. IN THIS ALTERNATE CANON, HE IS JUST NOW DIPPING HIS TOES INTO THE POTTER-VERSE. MIKE IDENTIFIES HIMSELF, AT THIS POINT, AS A "HUFFLEPUFF". MEGG ANNOUNCES TO BOOGER THAT SHE THINKS SHE'S PREGNANT, AT THIS POINT IN THE RUN I HAD NO IDEA WHERE I WAS GOING WITH THIS, I THINK AT SOME POINT SHE WAS MAYBE ACTUALLY GOING TO BE PREGNANT... IT'S ALL A BLUR, FRANKLY... OWL TAKES A ZOOM WITH HIS EMPLOYERS, 'BERNSTEIN & FINKEL', AND IS PROMPTLY FIRED FOR ALL THE WEIRD SHIT HE'S INVOLVED IN, AT THE END OF THE CALL SOMEONE SAYS "SHALOM", HEBREW FOR PEACE. A COUPLE OF PEOPLE IN THE COMMENTS STARTED COMPLAINING ABOUT THIS, SAYING IT WAS "RACIST" OR SOME SHIT. I DID NOT BOTHER ENGAGING WITH THESE VIRTUOUS TROLLS, WHY WOULD I? MY THOUGHTS, HERE, IN FASTIDIOUS HAND-WRITTEN COMMENTARY FORM? WHY WOULD IT BE ODD FOR A JEWISH-RUN BUSINESS TO END A CALL WITH A SHALOM? THE NATURE OF THEIR BUSINESS IS NEVER STATED BUT <u>YOU</u>, COMMENTERS, WENT STRAIGHT TO FINANCE. BIT WEIRD. ALSO: MY WIFE IS JEWISH, WE CELEBRATE HANUKKAH. SO I GUESS WHAT I'M SAYING IS "FUCK OFF WITH THAT SHIT, YOU OBSESSIVE FREAKS"... THE STRESS OF LOSING HIS JOB SEEMS TO EXACERBATE OWL'S COVID SYMPTOMS AND HE DONS HIS "HEISENBERG HAT", A REFERENCE TO THE POPULAR AMC DRAMA SERIES 'BREAKING BAD'. IT IS REVEALED THAT OWL DRINKS BONSOY. OF COURSE HE DOES.
54-57.	"EVERYTHING'S BOARDED UP". THIS WAS MAY 7TH, PRE-PEACEFUL PROTESTS AND RIOTS. IT WAS CRAZY HOW QUICKLY BUSINESSES STARTED SHUTTING DOWN AND HOW BRAZEN THE ROBBERIES WERE BECOMING. SHIT WAS FUCKING <u>TENSE</u>. MEGG AND BOOGER HAVE A TENSE CONVERSATION AND INSENSITIVE THINGS ARE SAID. I'VE COMPLETELY STOPPED CARING ABOUT ANY READERS TAKING OFFENSE TO MY ART, THE CAN WHINE AND MOAN INTO THEIR FAUX-ACADEMIC, SAFE SPACE ECHO CHAMBERS FOR ETERNITY FOR ALL I CARE, I WILL CONTINUE TO DO WHATEVER THE FUCK I WANT AND WRITE ABOUT ANYTHING I WANT. "ARTISTIC EXPLORATION", "DANCING ON THE EDGE OF A KNIFE". I'M TIRED OF THE CLIMATE OF NERVOUSNESS WE ALL LIVE IN, SCARED OF "TWITTER PILE-ONS". I JUST DON'T CARE ANYMORE. THAT'S THE SECRET. EMBARRASSING, SHRIEKING CLOWNS DESERVE NO RESPECT. BUT INDEED, WRITING ABOUT TRANS ISSUES IS DIFFICULT, IT'S A FIELD FULL OF CONSTANTLY SHIFTING LANDMINES... I'VE BEEN WRITING BOOGER FOR ALMOST A DECADE NOW AND I AM PROUD OF HER, I THINK SHE'S A COOL TRANS CHARACTER, SHE JUST DOES HER THING, JUST TRIES TO GET BY. SHE'S NOT AN ASSHOLE, SHE HAS SELF-DOUBT, SHE HAS DARK THOUGHTS, SHE'S SELF-AWARE, SHE'S SELF-DEPRECATING BUT SHE HAS INNER STRENGTH. SHE'S ALSO PRETTY HOT. HER DAYS OF DRINKING FOR CONFIDENCE ARE ALMOST BEHIND HER... JONES AND DIESEL HAVE A LOVELY INTERACTION IN THIS SEQUENCE, JONES IS ACTUALLY A PRETTY PRO-GRESSIVE FATHER. HE'S VERY ACCEPTING OF DIESEL'S DECLARATIONS AND CHOICES REGARDING HIS SEXUALITY, ALTHOUGH SOME MAY SAY HE'S PERHAPS A BIT <u>TOO</u> SUPPORTIVE AND IT VERGES ON BEING OBSESSIVE, OR CREEPY... ENTER OWL, WHO HAS DECIDED TO FORCE WEREWOLF JONES TO PERFORM ONLINE SEX ACTS AS HIS NEW CAREER. I'M WITH OWL HERE, IT <u>WAS</u> JONES'S FAULT THAT OWL LOST HIS JEW-JOB, WHAT'S AN OWL TO DO? IT WAS THE ONLY LOGICAL COURSE OF ACTION... AND ALSO HERE WE HAVE THE REVEAL THAT MEGG IS INDEED NOT PREGNANT. SHE IS MOST LIKELY JUST AN IDIOT AND HAS HER CYCLE DATES WRONG OR IS JUST SUPER UNHEALTHY OR HAS COVID. MOGG REALIZES MEGG IS CHEATING ON HIM AND FREAKS OUT AND BASHES HIS HEAD AGAINST THE WALL IN A STUNNING DISPLAY OF PATHETIC MANIPULATION. I ONCE HAD A PARTNER WHO WOULD BASH THEIR HEAD ON THE WALL AND THREATEN TO KILL THEMSELF IF I EVER LEFT THEM. IT'S NOT A GREAT THING TO DEAL WITH AND IT'S CERTAINLY THE OPPOSITE OF ENDEARING... SOMEHOW IT MAKES YOU WANT TO ESCAPE EVEN MORESO!
58-60.	WEREWOLF JONES IS DOING A BIT OF AN ALEX JONES BIT HERE, A NICE PIECE OF FUN WORDPLAY THAT I COULD NOT RESIST. THE GUEST ON HIS SHOW IS GRAHAM LINEHAN, DISGRACED EX-COMEDY WRITER. I MUST ADMIT TO BEING A HUGE FAN OF 'BIG TRAIN', 'BLACK BOOKS' AND 'THE IT CROWD'. IN 2014 FANTAGRAPHICS ACTUALLY ATTEMPTED TO PROCURE A LINEHAN QUOTE FOR THE BACK COVER OF 'MEGAHEX', LUCKILY FOR ME, HE WAS UN-AVAILABLE. LINEHAN HAS BECOME OBSESSED WITH TRANSGENDER POLITICS AND HAS BEEN BANNED FROM TWITTER, HOSTS A SAD YOUTUBE RANT-CHANNEL AND APPARENTLY HAS LOST ALL OF HIS FRIENDS AND HIS WIFE LEFT HIM. GIVE IT UP, GRAHAM, YOU'VE LOST! PEOPLE THINK YOU'RE A NUT JOB NOW. IT DOESN'T EVEN MATTER IF YOU'RE RIGHT OR WRONG, YOU'VE <u>LOST</u>. MEGG CALLS HER MOTHER AGAIN... MORE THINLY-VEILED AUTOBIOGRAPHY, HOUSE FULL OF CRACKHEADS, ZERO SOCIAL DISTANCING! PROBABLY A BUNCH OF FUCKING NEEDLE-SHARING GOING ON, "IT'S THE END OF THE WORLD, WHO CARES?!". AWESOME! OWL HAS SHUT THE POWER DOWN, HE WAS VERY UNCOMFORTABLE WITH THE CONVERSATION THAT JONES AND LINEHAN WERE CONDUCTING, IT APPEARS THERE IS A LIMIT TO FREE SPEECH FOR NERVOUS OWL, WHICH MAKES MEGG UNCOMFORTABLE... OWL DEMANDS THAT WEREWOLF JONES KEEP HIS CONTENT APOLITICAL. OWL IS "OLD SCHOOL", HE BELIEVES IN GENERALLY KEEPING YOUR OPINIONS TO ONESELF AND RESPECTING THE OPINIONS OF OTHERS (WITHIN LIMITS). WITHIN BUSINESS, HE DEFINITELY BELIEVES IN ATTEMPTING TO CATER TO AND PLEASE THE LARGEST DEMOGRAPHIC POSSIBLE. A FACADE OF BLAND LIKABILITY,

62-63.	MIKE IS ENJOYING THE SHIT OUT OF HIS HARRY POTTER AS THE COVID TAKES ITS HOLD ON THE HOUSE. MEGG AND OWL ARE MOVED INTO THE QUARANTINE SHED/PRISON. BOOGER REVEALS THAT SHE IS SEXUALLY ATTRACTED TO THONGS, AND ALLUDES TO A "THONG WEDDING". FOR A SHORT TIME THERE WAS TO BE AN ACTUAL THONG WEDDING SCENE TO GO ALONG WITH THE PREVIOUS THONG FUNERAL. MY WIFE, ONCE AGAIN, INFORMED ME THAT THIS WAS A SHIT IDEA AND NOT FUNNY.
64-65.	HERE WE DISCOVER THAT MOGG HAS SPLIT FROM THE HOUSE AND TAKEN OFF IN HIS CRASS "PUSSY WAGON" THAT HE PURCHASED ON CRAIGSLIST FOR $1400 IN 2018. IT RUNS FINE AND HAS A MATTRESS IN THE BACK. HE HAS SUDDENLY GOTTEN OVER HIS GERMOPHOBIA AND IS LIVING WILD AND FREE WITHOUT A CARE. HE HAS EMBRACED THE CHAOS. MOGG STATES TO OPHELIA THAT HE IS HEADING WEST, WHICH DOESN'T REALLY MAKE SENSE, ALTHOUGH I SUPPOSE HE COULD HAVE DRIVEN EAST FOR A WHILE AND THEN DECIDED TO JUST HEAD BACK WEST TO THE SEATTLE-ISH AREA THE STORY IS SET IN... I DON'T KNOW, GIVE ME A BREAK, I'M A HIGH SCHOOL DROPOUT... I'VE NEVER DONE METH OR CRACK OR ANYTHING LIKE THAT, I WONDER WHAT IT'S LIKE... I SHOULD ASK MY MOTHER, OR THE HOMELESS PEOPLE THAT CONGREGATE OUTSIDE THE SUPERMARKET THAT SHOUT HOMOPHOBIC SLURS AT ME...
66-78.	BACK TO THE HOUSE, EVERYBODY HAS SUCCUMBED TO THE COVID AND IT HAS FALLEN UPON JAXON'S SHOULDERS TO TAKE CARE OF EVERYONE, A REAL TEST OF HIS METTLE. HE'S BACK ON THE FAGS, HE NEEDS THAT SMOOTH NICOTINE RELIEF. OWL CONTINUES TO MONETIZE JONES'S SUFFERING, MUCH TO THE DELIGHT OF JIM HEMMINGFIELD, WHO HAS AT THIS POINT DONATED OVER 3000 BRITISH POUNDS IN SUPERCHATS. DRACULA JUNIOR, WITH THE ASSISTANCE OF WODDY, RETURNS TO EXACT REVENGE ON JONES FOR THE DEATH OF HIS SON. IAN RETURNS AND SPINS HIS LIE THAT JAXON STARTED THE FIRE AND ALSO HIS LIE THAT HE WAS AT THE BEACH, ALL PART OF DIESEL'S MANIPULATIVE PLAN TO SAVE HIS FATHER FROM CERTAIN DEATH. RATHER CLEVER, REALLY. JONES'S NIPPLE IS CHOPPED OFF, IT WAS A CHALLENGE TO REMEMBER THAT DURING EACH INSTALLMENT, JONES IS NAKED A LOT. MIKE APPEARS TO DIE HERE, A CASUALTY OF THE COVID, BUT THIS IS MERELY A FAKE-OUT AND MIKE SHALL BE REBORN... PAGE 78'S EPISODE HERE IS FROM JUNE 1ST AND THE CHARACTERS HAVE LEFT THE HOUSE TO DISCOVER THE CITY ON FIRE AND PROTESTERS AND RIOTERS RUNNING BUCK WILD THROUGH THE STREETS. OWL IS CONFUSED AS TO WHY EVERYONE IS OUTSIDE DURING A PANDEMIC...
79.	THIS EPISODE APPEARED ON INSTAGRAM ON JUNE 3RD... I TOOK A FEW DAYS OFF DUE TO THE WIDESPREAD ANGER AND CHAOS ACROSS THE COUNTRY IN THE WAKE OF THE MURDER OF GEORGE FLOYD, IT DIDN'T FEEL QUITE RIGHT TO BE POSTING THESE COMICS... I POSTED THE BLACK SQUARE THAT EVERYBODY WAS POSTING AS A SIGN OF SUPPORT FOR... SOMETHING. THE NEXT DAY EVERYBODY WAS MOANING ON ABOUT IT BEING RACIST TO POST THE BLACK SQUARE, SO I DELETED THE BLACK SQUARE... I BEGAN TO RECEIVE MESSAGES FROM UPPITY, IRATE INDIVIDUALS (MOSTLY WHITE NON-BINARY PEOPLE) DEMANDING THAT I "USE MY PLATFORM" TO PROMOTE "BAIL FUNDS" FOR "PROTESTERS". THIS ANNOYED ME, I FIND THESE KINDS OF PEOPLE INCREDIBLY ARROGANT AND AGGRESSIVE. MY "PLATFORM" IS LARGER THAN THEIRS PRECISELY BECAUSE I DON'T HARRASS AND INTIMIDATE MY "FANS" INTO THINKING "MY WAY". I RESPECT MY AUDIENCE AND DON'T GIVE A FUCK WHAT THEY DO OR DON'T DO, IT'S NONE OF MY FUCKING BUSINESS. AT THE SAME TIME I WAS RECEIVING A MUCH HIGHER VOLUME OF POLITE MESSAGES FROM REGULAR PEOPLE FROM ALL ACROSS THE GLOBE SAYING THEY MISSED CRISIS ZONE AND THAT IT HAD BEEN A HIGHLIGHT OF THEIR DAY. SO, I JUST GOT BACK TO WORK, FUCK IT. MY MAIN CONCERN WAS THE ONGOING PANDEMIC AND KEEPING MY FANS ENTERTAINED. A FRIEND TOLD ME THAT AN ARTIST WE BOTH KNOW HAD TOLD THEM THAT THEY WERE CUTTING PEOPLE OUT OF THEIR LIFE WHO "WEREN'T DOING ENOUGH FOR BLM". AFTER THE CALL WITH MY FRIEND I INSTANTLY UNFOLLOWED THE ARTIST WE HAD BEEN TALKING ABOUT. THAT'S SOME FUCKING CULT SHIT, I WAS NOT GOING TO BE FUCKING AROUND WITH THAT NONSENSE. MY WIFE AND I PRIVATELY DONATED SOME MONEY TO FOOD BANKS AND A TRANS-FRIENDLY SHELTER, NO RECEIPTS WERE POSTED, IT WAS JUST DONE... I HAD POSTED A PRO-BLM DRAWING I'D MADE ON TWITTER BUT I REMOVED IT ONCE THE MURDERS STARTED HAPPENING. THERE WAS SOME FUCKED UP SHIT GOING DOWN... I WANTED NOTHING TO DO WITH ANY SIDE...
80-89.	SO HERE WE ARE, CHAOS IN THE STREETS, TENSIONS RUNNING HIGH... GOTTA SAVE JAXON THOUGH. AFTER HIS LEGIT SUICIDE ATTEMPT AND SPAGHETTI COOK-UPS, PEOPLE HAD REALLY WARMED UP TO SWEET LIL JAXON AND WANTED THE BEST FOR HIM... FOR THIS CHUNK OF EPISODES CRISIS ZONE MORPHED INTO A SUPERHERO STORY, WHICH WAS FUN TO DO, PLAYING WITH GENRE... I GREW UP LOVING STUFF LIKE 'SUPERFRIENDS' AND 'DEFENDERS OF THE EARTH'... MIKE IS ALIVE... IN THE FIRST PANEL OF PAGE 81 YOU CAN SEE THE "UMBRELLA MAN", WHO WAS IN THE NEWS A LOT, I CAN'T REMEMBER EXACTLY WHAT ALL THAT WAS ABOUT, I THINK HE WAS SOME ANARCHIST RIGHT-WINGER WHO WAS CAUGHT SMASHING OUT THE WINDOWS AT AN AUTOZONE IN ORDER TO FRAME SOME PROTESTERS... IT'S DIFFICULT TO DECIPHER THE MECHANICS OF THIS SHIT, SO MUCH HAPPENED AND IS CONTINUING TO HAPPEN AND THERE'S SO MANY DIFFERENT NARRATIVES AND RUMORS AND LIES AND CONSPIRACIES FLYING AROUND. MAN, WHAT A HORRIBLE FUCKING TIME. PEOPLE SUCK. OH, TO NOT BE ADDICTED TO THE INTERNET AND JUST LIVE YOUR FUCKING LIFE IN IGNORANT BLISS!... ON PAGE 84 WE HAVE A DEPICTION OF SOME POLICE BRUTALITY FOR THE REMAINING LEFTISTS OF MY READERSHIP. THE COPS INDEED WERE DOING AN INCREDIBLY BAD JOB OF MANAGING THE RATHER JUSTIFIED ANGER AND FRUSTRATION THAT WAS BEING HURLED TOWARDS THEM, WE SEE DIESEL GETTING PEPPER SPRAYED IN THE FACE HERE. THIS ACTUALLY HAPPENED HERE IN SEATTLE, HORRIBLE BUSINESS, A KID GETTING MACED. I THINK IT WAS LIKE DAY 6 OR SOMETHING OF ALL THE CLASHES THAT WERE BREAKING OUT HERE, PROTESTERS AND THE COPS GETTING INTO IT, THROWING SHIT AT EACH OTHER. "HEY, LET'S TAKE THE KIDS DOWN!". PEOPLE WERE GETTING GASSED... MOGG'S OUT IN THE MIDDLE OF NOWHERE AND HAS A RUN-IN WITH A LOCAL, PARANOID, "PATRIOT" MILITIA. THE BOOGEYMANIFICATION OF "ANTIFA" AND "ANARCHISTS" WAS BEGINNING TO GROW LEGS... DURING THEIR MISSION TO FIND JAXON, THE SQUAD RUN INTO AN "AUTONOMOUS ZONE". I'VE BEEN TO CHRISTIANIA (FREETOWN), AN AUTONOMOUS ZONE IN SEATTLE THOUGH? YES. RIGHT WHERE I USED TO GO TO BAND PRACTICE, RIGHT NEXT TO ONE OF MY FAVORITE RESTAURANTS, IN CAPITOL HILL. IT WAS NOW COVERED IN A BUNCH OF RADICAL GRAFFITI AND THERE WERE WALLS OF TRASH EVERYWHERE... COOL? DURING THE DAY IT SEEMED INNOCENT ENOUGH BUT AT NIGHT IT REPORTEDLY DEVOLVED INTO CHAOS. AFTER BRANDING IT THE "SEATTLE SUMMER OF LOVE" THE INEPT MAYOR SHUT IT DOWN, MIGHT HAVE HAD SOMETHING TO DO WITH THE ACTUAL MURDERS THAT WENT ON DOWN THERE... WHO KNOWS? AFTER A FEW FOLLIES AND MISHAPS OUR HEROES FIND THEIR WAY TO DRACULA JUNIOR'S CRIME-WAREHOUSE AND FIND IT TO BE FULL OF ARMED, WISEGUY RABBITS. THESE RABBITS ARE ALL BASED ON MY ACTUAL, REAL, LIVING RABBITS THAT I TAKE CARE OF. MONTY, ROCKO AND "MISTER LINCOLN". THEY'RE NOT VERY NICE CHARACTERS, THESE CARTOON RABBITS, IT'S KEEPING WITH HOW A LOT OF RABBITS ARE, A BIT STROPPY AND MEAN, A BIT SCUMMY SOMETIMES (NOT MR. LINCOLN OR ROCKO THOUGH, THEY'RE VERY SWEET. IT'S MONTY WHO'S THE RUDE PRICK OF THE BUNCH. FUCKING SCUMBAG.) BUT YEAH, MOST OF MY RABBITS WERE FOUND ON THE STREETS. THEY'RE TOUGH, THEY'RE STREETWISE. THEY'VE PROBABLY DONE THINGS TO GET BY THAT YOU OR I COULDN'T EVEN BEGIN TO IMAGINE. IT'S TOUGH TO GET BY OUT THERE, YOU GOTTA DO WHAT YOU GOTTA DO... MAN, I FUCKING LOVE MY SCUMMY RABBITS SO MUCH. IT'S MY REWARD, AT THE END OF EACH DAY, TO HANG OUT WITH THESE LITTLE ANGELS.

90-100.	HERE WE SEGUE OUT OF SUPER-PASTICHE AND INTO AN "ACTION" MODE, A DOWN AND DIRTY, WORKING CLASS GUN FIGHT. IAN TAKES HIS FIRST OF FOUR BULLETS... RHDV, THE RABBIT DISEASE, IS A REAL THING AND IT AIN'T PRETTY. WE HAVE INSTITUTED A "NO SHOES IN THE HOUSE" POLICY TO PROTECT OUR RABBITS FROM FILTHY, DISEASE CARRYING BIRDS. YUCK!

NO ACTION SEQUENCE WOULD BE COMPLETE WITHOUT A SPEEDBOAT CHASE, SO I HAD TO THROW ONE OF THOSE IN... THE IDEA OF JONES WATCHING A JORDAN PETERSON LECTURE TO "CALM DOWN" IS, I BELIEVE, ONE OF THE FINEST JOKES IN THIS RUN. DRACULA JUNIOR APPEARS TO ACTUALLY BE TAKING PRETTY GOOD CARE OF JAXON WITH THE RACING CAR BED, PS4 PRO, BILLIE EILISH POSTER AND HOT POCKETS THAT PURPORT TO CONTAIN SOME FORM OF VEGETABLE... I BELIEVE THAT AXE BODY SPRAY IS KNOWN AS LYNX IN EUROPEAN TERRITORIES, IT IS HORRIBLE, HORRIBLE STUFF. I AM GLAD I NO LONGER HAVE TO SUFFER ITS ACRID STENCH IN RIDE-SHARE SITUATIONS. THE LOCKDOWN HAS ITS BLESSINGS. THE MIX OF AXE AND RECTAL GAS WAS THE STUFF OF NIGHTMARES.

101-102.	THE GANG RETURN HOME TO FIND MIKE ALIVE. MIKE APPEARS TO BE DRESSING A BIT FEMME NOW, WITH ONE OF HIS BALLS HANGING LOOSE AND DOING ITS OWN THING... I CAN'T REMEMBER IF AT THIS POINT I HAD CONCRETELY DECIDED TO HAVE MIKE TRANSITION INTO JENNIFER. MANY READERS HAVE ASKED WHAT BEARING THIS MIGHT HAVE ON MIKE'S CHARACTER IN THE MAIN CANON. CHECK OUT THE STORY 'LEGAL' IN SEEDS AND STEMS, THERE'S SOME CLUES IN THERE.

103.	HERE WE FIND MEGG IN THE MIDDLE OF THE AUTONOMOUS ZONE THAT POPPED UP IN SEATTLE, WHICH IN REAL LIFE WAS KNOWN AS THE "CHAZ." I HAVE DEPICTED IT HERE AS I SAW IT IN LIVESTREAMS, A BUNCH OF WELL-MEANING HIPPIES, RADICAL LEFT-WING GUN CLUBS, HOMELESS FOLK AND RANDOM ODDBALLS. I BELIEVE I ACTUALLY DID SEE A SOLICITATION

FOR A DOCUMENTARY SCREENING THAT REQUESTED "WHITES" BE SAT IN BACK, YOU CAN'T MAKE THIS SHIT UP. THERE WERE NUMEROUS SCUFFLES AND CONFLICTS DOWN THERE. BY DAY IT INTRIGUED "INTERNATIONAL TOURISTS" BUT BY NIGHT IT WAS PARANOIA AND GANG WARFARE. I HAD FRIENDS WHO WENT DOWN TO CHECK IT OUT BUT THERE WAS NO FUCKING WAY IN HELL I WAS GOING DOWN THERE. I AM A LAW-ABIDING, PERMANENT LEGAL RESIDENT, I DON'T FUCK WITH THIS CRAZY SHIT. I FEEL SOMEWHAT BAD FOR MY DEPICTION OF THE SHITTY LITTLE CHAZ "COMMUNITY GARDEN", I SAW AN INTERVIEW WITH THE DUDE WHO INITIATED IT AND HE SEEMED LIKE A REALLY SWEET, BIG HEARTED GUY, DOOMED TO FAIL THOUGH...

104-106.	MOGG FINDS HIMSELF WORKING AT AN AMAZON WAREHOUSE. WE WERE DRIVING TO THE SUPERMARKET ONE DAY AND I NOTICED THAT ALONG THE SIDE OF THE ROAD WERE AMAZON JOBS SIGNS EVERY 20FT OR SO. AMAZON WAS BEGINNING THEIR COMPLETE AND TOTAL DOMINATION OF LITERALLY EVERYTHING... MOGG IS SEEN PACKING A LARGE PILE OF DVD'S,

ALL OF THESE ARE TV SHOWS THAT WERE, AT THE TIME, GETTING YANKED OFF OF STREAMING SERVICES FOR BLACKFACE OR PERCEIVED RACIAL TRANSGRESSIONS. I MYSELF WENT OUT OF MY WAY TO PURCHASE HARD COPIES OF 'THE MIGHTY BOOSH', 'PEEP SHOW' AND 'THE LEAGUE OF GENTLEMEN' AND I'D IMAGINE MANY OTHER FANS OF THESE CLASSIC SHOWS DID THE SAME, IT'S FUNNY WATCHING 'THE GREAT BRITISH BAKEOFF' CURRENTLY, BOTH OF THE HOSTS HAVE HAD THEIR MOST FAMOUS AND POPULAR WORKS SCRUBBED FROM MOST STREAMING OUTLETS AND HAVE BEEN ACCUSED OF BEING RACISTS. THEY'RE BOTH STILL WORKING THOUGH, SO I GUESS THERE MAYBE IS SOMETHING TO THE ARGUMENT THAT "CANCEL CULTURE ISN'T REAL"... AS MOGG PACKS A SIR DICK™ DILDO (AN EIGHTBALL REFERENCE) HE ACCIDENTALLY PACKAGES HIS PISS-BOTTLE ALONG WITH IT. THIS PACKAGE WAS INTENDED TO ARRIVE AT THE HOUSE FOR WEREWOLF JONES, WHO WOULD EXPRESS SURPRISE AT THE MYSTERY BOTTLE OF CAT'S URINE, I NEVER MANAGED TO FIT THIS IN ANYWHERE... MITZI IS INTRODUCED, MOGG'S YOUNG, SOUNDCLOUD RAPPER "REPLACEMENT MEGG". THEY ARE LIVING IN LAS VEGAS WHERE TWO DOUBLE WHISKEYS WILL INDEED RUN YOU AT LEAST $68.00... I ACTUALLY DID RUN INTO ANDY DICK IN VEGAS ONCE, WE WERE STAYING AT THE SAME HOTEL, WHICH IS A SERIOUS INDICATION THAT HIS CAREER IS NOT GOING WELL... I WAS VERY, VERY PLEASED WITH MYSELF FOR COMING UP WITH THIS "CARROT BOTTOM" JOKE.

107.	"MY GOD, IT'S JUST POLITICS AND ACTIVISM EVERYWHERE!". YEP. IT WAS INESCAPABLE. FOR PEOPLE LIKE ME THAT HAVE NEVER REALLY CARED ABOUT POLITICS AND FOUND "ACTIVISTS" TO BE SMUG, SANCTIMONIOUS CUNTS, IT WAS A STRANGE TIME... I'D IMAGINE THIS EPISODE WOULD'VE PISSED OFF A LOT OF HARDLINE LEFTISTS. THEY DIDN'T LIKE IT

WHEN YOU POINTED OUT THAT A LOT OF BLACK-OWNED BUSINESSES WERE GETTING LOOTED AND DESTROYED, THEY DIDN'T LIKE CRITICISM OF THEIR TEARING DOWN OF STATUES THAT HAD NOTHING TO DO WITH ANYTHING THAT WAS HAPPENING, THEY DIDN'T WANT ANYBODY TO SEE ALL THE MOB BEATINGS AND EXTREME VIOLENCE IN THE STREETS. IT DIDN'T FIT THE NARRATIVE. WHAT CAN I SAY? IF YOU WERE WATCHING PROPERLY, WITH YOUR EYES WIDE OPEN, THERE WERE INSANE, PERPLEXING EVENTS UNFOLDING. I GUESS YOU COULD CALL ME POLITICALLY HOMELESS. I HATE THE EXTREME RIGHT, I HATE THE EXTREME LEFT. I JUST HATE EXTREMISM... IF I HAD TO PLACE A BET, I'D SAY WE'RE IN THE END TIMES, "POLITE SOCIETY" IS DEAD. NOBODY WILL EVER BE ALLOWED TO RELAX EVER AGAIN.

108-110.	HERE WE SEE OWL, WITH A PRESSURE-HOSE, CLEANING OFF THE POLITICALLY CHARGED GRAFFITI FROM HIS RESIDENCE. THIS WAS JULY 4TH. I GOT THE SENSE THAT A LOT OF PEOPLE MIGHT HAVE BEEN FEELING SLIGHTLY FATIGUED FROM ALL OF THE PREVIOUS MONTH'S INSANITY ON TOP OF THE ONGOING PANDEMIC, GOD FORBID YOU IMPLIED AS MUCH THOUGH, YOU

FUCKING RACIST! EVERYTHING'S FINE. "IT'S JUST PROPERTY AND PEOPLE'S LIVELIHOODS... FUCK 'EM!"... BOOGER IS PLAYING 'THE LAST OF US 2', A POPULAR VIDEOGAME THAT RELEASED A FEW WEEKS EARLIER. I PLAYED IT AND I ENJOYED IT. THERE WAS A LOT OF MOANING ONLINE FROM ALL STRIPES OF FUCKHEAD, BUT YEAH, I THOUGHT IT WAS FUCKING AWESOME. THE GAME FEATURES A POST-APOCALYPTIC SEATTLE RAVAGED BY A VIRUS, FULL OF ROVING GANGS AND CULTS, IT WAS INDEED VERY NOW. IT IS REVEALED THAT IAN IS A SHITTY, PRIVILEGED TRUST-PUNK. OF COURSE HE IS... AND HERE COMES JENNIFER. NO MORE MIKE. MY INTENTION HERE WAS TO TAKE A CHARACTER KNOWN FOR THEIR CHILL, RELAXED STYLE OF HANGING OUT AND TAKE THEM ON THIS TRANSITIONAL JOURNEY AND CHALLENGE THE OTHER CHARACTERS. MY HOPE WAS THAT CERTAIN READERS MIGHT ALSO BE CHALLENGED, IN A POSITIVE WAY. PERHAPS A LOVED ONE OR A FRIEND MAY JUST SUDDENLY "TRANSITION" TOMORROW, WHAT ARE YOU GONNA DO? I'D JUST RECENTLY HAD A FRIEND OF MINE SUDDENLY ANNOUNCE THEY WERE TRANS AND I'LL BE HONEST, IT WAS KIND OF WEIRD, THEY'D NEVER SHOWN ANY INKLING OF NEEDING TO DO THAT, DESPITE CONSTANTLY BEING SURROUNDED BY MY OWN GENDER-EXPLORATIONS AND THEIR VERY QUEER BROTHER. BUT YEAH, WHATEVER, WHY THE FUCK NOT? DURING THE QUARANTINE, I MYSELF HAD ALSO BEEN "DRESSING LIKE A WOMAN" A LOT MORE OFTEN, LIVING OUT ENTIRE WEEKS AND MONTHS IN "GIRL-MODE". AS JENNIFER STATES, "THE LOCKDOWN'S THE PERFECT TIME TO TRANSITION". IT'S NICE NOT HAVING TO LEAVE THE HOUSE TO BE EXPOSED TO THE JUDGEMENTAL GLARES AND THE MOCKING CHILDREN, IT'S COOL THAT YOU CAN WEAR A MASK TO HIDE YOUR MANLY JAW. GOOD OLD LOCKDOWN!... THE J.K. ROWLING THING WAS JUST THE ICING ON THE GAY CAKE, PERFECT TIMING FOR MIKE/JEN'S DEEP DIVE INTO HARRY POTTER, I COULDN'T HAVE PLANNED IT BETTER. THANKS, J.K.!

111,112.	JONES IS BLOWING UP ON "TIKTOK", A BIT META, AS CRISIS ZONE WAS BLOWING UP ON INSTAGRAM. NETFLIX SAW THAT THEY COULD MAKE SOME MONEY ON JONES AND A KNOCKING THEY CAME. DURING THIS PERIOD I WAS DEALING WITH SOME TV BULLSHIT MYSELF... FOR YEARS I'VE HAD PRODUCERS UP MY ASS, TRYING TO GET A SLICE OF THE MEGG AND MOGG PIE. I WAS NOT HAVING A GOOD TIME WITH IT. THE PRODUCERS I WAS WORKING WITH WERE BEING WEIRDLY EVASIVE AND I HAD A LOT OF CONCERNS ABOUT THE SCRIPT THAT WAS BEING WRITTEN...

ONE OF THOSE MILLIONAIRE HOLLYWOOD "COMEDIANS" WAS BROUGHT IN TO WRITE THE SCRIPT AND I ASSUMED IT WOULD BE ALRIGHT, BUT COMMUNICATION BROKE DOWN, WHICH SEEMED TO BE THE FAULT OF THE PRODUCERS AND EXECUTIVES. ONCE I FINALLY SAW THE SCRIPT, I WAS HORRIFIED. BLAND NEW CHARACTERS HAD BEEN INSERTED, OWL WAS TURNED INTO A GENERIC TINDER BRO, MEGG AND MOGG WERE NOW CUTESY MORONS THAT TALKED LIKE WOKE DRAG QUEENS. THE EDGE HAD BEEN DULLED. IT WAS NOT MEGG AND MOGG. THEY GAVE MEGG SUPERPOWERS AND MADE HER 400 YEARS OLD, A POLITICAL ACTIVIST WHO HAD "MARCHED AT SALEM". I RECALL SOME INCREDIBLY UNCOMFORTABLE ZOOMS... MY NOTES FOR THE SCRIPT WERE PERHAPS THE MOST IN-DEPTH AND ACADEMIC NOTES EVER PRODUCED IN THE WORLD OF SCRIPT NOTES. TEARING THAT SCRIPT APART WAS ONE OF THE MOST ENJOYABLE THINGS I'VE EVER DONE. IT'S A SHAME NOBODY WILL EVER GET TO READ BOTH THE HORRIBLE SCRIPT BY THE MILLIONAIRE HOLLYWOOD "COMEDIAN" AND MY INCREDIBLY HARSH NOTES. I'M CERTAIN THE SHOW WOULD HAVE BEEN PRODUCED, THEY WAVED A LOT OF MONEY UNDER MY NOSE, TOLD ME TO JUST SUCK IT UP AND FORGET MY ARTISTIC AND ETHICAL PRINCIPLES, BUT I TURNED IT ALL DOWN, GOT THE FUCK OUT OF THE DEAL AS QUICK AS I LEGALLY COULD. IF THEIR VERSION OF MEGG AND MOGG, OR ANYTHING LIKE IT, HAD MADE IT TO AIR, I WOULD'VE HAD TO KILL MYSELF. EVERYTHING I'D COMMITTED TO PAPER, LABORIOUSLY, FOR THE PAST DECADE, WOULD BE ECLIPSED BY TRITE, SACCHARINE PAP IN THE PUBLIC'S CONSCIOUSNESS. I COULD NOT ALLOW THAT TO HAPPEN. AND IT'S NOT ABOUT THE MONEY, IT'S ABOUT MAKING HONEST ART, IT'S ABOUT THE HORROR AND SQUALOR OF EXISTENCE! TV PEOPLE AREN'T INTERESTED IN THAT STUFF, THEY DON'T WANT THAT SHIT RIGHT NOW, AS MUCH AS THEY PRETEND THEY DO. I'M STILL TALKING TO TV PEOPLE. I HAD A MEETING A FEW WEEKS BACK WITH ONE OF THE MAJOR STUDIOS. IT WAS FINE. I POINT BLANK SAID THE ONLY WAY THERE WOULD EVER BE A MEGG AND MOGG TV SHOW IS IF I AM THE SOLE WRITER OF THE PRODUCTION, I'LL ACCEPT A VETERAN CO-WRITER IF I MUST, BUT THEY WOULD HAVE TO UNDERSTAND THAT THEY WOULD "BE MY BITCH", I WOULD BE IN CHARGE. THEY SENT ME AN EMAIL A WEEK OR SO AGO AND I JUST HAVEN'T GOTTEN BACK TO THEM... I THINK I JUST LIKE MAKING COMICS, I'M TOO USED TO HAVING FULL CONTROL. COMICS IS VERY LUXURIOUS IN ITS AUTONOMY, SO PURE AND UNCOMPLICATED. AIN'T ACTUALLY THAT MUCH MONEY IN TV EITHER, OVER THE YEARS I'VE SCOFFED AT MANY AN OFFER, LITERALLY LESS MONEY THAN WHAT I CAN MAKE YEARLY FLIPPING FUCKING ZINES ON BIGCARTEL. WHY THE FUCK WOULD I BOTHER? PUT UP WITH A BUNCH OF SOFT FUCKING HARVARD CUNTS WHO THINK THEY KNOW BETTER THAN ME? TELEVISION NEEDS TO BE TAKEN DOWN A PEG, IT'S NOT THE BE ALL, END ALL MEDIUM IT THINKS IT IS. I WANT A COMICS REVOLUTION. COMICS ARE BETTER THAN TV...

| 113-118. | HERE WE GO WITH 'ANUS KING'. I DON'T NEED A REAL TV SHOW, I CAN MAKE MY OWN TV SHOW, ALONE IN MY STUDIO, ON PAPER... MOGG GOES ALL SCORCHED EARTH AND DECIDES TO TAKE EVERYBODY DOWN AND SELL ALL OF THEIR SECRETS... I'M PRETTY SURE I DON'T WANT TO BE "FAMOUS" IN THIS DAY AND AGE. IT JUST OPENS YOU UP TO HARRASSMENT AND STALKING AND SMEARING. I'M CONSTANTLY SEEING PEOPLE CALLING JUSTIN ROILAND, FOR INSTANCE, A PEDOPHILE. IT'S JUST AWFUL. THE INTERNET IS HORRIBLE. I'M VERY |

HAPPY WITH MEGG AND MOGG BEING A "CULT" COMIC, IT SELLS WELL ENOUGH, I MAKE A LIVING AND I MOSTLY REMAIN UNHARRASSED BY PSYCHOTIC CONSERVATIVES AND UNHINGED UBER-LEFTISTS. I PRAY IT REMAINS THAT WAY... MITZI IS WEARING A "GOTH BOI CLIQUE (GBC)" SHIRT, THEY ARE A POPULAR UNDERGROUND "EMO HIP HOP" CREW OUT OF LOS ANGELES WHO CLAIMED LIL PEEP AS A MEMBER BEFORE HIS UNTIMELY DEATH IN 2017. R.I.P. LIL PEEP. FLAMIN' HOT CHEETOS ARE VERY POPULAR IN THE UNDERGROUND RAP WORLD. THE RAPPER 'LIL XAN' WAS HOSPITALIZED AT ONE POINT DUE TO HIS MASS CONSUMPTION OF THE PRODUCT. I FOUND THIS VERY AMUSING. LIL PEEP DIES OF A FENTANYL OVERDOSE, LIL XAN EATS TOO MANY HOT CHEETOS.

| 119-131. | ANUS KING IS AN INSTANT RATINGS JUGGERNAUT, A VIRAL SMASH... THE GANG HAVE FULL BANK ACCOUNTS AND EVERYBODY WANTS TO CANCEL THEM, SUPER GLAMOROUS STUFF, ALL THE COKE YOU CAN SNORT. IT BECOMES PUBLIC KNOWLEDGE THAT OWL ONCE MADE OUT (ACCIDENTALLY) WITH A CHILD CALLED PEYOTE. THIS OCCURRED IN THE MAIN CANON, MAIN SERIES OF BOOKS, IN 'MEGAHEX'. I FIGURED THAT THINGS THAT HAPPENED IN THAT REALITY MAY ALSO HAVE OCCURRED IN THIS ALTERNATE COVID-REALM. IN THE MAIN CANON, JONES |

DIES OF AN OVERDOSE IN 2017. IN THIS COVID-UNIVERSE, HE DID NOT DIE IN 2017. "SLIDING DOORS"... VALERIA IS INTRODUCED, SHE IS THE OFFICIAL "JONES FAMILY ENTERTAINMENT AGENT". SHE IS "LOOSELY" BASED ON MY REAL LIFE LITERARY AGENT, ALESSANDRA STERNFELD... I LOVE MY AGENT, SHE IS UTTERLY FANTASTIC AT HER JOB AND ALWAYS HAS THE FINEST ANECDOTES. I WAS ONE OF HER FIRST CLIENTS, I TOOK A CHANCE ON HER, I COULD SENSE A CERTAIN PASSION AND FIERY INTELLIGENCE. IT'S BEEN A PLEASURE OVER THE YEARS TO WATCH HER BUILD HER EMPIRE ACROSS THE GLOBE. I AM PROUD TO BE REPRESENTED BY 'AM BOOK'. SOME OF MY FAVOURITE HEATED ARGUMENTS I'VE EVER HAD HAVE BEEN WITH ALE. IN CRISIS ZONE I'VE REALLY PLAYED UP THE EUROTRASH ANGLE WITH VALERIA, I SHOULD HAVE DRESSED HER BETTER. REGULARLY, ALE WOULD TEXT ME, COMPLAINING ABOUT VALERIA'S LACKLUSTRE BUSINESS-CASUAL ATTIRE... THE CANCEL WARS BEGIN, WITH MEGG ATTEMPTING TO GET BACK AT MOGG BY LISTING A BUNCH OF HIS TRANSGRESSIONS. EVERYTHING SHE LISTS IS STUFF THAT HAPPENED IN 'MEGAHEX', FURTHER BLURRING THE LINES BETWEEN WORLDS... CHRIS HANSEN ARRIVES, WHO IS PERHAPS THE ENTERTAINMENT WORLD'S PREMIER PEDOPHILE HUNTER. IN OWL'S "FILE PHOTO" HE IS DRESSED AS FAMOUS MYSPACE EMO-PEDO DAHVIE VANITY OF THE TRULY AWFUL MUSICAL PROJECT 'BLOOD ON THE DANCEFLOOR'... KANYE WEST MAKES AN APPEARANCE. WHAT A FUCKING CLOWN... DRACULA JUNIOR RETURNS AND PROPOSES MARRIAGE TO JONES. DRAC' IS 100% LEGIT, THERE WAS NO FUNNY BUSINESS GOING ON, HE SERIOUSLY WANTED THE MARRIAGE TO WORK. HE MAY OR MAY NOT HAVE BEEN EXPERIENCING A MENTAL BREAKDOWN AT THE TIME... DIESEL ANNOUNCES SHE IS NOW "DESI" AND OF COURSE JONES IS UNBOTHERED BY THIS. I DEBATED WHETHER OR NOT TO GO IN THIS DIRECTION WITH DESI'S CHARACTER, WE ALREADY HAD BOOGER AND JENNIFER. I PULLED THE TRIGGER IN THE END THOUGH AND WENT WITH IT. IN A WAY IT'S A COMMENTARY ON POPULAR, MAINSTREAM MEDIA'S CURRENT "DIVERSITY PUSH". YOU SEE A LOT OF MOANING ONLINE FROM PEOPLE UPSET AT THE INCLUSION OF CERTAIN MINORITIES AND IDENTITIES CURRENTLY. SOME OF THESE PEOPLE ARE JUST ACTUALLY RACISTS OR TRANSPHOBES, SOME ARE MERELY PEOPLE WHO CAN SENSE WHEN SOMETHING IS BEING DONE ORGANICALLY VERSUS WHEN IT IS FOR SHOW OR "VIRTUE POINTS". I TRY TO MAKE MY WORK NATURALLY DIVERSE AND INCLUDE AN ARRAY OF DIFFERENT TYPES OF PEOPLE AND IDEOLOGIES, I CERTAINLY DON'T LOSE SLEEP OVER IT THOUGH... ANOTHER ASPECT TO MY INCLUSION OF THINGS LIKE DESI, A HORRIBLE PERSON, COMING OUT AS TRANS IS JUST THE TABOO NATURE OF SUCH THINGS CURRENTLY. SO MUCH TRANS MEDIA IS SO SHINY AND POSITIVE AND FUCKING FAKE. GENDER DYSPHORIA IS OFTEN QUITE DIFFICULT TO DEAL WITH (IN MY PERSONAL EXPERIENCE), IT'S A VARIED SPECTRUM OF EXPERIENCES... 'MEGG AND MOGG' IS AN ALTERNATIVE COMIC, IT IS MESSY AND FUCKED UP AND ALLOWS ITSELF TO MAKE MISTAKES. THERE ARE DIFFICULT CONVERSATIONS TO BE HAD, WITH OUR COMMUNITIES, OUR PEERS AND OURSELVES...

| 132. | MOGG HAS BEEN ABANDONED BY BOTH MITZI AND CARROT TOP AND RECEIVES TWO SEPERATE BREAKUP NOTES... I SPENT A LONG TIME TRYING TO COME UP WITH A CARROT TOP STYLE "PROP-BASED" BREAKUP NOTE. I LITERALLY HAD TO BECOME CARROT TOP, GET INSIDE HIS BRAIN... IT WAS A WEIRD MORNING... I GUESS I DID OKAY, IT'S AN ACCEPTABLE JOKE, BUT NOT THE GREATEST. I'M NOT SURE IF A BETTER JOKE EXISTS OR IS EVEN POSSIBLE, MATHEMATICALLY... I DEFINITELY HAVE A NEWFOUND RESPECT FOR CARROT TOP... |

133-140. IT'S WEDDING TIME! AS A CHILD I ACTUALLY SWALLOWED A GLASS MARBLE AND MY MOTHER SPENT SEVERAL DAYS MASHING UP MY TURDS WITH A FORK, TO MAKE SURE THAT THE MARBLE HAD PASSED THROUGH... SOME CREEPY LOSERS IN THE COMMENTS WERE TRYING TO IMPLY THAT SOMETHING UNTOWARD HAD HAPPENED WITH JAXON'S SWALLOWING OF THE WEDDING (COCK)RING; AS JONES TELLS CHRIS HANSEN "HOW DARE YOU?" KIDS SWALLOW STUFF. IT IS LATER SUGGESTED BY OWL THAT JAXON SWALLOWED THE RING ON PURPOSE IN AN ATTEMPT TO HALT THE WEDDING AND THIS IS INDEED WHAT HAPPENED... DAVID CHOE MAKES HIS FIRST APPEARANCE. HE BECAME A FAN OF MEGG AND MOGG AND WE BEGAN TALKING A BIT AND HE BOUGHT SOME ART FROM ME. HE FLOATED THE IDEA THAT I PERHAPS INCLUDE A CAMEO OF HIS "PIZZA MAN" CHARACTER, I DID NOT WANT TO DO THAT AND INSTEAD DECIDED TO WRITE IN CHOE HIMSELF AS A CHARACTER... SUSAN MAKES HER FIRST PHYSICAL APPEARANCE IN THE COMIC. SHE HAD PREVIOUSLY BEEN MENTIONED IN THE MAIN CANON AND I HAD PLANS FOR HER FIRST APPEARANCE TO BE IN "MEGG'S COVEN", I HEAVILY DEBATED WITH MYSELF HER INCLUSION HERE... I FIGURED I COULD GET AWAY WITH IT IN THIS DUE TO BEING ABLE TO HAVE HER FULLY MASHED AND NOT REVEAL HER IDENTITY... AROUND THIS TIME I SAID "FUCK IT" AND ALSO REVEALED HER "HUMAN FORM", BARE-FACED, IN 'SILK ROAD', A PROMOTIONAL "ZINE" THAT WAS INCLUDED AS A FREE PREMIUM ITEM WITH DIRECT PURCHASES OF 'SEEDS AND STEMS' FROM THE PUBLISHER, FANTAGRAPHICS BOOKS... VEJONIKA RETURNS AFTER HER APPEARANCE IN 'BAD GATEWAY' IN 2019... THE "POPCORN BOYS" RETURN TO EXACT REVENGE AFTER THE RHOV-DEATH OF WOODY. IAN IS SHOT FOR THE SECOND TIME AND I REALIZED THAT I WOULD HAVE TO COME UP WITH TWO OTHER WAYS FOR HIM TO BE SHOT. DAVID CHOE IS SHOT IN THE FACE AND DIES, REMOVING THE POSSIBILITY OF A CONSIDERED SUB-PLOT WHEREIN BOOGER BECOMES AN ONLINE "FINANCIAL DOMINATRIX" WHO "SERVICES" DAVID CHOE AND TAKES ALL OF HIS MONEY.

141-154. WITH THE WEDDING IN THE REARVIEW MIRROR, WEREWOLF JONES BECOMES OBSESSED WITH BEING A "PERFECT FAMILY" AND DECIDES TO HEAD ON DOWN TO A CONSERVATIVE, PRO LAW ENFORCEMENT DEMONSTRATION, WHICH WERE RATHER UNPOPULAR AT THE TIME... THERE ACTUALLY WAS AN EVENT IN SEATTLE WHERE A BUNCH OF RELIGIOUS NUTS SET UP A BAPTISM TUB IN THE PARK WHERE THE "CHAZ" WAS AND I'D IMAGINE A LOT OF COVID CASES CAME OUT OF THAT JESUS-WATER... JEN DESCRIBES "WOMANING ABOUT", THIS IS KIND OF HOW I FELT AROUND THIS TIME, ALL DOLLED UP IN MY WIGS AND MAKEUP, "MAKING A SANDWICH AS A WOMAN", "DRAWING A COMIC AS A WOMAN", A LOT OF DEEP, CONTEMPLATIVE THOUGHTS ON THE NATURE OF GENDER, FASHION AND IDENTITY... I TEND NOT TO CATEGORIZE MYSELF, I REJECT THE MODERN LANGUAGE AND LABELS, PERSONALLY. I AM A "HUMAN CREATURE" AND I WEAR AN ARRAY OF DIFFERENT MODERN STYLES OF DRESS, SOME "MALE" AND SOME "FEMALE", I HAVE CONSIDERED TRANSITIONING FULLY TO LIVING AS A WOMAN OVER THE PAST DECADE BUT I'M JUST NOT SURE THAT I PERSONALLY CARE ENOUGH... I'M JUST <u>LIVING</u>, THAT'S ENOUGH, CURRENTLY, AND I DON'T SEE LIFE GOING BACK TO "NORMAL" ANYTIME SOON. I DON'T LEAVE THE HOUSE, I DON'T SEE ANYONE, I DON'T SEE A POINT IN OBSESSING OVER MY "IDENTITY" AT THIS POINT IN TIME, IT HAS NO BEARING ON MY DAY TO DAY LIFE... DRACULA JUNIOR SETS THE FUNERAL EVENT IN MOTION, WHICH HAD BEEN PLANNED FOR A WHILE AND I HAD BEEN WORKING UP TO. AT THIS POINT IN THE COMIC I HAD A LOT OF FUTURE EVENTS PLANNED AND IT WAS JUST GETTING THERE AND CONNECTING ALL THE DOTS AND WRITING MY WAY OUT OF ALL THE HOLES I'D DUG FOR MYSELF... "PURITY TEENS" ARE A FASCINATING PHENOMENON, ULTRA-WOKE, OBSESSIVE AND CENSORIOUS, DUMBFUCK TEENAGERS, WHO DEMAND THAT ALL ART BE NEUTERED OF ANY AND ALL TRANSGRESSIVE ELEMENTS. THEY BRISTLE AT ANY DEPICTION OF TRAUMATIC EVENTS OF ANY KIND. THEY ARE NO DIFFERENT FROM THEIR UPTIGHT, RELIGIOUS FOREBEARS. THEY CAN ALL SUCK MY DICK. I WILL WRITE WHAT I WANT AND I WILL CONSUME WHAT I WANT, END OF STORY... MOGG WATCHES THE NEWS IN A SHITTY ROADSIDE MOTEL BAR. MITZI APPEARS ONSCREEN ALONGSIDE SWEDISH "CLOUD RAPPER" BLADEE. FOR A WHILE I HAD PLANS WITH BLADEE TO MAKE A SPLIT ART-ZINE THING BUT THE PROJECT FELL APART WHEN HE SCORED A BIG DESIGN GIG WITH CONVERSE AND STOPPED ANSWERING MY MESSAGES. I WAS UNBOTHERED BY THIS AS I MYSELF REGULARLY IGNORE MY EMAILS AND LET PROJECTS FALL APART. THERE'S ONLY SO MANY HOURS IN A DAY... JAXON TELLS EVERYONE TO GO AND FUCK THEMSELVES AND EXTRACTS HIMSELF FROM THE HORRIBLE SITUATION HE FINDS HIMSELF TRAPPED IN. THIS HAD BEEN PLANNED FOR A WHILE BUT I WAS STILL UNSURE OF WHERE EXACTLY HE WOULD END UP AND WHAT WOULD HAPPEN. SOMEHOW JAXON HAS BOUGHT INTO DESI AND IAN'S LIE THAT HE WAS RESPONSIBLE FOR THE TREEHOUSE/HOTEL FIRE AND THE 38 DEATHS. I'M GUESSING THAT HE DID IN FACT KNOCK OVER A CANDLE AROUND THE SAME TIME OF JONES STARTING THE HOT TUB FIRE... I GUESS WE'LL NEVER KNOW... JAXON "TAKES HIS SHIRT OFF IN THE YARD", AS NOTED BY MEGG, THIS IS A REFERENCE TO THE SONG "THE GLOW PT. 2" BY 'THE MICROPHONES' AKA PHIL ELVERUM. THE MICROPHONES/MOUNT EERIE IS MOST LIKELY MY FAVOURITE "BAND" EVER. I'D HAD THE PLEASURE OF HOSTING PHIL AT MY HOME IN HOBART, TASMANIA IN 2004, WHEN I WAS DABBLING IN GIG PROMOTION/BOOKING. WE HAVE PERIODICALLY KEPT IN TOUCH OVER THE YEARS AND HE IS INDEED A FAN OF THE DISGUSTING ADVENTURES OF MEGG AND MOGG. PHIL IS A VERY FUNNY GUY AND I'M CERTAIN HE COULD BE A CARLIN-LEVEL COMEDIAN IF HE SO CHOSE TO BE. "MICROPHONES IN 2020" IS MY CHOICE FOR RECORD OF THE YEAR IN 2020.

155 - 177. IT'S FUNERAL TIME! THE "DRACULA JUNIOR JR. FACSIMILE DOLL" SEEMED TO CREEP OUT A BUNCH OF PEOPLE, SO MISSION ACCOMPLISHED. I HAD A LOT OF FUN WRITING THE DOLL'S DIALOGUE THAT IS CLEARLY BEING RECORDED BY AN INEBRIATED WEREWOLF JONES... DESI BARGES IN AND PROCLAIMS SHE IS "SHE-RA, A RACIST LESBIAN". THIS WAS AN INTENSE ONLINE SHITSTORM. BASICALLY JUST A BUNCH OF PURITY TEENS FINDING PROBLEMS WHERE THERE REALLY WERE NO PROBLEMS, I WON'T BOTHER ATTEMPTING TO EXPLAIN IT, THIS KIND OF BULLSHIT DESERVES TO BE LOST TO HISTORY. JEN NAMEDROPS "BLAIRE WHITE" WHO IS A RIGHT-LEANING TRANS YOUTUBE "PERSONALITY" WHO IS REVILED BY LEFT-LEANING YOUTUBE "PERSONALITIES". OWL AND VALERIA ARE REVEALED TO BE IN A RELATIONSHIP AND OWL HAS FINALLY BROKEN OUT OF HIS DEPRESSION... A GROUP OF "ANARCHISTS" SHOW UP OUTSIDE THE HOUSE AND BERATE WEREWOLF JONES. THERE WAS A BIT OF A "KERFUFFLE" IN THE COMMENTS, A FEW ANGRY LEFT-LEANING INDIVIDUALS CLAIMING THAT THIS KIND OF BEHAVIOR DID NOT EXIST, A FEW OTHER (MOST LIKELY APOLITICAL SMARTASSES) COMMENTERS POINTED OUT THAT THE DIALOGUE AND ACTIONS OF THE CARTOON ANARCHISTS WAS BASICALLY DIRECTLY LIFTED FROM REAL LIFE, THERE WAS FOOTAGE FREELY CIRCULATING. HERE IN THE PACIFIC NORTHWEST IT WAS NOT UNCOMMON TO HEAR ABOUT ROVING BANDS OF ACTIVISTS WANDERING THE SUBURBS AT NIGHT, SHINING LIGHTS INTO PEOPLE'S WINDOWS AND SHOUTING SLOGANS AND PROFANITIES AT THE SLEEPING ELDERLY, CHILDREN AND EXHAUSTED FRONT LINE WORKERS. THERE WERE MANY INSTANCES OF OUTDOOR DINERS BEING BERATED AND FORCED AT MOB-POINT TO RAISE THEIR FISTS... OR ELSE (?). OFTEN THESE ROVING BANDS WOULD APPEAR TO BE MADE UP OF PREDOMINATELY WHITE INDIVIDUALS. I'VE SEEN NUMEROUS INTERVIEWS WITH <u>ACTUAL</u> BLACK LIVES MATTER PROTESTERS CONDEMNING THIS DUMB SHIT. I THINK IT'S HARD TO ARGUE WITH THE NOTION THAT PERHAPS THIS KIND OF AGGRESSIVE SHIT WAS MUDDYING THE PEACEFUL, INCLUSIVE MESSAGE OF THE BLACK LIVES MATTER PROTESTS... IT'S ALL VERY PLAINLY SPELLED OUT ON PAGE 160 FOR ANY OF THE PREVIOUS EPISODE'S MORONS WHO LACK BASIC READING COMPREHENSION SKILLS... WHILE ALL THIS SHIT WAS GOING DOWN IN THE COMMENTS MY WIFE CAME INTO MY STUDIO WITH A PLASTIC STICK COVERED IN HER URINE AND INFORMED ME THAT SHE WAS PREGNANT WITH OUR CHILD... WE HAD BEEN TRYING FOR A KID EARLIER IN THE YEAR, PUT A HOLD ON IT AT THE BEGINNING OF THE PANDEMIC, BUT HAD RECENTLY RESUMED OUR EFFORTS. WE WERE FUCKING <u>PUMPED</u>! ANY CONCERN OVER PEOPLE WHINING ABOUT POLITICS IN MY "COMMENTS SECTION" FULLY EVAPORATED. MY WIFE FORGOT THAT SHE WAS ANGRY AT ME FOR MAKING A POLITICALLY-CHARGED COMIC THAT SHE HAD WARNED ME NOT TO PRODUCE AND POST, IN THAT MOMENT, EVERYTHING CHANGED, I WAS TO BE A "FATHER", WE WERE STARTING A REAL FAMILY. EVERYBODY CAN SERIOUSLY JUST FUCH OFF, "NEVER TALK TO ME OR MY CHILD AGAIN".

IAN IS SHOT FOR THE THIRD TIME, THIS TIME IN HIS LEFT LEG, BY AN UNSEEN RACIST OLD MAN WHO WAS SPOOKED BY THE APPEARANCE OF THE RANTING ANARCHISTS ON HIS OTHERWISE QUIET STREET... THIS FUNERAL SEQUENCE WAS WRITTEN ALL TOGETHER, BACK TO BACK, BEFORE IT BEGAN. GENERALLY I WOULD JUST BE WRITING INDIVIDUAL EPISODES DAILY BUT FOR THIS SCENE I WANTED TO ATTEMPT TO REMAIN COHERENT... "PADDY O'REILLY'S DRY NIGHTS SANITARY PADS" IS AN OLD JOKE FROM MY NOISE MUSIC DAYS, I WOULD OFTEN OPEN MY PERFORMANCES WITH A LIST OF COMEDIC, FAKE SPONSORS. TACO BELL BEING A SPONSOR IS A REFERENCE TO THE OLD DANA CARVEY SKETCH SHOW THAT HAD A DIFFERENT STUPID SPONSOR EACH EPISODE. WEREWOLF JONES'S FEDORA JUST CRACKS ME THE FUCK UP, I CAN'T LOOK AT PANEL 4 OF PAGE 163 WITHOUT LAUGHING. JONES MAKES A NICE SPEECH ABOUT ACTOR CHADWICK BOSEMAN AND BLM AND THEN IMMEDIATELY RUINS IT BY ANNOUNCING HIS RIDICULOUS PRESIDENTIAL BID. THIS NEVER REALLY WENT ANYWHERE OR SERVED ANY PURPOSE IN THE STORY, I JUST HAD TO DO IT THOUGH, IT'S THE KIND OF OUT OF TOUCH, ARROGANT THING JONES WOULD DO. HIS POLICIES ARE ACTUALLY QUITE PROGRESSIVE AND HE HAS SOME GOOD IDEAS THOUGH!... IAN, DELIRIOUS FROM BEING SHOT AND ALLERGIC TO OWL'S SOY MILK, SPILLS THE BEANS ON WHAT ACTUALLY HAPPENED WITH THE FIRE. MONTHS HAD PASSED SINCE READERS HAD SEEN THESE FIRE SCENES AND MOST HAD PROBABLY FORGOTTEN WHAT HAD TRANSPIRED AND WERE CONFUSED, I ATTEMPTED TO SPELL IT ALL OUT AS CLEARLY AS POSSIBLE WITHOUT VEERING INTO BLAND, ROBOTIC EXPOSITION... WE THEN HAVE A SEVEN-PAGE-LONG FIGHT SCENE THAT WAS A WEEK-LONG SLOG FOR DAILY READERS. I WAS SOMEWHAT RIFFING ON BEN MARRA'S 'WHAT WE MEAN BY YESTERDAY' WEB SERIAL WHICH REVELS IN GLACIAL PACING... IAN IS SHOT FOR THE FOURTH TIME, THIS TIME HIS RIGHT LEG, BY A COKED-UP AND GRIEF-STRICKEN JONES... MOGG RETURNS AND FINDS THE HOUSEHOLD IN A STATE OF CHAOS.

178,179.	IT IS REVEALED THAT "JACK" HAS MADE HIS WAY TO LOS ANGELES AND IS WORKING AT A McDONALD'S. A LOT OF THIS IS AUTOBIOGRAPHICAL. I WORKED AT A MICKY D'S WHEN I WAS 14 AND REGULARLY FOUND MYSELF FISHING CONDOMS OUT OF THE WISHING WELL, COLLECTING DEAD RATS AND SCRAPING PICKLES OFF OF THE WINDOWS... READING THROUGH THIS COMIC AS A WHOLE I REALIZE THAT VERY LITTLE TIME HAS PASSED BETWEEN JAXON/JACK LEAVING AND HIS BEING SO ENSCONCED IN THIS JOB WITH EVERYBODY SEEMING TO KNOW HIM BY NAME. I GUESS HE JUST MAKES A STRONG IMPRESSION. HE'S A VERY VALUABLE TEAM MEMBER... THE EXTERIOR SHOT OF THE HOUSE HE IS LIVING AT IS ACTUALLY LOCATED IN HOBART, TASMANIA. KNOWN AS THE "WINTER PALACE", THIS WAS THE FIRST PLACE I LIVED WHEN I MOVED OUT OF MY MOTHER'S APARTMENT AND IT WAS ACTUALLY FILLED WITH A BUNCH OF "ALTERNATIVE CHRISTIANS" AT THAT TIME. THE HOUSE WAS ALSO PROMINENTLY FEATURED IN COMICS BY HOBART CARTOONIST LEIGH RIGOZZI IN THE EARLY 2000'S. HOBART WAS FUCKING AWESOME IN THE EARLY 2000'S...
180-194.	THE "FUCKTOWN" SIEGE BEGINS. THE POLICE DIDN'T SEEM TO CARE BEFORE ABOUT THE 38 DEATHS ON THE PROPERTY BUT THE ONSCREEN MURDER OF DRACULA JUNIOR SEEMS TO MOTIVATE THEM TO ACTION. PERHAPS THEY WERE FEELING DEMORALIZED AFTER THE ENTIRE COUNTRY WATCHED THEM NEEDLESSLY MURDER A BUNCH OF PEOPLE AND CALLED THEM OUT ON THEIR BULLSHIT? MAYBE THEY WERE PREOCCUPIED WITH RISING STREET VIOLENCE AND ROBBERIES? MAYBE A BIT OF BOTH... I DEFINITELY NEED TO PRODUCE SOME "FUCKTOWN" FLAGS AT SOME POINT IN THE FUTURE, THAT COULD BE A GREAT PIECE OF FUN MERCHANDISE THAT COULD HELP ME PAY FOR BABY FOOD AND RENT... MOGG HAS BEEN LOCKED UP IN THE NEWLY ESTABLISHED "FUCKTOWN PRISON". THIS WAS THE ONLY COURSE OF ACTION THAT MADE SENSE TO ME. WHY WOULD ANY OF THE GROUP ACCEPT MOGG BACK WITH OPEN ARMS? HE FUCKED EVERYONE OVER, HE PROBABLY SHOULD HAVE NEVER COME BACK... WEREWOLF JONES WAS INDEED BECOMING UNRELATABLE AT THIS POINT, I COULD SENSE THAT A LARGE PORTION OF THE AUDIENCE WAS GROWING TIRED OF HIS ESCALATING ANTICS... MITZI IS A GUEST ON "NO JUMPER", A DOUCHEY PODCAST THAT PREDOMINATELY HOSTS LOW TO MID-LEVEL SOUNDCLOUD RAPPERS... FINALLY, WITH THE SIEGE IN PLAY, MEGG HAS RUN OUT OF, AND IS UNABLE TO PROCURE, ANY MARIJUANA. SHE RESORTS TO DRINKING THE WATER OUT OF HER BONG. I HAD A FRIEND WHO USED TO DO THIS. HE WOULD CHILL IT IN THE FRIDGE AND ATTEMPT TO MASK THE ROTTEN TASTE WITH A DASH OF FRESH FRUIT JUICE. YUM!... IT IS REVEALED THAT ALL ALONG OTHER RESIDENTS HAVE BEEN SHARING THE HOUSE ALONGSIDE THE GANG. IT IS AN OLD HOUSE THAT HAS BEEN SPLIT INTO FOUR APARTMENTS. IT'S ACTUALLY A REAL HOUSE IN CARNEGIE, VICTORIA, AUSTRALIA. I LIVED THERE IN 2008 WITH MY FRIEND HTMLFLOWERS, HIS MOTHER AND HIS SISTER. WE HAD SOME GOOD TIMES IN THAT HOUSE... FUCKTOWN RESIDENT DAN IS MY FRIEND DAN CROSS, A HOBART MUSICIAN WHO NOW LIVES IN MELBOURNE. HE ACTUALLY DID COME UP WITH THE CHARACTER NAME "WEREWOLF JONES", WHICH I USED FIVE YEARS LATER FOR MY WEREWOLF CHARACTER AFTER DAN HAD NEVER DONE ANYTHING WITH HIS WEREWOLF CHARACTER. CHECK OUT THE GLASS HALO BANDCAMP, IT'S A REAL WEBSITE. SECRET VALLEY IS A QUALITY BAND... AS MEGG IS RUNNING OUT OF WEED SHE IS BECOMING MORE AND MORE PETULANT. I REMEMBER ACTING THIS WAY AS A TEENAGER. VERY PATHETIC STUFF... PAGE 191 IS A SLEAZY ADVERTISEMENT FOR A REAL-LIFE 'WEREWOLF JONES & SONS' HOT SAUCE THAT LAUNCHED THAT DAY, AND SOLD OUT IN LESS THAN AN HOUR. THE HOTSAUCE PROJECT WAS REALLY FUN AND I WAS "STOKED" ON THE FINAL PRODUCT HOSA PUT TOGETHER. HOSA IS A LOCAL WASHINGTON BOUTIQUE SAUCE COMPANY RUN BY FANTAGRAPHICS STAR-DESIGNER JACOB COVEY. IT'S FANTASTIC SAUCE, I EAT IT ALL THE TIME ON MY DADDY-BURGERS... DRACULA JUNIOR IS ALIVE. SURPRISE. ANOTHER TWIST. I WAS ATTEMPTING TO PULL OFF THE LARGEST AMOUNT OF CHEESY TWISTS POSSIBLE... I MUST ADMIT THAT I CHEW MY TOENAILS LIKE MEGG, I'VE NEVER ONCE USED CLIPPERS. YES, IT'S DISGUSTING, I KNOW. I ONLY DO IT AFTER A VIGOROUS, DETAILED SCRUBBING (A LIE)... THERE WAS A PLOT-HOLE WITH JONES'S MASERATI JUST DISSAPPEARING FROM THE STORY, SO THAT WAS RECTIFIED HERE ON PAGE 194 IN THE BONUS PANELS. THERE WE GO, PROBLEM SOLVED, IT WAS SMASHED UP BY THE COPS, STOP DMING ME ABOUT IT...
195-198.	MITZI IS IN L.A. FILMING "ANUS QUEEN", HER NEW ANUS KING SPIN-OFF. THE PERSON IN THE LIMO WITH HER IS LULO, A DJ, MODEL AND EVENT ORGANIZER PERHAPS MOST POPULAR FOR THEIR APPEARANCES IN MUSIC VIDEOS BY DORIAN ELECTRA AND LIL PEEP. MITZI IS DRESSED BY W.I.A., A FASHION LABEL WHOSE TAGLINE IS "COMFY AND EXPENSIVE"... POOR JACK IS RECOGNIZED BY MITZI IN THE DRIVE-THRU OF HIS McDONALD'S AND HIS COVER IS BLOWN. THE CHRISTIAN GUYS HERE ARE THE REAL CHRISTIAN GUYS I LIVED WITH AT THAT HOUSE, LEIGH, MATT AND BENNY. FOR A SHORT TIME I CONSIDERED HAVING JAXON SPEND A LOT MORE TIME AROUND MITZI, CULMINATING IN HER ACTUALLY MAKING A PASS AT HIM. MY WIFE WAS DISGUSTED BY THIS IDEA, I EXPLAINED THAT IT WAS A COMMENTARY ON THE PREVALENCE OF SUCH GOINGS ON IN THE WORLD OF SOUNDCLOUD RAPPERS, BUT SHE INSISTED IT WAS TOO DARK AND TOO HORRIBLE AND I LISTENED TO HER, ON THIS OCCASION...
199-212.	TEAR GAS CLOUDS ENVELOP THE HOUSE AS THE SIEGE CONTINUES. THERE WERE A LOT OF DISTURBING THINGS GOING AROUND ABOUT THE EFFECTS OF TEAR GAS ON VAGINA OWNERS. THE GAS WAS WAFTING OUT OF PROTEST ZONES AND INTO RESIDENTIAL AREAS AND CAUSING IRREGULAR PERIODS... KENNETH, THE ANUS KING BOOM OPERATOR IS REVEALED BY ALL THIS GAS TO BE A TRANSMAN, MAKING HIM CRISIS ZONE'S FOURTH TRANS CHARACTER. KENNETH IS A NICE

DUDE AND IT SUCKS FOR HIM TO BE PUBLICLY OUTED IN THIS FASHION... DAVID CHOE RETURNS A "CHOST". THIS IS 100%. MERELY A WEREWOLF JONES HALLUCINATION, CHOST IS NOT REAL. THERE IS NO SUCH THING AS CHOSTS. I WAS, HOWEVER, VERY HAPPY TO HEAR THAT IN REAL LIFE SOMEBODY SCREAMED "CHOST!" AT DAVID CHOE AS HE WAS WALKING DOWN THE STREET... DRAWING THIS DRUG TRIP SEQUENCE ON PAGE 202 WAS A FUCKING GRIND. THAT WAS A ROUGH FUCKING DAY. GOOD PAGE THOUGH... A FEW PEOPLE SEEMED TO GET UPSET ABOUT THIS DESI EPISODE WHEREIN THE HALLOWEEN SHOP KEEPER HAS HIS BUSINESS RUINED BY "POLITICAL YELPERS" DESPITE HIM DOING NOTHING WRONG AND IS CLEARLY NOT A "WHITE SUPREMACIST". BUT YEAH, SURE, NOTHING LIKE THAT HAS EVER HAPPENED IN THE REAL WORLD, IT'S TOTALLY IMPOSSIBLE FOR FALSE CLAIMS TO BE WEAPONIZED... DESI GOES IN HARD ON "ULTRA-WOKE" TRANS INDIVIDUALS, THE KIND THAT HAVE NOTHING ELSE GOING ON FOR THEM ASIDE FROM BEING TRANS AND NEVER SHUT THE FUCK UP ABOUT IT AND END UP SENDING DEATH-THREATS TO "CIS" WOMEN'S RAPE SHELTERS. DESI IS "ALTERNATIVE TRANS", I SUPPOSE. SHE'S JUST A GIRL, IN THE WORLD, SHE IS NOT DEFINED BY HER TRANSNESS, AND I PERSONALLY FIND HER INSPIRING... DESI'S "BUTT SLUTZ" DANCE TROUPE IS A REFERENCE TO THE FRENCH FILM 'MIGNONNES', WHICH CAUSED QUITE THE UPROAR IN 2020. I WATCHED THE NETFLIX TRAILER FOR IT AND IT DID INDEED APPEAR TO BE A PEDO-PHILE'S WET DREAM, TOTAL SOFTCORE PEDO-CATNIP. IN MY OPINION, THE OUTRAGE WAS JUSTIFIED. FUCKING HORRIBLE... JONES IS OBSESSED WITH GETTING ONTO THE "JOE ROGAN SHOW", MENTIONING HERE THAT HE HAS "DMT ANECDOTES". APPARENTLY JOE ROGAN IS ALWAYS GOING ON ABOUT DMT... I DID IT ONCE, WITH ALVIN BUENAVENTURA. FULLY PULLED BACK THE CURTAIN OF "REALITY", MET THE WOMAN ON THE MOON, THE ELVES, ALL OF IT. THE UNDULATING FRACTAL FIELDS. 10/10 WOULD RECOMMEND. R.I.P. ALVIN BUENAVENTURA... JONES SHUTS DOWN ANUS KING WITH THE USE OF "VIRTUOUS BLACKFACE". I'D THOUGHT OF THIS IDEA MONTHS EARLIER AND WAS WORKING UP TO IT. WHAT BETTER WAY TO GET YOUR SHOW INSTANTLY CANCELLED IN 2020? MY WIFE THOUGHT THIS WAS A TERRIBLE IDEA BUT I DID IT ANYWAY. NO ONE SEEMED TO GET TOO UPSET BY IT. I DIDN'T ACTUALLY SHOW THE BLACKFACE, MERELY SUGGESTED IT, AND I SUPPOSE AT THIS POINT IN THE RUN I'D DRIVEN AWAY ALL OF THE "SJW" AUDIENCE MEMBERS. THE COMMENTS WERE MORE RELAXED, THE GRIEVANCES AND BUZZWORDS HAD MIGRATED ELSEWHERE, MOST LIKELY BACK TO CHILDREN'S CARTOONS THAT WILL PANDER AND CAPITULATE... WITH THE SHOW CANCELLED AND THE SIEGE OVER, THE HOUSE IS MORE RELAXED. JAXON/JACK GETS GIVEN A BOX OF DUSTY OLD LEGO WHICH APPARENTLY MADE SOME READERS CRY. IT IS LEGITIMATELY HEARTWARMING... VERY EARLY AFTER JAXON'S RESCUE WE ACTUALLY SEE JAXON PLAYING WITH SOME LEGO ON THE LIVING ROOM FLOOR (ON INSTAGRAM), THIS WAS EDITED OUT FOR THIS BOOK IN ORDER TO NOT UNDERCUT THE EMOTIONAL HEFT OF THIS BEAUTIFUL LEGO MOMENT. AFTER I DREW THIS I ACTUALLY STARTED BUYING A BUNCH OF LEGO. IT'S REALLY RELAXING TO BUILD AND I ENJOY IT VERY MUCH. I BUILT A PIRATE ISLAND AND A TREEHOUSE AND A SHIP IN A BOTTLE. I KEPT TELLING MY WIFE THAT I WAS BUYING ALL THIS LEGO "FOR WHEN THE BABY'S OLD ENOUGH" BUT REALLY IT'S JUST FOR ME. ALTHOUGH I DO HOPE OUR DAUGHTER (OR WHATEVER SHE DECIDES TO BE) WILL ENJOY A BIT OF LEGO WITH HER WEIRD DAD. I HOPE WE CAN BUILD A LITTLE CITY TOGETHER... SET UP A TABLE IN THE BASEMENT AND GO FUCKING NUTS. TRAINS. A HARBOR. CASTLES. ETC...

213-219.	OWL FINALLY CLEANS UP THE BATHROOM, REMOVES THE TOILET-BRANCH AND PATCHES UP THE NUMEROUS HOLES. HE BURIES CHOE'S BODY IN THE BACKYARD AS JIANGUO WATCHES FROM HIS WINDOW... VALERIA HAS LEFT AND STOLEN ALL THE MONEY. MEANWHILE, MEGG HAS PROCURED SOME WEED AGAIN AND DUE TO HER TOLERANCE HAVING BEEN RESET, STARTS TO FUCKING LOSE IT... IAN GETS CYBERNETIC ARMS AND LEGS FROM ELON MUSK. FOR A LONG TIME I'D WANTED IAN TO HAVE CYBERNETIC ARMS ALA "JAXX" FROM 'MORTAL KOMBAT'... IT IS REVEALED THAT WHO WE THOUGHT WAS DAVID CHOE WAS NOT REALLY DAVID CHOE. I KIND OF REGRET DOING THIS, I PROBABLY SHOULD HAVE JUST LEFT IT ALONE... IT WAS VERY FUNNY SEEING CHOE ON 'THE 'MANDALORIAN'. I WONDER WHICH CAMEO HE PREFERS? I WOULD IMAGINE IT'S CRISIS ZONE... MOGG IS FINALLY RELEASED FROM THE FUCKTOWN PRISON AND MITZI GIVES BIRTH TO A LITTER OF KITTENS WHICH EVERYONE NATURALLY ASSUMES ARE MOGG'S... OR ARE THEY?...
220-222.	JONES IS IN PRISON. THE FIRST PAGE OF THIS SEQUENCE WAS ORIGINALLY PLACED EARLIER IN THE RUN, SANDWICHED IN BETWEEN THE SCENES OF MEGG PISSING IN THE HALLWAY. READING THROUGH EVERYTHING AS A WHOLE, IT JUST DIDN'T MAKE SENSE WHERE IT WAS, IN THE MIDDLE OF A SCENE, SO IT WAS MOVED UP TO BE WITH THE OTHER PRISON PAGES... WE SEE JONES, DRIED OUT, REVERTING TO HIS HUMAN FORM. WE'VE SEEN THIS BEFORE IN 'ONE MORE YEAR' AND 'BAD GATEWAY'. MOST READERS OF CRISIS ZONE, HOWEVER, WERE NEW OR CASUAL READERS, SO I WAS ABLE TO DEPLOY THIS HERE, ONCE AGAIN, TO MAXIMUM EFFECT... SOMEHOW DRACULA JUNIOR HAS ALSO ENDED UP IN PRISON AND HAS ATTEMPTED TO HAVE HIS FACE RECONSTRUCTED. WE NEVER SEE HOW THIS OCCURRED... I WOULD IMAGINE THAT AFTER DRAC' RAN OFF FROM THE SIEGE, HE RETURNED TO THE POPCORN BOYS, HAD HIS FACE DONE AND THEN COMMITTED SOME CRIMES. NOTHING TOO COMPLICATED. HE'S A MENTALLY DERANGED, UNSTABLE CRIMINAL AFTER ALL...
223-230.	EVERYONE HEADS OUT TO HIRE A WET-VAC TO GET RID OF THE PISS-STINK IN THE HOUSE... MEGG PASSES OUT FROM EATING TOO MANY ALMONDS, WHICH IS BASED ON THE TIME HTMLFLOWERS DID THIS. ME AND JMKE WERE HANGING OUT IN A RECORD STORE, DAY DRUNK, JUST LURKING, AND WE REALIZED WE'D LOST FLOWERS. WE FOUND HIM OUT IN THE STREET, LAYING ON A BENCH, MOANING AND GROANING. WE HAD TO BASICALLY CARRY HIM HOME, WE WERE REALLY SALTY ABOUT IT BECAUSE WE WERE HAVING A GOOD TIME AND IT WAS RUINED BY FLOWERS STUPIDLY EATING AN ENTIRE, GIANT BAG OF NUTS... ON THE WAY HOME THE GANG PASSES THE 'DOG BISCUITS' STOREFRONT. 'DOG BISCUITS' IS A RATHER FANTASTIC INSTAGRAM COMIC BY MY PAL ALEX GRAHAM. IF YOU ENJOYED CRISIS ZONE YOU WILL ALSO ENJOY 'DOG BISCUITS', CHECK IT OUT! ONE OF THE LAST PEOPLE I HUNG OUT WITH BEFORE QUARANTINE WAS ALEX. SHE AND HER PARTNER, PATRICK, AND I WENT AND SAW 'TIM AND ERIC' LIVE. I MISS HANGING OUT WITH ALEX AND PATRICK. PATRICK AND I WERE TRYING TO START A BAND AT THE BEGINNING OF 2020, I MISS MAKING LOTS OF NOISE AND GETTING DRUNK AND SHIT-TALKING IN OUR LITTLE RENTED PRACTICE SPACE... OWL IS ASSAULTED IN THE STREET BY ANARCHISTS WHO TOOK ISSUE WITH HIS APPEARANCE ON "THAT BLACKFACE SHOW". HIS CRIES FOR BLAND UNITY GO UNHEARD. HE IS ALSO DISGUSTED BY THE APPARENT SUPPORT FOR THE SHOW BY THE RIGHT-WING MAGA DOUCHEBAGS. HE IS CAUGHT BETWEEN A ROCK AND A HARD PLACE. A FEW WANKERS IN THE COMMENTS WOULD CLAIM THAT CRISIS ZONE WAS ATTRACTING AN "ALT-RIGHT" AUDIENCE. I HIGHLY DOUBT IT. AND DEFINE "ALT-RIGHT", YOU "ALT-LEFT" ZEALOTS. I WOULD BE VERY HAPPY TO HAVE "RIGHT-WING" PEOPLE ENJOY MY WORK, IT WOULD BE HEALTHY FOR THEM TO ENGAGE WITH MEDIA THAT FEATURES SO MANY PROMINENT TRANSGENDER AND QUEER CHARACTERS. BASICALLY EVERY CHARACTER IN THE MEGG AND MOGG WORLD IS QUEER, THEY'RE JUST NOT AGGRESSIVE CUNTS ABOUT IT. GOOD REPRESENTATIVES FOR THE MORE INTOLERANT AMONG US. I DON'T THINK MOST MODERN RIGHT-WINGERS HAVE A HUGE PROBLEM WITH "ALTERNATIVE LIFESTYLES", THEY JUST BRISTLE AT THE MILITANT ASPECTS OF THE CULTURE, A LOT OF ONLINE LGBTQI+ FOLKS ONLINE ARE VERY AGGRESSIVE AND EMBARRASSING. I SAY THIS AS A QUEER PERSON WHO "SUFFERS" FROM GENDER DYSPHORIA, CALM DOWN THE RHETORIC, LOSERS. MAYBE PEOPLE WOULD LIKE US MORE IF WE DIDN'T ACT LIKE DRAMATIC FUCKHEADS, CONSTANTLY ATTACKING PEOPLE. NOT TO DOWNPLAY ACTUAL BIGOTED AGGRESSION FROM SEGMENTS OF THE POPULATION BUT EVERYBODY NEEDS TO CHILL THE FUCK OUT AND CALM DOWN SO WE CAN CO-EXIST TOGETHER, TONE DOWN THE OBVIOUS OVEREXAGGERATION AND GANG-TACTICS... I JUST AVOID EVERYBODY THESE DAYS. I TRY NOT TO ENGAGE WITH PEOPLE ONLINE. EVERYONE'S EMBARRASSING... MOGG'S HAMBURGLAR MASK MAKES AN APPEARANCE. THIS MASK HAS BEEN FEATURED SEVERAL TIMES IN THE MAIN CANON AS A MEANS OF CONCEALING HIS FACE FROM MEGG WHEN SHE CAN'T STAND TO LOOK AT IT ANYMORE AND ALSO AS AN EROTIC SEX-MASK. THIS IS PARTLY BASED ON AN INJECTION-MOLDED BATMAN MASK I WORE FOR HALLOWEEN IN 1998 WHEN I WAS FAR TOO OLD FOR TRICK OR TREATING. YEARS LATER I FOUND THE MASK IN THE BACK OF MY CLOSET AND WORE IT WHILST MASTURBATING. JUST THE ONCE. I WAS EXPERIMENTING WITH "COMEDY MASTURBATION"...

| 231. | I THINK WE HAVE THE FIRST MENTION OF TRUMP HERE IN THE WHOLE COMIC (ASIDE FROM THE MIDWESTERN SEX-WORKER'S T-SHIRT WHICH I IMAGINE SHE WAS MOST LIKELY WEARING DUE TO A LACK OF BETTER OPTIONS). I FIGURED I WOULD LEAVE THE MONOTONOUS, UNFUNNY TRUMP-BASHING TO UNFUNNY LATE NIGHT "COMEDIANS" AND MENTALLY ILL LEFTISTS ON TWITTER. |

LET ME STATE THIS CLEARLY: I DETEST DONALD TRUMP. I THINK HE IS A CROOK, A MORON AND A DOUCHEBAG AND I AM SICK OF FUCKING HEARING ABOUT HIM AND ALL OF HIS UNPROFESSIONAL WORD-SALAD. END OF STORY. HE'S GONE NOW, PEOPLE, CALM DOWN. PEOPLE SEEMED VERY UPSET BY WHAT WAS HAPPENING TO JONES IN PRISON, WHICH I FOUND INTERESTING, AS PEOPLE HAD BEEN WISHING DEATH UPON HIM FOR MONTHS AS HE IS A HORRIBLE, ABUSIVE CHARACTER... HIS EXPERIENCE IN PRISON RANG TRUE TO ME. I GREW UP AROUND A LOT OF CRIMINALS AND HEARD A LOT OF INCREDIBLY DARK THINGS ABOUT THEIR EXPERIENCES. PRISON IS NOT A NICE PLACE! PRISONERS GROUP UP TOGETHER ALONG RACIAL LINES AND REVERT TO A PRIMAL MODE OF DOMINATION. IF I WERE TO EVER FIND MYSELF IN PRISON I AM 100% CERTAIN I WOULD BE BRUTALIZED AND PASSED AROUND, ENDLESSLY BEATEN AND RAPED. REALITY!

| 232-242. | THE GANG ARE OUT OF MONEY, MUCH MORE RELATABLE TO THE COMMON CITIZEN THAN HAVING A NETFLIX SHOW... IN MY YOUTH I WAS REGULARLY AT THE SUPERMARKET PAYING FOR A CAN OF BEANS WITH SEVERAL DIFFERENT CARDS AND A STACK OF RUSTY 1c. PIECES. I HAVE WORKED VERY HARD TO CLIMB MY WAY OUT OF THAT LEVEL OF POVERTY, I NEVER WANT TO GO BACK TO THAT... I DID CONSIDER HAVING OWL TOTALLY SNAP IN THE SUPERMARKET AND BEAT THE SHIT |

OUT OF THE MASKLESS FUCK STICK THAT WAS HARRASSING HIM, I DECIDED HOWEVER THAT OWL SHOULD TAKE THE ZEN APPROACH AND JUST LET IT WASH OVER HIM... BOOGER FINALLY REMOVES HERSELF FROM HER SHITTY "RELATIONSHIP" WITH LAME MEGG AND GETS A HAPPY ENDING IN HER RELATIONSHIP WITH SWEETHEART KENNETH, WHICH HAD BEEN PLANNED FOR A WHILE... I HAD BEEN WATCHING A LOT OF 'THE AMAZING RACE' AND IT VERY MUCH MADE ME SAD THAT SOMETHING LIKE THAT WILL MOST LIKELY NOT HAPPEN AGAIN FOR A VERY LONG TIME... DESI IS LURED BACK TO THE HOUSEHOLD BY OWL'S OFFER OF TENDER DISCIPLINE WITH THE FREEDOM TO BLOW OFF STEAM BY DENIGRATING LOSERS ONLINE... FOR MEGG, ANIMAL CROSSING IS STARTING TO LOSE ITS CHARM AND HAS BECOME A BORING, REPETITIVE GRIND, MUCH AS IT WAS IN REAL LIFE. AROUND THIS POINT MY WIFE AND I BOTH QUIT DOING IT. IT HAD SERVED ITS PURPOSE AND WE WERE DONE WITH IT... OWL'S 'PHANTOM OF THE OPERA' MASK VERILY CRACKS ME UP. JACK WINCES AT THIS SCENE, FEARING THAT OWL IS BECOMING WEREWOLF JONES. JACK SELFLESSLY, HEROICALLY SACRIFICES HIS LEGO TO HELP THE HOUSEHOLD, RIGHT IN TIME FOR THE RETURN OF SUSAN, THE "FINAL BOSS".

| 243-248. | SUSAN ARRIVES WITH VEJONIKA, TO COLLECT HER OTHER CHILDREN. I DIDN'T REALLY WANT TO GIVE AWAY HER WERE-WOLF FORM IN THIS FREE STORY BUT I ALSO HAD TO... THE WHOLE GANG LOVES THE KIDS NOW AND THERE'S NO WAY THEY WERE LETTING THEM GO. EVERYONE BANDS TOGETHER AND STANDS UP TO SUSAN AND MEGG IS BROUGHT OUT OF HER FUNK, JUST IN TIME, HER DEPRESSED INDIFFERENCE TO THE SITUATION IS HER STRENGTH. SUSAN TOOK THE MONEY. |

| 249-259. | THE LONG PLANNED 'ANUS KING' REUNION FINALLY OCCURS, HOSTED BY JOEL McHALE, WHO HAD PREVIOUSLY DONE A POOR JOB OF HOSTING THE 'TIGER KING' REUNION SPECIAL. RATHER BORING PAGES, NO ACTION, ALL TALKING HEADS, HEAVY DIALOGUE. THIS IS HOW A LOT OF US EXPERIENCED 2020 THOUGH, IT WAS THE ONLY WAY WE COULD INTERACT WITH OTHER PEOPLE... I SYMPATHIZE WITH BOTH MEGG AND BOOGER HERE, NOTHING FEELS NATURAL ANYMORE AND ONLINE CULTURE |

AND THE CULTURE AT LARGE IS FRACTURED AND DEPRESSING (IF YOU'RE A SANE, NORMAL PERSON)... I PERSONALLY THINK JENNIFER IS A GOOD TRANS ROLE MODEL. SHE IS RELAXED, CONFIDENT IN HERSELF AND UNAFRAID TO ACKNOWLEDGE HER PAST, IT WOULD BE NICE TO SEE MORE OF THAT... IT IS REVEALED THAT "DAVID CHOE" WAS ALL ALONG AN "ADVANCED CHOEBOT" WHO WAS THERE TO PROMOTE A PRANK SHOW ON APPLETV+. THIS BARELY MAKES SENSE BUT IT WAS THE BEST I COULD COME UP WITH AFTER STUPIDLY INTRODUCING THE MYSTERY OF WHO THE FAKE CHOE ACTUALLY WAS... WHY WOULD NETFLIX ALLOW THE PROMOTION OF A SHOW ON A RIVAL STREAMING PLATFORM?... JIM HEMMINGFIELD MAKES A PHYSICAL APPEARANCE AS HE WAS ALWAYS INTENDED TO FROM THE FIRST MENTION OF HIS NAME. IN THE BONUS PANELS WE ALSO SEE HIS WIFE MICHELLE AND THEIR DOG... PEOPLE SEEMED VERY TURNED OFF BY WEREWOLF JONES'S "PINK BLOOD", MY DEEPEST APOLOGIES... IT'S OFFICIAL, OWL IS THE LEGAL GUARDIAN OF THE JONES CHILDREN. OWL IS A GOOD GUY, IN MY OPINION, I THINK HE TRIES HIS BEST AND HE WILL DO A GOOD JOB.

| 260-270. | THE FINAL STRETCH... I HAD TO SHUT THIS THING DOWN, I'D INTENDED TO STOP WEEKS EARLIER BUT I FOUND IT DIFFICULT TO BREAK AWAY FROM IT, I WAS IN THE ZONE... WITH THEIR MONEY FROM THE NETFLIX REUNION POOLED, THE GANG BUYS THE HOUSE AND KICKS OUT ALL THE OTHER RESIDENTS ON CHRISTMAS DAY... THE KIDS HAVE THEIR FIRST PROPER CHRISTMAS EVER... DESI IS RIGHT TO BE UPSET BY 'CYBERPUNK 2077', I BOUGHT IT AND PLAYED IT FOR A FEW HOURS |

BEFORE TURNING IT OFF IN DISGUST. WHAT A STEAMING PILE OF SHIT... MEGG FINALLY CALLS HER MOTHER AFTER SEVERAL MONTHS. I HAD DONE THIS IN REAL LIFE. FOR A WHILE I JUST COULDN'T FACE MY MOTHER, IT WAS TOO DEPRESSING, SHE WAS REFUSING TO DO ANYTHING TO HELP HERSELF AND HAD ENDED UP IN THE HOSPITAL A FEW TIMES. I HAVE GIVEN HER THOUSANDS UPON THOUSANDS OF DOLLARS OVER THE PAST DECADE AND IT HAS ALL GONE UP HER ARM. WE ARE TALKING AGAIN CURRENTLY BUT I REFUSE TO SEND HER CASH, I WILL ONLY BUY HER ONLINE FOOD DELIVERIES, WHICH IN A WAY, STILL ENABLES HER ADDICTION. IT IS VERY TOUGH WATCHING SOMEONE YOU LOVE CONTINUE TO HURT THEMSELF, I UNDERSTAND IT, BUT IT IS FUCKING DEPRESSING. I KEEP PRAYING SHE'LL GET BETTER BUT AT THIS POINT I DON'T KNOW IF THAT'S EVEN A REALISTIC HOPE TO CLING TO... I JUST WANT HER TO BE HAPPY AND NOT HAVE TO WORRY ABOUT HER. I WANT TO BE THE CHILD. I DO NOT WANT TO BE HER PARENT. I'LL BE EXPLORING ALL OF THIS SHIT IN DETAIL IN THE BOOK 'MEGG'S COVEN', WHEN I FINALLY FUCKING GET AROUND TO IT... IF YOU ARE READING THIS, MA, I LOVE YOU. SERIOUSLY, I LOVE YOU, BUT YOU GOTTA TAKE A LOOK IN THE MIRROR SOMETIMES AND COME DOWN TO EARTH AND REALIZE ALL THE SHIT YOU'VE PUT ME THROUGH OVER THE YEARS... I DON'T BLAME YOU. I BLAME THE DRUGS. ... OWL TURNS JONES AWAY. HE'S GIVEN HIM ALL THE CHANCES HE'S GOING TO GIVE HIM AND ESSENTIALLY SENTENCES HIM TO DEATH. OWL WILL HAVE TO LIVE WITH THIS DECISION FOR THE REST OF HIS LIFE... WITH JONES'S DEATH THOUGH, COMES A CERTAIN CALM... A NEW DAY DAWNS. A HOPEFUL DAY WITH NEW OPPORTUNITIES. THE OUTSIDE WORLD MIGHT BE FALLING APART, BUT THE GANG OWNS THEIR LITTLE PIECE OF LAND AND THERE IS MUCH WORK TO BE DONE... THE FINAL SCENE IS INTENDED TO ECHO THE FINAL SCENE IN 'THE EMPIRE STRIKES BACK'. I VERY MUCH INTENTIONALLY INSERTED A FUCKLOAD OF CLASSIC POP-CULTURAL AND SHAKESPEARIAN THEMES INTO CRISIS ZONE, I WANTED IT TO BE AS "MAINSTREAM" AS POSSIBLE, IT WAS MADE "FOR THE PEOPLE" AND "THE PEOPLE" LIKE WALLOWING AROUND IN THE SAME OLD, SAFE SHIT THEY'VE ALWAYS WALLOWED IN. SECURITY IN REPETITION AND ROUTINE... WAS THIS A SATISFYING ENDING? IT DID FEEL LIKE THE END, NOT ONLY FOR THE ARCS OF THE CHARACTERS BUT ALSO WHAT WE CONSIDERED "NORMAL", MODERN LIFE... EVERYTHING HAS CONTINUED TO MUTATE AND FLARE UP GOING INTO 2021, WE'RE NOT OUT OF THE WOODS YET, WHO KNOWS WHAT WILL HAPPEN? ALL I KNOW, IS THAT I WILL BE WATCHING IT ALL FROM MY WINDOW AND TRYING TO AVOID AS MANY PEOPLE AS I POSSIBLY CAN. "THE OLD WORLD IS DEAD", GOOD LUCK TO YOU ALL. ENJOY YOUR MOBS AND YOUR CANCELLINGS AND YOUR RIOTS AND LEAVE ME THE FUCK ALONE. I WILL BE BUSY WORKING AS HARD AS I CAN TO SUPPORT MY FAMILY AND LIVE A GOOD LIFE... I DON'T USE SPOTIFY, DUE TO IT BEING FOR CUNTS, BUT IF SOMEBODY WANTS TO MAKE A "PLAYLIST" OR WHATEVER OUT OF THE SONG LIST IN THE CREDITS, I WOULD LIKE THAT VERY MUCH... THANK YOU TO ALL THE PUBLISHERS WHO SIGNED ON TO PUBLISH THIS GARBAGE. EAGLE-EYED READERS WILL NOTICE THAT FRENCH DUTIES ARE BEING CARRIED OUT BY DUPUIS IN PLACE OF MY USUAL MISMA EDITIONS, THIS WAS ONE OF THE HARDEST DECISIONS OF MY PROFESSIONAL CAREER. MISMA WAS ONE OF MY EARLIEST PUBLISHERS AND HAVE ALWAYS BEEN FANTASTIC. HOWEVER, WITH A CHILD ON THE WAY, I COULDN'T TURN DOWN THE LARGER ADVANCE AND WIDER DISTRIBUTION OFFERED BY DUPUIS. NOT AN EASY DECISION TO MAKE. DAMIEN & GUILLAUME, I LOVE YOU AND I AM SORRY... POST-CREDITS WE SEE IAN TAKEN UP BY A U.F.O., ORIGINALLY IT WAS GOING TO BE DESI, BUT THAT WAS TOO SILLY... I WAITED ALL 2020 FOR THE ALIENS TO COME... MAYBE IN 2021... WHY THE FUCK DID I WRITE ALL THESE NOTES? WHAT IS WRONG WITH ME? ALRIGHT... FUCK OFF.

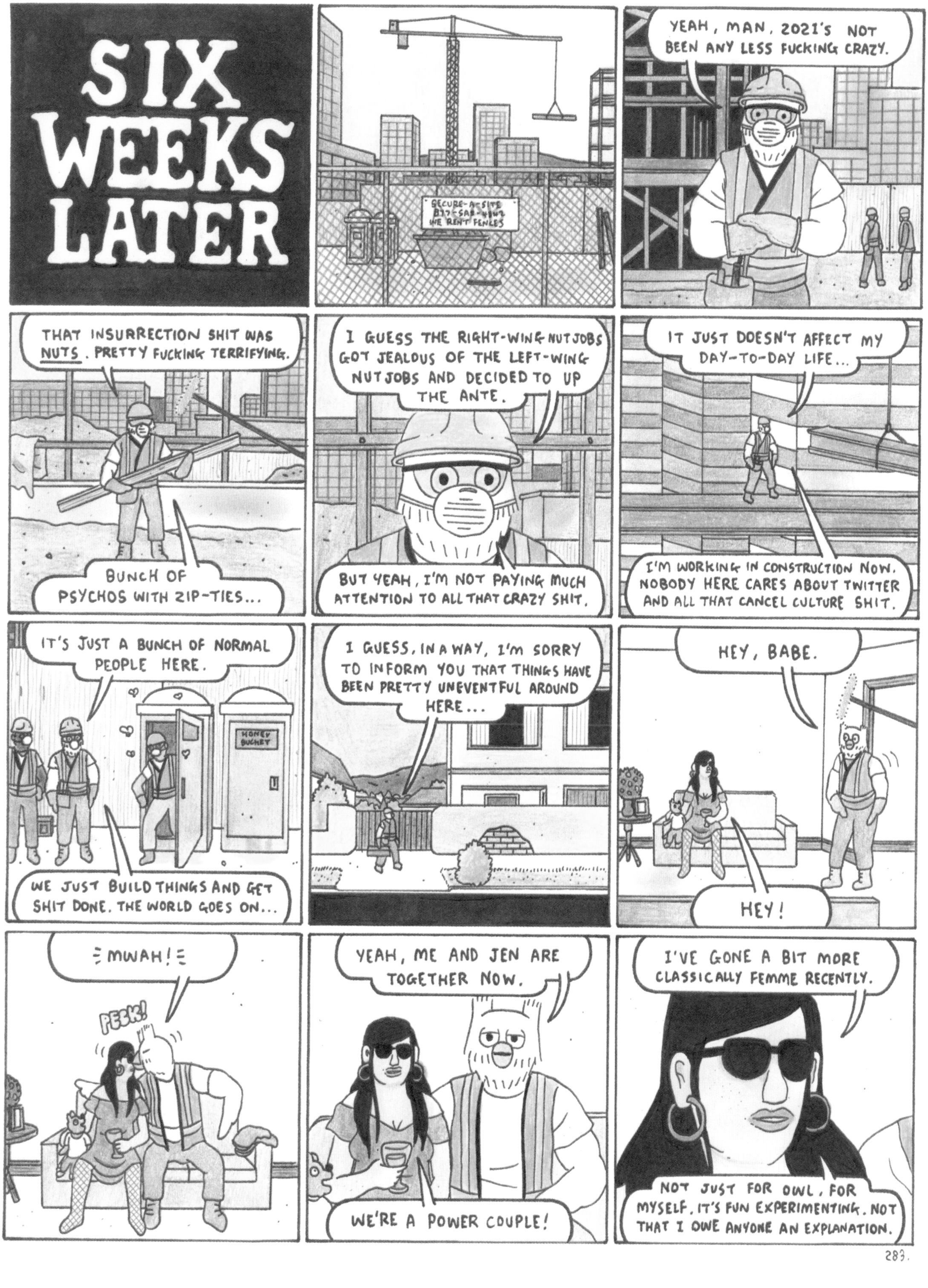
SIX WEEKS LATER
SECURE-A-SITE
WE RENT FENCES
YEAH, MAN, 2021'S NOT BEEN ANY LESS FUCKING CRAZY.
THAT INSURRECTION SHIT WAS NUTS. PRETTY FUCKING TERRIFYING.
BUNCH OF PSYCHOS WITH ZIP-TIES...
I GUESS THE RIGHT-WING NUTJOBS GOT JEALOUS OF THE LEFT-WING NUTJOBS AND DECIDED TO UP THE ANTE.
BUT YEAH, I'M NOT PAYING MUCH ATTENTION TO ALL THAT CRAZY SHIT.
IT JUST DOESN'T AFFECT MY DAY-TO-DAY LIFE...
I'M WORKING IN CONSTRUCTION NOW. NOBODY HERE CARES ABOUT TWITTER AND ALL THAT CANCEL CULTURE SHIT.
IT'S JUST A BUNCH OF NORMAL PEOPLE HERE.
HONEY BUCKET
WE JUST BUILD THINGS AND GET SHIT DONE. THE WORLD GOES ON...
I GUESS, IN A WAY, I'M SORRY TO INFORM YOU THAT THINGS HAVE BEEN PRETTY UNEVENTFUL AROUND HERE...
HEY, BABE.
HEY!
MWAH!
PECK!
YEAH, ME AND JEN ARE TOGETHER NOW.
WE'RE A POWER COUPLE!
I'VE GONE A BIT MORE CLASSICALLY FEMME RECENTLY.
NOT JUST FOR OWL, FOR MYSELF. IT'S FUN EXPERIMENTING. NOT THAT I OWE ANYONE AN EXPLANATION.

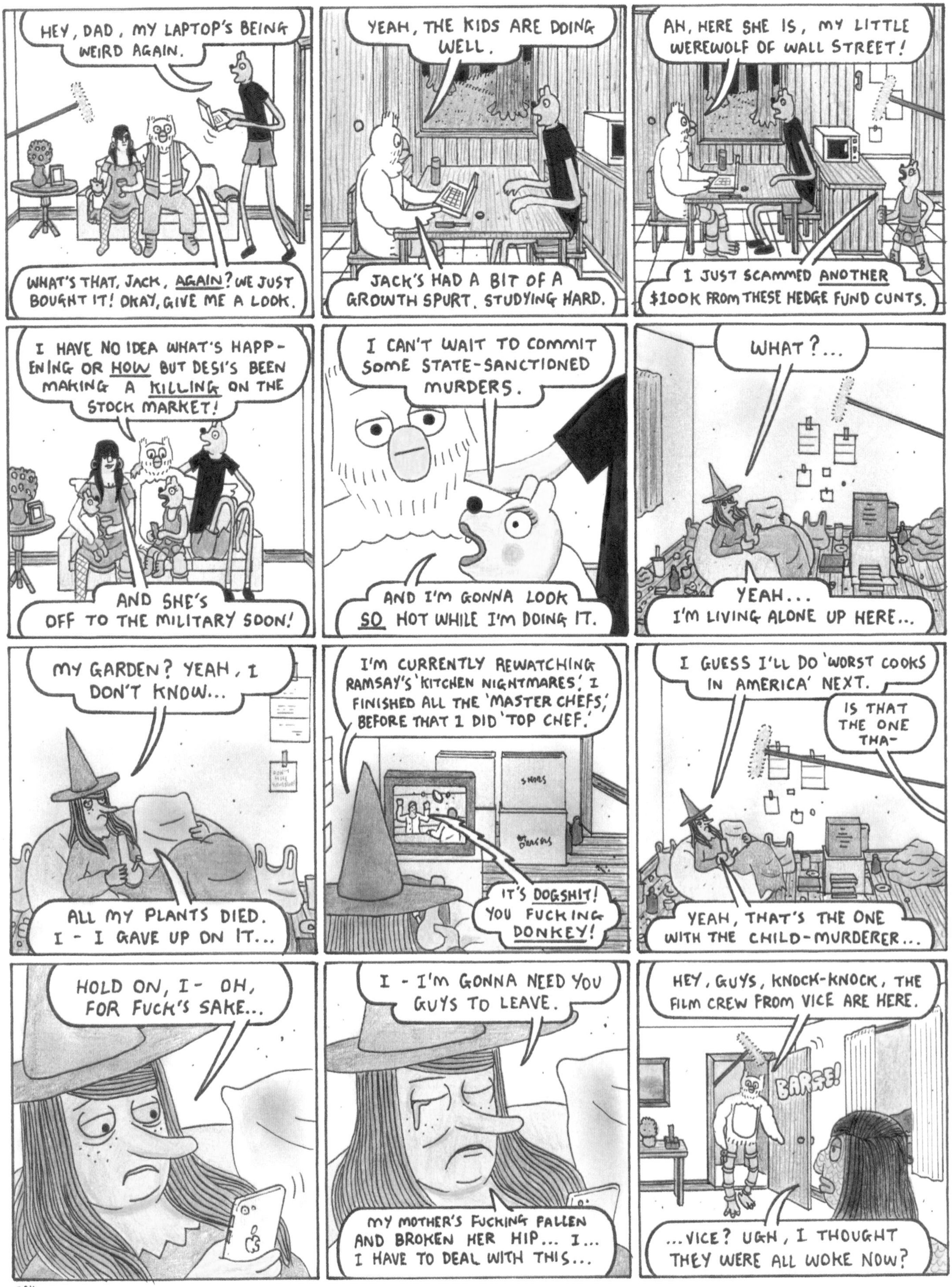
HEY, DAD, MY LAPTOP'S BEING WEIRD AGAIN.
WHAT'S THAT, JACK, AGAIN? WE JUST BOUGHT IT! OKAY, GIVE ME A LOOK.
YEAH, THE KIDS ARE DOING WELL.
JACK'S HAD A BIT OF A GROWTH SPURT. STUDYING HARD.
AH, HERE SHE IS, MY LITTLE WEREWOLF OF WALL STREET!
I JUST SCAMMED ANOTHER $100K FROM THESE HEDGE FUND CUNTS.
I HAVE NO IDEA WHAT'S HAPPENING OR HOW BUT DESI'S BEEN MAKING A KILLING ON THE STOCK MARKET!
AND SHE'S OFF TO THE MILITARY SOON!
I CAN'T WAIT TO COMMIT SOME STATE-SANCTIONED MURDERS.
AND I'M GONNA LOOK SO HOT WHILE I'M DOING IT.
WHAT?...
YEAH... I'M LIVING ALONE UP HERE...
MY GARDEN? YEAH, I DON'T KNOW...
ALL MY PLANTS DIED. I - I GAVE UP ON IT...
I'M CURRENTLY REWATCHING RAMSAY'S 'KITCHEN NIGHTMARES', I FINISHED ALL THE 'MASTER CHEFS', BEFORE THAT I DID 'TOP CHEF.'
IT'S DOGSHIT! YOU FUCKING DONKEY!
I GUESS I'LL DO 'WORST COOKS IN AMERICA' NEXT.
IS THAT THE ONE THA-
YEAH, THAT'S THE ONE WITH THE CHILD-MURDERER...
HOLD ON, I- OH, FOR FUCK'S SAKE...
I - I'M GONNA NEED YOU GUYS TO LEAVE.
MY MOTHER'S FUCKING FALLEN AND BROKEN HER HIP... I... I HAVE TO DEAL WITH THIS...
HEY, GUYS, KNOCK-KNOCK, THE FILM CREW FROM VICE ARE HERE.
BARGE!
...VICE? UGH, I THOUGHT THEY WERE ALL WOKE NOW?

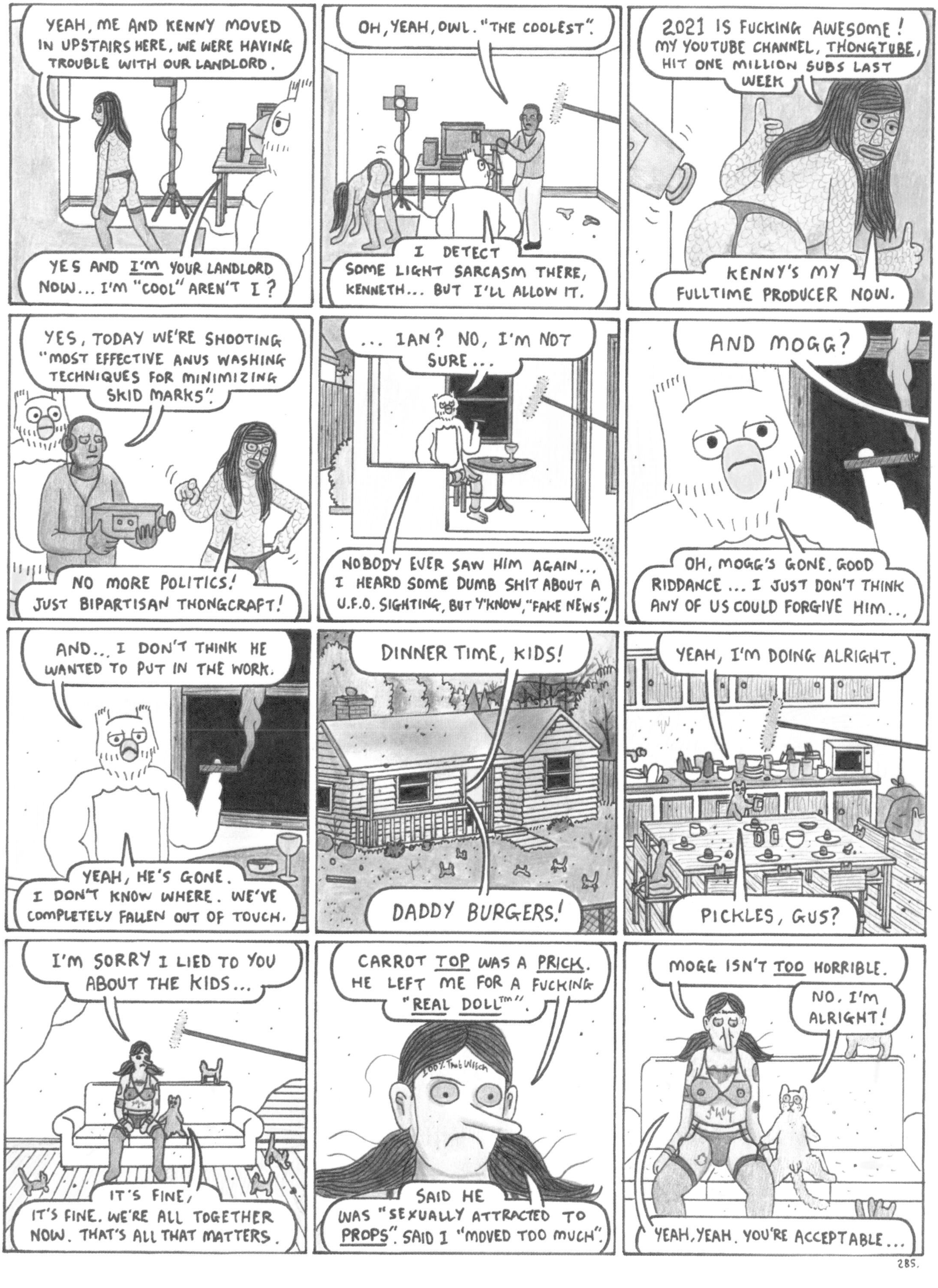
YEAH, ME AND KENNY MOVED IN UPSTAIRS HERE, WE WERE HAVING TROUBLE WITH OUR LANDLORD.
YES AND I'M YOUR LANDLORD NOW... I'M "COOL" AREN'T I?
OH, YEAH, OWL. "THE COOLEST".
I DETECT SOME LIGHT SARCASM THERE, KENNETH... BUT I'LL ALLOW IT.
2021 IS FUCKING AWESOME! MY YOUTUBE CHANNEL, THONGTUBE, HIT ONE MILLION SUBS LAST WEEK
KENNY'S MY FULLTIME PRODUCER NOW.
YES, TODAY WE'RE SHOOTING "MOST EFFECTIVE ANUS WASHING TECHNIQUES FOR MINIMIZING SKID MARKS".
NO MORE POLITICS! JUST BIPARTISAN THONGCRAFT!
... IAN? NO, I'M NOT SURE...
NOBODY EVER SAW HIM AGAIN... I HEARD SOME DUMB SHIT ABOUT A U.F.O. SIGHTING, BUT Y'KNOW, "FAKE NEWS".
AND MOGG?
OH, MOGG'S GONE. GOOD RIDDANCE... I JUST DON'T THINK ANY OF US COULD FORGIVE HIM...
AND... I DON'T THINK HE WANTED TO PUT IN THE WORK.
YEAH, HE'S GONE. I DON'T KNOW WHERE. WE'VE COMPLETELY FALLEN OUT OF TOUCH.
DINNER TIME, KIDS!
DADDY BURGERS!
YEAH, I'M DOING ALRIGHT.
PICKLES, GUS?
I'M SORRY I LIED TO YOU ABOUT THE KIDS...
IT'S FINE, IT'S FINE. WE'RE ALL TOGETHER NOW. THAT'S ALL THAT MATTERS.
CARROT TOP WAS A PRICK. HE LEFT ME FOR A FUCKING "REAL DOLL™".
100% That Witch
SAID HE WAS "SEXUALLY ATTRACTED TO PROPS". SAID I "MOVED TOO MUCH".
MOGG ISN'T TOO HORRIBLE.
NO, I'M ALRIGHT!
YEAH, YEAH. YOU'RE ACCEPTABLE...

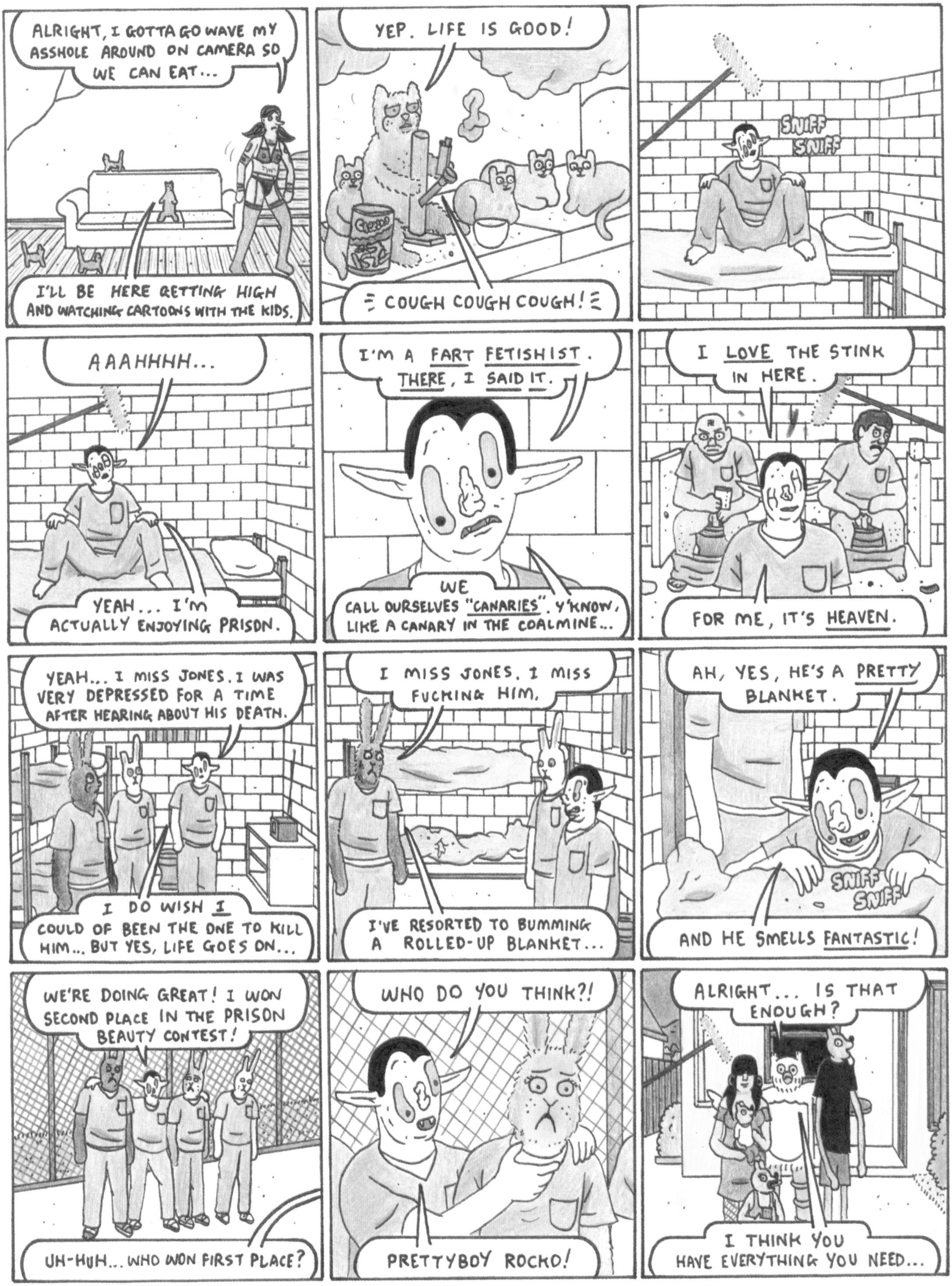

ALRIGHT, I GOTTA GO WAVE MY ASSHOLE AROUND ON CAMERA SO WE CAN EAT...
I'LL BE HERE GETTING HIGH AND WATCHING CARTOONS WITH THE KIDS.
YEP. LIFE IS GOOD!
COUGH COUGH COUGH!
SNIFF
SNIFF
AAAHHHH...
YEAH... I'M ACTUALLY ENJOYING PRISON.
I'M A FART FETISHIST. THERE, I SAID IT.
WE CALL OURSELVES "CANARIES". Y'KNOW, LIKE A CANARY IN THE COALMINE...
I LOVE THE STINK IN HERE.
FOR ME, IT'S HEAVEN.
YEAH... I MISS JONES. I WAS VERY DEPRESSED FOR A TIME AFTER HEARING ABOUT HIS DEATH.
I DO WISH I COULD OF BEEN THE ONE TO KILL HIM... BUT YES, LIFE GOES ON...
I MISS JONES. I MISS FUCKING HIM.
I'VE RESORTED TO BUMMING A ROLLED-UP BLANKET...
AH, YES, HE'S A PRETTY BLANKET.
SNIFF
SNIFF
AND HE SMELLS FANTASTIC!
WE'RE DOING GREAT! I WON SECOND PLACE IN THE PRISON BEAUTY CONTEST!
UH-HUH... WHO WON FIRST PLACE?
WHO DO YOU THINK?!
PRETTYBOY ROCKO!
ALRIGHT... IS THAT ENOUGH?
I THINK YOU HAVE EVERYTHING YOU NEED...

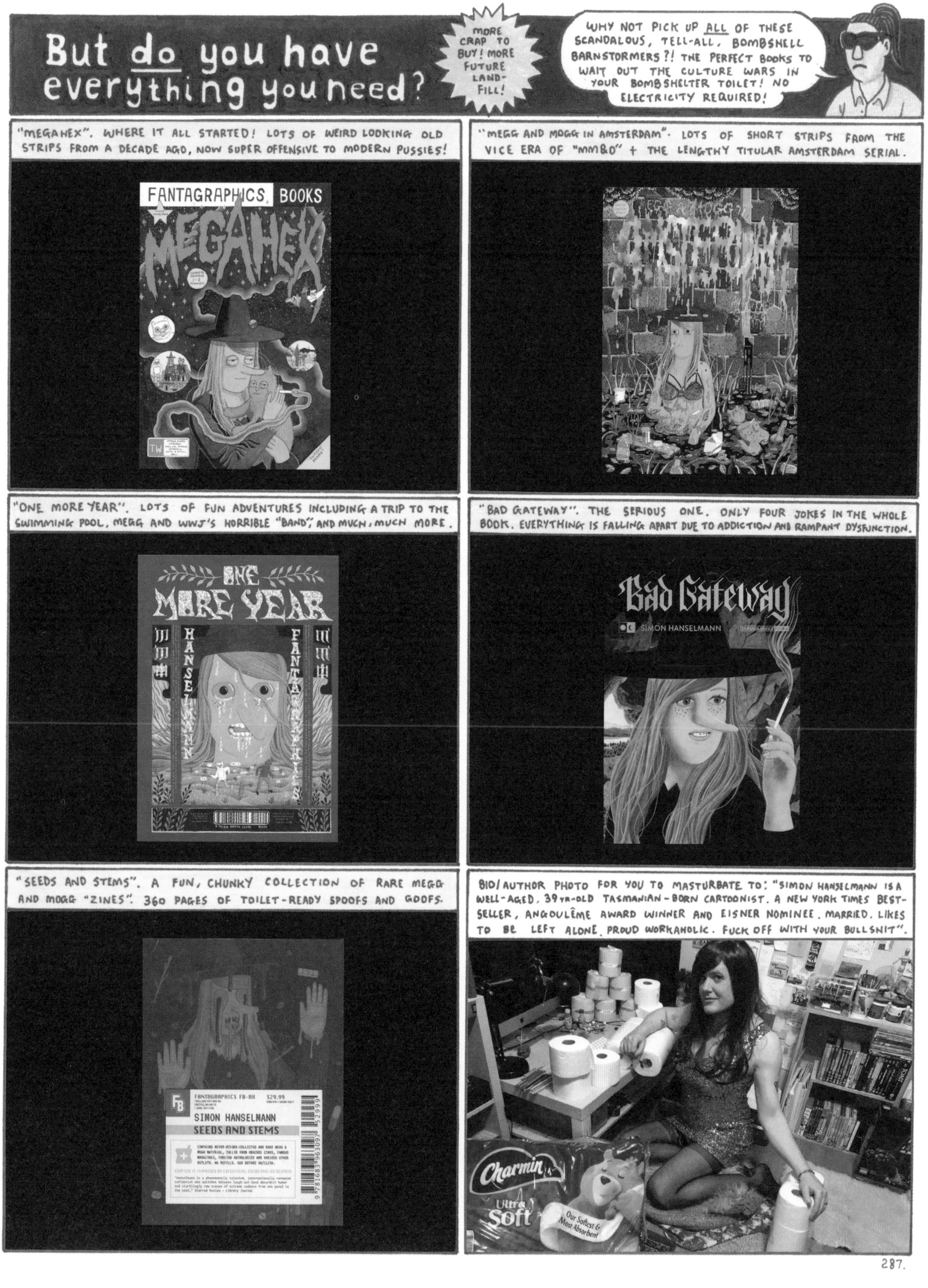

But do you have everything you need?
MORE CRAP TO BUY! MORE FUTURE LAND-FILL!
WHY NOT PICK UP ALL OF THESE SCANDALOUS, TELL-ALL, BOMBSHELL BARNSTORMERS?! THE PERFECT BOOKS TO WAIT OUT THE CULTURE WARS IN YOUR BOMBSHELTER TOILET! NO ELECTRICITY REQUIRED!
"MEGAHEX". WHERE IT ALL STARTED! LOTS OF WEIRD LOOKING OLD STRIPS FROM A DECADE AGO, NOW SUPER OFFENSIVE TO MODERN PUSSIES!
FANTAGRAPHICS BOOKS
MEGAHEX
"MEGG AND MOGG IN AMSTERDAM". LOTS OF SHORT STRIPS FROM THE VICE ERA OF "MM&O" + THE LENGTHY TITULAR AMSTERDAM SERIAL.
"ONE MORE YEAR". LOTS OF FUN ADVENTURES INCLUDING A TRIP TO THE SWIMMING POOL, MEGG AND WWJ'S HORRIBLE "BAND", AND MUCH, MUCH MORE.
ONE MORE YEAR
HANSELMANN
FANTAGRAPHICS
"BAD GATEWAY". THE SERIOUS ONE. ONLY FOUR JOKES IN THE WHOLE BOOK. EVERYTHING IS FALLING APART DUE TO ADDICTION AND RAMPANT DYSFUNCTION.
Bad Gateway
SIMON HANSELMANN
"SEEDS AND STEMS". A FUN, CHUNKY COLLECTION OF RARE MEGG AND MOGG "ZINES". 360 PAGES OF TOILET-READY SPOOFS AND GOOFS.
FANTAGRAPHICS FB-RH $29.99
SIMON HANSELMANN
SEEDS AND STEMS
BIO/AUTHOR PHOTO FOR YOU TO MASTURBATE TO: "SIMON HANSELMANN IS A WELL-AGED, 39 YR-OLD TASMANIAN-BORN CARTOONIST. A NEW YORK TIMES BEST-SELLER, ANGOULÊME AWARD WINNER AND EISNER NOMINEE. MARRIED. LIKES TO BE LEFT ALONE. PROUD WORKAHOLIC. FUCK OFF WITH YOUR BULLSHIT".
Charmin
Ultra Soft
Our Softest & Most Absorbent

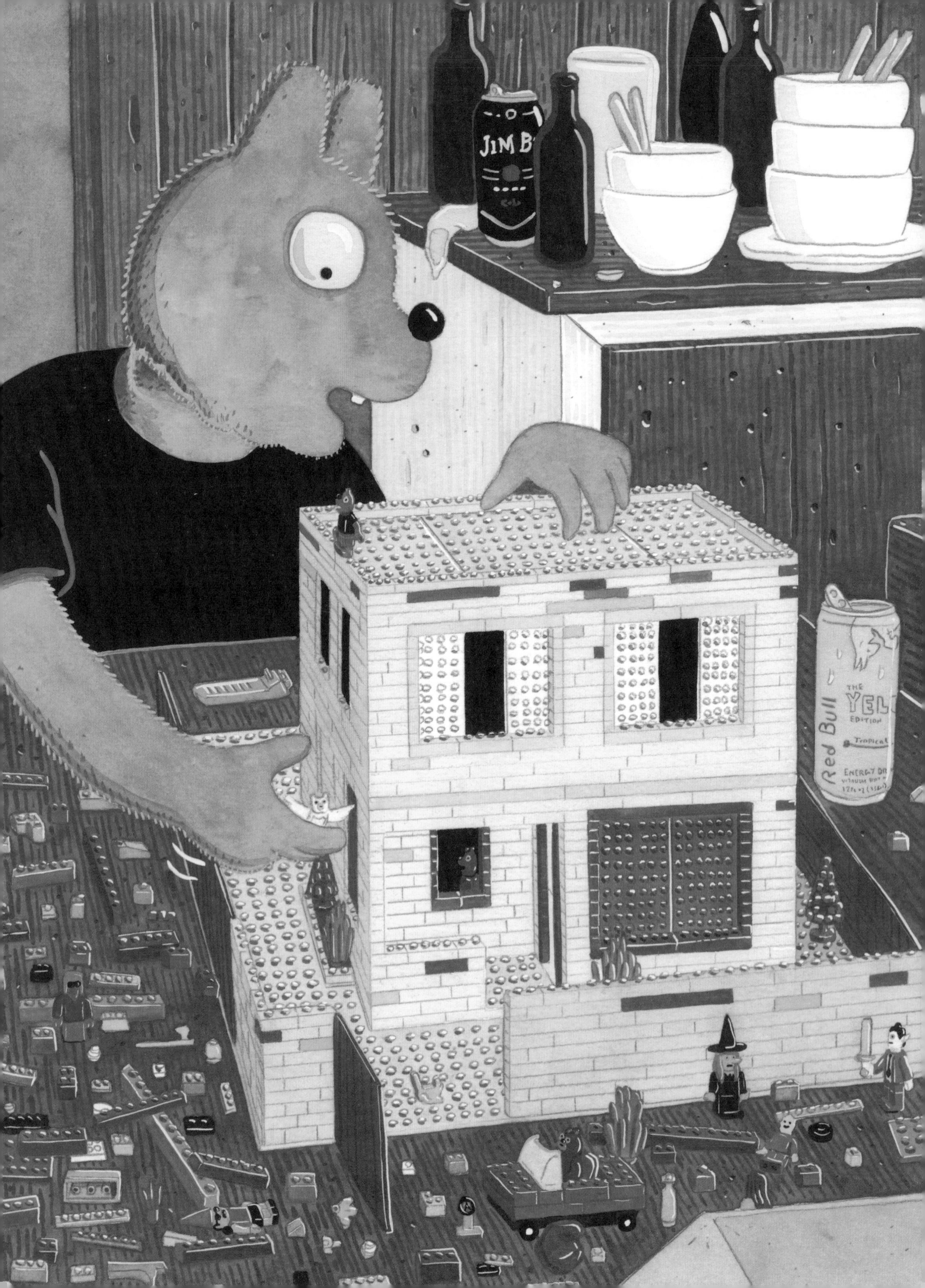
Red Bull
THE
EDITION

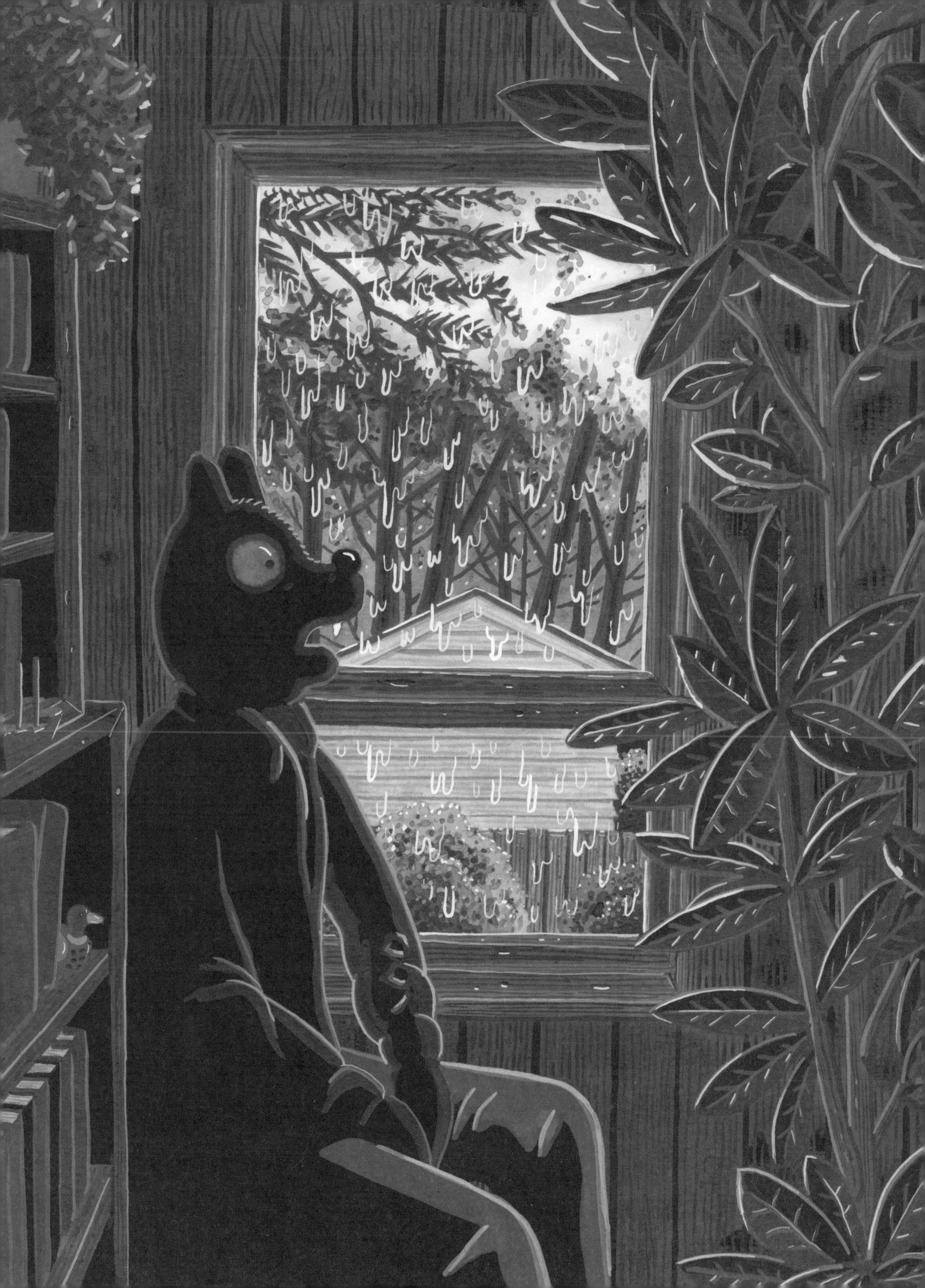

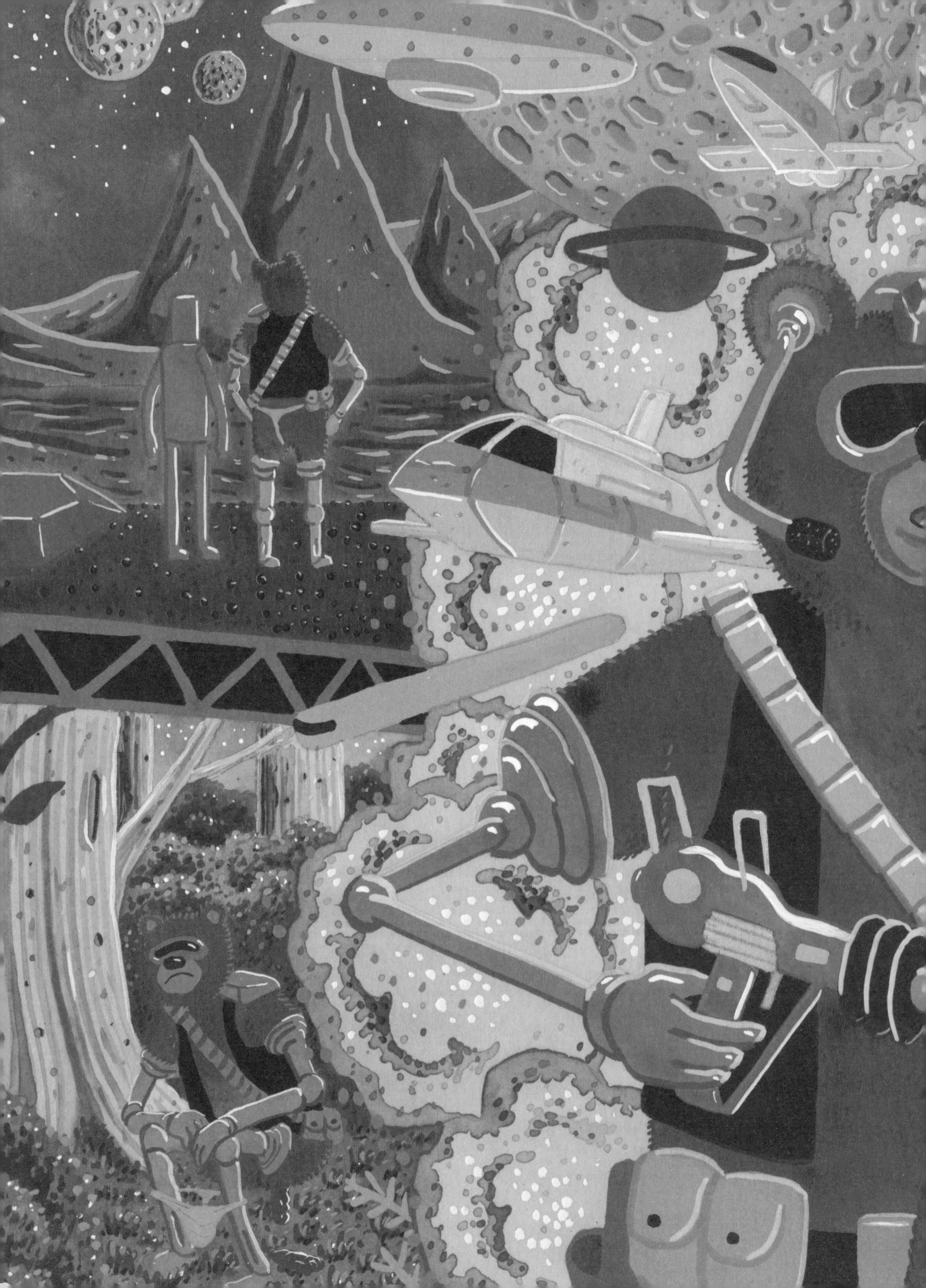